Fodor's 2001

Walt Disney World Resort, Universal Orlando, and Central Florida

USED

The complete guide, thoroughly up-to-date

Packed with details that will make your trip

The must-see sights, off and on the beaten path

What to see, what to skip

Mix-and-match vacation itineraries

City strolls, countryside adventures

Smart lodging and dining options

Essential local do's and taboos

Transportation tips, distances and directions

Key contacts, savvy travel tips

When to go, what to pack

Clear, accurate, easy-to-use maps

II

Fodor's Walt Disney World® Resort, Universal Orlando, and Central Florida

EDITOR: David Cashion

Editorial Contributors: Pam Acheson, Gary McKechnie, Valerie Meyer, Rowland Stiteler

Editorial Production: Brian Vitunic, Ira-Neil Dittersdorf

Maps: David Lindroth, *cartographer*; Bob Blake and Steven Amsterdam, *map editors*

Design: Fabrizio La Rocca, *creative director*; Guido Caroti, *art director*; Jolie Novak, *photo editor*

Cover Design: Pentagram

Cover Photograph: © Disney Enterprises, Inc. (Splash Mountain)

Production/Manufacturing: Robert Shields

Copyright

Important Tip

Although all prices, opening times, and other details in this book are based on information supplied to us at press time, changes occur all the time in the travel world, and Fodor's cannot accept responsibility for facts that become outdated or for inadvertent errors or omissions. So **always confirm information when it matters,** especially if you're making a detour to visit a specific place.

Special Sales

Fodor's Travel Publications are available at special discounts for bulk purchases for sales promotions or premiums. Special editions, including personalized covers, excerpts of existing guides, and corporate imprints, can be created in large quantities for special needs. For more information, contact your local bookseller or write to Special Markets, Fodor's Travel Publications, 280 Park Avenue, New York, NY 10017. Inquiries from Canada should be directed to your local Canadian bookseller or sent to Random House of Canada, Ltd., Marketing Department, 2775 Matheson Boulevard East, Mississauga, Ontario L4W 4P7. Inquiries from the United Kingdom should be sent to Fodor's Travel Publications, 20 Vauxhall Bridge Road, London SW1V 2SA, England.

PRINTED IN THE UNITED STATES OF AMERICA

10 9 8 7 6 5 4 3 2 1

CONTENTS

ON THE ROAD WITH FODOR'S

MANY YEARS AGO, I wrote the *Official Guide to Walt Disney World*. But not until we at Fodor's produced the volume you now hold in your hands have I ever felt that there was a perfect guidebook to the most unusual of vacation kingdoms.

In the first place, it's now the only Disney guide that's updated twice a year, to fill you in on all that's new in fast-changing Orlando. Beyond that, it's also the best book for visiting with kids. If a ride routinely scares toddlers, we say so. But it's also great for grown-ups. And it's also the book for people who can't stand waiting in line. We're completely impartial—the information in this guide originated with the authors and revisers and is their opinion and mine—of what's worth your time. We also cover all of Orlando's many attractions with equal care, including Universal Studios Escape and SeaWorld, to help you decide how you want to spend your time.

About Our Writers

Our success in helping to make your trip the best of all possible vacations is a credit to the hard work of our extraordinary writers.

Val Meyer has been a Disney aficionado since birth. A resident of Fort Myers, Florida, Val has put many, many miles on her car for pilgrimages to Orlando with her daughter, Mandy.

On her way to the Caribbean, former New York publishing exec **Pamela Acheson** stopped in the Sunshine State and fell in love. She likes nothing better than to drive around to neat little towns, undiscovered beaches, and other less-traveled places of her adopted home.

Florida native **Gary McKechnie** has encyclopedic knowledge of what he thinks of as the greatest state in the Union and, while a student, worked as a Walt Disney World ferryboat pilot, Jungle Cruise skipper, steam train conductor, doubledecker bus driver, and improv comedian at Epcot.

Good meals stick to your ribs; great meals stick in your mind. That's the belief of **Rowland Stiteler,** who has served as editor and dining critic of *Orlando* and *Central Florida* magazines. In his effort to beat the buffet blahs, he always has an eye peeled for the next hot thing in Floridian cuisine.

Audiences and Ratings

Every visitor leaves the theme parks with a different opinion about what was "the best." To take this into account, our descriptions rate each attraction with ★, ★★, or ★★★, depending on its appeal to the audience noted. In audience designations, "young children" refers to kids ages 5–7; "very young children" are those (ages 4 and under) who probably won't meet the height requirements of most thrill rides anyway. Since youngsters come with different confidence levels, exercise your own judgment when it comes to the scarier rides.

Don't Forget to Write

Keeping a travel guide up-to-date is a big job. So we love your feedback—positive and negative—and follow up on all suggestions. Contact the Walt Disney World editor at editors@fodors.com or c/o Fodor's, 280 Park Avenue, 10th Floor, New York, NY 10017. Have a wonderful trip!

Karen Cure
Editorial Director

The Florida Peninsula

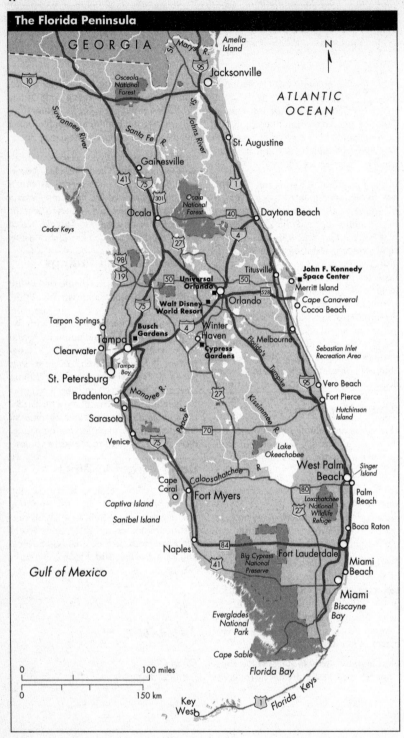

GEORGIA

10

Osceola
National
Forest

Suwannee River

Santa Fe R.

St. Marys R.

Amelia
Island

95

Jacksonville

ATLANTIC
OCEAN

St. Johns River

St. Augustine

Gainesville

41

75

301

Ocala
National
Forest

Cedar Keys

Ocala

27

40

Daytona Beach

4

98

19

50

Universal
Orlando

75

Walt Disney
World Resort

Busch
Gardens

Tarpon Springs

Tampa

Clearwater

4

Winter
Haven

Cypress
Gardens

Titusville

50

528

Orlando

Melbourne

John F. Kennedy
Space Center

Merritt Island

Cape Canaveral
Cocoa Beach

Florida's Turnpike

Sebastian Inlet
Recreation Area

St. Petersburg

Tampa
Bay

Bradenton

Manatee R.

Sarasota

Venice

75

Peace R.

27

70

Kissimmee R.

95

Vero Beach

Fort Pierce

Hutchinson
Island

Lake
Okeechobee

West Palm
Beach

Singer
Island

Cape
Coral

Caloosahatchee R.

Fort Myers

80

Loxahatchee
National
Wildlife
Refuge

27

Palm
Beach

Boca Raton

Captiva Island

Sanibel Island

Naples

84

41

Big Cypress
National
Preserve

Fort Lauderdale

Miami
Beach

Gulf of Mexico

Everglades
National
Park

Miami

Biscayne
Bay

Cape Sable

Florida Bay

0   100 miles

0   150 km

Key
West

1   Florida Keys

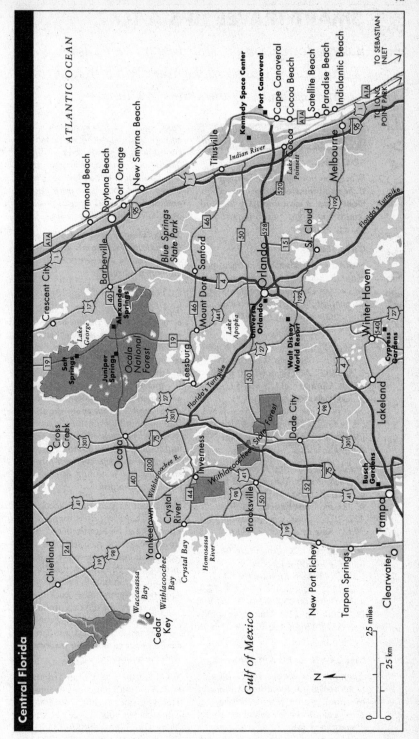

Central Florida

SMART TRAVEL TIPS A TO Z

Basic Information on Traveling in Walt Disney World, Savvy Tips to Make Your Trip a Breeze, and Companies and Organizations to Contact

AIR TRAVEL TO AND FROM WALT DISNEY WORLD

BOOKING

When you book **look for nonstop flights** and **remember that "direct" flights stop at least once.** Try to avoid connecting flights, which require a change of plane.

CARRIERS

More than 20 scheduled airlines and more than 30 charter firms operate in and out of Orlando International Airport, providing direct service to more than 100 cities in the United States and overseas.

➤ MAJOR AIRLINES: **Air Tran** ☎ 800/247–8726). **America West** (☎ 800/235–9292). **American** (☎ 800/433–7300). **Continental** (☎ 800/523–3273). **Delta** (☎ 800/221–1212). **Northwest** (☎ 800/225–2525). **TWA** (☎ 800/221–2000). **United Airlines** (☎ 800/241–6522). **US Airways** (☎ 800/428–4322).

➤ SMALLER AIRLINES: **Frontier** (☎ 800/432–1359). **Metro Jet** (☎ 888/638–7653). **Midway** (☎ 800/446–4392). **Midwest Express** (☎ 800/452–2022). **Southwest** (☎ 800/435–9792). **Spirit** (☎ 800/772–7117).

➤ FROM THE U.K.: **American** (☎ 0345/789–789) via Miami or Chicago. **British Airways** (☎ 0345/222–111). **Continental** (☎ 0800/776–464). **Delta** (☎ 0800/414–767). **TWA** (☎ 0800/222–222). **United** (☎ 0800/888–555). **Virgin Atlantic** (☎ 01293/747–747).

CHECK-IN & BOARDING

Assuming that not everyone with a ticket will show up, airlines routinely overbook planes. When everyone does, airlines ask for volunteers to give up their seats. In return, these volunteers usually get a certificate for a free flight and are rebooked on the next flight out. If there are not enough volunteers, the airline must choose who will be denied boarding. The first to get bumped are passengers who checked in late and those flying on discounted tickets, so **get to the gate and check in as early as possible,** especially during peak periods.

Always **bring a government-issued photo I.D. to the airport.** You may be asked to show it before you are allowed to check in.

CUTTING COSTS

You can get some terrific deals as a result of the large volume of travelers and the number of airlines that serve Orlando. The least-expensive airfares to Orlando must usually be purchased in advance and are non-refundable. It's smart to **call a number of airlines, and when you are quoted a good price, book it on the spot**—the same fare may not be available the next day. Always **check different routings** and look into using different airports. Travel agents, especially low-fare specialists (☞ Discounts & Deals, *below*), are helpful.

Consolidators are another good source. They buy tickets for scheduled international flights at reduced rates from the airlines, then sell them at prices that beat the best fare available directly from the airlines, usually without restrictions. Sometimes you can even get your money back if you need to return the ticket. Carefully read the fine print detailing penalties for changes and cancellations, and **confirm your consolidator reservation with the airline.**

➤ CONSOLIDATORS: **Cheap Tickets** (☎ 800/377–1000). **Discount Airline Ticket Service** (☎ 800/576–1600). **Unitravel** (☎ 800/325–2222). **Up & Away Travel** (☎ 212/889–2345). **World Travel Network** (☎ 800/409–6753).

ENJOYING THE FLIGHT

For more legroom, **request an emergency-aisle seat.** Don't sit in the row in front of the emergency aisle or in front of a bulkhead, where seats may not recline. If you have dietary concerns, **ask for special meals when booking.** These can be vegetarian, low-cholesterol, or kosher, for example. On long flights, try to maintain a normal routine, to help fight jet lag. At night, **get some sleep.** By day, **eat light meals, drink water** (not alcohol), and **move around the cabin** to stretch your legs.

En route to Orlando, wear lighter clothing and carry a mid-weight jacket if you're coming from a colder climate. If you're traveling with children, be sure to bring snacks, games, toys, and books to keep them entertained during the flight.

FLYING TIMES

Flying time is 2½ hours from New York, 3½ hours from Chicago, and 5 hours from Los Angeles.

HOW TO COMPLAIN

If your baggage goes astray or your flight goes awry, complain right away. Most carriers require that you **file a claim immediately.**

➤ AIRLINE COMPLAINTS: U.S. Department of Transportation **Aviation Consumer Protection Division** (✉ C-75, Room 4107, Washington, DC 20590, ☎ 202/366–2220, airconsumer@ost.dot.gov, www.dot.gov/airconsumer). **Federal Aviation Administration Consumer Hotline** (☎ 800/322–7873).

AIRPORTS & TRANSFERS

The Orlando airport (MCO on your baggage tag) is ultramodern, huge, and growing all the time. Monorails shuttle you from gate areas to the core area, where you'll find baggage claim. The complex is south of Orlando and northeast of Walt Disney World.

➤ AIRPORT INFORMATION: **Orlando International Airport** (☎ 407/825–2001).

AIRPORT TRANSFERS

Taxis take only a half hour to get from the airport to most hotels used by WDW visitors; they charge about $25 plus tip to the International Drive area, about $10 more to the U.S. 192 area. Depending on the number of people in your party, this will cost more or less than paying by the head for an airport shuttle. **Mears Transportation Group** meets you at the gate, helps with the luggage, and whisks you away, in either an 11-passenger van, a town car, or a limo. Vans run to Walt Disney World and along U.S. 192 every 30 minutes; prices range from $12.50 one-way for adults ($8.50 for children 4–11) to $22 round-trip for adults ($16 children 4–11). Limo rates run $50–$60 for a town car that accommodates three or four to $90 for a stretch limo that seats six. **Town & Country Transportation** charges $30–$40 one-way for up to seven people, depending on the hotel.

Lynx operates public buses between the airport and the main terminal downtown. Though the cost is $1, other options are more convenient because center-city Orlando is far from most theme-park area hotels.

➤ BUSES & LIMOS: **Lynx** (✉ 1200 W. South St., Orlando, ☎ 407/841–8240). **Mears Transportation Group** (☎ 407/423–5566). **Town & Country Transportation** (☎ 407/828–3035).

BUS TRAVEL

If you are staying along International Drive, in Kissimmee, or in Orlando proper, public buses can get you around the immediate area. To find out which bus to take, ask your hotel clerk or call the Lynx public transportation office. **Lymmo,** operated by Lynx, circles downtown daily until 10 PM (until midnight on Friday and Saturday), connecting most area entertainment and sports venues. **Lynx** also runs limited service between Sanford and Daytona Beach. (Note, however, that it can take you as much as three hours to make the short trip, so if Daytona is a destination, you would be better off renting a car unless you have plenty of time.)

In addition, many hotels run their own shuttles especially for guests. To arrange a ride, all you have to do is ask your hotel's concierge, inquire at

THE GOLD GUIDE / SMART TRAVEL TIPS

the front desk, or phone the operator directly. However, these buses may not run to the places you want to see on the days or at the times you prefer, whether that's back to your hotel at midday or out to the theme parks in late afternoon. Some buses also pick up or drop off guests at several hotels, adding to your ride time and delaying your arrival at your destination.

One-way fares are usually $8–$10 per adult, and a couple of dollars less for children ages 4–11, between major hotel areas and the Disney parks. Excursion fares to Busch Gardens and Cypress Gardens, which are more than a half hour's drive, are $27 per person, including admission as well as round-trip fare. Sometimes you can negotiate a room rate that includes free transportation, even when it's not routinely available.

➤ BETWEEN HOTELS AND ATTRACTIONS: **Lynx Information Office** (⌧ 1200 W. South St., Orlando, ☎ 407/841–8240). **Gray Line of Orlando** (☎ 407/422–0744). **Mears Transportation Group** (☎ 407/423–5566). **Phoenix Tours** (☎ 407/859–4211). **Rabbit Bus Lines** (☎ 407/291–2424).

CAMERAS & PHOTOGRAPHY

➤ PHOTO HELP: **Kodak Information Center** (☎ 800/242–2424). *Kodak Guide to Shooting Great Travel Pictures,* available in bookstores or from Fodor's Travel Publications (☎ 800/533–6478; $16.50 plus $5.50 shipping).

EQUIPMENT PRECAUTIONS

Always **keep your film and tape out of the sun.** Carry an extra supply of batteries, and **be prepared to turn on your camera or camcorder** to prove to security personnel that the device is real. Always **ask for hand inspection of film,** which becomes clouded after repeated exposure to airport X-ray machines, and **keep videotapes away from metal detectors.**

CAR RENTAL

If you want to visit major theme parks outside Walt Disney World, or move from park to resort to park on Disney property in a single day, or stay in a Disney resort that's served only by buses, or venture off the beaten track, or eat where most tourists don't, it's nearly essential in Orlando to **rent a car.**

Rates are among the lowest in the United States. They begin at $30 a day and $149 a week for an economy car with air-conditioning, an automatic transmission, and unlimited mileage. This does not include tax on car rentals, which is 6%. Avis is particularly convenient, since the car lot is on airport property, a short walk from baggage claim.

➤ MAJOR AGENCIES: **Alamo** (☎ 800/327–9633; 020/8759–6200 in the U.K.). **Avis** (☎ 800/331–1212; 800/879–2847 in Canada; 02/9353–9000 in Australia; 09/525–1982 in New Zealand). **Budget** (☎ 800/527–0700; 0144/227–6266 in the U.K.). **Dollar** (☎ 800/800–4000; 020/8897–0811 in the U.K., where it is known as Eurodollar; 02/9223–1444 in Australia). **Hertz** (☎ 800/654–3131; 800/263–0600 in Canada; 020/8897–2072 in the U.K.; 02/9669–2444 in Australia; 03/358–6777 in New Zealand). **National InterRent** (☎ 800/227–7368; 0345/222525 in the U.K., where it is known as Europcar InterRent).

CUTTING COSTS

To get the best deal, **book through a travel agent who will shop around.** Also **price local car-rental companies,** although the service and maintenance may not be as good as those of a major player. Remember to ask about required deposits, cancellation penalties, and drop-off charges if you're planning to pick up the car in one city and leave it in another. If you're traveling during a holiday period, also make sure that a confirmed reservation guarantees you a car.

Do **look into wholesalers,** companies that do not own fleets but rent in bulk from those that do and often offer better rates than traditional car-rental operations.

➤ WHOLESALERS: **Auto Europe** (☎ 207/842–2000 or 800/223–5555, FAX 800–235–6321, www.autoeurope.com). **Kemwel Holiday Autos** (☎ 800/678–0678, FAX 914/825–3160, www.kemwel.com).

INSURANCE

When driving a rented car you are generally responsible for any damage to or loss of the vehicle as well as for any property damage or personal injury that you may cause. Before you rent see what coverage your personal auto-insurance policy and credit cards already provide.

For about $15 to $20 per day, rental companies sell protection, known as a collision- or loss-damage waiver (CDW or LDW), that eliminates your liability for damage to the car. In most states you don't need a CDW if you have personal auto insurance or other liability insurance. However, **make sure you have enough coverage to pay for the car.** If you do not have auto insurance or an umbrella policy that covers damage to third parties, purchasing liability insurance and a CDW or LDW is highly recommended.

REQUIREMENTS & RESTRICTIONS

In Florida you must be 21 to rent a car, and rates may be higher if you're under 25. You'll pay extra for child seats (about $3 per day), which are compulsory for children under five, and for additional drivers (about $2 per day). Non-U.S. residents will need a reservation voucher, a passport, a driver's license, and a travel policy that covers each driver, when picking up a car.

SURCHARGES

Before you pick up a car in one city and leave it in another, **ask about drop-off charges or one-way service fees,** which can be substantial. Note, too, that some rental agencies charge extra if you return the car before the time specified in your contract. To avoid a hefty refueling fee, **fill the tank just before you turn in the car,** but be aware that gas stations near the rental outlet may overcharge.

CAR TRAVEL

If you arrive by plane, **use the Beeline Expressway (Rte. 528) to get to the hotels from the airport.** Follow the expressway west to International Drive, and exit at SeaWorld. Or stay on the Beeline to I–4, and head either west to Walt Disney World and U.S. 192/Kissimmee or east to downtown

Orlando. Call your hotel for the best route.

The most important artery in the Orlando area is I–4, which links the Atlantic Coast to Florida's Gulf of Mexico. However, the interstate actually runs north and south in the Orlando area. So **think north when I–4 signs say east and think south when the signs say west.**

Two other main roads you're likely to use are International Drive, also known as I–Drive, and U.S. 192, sometimes called the Spacecoast Parkway or Irlo Bronson Memorial Highway. You can get onto International Drive from I–4 Exits 28, 29, and 30B. U.S. 192 cuts across I–4 at Exits 25A and 25B.

In Walt Disney World, there is a **Car Care Center** (☞ Walt Disney World A to Z *in* Chapter 2).

CHILDREN IN ORLANDO

Are your children old enough for a Central Florida vacation? Thinking about this question is not unlike considering whether to take your youngsters to New York City or Paris. There's no question that at 10, or even 8 or 9, many children have the maturity to understand and enjoy the information and entertainment at the theme parks. Younger children are another matter. It's not that they won't enjoy it, because all the theme parks get high marks from young travelers. Hotel facilities for children range from okay to fabulous. But for Orlando, as for Paris and New York, you'll be spending a lot of money and probably battling huge crowds to see the place yourself, and you and your children may have totally different ideas about what's fun. While you're envisioning the Twilight Zone Tower of Terror, ExtraTERRORestrial Alien Encounter, Space Mountain, *Earthquake, JAWS,* and *Back to the Future . . .* The Ride, your youngsters may want to ride Dumbo 100 times, splash in the fountains outside Ariel's Grotto, and collect signatures from people dressed up in funny outfits. And they may well be terrified by the very attractions that adults typically travel to the Orlando area to experience. Although the Baby Swap (☞ *below*) can be helpful, allowing you and your spouse to take turns experiencing an attraction, it's not a real answer. There's the issue of how you feel about forcing your youngsters to wait repeatedly in the hot Florida sun while you ride, or making them go on rides that are scary for them. There's also an issue of cost: Do you really want to spend $40 for your child to be doing this? And then there's the issue of who you ride with: When you use Baby Swap, you end up experiencing the attractions with total strangers, while your significant other baby-sits back in the queue area. Add to the equation the fact that having young children along slows you down and effectively increases the time you spend waiting in line, and you may well decide to wait until your youngsters are older, when their Central Florida agenda will more closely resemble yours.

The alternative, of course, is to bite the bullet and go anyway. Do **create an itinerary that builds in your children's interests as well as your own**, understanding that they will delight in details that you might overlook; allow yourself to appreciate the park from their point of view. Also **plan for plenty of family time away from the theme parks.** For a night or two, step out for the fireworks or some other after-dark thrills in or away from the theme parks (☞ Baby-Sitting, *below*). Give yourself more time than you think you need, and buy passes rather than tickets so that you can always go back and see what you've missed another day. (Passes, in theme park lingo, allow you to visit a number of theme parks on any given day as long as the pass is valid.) Or, alternatively, **understand in advance that you will probably not see all the attractions.**

Crowds are often a problem and can overwhelm preschoolers. Do what you can to **avoid the times of the year that are likely to be the most crowded** (☞ When to Go, *below*), and then **plan your itinerary around the days of the week and times of day when the parks and attractions are the least busy** (☞ Strategies for Your Visit to each park *in* Chapters 2, 3, and 4).

So that you won't have to concern yourself with lugging items such as strollers, cribs, high chairs, and backpack carriers, be sure to ask your hotel whether what you need can be provided. If it can't, consider calling **A Baby's Best Friend** before you leave. The company's employees will deliver high-quality equipment to your accommodations prior to your arrival and pick them up after your departure. If you are renting a car, don't forget to **arrange for a car seat** when you reserve.

BABY-SITTING

At Walt Disney World, there are strong children's facilities and programs at the BoardWalk, Contemporary, Dolphin, Grand Floridian, Polynesian, Swan, Wilderness Lodge, and Yacht and Beach Resorts; the Polynesian Resort's Never Land Club will enchant you and your offspring with its Peter Pan–theme clubhouse and youngsters-only dinner show. Parents also rave about the Sand Castle Club at the Yacht and Beach Resorts. The Hilton, near Downtown Disney's Marketplace, has the Vacation Station, a hotel within a hotel for the little ones. The BoardWalk's child-care facility, Harbor Club, provides late-afternoon and evening baby-sitting.

Off-site, many hotels have supervised children's programs (☞ Chapter 7), with trained counselors and planned activities as well as attractive facilities; some even have mascots. Standouts are at the Hyatt Regency Grand Cypress, near Downtown Disney, and the Camp Holiday programs at the Holiday Inn SunSpree Resort Lake Buena Vista and Holiday Inn Hotel & Suites Main Gate East (☞ Lodging, *below*).

Walt Disney World has KinderCare preschool and drop-off day-care facilities in the Lake Buena Vista area. It will also send baby-sitters to your hotel room. The KinderCare center proper accepts children who are potty trained and walking and is open daily 6 AM–8 PM; you don't have to stay at Disney to use the program.

All programs charge between $5 and $10 an hour, depending on the ages and number of children and the type of service provided.

➤ AGENCIES: **KinderCare** (☎ 407/827-5437).

BABY SWAP

Parents with small children under the height limit for major attractions have to take turns waiting in the long lines, right? Wrong. In what's unofficially known as the Baby Swap, both of you queue up, and when it's your turn to board, one stays with the youngsters until the other returns; the waiting partner then rides without waiting again. Universal Studios calls it a Baby Exchange and has Baby Exchange areas at most rides.

CHARACTER MEALS

At special breakfasts, brunches, lunches, and dinners in many Walt Disney World restaurants, Mickey, Donald, Goofy, Chip 'n' Dale, Cinderella, and other favorite characters sign autographs and pose for snapshots. Universal's Islands of Adventure has a character luncheon, so your children can enjoy pizza or chicken fingers with their favorite Seuss characters. With your children, determine which characters they most want to see; then call the Disney dining reservations line and speak with the representative about what's available. Reservations are not always necessary, but these hugging-and-feeding frenzies are wildly popular, so **show up early if you don't like to wait.** It's a good idea to **plan your character meal for toward the end of your visit,** when your little ones will be used to seeing these large and sometimes frightening figures; they're also a good way to spend the morning on the day you check out (☞ Chapter 6).

DINING

Many Central Florida restaurants have children's menus. And franchised fast-food eateries abound, providing that reassuring taste of home. The McDonald's on International Drive has an elaborate multilevel playground that seems almost bigger than the restaurant. The Rainforest Café chain, with its rainstorms and exotic jungle decor, is another child-pleaser. Stagestruck girls like the belly-dancer in the Marrakesh Restaurant, in Morocco in Epcot's World Showcase. Whispering Canyon Café in Disney's Wilderness Lodge and 'Ohana in the Polynesian have what it takes to please both parents and their offspring (☞ Chapter 6).

EDUCATIONAL PROGRAMS

For any behind-the-scenes tours and programs **be sure to reserve ahead.**

SeaWorld's Sea Safari programs ($5.95 adults, $4.95 children 3–9) offer behind-the-scenes looks at park operations that are great for kids, though not designed specifically for them (☞ Chapter 4). For a wide selection of age-specific classes on wildlife and ecology, you'll have to wait for summer, when the calendar is chockablock with programs ranging from one day to one week in length; most cost $15–$60. In addition, the bring-your-own-sleeping-bag "Education Sleepovers," offered exclusively to school groups in winter, are open to individual visitors. How about bedding down in the shark exhibit at Terrors of the Deep? Or try "Cool Nights with Penguins" to see the nightlife of the tuxedoed masses.

Busch Gardens' Multiday Zoo Camps keep children learning here from June through October. There's a different program for each age group, from kindergartners through 10th graders, and each program lasts several days ($80–$100 per session). Youngsters can also sign up for classes that last just a few hours ($15–$20), from a hands-on introduction to wildlife for toddlers to a night hike for preteens.

➤ EDUCATIONAL PROGRAMS:: **SeaWorld** (☎ 407/363-2380 or 800/406-2244). **Busch Gardens** (☎ 813/987-5555).

LODGING

In all but the smallest motels there is little or no charge for children under 18 who share a room with an adult.

All hotels on Disney property and many others in the area have playgrounds and arcades with video games and pinball machines. The one in Disney's Contemporary Resort is, hands down, the biggest game room in any hotel in the area. Parrot Cay, a little island in the Caribbean Beach Resort's lagoon, is anchored by a winning little playground with soft white sand underfoot. Swimming pools are long on Disney charm, with such special touches as a pirate stronghold and a cannon that lets out periodic booms, the Stormalong Bay area between Disney's Yacht and Beach Club, the lagoon at Disney's Dixie Landings Resort, and the roller coaster–theme water slide at the BoardWalk. Away from Disney property, many lodgings also offer special facilities for kids. The Holiday Inn SunSpree Resort Lake Buena Vista features Kidsuites, theme playhouses within guest rooms that contain bunk beds and their own TV with video games.

➤ RENTAL BABY EQUIPMENT: **A Baby's Best Friend** (☎ 407/382–9267 or 888/461–2229).

STROLLER RENTALS

Stroller rentals are available in theme parks, but you may want to bring your own, since fees run $5–$7 per day (plus a deposit). Also, you will probably need a stroller in places where you can't rent one—to tour Orlando off the beaten track, to explore Orlando's malls, even just to get around your hotel, if it's big. Theme parks' strollers are sturdy but unyielding, and not optimal for infants.

If you do rent a stroller, there is always the possibility that it will be taken. A word to the wise: Although it is tempting, **don't leave packages in your stroller.** Experienced park visitors have long been taping a large card with their name to the stroller; now many of the parks themselves provide the tags. In addition, you might have some small personal item to mark yours, such as a bandanna, a T-shirt, even a clear plastic bag with diapers inside; the theory is that people who wouldn't think twice about purloining theme-park property that they will subsequently return hesitate to make off with something that belongs to a fellow parent. If your stroller does disappear, you can easily pick up a replacement; ask any park staffer for the nearest location. If you wish to park hop on the same day there is no need to rent another stroller. Simply turn the old one in

when leaving the first park and get a new one upon entrance to the next park. Your deposit receipt is good all day at all the theme parks at Disney.

WHAT TO BRING

A backpack is a good idea. In hot weather, bring sunscreen, a water bottle that you can refill at drinking fountains, and an assortment of small, uncrushable snacks to tide you over between meals (or even meals themselves). Some parents bring frozen juice boxes—they'll thaw out by the time your children are ready for them and keep your back cool in the meantime. A bathing suit or a change of clothes can also be helpful, since youngsters like to splash around in theme-park fountains. Clean, dry socks are incredibly soothing to sore feet in the middle of the day. And a pen is essential for gathering precious character autographs—buy an autograph book at your hotel or as soon as you arrive in the theme park.

CONCIERGES

Concierges, found in many hotels, can help you with theater tickets and dinner reservations: a good one with connections may be able to get you seats for a hot show or prime-time dinner reservations at the restaurant of the moment. You can also turn to your hotel's concierge for help with travel arrangements, sightseeing plans, services ranging from aromatherapy to zipper repair, and emergencies. Always, **always tip** a concierge who has been of assistance (☞ Tipping, *below*).

CONSUMER PROTECTION

Whenever shopping or buying travel services in Orlando, **pay with a major credit card** so you can cancel payment or get reimbursed if there's a problem. If you're doing business with a particular company for the first time, **contact your local Better Business Bureau and the attorney general's offices** in your own state and the company's home state, as well. Have any complaints been filed? Finally, if you're buying a package or tour, always **consider travel insurance** that includes default coverage (☞ Insurance, *below*).

➤ BBBs: **Council of Better Business Bureaus** (✉ 4200 Wilson Blvd., Suite 800, Arlington, VA 22203, ☎ 703/276–0100, FAX 703/525–8277 www.bbb.org).

CUSTOMS & DUTIES

When shopping, **keep receipts** for all purchases. Upon reentering the country, **be ready to show customs officials what you've bought.** If you feel a duty is incorrect or object to the way your clearance was handled, note the inspector's badge number and ask to see a supervisor. If the problem isn't resolved, write to the appropriate authorities, beginning with the port director at your point of entry.

IN AUSTRALIA

Australian residents who are 18 or older may bring home $A400 worth of souvenirs and gifts (including jewelry), 250 cigarettes or 250 grams of tobacco, and 1,125 ml of alcohol (including wine, beer, and spirits). Residents under 18 may bring back $A200 worth of goods. Prohibited items include meat products. Seeds, plants, and fruits need to be declared upon arrival.

➤ INFORMATION: **Australian Customs Service** (Regional Director, ✉ Box 8, Sydney, NSW 2001, ☎ 02/9213–2000, FAX 02/9213–4000).

IN CANADA

Canadian residents who have been out of Canada for at least 7 days may bring home C$500 worth of goods duty-free. If you've been away less than 7 days but more than 48 hours, the duty-free allowance drops to C$200; if your trip lasts 24–48 hours, the allowance is C$50. You may not pool allowances with family members. Goods claimed under the C$500 exemption may follow you by mail; those claimed under the lesser exemptions must accompany you. Alcohol and tobacco products may be included in the 7-day and 48-hour exemptions but not in the 24-hour exemption. If you meet the age requirements of the province or territory through which you reenter Canada, you may bring in, duty-free, 1.14 liters (40 imperial ounces) of wine or liquor *or* 24 12-ounce cans or bottles of beer or ale. If you are 16 or older you may bring in, duty-free, 200 cigarettes and 50 cigars. Check ahead of time with Revenue Canada or the Department of Agriculture for policies regarding meat products, seeds, plants, and fruits.

You may send an unlimited number of gifts worth up to C$60 each duty-free to Canada. Label the package UNSOLICITED GIFT—VALUE UNDER $60. Alcohol and tobacco are excluded.

IN NEW ZEALAND

Homeward-bound residents 17 or older may bring back $700 worth of souvenirs and gifts. Your duty-free allowance also includes 4.5 liters of wine or beer; one 1,125-ml bottle of spirits; and either 200 cigarettes, 250 grams of tobacco, 50 cigars, or a combination of the three up to 250 grams. Prohibited items include meat products, seeds, plants, and fruits.

➤ INFORMATION: **New Zealand Customs** (Custom House, ✉ 50 Anzac Ave., Box 29, Auckland, New Zealand, ☎ 09/359–6655, FAX 09/359–6732).

IN THE U.K.

From countries outside the EU, including the United States, you may bring home, duty-free, 200 cigarettes or 50 cigars; 1 liter of spirits or 2 liters of fortified or sparkling wine or liqueurs; 2 liters of still table wine; 60 ml of perfume; 250 ml of toilet water; plus £136 worth of other goods, including gifts and souvenirs. If returning from outside the EU, prohibited items include meat products, seeds, plants, and fruits.

➤ INFORMATION: **HM Customs and Excise** (✉ Dorset House, Stamford St., Bromley, Kent BR1 1XX, ☎ 020/7202–4227).

IN THE U.S.

➤ INFORMATION: **U.S. Customs Service** (✉ 1300 Pennsylvania Ave. NW, Washington, DC 20229, www.customs.gov; inquiries ☎ 202/354–1000; complaints c/o ✉ Office of Regulations and Rulings; registration of equipment c/o ✉ Resource Management, ☎ 202/927–0540).

THE GOLD GUIDE / SMART TRAVEL TIPS

DINING

The restaurants we list in the Dining chapter and in the Cocoa Beach chapter are the cream of the crop in each price category. There are many more. Properties indicated by an ✕▦ are lodging establishments whose restaurant warrants a special trip.

CATEGORY	COST*
$$$$	over $50
$$$	$35–$50
$$	$20–$35
$	under $20

per person, excluding drinks, service, and 6% sales tax

RESERVATIONS & DRESS

Reservations are always a good idea: we mention them only when they're essential or not accepted. Book as far ahead as you can, and reconfirm as soon as you arrive. We mention dress only when men are required to wear a jacket or a jacket and tie.

DISABILITIES & ACCESSIBILITY

Central Florida attractions are among the most accessible destinations in the world for people who have disabilities. The hospitality industry continues to spend millions on barrier-removing renovations. Though some challenges remain, most can be overcome with planning.

The main park-information centers (☞ Chapters 2, 3, and 4) can answer specific questions and dispense general information for guests with disabilities. Both Walt Disney World and Universal Studios publish guidebooks for guests with disabilities; allow six weeks for delivery.

LODGING

Hotels and motels here are continually being renovated to comply with the Americans with Disabilities Act. Call the WDW Special Request Reservations for up-to-the-minute information.

For guests using wheelchairs, staying at Disney-owned resort hotels is particularly convenient, since the Disney transportation system has dozens of lift-equipped vehicles. Most resorts here in every price range have rooms with roll-in showers or transfer benches in the bathrooms.

You will be comfortable at any number of on-property Disney resorts. Especially worthwhile and convenient is the Grand Floridian, a luxurious monorail resort, and Port Orleans, which has all the advantages of Dixie Landings but a much more intimate feel. One of the most accommodating off-site resorts is the Marriott Orlando World Center; its level of commitment is especially apparent on Sunday morning, when the Garden Terrace Restaurant hosts one of the most delicious and hospitable Sunday brunches in Central Florida.

In most properties, only elevators are braille-equipped, but some have programs to help employees understand how best to assist guests with visual impairments. Particularly outstanding is the Wyndham Resort and Spa at WDW Resort, on Hotel Plaza Boulevard. The Embassy Suites resorts at Lake Buena Vista and International Drive offer services such as talking alarm clocks and braille or recorded menus.

Most area properties have purchased the equipment necessary to accommodate guests with hearing impairments. Telecommunications devices for the deaf, flashing or vibrating phones and alarms, and closed captioning are common; an industry-wide effort to teach some employees sign language is under way. The Grosvenor Resort, on Hotel Plaza Boulevard, has excellent facilities but no teletype reservations line.

➤ WDW Wheelchair-Accessible Lodgings: **Yacht Club** (☎ 407/934–7000). **Beach Club** (☎ 407/934–8000). **Dixie Landings** (☎ 407/934–6000). **Port Orleans** (☎ 407/934–5000). **Grand Floridian** (☎ 407/824–3000; 407/934–7639 Walt Disney World Central Reservations; 407/939–7670 TTY). **All-Star Sports Resort** (☎ 407/939–5000). **All-Star Music Resort** (☎ 407/939–6000). **All-Star Movies Resort** (☎ 407/939–7000). **Wilderness Lodge** (☎ 407/824–3200). **BoardWalk** (☎ 407/939–5100). **Coronado Springs Resort** (☎ 407/939–0300).

➤ Wheelchair-Accessible Lodgings Elsewhere: **Embassy Suites Resorts Lake Buena Vista** (☎ 407/239–1144 or 800/362–2779; 800/451–4833 TTY). **Embassy Suites International Drive South** (☎ 800/433–7275; 407/352–1400 TTY).

➤ GOOD HOTELS FOR VISION-IMPAIRED GUESTS: **Wyndham Resort and Spa at WDW Resort** (☎ 407/827–2727 or 800/327–2990). **Embassy Suites Resorts** (☞ *above*).

➤ RESERVATIONS: **WDW Special Request Reservations** (☎ 407/354–1853).

RESERVATIONS

When discussing accessibility with an operator or reservations agent, **ask hard questions.** Are there any stairs, inside *or* out? Are there grab bars next to the toilet *and* in the shower/tub? How wide is the doorway to the room? To the bathroom? For the most extensive facilities meeting the latest legal specifications, **opt for newer accommodations.**

THEME PARKS

Guests with disabilities can **take advantage of a wide variety of discounts:** 50% at Busch Gardens for wheelchair users and the visually or hearing impaired; at least 50% at Cypress Gardens and SeaWorld for guests with visual or hearing impairments; and 20% at Universal Studios for those with a disability that limits enjoyment of the park.

Accessibility in the area is constantly improving for people who use wheelchairs. At Walt Disney World, a new standard of access was set with the opening of Disney's Animal Kingdom; all attractions, restaurants, and shops are wheelchair accessible. Disney–MGM Studios comes in a close second, followed by Epcot, some of whose rides have a tailgate that drops down to provide a level entrance to the ride vehicle. Though the Magic Kingdom, now in its third decade, was designed before architects gave consideration to access issues, renovation plans are under way. Even so, the 20 or so accessible attractions combine with the live entertainment around the park to provide a memorable experience. For specific accessibility information, *see* the For Travelers with Disabilities section for each park.

Universal Studios and SeaWorld are both substantially barrier-free. Cypress Gardens is also mostly wheelchair-accessible.

In some attractions, you may be required to transfer to a wheelchair if you use a scooter. In others, you must be able to leave your own wheelchair to board the ride vehicle and must have a traveling companion assist, as park staff cannot do so. Attractions with emergency evacuation routes that have narrow walkways or steps require additional mobility. Turbulence on other attractions poses a problem for some guests.

Rest rooms at all of these parks have standard accessible stalls. More spacious facilities are available in first-aid stations.

WDW and Universal have produced descriptive cassette tapes that can be borrowed, along with portable tape recorders (deposit required); SeaWorld, with a week's notice, provides an escort or interpreter to take people with visual or hearing impairments through the park. The other parks have no services for the people with visual impairments. Service animals, while welcome, must be leashed or in a harness; they may board many rides, but not all—usually not those with loud noises, pyrotechnics, and other intense effects.

Walt Disney World publishes a special guidebook describing the theme and story of various attractions in the three parks. At Epcot, you can rent personal translator units that amplify the sound tracks of seven shows ($4; $40 deposit). There and in the Magic Kingdom (and in Disney–MGM Studios by special arrangement), four-hour guided tours in sign language are available. Advance reservations are a must; provide two weeks' notice if possible ($5 adults, $3.50 children 3–9).

Both Universal Studios and SeaWorld can also provide guides fluent in sign language with advance notice; Universal also has scripts available for all its shows. Busch Gardens and Cypress Gardens do not offer assistance in sign.

➤ THEME-PARK INFORMATION FOR GUESTS WITH DISABILITIES: **Walt Disney World** (☎ 407/560–6233; 407/827–

5141 TTY). **Universal Studios** (☎ 407/354–6356; 407/363–8265 TTY). **SeaWorld** (☎ 407/351–3600; 407/363–2617 TTY).

TRANSPORTATION

Outside of Disney property there are some lift-equipped vans for rent and some shuttle services available, but you'll need to plan your itinerary beforehand. Inside Disney, every other bus on each route is lift-equipped and there's never more than a 30-minute wait for hotel-to-theme-park trips. Consult transportation companies for more information.

Designated parking is available for guests with disabilities. It's near the turnstile area for most parks. The Magic Kingdom's special lot is near the Transportation and Ticket Center, where ferries depart for the Magic Kingdom and monorails travel there and to Epcot. Monorail entrances are level, but the ramp is quite steep.

➤ COMPLAINTS: **Disability Rights Section** (⊠ U.S. Department of Justice, Civil Rights Division, Box 66738, Washington, DC 20035-6738, ☎ 202/514–0301 or 800/514–0301; TTY 202/514–0301 or 800/514–0301, FAX 202/307–1198) for general complaints. **Aviation Consumer Protection Division** (☞ Air Travel, *above*) for airline-related problems. **Civil Rights Office** (⊠ U.S. Department of Transportation, Departmental Office of Civil Rights, S-30, 400 7th St. SW, Room 10215, Washington, DC 20590, ☎ 202/366–4648, FAX 202/366–9371) for problems with surface transportation.

➤ TRANSPORTATION: **Go Special Coach** (⊠ 7103 Burnway Dr., Orlando 32819, ☎ 407/345–1600 or 877/345–1600).

TRAVEL AGENCIES

In the United States, the Americans with Disabilities Act requires that travel firms serve the needs of all travelers. Some agencies specialize in working with people with disabilities.

➤ TRAVELERS WITH MOBILITY PROBLEMS: **Access Adventures** (⊠ 206 Chestnut Ridge Rd., Rochester, NY 14624, ☎ 716/889–9096,

dltravel@prodigy.net), run by a former physical-rehabilitation counselor. **CareVacations** (⊠ 5-5110 50th Ave., Leduc, Alberta T9E 6V4, ☎ 780/986–6404 or 877/478–7827, FAX 780/986–8332, www.carevacations.com), for group tours and cruise vacations. **Flying Wheels Travel** (⊠ 143 W. Bridge St., Box 382, Owatonna, MN 55060, ☎ 507/451–5005 or 800/535–6790, FAX 507/451–1685, thq@ll.net, www.flyingwheels.com). **Hinsdale Travel Service** (⊠ 201 E. Ogden Ave., Suite 100, Hinsdale, IL 60521, ☎ 630/325–1335, FAX 630/325–1342, hinstrvl@interaccess.com).

➤ TRAVELERS WITH DEVELOPMENTAL DISABILITIES: **New Directions** (⊠ 5276 Hollister Ave., Suite 207, Santa Barbara, CA 93111, ☎ 805/967–2841 or 888/967–2841, FAX 805/964–7344, newdirec@silcom.com, www.silcom.com/ậnewdirec/). **Sprout** (⊠ 893 Amsterdam Ave., New York, NY 10025, ☎ 212/222–9575 or 888/222–9575, FAX 212/222–9768, sprout@interport.net, www.gosprout.org).

WHEELCHAIRS

Probably the most comfortable course is to bring your wheelchair from home. However, except in theater-style shows, access may be difficult if it's wider than 24½ inches and longer than 32 inches (44 inches for scooters); consult attraction hosts and hostesses. Thefts of personal wheelchairs while guests are inside attractions are rare but have been known to occur. Take the precautions you would in any public place.

Wheelchair rentals are available from area medical-supply companies that will deliver to your hotel and let you keep the chair for the duration of your vacation. You can also rent by the day in major theme parks ($6 a day for wheelchairs, $25–$30 daily for the limited number of scooters, plus a deposit; *see* Chapters 2, 3, and 4 for specifics).

In Disney parks, since rental locations are relatively close to parking, it may be a good idea to send someone ahead to get the wheelchair and bring it back to the car; at day's end, a Disney host or hostess may escort you to your car and then return the wheelchair for you. Here and at the other major area theme parks, rented wheelchairs that disappear while you're in a ride can be replaced throughout the parks—ask any staffer for the nearest location. Attaching some small personal item to the wheelchair may prevent other guests from taking yours by mistake.

DISCOUNTS & DEALS

There are plenty of ways to save money while you're in the Orlando area. Be a smart shopper and **compare all your options** before making decisions. Always keep in mind that what you get is just as important as what you save.

A plane ticket bought with a promotional coupon from travel clubs, coupon books, and direct-mail offers may not be cheaper than the least expensive fare from a discount ticket agency. And always keep in mind that what you get is just as important as what you save.

BEST WAYS TO SAVE

1. Shop around carefully for theme-park tickets. Discounted theme-park tickets are widely available. Be sure to **look into combination tickets** and **second-day free tickets** that get you admission to multiple theme parks or two days' admission for the price of one to a single park. The Orlando FlexTicket is just one example of the various combination tickets out there (☞ Admission sections for each theme park). You can also visit the **Orlando/Orange County Convention and Visitors Bureau** on International Drive (☞ Visitor Information, *below*) or stop in one of the many ticket booths around town, including the **Tourism Bureau of Orlando, Know Before You Go,** and the **Tourist Information Center of Orlando.** Do watch out for extra-cheap tickets (they may be expired) and discounts that require you to take time-share tours—unless you're interested in a time-share, that is. If you're a member of the **American Automobile Association,** be sure to ask at your local club about getting discounted tickets. Find out if your company belongs to the **Universal Fan Club** or the **Magic Kingdom Club,** which offer discount

schemes to members' employees. Take advantage of next-day free offers on tickets, which are often available. You'll get into a theme park a second day for the price of a one-day ticket. At Busch Gardens Tampa, go for the Twilight Tickets, available after 3 PM.

2. Buy your tickets as soon as you know you're going. Prices typically go up two or three times a year, so you might beat a price hike—and save a little money.

3. Stay at hotels on U.S. 192 around Kissimmee and on International Drive that offer free transportation to and from the park. Getting to and from the parks may take a little extra time, but you won't have to pay to rent a car—or to park it.

4. In deciding whether or not to rent a car, do the math. Weigh the cost of renting against what it will cost to get your entire party to and from the airport and the theme parks and any other places you want to go. If you are traveling with a group of more than four, you may actually save money by renting a car.

5. Choose accommodations with a kitchen. You can stock up on breakfast items in a nearby supermarket, and save time—and money—by eating your morning meal in your hotel.

6. Watch your shopping carefully. Theme-park merchandisers are excellent at displaying the goods so that you can't resist them. You may find that some of the items for sale are also available at home—for quite a bit less. One way to cope is to give every member of your family a souvenir budget—adults and children alike.

7. Shop around for vacation packages. But when you do, buy a package that gives you exactly the features you want. Don't go for one that includes admission parks or other sites you don't care about.

8. Go off-season. You can see more in less time and lodging rates are lower.

9. If you fly to Orlando, book your flights well in advance so that you

THE GOLD GUIDE / SMART TRAVEL TIPS

have the best selection of the airlines' extra-low fares.

10. If you plan to eat in a full-service restaurant, have a large, late breakfast, then eat lunch late in the day in lieu of dinner. Lunchtime prices are almost always lower than dinnertime prices.

➤ DISCOUNT TICKET OFFICES: **Orlando/Orange County Convention and Visitors Bureau** (☞ Visitor Information, *below*) on International Drive. **Tourism Bureau of Orlando** (☎ 407/363–5800). **Know Before You Go** (☎ 407/352–9813). **Tourist Information Center of Orlando** (☎ 407/363–2901).

For further discount information, if applicable, *see* Disabilities & Accessibility, *above,* and Senior-Citizen Travel, *below.*

DISCOUNT RESERVATIONS

To save money, **look into discount reservations services** with toll-free numbers, which use their buying power to get a better price on hotels, airline tickets, even car rentals. When booking a room, always **call the hotel's local toll-free number** (if one is available) rather than the central reservations number—you'll often get a better price. Always ask about special packages or corporate rates.

➤ AIRLINE TICKETS: ☎ **800/FLY–4–LESS.** ☎ **800/FLY–ASAP.**

➤ HOTEL ROOMS: **Accommodations Express** (☎ 800/444–7666, www.accommodationsexpress.com). **Central Reservation Service (CRS)** (☎ 800/548–3311). **Hotel Reservations Network** (☎ 800/964–6835, www.hoteldiscounts.com). **Players Express Vacations** (☎ 800/458–6161, www.playersexpress.com). **RMC Travel** (☎ 800/245–5738, www.rmcwebtravel.com). **Steigenberger Reservation Service** (☎ 800/223–5652, www.srs-worldhotels.com). **Turbotrip.com** (☎ 800/473–7829, www.turbotrip.com).

PACKAGE DEALS

Don't confuse packages and guided tours. When you buy a package, you travel on your own, just as though you had planned the trip yourself. Fly/drive packages, which combine airfare and car rental, are often a good deal.

EMERGENCY SERVICES

All the area's major theme parks have first-aid centers. Hospital emergency rooms are open 24 hours a day. For minor emergencies visit the Housemed clinic (open daily 9–9) or its minor-emergency mobile service, which offers hotel-room visits by physicians for minor medical care and dispenses nonnarcotic medication. Centra Care, closer to Orlando (a block east of Kirkman Road), is open daily 8 AM–midnight. Near WDW, the most convenient facility is the Buena Vista Walk-in Medical Center, near Downtown Disney, open daily 8–8; it also provides free shuttle service from any of the Disney theme park's first-aid stations.

➤ CONTACTS: **Police or ambulance** (☎ 911).

➤ DOCTORS & DENTISTS: **Emergency Dental Referral** (☎ 407/847–7474).

➤ HOSPITALS & CLINICS: **Orlando Regional Medical Center/Sand Lake Hospital** (☎ 407/351–8500), near International Drive. **Housemed** (✉ 2901 Parkway Blvd., Kissimmee, ☎ 407/396–1195, 407/648–9234, or 407/846–2093). **Centra Care** (☎ 407/660–8118). **Buena Vista Walk-in Medical Center** (☎ 407/828–3434).

➤ 24-HOUR PHARMACIES: **Eckerd Drugs** (✉ 670 Lee Rd., Orlando, ☎ 407/628–4550), off I–4 at the Lee Road exit. **Walgreens** (✉ 6201 International Dr., Orlando, ☎ 407/345–8311 or 407/345–8402, opposite Wet 'n Wild; 4578 S. Kirkman Rd., Orlando, ☎ 407/293–8458, just north of Universal Studios; 5935 W. Irlo Bronson Memorial Hwy., Kissimmee, ☎ 407/396–2002 or 407/396–1006, next to the Old Town shopping center).

GAY & LESBIAN TRAVEL

June's annual Gay Days Orlando, sponsored by many national corporations, includes a week's worth of activities. Contact the Gay and Lesbian Community Services (GLCS) for more information.

➤ LOCAL INFORMATION: **Gay and Lesbian Community Services** (✉ 714

E. Colonial Dr., Orlando, FL 32803
(☎ 407/843–4297).

HOLIDAYS

Major national holidays include New
Year's Day (Jan. 1); Martin Luther
King, Jr., Day (3rd Mon. in Jan.);
President's Day (3rd Mon. in Feb.);
Memorial Day (last Mon. in May);
Independence Day (July 4); Labor
Day (1st Mon. in Sept.); Thanksgiving
Day (4th Thurs. in Nov.); Christmas
Eve and Christmas Day (Dec. 24 and
25); and New Year's Eve (Dec. 31).

INSURANCE

The most useful travel insurance plan
is a comprehensive policy that includes coverage for trip cancellation
and interruption, default, trip delay,
and medical expenses (with a waiver
for preexisting conditions).

Without insurance you will lose all or
most of your money if you cancel
your trip, regardless of the reason.
Default insurance covers you if your
tour operator, airline, or cruise line
goes out of business. Trip-delay
covers expenses that arise because of
bad weather or mechanical delays.
Study the fine print when comparing
policies.

British and Australian citizens need
extra medical coverage when traveling overseas. Always **buy travel
policies directly from the insurance
company**; if you buy them from a
cruise line, airline, or tour operator
that goes out of business you probably will not be covered for the agency
or operator's default, a major risk.
Before making any purchase, **review
your existing health and home-
owner's policies** to find what they
cover away from home.

➤ TRAVEL INSURERS: In the U.S.:
Access America (✉ 6600 W. Broad
St., Richmond, VA 23230, ☎ 804/
285–3300 or 800/284–8300, FAX 804/
673–1583, www.previewtravel.com).
Travel Guard International (✉ 1145
Clark St., Stevens Point, WI 54481,
☎ 715/345–0505 or 800/826–1300,
FAX 800/955–8785,
www.noelgroup.com). In Canada:
Voyager Insurance (✉ 44 Peel Center
Dr., Brampton, Ontario L6T 4M8, ☎
905/791–8700; 800/668–4342 in
Canada).

➤ INSURANCE INFORMATION: In the
U.K.: **Association of British Insurers**
(✉ 51–55 Gresham St., London
EC2V 7HQ, ☎ 020/7600–3333, FAX
020/7696–8999, info@abi.org.uk,
www.abi.org.uk). In Australia: **Insurance Council of Australia** (☎ 03/
9614–1077, FAX 03/9614–7924).

LODGING

The lodgings we list in the Lodgings
and Cocoa Beach chapters are the
cream of the crop in each price category. We always list the facilities that
are available—but we don't specify
whether they cost extra: When pricing
accommodations, always ask what's
included and what costs extra. Properties indicated by an ✕🏠 are lodging establishments whose restaurant
warrants a special trip.

CATEGORY	COST*
$$$$	over $200
$$$	$100–$200
$$	$60–$100
$	under $60

*All rates for two adults traveling with
up to two children during high season
plus 10% tax.*

Assume that hotels operate on the
European Plan (EP, with no meals).

APARTMENT RENTALS

If you want a home base that's roomy
enough for a family and comes with
cooking facilities, **consider a furnished
rental.** These can save you money,
especially if you're traveling with a
group. Home-exchange directories
sometimes list rentals as well as
exchanges.

➤ INTERNATIONAL AGENTS: **Interhome**
(✉ 1990 N.E. 163rd St., Suite 110,
N. Miami Beach, FL 33162, ☎ 305/
940–2299 or 800/882–6864, FAX 305/
940–2911, interhomeu@aol.com,
www.interhome.com).

B&BS

Though inns aren't as plentiful in the
immediate Walt Disney World and
Orlando area as are big resorts, you'll
find some charming B&Bs away from
tourism central, such as in the quaint
town of Mount Dora.

CAMPING

Camping opportunities range from
Walt Disney World's own Fort

Wilderness (☞ Chapter 7) to the lakeside campgrounds of local fishing camps (☞ Chapter 9).

HOME EXCHANGES

If you would like to exchange your home for someone else's, **join a home-exchange organization,** which will send you its updated listings of available exchanges for a year and will include your own listing in at least one of them. It's up to you to make specific arrangements.

➤ EXCHANGE CLUBS: **HomeLink International** (✉ Box 650, Key West, FL 33041, ☎ 305/294–7766 or 800/638–3841, FAX 305/294–1448, usa@homelink.org, www.homelink.org; $98 per year). **Intervac U.S.** (✉ Box 590504, San Francisco, CA 94159, ☎ 800/756–4663, FAX 415/435–7440, www.intervac.com; $89 per year includes two catalogues).

HOSTELS

No matter what your age, you can **save on lodging costs by staying at hostels.** In some 5,000 locations in more than 70 countries around the world, Hostelling International (HI), the umbrella group for a number of national youth-hostel associations, offers single-sex, dorm-style beds, and, at many hostels, rooms for couples and family accommodations. Membership in any HI national hostel association, open to travelers of all ages, allows you to stay in HI-affiliated hostels at member rates; one-year membership is about $25 for adults (C$26.75 in Canada, £9.30 in the U.K., $30 in Australia, and $30 in New Zealand); hostels run about $10–$25 per night. Members have priority if the hostel is full; they're also eligible for discounts around the world, even on rail and bus travel in some countries.

➤ ORGANIZATIONS: **Hostelling International—American Youth Hostels** (✉ 733 15th St. NW, Suite 840, Washington, DC 20005, ☎ 202/783–6161, FAX 202/783–6171, www.hiayh.org). **Hostelling International—Canada** (✉ 400–205 Catherine St., Ottawa, Ontario K2P 1C3, ☎ 613/237–7884, FAX 613/237–7868, www.hostellingintl.ca). **Youth Hostel Association of England and Wales** (✉ Trevelyan House, 8 St. Stephen's Hill, St. Albans, Hertfordshire AL1 2DY, ☎ 01727/855215 or 01727/845047, FAX 01727/844126, www.yha.uk). **Australian Youth Hostel Association** (✉ 10 Mallett St., Camperdown, NSW 2050, ☎ 02/9565–1699, FAX 02/9565–1325, www.yha.com.au). **Youth Hostels Association of New Zealand** (✉ Box 436, Christchurch, New Zealand, ☎ 03/379–9970, FAX 03/365–4476, www.yha.org.nz).

HOTELS

Every major hotel chain has at least one link in the Orlando area, and many have several. Because of the huge number of tourists visiting Orlando, hoteliers tend to put their best foot forward, resulting in accommodations better than what you might expect. In addition, the best independents meet the competition head on, offering many of the same amenities as the chains.

➤ TOLL-FREE NUMBERS: **Adam's Mark** (☎ 800/444–2326, www.adamsmark.com). **Baymont Inns** (☎ 800/428–3438, www.baymontinns.com). **Best Western** (☎ 800/528–1234, www.bestwestern.com). **Choice** (☎ 800/221–2222, www.hotelchoice.com). **Clarion** (☎ 800/252–7466, www.choicehotels.com). **Comfort** (☎ 800/228–5150, www.comfortinn.com). **Days Inn** (☎ 800/325–2525, www.daysinn.com). **Doubletree and Red Lion Hotels** (☎ 800/222–8733, www.doubletreehotels.com). **Embassy Suites** (☎ 800/362–2779, www.embassysuites.com). **Fairfield Inn** (☎ 800/228–2800, www.marriott.com). **Four Seasons** (☎ 800/332–3442, www.fourseasons.com). **Hilton** (☎ 800/445–8667, www.hiltons.com). **Holiday Inn** (☎ 800/465–4329, www.holiday-inn.com). **Howard Johnson** (☎ 800/654–4656, www.hojo.com). **Hyatt Hotels & Resorts** (☎ 800/233–1234, www.hyatt.com). **La Quinta** (☎ 800/531–5900, www.laquinta.com). **Marriott** (☎ 800/228–9290, www.marriott.com). **Omni** (☎ 800/843–6664, www.omnihotels.com). **Quality Inn** (☎ 800/228–5151, www.qualityinn.com). **Radisson** (☎ 800/333–3333, www.radisson.com). **Ramada** (☎ 800/228–2828, www.ramada.com).

Renaissance Hotels & Resorts (☎ 800/468–3571, www.hotels.com). **Sheraton** (☎ 800/325–3535, www.sheraton.com). **Sleep Inn** (☎ 800/753–3746, www.sleepinn.com). **Westin Hotels & Resorts** (☎ 800/228–3000, www.starwood.com). **Wyndham Hotels & Resorts** (☎ 800/822–4200, www.wyndham.com).

MONEY MATTERS

Be prepared to spend and spend—and spend some more. Despite relatively low airfares and car-rental rates, cash seems to evaporate out of wallets and credit cards seem to melt in the hot Orlando sun. Theme-park admission averages $40 per day per person—not counting all the $2 soft drinks and $10–$20 souvenirs. Hotels range so wildly—from $30 a night to 10 or more times that—that you'll have to do some hard thinking about just how much you want to spend. Meals away from the theme parks cost about as much as they do in the average city.

Prices throughout this guide are given for adults. Substantially reduced fees are almost always available for children, students, and senior citizens. For information on taxes, *see* Taxes, *below.*

ATMS

There are ATMs in the entry areas of all theme parks as well as here and there around town. Often there is a $1–$1.50 charge if you're not a customer of the specific bank that maintains the ATM.

CREDIT CARDS

Credit cards are almost universally accepted in the Orlando and Kissimmee area.

Throughout this guide, the following abbreviations are used: **AE,** American Express; **D,** Discover; **DC,** Diner's Club; **MC,** MasterCard; and **V,** Visa.

PACKING

Comfortable walking shoes or sneakers are essential. The entire area is extremely casual, day and night, so men need a jacket and tie in only a handful of restaurants. For sightseeing and theme-park visits, pack cool, comfortable clothing. The perfect theme-park outfit begins with shorts with large pockets made of a breathable, quick-drying material, topped either by a T-shirt of similar material or, for women, a bathing suit top. Most theme parks either have water rides that leave you drenched or interactive fountains that are so tempting on hot days—that is, most of the time—that you're hard put to pass them by. Experienced theme-park visitors also suggest using fanny pack rather than a tote bag or purse. Sunglasses are a must—as is sunscreen. Don't ruin your trip by getting sunburned on the first day.

In winter, be prepared for a range of temperatures: Take clothing that you can layer, including a sweater and warm jacket. It can get quite cool in December and January. For summer, you'll want a sun hat, and a poncho and folding umbrella in case of sudden thunderstorms (a daily occurrence in summer). In your carry-on luggage, **pack an extra pair of eyeglasses or contact lenses** and **enough of any medication you take** to last the entire trip. You may also ask your doctor to write a spare prescription using the drug's generic name, since brand names may vary from country to country. In luggage to be checked, **never pack prescription drugs or valuables.** To avoid customs delays, carry medications in their original packaging. And don't forget to carry with you the addresses of offices that handle refunds of lost traveler's checks.

CHECKING LUGGAGE

How many carry-on bags you can bring with you is up to the airline. Most allow two, but not always, so make sure that everything you carry aboard will fit under your seat or in the overhead bin, and get to the gate early. Note that if you have a seat at the back of the plane, you'll probably board first, while the overhead bins are still empty.

If you are flying internationally, note that baggage allowances may be determined not by piece but by weight—generally 88 pounds (40 kilograms) in first class, 66 pounds (30 kilograms) in business class, and 44 pounds (20 kilograms) in economy.

THE GOLD GUIDE / SMART TRAVEL TIPS

Airline liability for baggage is limited to $1,250 per person on flights within the United States. On international flights it amounts to $9.07 per pound or $20 per kilogram for checked baggage (roughly $640 per 70-pound bag) and $400 per passenger for unchecked baggage. You can buy additional coverage at check-in for about $10 per $1,000 of coverage, but it excludes a rather extensive list of items, shown on your airline ticket.

Do remember to **pack any toy guns, toy knives, and the like that you buy in theme parks in your checked luggage.** Security may give you a hard time if you try to carry them on board.

Before departure, **itemize your bags' contents** and their worth, and label the bags with your name, address, and phone number. (If you use your home address, cover it so potential thieves can't see it readily.) Inside each bag, **pack a copy of your itinerary.** At check-in, **make sure that each bag is correctly tagged** with the destination airport's three-letter code. If your bags arrive damaged or fail to arrive at all, file a written report with the airline before leaving the airport.

PASSPORTS & VISAS

➤ CONTACTS: **U.S. Embassy Visa Information Line** (☎ 01891/200–290; calls cost 49p per minute, 39p per minute cheap rate) for U.S. visa information. **U.S. Embassy Visa Branch** (⊠ 5 Upper Grosvenor Sq., London W1A 1AE) for U.S. visa information; send a self-addressed, stamped envelope. **U.S. Consulate General** (⊠ Queen's House, Queen St., Belfast BTI 6EO) if you live in Northern Ireland. **Office of Australia Affairs** (⊠ 59th floor, MLC Centre, 19–29 Martin Pl., Sydney, NSW 2000) if you live in Australia. **Office of New Zealand Affairs** (⊠ 29 Fitzherbert Terr., Thorndon, Wellington) if you live in New Zealand.

PASSPORT OFFICES

The best time to apply for a passport or to renew is in fall and winter. Before any trip, check your passport's expiration date, and, if necessary, renew it as soon as possible.

➤ AUSTRALIAN CITIZENS: **Australian Passport Office** (☎ 131–232, www.dfat.gov.au/passports).

➤ CANADIAN CITIZENS: **Passport Office** (☎ 819/994–3500 or 800/567–6868, www.dfait-maeci.gc.ca/passport).

➤ NEW ZEALAND CITIZENS: **New Zealand Passport Office** (☎ 04/494–0700, www.passports.govt.nz).

➤ U.K. CITIZENS: **London Passport Office** (☎ 0990/210–410) for fees and documentation requirements and to request an emergency passport.

PETS

It's really best to leave Rover at home, but if you just can't part with your best friend, all the parks have kennel facilities. They will provide a cage, water and food, but you have to do the walking, which, of course, takes up valuable vacation time. On-site Disney resort guests may board their pets for $9 per night; others pay $11 per night. The daily rate is $6.

PLANNING YOUR TRIP

Careful planning is key to the most hassle-free visit to the Orlando area. The first step is to **figure out everything you want to see and do in the area.** Will you be staying put, or do you want to spend some time at the beach? Once you've settled on your sightseeing priorities, you can figure out how long you want to stay, make reservations, and buy tickets.

HOW LONG TO STAY

There are a couple of ways to approach this question. If your objective is to enjoy the complete Orlando resort experience, seven days is a comfortable period to allow; this gives you time to see all of the parks at Universal and WDW and to take in one water park, to sample the restaurants and entertainment, and to spend a bit of time around the pool. Eight days would be better. Figure on an additional day for every other area theme park you want to visit, and then add your travel time to and from home.

If you're coming to the area mostly to go on the rides and see the theme parks, allow one day per theme park. This supposes that you're willing to start out early every day, move quickly, breeze through shops, and hurry through meals. Then add your travel time to and from home.

In either case, add time for exploring Orlando off the beaten track, and for shopping in Orlando's flea markets and discount malls. In addition, **add an extra day or two if you're traveling with small children,** who may have limited patience for marathon touring; if you want to linger during your stays; if you're staying off Disney property or using local shuttle transportation rather than your own or a rental car to accommodate the extra time you will spend just getting to and from your destinations; or if you're visiting during a busy period, when long lines will make it nearly impossible to see all the most popular attractions—unless you have a lot of stamina for long days on your feet and are willing to be on the go from early in the morning until park closing. You could easily spend more than two weeks in the area and still not see it all.

CREATING AN ITINERARY

Once you know what you want to see and do, the first step is to **lay out a day-by-day touring plan,** using the Strategies for Your Visit sections of our theme-parks sections in Chapters 2, 3, and 4 and the italicized Crowds and Strategy information following each review. Don't try to plot your route from hour to hour; instead break the day up into morning, afternoon, and evening sections. Make a note of the busiest days in each park you've planned to visit, and schedule yourself accordingly. Then, beginning with the dates on which you plan to visit, **decide which parks you will see on each day.**

Think creatively. If you're staying on Walt Disney World property in a not-too-busy period and have at least five days, **consider spending afternoons at one of the water parks,** at your hotel swimming pool, or at a spa or sports facility. If you buy a multiday park-hopper pass, which is good for unlimited visits to WDW's major parks, you can also **visit two or more theme parks in a day**—say, do the Magic Kingdom in the morning, when the park isn't crowded, and spend an afternoon in Epcot's Future World, that area's least busy time.

Put each day's plan on a separate index card, and carry the card with you as you explore Orlando.

Finally, **make a schedule for calling for any reservations** you will need. Make a list of all the things you want to do that require reservations. Note on the list how far in advance you can book for each. Then, based on your travel schedule, designate the date on which you should call for the reservations you want. Some reservations can be made as soon as you book your hotel or before; others will have to wait until you're in the area.

BUYING YOUR TICKETS

If you aren't signing up for an escorted tour or travel package, buy your tickets in advance. This will save you time in Orlando, and you may beat a price hike and save a little money as well.

The Orlando airport has Universal Studios, SeaWorld, and Walt Disney World gift shops, where tickets, maps, and information are available. Buying tickets here while waiting for your bags to be unloaded will save time later. Local Disney Stores also sell certain multiday passes. Plenty of other outlets around Orlando sell theme-park tickets, including stores and, most likely, your hotel.

SENIOR-CITIZEN TRAVEL

Bear in mind that school vacation times can spell ordeal rather than adventure if you have limited energy or patience. What endurance you have will go further if you arrive in the theme parks at opening time or even before. Do a little homework about your destination, and have a plan of action. In the morning take in first those attractions that you most want to see. This way you can take it easy when the day warms up. Then relax in the shade, have a nice long lunch, see some shows in air-conditioned theaters, and maybe even go back to your hotel to relax around the pool, read, or nap. Refreshed, you can return to one of the theme parks, when they're open late, or explore Pleasure Island, Church Street Station, or Orlando's other after-dark options. Don't overdo it.

To qualify for age-related discounts, **mention your senior-citizen status up front** when booking hotel reservations (not when checking out) and before you're seated in restaurants (not when paying the bill). When renting a car, ask about promotional car-rental discounts, which can be cheaper than senior-citizen rates.

➤ EDUCATIONAL PROGRAMS: **Elderhostel** (✉ 75 Federal St., 3rd floor, Boston, MA 02110, ☎ 877/426–8056, FAX 877/426–2166, www.elder-hostel.org).

SIGHTSEEING TOURS

IN THE THEME PARKS

Guided tours are available in all the area's major theme parks (☞ A to Z sections *in* individual theme-park descriptions *in* Chapters 2, 3, and 4).

AROUND ORLANDO

Quick, look up! Any morning in Orlando chances are fair to good that you'll spot a brightly colored hot-air balloon floating through the skies. You don't have to have your own gear to experience these silent, beautiful craft. Several operators offer hot-air balloon rides, which usually include a Continental-breakfast picnic with champagne or a gala restaurant meal. They'll take children as well as adults, though most discourage parents from bringing babies and toddlers, who may be frightened by the experience. Helicopter rides are another way to take in the scenery from high above the city; costs range from $20 to $399.

➤ BALLOON RIDES: **Rise & Float Balloon Tours** (✉ 5767 Major Blvd., opposite Universal Studios at the Mystery Fun House, Orlando, ☎ 407/352–8191).

➤ HELICOPTER RIDES: **Air Orlando** (✉ 8990 International Dr., Orlando, ☎ 407/354–1400).

STUDENTS

➤ I.D.S & SERVICES: **Council Travel** (CIEE; ✉ 205 E. 42nd St., 14th floor,

New York, NY 10017, ☎ 212/822–2700 or 888/268–6245, FAX 212/822–2699, info@councilexchanges.org, www.councilexchanges.org) for mail orders only, in the U.S. **Travel Cuts** (✉ 187 College St., Toronto, Ontario M5T 1P7, ☎ 416/979–2406 or 800/667–2887, www.travelcuts.com) in Canada.

TAXES

Tourists pay a 5% bed tax as well as a restaurant tax ranging from 6% to 7%, depending on which county they're in. There are no airport departure taxes.

SALES TAX

Orlando-area sales tax varies from 6% to 7%; it is 6% in Orange County, 7% in Osceola and Seminole counties. You will pay different sales tax within Walt Disney World depending on where you are in the complex. At other major area theme parks, which are all in Orange County, you pay 6%. Sales taxes are levied on clothing, souvenirs, and snack items.

TAXIS

Taxi fares start at $2.45 and cost $1.40 for each mile thereafter. Sample fares: To WDW's Magic Kingdom, about $20 from International Drive, $11–$15 from U.S. 192. To Universal Studios, $6–$11 from International Drive, $25–$30 from U.S. 192. To Church Street Station, downtown, $20–$25 from International Drive, $30–$40 from U.S. 192.

For information on getting to or from the airport by taxi, *see* Airports & Transfers, *above.*

TIPPING

Whether they carry bags, open doors, deliver food, or clean rooms, hospitality employees work to receive a portion of your travel budget. In deciding how much to give, **base your tip on what the service is and how well it's performed.**

In transit, tip an airport valet $1–$3 per bag, a taxi driver 15%–20% of the fare.

For hotel staff, recommended amounts are $1–$3 per bag for a bellhop, $1–$2 per night per guest for chambermaids, $5–$10 for special concierge service, $1–$3 for a doorman who hails a cab or parks a car, 15% of the greens fee for a caddy, 15%–20% of the bill for a massage, and 15% of a room service bill.

In a restaurant, give 15%–20% of your bill before tax to the server, 5%–10% to the maître d', 15% to a bartender, and 15% of the wine bill for a wine steward who makes a special effort in selecting and serving wine.

TOURS & PACKAGES

Because everything is prearranged on a prepackaged tour or independent vacation, you'll spend less time planning—and often get it all at a good price.

BOOKING WITH AN AGENT

Travel agents are excellent resources. But it's a good idea to collect brochures from several agencies as some agents' suggestions may be influenced by relationships with tour and package firms that reward them for volume sales. If you have a special interest, **find an agent with expertise in that area**; ASTA (☞ Travel Agencies, *below*) has a database of specialists worldwide.

Make sure your travel agent knows the accommodations and other services of the place they're recommending. Ask about the hotel's location, room size, beds, and whether it has a pool, room service, or programs for children, if you care about these. Has your agent been there in person or sent others whom you can contact?

Do some homework on your own, too: local tourism boards can provide information about lesser-known and small-niche operators, some of which may sell only direct.

BUYER BEWARE

Each year consumers are stranded or lose their money when tour operators—even large ones with excellent reputations—go out of business. So **check out the operator.** Ask several travel agents about its reputation, and try to **book with a company that has a consumer-protection program.** (Look for information in the company's brochure.) In the United

States, members of the National Tour Association and the United States Tour Operators Association are required to set aside funds to cover your payments and travel arrangements in the event that the company defaults. It's also a good idea to choose a company that participates in the American Society of Travel Agents' Tour Operator Program (TOP); ASTA will act as mediator in any disputes between you and your tour operator.

Remember that the more your package or tour includes the better you can predict the ultimate cost of your vacation. Make sure you know exactly what is covered, and **beware of hidden costs.** Are taxes, tips, and transfers included? Entertainment and excursions? These can add up.

➤ TOUR-OPERATOR RECOMMENDATIONS: **American Society of Travel Agents** (☞ Travel Agencies, *below*). **National Tour Association** (NTA; ✉ 546 E. Main St., Lexington, KY 40508, ☎ 606/226–4444 or 800/682–8886, www.ntaonline.com). **United States Tour Operators Association** (USTOA; ✉ 342 Madison Ave., Suite 1522, New York, NY 10173, ☎ 212/599–6599 or 800/468–7862, FAX 212/599–6744, ustoa@aol.com, www.ustoa.com).

TRAIN TRAVEL

If you want to have your car in Florida without driving it there, consider the **Auto-Train,** which departs for Florida from Lorton, Virginia, near Washington, D.C. Its southern terminus—Sanford, Florida—is 23 mi north of Orlando.

FARES & SCHEDULES

Auto-Train (☎ 703/690–3355 or 407/323–4800).

TRAVEL AGENCIES

A good travel agent puts your needs first. Look for an agency that has been in business at least five years, emphasizes customer service, and has someone on staff who specializes in your destination. In addition, **make sure the agency belongs to a professional trade organization.** The American Society of Travel Agents (ASTA), with 27,000 agents in some 170

THE GOLD GUIDE / SMART TRAVEL TIPS

countries, is the largest and most influential in the field. Operating under the motto "Integrity in Travel," it maintains and enforces a strict code of ethics and will step in to help mediate any agent-client disputes if necessary. ASTA also maintains a Web site that includes a directory of agents. (If a travel agency is also acting as your tour operator, *see* Buyer Beware *in* Tours & Packages, *above*.)

➤ LOCAL AGENT REFERRALS: **American Society of Travel Agents** (ASTA; ☎ 800/965–2782 24-hr hot line, FAX 703/684–8319, www.astanet.com). **Association of British Travel Agents** (✉ 68–71 Newman St., London W1P 4AH, ☎ 020/7637–2444, FAX 020/7637–0713, information@abta.co.uk, www.abtanet.com). **Association of Canadian Travel Agents** (✉ 1729 Bank St., Suite 201, Ottawa, Ontario K1V 7Z5, ☎ 613/521–0474, FAX 613/521–0805, acta.ntl@sympatico.ca). **Australian Federation of Travel Agents** (✉ Level 3, 309 Pitt St., Sydney 2000, ☎ 02/9264–3299, FAX 02/9264–1085, www.afta.com.au). **Travel Agents' Association of New Zealand** (✉ Box 1888, Wellington 10033, ☎ 04/499–0104, FAX 04/499–0827, taanz@tiasnet.co.nz).

VISITOR INFORMATION

For Disney parks, hotels, dining, and entertainment reservations, contact Walt Disney World Information and Disney Reservation Center. To sit in the audience at a show being taped at Disney–MGM Studios call Production Information. Contact the numbers below for general information on the area's other theme parks. To get general information packages on the attractions of the greater Orlando area, contact the convention and visitors bureaus below. For information on destinations outside the immediate Orlando-Kissimmee area, contact the Florida Tourism Industry Marketing Corporation.

➤ DISNEY INFORMATION: **Walt Disney World Information** (✉ Box 10000, Lake Buena Vista, FL 32830, ☎ 407/824–4321; 407/827–5141 TDD). **Disney Reservation Center** (☎ 407/

934–7639; 407/939–3463 for dining). **Production Information** (☎ 407/560–4651).

➤ DETAILS ON OTHER THEME PARKS: **Universal Studios Escape** (✉ 1000 Universal Studios Plaza, Orlando, FL 32819-8000, ☎ 407/363–8000; 407/363–8265 TDD). **SeaWorld Orlando** (✉ 7007 SeaWorld Dr., Orlando, FL 32821, ☎ 407/351–3600). **Busch Gardens** (✉ Box 9158, Tampa, FL 33674, ☎ 813/987–5283).

➤ ABOUT GREATER ORLANDO: **Orlando/Orange County Convention & Visitors Bureau** (✉ 8723 International Dr., Orlando, FL 32819, ☎ 407/363–5871). **Kissimmee/St. Cloud Convention and Visitors Bureau** (✉ 1925 Bill Beck Blvd., Kissimmee, FL 34744, ☎ 407/847–5000 or 800/327–9159). **Winter Park Chamber of Commerce** (✉ Box 280, Winter Park, FL 32790, ☎ 407/644–8281).

➤ ABOUT THE STATE OF FLORIDA: **Florida Tourism Industry Marketing Corporation** (✉ Box 1100, 661 E. Jefferson St., Suite 300, Tallahassee, FL 32302, ☎ 904/487–1462, FAX 904/224–2938). In the U.K.: **ABC Florida** (✉ Box 35, Abingdon, Oxon. OX14 4TB; enclose £2 for a vacation pack, or call 0891/600–555, at 50p per minute).

FURTHER READING

Still the most perceptive book on Disney is *The Disney Version,* by Richard Schickel (Simon & Schuster, 1985). Disney's art is featured in *Disneyland: The Inside Story,* by Randy Bright (Harry N. Abrams), and a comprehensive history of the great Disney animation tradition is provided in *Disney Animation: The Illusion of Life,* by Frank Thomas and Ollie Johnston (Abbeville, 1981). For a good read about Disney and other animators, look for *Of Mice and Magic* (NAL Dutton, 1987), by Leonard Maltin. *Walt Disney: An American Original* (Pocket Books, 1980), by Bob Thomas, is full of anecdotes about the development of WDW, and Marc Elliot's *Walt Disney: Hollywood's Dark Prince* (Birch Lane Press, 1993) is a controversial look at the life of WDW's creator.

WEB SITES

Do check out the World Wide Web when you're planning. You'll find everything from current weather forecasts to virtual tours of famous cities. Fodor's Web site, www.fodors.com, is a great place to start your on-line travels. When you see a ✎ in this book, go to www.fodors.com/urls for an up-to-date link to that destination's site.

Each theme park has its own Web site: www.disney.com for Walt Disney World, www.uescape.com, for Universal Orlando www.seaworld.com, and www.buschgardens.com. These are the places to get the latest prices and operating hours and the latest information on rides and attractions. To get feedback from fellow visitors who have been there, done that, before you, check out the lively bulletin boards at www.disneyinfo.com and at www.fodors.com. To tap into the thrill-riding community, check out www.thrillride.com. Orlando is heavily represented, although you can also read about other theme parks nationwide.

WEDDINGS

Planning on living happily ever after? Then maybe you should tie the knot at Walt Disney World, as do some 1,000 couples every year. At the Fairy Tale Wedding Pavilion near the Grand Floridian Resort, the bride can ride in a Cinderella coach, have rings borne to the altar in a glass slipper, and invite Mickey and Minnie to attend the reception. Or exchange vows in the presence of sharks and dolphins at SeaWorld's *Ports of Call* events and banquet complex. While it might be impossible for Shamu to make a guest appearance, the ocean atmosphere surrounding the pavilion is tranquil.

➤ WDW WEDDING INFORMATION: **Fairy Tale Wedding Pavilion** (☎ 407/828–3400, ℻ 407/828–3744). **Ports of Call** (☎ 407/363–2200). **SeaWorld Weddings** (☎ 407/363–2273).

WHEN TO GO

Timing can spell the difference between a good vacation in the theme parks and a great one. Since the Orlando area is an obvious destination for families, the area is at its most crowded during school vacation periods. (The exception is Cypress Gardens, which, because it attracts older travelers, is busy throughout the winter.)

If you're traveling without youngsters or with just preschoolers, **avoid school holidays.** Attendance is light— i.e., the parks are busy but not packed—from early September until just before Thanksgiving. Another excellent time is January. The least crowded period of all is from just after the Thanksgiving weekend until the beginning of the Christmas holidays. If you have school-age children, however, the question of when to go is more complicated.

With schoolchildren, it's nice to avoid prime break times, but it's not always possible—or necessary. During certain periods, especially Christmas to New Year's Day, the parks are oppressively crowded, with discouraging lines. However, bigger crowds do not *always* mean longer lines, as the parks staff up and run rides at full capacity to accommodate the larger number of visitors. In addition, busy periods bring longer hours and added entertainment and parades, such as the evening Parade in Disney's Magic Kingdom, that you can't see in quiet seasons. For many children, it's more fun to be in a park with plenty of other children around.

So if possible, avoid Christmas, March (when most colleges have spring break), the Easter weeks, and mid-June to mid-August, especially around July 4 (it's not fun waiting on lines in the hot sun, anyway). Try to vacation in late May or early June (excluding Memorial Day weekend), as soon as the school year ends; in late August, if you must go in summer; or at Thanksgiving, which is not as busy as other holidays. If your children are good students, consider taking them out of school to visit during a less-congested period. Educational programs and the broadening experience of travel itself may persuade your children's teachers to

THE GOLD GUIDE / SMART TRAVEL TIPS

excuse the absence. Teachers may also arrange special study assignments relating to the trip.

Finally, before you finalize your travel schedule, call the theme parks you plan to visit in order to find out about any planned maintenance that will close major attractions you want to see.

CLIMATE

The following are average daily maximum and minimum temperatures for Orlando.

CLIMATE IN ORLANDO

Jan.	70F	21 C	May	88F	31C	Sept.	88F	31C
	49	9		67	19		74	23
Feb.	72F	22C	June	90F	32C	Oct.	83F	28C
	54	12		74	23		67	19
Mar.	76F	24C	July	90F	32C	Nov.	76F	24C
	56	13		74	23		58	14
Apr.	81F	27C	Aug.	90F	32C	Dec.	70F	21C
	63	17		74	23		52	11

➤ FORECASTS: **Weather Channel Connection** (☎ 900/932–8437), 95¢ per minute from a Touch-Tone phone.

1 DESTINATION: WALT DISNEY WORLD® RESORT, UNIVERSAL ORLANDO, AND CENTRAL FLORIDA

IT'S A NEW, NEW, NEW, NEW WORLD

S DUSK FALLS on Walt Disney World, the sky over Cinderella Castle turns a perfect pink. It is the end of your first day in Never Land, and you've racked up an Indiana Jones–worthy number of accomplishments. Suppressing the urge to squeeze just one more attraction into the day's itinerary, you beckon to your brood, who by now are moving like a trained corps de ballet, and all plunk down onto a bench. Voilà! A flock of doves wheels from the heights of the marzipan-like enchanted castle into the clouds overhead, and you realize that "Once Upon a Time" is happening this very moment.

The key to entering this sweet zone is a combination of canny strategizing and good luck—and this guide is here to get you started.

WHAT'S WHERE

Orlando is a pretty bewildering place, with its endless stream of attractions. Walt Disney World alone can flummox the planner in you, with its 46 square mi (that's twice the area of Manhattan). But don't let the selection and the enormity of it all stop you in your tracks.

Walt Disney World

Many people are surprised to learn that Walt Disney World is not a theme park. Instead, it's a huge complex of assorted diversions, including not one theme park but several, along with resort hotels, shopping and entertainment complexes, golf courses, and water parks—several of each genre. And technically, just in case you're talking within earshot of any Disney lawyers or officials, the proper name for this fantastic conglomeration in central Florida is Walt Disney World® Resort.

THE MAGIC KINGDOM➤ What most people imagine to be Walt Disney World—the Magic Kingdom—is actually just a small part of it. Similar to California's Disneyland, the Magic Kingdom is the well-spring of Mickeymania and the most popular individual theme park in the United States, welcoming millions of visitors every year. For so many of us who have grown up with Cinderella, Peter Pan, Dumbo, Davy Crockett, and Pinocchio, it's one of those magical places "so full of echoes, allusions, and half-memories as to be almost metaphysical," according to renowned travel writer Jan Morris. It's the site of such world-famous attractions as **Space Mountain, Pirates of the Caribbean, Splash Mountain,** and **It's a Small World.**

EPCOT: EXCELLENT EDUTAINMENT➤ Designed to promote enthusiasm for knowledge, Epcot is packed with multi-million-dollar attractions—rides that are sure to turn on every family's curiosity quotient and ignite every child's Jurassic spark. Epcot covers everything from dinosaurs and energy to the cultures of various nations and is more like a huge world's fair than an amusement park, a subtle blend of the entertaining and the edifying. The 40-acre World Showcase Lagoon separates its two main segments: **Future World**—anchored by the trademark 17-story silver geosphere known as **Spaceship Earth**—where the focus of activities inside the pavilions is on discovery and the fascination of science. Don't miss the funny 3-D film *Honey, I Shrunk the Audience* in the **Journey into Your Imagination** pavilion. In the second major area of Epcot, **World Showcase,** you can tour a good part of the world, minus jet lag, via exhibition pavilions that represent nations around the world.

DISNEY–MGM STUDIOS: REEL LIFE➤ With a cast that reads like the credits of the biggest blockbuster ever made—to Walt's name, add George Lucas, Jim Henson, the Duke, Bogie, and Marilyn—this is Disney's attempt to bring Hollywood to Florida. Here, more than a dozen top attractions marry movies to the latest in Disney ride technology; grace notes are the fully operational film and television production center and nostalgia tours of the "Hollywood that never was and always will be."

Disney–MGM's amazing attractions are the key to its success: there's that stunt artist's showcase, the **Indiana Jones Epic Stunt Spectacular!**; **Star Tours**, a *Star Wars* simulator adventure; **Jim Henson's Muppet*Vision 4-D**; and the **Magic of Disney Animation,** a behind-the-scenes look at Disney animators animating. The park is also home to the 13-story **Twilight Zone Tower of Terror,** the free-falling elevator that plunges more than 160 ft toward terminal velocity. Disney's first honest-to-goodness roller coaster, the **Rock 'n' Roller Coaster,** is also here.

DISNEY'S ANIMAL KINGDOM➤ Opened in spring 1998, this is the largest of all Disney parks, five times the size of the Magic Kingdom, with thrilling rides, dramatic landscapes, and close encounters with exotic animals. Its centerpiece is the wonderfully detailed 145-ft **Tree of Life,** which houses a 3-D film, *It's Tough to Be a Bug!* The park has seven major lands. The **Oasis,** the colorful entrance area, is full of exotic flora. In **Africa,** elephants, zebras, lions, and other animals roam freely, not far from the village of Harambe, which has a bustling marketplace and architecture typical of a coastal African village. In **Asia,** you can experience Bengal tigers and a high-speed white-water raft ride.

THE WETTER, THE BETTER!➤ What could be better than an entire park devoted to water rides? How about three water parks? Since the opening of the first of these, **River Country,** Disney has been uniting humans and water in a tumultuously semi-amphibious state of cohabitation. **Typhoon Lagoon** came next, followed by **Blizzard Beach.** And they're always jam-packed when the weather's steamy. The best—or is it the worst?—is the wild, 55-mph dead-drop to a splashy landing from the Summit Plummet, which feels as fast as it sounds. If you have water babies in your party, look for Typhoon Lagoon's scaled-down Ketchakiddie Creek, Blizzard Beach's Tyke's Peak, and its River Country counterpart.

SO MUCH DISNEY, SO LITTLE TIME➤ The sheer scope of Walt Disney World makes the "World" highly appropriate. Beyond the theme parks and the water parks, there's also **Downtown Disney,** a shopping and entertainment complex that encompasses **Disney's Marketplace,** an intimate open-air shopping complex; **Pleasure Is-**land, a pay-one-price nightlife complex with a sprinkling of restaurants and shops; and **Disney's West Side,** with its own blockbuster entertainment options (including a resident troupe of Cirque du Soleil acrobats and clowns as well as several theme restaurants). If you're among the lucky ones who can afford it, **Disney's VIP Tour Services** enable you to experience Walt Disney World in a new and carefree way. All the magic and adventure of the four parks awaits you with a VIP Tour Guide as your personal ambassador. If it is scheduled more than 48 hours in advance the cost is $65 per hour; otherwise, it's $85. There is a four-hour minimum tour requirement; call ☎ 407/560–6233 for information.

Universal Orlando

Up until now, Universal has been just the *other* movie park on the block. Now, though, it's reinventing itself as another destination resort. The original park was joined in May 1999 by Islands of Adventure, a blockbuster new park. In the fall of 1999, the first of five hotels to be linked together by lushly landscaped canals and walkways, Portofino Bay, opened.

UNIVERSAL STUDIOS–RIDE THE MOVIES➤ Far from being a "me-too" version of Disney–MGM Studios, Universal Studios has long been a theme park with plenty of hip originality and a saucy, sassy personality of its own, not to mention *Back to the Future* . . . The Ride, a simulator ride to end all simulator rides, and the long-time special effects star among theme-park rides—*Terminator 2* 3-D, which combines a spectacular 3-D film, live Arnold look-alikes whizzing around on bruiser Harley-Davidsons, bone-chilling fog, and more. Screams are also the order of the day at *Jaws,* where 40 ft of teeth come in for the kill and almost wind up in your lap, and *Twister: Ride It Out, Earthquake—The Big One,* and **Kongfrontation. A Day in the Park with Barney,** a boppin' musical revue and a hands-on educational playground is part of **Woody Woodpecker's KidZone,** which opened in summer 1999, giving toddlers and elementary-school-age children something else to get excited about.

ISLANDS OF ADVENTURE➤ The screams of terror and delight produced by Universal's newest theme park have been heard all the way down I-4 to Walt Disney World. Tops on the scream meter are the **Incredible Hulk Coaster**; the double coaster known as **Dueling Dragons**; and the **Amazing Adventures of Spider-Man**, the most technically complex attraction in Orlando—amazing is the operative word. There are plenty of opportunities to get wet, too: **Jurassic Park River Adventure** climaxes in a splashy 85-ft plunge; **Dudley Do-Right's Ripsaw Falls**, the first flume ride with an underwater portion, soaks every rider to the skin, as does **Popeye & Bluto's Bilge-Rat Barges**. Little ones have a land all to themselves: **Seuss Island**, where they can enter the world of *One Fish, Two Fish, Red Fish, Blue Fish* and the *Cat in the Hat.*

SeaWorld Orlando

It's the animals who are the stars here. Sleek dolphins perform like Kerri Strug, and orca whales sail through the air like featherweight Nijinskys. The world's largest zoological park, SeaWorld is entirely devoted to mammals, birds, fish, and reptiles that live in the oceans and their tributaries. Every attraction is designed to teach visitors about the marine world and its vulnerability to human use. Yet the presentations are always enjoyable, and almost always memorable. The highlight is **Shamu Stadium**, where you can see Shamu and his sidekicks propel their trainers into the air like Saturn missiles.

Busch Gardens

Wildlife at its chest-thumping best is the specialty here: Busch Gardens Tampa is one of America's leading legitimate zoos as well as a great theme park. Going eyeball-to-eyeball with a Western Lowland gorilla will please any budding Jane Goodall. Plus, there are spectacular roller coasters and other thrill rides: the twisting **Kumba**; the inverted **Montu**, whose cars are suspended from the track rather than placed on top of it; the **Tanganyika Tidal Wave**, whose 55-ft drop is an outrageous way to test zero gravity; and the new **Gwazi**, twin racing wooden coasters.

Cypress Gardens

A botanic garden, amusement park, and waterskiing circus rolled into one, Cypress Gardens is uniquely Floridian. Here flowers bloom in colors as kitschy as those of vintage tinted postcards. A 45-minute drive from Walt Disney World, the park encompasses 233 acres and contains more than 8,000

varieties of plants gathered from 75 countries. Amid all these sylvan glades is a bevy of hoop-skirted southern belles, a mammoth walk-through butterfly conservatory, and the **Water Ski Stadiums**, home to those amazing aquatic revues. Even the cerise-and-cerulean sunsets look color-coordinated with the cypress-draped canals. For fans, this is Florida at its Technicolor best.

The Space Coast

Exploration of the last remaining frontier—outer space—first became a reality at the Kennedy Space Center, an hour's drive east of Orlando. It's an hour well spent, as much for the distinctive Florida-scrub scenery en route as for the fascinating experience of the Space Center, at your journey's end. Here, at the home-launch base of America's Space Shuttle program, the history of travel was rewritten when astronauts blasted off to the moon. Highlights of a visit to the **Kennedy Space Center Visitor Complex** include two-hour bus tours that offer camera stops near Space Shuttle Launch Pads, the massive Vehicle Assembly Building, a 365-ft *Saturn V* moon rocket, and a trio of IMAX movies.

GREAT ITINERARIES

If You Have 4 Days

Most people begin by tackling the **Magic Kingdom**—the park that started it all. Go ahead and follow their lead. Then take your pick of the theme parks. **Epcot** is a must, but if you want to experience the state of the art in attraction design, head for Universal Orlando's **Islands of Adventure**. On day three, see **Universal Studios** or the smaller and more manageable **Disney–MGM Studios** if you like your theme parks tamer. On your fourth day, go for **Disney's Animal Kingdom** or **SeaWorld**. Be sure to shuffle the days around according to early entry days and other factors (☞ When to Go *in* Strategies for Your Visit *in* every theme-park section in Chapters 2, 3, and 4).

If You Have 7 Days

Spend your first four days exploring theme parks: **Magic Kingdom**, Universal Orlando's **Islands of Adventure, Epcot,** and

Animal Kingdom or **Universal Studios.** (Shuffle the days around according to the advice in When to Go; *see* Strategies for Your Visit, which ends every theme-park description in Chapters 2, 3, and 4.) Rest up on day five with a trip to **Kennedy Space Center, Cocoa Beach,** or your hotel pool. After all that theme-parking, you'll need a rest. Use day six as a chance to see **Disney-MGM Studios** or to take in Orlando beyond the theme parks—check out the **downtown area** or **Winter Park.** On day seven, visit either **SeaWorld** or one of the **Disney water parks.** If you have small children, do the beach on day three instead of day five, and consider SeaWorld instead of Epcot.

FODOR'S CHOICE

No two people agree on what makes a perfect vacation, but it's fun and helpful to know what others think. Here's a compendium compiled from the must-see lists of hundreds of Florida travelers.

WDW's Magic Kingdom

★ **Haunted Mansion.** The portrait busts bespeak the world's greatest "ghost writers" here where ghoulish wit and Victorian decor add up to a delightful scarefest.

★ **it's a small world.** Walt Disney believed we are all children at heart, and this attraction proves it. With hundreds of dancing babies—Dutch moppets in clogs, Russian balalaika players, tiny Tower of London guards, Polynesian hip-twitchers—even grumps exit grinning. It will take you a while to forget the music.

★ **Splash Mountain.** With one of the steepest drops of any flume ride in existence, you'll feel like Wile E. Coyote as you head over that final hang-on-to-your-hat moment.

Disney's Epcot

★ **Honey, I Shrunk the Audience.** The funniest 3-D show in the world, this is the wildest sensation at Epcot's Journey into Your Imagination. It remains one of Orlando's top attractions.

★ **Journey Into Your Imagination.** Let Dr. Szalinski show you how to use your senses to create a magical world after you see the *Honey, I Shrunk the Audience* show.

Disney-MGM Studios

★ **Magic of Disney Animation.** Take a behind-the-scenes look at the making of Disney's great animated cartoons.

★ **Rock 'n' Roller Coaster.** WDW's first attempt at a high-speed, multiple-inversion roller coaster is a great one.

★ **Twilight Zone Tower of Terror.** Flout every law of gravitation at this deserted hotel, where you'd be better off taking the stairs—if there were any.

Animal Kingdom

★ **Kilimanjaro Safaris.** You really do see wild animals on this lurching ride through Disney's own savanna.

★ **Tarzan Rocks!** This live show keeps the energy high with its roller-blading acrobatics, loud rock soundtrack, and amazing costumes.

Other Disney Delights

★ **Blizzard Beach.** It's the freshest and most creative of Orlando's great water parks.

★ **Disney Character Breakfasts.** Get a paw autograph from Goofy or collect a signature from any other favorite character and feast on Mickey Mouse–shape pancakes.

★ **Hoop-Dee-Doo Revue.** Stomp your feet and chow down on all the fixin's at Disney's most popular dinner show, staged several times nightly at Fort Wilderness's rustic Pioneer Hall.

★ **Main Street Electrical Parade and IllumiNations.** For a true "When You Wish Upon A Star" finale, cap it all off with the best Disney evening extravaganzas: the show in Epcot or the dazzling parade in the Magic Kingdom.

Universal Studios

★ **Back to the Future . . . The Ride.** Thrill zealots race to this ride, where Doc Brown captains a time-traveling trip covering everything from dinosaurs to the Wright Brothers at Kitty Hawk. It's the ne plus ultra of simulator rides.

★ **Terminator 2 3-D.** Join Arnold Schwarzenegger in a fierce galactic battle starring effects that are spectacular even by Orlando standards.

Universal Orlando Islands of Adventure

★ **The Amazing Adventures of Spider-Man.** Join the Marvel comics superheroes in this attraction, which combines a speed ride, simulator technology, fire and fog special effects, and more—this may well be the best theme-park ride in Orlando.

★ **Cat in the Hat.** This puts you right in the middle of that chaotic day when the cat came to play. It's great fun for children and adults alike—until Mom comes home.

★ **Dueling Dragons.** These dual multiple inversion coasters give you such a smooth, elegant ride that even those ambivalent about such rides come out wanting to go back for more.

★ **Incredible Hulk Coaster.** Hang on to everything you own, including your voice.

SeaWorld Orlando

★ **Kraken.** The park's most thrilling roller coaster, which opened in June 2000, packs in seven high-speed loops, three underground plunges, and plenty of water—all experienced in open-side seats.

★ **Shamu Stadium.** It would be unthinkable to visit SeaWorld and not pay homage to its first family.

The Space Coast

★ **Canaveral National Seashore.** Head for this vast and uncrowded stretch of natural coastline with great beaches and miles of grassy marshes.

★ **Kennedy Space Center.** Take one of the bus tours here and get a close-up view of the enormous shuttle.

Restaurants

★ **California Grill.** Dine atop the World at this chic restaurant in Disney's Contemporary Resort, where you'll enjoy a truly magical view of Cinderella Castle and the evening fireworks. $$–$$$$

★ **Enzo's on the Lake.** A former private home on a lake north of Orlando provides the setting for this Italian bistro, a local favorite for years. $$–$$$$

★ **Spoodles.** Appetizers, and lots of them, are the rule at this restaurant on Disney's BoardWalk. $$–$$$$

★ **Le Coq au Vin.** Locals and visitors alike rave about the excellent French country fare at this quiet little bistro in a small house in south Orlando. $$

★ **Artist Point.** The smoked elk, salmon, and venison on the menu here complement the rustic and original setting in Disney's could-it-be-Florida Wilderness Lodge. $–$$$

★ **Rainforest Café.** A totally fake rain-forest canopy forms the ceiling in one of Orlando's most popular restaurants. Periodic thundershowers keep things interesting. There are branches in Disney's Animal Kingdom and at Downtown Disney's Marketplace. $–$$

Hotels

★ **Disney's BoardWalk Inn and Villas.** The architectural innovations here even extend to the swimming pool, whose 200-ft water slide looks like a turn-of-the-20th-century wooden roller coaster. $$$$

★ **Hyatt Regency Grand Cypress Resort.** The word "grand" in the hotel's name is no misrepresentation. $$$$

★ **Peabody Orlando.** The hotel's flock of trained ducks parade back and forth through the lobby every morning and afternoon. $$$$

★ **Walt Disney World Dolphin.** Twin 56-ft-tall sea creatures adorn this lavish hotel next to Epcot. $$$$

★ **Walt Disney World Wilderness Lodge.** This majestic hotel is patterned after the Rocky Mountain lodges of the Teddy Roosevelt era. The mountainlike landscaping is oddly jarring in sunny Central Florida. $$$–$$$$

★ **Coronado Springs Resort.** You get considerable bang for your buck in this Southwestern on-property option. $$$

★ **Disney's All-Star Sports, Music, and Movies Resorts.** Baseball bats the size of giant sequoia trees, three-story bongos, a huge piano keyboard, and 30-ft tennis rackets give you the most fantasy for your Orlando lodging dollar. $$

FESTIVALS AND SEASONAL EVENTS

WINTER

➤ JAN.: The **CompUSA Florida Citrus Bowl Football Classic** (☎ 407/423–2476) takes place at the Orlando Citrus Bowl on January 1. Early in the month, the **Walt Disney World Marathon** sends runners on a 26.25-mi odyssey around the World (☎ 407/363–6100). At the end of January, **Scottish Highland Games** are played at Orlando's Central Florida Fairgrounds (☎ 407/672–1682). January marks the running of the **Indy 200 at Walt Disney World** (☎ 407/363–6100).

➤ FEB.: Early in February, the **Walt Disney World Village Food and Wine Festival** (☎ 407/934–6743) showcases the vintages of 60 participating wineries from all over the country, and well-known international chefs offer samplings of their latest inventions. On the first weekend of February, the **Mount Dora Art Festival** (☎ 352/383–2165) opens Central Florida's spring art fair season; attracting more than 200,000 visitors over three days, it is one of Central Florida's major outdoor events. Reenact the events of the Civil War at the **Battle of Townsend's Plantation and Civil War Festival** in Mount Dora (☎ 407/422–5560). February is the month of the Orlando Museum of Art's annual **Antiques Show and Sale** (☎ 407/672–3838),

which features exquisite paintings, furniture, and jewelry from more than 30 dealers from throughout the United States. The **National Championship Rodeo Finals** at the TD Waterhouse Centre (☎ 407/849–2020) give cowboys from all over a chance to compete. Kissimmee's **Silver Spurs Rodeo** (☎ 407/847–5000) is one of the oldest and largest events of its kind in the South, drawing cowboys from all over the United States and Canada.

SPRING

➤ MAR.: Early in March, the **Annual Central Florida Fair** is held at Orlando's Central Florida Fairgrounds (☎ 407/295–3247), with shows, rides, exhibits, and entertainment. **Universal Studios' Mardi Gras** (☎ 407/363–8000) is one of the events that has given Universal the reputation for being the best place around Orlando. You'll find Hurricane cocktails, loads of shrimp creole, lots of live music, and the largest parade east of the Louisiana Bayou, complete with beads, beads, and more beads. For its part, **Pleasure Island Mardi Gras** (☎ 407/939–7814) calls itself the biggest, most authentic Mardi Gras festival outside New Orleans. It's baseball **spring training time** all over Florida (☞ Chapter 9). Cypress Gardens kicks off its **Spring Flower Festival** (☎

813/324–2111), which runs through May and features extraordinary floral topiaries and a profusion of spring blossoms. One weekend in early March, the **Kissimmee Bluegrass Festival** showcases bluegrass bands and gospel music at the Silver Springs Arena (☎ 407/856–0246). On March 17, the **St. Patrick's Day Street Party** encourages the "wearin' o' the green" at Church Street Station (☎ 407/422–2434). Mid-month, the **Bay Hill Invitational,** a regular PGA Tour event, stops at Orlando's Bay Hill Club (☎ 407/876–2888), and the **Winter Park Sidewalk Art Festival** (☎ 407/644–8281) draws thousands of art enthusiasts to trendy Park Avenue.

➤ APR.: From early April through early May, the **Orlando Shakespeare Festival** pays tribute to the Bard at Orlando's Lake Eola Amphitheater (☎ 407/423–6905). The **Dr. Pepper Annual Surf Festival** (☎ 407/783–5813) draws professional and amateur surfers to Cocoa Beach early in April. On Easter Sunday there are **Easter Sunrise Services** at SeaWorld's Atlantis Theater (☎ 407/351–3600). During mid-April the **Easter Parade** down Main Street in the Magic Kingdom at Walt Disney World (☎ 407/939–7814) shows a whole new side to Mickey Mouse. From the end of April until early May, the **Orlando International Fringe Festival** brings 200 artists and theater troupes to perform in downtown Orlando. Cypress Gardens's **Spring**

Flower Festival wraps up in early May.

➤ MAY: Topiaries of characters and beautiful floral designs grace Epcot during its **Flower and Garden Show** (☎ 407/824–4321), which also features nightly entertainment. Mother's Day brings a special weekend for moms. The annual **"Up, Up, and Away" Airport Art Show** takes place at Orlando International Airport (☎ 407/825–2055) the third weekend of the month.

SUMMER

➤ JUNE: The city of Orlando hosts the **Cultural Heritage Festival** (☎ 407/423–6905) during the first weekend in June. **Summer Nights** kick off at Wet 'n Wild (☎ 407/351–9453) with late park hours and entertainment by live bands, contests, and hundreds of prizes. June 3 is **Gay Day** in the Magic Kingdom. Although not an official WDW event, it has grown exponentially since 1991, attracting more than 100,000 gay and lesbian visitors for events in all the Disney parks for as long as a week. Late in June and early in July is the **Silver Spurs Rodeo** (☎ 407/847–5000); there's another in early February.

➤ JULY: The Fourth of July is a big day in and around Orlando with **fireworks** everywhere. WDW's Independence Day pyrotechnic displays are legendary; recent years have brought record crowds (☎ 407/939–

7814). In downtown Orlando, the masses gather around Lake Eola for the city's fireworks (☎ 407/363–5871). Lakefront Park in Kissimmee has fireworks as part of an old-fashioned celebration that also features games, rides, entertainment, and food (☎ 407/932–7223).

➤ AUG.: The **World Precision Hang Gliding Tournament** at Cypress Gardens (☎ 941/984–2111) features the best talents in this sport. The 10th annual **Christmas in August Craft Fair** is held at the Central Florida Fairgrounds (☎ 407/860–0092).

AUTUMN

➤ SEPT.: **Oktoberfest at Church Street Station** (☎ 407/422–2434) means oompah bands and German folk dancers, food, and beer.

➤ OCT.: Cypress Gardens hosts its month-long **Chrysanthemum Festival** (☎ 813/324–2111) beginning in October, featuring more than 3 million brilliant blooms in magnificent arches, "poodle" baskets, and various other eye-popping arrangements. With a 35-ft cascading waterfall as its centerpiece, the festival also includes chrysanthemum-filled gazebos and acres of flowing mum beds. SeaWorld devotes the entire month to man's best friend with its **PetFest** (☎ 407/351–3600). A variety of shows, including a "doggie social" and pet-care seminars led by

"old time" television stars such as Jerry Mathers (*Leave It To Beaver*) and Donna Douglas (*The Beverly Hillbillies*), rounds out the event. Legendary bull riders and cowboys compete at the 104th **Silver Spurs Rodeo and RibFest**, held the first weekend in October in Kissimmee (☎ 407/847–4052 or 407/847–3174). The **Grand Reserve Dinner and Wine Tasting** at Church Street Station (☎ 407/422–2434, ext. 405) includes a six-course Grand Reserve Dinner, with reserve vintage wines introduced by winery owners. Early in October, the **Universal Art Show** is held on Orlando's Central Florida Fairgrounds (☎ 407/295–3247). Mid-October is the time for the **Walt Disney World Oldsmobile Golf Classic,** played on three of Walt Disney World's 18-hole golf courses (☎ 407/824–2729). The **National Senior Games,** slated for October 19–29, will bring some 10,000 senior athletes to WDW's Wide World of Sports complex (☎ 407/824–4321). They will compete in 18 sports, including softball, volleyball, tennis, and archery. Cypress Gardens' **Annual Mustang Roundup** (☎ 800/282–2123) draws aficionados of that most famous Ford to exhibit and ogle models from 1965 to the present. The **Winter Park Autumn Art Festival** takes place at Rollins College (☎ 407/644–8281). The **Pioneer Days Folk Festival** brings craftspeople and musicians to the grounds of the Folk Art Center on East Fairlane Avenue in suburban Pine Castle (☎ 407/855–7461). For Halloween, there are several October weekends of **Halloween Horror Nights** at Universal Studios, one of the top events of the year in Orlando. Universal creative talents exercise the dark side of their imagination, and there are truly frightening haunted houses here and there on the park grounds, open during the special ticketed events. At Church Street Station (☎ 407/422–2434) the holiday inspires yet another high-spirited **Halloween Party.**

➤ NOV.: Early in the month, there's **Festival in the Park,** an arts-and-crafts show around the shores of downtown Orlando's Lake Eola. The **American Indian Powwow** (☎ 407/295–3247) kicks off the month at the Central Florida Fairgrounds. **The Space Coast Birding & Wildlife Festival** in Titusville occurs November 9–12 and features field trips, seminars, and art exhibits (☎ 321/268–5000). Mid-November is the **Festival of the Masters,** with 230 top artists exhibiting their creations at Downtown Disney's Marketplace (☎ 407/934–6743). Starting

at Thanksgiving, the **Osborne Family Lights,** an amazing neighborhood light display that started out in Little Rock, Arkansas, comes to Residential Street on the backlot of Disney–MGM Studios (☎ 407/824–4321)—all 4 million lights of it. Universal's CityWalk hosts its annual **BeerFest** (☎ 407/363–8000), complete with lager tastings from throughout the world.

➤ DEC.: Early in the month, Orlando's Loch Haven Park stages a **Pet Fair & Winterfest** (☎ 407/644–2739). **Christmas in the Park** (☎ 407/644–8281) takes place in downtown Winter Park the first weekend in December. The city's main shopping area is a brilliant setting for holiday music provided by the Bach Festival adult and children's choirs. December 4–11, **Disney's Wide World of Sports** (☎ 407/839–3900) hosts the Pop Warner Super Bowl and the Pop Warner National Cheer & Dance Championships. These events bring hundreds of aspiring young football players

and cheerleaders to Orlando from across the nation. The lighting of the **Great American Christmas Tree** is held every year at Church Street Station (☎ 407/422–2434). For a **Disney Christmas,** Walt Disney World gears up by decorating Main Street in perfect Victorian style, complete with a magnificent Christmas tree in Town Square, strolling characters, special afternoon parades, and entertainment. Every weekend in December before Christmas, **Mickey's Very Merry Christmas Party** in the Magic Kingdom can really get you into the holiday spirit. At Epcot, the **Candlelight Processional** and **Holidays Around the World** keep things festive. At **Downtown Disney's Marketplace** (☎ 407/824–4321) you will find a Nativity Pageant, *Mickey's Christmas Carol* stage show, and appearances by the North Pole's most important citizen. Cypress Gardens mounts its annual **Poinsettia Festival** (☎ 813/324–2111), featuring 48,000 multicolored blooms.

2 EXPLORING WALT DISNEY WORLD® RESORT

No moss ever grows under the Mouse's paws (unless it's artfully re-created moss for some lush forest landscape). Walt Disney World® Resort is always changing, adding a new theme park here, revamping an out-of-date ride there. Yet amid all the hoopla, much remains reassuringly unchanged since the Magic Kingdom opened in 1971, rekindling fond memories among parents returning with their children.

By Catherine
Fredman

Updated by
Val Meyer

MILLIONS OF VISITORS, even those who place Pirates of the Caribbean and Space Mountain among the wonders of the world, are hard-pressed to define Walt Disney World. When you take a Walt Disney World exit off I–4, you're almost on the grounds, even though there's no Cinderella Castle in sight—it's a very big place. And it's crammed with pleasures: from swooping above a starlit London in the Magic Kingdom's Peter Pan's Flight to simply sitting under the shade of a Callary pear tree frosted with blooms in Epcot, from enjoying jazz at Pleasure Island and cheering for your favorite team at the ESPN sports bar at Disney's BoardWalk to whooping and hollering down water slides at the ultracreative water parks.

The sheer enormity of the property—27,400 acres near Kissimmee, Florida—suggests that WDW is more than a single theme park with a fabulous castle in the center. The property's acreage translates to 43 square mi—twice the size of Manhattan or Bermuda, 60 times larger than Monaco, and just a shade smaller than Nantucket or Liechtenstein. If you were to drive at 60 mph from one side of the property to the other, it would take close to 45 minutes. On a tract that size, 98 acres is a mere speck, yet that is the size of the Magic Kingdom. When most people imagine Walt Disney World, they think only of those 98 acres, but there is much, much more.

More than 2,500 acres of the property are occupied by hotels and villa complexes, each with its own theme and swimming pools and other recreational facilities. Epcot, a little more than twice the size of the Magic Kingdom, is the second major theme park. A combination of a science exploratorium and a world's fair, Epcot looks at the future and celebrates the world's cultural diversity. Disney–MGM Studios Theme Park, devoted to the film business and also known familiarly as the "Studios," is nearby. In 1998, WDW opened its fourth major theme park, Disney's Animal Kingdom, devoted to fauna real, imaginary, and extinct. Thousands of acres are still undeveloped—grassy plains and pine forests patrolled by deer, swamps patched by thickets of palmettos and fluttering with white ibis.

Recently, Disney introduced a new way to experience the most popular attractions with little or no wait. **FASTPASS** allows guests to schedule appointments to avoid the long lines that are so commonplace. All you have to do is step up to the front of the line and book your time, with your admission ticket in your hand. Eventually you will be able to plan your entire vacation in advance, including time at the attractions.

As Walt Disney himself decreed, WDW has never been completed; as one new confection welcomes its first guests, another begins construction, and still others are under study. So do plenty of research before you go, make a plan, then relax—and have a wonderful time.

MAGIC KINGDOM

The Magic Kingdom is the heart and soul of the Disney empire. Comparable to California's Disneyland, it was the first Disney outpost in Florida when it opened in 1971, and it is the park that traveled, with modifications, to France and Japan.

For a park that wields such worldwide influence, the Magic Kingdom is surprisingly small: at barely 98 acres, it is also the tiniest of Walt Disney World's Big Four. However, the unofficial theme song—"It's a Small World After All"—doesn't hold true when it comes to the Magic Kingdom's attractions. Packed into seven different "lands" are nearly

Walt Disney World

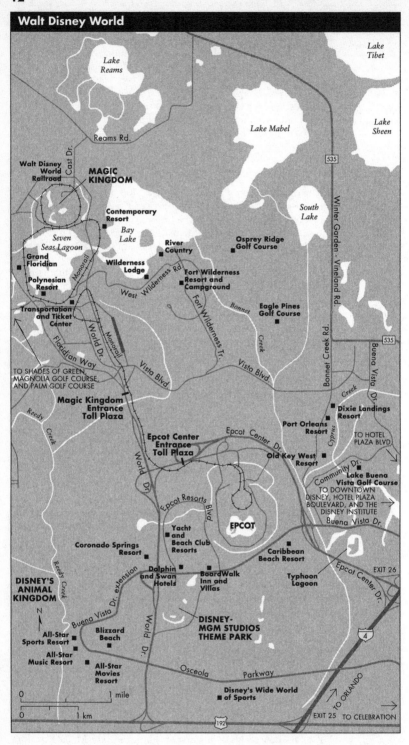

50 major crowd pleasers, and that's not counting all the ancillary attractions: shops, eateries, live entertainment, cartoon characters, fireworks, parades, and, of course, the sheer pleasure of strolling through the beautifully landscaped and manicured grounds.

Many rides are geared for the young, but the Magic Kingdom is anything but a kiddie park. The degree of detail, the greater vision, the surprisingly witty spiel of the guides, and the tongue-in-cheek signs that crop up in the oddest places—for instance, in Fantasyland, the rest rooms are marked "Prince" and "Princess"—all contribute to a delightful sense of discovery that's far beyond the mere thrill of a ride.

The park is laid out on a north–south axis, with Cinderella Castle at the epicenter and the various lands surrounding it in a broad circle. Upon passing through the entrance gates, you immediately discover yourself in **Town Square,** containing City Hall, the park's main information center. Town Square directly segues into **Main Street, U.S.A.,** a boulevard filled with Victorian-style stores and snack spots. Main Street runs due north and ends at the Hub, a large tree-lined circle, properly known as Central Plaza, in front of Cinderella Castle. Rope Drop, the ceremonial stampede that kicks off each day, occurs at the various points where the end of Main Street intersects the Hub.

As you move clockwise from the Hub, the Magic Kingdom's various lands begin with **Adventureland**—home of Pirates of the Caribbean, the Jungle Cruise, and the Swiss Family Treehouse. Next come **Frontierland** and **Liberty Square,** containing Splash Mountain, Big Thunder Mountain Railroad, and the Haunted Mansion. **Fantasyland** is directly behind Cinderella Castle—in the castle's rear courtyard, as it were. **Mickey's Toontown Fair** is set off the upper right-hand corner—that's northeast to those who know their geography—of Fantasyland. **Tomorrowland,** directly to the right of the Hub, rounds out the circle.

Numbers in the margin correspond to points of interest on the Magic Kingdom map.

Main Street, U.S.A.

With its pastel Victorian-style buildings, antique automobiles oohga-oohga-ing, sparkling sidewalks, and atmosphere of what one writer has called "almost hysterical joy," Main Street is more than a mere conduit to the other enchantments of the Magic Kingdom. It is where the spell is first cast.

Like Dorothy waking up in a Technicolor Oz or Mary Poppins jumping through the pavement painting, you emerge from the tunnel beneath the Walt Disney World Railroad Station into a realization of one of the most tenacious American dreams. The perfect street in the perfect small town in a perfect moment of time is burnished to jewel-like quality, thanks to a ⅝-scale reduction, nightly cleanings with high-pressure hoses, and constant repainting; neither life-size nor so small as to appear toylike, the carefully calculated size is meant to make you feel as though you're looking through a telescope into another world.

Everyone's always happy in this world, spirits kept sunny thanks to outpourings of music: Dixieland jazz, barbershop quartets, brass-band parades, and scores of Disney films and American musicals played over loudspeakers. Old-fashioned horse-drawn trams and omnibuses—horns a-tootle—chug along the street. Street vendors in Victorian costumes sell balloons and popcorn. And the Cinderella Castle floats at the end of Main Street.

14

The Magic Kingdom

Fort Sam
Clemens

Rivers of America

WDW
Railroad
Frontierland
Depot

Columbia
Harbour
House

Aunt
Polly's
Dockside
Inn

FRONTIERLAND

LIBERTY

SQUARE

Liberty Tree
Tavern

ATM

Caribbean
Plaza

Adventureland
Bazaar

Crystal
Palace

First Aid

ADVENTURELAND

N

KEY

🛉 Restaurants

🚻 Rest rooms

—— Rail Line

••••• Skyride

≈≈≈ Monorail

Newsstand

Monorail

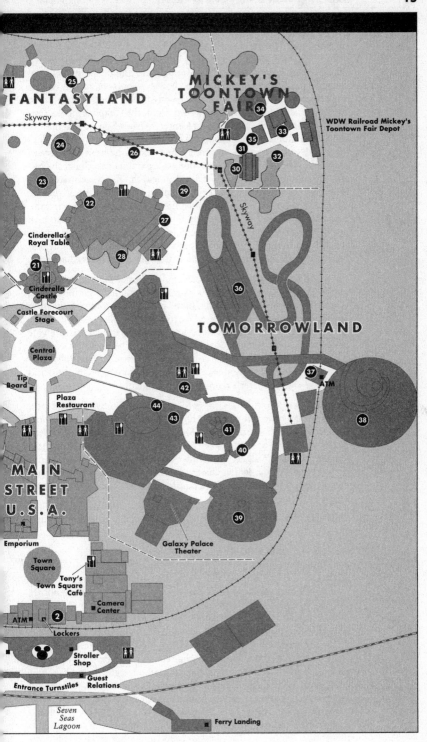

FANTASYLAND

MICKEY'S TOONTOWN FAIR

WDW Railroad Mickey's Toontown Fair Depot

Skyway

Cinderella's Royal Table

Cinderella Castle

Castle Forecourt Stage

Central Plaza

Tip Board

Plaza Restaurant

TOMORROWLAND

ATM

MAIN STREET U.S.A.

Emporium

Town Square

Tony's Town Square Café

Camera Center

Galaxy Palace Theater

ATM

Lockers

Stroller Shop

Entrance Turnstiles

Guest Relations

Seven Seas Lagoon

Ferry Landing

Although attractions with a capital "A" are minimal on Main Street, there are plenty of inducements—namely, shops—to while away your time and part you from your money. The **Main Street Gallery,** a bright yellow, Victorian-style gingerbread building, is filled with animation art and other memorabilia. The **Main Street Athletic Shop** sells a variety of "Team Mickey" clothing and houses a sports memorabilia museum and small eating area. The **Harmony Barber Shop** is the place to have yourself shorn. A milliner's emporium, the **Chapeau** stocks Cat-in-the-Hat fantasies. The **Camera Center** in Town Square is actually a shop and exhibit in one; inside the door on the far right are displays of cameras of yesteryear and today, and you can e-mail a picture of yourself to loved ones at home. Alongside exhibits describing the history of animation, you can catch a full-length Disney animated feature film such as *Fantasia* in a delightfully air-conditioned theater, which can come in very handy when the approaching afternoon thunderstorms give way to downpours in the summer. You can also pick up batteries, film, and disposable cameras. If the weather looks threatening, head for the **Emporium** to purchase a signature mouse-ear umbrella or a yellow poncho with Mickey emblazoned on the back.

The **Main Street Cinema,** once a small movie theater that screened back-to-back vintage Mickey cartoons, is stocked with items promoting the current Disney animated feature. In the back, you can catch clips from *Steamboat Willie,* the first sound cartoon and Mickey's debut. In his silver-screen premier, Mickey met Minnie and was inspired to serenade her using a cow's udder. (Walt Disney said that he loved his creation more than any woman, which could make one wonder how Lilly Belle felt about this, especially since it was she who convinced her husband to change the character's name from Mortimer.)

Main Street is also full of in-jokes for those in the know. For instance, check out the proprietors' names above the shops: **CrystalArts** honors Roy Disney, Walt's brother. The **Shadow Box** is the domain of Dick Nunis, chairman of Walt Disney Attractions. At the **Main Street Athletic Shop,** Card Walker—the "Practitioner of Psychiatry and Justice of the Peace"—is the former chairman of the company's executive committee. At last glance, today's Head Mouseketeer, Michael Eisner, still didn't have his own shop.

❶ City Hall. This is information central, where you can pick up maps and guidebooks and inquire about all things Disney.

❷ Walt Disney World Railroad. Step right up to the elevated platform above the Magic Kingdom's entrance for a ride into living history. Walt Disney was a railroad buff of the highest order—he constructed a ⅛-scale train in his backyard and named it *Lilly Belle,* after his wife. Another *Lilly Belle* rides the rails here, as do *Walter E. Disney, Roy O. Disney* (named for Walt's brother), and *Roger Broggie* (named for a Disney Imagineer and fellow railroad aficionado). All the locomotives date from 1928, coincidentally the same year Mickey Mouse was created. Disney scouts tracked down these vintage carriers in Mexico, where they were used to haul sugarcane in the Yucatán, brought them back, and completely overhauled them to their present splendor. And splendid they are, with striped awnings, brightly painted benches, authoritative "choo-choo," and hissing plumes of steam. Their 1½-mi track runs along the perimeter of the Magic Kingdom, with much of the trip through the woods. You'll pass Tom Sawyer Island and other attractions; stops are in Frontierland and Mickey's Toontown Fair. Although the ride provides a good introduction to the layout of the park, it's better as relief for tired feet and dragging legs later in the day. The four trains run at five- to seven-minute intervals. *Duration: 21 mins. Crowds: Can be* substantial beginning in late morning through late afternoon. *Strategy:* Go in mid-afternoon if you don't see a line; otherwise, skip on a first-time visit. Ride to Frontierland in the early morning to get a jump-start on the Splash Mountain line. *Audience:* All ages. *Rating:* ★

Adventureland

From the scrubbed brick, manicured lawns, and meticulously pruned trees of the Central Plaza, an artfully dilapidated wooden bridge leads to Adventureland, Disney's version of jungle fever. The landscape artists went wild here: South African cape honeysuckle droops, Brazilian bougainvillea drapes, Mexican flame vines cling, spider plants clone, and three different varieties of palm trees sway, all creating a seemingly spontaneous mess. The bright, all-American sing-along tunes that fill the air along Main Street and Central Plaza are replaced by the recorded repetitions of trumpeting elephants, pounding drums, and squawking parrots. The architecture is a mishmash of the best of Thailand, the Caribbean, Africa, and Polynesia, arranged in an inspired disorder that recalls comic-book fantasies of far-off places. The message is that, although the natives may be restless, the kids are all right.

Adventureland surrounds its own oblong central plaza. To your right as you cross the bridge from the Hub is the **Adventureland Bazaar,** whose six shops have names like Bwana Bob's, Traders of Timbuktu, Zanzibar Shell Company, and Elephant Tales. They sell exotic—and generally quite affordable—safari-theme clothing, sharks'-teeth jewelry, elephant-hair bracelets, and other trinkets from the erstwhile Dark Continent as well as a menagerie's worth of life-size tropical critters. To your left are the spreading branches of the Swiss Family Robinson's banyan tree. As you continue around the plaza you'll see the entrances to the **Jungle Cruise, the Pirates of the Caribbean,** and the Polynesian great house containing the **Enchanted Tiki Room Under New Management.** In the far end of the plaza is another conglomeration of shops, the **Caribbean Plaza,** selling treasures inspired by the Pirates of the Caribbean: most notably tropical clothing, costume jewelry (how about some pineapple earrings?), pirates' swords, and hats embroidered with skulls and crossbones. At **Lafitte's Portrait Deck,** you can stick your head through a pirate cutout and bring home a picture of yourself as the Scourge of the Spanish Main.

❸ **Swiss Family Treehouse.** Few New York City apartments can boast the light, the airiness, the number of rooms, and all the services of this arboreal abode. In fact, the only thing lacking here is an elevator. Based on the classic novel by Johann Wyss about the adventures of the Robinson family, who were shipwrecked on the way to America, the tree house shows what you can do with a big banyan and a lot of imagination. The rooms are furnished with patchwork quilts and mahogany furniture. Disney detail abounds: the kitchen sink is made of a giant clamshell; the boys' room, strewn with clothing, has two hammocks instead of beds; and an ingenious system of rain barrels and bamboo pipes provides running water in every room. Small wonder that in the 1960 film, when offered the chance to leave their island, all but one Robinson decided to stay on. As you clamber around the narrow wooden steps and rope bridges that connect the rooms in this split-level dwelling, take a look at the Spanish moss. It is real, but the tree itself—some 90 ft in diameter, with more than 600 branches—was constructed by the props department. The 800,000 leaves are made of vinyl and cost $1 per leaf in the early 1970s. It all adds up to a species of tree unofficially called *Disneyodendron eximus,* or "out-of-the-ordinary Disney tree." *Duration: Up to you. Crowds: Artfully camouflaged so you may not see them—and the lines move slowly. Strategy: Go first thing in the morning or after dark. Audience: All ages; toddlers unsteady on their feet may have trouble with the stairs. Rating:* ★★

❹ **Jungle Cruise.** On this Disney favorite, you cruise through three continents and along four rivers: the Congo, the Ni le, the Mekong, and the Amazon. The canopied launches are loaded, the safari-suited guides make a point of checking their pistols, and the *Irrawady Irma* or *Mongala Millie* is off for another "perilous" journey. The guide's shtick is surprisingly funny, with just the right blend of cornball humor and the gently snide, although some guides seem to be trying to deliver their lines with a Chuck Yeager drawl patented by airline pilots that makes what they're saying almost unintelligible. Along the way, you'll encounter animals of the African veldt, elephants bathing, slinky pythons, an irritated rhinoceros, a tribe of hungry headhunters, and a bunch of hyperactive hippos (good thing the guide's got a pop pistol). Then there's Old Smiley, the crocodile, who's always waiting for a handout—or, as the guide quips, "a foot out." Be sure to give him your left hand, the guide advises, and you'll be "all right." Kids who might be terrified by Pirates of the Caribbean will love this ride, and adults love the patter and all the detail—listen for what's playing on the radio of the overturned Jeep. *Duration: 10 mins. Crowds: Huge, from late morning until dinnertime. Strategy: Use the FASTPASS. Otherwise go first thing in the morning or during the afternoon parade, but not after dark—you miss too much. Audience: All ages. Rating:* ★★★

❺ **Shrunken Ned's Junior Jungle Boats.** These remote-controlled boats, although cleverly named, are nothing more than remote-controlled miniatures of the Jungle Cruise boats. Look for them to your immediate right as you exit the Jungle Cruise (they're easy to miss on a crowded day). A change machine spits out tokens, which you must purchase in order to play with them. Cost is $1 for one token, $5 for 6. *Duration: As long as you like and your money holds out. Crowds: Can get thick during mid-afternoon. Strategy: If you can talk the kids out of it, skip this attraction. Audience: Older children and adults. Rating:* ★

NEED A BREAK?   Among the fast munchies here, some of the best are the fresh pineapple spears at Adventureland's **Aloha Isle.**

❻ **Enchanted Tiki Room Under New Management.** In its original incarnation as the Enchanted Tiki Birds, this was Disney's first Audio-Animatronics attraction. Now updated, it includes the avian stars of recent Disney animated films: Zazu from *The Lion King* and *Aladdin*'s Iago. The boys take you on a tour of the original attraction while cracking lots of jokes. A holdover from the original is the ditty "In the Tiki, Tiki, Tiki, Tiki, Tiki Room," which is second only to "It's a Small World" as the Disney song you love to hate. *Duration: 12 mins. Crowds: Waits seldom exceed 30 mins. Strategy: Go when you need to sit in an air-conditioned room. Audience: All ages. Rating:* ★

❼ **Pirates of the Caribbean.** This boat ride is classic Disney: memorable vignettes, incredible detail, a gripping story, and catchy music whose relentless yo-ho-ing can be eradicated only by "It's a Small World." One of the pirate's "Avast, ye scurvy scum!" is the sort of greeting your children will proclaim for the next week—which gives you an idea of the ride's impact.

The gracious arched entrance soon gives way to a dusty dungeon, redolent of damp and of a spooky, scary past. Lanterns flicker as you board the boats and a ghostly voice intones, "Dead men tell no tales." Usually, at this point, a much higher, younger voice quavers, "Mommy, can we get off?" A deserted beach, strewn with shovels, a skeleton, and a disintegrating map indicating buried treasure, is the preface to this story of greed, lust, and destruction.

Emerging from a pitch-black time tunnel, you're literally in the middle of a furious battle. A pirate ship, cannons blazing, is attacking a stone fortress. Cannonballs splash into the water just off your bow, and Audio-Animatronics pirates hoist the Jolly Roger while brave soldiers scurry to defend the fort—to no avail. Politically correct nerves may twinge as the women of the town are rounded up and auctioned. "Strike your colors, ye brazen wench, no need to expose your superstructure!" shouts one pirate, but the scene is terrific: pirates chasing chickens, dunking the town mayor in the well, and collapsing into a snoring stupor with a couple of pigs. Check out the hairy legs of the two carousers straddling the wall. The wild antics of the pirates result in a conflagration; the town goes up in flames, and all go to their just reward amid a chorus of "Yo-ho! Yo-ho! A pirate's life for me." There's a moral in there somewhere, if you want to look for one—or you can just enjoy the show. *Duration: 10 mins. Crowds: Waits seldom exceed 30 mins, despite the ride's popularity. Strategy: A good destination even during the busy afternoons. Audience: All ages. Rating:* ★★

Frontierland

Frontierland, in the northwest quadrant of the Magic Kingdom, invokes the American frontier. The period seems to be the latter half of the 19th century, and the West is being won by Disney staffers dressed in checked shirts, leather vests, cowboy hats, and brightly colored neckerchiefs. Banjo and fiddle music twang from tree to tree, and guests walk around munching on the biggest drumsticks you've ever seen.

The screams that periodically drown out the string-sawing are not the result of a cowboy surprising an Indian. They come from two of the Magic Kingdom's more thrilling rides, **Splash Mountain,** an elaborate flume ride, and **Big Thunder Mountain Railroad,** one of the park's two roller coasters. The rust-red rock spires of Thunder Mountain and Splash Mountain serve as local landmarks and set a landscaping tone best described as "Arid, Extra Dry." In contrast to lush Adventureland, Frontierland is planted with mesquite, twisted Peruvian pepper trees, slash pines, and many cacti. The unpainted buildings and wooden sidewalks have a ramshackle quality, and even though you know that no dust is allowed in Walt Disney World, the setting evokes dusty thoughts.

Shops and eateries are along the avenue bordering the southern curve of a body of water that looks like a lake but because it variously represents the Mississippi and Missouri rivers and their tributaries is called Rivers of America. Emporia here are generally referred to as "posts," as in the **Frontier Trading Post** and **Prairie Outpost,** which sell sheriff badges, leather work, cowboy hats, and Southwestern, Native American, and Mexican crafts. Then there's **Big Al's,** for genuine Davy Crockett coonskin hats. Yee-haw!

The Walt Disney World Railroad makes a stop at Frontierland. It tunnels through Splash Mountain and drops you off between Splash Mountain and Thunder Mountain.

8 **Splash Mountain.** At Rope Drop, one of the attractions to which the hordes are dashing is this incredibly popular log-flume ride. Based on the animated sequences in Disney's 1946 film *Song of the South,* it features Audio-Animatronics creations of Br'er Rabbit, Br'er Bear, Br'er Fox, and a menagerie of other Br'er beasts (including Br'er Frog and a Heckle-and-Jeckle duo of Br'er Crows) frolicking in bright, cartoonlike settings. No matter what time you get there, you *will*, repeat *will*, wait in line. So the Disney folks have made the waiting area here as entertaining and comfortable as possible, with trees to shade you and, to entertain you, little critters in tiny houses and toe-tappin' country music wafting from speakers hidden in rocks. When you finally do settle into the eight-person hollowed-out logs, Uncle Remus's voice growls, "Mark mah words, Br'er Rabbit gonna put his footin Br'er Fox's mouth one of these days." And this just might be the day.

As the boat carries you through a lily pond—just bopping with Br'er Frogs merrily singing the ride's theme song, "Time to Be Moving Along"—past signs for Br'er Fox's lair and Br'er Bear's den, Br'er Rabbit's silhouette hops along in front, always just ahead of you. Every time some critter makes a grab for the bunny, the log boats drop out of reach. But Br'er Fox has been studying his book *How to Catch a Rabbit,* and our lop-eared friend looks as if he's destined for the pot. Things don't look so good for the flumers either, as the boats creak up and up the mountain, past a pair of pessimistic crows. You get one heart-stopping pause at the top—just long enough to grab the safety bar—and then the boat plummets down a long, sharp flume drop right into a gigantic briar patch. In case you want to know what you're getting into, the drop is 52½ ft—that's about five stories—at a 45° angle, enough to reach speeds of 40 mph and make you feel weightless. From the boat—especially if you are in the front seat—it looks truly as if you are going to be impaled on those enormous spikes. Try to smile through your clenched teeth: as you begin to drop, a flashbulb pops, so you can purchase a photographic memento of the experience before exiting the ride. Br'er Rabbit escapes—and so do you, wet and exhilarated—to the tune of "Zip-a-Dee-Doo-Dah," whose bouncy melody has become something of a Disney theme song. If you want to get really wet—and you will get splashed from almost every seat—ask the ride attendant to seat you in the front row.

Duration: 11 mins. Crowds: Yes! Strategy: If you're not in line by 9:45, your only hope is during meals or a parade, unless you have made your appointment using the FASTPASS system. Parents who need to baby-swap can take the young ones to a play area in a cave under the ride. Audience: All except very young children; they would like the music and scenery but may be terrified by the final drop. No pregnant women or guests wearing back, neck, or leg braces. Minimum height: 40″. Rating: ★★★

❾ Big Thunder Mountain Railroad. As any true roller-coaster lover can tell you, this three-minute ride is relatively tame; despite the posted warnings, you won't stagger off, you won't throw up, and you won't vow never to subject yourself to the experience again. The thrills are there, however, thanks to the intricate details and stunning scenery along every inch of the 2,780-ft track.

Set in gold-rush days, the runaway train rushes and rattles past 20 Audio-Animatronics figures—including donkeys, chickens, a goat, and a grizzled old miner surprised in his bathtub—$300,000 of genuine antique mining equipment, tumbleweeds, a derelict mining town, hot springs, and a flash flood.

The ride was 15 years in the planning and took two years and close to $17 million to build. This price tag, give or take a few million, equaled the entire cost of erecting California's Disneyland in 1955. The 197-ft mountain is based on the monoliths of Utah's Monument Valley, and thanks to 650 tons of steel, 4,675 tons of cement, and 16,000 gallons of paint, it closely resembles the real thing. *Duration: 4 mins. Crowds: Large. Strategy: Frequent Disney visitors swear that the ride is even better at night, when you can't anticipate the curves and the track's rattling sounds as if something's about to give. But then you miss the scenic details. The solution—go twice. Audience: All except young children, though it's a good starter coaster for kids who have mastered Toontown's Barnstormer. No pregnant women or guests wearing back, neck, or leg braces. Minimum height: 40". Rating:* ★★★

🔟 **Tom Sawyer Island.** An artfully misspelled sign, signed by Tom Sawyer, tells you what to expect: "IF'N YOU LIKE DARK CAVES, MYSTERY MINES, BOTTOMLESS PITS, SHAKY BRIDGES 'N' BIG ROCKS, YOU HAVE CAME TO THE BEST PLACE I KNOW." Aunt Polly would have walloped Tom for his orthography, but she couldn't have argued with the truth. Actually two tiny islands connected by an old-fashioned swing bridge, Tom Sawyer Island is a natural playground, all hills and trees and rocks and shrubs. You could always sit this one out on the porch of Aunt Polly's Dockside Inn, sipping lemonade—but why let the kids have all the fun?

The main island, where the boats dock, is where you'll find most attractions. The Mystery Cave is an almost pitch-black labyrinth where the wind wails in a truly spooky fashion. Injun Joe's Cave is all pointy stalactites and stalagmites and is endowed with lots of columns and crevices from which to jump out and startle younger sisters and brothers. Harper's Mill is an old-fashioned gristmill. And, in a clearing at the top of the hill, there's a rustic playground. As you explore the shoreline on the dirt paths, keep an eye out for the barrel bridge—every time someone takes a step, the whole contraption bounces.

On the other island is Fort Sam Clemens, a log fortress from which you can fire air guns with great booms and cracks at the soporific passengers on the *Liberty Belle* Riverboat. It's guarded by an equally soporific Audio-Animatronics sentry, loudly snoring off his last bender. Both islands are sprinkled with lookouts for great views to Thunder Mountain and Frontierland, as well as with nice natural niches—often furnished with benches and water fountains. On Saturdays and busier days, you can help Tom find some of his daily necessities in a scavenger hunt on the Mighty Mississippi and do arts and crafts at Hickory Switch Hill. *Duration: Up to you. Crowds: Seldom overwhelming, but it wouldn't matter—here, the more the merrier. Strategy: Try it as a refreshing afternoon getaway. Audience: All ages. Rating:* ★★★

1️⃣1️⃣ **Country Bear Jamboree.** Wisecracking, cornpone Audio-Animatronics bears joke, sing, and play country music and 1950s rock-and-roll in this stage show. The emcee, the massive but debonair Henry, leads a stellar cast that includes the robust Trixie, the Tampa Temptation, who laments a love lost while perched in a swing suspended from the ceiling; Bubbles, Bunny, and Beulah, harmonizing on "All the Guys That Turn Me On Turn Me Down"; and Big Al, a cult figure who has inspired postcards, stuffed animals, and his own shop next door. *Duration: 16 mins. Crowds: Large, considering the relatively small theater. Strategy: Visit before 11 AM, during the afternoon parade, or after most small children have left for the day. Stand to the far left in the anteroom where you wait to end up in the front rows; to the far right if you want to sit in the last row, where small children can perch on top of the seats to see better. Audience: All ages; even timid youngsters love the bears. Rating:* ★★★

1️⃣2️⃣ **Frontierland Shootin' Arcade.** At this classic shooting arcade, laser beams sub for bullets, as genuine Hawkins 54-caliber buffalo rifles have been refitted to emit electronic beams. When they strike, tombstones spin and epitaphs change, ghost riders gallop out of clouds, and skulls pop out of graves, accompanied by the sounds of howling coyotes, creaking bridges, and the cracks of the rifles blasted over the digital audio system. *Cost: 25¢ per 5 shots. Strategy: Bring a pocketful of change. Audience: Older children and adults. Rating:* ★★

⑬ Diamond Horseshoe Saloon Revue. "Knock, knock." "Who's there?" "Ya." "Ya who?" "Yaaahooo!" And they're off, with another rip-roaring, raucous, corny, nonstop, high-kicking, elbow-jabbing, song-and-dance-and-fiddling show staged in a re-creation of an Old West saloon. The show features a sextet of dance-hall girls and high-spirited cowboys; Sam, the stagestruck and lovelorn saloon keeper; and Lily, a shimmying, feather-boa-toting reincarnation of Mae West, whose throaty version of "A Good Man Is Hard to Find" brings down the house. At other times, Lily swishes around the hall, tickling noses with her boa and uttering such lines as "Watch it, honey, this is Frontierland, not Fantasyland!" The cowboys leap from the balconies and swing around columns; Lily's Girls perform an exuberant cancan; and everyone has a hand-clapping good time. Snacks and light refreshments may be purchased. *Show times: Continuously, starting just after opening. Seating is on a first-come, first-served basis. Duration: 30 mins. Crowds: Busy for all shows. Strategy: Go early. You can kill two birds with one stone by eating here—light refreshments such as salads and sandwiches are served. But give it a miss if you're on a tight schedule and have plans to see the Hoop-Dee-Doo Revue at Fort Wilderness Resort (☞ Chapter 10). Audience: All ages. Rating:* ★★

Liberty Square

The weathered siding gives way to neat clapboard and solid brick; the mesquite and cactus are replaced by stately oaks and masses of azalea; and the rough-and-tumble Western frontier gently slides into colonial America. Liberty Square picks up where Frontierland leaves off, continuing around the shore of Rivers of America and forming the western boundary of Fantasyland.

The theme is colonial history, which Northerners will be happy to learn is solid Yankee. The small buildings topped with weather vanes and exuding comfortable prosperity from every rosy brick and every spiffy shutter are pure New England. A replica of the Liberty Bell, complete with the famous crack, seems an appropriate prop to separate Liberty Square from Frontierland. There's even a **Liberty Tree,** a 150-year-old live oak actually found on Walt Disney World property and moved to the Magic Kingdom. Just as the Sons of Liberty hung lanterns on trees as a signal of solidarity after the Boston Tea Party, the Liberty Tree's branches are decorated with 13 lanterns representing the 13 original colonies.

As you wander through this area, look into the **Yankee Trader** for fancy food and cooking items, and stop at the **Silhouette Cart** for profiles, hand-cut and framed while you wait. The **Umbrella Cart** sells personalized products that are sure to come in handy during the daily summer afternoon thundershower. There are plenty of tree-shaded tables for alfresco meals and plenty of carts and fast-food eateries supplying the goods.

⑭ Hall of Presidents. This multimedia tribute to the Constitution caused quite a sensation when it opened, because it was here that the first refinements of the Audio-Animatronics system of computerized robots could be seen. Now surpassed by Epcot's American Adventure, it's still well worth attending, as much for the spacious, air-conditioned theater as for the two-part show.

It starts with a film, narrated by writer Maya Angelou, that discusses the Constitution as the codification of the spirit that founded America. You learn about threats to the document, ranging from the 18th-century Whiskey Rebellion to the Civil War, and hear such famous speeches as Benjamin Franklin's plea to the Continental Congress delegates for ratification and Abraham Lincoln's warning that "a house divided against itself cannot stand." The shows conveying Disney's brand of patriotism may be ponderous, but they're always well researched and lovingly presented; this film, for instance, was revamped to replace a lingering subtext of Cold War paranoia with the more progressive assertion that our democracy is a work in progress, that liberty and justice still do not figure equally in the lives of all Americans.

The second half is a roll call of all 42 U.S. presidents. Each chief executive rises and responds with a nod—even those who blatantly attempted to subvert the Constitution. The detail is lifelike, right down to the brace on Franklin Delano Roosevelt's leg. The robots can't resist nodding, fidgeting, and even whispering to each other while waiting for their names to come up. The last to be called is Bill Clinton, who, unlike other contemporary presidential robots, has a speaking part. Audio-Animatronics Clinton's speech was written for Disney by *The Lion King* lyricist Tim Rice, of *Jesus Christ Superstar* and *Evita*, in collaboration with the President's chief speechwriter; the audio was provided—in one take—by Bill Clinton himself. *Duration: 30 mins. Crowds: Usually moderate. Strategy: Go in the afternoon, when you'll appreciate the air-conditioning. Audience: Older children and adults. Rating:* ★★★

NEED A   **Sleepy Hollow** carts sell fresh fruit—a welcome change from the Magic
BREAK?   Kingdom's ubiquitous french fries and burgers.

⑮ *Liberty Belle* **Riverboat.** A real old-fashioned steamboat, named after Walt's wife, the *Liberty Belle* is authentic, from its calliope whistle and the gingerbread trim on its three decks to the boilers that produce the steam that drives the big rear paddle wheel. In fact, the boat misses authenticity on only one count: there's no mustachioed captain to guide it during the ride around the Rivers of America. That task is performed by an underwater rail. The trip is slow and not exactly thrilling, except, perhaps, to the kids getting shot at by their counterparts at Fort Sam Clemens on Tom Sawyer Island. But it's a relaxing break for all concerned, and children like exploring the boat. *Duration: 15 mins. Crowds: Moderate, but capacity is high so waits are seldom trying. Strategy: Go when you need a break from the crowds. Audience: All ages. Rating:* ★

⑯ **Mike Fink Keelboats.** They're short and dumpy and you have to sit on a bench, wedged tightly between fellow visitors, and listen to a heavy-handed, noisy gag about those roistering, roustabout days along the Missouri. And the Tom Sawyer Island crowd doesn't even bother to shoot you. Just for that we're going to tell you the answer to the guide's extraordinarily lackluster joke: "Firewood." *Duration: 10–15 mins. Crowds: Lines move slowly because of boats' low passenger capacity. Strategy: Skip this on your first visit. Audience: All ages. Rating:* ★

⑰ **Haunted Mansion.** The special effects here are a howl. Or should we say a scream? You are greeted at the creaking iron gates of this Hudson Gothic mansion by a lugubrious attendant, who has the only job at Walt Disney World for which smiling is frowned upon, and ushered into a spooky picture gallery. A disembodied voice echoes from the walls: "Welcome, foolish mortals, to the Haunted Mansion. I am your ghost host." A scream shivers down, and you're off into one of the best attractions at Walt Disney World.

Consisting mainly of a slow-moving ride in a black, cocoonlike "doom buggy," the Haunted Mansion is scary but not terrifying for adults, and moderately scary for younger children, mostly because of the darkness throughout. Certainly, the special effects are delightful. Catch the glowing bats' eyes on the wallpaper; the suit of armor that comes alive; the shifting walls in the portrait gallery that make you wonder if they are moving up or if you are moving down; the strategically placed gusts of damp, cold air; the marble busts of the world's greatest ghost writers in the library; the wacky inscriptions on the tombstones as you wait in line; the spectral xylophone player who enlivens the graveyard shift with bones instead of mallets; the ghostly ballroom dancers; and, of course, the chattering head of the woman in the crystal ball. If you look at her hard enough, you'll see she's a hologram. Just when you think the Imagineers have exhausted their bag of ectoplasmic tricks, along comes another one. They've saved the best for last, as you suddenly discover that your doom buggy has gained an extra passenger. As you approach the exit, your ghoulish guide intones, "Now I will raise the safety bar and the ghost will follow you home." Thanks for the souvenir, pal.

An interesting piece of Disney trivia: one of the biggest jobs for the maintenance crew here is not cleaning up but keeping the 200-odd trunks, chairs, harps, dress forms, statues, rugs, and other knickknacks appropriately dusty. Disney buys its dust in 5-pound bags and scatters it throughout the mansion with a special gadget resembling a fertilizer spreader. According to local lore, enough dust has been dumped since the park's 1971 opening to completely bury the mansion. Where does it all go? Perhaps the voice is right in saying that something will follow you home. *Duration: 8 mins. Crowds: Substantial, but high capacity and fast loading usually keep lines moving. Strategy: Go early, late, or during the nighttime parade; at any other time, check the line and go back later if it's long. And always check out the space to the left—you can walk wherever there's no velvet rope barring your passage. Audience: All but young children, who may be frightened. Rating:* ★★★

Fantasyland

Walt Disney called this "a timeless land of enchantment." Fantasyland does conjure up pixie dust. Perhaps that's because the fanciful gingerbread houses, gleaming gold turrets, and, of course, rides based on Disney-animated movies are what the Magic Kingdom is all about.

With the exception of the slightly spooky **Snow White's Scary Adventures**, the attractions here are imaginative rather than heart-stopping. Like the animated classics on which they are based, these rides—which could ostensibly be classified as rides for children—are packed with enough delightful detail to engage the adults who accompany them. Although the youngsters are awed by the bigger picture, their parents take a quick trip back to their childhoods via rides that conjure up favorite images of Winnie the Pooh, Peter Pan, and others, and it's hard to remain unmoved by the view of moonlit London in **Peter Pan's Flight**. If you're traveling without children, stick with Peter Pan and the unforgettable **it's a small world** and enjoy the rest of the scenery as you pass through, or save the rides for evening, when a sizable number of the little ones will have departed for their own private dreamland. Unfortunately, Fantasyland is always the most heavily trafficked area in the park, and its rides are almost always crowded.

You can enter Fantasyland on foot from Liberty Square, but the classic introduction is through the **Cinderella Castle.** To get in an appropriately magical mood—and to provide yourself with a cooling break—turn left immediately after you exit the castle's archway. Here you'll find one of the most charming and most overlooked touches in Fantasyland: **Cinderella Fountain,** a lovely brass casting of the castle's namesake, who's dressed in her peasant togs and surrounded by her beloved mice and bird friends. Water splashing from the fountain provides a cooling sensation on a hot day—as do the very welcome brass drinking fountains at the statue's base. Don't forget to toss in a coin and make a wish; after all, you're in Fantasyland, where dreams do come true.

Photographers will want to take advantage of one of the least-traveled byways in the Magic Kingdom. If you're coming to Fantasyland from the southern end of Liberty Square, turn left at the Sleepy Hollow snack shop. Just past the outdoor tables you'll find a shortcut that provides about the best unobstructed ground-level view of Cinderella Castle. It's a great spot for a family photo.

⑱ it's a small world. Visiting Walt Disney World and not stopping for this tribute to terminal cuteness—why, the idea is practically un-American. Disney raided the remains of the 1964–65 New York World's Fair for this boat ride and then appropriated the theme song of international brotherhood and friendship for its own.

The ride strains the patience more than the adrenal glands. Moving somewhat slower than a snail, your barge inches through several brightly colored barnlike rooms, each representing a continent and each crammed with musical moppets, all madly singing the theme song, "It's a Small World After All." It's the revenge of the Audio-Animatrons, you think, as simplistic dolls differentiated only by their national costumes—Dutch babies in clogs, Spanish flamenco dancers, German oompah bands, Russian balalaikas, sari-wrapped Indians waving temple bells, Tower of London guards in scarlet Beefeater uniforms, yodelers and goatherds, Japanese kite fliers, and juvenile cancan dancers, to name just a few—parade past, smiling away and wagging their heads in time to the song. But somehow, by the time you reach the end of the ride, you're grinning and wagging, too. You just can't help it— and small children can't wait to ride again. By the way, there is only one verse to the song, and it repeats incessantly, tattooing itself indelibly into your brain. Now all together: "It's a world of laughter, a world of tears. It's a world of hope and a world of fears . . ." *Duration: 11 mins. Crowds: Steady, but lines move fast. Strategy: Check out all available queues before you line up—one line is sometimes shorter. Go back later if there's a wait, since crowds ebb and flow here. Audience: All ages. Rating:* ★★

⑲ Peter Pan's Flight. This truly fantastic indoor ride was inspired by Sir James M. Barrie's story about the boy who wouldn't grow up, which Disney animated in 1953. Aboard two-person magic sailing ships with brightly striped sails, you soar into the skies above London en route to Never Land. Along the way you see Wendy, Michael, and John get sprinkled with pixie dust while Nana barks below, wave to Princess Tiger Lily, meet the evil Captain Hook, and cheer for the tick-tocking, clock-swallowing crocodile who's breakfasted on Hook's hand and is more than ready for lunch. Despite the absence of high-tech special effects, children love this ride. Adults enjoy the dreamy views of London by moonlight, a galaxy of twinkling yellow lights punctuated by

Big Ben, London Bridge, and a moonlit Thames River. There's so much to see that the ride seems much longer than it is. *Duration: 2½ mins. Crowds: Always heavy, except in the evening and early morning. Strategy: Go early, during the afternoon parade, or after dark. Audience: All ages. Rating:* ★★

⑳ **Legend of the Lion King.** Featuring an advanced form of puppetry, the elaborate stage show based on Disney's 32nd animated feature gets some extra pizzazz from good special effects and Elton John's lyrical music. Unlike many of the stage shows in the Magic Kingdom, this one does not draw on human talent; here, Simba, Mufasa, Scar, and the rest of the characters are played by "humanimals," Disneyspeak for bigger-than-life-size figures that are manipulated by human "animateers" hidden from the audience's view. The preshow consists of the opening "Circle of Life" overture from the film. *Duration: 15 mins. Crowds: Rendered insignificant by large theater capacity. Strategy: Save this for mid- or late afternoon, when you want to sit down and cool off. Audience: All ages. Note that last show is 30 mins to 1 hr before park closing; check with show attendant. Rating:* ★★

㉑ **Cinderella Castle.** This quintessential Disney icon, with its royal blue turrets, gold spires, and glistening white towers, was inspired by the castle built by the mad Bavarian king Ludwig at Neuschwanstein, as well as by drawings prepared for Disney's animated film of the classic French fairy tale. Although often confused with Disneyland's Sleeping Beauty Castle, at 180 ft this castle is more than 100 ft taller; and with its elongated towers and lacy fretwork, it is immeasurably more graceful. It's easy to bypass the elaborate murals on the walls of the archway as you rush toward Fantasyland from the Hub, but they are worth a stop. The five panels, measuring some 15 ft high and 10 ft wide, were created by Disney artist Dorothea Redmond and realized in a million bits of multicolor Italian glass, real silver, and 14-karat gold by mosaicist Hanns-Joachim Scharff. Following the images drawn for the Disney film, the mosaics tell the story of the little cinder girl from pumpkin to prince and happily ever after.

The fantasy has feet, if not of clay, then of solid steel beams, fiberglass, and 500 gallons of paint. Instead of dungeons, there are service tunnels for the Magic Kingdom's less-than-magical quotidian operations. These are the same tunnels that honeycomb the ground under much of the park. And upstairs does not hold, as rumor has it, a casket containing the cryogenically preserved body of Walt Disney but instead mundane broadcast facilities, security rooms, and the like (which you don't see).

Within the castle's archway, on the left as you face Fantasyland, is the **King's Gallery,** one of the Magic Kingdom's priciest shops. Here you'll find exquisite hand-painted models of carousel horses, delicate crystal castles, and other symbols of fairy-tale magic, including Cinderella's glass slipper in a variety of colors and sizes.

㉒ **Snow White's Scary Adventures.** What was previously an unremittingly scary indoor spook-house ride where the dwarves might as well have been named Anxious and Fearful is now a kinder, gentler experience with six-passenger cars and a miniversion of the movie. There's still the evil queen, the wart on her nose, and her cackle, but joining the cast at long last are the prince and Snow White herself. Although the trip is packed with plenty of scary moments, an honest-to-goodness kiss followed by a happily-ever-after ending might even get you heigh-ho-ing on your way. *Duration: 3 mins. Crowds: Steady from late morning until evening. Strategy: Go very early, during the afternoon* *parade, or after dark. Audience: All ages; may be frightening for young children. Rating:* ★★

㉓ Cinderella's Golden Carrousel. This is the whirling, musical heart of Fantasyland. This ride encapsulates the Disney experience in 90 prancing horses and then hands it to you on a 60-ft platter. Seventy-two of the dashing wooden steeds date from the original carousel built in 1917 by the Philadelphia Toboggan Company; 12 additional mounts were made of fiberglass. All are meticulously painted—at a rate of about 48 hours per horse—and each one is completely different. One steed wears a collar of bright yellow roses, another a quiver of Native American arrows, and yet another, for some completely mysterious reason, a portrait of Eric the Red. They gallop ceaselessly beneath a wooden canopy, gaily striped on the outside and decorated on the inside with 18 panels depicting scenes from Disney's 1950 film *Cinderella*. As the platter starts to spin, the mirrors sparkle, the fairy lights glitter, and the rich notes of the band organ—no calliope here—play favorite tunes from Disney movies. If you wished upon a star, it couldn't get more magical. *Duration: 2 mins. Crowds: Lines during busy periods. Strategy: Go early, during the afternoon parade, or after dark. Audience: All ages. Rating:* ★★

㉔ Dumbo the Flying Elephant. Hands down, this is one of Fantasyland's most popular rides. Although the story has one baby elephant with gigantic ears who accidentally downs a bucket of champagne and learns he can fly, the ride has 16 jolly Dumbos flying around a central column, each pachyderm packing a couple of kids and a parent. A joystick controls each of Dumbo's vertical motions, so you can make him ascend or descend at will. Alas, the ears do not flap. *Duration: 2 mins. Crowds: Perpetual, except in very early morning, and there's no shade—in summer, the wait is truly brutal. Strategy: If accompanying small children, make a beeline here at Rope Drop; otherwise, skip it. Audience: Young children—the modest thrills are just perfect for them. Rating:* ★

㉕ Ariel's Grotto. This starfish-scattered, pink-and-purple-character meet-and-greet locale carries out an "Under the Sea" motif. Ariel the Little Mermaid is always here in person, her dark carrot-red tresses cascading onto her glittery green tail. Just across the ropes from the queue area are a group of wonderfully interactive fountains that little kids love splashing around in. *Duration: Up to you. Strategy: Check your map for appearance times, and arrive at least 20 mins ahead. Audience: Young children. Rating:* ★

㉖ Fantasyland Character Festival. In the former queue-up area of 20,000 Leagues Under the Sea, you can collect autographs from and have your picture taken with Pinocchio, Pluto, Goofy, and other popular characters. *Duration: Up to you. Strategy: Check your map for appearance times and arrive at least 20 mins ahead. Lines tend to be longer in later morning and early afternoon, when toddlers are at their best. Audience: Young children. Rating:* ★

㉗ The Many Adventures of Winnie the Pooh. The famous honey-lover and his exploits in the Hundred Acre Wood are the theme for this newcomer on the site of the late lamented Mr. Toad's Wild Ride, and you can read passages from A. A. Milne's famous stories as you wait in line. Once you board your honey pot, Pooh and his friends wish you a "happy windsday." Pooh flies through the air, held aloft by his balloon, in his perennial search for "hunny," and you bounce along with Tigger, ride with the Heffalumps and Woozles, and experience a cloudburst. When the rain ends at last, everyone gathers again to say "Hurray!" *Dura-*

tion: About 3 mins. Crowds: To be expected—new attractions always draw crowds. Strategy: Use the FASTPASS setup; if the youngsters favor immediate gratification, go early in the day, late in the afternoon, or after dark. Audience: All ages. Rating: ★★★

㉘ Fairytale Garden. Belle makes an appearance here and brings *Beauty and the Beast* to life, using park guests as members of the cast. Storytelling was never made to be so much fun. *Duration: 25 minutes. Crowds: Heaviest in midday. Strategy: See during the Fantasyland stage show or during the parade. Audience: All ages. Rating:* ★

㉙ Mad Tea Party. A staple in carnivals, where it's known as "Tubs o' Fun," this Fantasyland icon is for the vertigo addict looking for a fix. The Disney version is based on the 1951 film *Alice in Wonderland,* in which the Mad Hatter hosts a tea party for his un-birthday. You hop into oversize, pastel-color teacups and whirl around a giant platter. Add your own spin to the teacup's orbit with the help of the steering wheel in the center. If the centrifugal force hasn't shaken you up too much, check out the soused mouse that pops out of the teapot centerpiece and compare his condition to your own. *Duration: 2 mins. Crowds: Steady from late morning on, with slow-moving lines. Strategy: Skip this on your first Magic Kingdom visit. Rating:* ★

Mickey's Toontown Fair

This concentrated dose of adulation for the big-eared mighty one was built in 1988 as Mickey's Birthdayland to celebrate the Mouse's Big Six-O. Then, owing to its popularity with the small-fry set, it was retained, first as Mickey's Starland and now as an official Magic Kingdom land, a 3-acre niche set off to the side of Fantasyland. As in a scene from a cartoon, everything is child size. The pastel houses are positively Lilliputian, with miniature driveways, toy-size picket fences, and signs scribbled with finger paint. The best way to arrive is on the Walt Disney World Railroad, the old-fashioned choo-choo that also stops at Main Street and Frontierland.

㉚ Barnstormer at Goofy's Wiseacres Farm. Traditional red barns and farm buildings form the backdrop here. The real attraction is the Barnstormer, a roller coaster whose ride vehicles are 1920s crop-dusting biplanes—designed for children but large enough for adults as well. If there are any questions in your mind as to whether your offspring are up to Big Thunder Mountain, stop here first. *Duration: 1 min. Crowds: Heaviest in mid-morning. Strategy: Visit in the evening when tykes have gone home. Audience: Younger children. Minimum height: 36". Rating:* ★★

㉛ Toon Park. This spongy green area is filled with foam topiary in the shapes of goats, cows, pigs, and horses. Children can jump and hop on interactive lily pads to hear animal topiaries moo, bleat, and whinny. *Duration: Up to you. Crowds: Moderate and seldom a problem. Strategy: Go anytime. Audience: Young children mainly, but everyone enjoys watching them. Rating:* ★

㉜ Donald's Boat. A cross between a tugboat and a leaky ocean liner, the *Miss Daisy* is actually a water play area, with lily pads that spout jumping streams and spray without warning. Although it's intended for kids, there's no reason for grown-ups not to take the opportunity to cool off here on a humid Central Florida afternoon, too. *Duration: Up to you. Crowds: Can get heavy in late morning and early afternoon. Strategy: Go first thing in the morning or after the toddlers have gone home. Audience: Young children and their families. Rating:* ★★

Toontown Market sells hot dogs and soft drinks. If you're lucky, you can find a place on the park bench next to the cart and give your feet a break.

㉝ Mickey's Country House. As you walk through this slightly goofy piece of architecture right in the heart of Toontown Fairgrounds, notice the radio in the living room, "tooned" to scores from Mickey's favorite football team, Duckburg University. Down the hall, Mickey's kitchen shows the ill effects of Donald and Goofy's attempt to win the Toontown Home Remodeling Contest—with buckets of paint spilled and stacked in the sink and paint splattered on the floor and walls. The flowers in the garden, just outside the kitchen, are shaped like Mickey's familiar silhouette, and Mickey's Mousekosh overalls are drying on the clothesline next to oversize tomato plants, cactus plants, and pumpkins (complete with ears, of course). *Duration: Up to you. Crowds: Moderate. Strategy: Go first thing in the morning or during the afternoon parade. Audience: All ages, although teens may be put off by the terminal cuteness of it all. Rating:* ★★

㉞ Toontown Hall of Fame. Stop here to collect an autograph and a hug from Disney characters and check out the blue-ribbon-winning entries from the Toontown Fair. **County Bounty** sells stuffed animals and all kinds of Toontown souvenirs. *Duration: Up to you. Crowds: Can get heavy in late morning and early afternoon. Strategy: Go first thing in the morning or after the toddlers have gone home. Audience: Young children. Rating:* ★★

㉟ Minnie's Country House. Unlike Mickey's house, where ropes keep you from going into the rooms, this baby-blue and pink house is a please-touch kind of place. In this scenario, Minnie is editor of *Minnie's Cartoon Country Living* magazine, the Martha Stewart of the mouse set. While touring her office, crafts room, and kitchen you can check the latest messages on her answering machine, bake a "quick rising" cake at the touch of a button, and, opening the refrigerator door, get a wonderful blast of arctic air. *Duration: Up to you. Crowds: Moderate. Strategy: Go first thing in the morning or during the afternoon parade. Audience: All ages, although teens may be put off. Rating:* ★★

Tomorrowland

The stark, antiseptic future predicted by the original Tomorrowland had become embarrassingly passé by the mid-'90s: bare concrete and plain white walls, plus such outdated rides as Starjets and Mission to Mars, said more about Eisenhower-era aesthetics, or lack thereof, than about third-millennium progress. So to revitalize what had become the least appealing area of the Magic Kingdom, Disney artists and architects created new facades, restaurants, and shops for an energized Future City, which is more similar in mood to the theme villages of other lands. And this time around the creators showed that they had learned their lesson: rather than forecast a tomorrow destined for obsolescence, they focused on "the future that never was," the future envisioned by sci-fi writers and moviemakers in the '20s and '30s, when space flight, laser beams, and home computers belonged in the world of fiction, not fact. As the millennium dawns, the Jetsonesque styling has a retro feel that lends it fresh chic—at least for now.

The ATM near the **Tomorrowland Arcade** is useful when the games begin to deplete your stash of cash.

㊱ Tomorrowland Indy Speedway. This is one of those rides that incites instant addiction among children and immediate antipathy among parents. The reasons for the former are easy to figure out: the brightly colored Mark VII model, gasoline-powered cars that swerve around the four 2,260-ft tracks with much vroom-vroom-vrooming. Kids will feel like they are Mario Andretti as they race around the track. Like real sports cars, the vehicles are equipped with rack-and-pinion steering and disc brakes; unlike the real thing, these run on a track. However, the track is so twisty that it's hard to keep the car on a straight course—something the race car fanatics warming the bleachers love to watch. If you're not a fanatic, the persistent noise and pervasive smell of high-test on a muggy Central Florida afternoon can quickly rasp your nerves into the danger zone. Furthermore, there's a lot of waiting: you can wait up to an hour to get on the track; you wait again for your turn to climb in a car; then you wait one more time to return your vehicle after your lap. All this for a ride in which the main thrill is achieving a top speed of 7 mph. *Duration: 5 mins. Crowds: Steady and heavy from late morning to evening. Strategy: Go in the evening or during a parade; skip on a first-time visit until you've been through all the major attractions. Audience: Older children. Minimum height: 52" to drive. Rating:* ★

㊲ Tomorrowland Arcade. Main Street's Penny Arcade has been moved to a new locale inside the Tomorrowland Light and Power Company and updated to reflect its new surroundings. With the move, however, much of the charm of the Main Street digs has been lost; gone are the antique Mute-o-scopes and Cail-o-scopes that cost a nickel. In their place are a bank of video games, with a heavy emphasis on Formula One racing. There is one tribute to the past left—an antique Candy Crane, where youngsters can fish for toys. Alas, it never has a line. *Duration: Up to you. Crowds: Not usually a problem. Strategy: Give it a wide berth unless you love arcade games. Audience: Teens. Rating:* ★

㊳ Space Mountain. The needlelike spires and gleaming white concrete cone of this attraction are almost as much of a Magic Kingdom landmark as Cinderella Castle. Towering 180 ft high, the structure has been called "Florida's third-highest mountain." Inside is arguably the world's most imaginative roller coaster—still. Although there are no loop-the-loops, gravitational whizbangs, or high-speed curves, the thrills are amply provided by Disney's masterful brainwashing as you take a trip into the depths of outer space—in the dark.

The mood for your space shot is set in the waiting area, where a dim blue light reflects off the mirror-and-chrome walls, while above planets and galaxies and meteors and comets whirl past; strobe lights flash, and the fluorescent panels on the six-passenger rockets streak by, leaving phosphorescent memories. Screams and shrieks echo in the chamber, piercing the rattling of the cars and the various otherworldly beeps and buzzes. Meanwhile, you can't help overhearing gossip about how earrings have been known to be ripped out of earlobes by the centrifugal force, pocketbooks shaken open and upended, and so on.

Finally, you get your chance to wedge yourself into the seat. The blinking sign in front switches from "boarding" to "blast off," and you do. The ride lasts only 2 minutes and 38 seconds and attains a top speed of 28 mph, but the devious twists and invisible drops, and the fact that you can't see where you're going, make it seem twice as long and many more times as thrilling. People of all ages adore this ride.

For the significant number who dislike it or are afraid they will, there's a bail-out area just before boarding. Keep in mind, though, that although the ride *is* rough, and it's a good idea to stow personal belongings securely, Disney staffers in a control booth constantly monitor the ride on a battery of closed-circuit televisions; at the first sign of any guest having trouble, the ride can be stopped. And that seldom happens. *Duration: 2½ mins. Crowds: Large and steady, with long lines from morning to night despite high capacity. Strategy: Sign up for a FASTPASS time and ride when you have your appointment. Or go either at the end of the day, during a parade, or at Rope Drop (in which case you should wait at the Plaza Restaurant to give yourself a 120-yard head start on the crowd). Audience: All except young children. No pregnant women or guests wearing back, neck, or leg braces. Minimum height: 44". Rating:* ★★★

③⑨ Carousel of Progress. Originally seen at New York's 1964–65 World's Fair, this revolving theater traces the impact of technological progress on the daily lives of Americans from the turn of the 20th century into the near future. Representing each decade, an Audio-Animatronics family sings the praises of the new gadgets that technology has wrought. Fans of the holiday film *A Christmas Story* will recognize the voice of its narrator, Jean Shepard, who injects his folksy, all-American humor as father figure through the decades. A preshow, which you see on overhead video monitors while waiting to enter the theater, details the design of the original carousel and features Walt himself singing the theme song. Speaking of which, the irritating theme of years past, "The Best Time of Your Life," has been replaced by the ride's original ditty, "There's a Great Big Beautiful Tomorrow"—very fitting in the new Tomorrowland. *Duration: 20 mins. Crowds: Moderate. Strategy: Skip on a first-time visit. Audience: All ages. Rating:* ★

④⓪ Tomorrowland Transit Authority. A reincarnation of what Disney old-timers may remember as the WEDway PeopleMover, the TTA takes a nice, leisurely ride around the perimeter of Tomorrowland, circling the Astro-Orbiter and eventually gliding through the middle of Space Mountain. Some fainthearted TTA passengers have no doubt chucked the notion of riding the roller coaster after being exposed firsthand to the screams emanating from the dark of the mountain—although these make the ride sound worse than it really is. Disney's version of future mass transit is smooth and noiseless, thanks to an electromagnetic linear induction motor that has no moving parts, uses little power, and emits no pollutants. *Duration: 6 mins. Crowds: Not one of the park's popular attractions, so lines are seldom long. Strategy: Go if you want to preview Space Mountain, but skip on a first-time visit until you've been through all the major attractions. Audience: All ages. Rating:* ★

④① Astro-Orbiter. This gleaming superstructure of revolving planets has come to symbolize the new Tomorrowland as much as Dumbo represents Fantasyland. The ride itself, however, hasn't changed much since it was Starjets. Passenger vehicles, on arms projecting from a central column, sail past whirling planets; you control your car's altitude if not the velocity. The entrance is directly across from the entrance to the TTA. *Duration: 2 mins. Crowds: Humongous, and the line moves slowly. Strategy: Skip on your first visit if time is short, unless there's no line. Audience: All ages. Rating:* ★★

④② ExtraTERRORestrial Alien Encounter. This ride is probably the single scariest attraction in all of Walt Disney World, engendering start-to-finish screams among teens and ashen faces and tears among younger children who decide to brave it despite the warnings posted throughout the queuing area. Playing on Tomorrowland's new Future City theme, the story line is that you're entering the city's convention center to watch a test of a new teleportation system. Representatives from the device's manufacturer, an alien corporation called XS-Tech (pronounced "excess")—whose motto is "If something can't be done with XS, it can't be done at all"—try to transport the company's CEO from their planet to Earth. The attempt fails, however, and the resulting catastrophe consists of a very close encounter with an "extraTERRORestrial" creature, complete with realistic sound effects, smoke, and several seconds of complete, seriously inky darkness. *Duration: 20 mins. Crowds: Expect lines. Strategy: Go first thing in the morning or during a parade or the fireworks. Audience: All but young children, who will be absolutely terrified, and those afraid of the dark. Rating:* ★★

43 **Buzz Lightyear's Space Ranger Spin.** Based on the wildly popular *Toy Story II*, this ride pits you and Buzz against the world. You're seated in a fast-moving two-passenger vehicle with a laser gun in front of each rider. You shoot at targets throughout the ride to help Disney's macho space man defeat Emperor Zurg and save the universe—you have to hit the targets marked with a "Z" to score, and the rider with the most points wins. As Buzz likes to say, "To infinity—and beyond!" Be sure to take note of the much larger-than-life-size toys in the queue area. *Duration: 5 mins. Crowds: Substantial, but lines move fast. Go first thing in the morning, get your FASTPASS appointment time, then return when scheduled. Audience: Mainly young children age 3 and above who are in love with Buzz, although it's really fun for everybody. Rating:* ★★★

44 **Timekeeper.** Disney World trivia buffs may remember this attraction as the former "America the Beautiful," a CircleVision 360° tribute to the natural wonders of the United States. It's now a time-traveling adventure hosted by TimeKeeper, a C-3PO clone whose frenetic personality is given voice by the great Robin Williams, and Nine-Eye, a slightly frazzled droid, who's a graduate of MIT (the Metropolis Institute of Time Travel). Along the way, you meet famous inventors and visionaries of the machine age, such as Jules Verne and H. G. Wells. Don't plan on a relaxing voyage, however; there are no seats in the theater—only lean rails. *Duration: 11 mins. Crowds: Moderate but lines move steadily, since theater capacity is nearly 900. Strategy: Go when the lines at ExtraTERRORestrial Alien Encounter are long. Audience: All ages, although you'll have to hold youngsters or piggyback them so they can see. Rating:* ★★

Strategies for Your Visit to the Magic Kingdom

When to Go

Most families hit the Magic Kingdom early in their visit, so try to go toward the end of the week instead. Although tourists use weekends as travel days, local residents use them to visit the park. If you're staying in a Disney hotel, visit on one of the early admission days, which are Saturdays, Mondays, and Thursdays. Be sure to arrive at the turnstiles about 15 minutes before the appointed hour so that you can take full advantage of this special perk. If you're *not* staying at a Disney hotel, make sure that you don't make your Magic Kingdom visit on the early admission day—otherwise you'll go to a lot of trouble to show up early only to find that privileged Disney guests have already been there for an hour.

Blitz Tours

WITH SMALL CHILDREN

Go directly to Fantasyland and start your day by making your FAST-PASS appointment at the **Many Adventures of Winnie the Pooh.** Then, go on a ride with **Dumbo the Flying Elephant.** Check your character-greeting location guide and modify the rest of your visit accordingly. Probably, your next stops should be **Cinderella's Golden Carrousel** and, moving clockwise, the other attractions. By now, it will probably be time to ride the **Many Adventures of Winnie the Pooh,** using your FAST-

PASS. Then, check the line at **Legend of the Lion King**; if it's moving briskly, join the crowd. You'll get into the next show. Next visit **Ariel's Grotto** to pose for snapshots with the Little Mermaid. Leave **it's a small world** until last; its continuously moving lines keep crowds shuffling along, and it's a nice end to a Fantasyland visit.

Proceed to Cinderella Castle for lunch at Cinderella's Royal Table, or head to Liberty Square and have an early lunch at Liberty Tree Tavern (be sure to make reservations in advance). Take an after-lunch tour of **Tom Sawyer Island** and follow it up with the next show at Frontierland's **Country Bear Jamboree**. Before queuing up for the line there, though, pick up your ticket for your FASTPASS appointment for **Splash Mountain**. Return to the **Country Bears**, then claim a piece of pavement for the three o'clock parade in front of the Bears. Then you'll be free to make a quick exit to line up for **Big Thunder Mountain Railroad**— if your kids can handle the thrills and are tall enough. For the shortest lines, go *during* the parade; make sure you're on the appropriate side of the parade route before it starts. By now, your FASTPASS ticket should be indicating that it's time to wait for **Splash Mountain**.

From the far corner of Frontierland, make a right at Frontier Woodcarving at the end of the row of false-front shops and take the shortcut to Adventureland. Proceed directly across the Adventureland plaza to the **Jungle Cruise**. Pick up another FASTPASS here if the line is more than 45 minutes long. If your arms and legs are up to it, scramble around the **Swiss Family Treehouse** as a time-killer, then do **Pirates of the Caribbean**, and head back for your "VIP" entry to the **Jungle Cruise**.

Now stroll through the rest room arch next to Plaza del Sol Caribe by the **Pirates of the Caribbean** back to Frontierland, round the corner of Splash Mountain to the **Walt Disney Railroad** station. Take the train to **Mickey's Toontown Fair**. From here, depending on your stamina, either proceed to Tomorrowland for the **Carousel of Progress** or hop back on board the train to Main Street.

If you're really determined to see it all, leave the park for your hotel. Come back for dinner at the **Crystal Palace** and claim a piece of pavement about an hour before the **evening parade.** (Check to see when it is; times change depending on the day and season.)

FOR EVERYONE ELSE

Arrive at the parking lot 45 minutes before scheduled opening, and once in the park, head for the **Walt Disney Railroad**, getting off at Frontierland to claim an early FASTPASS time for **Splash Mountain**. After you've received your ticket, head over for **Big Thunder Mountain Railroad**. Then, catch the next **Country Bears Jamboree show.** By now, if things are going well, your FASTPASS ticket should be valid to ride **Splash Mountain.** Now head over to Adventureland to the **Jungle Cruise** and pick up another FASTPASS. Use the 45-minute time allotment to do **Pirates of the Caribbean** and the **Swiss Family Treehouse.** If the time is still not right to do the Jungle Cruise, grab a bite to eat at **El Pirata Y el Perico Restaurante,** where you can get tacos, nachos and hot dogs, or some fat-free yogurt at the **Sunshine Tree Terrace.** By now, it should be time to take the **Jungle Cruise.** When you're done, sprint over to Tomorrowland and pick up your next FASTPASS, this time for **Space Mountain.** Take in the **Carousel of Progress,** where there is seldom a wait, and then ride the **Tomorrowland Transit Authority (TTA).** Experience the **ExtraTERRORestrial Alien Encounter** and, if there's time, **The Timekeeper.** By now, it will be time for you to ride **Space Mountain.** Now, pick up your next FASTPASS—this time for **Buzz Lightyear's Space Ranger Spin.** If you haven't done some of the attractions above, now's the time to squeeze them in before returning to help Buzz in his attempt to save the planet.

By now, it should be time to grab a piece of pavement for the three o'-clock parade. Send a member of your group to pick up the next set of FASTPASS tickets for **The Many Adventures of Winnie the Pooh.** Treat yourself to some ice cream at the **Plaza Ice Cream Parlor** or stop for a more substantial lunch at the **Plaza Restaurant,** a sit-down restaurant that serves sandwiches, burgers, and ice cream sundaes. If the crowds are not too thick, a real nice viewing spot is on the second floor of the train station. Now, take the train to **Mickey's Toontown Fair** and look at the cute houses there. From there, you'll run right into Fantasyland, where you can hit many of the attractions that were too crowded be-fore, now that the little ones are heading home. Take a ride on **Snow White's Scary Adventures,** then see the **Legend of the Lion King.** Treat the family to dinner at **Cinderella's Royal Table,** where you can get a magical view of Fantasyland as the sky turns to dusk. By now, your FASTPASS time should be valid for **The Many Adventures of Winnie the Pooh.** This attraction is so popular that when you retrieve your FAST-PASS appointment, you could have as much as a seven-hour wait to use it. If the lines aren't too long, you may want to forego utilizing the FASTPASS, depending on where you are at the moment.

Now is the time to take in the other Fantasyland attractions. **Cin-derella's Golden Carrousel** provides a magical touch to a Fantasyland visit when it's ridden in darkness. Then, head over to **it's a small world.** It's a nice way to end a Fantasyland stay.

Meander over to Liberty Square now. Take in the next **Hall of Presi-dents** show. It should be a good time to do the **Haunted Mansion** now. See if there's another performance of the **Diamond Horseshoe Saloon Revue.** During off-season, the last show is usually at 5:00. During the holidays, there is almostalways an evening show.

Upon your exit, sit down on a curb to see the **evening parade.** You can then meander your way to the exit through Adventureland and then to Main Street for the perfect viewing spot of the evening fireworks.

On Rainy Days
If you visit during a busy time of year, pray for rain. Rainy days dis-solve the crowds here. Unlike those at Disney–MGM and Epcot's Fu-ture World, however, many of the Magic Kingdom's attractions are outdoors. If you don't mind getting damp, pick up a brightly colored poncho on Main Street ($5 adults, $4 children) and soldier on.

Other Tips
- Arrive at least 30 minutes before Rope Drop to get your bearings and explore the shops on Main Street. On early admission days, there is no rope drop in Fantasyland or Tomorrowland.

- If you are staying at a Disney resort, check your pass to see whether you are entitled to early admission; this is vital, especially for parents with small children, who will be able to visit most of the Fantasyland rides before the park officially opens, thereby offering an opportunity to rest or do a water park.

- If you plan to spend time shopping, do it in mid-afternoon, when lines at rides resemble a malevolent anaconda taking a nap. During the af-ternoon parade, store clerks have actually been seen twiddling their thumbs; if you're looking for a hard-to-find item, this is the time to ask for sales assistance. If you go at the end of the day, you'll be en-gulfed by rush-hour crowds.

- For a similar reason, if you're willing to miss the parade, hit one of the star attractions, since lines will ease considerably. But be careful not to get stuck on the wrong side of the parade route when the hoopla starts, or you may never get across.

- Designate a very specific meeting place, such as a particular bench, after rest room stops, when it's easy to miss someone.

- Set up a rendezvous point and time at the start of the day, just in case you and your companions get separated. Good places are by the Cinderella Fountain in Fantasyland, the bottom of the staircase at the Main Street railroad station, and the archway entrance to Adventureland.

Magic Kingdom A to Z

Baby Care

The Magic Kingdom's soothing, quiet **Baby Care Center** is next to the Crystal Palace at the end of Main Street. Furnished with rocking chairs, it has a low lighting level that makes it comfortable for nursing. There are adorable toddler-size toilets (these may be a high point for your just-potty-trained offspring) as well as supplies such as formula, baby food, pacifiers, and disposable diapers. You'll find changing tables here, as well as in all women's rooms and some men's rooms. You can also buy disposable diapers in the Emporium on Main Street. The Stroller Shop near the entrance to the Magic Kingdom, on the east side of Main Street, is the place for stroller rentals ($7 fee; $1 deposit).

Barbershop

Tucked in a corner just off Main Street, where the Emporium ends, the **Harmony Barber Shop** isn't just for show—it's a for-real place to get a haircut from Disney cast members dressed in 19th-century costumes.

Cameras and Film

Kodak's disposable Fun Saver cameras are widely available in shops throughout the theme parks and hotels. The **Camera Center,** at Town Square, is staffed by cast members who will pose you and your group for a photo in front of Cinderella Castle. A 5″ x 7″ photo costs $7. This is also the place for minor camera repairs.

For two-hour film developing, look for the **Photo Express** sign throughout the park; drop your film in the container, and you can pick up your pictures at the Camera Center as you leave the park—instant gratification.

Dining

The gustatory offerings are mostly fast food—and every land has its share of restaurants serving burgers, hot dogs, grilled chicken sandwiches, and nachos, with a token salad or two thrown in for the on-the-go crowd. In addition, the walkways are peppered with carts dispensing popcorn, lemonade, and soda. If you want ice cream before afternoon and evening parades, stop at the ice-cream parlor on Main Street or at the Diamond Horseshoe.

FULL-SERVICE RESTAURANTS

Reservations are essential for the three full-service restaurants in the Magic Kingdom. You can make them at all restaurants or through the **Disney dining reservations hot line** (☎ 407/939–3463).

In **Cinderella's Royal Table,** the choices are basic: seafood salad or roast beef sandwiches at lunch; chicken, seafood, or prime rib at dinner. But the real attraction is that you get to eat inside Cinderella Castle in an old mead hall, where Cinderella herself is sometimes on hand in her truly magically shiny blue gown—sometimes escorted by her equally glittering fairy godmother—and serving wenches whisk around in medieval gowns and 13th-century-style wimples. How they keep their veils from dragging in the mayonnaise is one of those secrets revealed only to the adepts. A character breakfast here is a mighty special treat for the entire family—and a good way to get a jump on the Rope Drop stampede. *In Fantasyland.*

Decorated in lovely Williamsburg colors, with Early American antiques and lots of brightly polished brass, **Liberty Tree Tavern** is a pleasant place even when jammed to the gills. The menu is all-American, with oversize salads and assorted sandwiches a good bet at lunch, and fresh fish, prime rib, and chicken the best choices at dinner. You can also order a full Thanksgiving turkey feast with all the trimmings—even in July. But then you'd miss out on the idiosyncratic garnish that decorates the sandwiches: a slice of watermelon cut to resemble Mickey Mouse's profile, ears and all. Here at dinnertime, you can experience a "revolutionary" meal with the Disney characters. *In Liberty Square.*

Tony's Town Square Café is named after the Italian restaurant in *Lady and the Tramp,* where Disney's most famous canine couple share their first kiss over a plate of spaghetti. In fact, the video plays on a TV in the restaurant's waiting area. Lunch and "Da Dinner" menus offer pasta, of course, along with seafood, steak, and chicken. You can also have breakfast here beginning at 8:30. *Main Street.*

SELF-SERVICE RESTAURANT

In the **Crystal Palace,** the "buffets with character" are pleasant. Winnie the Pooh and his pals from the Hundred Acre Wood visit tables in this glass-roof conservatory, and the offerings at breakfast, lunch, and dinner are varied, generous, and surprisingly good. The black-bean soup is especially noteworthy, as are the burritos; both are regulars, and there's a sizable choice of pastas and salads that varies from day to day. The place is huge but charming with its numerous nooks and crannies, comfortable banquettes, cozy cast-iron tables, and abundant sunlight. It's also one of the few places in the Magic Kingdom that serves breakfast. *At the Hub end of Main Street facing Cinderella Castle.*

For Travelers with Disabilities

ATTRACTIONS

At monitor-equipped attractions, there is at least one television that has close-captioning for the hearing-impaired.

To board the **Walt Disney World Railroad** at the Main Street Station, you must transfer from your wheelchair, which can be folded to ride with you or left in the station. Alternatively, board at Frontierland or Mickey's Toontown Fair. The **Main Street Vehicles** can be boarded by guests with limited mobility who can fold their wheelchair and climb into a car. There are curb cuts or ramps on each corner.

In Adventureland, the **Swiss Family Treehouse,** with its 100 steps and lack of narration, gets low ratings among those with mobility and visual impairments. At the **Jungle Cruise,** boarding requires that a guest step down into the boat; those who can lip-read will find the skippers' punny narration, delivered with a handheld mike, difficult to follow, although sitting up front may make it easier to see. Boarding **Pirates of the Caribbean** requires transferring from a nonfolding to a folding wheelchair, available at the entrance; the flume drop may make the attraction inappropriate for those with limited upper-body strength or who wear neck or back braces, and because of gunshot and fire effects, service animals should stay behind.

Frontierland is the only area of the park, aside from Main Street, that has sidewalk curbs; there are ramps by the Mile Long Bar and east of Frontierland Trading Post. To ride **Big Thunder Mountain Railroad** and **Splash Mountain,** you must be able to step into the ride vehicle and walk short distances, in case of an emergency evacuation; those with limited upper-body strength should assess the situation on site, and those wearing back, neck, or leg braces should not ride. The same holds true for service animals. **Tom Sawyer Island,** with its stairs, bridges, inclines, and narrow caves, is not negotiable by those using a wheelchair. The **Diamond Horseshoe Saloon Revue** and the **Country Bear Jamboree** are completely wheelchair accessible; if you lip-read, ask to sit up front, especially at the Diamond Horseshoe (its script is not in the guide for guests with hearing impairments). The **Frontierland Shootin' Arcade** has two guns at wheelchair level.

The **Hall of Presidents** and *Liberty Belle* Riverboat, in Liberty Square, are completely wheelchair accessible. To ride the **Mike Fink Keelboats,** you must negotiate two steep steps. At the **Haunted Mansion,** guests using wheelchairs must transfer to the "doom buggies" and take one step; however, if you can walk as much as 200 ft, you will enjoy the great preshow as well as the sensations and eerie sounds of the rest of the ride.

The stage show **Legend of the Lion King** has wheelchair seating; for guests with visual impairments, the chief attraction is the music by Elton John. **it's a small world** can be boarded without leaving your wheelchair, but only if it's a standard-size one; guests using a scooter or an oversize chair must transfer to one of the attraction's standard chairs, available at the ride entrance. To board **Peter Pan's Flight, Dumbo the Flying Elephant, Cinderella's Golden Carrousel,** the **Mad Tea Party,** and **Snow White's Scary Adventures,** guests using wheelchairs must transfer to the ride vehicles. Dumbo and Peter Pan's are inappropriate for service animals. For **Winnie the Pooh,** people who use wheelchairs wait in the main queue, and then are able to roll right onto an individual honey pot to ride, with one member of their party accompanying them. There are amplifiers for guests with hearing impairments.

Mickey's Toontown Fair is completely accessible.

Of the Tomorrowland attractions, **ExtraTERRORestrial Alien Encounter, Timekeeper,** and the **Carousel of Progress** are barrier-free for those using wheelchairs. To board **Buzz Lightyear's Space Ranger Spin, Astro-Orbiter,** and the **Tomorrowland Transit Authority,** you must be able to walk several steps and transfer to the ride vehicle. The TTA has more appeal to guests with visual impairments. To drive **Tomorrowland Indy Speedway** cars, you must have adequate vision and be able to steer, press the gas pedal, and transfer into the low car seat. The cautions for Big Thunder Mountain Railroad and Splash Mountain (☞ *above*) also apply to **Space Mountain.** In the **Tomorrowland Arcade,** the machines may be too high for guests using wheelchairs and not of much interest for some guests with visual impairments.

RESTAURANTS AND SHOPS
All restaurants and shops throughout the park have level entrances or are accessible by ramps.

WHEELCHAIR RENTALS
Go to the gift shop to the left of the ticket booths at the **Transportation and Ticket Center** or the **Stroller Shop** inside the main entrance to your right ($7; $1 deposit); the latter also has motor-powered chairs ($30; $10 deposit). Electric scooters are also available ($30; $20 deposit). If your rental needs replacing, ask any host or hostess.

Entertainment

The main events are the **Disney characters,** especially if you're travel-ing with children, but even if you're not. In what Disney calls "char-acter greetings," these lovable creatures sign autographs and pose for snapshots throughout the park—line up at City Hall for your turn to pose for a picture, or snag Mickey's autograph in Mickey's Toontown Fair. Ariel's Grotto and the Fantasyland Character Festival in Fanta-syland are prime spots for character autographs. Pick up a character-greeting location guide at City Hall or in any shop for times and locations of these and other opportunities in the park.

Particularly along Main Street, you'll come upon all sorts of shows and happenings: a barbershop quartet, ragtime pianist, brass bands, banjo pickers. Every day just after 5 PM, homing pigeons wing their way to Cinderella Castle from Town Square as part of a **Flag Retreat.** There are usually **song-and-dance revues** in the Cinderella Castle forecourt and in Fantasyland and Tomorrowland as well.

You can get another eyeful of characters at the 15-minute-long **Daily Parade,** which proceeds through Frontierland and down Main Street beginning at 3 PM. It shows off floats, balloons, cartoon characters, dancers, and singers, who are usually lip-synching to music played over the public-address system. It's almost as good as the Macy's Thanks-giving Day Parade—and the streets are cleaner. There's usually some thematic rubric attached. Note that lines at popular attractions often disappear during the parade.

Times for after-dark entertainment depend on the day of the week, hol-idays and peak times, and, of course, when it gets dark. Check the sched-ule when you enter the park or even before.

The big deal is **Main Street Electrical Parade,** a 20-minute extravaganza that runs only during holiday periods and in summer. To the merry ac-companiment of a toe-tapping piece of blipping and bleeping music that's aptly named "Baroque Hoedown," Alice, Cinderella, and Mickey, among others, wave from their individualized perches that are outlined by thousands of twinkling lights. Even some of the characters and their human escorts are adorned with the tiny lights. It's a wondrous and shimmering spectacle you won't want to miss. At press time, though, the parade's fate after summer 2000 was up in the air.

For a blast, be sure to see **Fantasy in the Sky,** the Magic Kingdom fire-works display, heralded by a dimming of all the lights along Main Street and the strains of "When You Wish Upon A Star" playing over cam-ouflaged loudspeakers. A single spotlight illuminates the top turret of the Cinderella Castle and—poof!—Tinker Bell emerges in a shower of pixie dust. Thanks to an almost-invisible guy wire, she appears to fly over the treetops and the crowds, on her way to a Never Land touch-down located, appropriately enough, in Tomorrowland. Her disap-pearance signals the start of the fireworks, which fill the sky with some pixie dust of their own.

First Aid

The Magic Kingdom's First Aid Center, staffed by registered nurses, is alongside the Crystal Palace.

Getting Around

Once you're in the Magic Kingdom, distances are generally short, and the best way to get around is on foot. The Walt Disney World Rail-road, the Main Street vehicles, the Skyway between Fantasyland and

Tomorrowland, and the Tomorrowland Transit Authority do help you cover some territory and can give your feet a welcome rest, but they're primarily entertainment, not transportation.

Guided Tours

A number of **guided tours** are available; for information and reservations, call ☎ 407/939–8687. The 4½-hour **Keys to the Kingdom Tour** is good way to get a feel for the layout of the Magic Kingdom and what goes on behind the scenes ($45 adults and children 16 and up, not including park admission; no younger children allowed). Tours leave from City Hall four times daily at 9:30, 10:30, 1:30, and 2. Included are visits to some of the "backstage" zones: the parade staging area and parts of the tunnels that spiderweb the ground underneath the Magic Kingdom, including the wardrobe area.

The **Family Magic Tour** is a two-hour scavenger hunt in which your tour guide encourages you to find things that have disappeared. Disney officials don't want to reveal the tour's components—after all, it is the Family "Magic" Tour—but they can say that a special character greeting session and the opportunity for a no-wait ride on a favorite Fantasyland attraction await you at the end of the adventure. Meet at City Hall at 9:30 AM daily ($25 adults, $15 children).

Backstage Magic is a behind-the-scenes tour of the Magic Kingdom, Epcot, and MGM Studios. The cost is $199 per person, and theme park admission is not required.

Railroad enthusiasts will love **The Magic Behind Our Steam Trains,** which gives you an inside look at the daily operation of the WDW railroad. Beginning at 7:30 AM on Thursday, the tour is two hours long. Children over 10 years old may participate. Cost is $25 per person, plus park admission.

Lockers

You'll find lockers in an arcade underneath the Main Street Railroad Station ($5; $2 deposit). If what you need to store won't fit in the larger lockers, inquire at City Hall.

Lost Things and People

If you're worried about your children getting lost, you can get name tags at City Hall or at the Baby Center next to the Crystal Palace. Instruct them to talk to anyone with a Disney name tag if they lose you. If that does happen, immediately ask any cast member and try not to panic; children who are obviously lost are usually taken to City Hall or the Baby Care Center, where lost-children logbooks are kept, and everyone is well trained to effect speedy reunions. City Hall also has a lost and found and a computerized Message Center, where you can leave notes for your traveling companions, both those in the Magic Kingdom and those visiting other parks.

Money Matters

ATMs are located by the lockers underneath the Main Street railroad station, inside the Tomorrowland Arcade, and in the breezeway between Adventureland and Frontierland. For currency exchange, go to the Guest Relations window in the turnstile area, or to City Hall.

Package Pickup

Ask the shop clerk to send any large purchase you make to Guest Relations, so you won't have to carry it around all day. Allow three hours. The package pickup area is next to the Emporium, at the Town Square entrance.

Shopping

Everywhere you turn in the Magic Kingdom there are shops and stalls urging you to take home a little piece of the magic. Many of the trinket and treasure troves carry items themed to the area where they're found.

The big daddy of all Magic Kingdom shops is the enormous **Emporium,** which stocks thousands of Disney character products, f rom key chains to T-shirts to sunglasses and stuffed animals. Although perpetually crowded and absolutely mobbed at closing time, the Emporium is, hands down, one of the best sources for souvenirs, especially for hard-to-buy-for Aunt Tilly. Hang on to your kids in here; they're likely to wander away as they spot yet another trinket they have to have—and near park closing, the crowds are so thick that you'll be hard pressed to find them before you panic.

The **Main Street Athletic Shop** is a source for all things sports-related with character logos. **Ye Olde Christmas Shoppe** has a wonderful collection of holiday items. Serious collectors of Disney memorabilia stop at **Main Street Gallery,** next to City Hall. Limited-edition sculptures, dolls, posters, and sometimes even park signs are available, and you can have your portrait sketched by Disney character artists. The **Main Street Market House** sells fine cigars and cooking accessories of all types. **Uptown Jewelers** offers Mickey Mouse jewelry and collectibles.

Inside Cinderella Castle is the **King's Gallery,** where you can buy imported European clocks, chess sets, and tapestries while artisans perform intricate metalwork that will look just right in your house if you're going for that Olde Europe look. Another nifty nook is **Harmony Barber Shop,** on the west side of Main Street, where such old-time shaving items as mustache cups are sold. At **Heritage House,** in Liberty Square, history buffs can find presidential and Civil War memorabilia.

Among the all-time best Magic Kingdom souvenirs are the pirate hats, swords, and plastic hooks-for-hands at the **House of Treasure,** just outside Pirates of the Caribbean in Adventureland. Creepy-crawly rubber snakes and lizards, available at **Bwana Bob's** kiosk next to the entrance to the Jungle Cruise in Adventureland, are just the sort of thing to spook a younger sibling. For Davy Crockett coonskin hats, personalized sheriff badges, and Big Al memorabilia, check out **Big Al's,** across from the Country Bear Jamboree in Frontierland.

To get monogrammed mouse ears, stop at the **Chapeau,** on the east side of Main Street; the Fantasyland source for the famous black Mouseketeer toppers hats is **Sir Mickey's.** You'll find children's clothing with Disney characters at **Tinker Bell's Treasures,** in Fantasyland. The best collection of character pins can be found at the pushcart in front of the Fantasyland Character Carnival, across from the Winnie the Pooh ride. The **Briar Patch,** next door to Splash Mountain, handles all things Winnie the Pooh, and it's among several places where you can buy those signature yellow ponchos with Mickey smiling on the back—$5 for adults and $4 for kids.

Visitor Information

City Hall (☎ 407/824–4521) is the Magic Kingdom's principal information center. Here you can search for misplaced belongings or companions, ask questions of the omniscient staffers, and pick up the *Magic Kingdom Guide Book* and a schedule of daily events and character greetings (if you haven't requested one by mail in advance).

At the end of Main Street, on the left as you face Cinderella Castle, just before the Hub, is the **Tip Board,** a large chalkboard with constantly updated information about attractions' wait times—fairly reliable except for those moments when everyone follows the "See It Now!" advice and the line immediately triples.

Signs at the centrally located WDW Ticket and Transportation Center keep you posted about park hours and activities such as parades and fireworks. And cast members are available at almost every turn to help you. In fact, providing information for visitors is part of the job description of the young men and women who sweep the pavement and faithfully keep litter in its place.

EPCOT

Walt Disney World was created because of Walt Disney's dream of EPCOT, an "Experimental Prototype Community of Tomorrow." Disney envisioned a future in which nations coexisted in peace and harmony, reaping the miraculous harvest of technological achievement. He suggested the idea as early as October 1966, saying, "EPCOT will be an experimental prototype community of tomorrow that will take its cue from the new ideas and new technologies that are now emerging from the creative centers of American industry." He wrote of the never completed, always improving Epcot, "Epcot . . . will never cease to be a living blueprint of the future . . . a showcase to the world for the ingenuity and imagination of American free enterprise."

But with Disneyland hemmed in by development, Disney had to search for new lands in which to found his new world. He found it in Central Florida. Many of the technologies incorporated into the Walt Disney World infrastructure were cutting-edge at the time. But the permanent community that he envisioned wasn't to be and is only now taking shape, in a '90s way, in Disney's Celebration, an urban planner's dream of a town near grown-like-Topsy Kissimmee. Until the debut of Celebration, the closest entity to Walt's vision was Epcot, which opened in 1982, 16 years after Disney's death—a showcase, ostensibly, for the concepts that would be incorporated into the real-life Epcots of the future. Then, as now, it was composed of two parts: **Future World,** where the majority of pavilions are sponsored by major U.S. corporations and demonstrate their technological advances; and **World Showcase,** where exhibition areas each represent a different country.

Epcot today is both more and less than Walt Disney's original dream. Less because some of the Future World pavilions are stuck in a 1965 World's Fair mentality. Less because World Showcase presents views of its countries that are, as an Epcot guide once put it, "as Americans perceive them"—highly idealized. Less because the missionary zeal that infuses the park backfires occasionally; young children get bored and adults start to wonder if they have to take a short test at the exit.

But these are minor quibbles in the face of the major achievement: Epcot is that rare paradox—an educational theme park—and a very successful one, too. The amount of imagination concentrated in its 230 acres is astounding. Through ingenious architecture, intriguing exhibits, amusing and awe-inspiring movies, and lively rides, Epcot inspires curiosity, rewards discovery, and encourages the creative spark in each of us. Something as simple as the leapfrogging fountains outside the Journey into Your Imagination pavilion can be as entrancing as the attractions themselves. As the park ages and the plantings mature, Epcot is also taking on a very real charm and even tranquility.

As a result, although rides have been added over the years, the thrills are mostly for the mind. Consequently, Epcot is best for older children and adults. (If you do bring young ones, don't miss the Kid Zones sprin-

42

20 ROMANTIC THINGS TO DO AT WALT DISNEY WORLD®

NOT EVERYTHING AT DISNEY World involves children. Get a baby-sitter and enjoy some private time, just the two of you.

1. Have dinner at the very grand Victoria and Albert's restaurant in the Grand Floridian (☞ Walt Disney World *in* Chapter 6).

2. Have dinner at the California Grill and watch the Magic Kingdom fireworks (☞ In Walt Disney World: Disney-Owned Hotels *in* Chapter 7; In Walt Disney World *in* Chapter 6).

3. Rent a boat to take a cruise on the Seven Seas Lagoon or the waterways leading to it. Bring champagne, and glasses (☞ Watersports *in* Chapter 9).

4. Take a nighttime whirl on Cinderella's Golden Carrousel in Fantasyland. Sparkling lights make it magical (☞ Fantasyland *in* Magic Kingdom, *above*).

5. Have your picture taken and grab a kiss in the heart-shaped gazebo in the back of Minnie's Country House (☞ Magic Kingdom, *above*).

6. Sit on the beach at the Grand Floridian at sunrise or at dusk—a special time (☞ In Walt Disney World: Disney-Owned Hotels *in* Chapter 7).

7. Have a massage day at the Disney Institute (☞ Smart Travel Tips A to Z).

8. Buy a faux diamond ring at the Emporium on Main Street in the Magic Kingdom (☞ Magic Kingdom A to Z *in* Magic Kingdom, *above*). Propose to your sweetheart at your favorite spot in the World.

9. Have a caricature drawn of the two of you at the Marketplace (☞ Walt Disney World *in* Chapter 8).

10. Sit by the fountain in front of Epcot's France pavilion and have some wine or a pastry and coffee (☞ Epcot, *above*).

11. Have a drink at the cozy Yachtsman's Crew bar in the Yacht Club hotel.

12. After dinner at Narcoosee's in the Grand Floridian, watch the Electrical Water Pageant outside (☞ Walt Disney World *in* Chapter 10).

13. Take a walk on the BoardWalk. Watch IllumiNations from the bridge to the Yacht and Beach Club. Then boogie at Atlantic Dance (☞ Walt Disney World *in* Chapter 10).

14. Tie the knot all over again at the Wedding Pavilion. Invite Mickey and Minnie to the reception (☞ Weddings *in* Smart Travel Tips A to Z).

15. Rent a hot-air balloon for a magical tour of Walt Disney World (☞ Sightseeing Tours *in* Smart Travel Tips A to Z).

16. Every night is New Year's Eve at Pleasure Island. Declare your love amid confetti and fireworks (☞ Walt Disney World *in* Chapter 10).

17. Enjoy a British lager outside at Epcot's Rose & Crown Pub—a perfect IllumiNations viewing spot. Book ahead and ask for a table with a view (☞ In Walt Disney World *in* Chapter 6).

18. Have your picture taken with Mickey at Toontown Fair (☞ Magic Kingdom, *above*).

19. Have dinner at Alfredo's in Epcot, right after IllumiNations—request an 8:55 reservation. After dinner, since the park is officially closed, it's incredibly lovely (☞ Walt Disney World *in* Chapter 6).

20. Have dinner at the Brown Derby in Disney–MGM Studios and book ahead for priority *Fantasmic!* seating (☞ Disney–MGM Studios Theme Park, *below*).

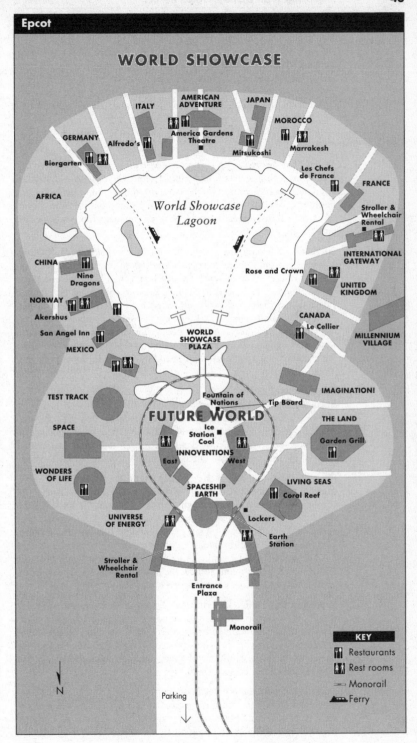

Epcot

WORLD SHOWCASE

ITALY
AMERICAN ADVENTURE
JAPAN
MOROCCO
GERMANY
Alfredo's
America Gardens Theatre
Mitsukoshi
Marrakesh
Biergarten
Les Chefs de France
FRANCE
AFRICA
Stroller & Wheelchair Rental
World Showcase Lagoon
INTERNATIONAL GATEWAY
CHINA
Nine Dragons
Rose and Crown
UNITED KINGDOM
NORWAY
Akershus
San Angel Inn
CANADA
Le Cellier
MILLENNIUM VILLAGE
MEXICO
WORLD SHOWCASE PLAZA
IMAGINATION!
TEST TRACK
Fountain of Nations
Tip Board
FUTURE WORLD
THE LAND
SPACE
Ice Station Cool
Garden Grill
INNOVENTIONS
East
West
WONDERS OF LIFE
LIVING SEAS
Coral Reef
SPACESHIP EARTH
Lockers
UNIVERSE OF ENERGY
Earth Station
Stroller & Wheelchair Rental
Entrance Plaza
N
Monorail
Parking

KEY

🚻	Restaurants
🚹🚺	Rest rooms
⊶	Monorail
⛴	Ferry

kled throughout World Showcase, where they can make puppets, draw pictures, use chalk on the pavement, and make a Moroccan fez.)

The two parts of Epcot are separated by the 40-acre World Showcase Lagoon. The northern half, Future World, is where the monorail drops you off and is the official entrance. The southern half is World Showcase—this is where you'll find the International Gateway, where the trams from the Dolphin and Swan hotels and Disney's Yacht and Beach Club and BoardWalk resorts drop you off.

Future World

Future World is made up of two concentric circles of pavilions. The inner core is composed of the **Spaceship Earth** geosphere and, just beyond it, a plaza anchored by the wow-generating computer-animated Fountain of Nations, which is as mesmerizing as many a more elaborate ride or show. Bracketing it are the crescent-shape **Innoventions East and West.**

Six pavilions (excluding **Space,** scheduled for a spring 2001 opening) compose the outer ring. On the east side they are, in order, the **Universe of Energy, Wonders of Life,** and **Test Track.** With the exception of the Wonders of Life, the pavilions present a single, self-contained ride and an occasional postride showcase; a visit rarely takes more than 30 minutes, but it depends on how long you spend in the postride area. On the west side there are **Living Seas, The Land,** and **Imagination!** Like the Wonders of Life, these blockbuster exhibits contain both rides and interactive displays; count on spending at least 1½ hours per pavilion.

Spaceship Earth

Balanced like a giant golf ball waiting for some celestial being to tee off, the multifaceted silver geosphere of Spaceship Earth is to Epcot what Cinderella Castle is to the Magic Kingdom. As much a landmark as an icon, it can be seen on a clear day from an airplane flying down either coast of Florida. Spaceship Earth contains the **Spaceship Earth Ride.**

Everyone likes to gawk at the golf ball, but there are some truly jaw-dropping facts about it: it weighs 1 million pounds and measures 164 ft in diameter and 180 ft in height ("Aha!" you say. "It's not really a sphere!"). Altogether it encompasses more than 2 million cubic ft of space, and it is balanced on six pylons sunk 100 ft into the ground. The anodized aluminum sheath is composed of 954 triangular panels, not all of equal size or shape. And, last, because it is not a geodesic dome, which is only a half sphere, the name "geosphere" had to be invented; no other like it existed when it was built.

Spaceship Earth Ride. This ride conveys you past a series of tableaux that explores human progress and the continuing search for better forms of communication. Scripted by science fiction writer Ray Bradbury and narrated by Jeremy Irons (who replaced Walter Cronkite), the journey begins in the darkest tunnels of time, proceeds through history, and ends poised on the edge of the future.

Audio-Animatronics figures present in astonishing detail Cro-Magnon man daubing mystic paintings on cave walls, Egyptian scribes scratching genuine hieroglyphics on papyrus, Roman centurions building roads, Islamic scholars mapping the heavens, and 11th- and 12th-century Benedictine monks hand-copying ancient manuscripts in order to preserve the wisdom of the past. One monk, not as tireless as history would have us believe, is conked out at his carrel, his candle smoking in the gusts of his snores. As you move into the Renaissance, Michelangelo paints the Sistine Chapel, Gutenberg invents the printing press, and in rapid succession, the telegraph, radio, television, and computer come into being. The pace speeds up, you're bombarded with images from our communication age, and, just as you begin to think you can't absorb another photon, you're shot through a tunnel of swirling lights into serene space, its velvety darkness sparkling with thousands of stars. In one corner, hanging like the jeweled toy envisioned by Milton in *Paradise Lost,* is our own Earth as photographed by the astronauts on one of the *Apollo* moon shots. It's breathtaking. Toward the conclusion of the ride, you arrive in a "Global Neighborhood," updated for the millennium, that ties all of the peoples of the earth together through an interactive global network. Special effects, animated sets, and audience-enclosing laser beams are used to create the experience. *Duration: 15 mins. Crowds: Longest during the morning and shortest just before closing. Strategy: Ride first thing in the morning or just before leaving. Audience: All ages. The portion of the ride in total darkness may frighten children or others who are anxious in dark, narrow, or enclosed spaces, but the ride vehicles move slowly and the subject matter is completely educational, so the scare factor is low. Rating:* ★★★

Innoventions

In Innoventions—the two-building, 100,000-square-ft attraction at the center of Future World—new technology that affects daily living is highlighted by exhibits, live stage demonstrations, and hands-on displays. Each major exhibition area is presented by a leading manufacturer. **Innoventions East** appeals most strongly to adults, focusing on products for the home of the not-too-distant future. **Innoventions West,** hugely popular with preteens, features an enormous display of Sega toys and games. One of the most popular is an eight-car Formula One Grand Prix race in which you get to drive a full-size car through a turn-filled course that's projected onto a huge screen in front of each vehicle. You'll be hard-pressed to pull your kids out of here. *Duration: Up to you. Crowds: Largest around the popular computer displays. Strategy: Go first thing in the morning or after dark during IllumiNations. Audience: All but toddlers and preschoolers. Rating:* ★★★

NEED A BREAK? The **Fountain View Espresso and Bakery** purveys freshly ground coffees, scrumptious croissants, fruit tarts, crème brûlée, and éclairs. You can eat at the circular counter or perch on a chair at one of the high tables. The umbrella-covered tables on the patio have a fine view of the fountain. In the afternoon, this is a great place to sip wine and watch the Fountain of Nations water ballet show without having to stand in the blazing sun and crane your neck.

Ice Station Cool

Stooping low in the tunnel-like entrance to this re-created igloo, you see statues of one Refreshus Maximus, frozen in his hunt for refreshment. Beyond, you come to a room full of soda machines where you can sample Coca-Cola products from around the world, such as Vegitabeta from Japan, Smart Watermelon from China, and Kinley Lemon from Israel. There's no free American Coca-Cola to sample, but there's plenty of Coca-Cola memorabilia to buy. *Duration: As long as you like. Crowds: Move pretty quickly. Strategy: Visit in mid-afternoon on a very hot day. Audience: All ages. Rating:* ★

Universe of Energy

The first of the pavilions on the left, or east, side of Future World, the Universe of Energy occupies a large, lopsided pyramid sheathed in thousands of mirrors—solar collectors that power the attraction inside. It's one of the most technologically complex shows at Epcot, combining one ride, film, the largest Audio-Animatronics animals ever built, 250 prehistoric trees, and enough cold, damp fog to make you think you've been transported to the inside of a defrosting refrigerator. ("We don't want to go through that fog again," one child announced after emerging from a particularly damp vision of the Mesozoic era.)

Ellen's Energy Adventure. In the Universe of Energy show, popular comedienne Ellen DeGeneres portrays a woman who dreams she's a contestant on *Jeopardy!* only to discover that all the categories are about a subject she knows nothing about—energy. Her challengers on the show, hosted by Alex Trebek himself, are Ellen's know-it-all former college roommate (played to the irritating hilt by Jamie Lee Curtis) and Albert Einstein. Enter Bill Nye, the Science Guy, Ellen's nice-guy neighbor and all-around science whiz, who guides Ellen (and you) on a crash course in Energy 101.

First comes the history of the universe—in one minute—on three 70-mm screens, 157 ft wide by 32 ft tall. Next the theater separates into six 96-passenger vehicles that lurch into the forest primeval. Huge trees loom out of the mists of time, ominous blue moonbeams waver in the fog, sulfurous lava burbles up, and the air smells distinctly of Swamp Thing. Through this unfriendly landscape brontosauruses wander trailing mouthfuls of weeds, a tyrannosaurus fights it out with a triceratops, pterodactyls swoop through the air, and a truly nasty sea snake emerges from the swamp to attack the left side of the tram. A terrified Ellen is even cornered by a menacing elasmosaurus.

The ride concludes with another film in which Ellen learns about the world's present-day energy needs, resources, and concerns. It's shown on three screens, each 30 ft tall, 74 ft wide, and curved to create a 200° range of vision. And she wins! An interesting fact here: the 96-passenger, 30,000-pound "traveling theaters" are guided along the concrete floor by a wire only ⅛-inch thick and are powered by the 80,000 solar cells on the roof so that you have been, as they say, "riding on sunshine." *Duration: 30 mins. Crowd: Steady but never horrible; 600 people enter every 15 mins. Strategy: To be at the front of the ride and have your experience of the primeval landscape unspoiled by rows of modern heads in front of you, sit in the seats to the far left and front of the theater; to get these seats, be sure to position yourself similarly in the preshow area. Audience: All ages. Rating: ★★★*

Wonders of Life

A towering statue of a DNA double helix outside the gold-crowned dome of the Wonders of Life welcomes you to one of Epcot's most popular attractions. Truly among the wonders of Epcot, it takes an amusing but serious and educational look at health, fitness, and modern lifestyles. The messages are delivered via an ultracharming improvisational theater revue that youngsters can watch over and over again, in two films, on Disney's first flight-simulator ride, during a multimedia presentation, and at dozens of interactive gadgets that whiz, bleep, and blink.

Body Wars. The flight-simulator technology that is used to train commercial and military pilots adapts perfectly to thrill rides. By synchronizing the action on a movie screen with the movement of a ride vehicle, you're tricked into thinking you're moving in wild and crazy fashion even though you never leave your seat. Probably the mildest flight simulator in Central Florida, Body Wars still offers a nifty experience, thanks to the fascinating film and the ingenious idea. You and your fellow scientists enter a simulator chamber that, like something out of *Honey, I Shrunk the Kids,* will be miniaturized and injected into the body's bloodstream to remove a splinter, which appears on-screen like a massive rock formation. "How's the weather in there?" calls out one of the specialists on the screen. "Clear and warm, temperature about 98.6" comes the reply from within. And in a couple of seconds, you feel it yourself: shooting through the heart, wheezing through the lungs, and picking up a jolt of energy in the brain. *Duration: 5 mins. Crowds: Sometimes discouraging, with occasional 45-min waits. Strategy: Go as soon as the park opens, during the hr before closing, or between 6 and 7 PM, the peak dinnertime in World Showcase. Audience: All but some young children, who may be frightened by the sensation of movement the film induces and by the lurching and pitching of the simulator chamber. Not recommended for pregnant women or guests with heart, back, or neck problems or motion sickness. Minimum height: 40". Rating:* ★★★

The Making of Me. Show times at Wonders of Life are staggered to pick up as soon as another lets out, so with a little luck you can segue right into this valuable film on human conception and childbearing. Starring Martin Short as a man who, in search of his origins, journeys back in time to his parents' childhood, youth, marriage, and, eventually, their decision to have him, the film uses both animation and actual footage from a live birth to explain where babies come from. Some scenes are explicit, but all the topics are handled with gentle humor—as when the sperm race for the egg to the tune of "The Ride of the Valkyries"—and with great delicacy. Children tend to be dumbstruck; many adults find the film affecting enough to get out the handkerchiefs for a quick swipe at overflowing eyes. *Duration: 14 mins. Crowds: Long lines all day in busy periods because the theater is so small. Strategy: Save this one for after 6 PM. Audience: All ages. Rating:* ★★★

Cranium Command. Combining a fast-pace movie with an elaborate set, this engaging show looks at how the cranium manages to make the heart, the uptight left brain, the laid-back right brain, the stomach, and an ever-alert adrenal gland all work together as their host, a 12-year-old boy, surmounts the slings and arrows of a typical day. The star is Buzzy, a bumbling Audio-Animatronics Cranium Commando for whom adolescent boys are the last chance before being consigned to run the brain of a chicken. Buzzy's is not an easy job; as the sign on the way to the theater warns, you are entering THE HOME OF THE FLYING ENDORPHINS. In the flick, Buzzy's 12-year-old wakes up late, dashes off without breakfast, meets the new girl in school, fights for her honor, gets called up before the principal, and, finally, returns home and has a much-needed snack. Buzzy attempts to coordinate a heart, operated by *Saturday Night Live*'s muscle team, Hans and Franz; a stomach, run by George Wendt, formerly of *Cheers,* in a sewer worker's overalls and rubber boots; and all the other body parts. Buzzy succeeds—but just barely. *Duration: 20 mins. Crowds: Long lines, but they're quickly erased by the big theater, which seats 200 at a shot. Strategy: Go when everyone else is at Body Wars. Audience: All ages. Rating:* ★★★

Fitness Fairground. This educational playground, which teaches both adults and children about good health, takes up much of Wonders of Life. There are games in which you can test your golf and tennis prowess, pedal around the world on a stationary bicycle while watching an ever-changing view on video, and guess your stress level at an interactive computer terminal. "Goofy about Health," an eight-minute multiscreen montage, follows Goofy's conversion from a foul-living dog to a fun-loving guy. The **AnaComical Players Theater,** seating 100 people, is a corny but funny improvisational show with lots of audience participation. The **Frontiers of Medicine,** the only completely serious section of the pavilion, demonstrates leading-edge developments in medicine. *Duration: Up to you. Crowds: Shifting, but they don't affect your visit. Strategy: Hang loose and take turns while you're in the Fitness Fairground. Audience: All ages. Rating:* ★★★

NEED A
BREAK?

Pure & Simple, which offers healthful snacks and full meals that you can eat at nearby tables, proves that nutritious can also be delicious. If you take the Wonders of Life message to heart, sample the vegetarian chili spiked with fresh herbs or a yogurt smoothie. The whole wheat waffles with berry toppings are nice, too. Nor will the prices give you indigestion, although overhearing the AnaComical Players ask—and answer—as you eat, "Why do some people pick their nose?" may give you pause.

Space

This pavilion, which opens in the spring of 2001, is dedicated to the men and women who gave of themselves in our nation's space program. It is specifically approved by NASA, and will feature astronaut memorabilia and displays of the universe. *Duration: Due to the newness of the attraction, service information is unavailable at this time.*

Test Track

This small-scale, just-for-show version of a General Motors test track takes you behind the scenes of automobile testing. The queue area showcases many of these tests in informative, action-packed exhibits—if you don't have to wait, you'll miss a lot that's interesting here.

The main draw, however, is the ride itself, billed as "the longest and fastest ride in Walt Disney World's history." The ride is so complex that its opening was delayed several times. Now, sporty Test Track vehicles take you and five other passengers through seven different performance tests. In the Brake Test your ride vehicle makes two passes through a circular setup of traffic cones, and you learn how antilock brakes can make a wildly out-of-control skid become manageable. In the Environmental Chamber, the ride vehicle is exposed to extreme heat, bone-chilling cold, and a mist sprayed by industrial robots that simulates most vehicles' exposure to corrosive substances. After leaving these test chambers, vehicles accelerate quickly up a switchback "mountain road" in the Ride Handling Test. There's also a too-close-for-comfort view of a Barrier Test. The best part, the High-Speed Test, is last: your vehicle goes outside the Test Track building to negotiate a steeply banked loop at a speed of nearly 60 mph. As you leave the pavilion, kids can get a soaking in the Cool Wash, an interactive water area that lets them pretend they are in a car wash. *Duration: 5 mins. Crowds: Expect long lines, as at all newer attractions. Strategy: Go first thing in the morning and make a FASTPASS appointment, or you will wait—a long time. Audience: All but young children; the queue-area message will be lost on them, and the speeds and other effects may prove frightening. No pregnant women or guests wearing back, neck, or leg braces. Minimum height: 40". Rating:* ★★★

Living Seas

Epcot is known for its imaginative fountains; the one at Living Seas, the first satellite pavilion on the western outer ring, flings surf in a never-ending wave against a rock garden beneath the stylized marquee. The pavilion itself is a favorite among children. Time and technology have caught up with the 5.7 million-gallon aquarium at the pavilion's core—thrilling when it first opened—so that what was once revolutionary has now been equaled by top aquariums around the country. Still, the collection of sea life looks quite impressive when you circle the tank on the outside, even more so when you take advantage of the opportunity to scuba dive within it (☞ Guided Tours *in* Epcot A to Z, *below*). After the short **Seacabs** ride, you may want to circumnavigate the tank at your own speed on an upper level, pointing out barracudas, stingrays, parrot fish, sea turtles, and even sharks.

Seacabs. Think of this ride with a view of the big acrylic tank as just a shuttle to Sea Base Alpha, or up-front crowd control for the pavilion's interactive exhibits, and you won't be disappointed by its brevity. En route, in addition to spotting the aquarium's full-time denizens, you'll sometimes catch sight of a diver testing out the latest scuba equipment. Surrounded by a cloud of parrot fish, the diver may scatter Disney fish food—a mixture of dry dog food, chicken's laying pellets, amino-acid solution, and B-complex vitamins—or you may see him carefully place a head of lettuce within reach of a curious sea turtle. *Duration: 3 mins. Crowds: Large, all day long. Strategy: Go early or late. Audience: All but young children. Rating:* ★★★

Sea Base Alpha. This typical Epcot playground, on two levels, contains six modules, each dedicated to a specific subject: the history of robotics, ocean exploration, ocean ecosystems, dolphins, porpoises, and sea lions. Fully interactive, these contain films, touchy-feely sections, miniaquariums, and video quizzes. Unfortunately, SeaBase Alpha is accessible only via Seacab, so access can be difficult when it's busy. *Duration: 30 mins and up, depending on how long you play Diver Dan at the modules. Crowds: Large, all day long. Strategy: Stop in first thing in the morning or after 5. Audience: All but young children. Rating:* ★★★

The Land

Shaped like an intergalactic greenhouse, the enormous, skylighted Land pavilion dedicates 6 acres and a host of different attractions to everyone's favorite topic: food. You can easily spend two hours exploring here, more if you take one of the guided greenhouse tours available throughout the day (☞ Guided Tours *in* Epcot A to Z, *below*).

Living with the Land. Piloted by an informative, overalls-clad guide, you cruise through three biomes—rain forest, desert, and prairie ecological communities—and into an experimental greenhouse that demonstrates how food sources may be grown in the future, not only on the planet but also in outer space. Shrimp, sunshine bass, tilapia, and pacu—the piranha's vegetarian cousin—are raised in controlled aquacells, and tomatoes, peppers, and squash thrive in the Desert Farm area through a system of drip irrigation that delivers just the right amount of water and nutrients to their roots. Gardeners are usually interested in the section on integrated pest management, which relies on such "good" bugs as ladybugs to control insect predators. Many of the growing areas are actual experiments-in-progress, in which Disney and the U.S. Department of Agriculture have joined forces to produce, say, a sweeter pineapple or a faster-growing pepper. Interestingly, although the plants and fish in the greenhouse are all quite real—and are regularly harvested for use in The Land's restaurants—those in the biomes are artful fakes, manufactured by Disney elves out of flexible, lightweight plastic. The grass is made out of glass fibers that have been implanted in rubber mats—a useful deterrent to barefoot trespassers, perhaps. *Duration: 14 mins. Crowds: Large, all day. Strategy: Go during mealtimes. Audience: Teens and adults. Rating:* ★★★

Food Rocks. In this rowdy concert, recognizable rock-and-roll performers take the shape of favorite foods and sing about the joys of nutrition. There are performances by the Peach Boys, Chubby Cheddar, and Neil Moussaka, among others. *Duration: 20 mins. Crowds: A large theater* *erases them. Strategy: Go when the line at Living with the Land is too long. Audience: Children and parents who like classic rock. Rating:* ★

Circle of Life. Featuring three stars of *The Lion King*—Simba the lion, Timon the meerkat, and Pumbaa the waddling warthog—this film delivers a powerful message about protecting the world's environment for all living things. Part animation, part *National Geographic*–like film using spectacular 70-mm live-action footage, *Circle of Life* tells a fable about a "Hakuna Matata Lakeside Village" that Timon and Pumbaa are developing by clearing the African savanna. Simba cautions about mistreating the land by telling a story of a creature who occasionally forgets that everything is connected in the great Circle of Life. "That creature," he says, "is man." The lilting accompaniment, of course, is Elton John's award-winning song, and the narration is provided by James Earl Jones. *Duration: 20 mins. Crowds: Large, all day. Strategy: Hit this first in the Land. Audience: Enlightening for children and adults; a nap opportunity for toddlers. Rating:* ★★

NEED A
BREAK?

Talk about a self-contained ecosystem: the pavilion grows its own produce and houses the **Sunshine Season Food Fair,** a food court composed of a dozen or so stands—a soup-and-salad spot, bakery (with great jumbo-size cinnamon rolls and corn muffins before 11 AM), barbecue store, sandwich counter, ice-cream outlet, potato purveyor, and beverage house, which bolsters the usual soft drinks with milk shakes, buttermilk, vegetable juice, and exotic fruit nectars. Pause for a healthful snack. (Between noon and 2, lines are huge and tables hard to come by.) The bakery's brownies are legendary, and Epcot staffers have been known to make a special trip to pick up some of its chocolate chip cookies. Just remember that at this pavilion, you must eat all your vegetables.

Imagination!

The theme here is the imagination and the fun that can be had when you let it loose. The imaginative leaping fountains outside are a perfect example of the point being made, as is the big attraction here, the 3-D film *Honey, I Shrunk the Audience.* The **Image Works,** an Epcot interactive fun house devoted to music and art, has also been refurbished as part of WDW's Millennium celebration.

Honey, I Shrunk the Audience. Don't miss this 3-D adventure, one of WDW's best, about the futuristic "shrinking" technologies demonstrated in the hit films that starred Rick Moranis. Moranis reprises his role as Dr. Wayne Szalinski, who is about to receive the Inventor of the Year Award from the Imagination Institute. While Dr. Szalinski is demonstrating his latest shrinking machine, though, things go really, really wrong. Be prepared to laugh and scream your head off, courtesy of the special in-theater effects, moving seats, and 3-D film technology that are ingeniously used, from start to finish, to dramatize a hoot of a story. *Duration: 14 mins. Crowds: Large theater capacity should mean a relatively short wait, but the film's popularity can make for big crowds. Strategy: Go first thing in the morning or just before closing, or utilize the FASTPASS scheme. Audience: All but easily frightened children. Though some will be scared, you might want to try taking even generally timid youngsters, since the humor quotient outweighs the few scary moments. Rating:* ★★★

Journey Into Your Imagination. Returning guests may remember Figment, the host of the Journey to Imagination ride. He is still in this updated version, but not as prominent. Now, Dr. Nigel Channing, the presenter of Dr. Szalinski's award in *Honey, I Shrunk the Audience,* is your host in a rehabilitated newcomer. He makes you a test subject in a new invention, the Imagination Scanner, which will measure your "I.Q." (Imagination Quotient). After travelling on a sensory adventure through sound, illusion, gravity, dimensions, and color, you can try out your newly enhanced imagination at the **Image Works,** where a bunch of "What if" questions can be answered through interactive displays. The ride takes you on a behind-the-scenes tour of what you saw in the *Honey, I Shrunk the Audience* film. *Duration: 8 mins. Crowds: The ride's newcomer status means that they'll be big. Strategy: Ride first thing in the morning, or make a FASTPASS appointment. Audience: Older children and adults. Younger children may be frightened by the scanner at the end of the ride and also during the brief period of darkness. Rating:* ★★

World Showcase

The 40-acre World Showcase Lagoon is 1⅓ mi around, but in that space, you circumnavigate the globe, or at least explore it, in pavilions representing 11 different countries in Europe, Asia, North Africa, and the Americas. In each pavilion, restaurants and snack spots peddling native food as well as entertainment, art and handicrafts, and usually a multimedia presentation showcase the particular culture and people, and well-known landmarks have been re-created. France has a scaled-down model of the Eiffel Tower, America's display is housed in an ersatz Liberty Hall, Japan glories in a pagoda, Italy has a reproduction of Venice's Piazza San Marco, and Morocco's minaret is an architectural tour de force in its own right. Impressive as they are by day, the structures are truly amazing at night, when they are outlined in literally miles of tiny lights. Instead of rides, you have breathtaking films at the Canadian, Chinese, and French pavilions; several art exhibitions; and the chance to chat in the native language of the friendly foreign staff, all of whom are part of a Disney exchange program. Each pavilion also has a designated **Kid Zone,** where youngsters can try their hands at crafts projects—they might make a Moroccan fez or a Norwegian troll, for instance. Live entertainment is an integral part of the pavilions' presentations.

The focal point of World Showcase is the **American Adventure,** directly opposite Spaceship Earth on the far side of the lagoon. The pavilions of other countries fan out from both sides, encircling the lagoon. Counterclockwise from World Showcase Plaza as you enter from Future World are **Canada,** the **Millennium Village,** the **United Kingdom, France, Morocco, Japan,** the **American Adventure, Italy, Germany, China, Norway,** and **Mexico.**

Canada

"Oh, it's just our Canadian outdoors," said a typically modest native guide upon being asked the model for the striking rocky chasm and tumbling waterfall that represent just one of the high points of Canada. The beautiful formal gardens do have an antecedent: Butchart Gardens, in Victoria, British Columbia. And so does the Hôtel du Canada, a French Gothic mansion with spires, turrets, and a mansard roof; anyone who's ever stayed at Québec's Château Frontenac or Ottawa's Château Laurier will recognize the imposing style favored by architects of Canadian railroad hotels. Like the size of the Rocky Mountains and the Great Canadian North, the scale of the structures seems immense; unlike the real thing, it's managed with a trick called forced perspective, which exaggerates the smallness of the distant parts to make the entire thing look humongous. Another bit of design legerdemain: the World Showcase Rockies are made of chicken wire and painted concrete mounted on a movable platform similar to a parade float. Ah, wilderness!

Canada also contains shops selling maple syrup, lumberjack shirts, and other trapper paraphernalia.

O Canada! That's just what you'll say after seeing this CircleVision film's stunning opening shot—footage of the Royal Canadian Mounted Police surrounding you as they circle the screen. From there, you whoosh over waterfalls, saunter through Montréal and Toronto, sneak up to bears and bison, mush behind a husky-pulled dogsled, and land pluck—or, should we say, puck—in the middle of a hockey game. This is a standing-only theater, with lean rails. *Duration: 17 mins. Crowds: Can be thick in late afternoon. Strategy: Go when World Showcase opens or in the evening. Audience: All ages, but no strollers permitted, and toddlers and small children can't see unless they're held aloft. Rating:* ★★★

Millennium Village

This pavilion between Canada and the United Kingdom emphasizes the customs of some of our neighboring countries, and is a result of a friendship between Epcot and the Expo 2000 Hannover, which was held in Germany. It was opened in October 1999 to celebrate the Millennium, and is presently scheduled to remain a permanent attraction. *Duration: Up to you. Crowds: Steady all day long. Strategy: Visit while most everyone else is staking a spot for IllumiNations. Audience: All ages. Rating:* ★

United Kingdom

Never has it been so easy to cross the English Channel. A pastiche of there-will-always-be-an-England architecture, the United Kingdom rambles between the elegant mansions lining a London square to the bustling, half-timber shops of a village High Street to the thatched-roof cottages from the countryside. (The thatch is made of plastic broom bristles in consideration of local fire regulations.) And of course there's a pair of the scarlet phone booths that used to be found all over the United Kingdom, now on their way to being relics. The pavilion has no single major attraction. Instead, you can wander through shops selling tea and tea accessories, Welsh handicrafts, Royal Doulton figurines, and woolens and tartans from **Pringle of Scotland**; the **Magic of Wales** sells delicate British china and fragile collectibles. Outside, the strolling World Showcase Players coax audience members into participating in their definitely low-brow versions of Shakespeare. There's also a lovely garden and park with benches in the back that's easy to miss. It's a scene right out of the street on which Mary Poppins lived; in fact, Ms. Poppins often makes appearances here along with another lovely English lass, Alice from Wonderland.

....

NEED A BREAK?

Revive yourself with a pint of the best—although you'll be hard-put to decide among the offerings—at the **Rose and Crown Pub,** which also offers traditional afternoon tea outside. The adjacent dining room serves more substantial fare (reservations required). The terrace outside is one of the best spots to watch IllumiNations; arrive early.

....

France

You don't need the scaled-down model of the Eiffel Tower to tell you that you've arrived in France, specifically Paris. There's the poignant accordion music wafting out of concealed speakers, the trim sycamores pruned in the French style to develop signature knots at the end of each branch, and the delicious aromas surrounding the Boulangerie Pâtisserie bake shop. This is the Paris of dreams, a Paris without parking problems and all those irascible French shopkeepers. It's a Paris of the years just before World War I, when solid mansard-roof mansions were crowned with iron filigree, when the least brick was drenched in romanticism. Here's a replica of the conservatorylike Les Halles—the iron-and-glass barrel-roof market that no longer exists in the City of Light; there's an arching footbridge, and all around, of course, there are shops. You can inspect artwork, Limoges porcelain, and crystal in the exquisite **Plume et Palette**; sample perfume and cosmetics at the **Guerlain Boutique**; pick up a baking pan to make those famous madeleine cookies at **La Casserole**; and acquire a bottle of Bouzy Rouge to wash it all down at **Les Vins de France**, where wine tastings are frequently held for a small charge.

Impressions de France. The intimate **Palais du Cinema**, inspired by the royal theater at Fontainebleau, screens this homage to the glories of the country. Shown on five screens spanning 200° in an air-conditioned, sit-down theater, the film takes you to vineyards at harvest time, Paris on Bastille Day, the Alps, Versailles, Normandy's Mont-St-Michel, and the stunning châteaus of theLoire Valley. The musical accompaniment also hits high notes, with familiar segments from Offenbach, Debussy, and Saint-Säens, all woven together by longtime Disney musician Buddy Baker. *Duration: 18 mins. Crowds: Considerable from World Showcase opening through late afternoon. Strategy: Come before noon or after dinner. Audience: Adults. Rating:* ★★★

NEED A BREAK? Bring your patience—there are almost always lines at the times you're hungry—and stop in for a French pastry at **Boulangerie Pâtisserie,** a small Parisian-style sidewalk café. Sandwiches and omelets are available at the nearby **Bistro de Paris,** a full-service restaurant.

Morocco

You don't need a magic carpet to be instantaneously transported into an exotic culture—just walk through the pointed arches of the Bab Boujouloud gate into Morocco. A gift from the kingdom of Morocco, they are ornamented with beautiful wood carvings and encrusted with intricate mosaics made of 9 tons of handmade, hand-cut tiles; 19 native artisans were sent to Epcot to install them and to create the dusty, stucco walls that seem to have withstood centuries of sandstorms. Look closely and you'll see that every tile has a small crack or some other imperfection, and no tile depicts a living creature—in deference to the Muslim belief that only Allah creates perfection and life.

Koutoubia Minaret, a replica of the prayer tower in Marrakesh, acts as Morocco's landmark. Traditional winding alleyways, each corner bursting with carpets, brasses, leather work, and other North African craftsmanship, lead to a beautifully tiled fountain and lush gardens. Check out the ever-changing exhibit in the **Gallery of Arts and History,** and entertain yourself examining the wares at such shops as **Casablanca Carpets, Jewels of the Sahara, Brass Bazaar,** and **Fez House.** You can take a guided tour of the pavilion by inquiring of any cast member.

Japan

A brilliant vermilion torii gate, derived from the design of Hiroshima Bay's much-photographed Itsukushima Shrine, frames the World Showcase Lagoon and stands as the striking emblem of Disney's serene version of Japan. Disney horticulturists deserve a hand here for their achievement in constructing out of all-American plants and boulders a very Japanese landscape, complete with rocks, pebbled streams, pools, and hills. At sunset, or during a rainy dusk, the sharp edges of the evergreens and twisted branches of the corkscrew willows frame a perfect Japanese view of the five-story winged pagoda that is the heart of the pavilion. Based on the 8th-century Horyuji Temple in Nara, the brilliant blue pagoda has five levels, symbolizing the five elements of Buddhist belief—earth, water, fire, wind, sky. As you wander along the twisting paths, listen for the wind chimes and the soothing clack of the water mill, and watch a fiery sunset—Walt Disney World seems a million miles away.

The peace is occasionally disturbed by performances on drums and gongs. Other entertainment is provided by demonstrations of traditional Japanese crafts, such as kite making and the snipping of brown rice toffee into intricate shapes; these take place outdoors on the pavilion's plaza or in the **Bijutsu-Kan Gallery,** where there are also changing art exhibitions. **Mitsukoshi** department store, an immense three-centuries-old retail firm known as Japan's Sears Roebuck, carries everything from T-shirts to kimonos and row upon row of Japanese dolls.

American Adventure

In a Disney version of Philadelphia's Liberty Hall, the Imagineers prove that their kind of fantasy can beat reality hands down. The 110,000 bricks, made by hand from soft pink Georgia clay, sheathe the familiar structure, which acts as a beacon for Epcot visitors across the lagoon. Talk about symbolism. And when those colored lights start flashing and the lasers zing between here and Spaceship Earth during the sound-and-light-and-fireworks IllumiNations show after dark, the patriotism in the air is palpable. The pavilion includes an all-American fast-food restaurant, a shop, an outdoor theater, lovely rose gardens, and a show.

American Adventure Show. The pavilion's key attraction is this 100-yard dash through history. To the music of a piece called "The Golden Dream," performed by the Philadelphia Orchestra, it combines evocative sets, the world's largest rear-projection screen (72 ft wide), enormous movable stages, and 35 Audio-Animatronics players, which are some of the most lifelike ever created—Ben Franklin even climbs up stairs. Beginning with the arrival of the Pilgrims at Plymouth Rock and their grueling first winter, Ben Franklin and a wry, pipe-smoking Mark Twain narrate the episodes, both praiseworthy and shameful, that have shaped the American spirit. Disney detail is so painstaking that you never feel rushed, and, in fact, each speech and each scene seems polished like a little jewel. You feel the cold at Valley Forge and the triumph when Charles Lindbergh flies the Atlantic; are moved by Nez Percé chief Joseph's forced abdication of Native American ancestral lands and by women's rights campaigner Susan B. Anthony's speech; laugh with Will Rogers's aphorisms and learn about the pain of the depression through an affecting radio broadcast by Franklin Delano Roosevelt; and recognize such popular figures as John Wayne, Lucille Ball, Muhammad Ali, and, yes, Mickey Mouse epitomizing the American spirit. *Duration: 30 mins. Crowds: Large, but the theater is huge, so you can almost always get into the next show. Strategy: Go when everything else is busy and you want to sit down and cool off. Audience: All ages. Rating:* ★★★

America Gardens. On the edge of the lagoon, directly opposite Disney's magnificent bit of colonial fakery, is this venue for concerts and shows of the "Yankee Doodle Dandy" variety. This is also the spot for the annual yuletide Candlelight Processional—a not-to-be-missed event if you're at WDW during the holidays. The special Candlelight Dinner Package (available through Disney's dining reservations hot line, ☞ *above*) includes a special after-4 admission to Epcot, dinner in any World Showcase restaurant, and preferred seating for IllumiNations.

NEED A
BREAK?
What else would you order at the counter-service **Liberty Inn** but apple pie and other all-American fare? If your youngsters want an ice-cream sundae to eat before IllumiNations, this is the place to get it.

Italy

In WDW's Italy, the star is the architecture: a reproduction of Venice's Piazza San Marco; a re-creation of Venice's Doge's Palace that's accurate right down to the gold leaf on the ringlets of the angel perched 100 ft atop the campanile; the seawall stained with age, with barbershop-stripe poles to which two gondolas are tethered; and the Romanesque columns, Byzantine mosaics, Gothic arches, and stone walls that have all been carefully "antiqued" to look historical. Mediterranean plantings such as cypress, kumquat, and olive trees add verisimilitude. Inside, shops sell Venetian beads and glasswork, leather purses and belts, and Perugina cookies and chocolate kisses.

Germany

Germany, a make-believe village that distills the best folk architecture from all over that country, is so jovial that you practically expect the Seven Dwarfs to come "heigh-ho"-ing out to meet you. Instead, you'll hear the hourly chimes from the specially designed glockenspiel on the clock tower, musical toots and tweets from multitudinous cuckoo clocks, folk tunes from the spinning dolls and lambs sold at **Der Teddybär,** and the satisfied grunts of hungry visitors chowing down on hearty German cooking. An oompah band performs four times a day in the Biergarten restaurant and twice a day in the courtyard, and there are shops aplenty—more than in any other pavilion. The most irresistible are **Die Weinachts Ecke,** where you'll find nutcrackers and other old-world Christmas ornaments; **Süssigkeiten,** for cookies and animal crackers; and **Volkskunst,** whose folk-crafts collection includes cuckoo clocks ranging from hummingbird scale to the size of an eagle.

NEED A
BREAK?
The **Sommerfest** pretzel-and-bratwurst cart is the heartiest snacking option in this part of the World.

China

A shimmering red-and-gold, three-tier replica of Beijing's Temple of Heaven towers over a serene Chinese garden, an art gallery displaying treasures from the People's Republic, a spacious emporium devoted to Chinese goods, and two restaurants. The garden, planted with rosebushes native to China, a 100-year-old mulberry tree, and water oaks whose twisted branches look Asian but are actually Florida homegrown, is one of the most peaceful spots in World Showcase, with its piped-in traditional Chinese music.

Wonders of China. Think of the Temple of Heaven as an especially fitting setting for a movie whose sensational panoramas of the land and people are dramatically portrayed on a 360° CircleVision screen. The only drawback is that the theater has no chairs; lean rails are provided. *Duration: 19 mins. Crowds: Steady from World Showcase opening through late afternoon, but the theater's high capacity means you can usually get into the next show. Strategy: Go anytime. Audience: All ages, but no strollers permitted, and small children have to be held aloft to see. Rating:* ★★★

NEED A
BREAK?
Lotus Blossom Café has egg rolls and not-too-exotic stir-fries that you can wash down with cold Tsing Tao beer.

Norway

Here there are rough-hewn timbers and sharply pitched roofs—softened and brightened by bloom-stuffed window boxes, figured shutters, and lots of smiling, blond and blue-eyed young Norwegians, all eager to speak English and show off their country. The pavilion complex contains a 14th-century stone fortress that mimics Oslo's Akershus, cobbled streets, rocky waterfalls, and a stave church, modeled after one built in 1250, with wood dragons glaring from the eaves. The church houses an exhibit called "To the Ends of the Earth," which tells the story of two early 20th-century polar expeditions by using vintage artifacts. It all puts you in the mood for the pavilion's shops, which feature wood carvings, glass artwork, and beautifully embroidered woolen sweaters, which sell briskly despite Florida's heat.

Maelstrom. In Norway's dandy boat ride, you pile into 16-passenger, dragon-headed longboats for a voyage through time that, despite its scary name and encounters with evil trolls, is actually more interesting than frightful. The journey begins in a 10th-century village, where a boat, much like yours and the ones used by Eric the Red, is being readied for a Viking voyage. You glide steeply up through a mythical forest populated by trolls, who cause the boat to plunge backward down a mild waterfall, then cruise amid the grandeur of the Geiranger fjord, following which you experience a storm in the North Sea and, as the presence of oil rigs signals a return to the 20th century, end up in a peaceful coastal village. Disembarking, you proceed into a theater for a quick and delightful film about Norway's scenic wonders, culture, and people. *Duration: 10 mins. Crowds: Steady, with slow-moving lines from late morning through early evening. Strategy: Go in the evening. Audience: All ages. Rating:* ★★

Age of the Viking Ship. Children adore this replica of a Viking ship, an interactive playground filled with ropes and climbing adventures from bow to stern. *Duration: As long as you want. Crowds: Not that bad. Strategy: Go anytime. Audience: Toddlers and elementary-school-age children. Rating:* ★

NEED A BREAK? | Open-face sandwiches can be washed down with Norwegian Ringnes beer at **Kringla Bakeri og Kafe.** Go early or late for speediest service.

Africa

The area between China and Germany celebrates the cultural life of the African continent by showcasing its shopping and entertainment. Throughout the day **Mdundo Kibandu** perform traditional song and dance, while **Village Traders** sells handicrafts and—you guessed it—souvenirs relating to *The Lion King*.

Mexico

Housed in a spectacular Maya pyramid surrounded by a tangle of tropical vegetation, Mexico contains the **El Río del Tiempo** boat ride, an exhibit of pre-Columbian art, a restaurant, and, of course, a shopping plaza, where you can unload many, many pesos.

Modeled on the market in the town of Taxco, **Plaza de los Amigos** is well named: there are lots of friendly people—the women dressed in ruffled off-the-shoulder peasant blouses and bright skirts, the men in white shirts and dashing sashes—all eager to sell you trinkets from a cluster of canopied carts. The perimeter is rimmed with stores with tile roofs, wrought-iron balconies, and window boxes drooling flowers. What to buy? Brightly colored paper blossoms, sombreros, baskets, pottery, leather goods, and colorful papier-mâché piñatas, which Epcot imports by the truckload.

El Río del Tiempo. True to its name, this attraction takes you on a trip down the River of Time. Your journey from the jungles of the Yucatán to modern-day Mexico City is enlivened by video images of feathered Toltec dancers; by Spanish-colonial Audio-Animatronics dancing puppets; and by film clips of cliff divers in Acapulco, speed boats in Manzanillo, and snorkeling around Isla Mujeres. The puppets are garish and reprise "It's a Small World" without the brain-numbing ditty. But this ride is still one of the major attractions in World Showcase. *Duration: 9 mins. Crowds: Long, slow-moving lines from late morning through late afternoon. Strategy: Skip this one on a first-time visit. Audience: All ages. Rating:* ★

Strategies for Your Visit to Epcot

When to Go

Epcot is now so vast and varied that a dedicated visitor really needs two days to explore it all. The best days are those early in the week, since visitors tend to go to Disney's Animal Kingdom and the Magic Kingdom first. It's a good idea to time your visit according to Epcot Center's early-admission days—Tuesday and Friday. If you are staying in a Disney resort, be sure to arrive at the turnstiles about 15 minutes before the appointed hour so that you can take full advantage of this special perk. If you're *not* staying at a Disney hotel, make sure that you don't make your Epcot visit on either early admission day—otherwise you'll go to a lot of trouble to show up early only to find that privileged Disney guests have already been there for an hour.

Blitz Tour

Plan to arrive in the parking lot 45 minutes before the official park opening. As soon as you're admitted, race over to **Test Track.** Get your FASTPASS appointment time, and then backtrack to **Spaceship Earth** with nothing more on your mind than to have it expanded.

Upon leaving Spaceship Earth, people naturally head for the first pavilion they see: either Universe of Energy or the Living Seas. Skip them for now and go directly to the **Wonders of Life** and segue without a pause from Body Wars to *The Making of Me* to Cranium Command. Skip the Fitness Fairground area.

If your timing is right, go back to **Test Track,** FASTPASS ticket in hand. Then head to **Future World**'s western pavilions. Visit the **Imagination!** pavilion and make another FASTPASS appointment for *Honey, I Shrunk the Audience.* Visit Journey into Your Imagination and if you have a short amount of time left, meander through Image Works before returning to *Honey, I Shrunk the Audience.*

Now enter **The Land**; take the boat ride and see *Circle of Life* and Food Rocks. By this time there may be a line at Living Seas, but if there isn't, go on in and stay as long as you like. Outside, things should be getting crowded.

Head counterclockwise into World Showcase, toward **Canada,** while everyone else is hoofing it toward Mexico. Then see **France** and the **American Adventure.** If there are lines at **Norway** by the time you get there, head for **Innoventions,** the **Image Works,** and **Wonders of Life's Fitness Fairground.**

After dinner at Alfredo's or in the food court in the Land pavilion, see any World Showcase attractions you missed, plus the **Universe of Energy,** remembering that parts of Future World sometimes close ahead of the rest of the park. Stick around for IllumiNations and take your time on the way out—there's a truly magical quality to the whole park after dusk.

On Rainy Days

Although attractions at Future World are largely indoors, Epcot's expansiveness and the pleasures of meandering around World Showcase on a sunny day make the park a poor choice in inclement weather. Still, if you can't go another day, bring a poncho and muddle through. You'll feel right at home in the United Kingdom.

Other Tips

- Don't sleep late, especially if you're attempting to see the park in one day. Count on arriving in the parking lot at least 45 minutes to an hour ahead of opening. It's the best way to squeeze the most in and to avoid some of the lines.

- Don't spend time eating a big lunch. Instead, have a big breakfast and tote a snack to tide you over to an early dinner or a quick late lunch. (This is a *blitz* tour, after all.)

- Before you arrive at Epcot (either the night before or even before you leave home), make reservations for a 5:30 dinner (☞ Dining *in* Epcot A to Z, *below*), because by that time in your marathon day, you'll be ready to sit down. Later, while everyone else is dawdling over dinner, you can zip through the attractions you've missed.

- Walk fast, see the exhibits when the park is its emptiest, and slow down and enjoy the shops and the live entertainment when the crowds thicken.

- Set up a rendezvous point and time at the start of the day, just in case you and your companions get separated. Be specific—deciding on a particular bench or table is a smart idea. Some good places in Future World include in front of Gateway Gifts near Spaceship Earth and in front of the Fountain of Nations; in World Showcase, meet at one of the boat ramp entrances.

Epcot A to Z

Baby Care

Epcot has a **Baby Care Center** as peaceful as the one in the Magic Kingdom; it's near the Odyssey Restaurant in Future World. Also furnished with rocking chairs, it has a low lighting level that makes it comfortable for nursing, and cast members have supplies such as formula, baby food, pacifiers, and disposable diapers for sale. You'll find changing tables here, as well as in all women's rooms and some men's rooms. You can also buy disposable diapers near the park entrance at Baby Services. For stroller rentals ($7 a day; $1 deposit required), look for the special stands on the east side of the Entrance Plaza and at World Showcase's International Gateway.

Cameras and Film

Kodak's disposable Fun Saver cameras are widely available, and you can get assistance with minor camera problems at the **Kodak Camera Center,** in the Entrance Plaza, and at **Cameras and Film,** at Journey into Your Imagination. Remember when you had your picture taken in front of Spaceship Earth when you entered the park? Pick up your photo at the **Kodak Camera Center** as you exit, or send someone from your group over to pick it up while you are waiting in line at Spaceship Earth.

For two-hour film developing, look for the **Photo Express** signs throughout the park: in Future World at the Kodak Camera Center as well as Cameras and Film and in World Showcase at Northwest Mercantile in Canada; World Traveler at International Gateway; Heritage Manor Gifts in the American Adventure; at the booth on the right as you enter Norway; and at Artesanias Mexicanas in Mexico. Drop your film in the container, and you can pick up your pictures at the Kodak Camera Center as you leave.

Dining

In World Showcase every pavilion sponsors at least one and often two or even three eateries. Where there's a choice, it is among a full-service restaurant with commensurately higher prices, a more affordable, ethnic fast-food spot, and carts and shops selling snacks ranging from French pastries to Japanese ices—whatever's appropriate to the pavilion. Lunch and dinner reservations are essential at the full-service restaurants; you can make them up to 60 days in advance by calling ☎ 407/939–3463 or in person at the WorldKey terminals at the park (only on the day of the meal) or at the restaurants themselves when they open for lunch, at 11. Many of these are so good that they warrant their own review in this book as among Orlando's best dining options (☞ Chapter 6).

In Future World, two large fast-food emporiums dominate the Innoventions Plaza area. In Innoventions East you'll find the **Electric Umbrella.** The fare here is chicken sandwiches, burgers, and salads. Innoventions West offers the **Pasta Piazza Ristorante.** As its name suggests, it's heavy on the Italian, with pizza, pasta, and salads. (The kids will love the pizza shaped like Mickey Mouse.) It's also one of the few places in Epcot that serves breakfast. Morning fare includes omelets and the Sunrise Scramble, a tasty Egg McMuffin clone. At The Land's **Garden Grill,** you can eat solid American fare with a twist as the restaurant revolves, giving you an ever-changing view of each biome on the boat ride. Living Seas' **Coral Reef** serves a finny menu, and there's a 600-gallon aquarium full of interesting critters. The character breakfast, starring Ariel, is a big draw.

For Travelers with Disabilities

Accessibility standards in this park are high. Many attractions and most restaurants and shops are fully wheelchair accessible. Not only does the *Guidebook for Guests with Hearing Impairments* give scripts and story lines for all Epcot attractions with sound tracks, but personal translator units can be rented ($40 deposit) to amplify sound in some of the theater shows. Closed-captioning is available on TV monitors at attractions that have preshows.

ATTRACTIONS

At Future World, to go on the **Spaceship Earth ride,** you must be able to walk four steps and transfer to a vehicle; in the unusual case that emergency evacuation may be necessary, it is by way of stairs. Service animals are not appropriate. Although much of the enchantment is in the visual details, the narration is interesting as well. The Epcot Discovery Center here is wheelchair accessible. **Innoventions** is completely wheelchair accessible. **Universe of Energy** is accessible to guests using standard wheelchairs and those who can transfer to them; especially because this is one of the attractions that has sound tracks amplified by rental personal translator units, it is slightly more interesting to those with hearing impairments than to those with visual impairments. **Wonders of Life,** including Cranium Command, *The Making of Me,* "Goofy about Health," and the AnaComical Theater, is totally wheelchair accessible, with special seating sections for guests using wheelchairs. Guests with visual impairments may wish to skip "Goofy about Health"; Cranium Command and *The Making of Me* are both covered in the *Guidebook for Guests with Hearing Impairments.* To ride the turbulent Body Wars, you must transfer to a ride seat; if you lack upper-body strength, request extra shoulder restraints. It's inappropriate for service animals. At **Test Track,** one TV monitor in the preshow area is close-captioned for people with hearing impairments. In **Living Seas,** guests using wheelchairs typically bypass the three-minute ride—no loss— and move directly into the Sea Base Alpha and aquarium area, the best part of the pavilion. In **The Land,** *Circle of Life,* Food Rocks, and the greenhouse tour are completely wheelchair accessible. Reflective captioning is available at the *Circle of Life,* and if you can read lips, you will enjoy the greenhouse tour. As for the Living with the Land boat ride, guests using an oversize wheelchair or a scooter must transfer to a Disney chair. Boarding the **Journey into Your Imagination** ride requires guests to take three steps and step up into a ride vehicle. The theater that screens *Honey, I Shrunk the Audience* is completely accessible, although you must transfer to a theater seat to experience some of the special effects. The preshow area has one TV monitor that is close-captioned. The hands-on activities of Image Works have always been wheelchair accessible and should continue to be; there's something for everyone in here. **Ice Station Cool** is not wheelchair accessible.

At World Showcase, most people stroll about, but there are also Friendship boats, which require guests using oversize wheelchairs or scooters to transfer to Disney chairs; the **American Adventure, France, China,** and **Canada** are all wheelchair accessible; personal translator units amplify the sound tracks here. **Germany, Italy, Japan, Morocco,** and the **United Kingdom** all have live entertainment, most with strong aural as well as visual elements; the plaza areas where the shows are presented are wheelchair accessible. In **Norway,** you must be able to step down into and up out of a boat to ride the Maelstrom, and an emergency evacuation would require the use of stairs; service animals should not ride. In **Mexico,** the El Río del Tiempo boat ride is accessible to guests using wheelchairs, but those using a scooter or oversize chair must transfer to a Disney model. **Millennium Village** is fully wheelchair accessible.

ENTERTAINMENT
Certain areas along the lagoon's edge at Showcase Plaza, the United Kingdom, and Italy are reserved for guests using wheelchairs during IllumiNations.

INFORMATION
See For Travelers with Disabilities *in* Walt Disney World A to Z, *below.*

RESTAURANTS AND SHOPS
With a few exceptions, all are wheelchair accessible. In both the Garden Grill and Living Seas' Coral Reef restaurant, only one level is accessible to guests using wheelchairs.

WHEELCHAIR RENTALS
You'll find them inside the Entrance Plaza on the left, to the right of the ticket booths at the Gift Stop, and at World Showcase's International Gateway. Standard models are available ($6; $1 deposit); you can also rent an electric scooter ($30; $10 deposit).

Entertainment

ABOVE THE LAGOON
First there are the all-out spectaculars we've come to expect at the Disney parks. Figuring "Why waste a perfectly good lagoon?," Walt Disney World uses its watery stage for the spectacular **IllumiNations** show every night before closing. Be sure to stick around for the lasers, lights, fireworks, fountains, and music from every host nation that fill the air over the lagoon. Although there's generally good viewing from all

around the lagoon, the best spots are on the bridge between France and the United Kingdom, the promenade in front of Canada and Norway, and the bridge between China and Germany, which will give you a clear shot, unobstructed by trees. After the show, concealed loudspeakers play the theme music manipulated into salsa, polka, waltz, and even—believe it or not—Asian rhythms.

AT THE PAVILIONS

Some of the most enjoyable entertainment takes place outside the pavilions and along the promenade. Live shows with actors, dancers, singers, mime routines, and demonstrations of folk arts and crafts are presented at varying times of day; get times in your Epcot Map Guide or at the WorldKey terminals at Guest Relations and Germany. Or look for signs posted at the pavilions. Wonders of Life's **AnaComical Players,** Italy's farcical **Nova Era,** Morocco's **MoRockin',** and the United Kingdom's **World Showcase Players** each enlist audience members as heroes and villains, princes and princesses, to the hilarity of all. The United Kingdom also has an illusionist and a '60s rock group, the **British Invasion.** A group that calls itself the **JAMMitors** plays up a storm in Epcot using the tools of the janitorial trade—garbage cans, waste baskets, brooms, mops, and dustpans. By the Fountain of Nations, check out **Cast in Bronze,** which makes music on an unusual eight-tier organ, if it's still on when you visit. The **Alpine Trio** oompahs away in Germany. If you hear drumming from the vicinity of Japan, scurry on over.

First Aid

The park's First Aid Center, staffed by registered nurses, is near the Odyssey Restaurant in Future World.

Getting Around

It's a big place; a local joke suggests that Epcot is an acronym for "Every Person Comes Out Tired." But still, the most efficient way to get around is to walk. Just to vary things, you can cruise across the lagoon in one of the air-conditioned, 65-ft water taxis that departs every 12 minutes from World Showcase Plaza at the border of Future World. There are two docks: Boats from the one on the left zip to the Germany pavilion, from the right to Morocco. You may have to stand in line for your turn to board, however.

If you think the huge distances involved may be a problem, start out by renting a stroller or wheelchair.

Guided Tours

Reserve up to six weeks in advance for a behind-the-scenes tour (☏ 407/939–8687), led by a knowledgeable Disney cast member and open to guests 16 and older. Several tours offer close-up views of the phenomenal detail involved in the planning and maintenance of Epcot. **Hidden Treasures Plus** (✉ $85, including park admission and lunch) is a comprehensive guide to all 11 international pavilions. You'll learn everything from the provenance of the boulders in Japan's garden to the number of bricks in the U.S. pavilion. The four-hour **Hidden Treasures of World Showcase** (✉ $69; park admission included), which runs on Tuesday, Thursday, and Saturday, offers a look at all 11 nations in World Showcase. The three-hour **Gardens of the World Tour** (✉ $49 plus park admission) runs Tuesday and Thursday; it explains World Showcase's realistic replicas of exotic plantings.

Behind the Seeds (✉ $6 adults, $4 children), 60-minute guided tours of the greenhouses and aquacell areas in Future World's The Land pavilion, covers the same topics as the Living with the Land boat ride but in much more detail—and you have the chance to ask questions. Tours run every half hour 9:30 to 4:30, and reservations are essential; they can be made on The Land's lower floor, in the corner opposite the boat ride entrance, behind the Green Thumb Emporium. This is a good activity for busy times of day.

If you want to get into the swim—and you have scuba open-water adult certification and can prove it—try Living Seas' **Epcot Divequest** (🖰 $140, park admission not required). Under the supervision of one of the Living Seas' master divers you can spend three hours underwater in the aquarium. The tours take place Sundays through Saturdays at either 4:30 or 5:30. **Dolphins in Depth** (🖰 $140, park admission not required) is an experience that encourages interaction with your favorite water friends. Tours meet weekdays at 9:30 AM at the Living Seas pavilion and last about 3½ hours. All tours are open only to those 16 years of age and over.

Lockers
You'll find them ($3, plus $2 refundable deposit) to the west of Spaceship Earth, outside the Entrance Plaza, and in the Bus Information Center by the bus parking lot. If what you need to store won't fit into the larger lockers, go to Guest Relations in the Entrance Plaza or at Earth Station.

Lost Things and People
If you're worried about your children getting lost, get name tags for them at either Guest Relations or the Baby Care Center. Instruct them to speak to someone with a Disney name tag if you become separated. And if you do, immediately report your loss to any cast member and try not to panic; the staff here is experienced at reuniting families, and there are lost-children logbooks at Earth Station and the Baby Care Center. Earth Station also has a computerized Message Center, where you can leave notes for your traveling companions in any of the parks. For the lost and found, go to the west edge of the Entrance Plaza. If nobody claims what you turn in, you may get to keep it.

Money Matters
For cash and currency exchange, go to the SunTrust branch at Epcot (open daily 9–4) or the Guest Relations window. There are ATMs on the Mexico side of the walkway between Future World and World Showcase as well as near the rest rooms in the Italy pavilion, and there is an American Express ExpressCash machine on the left side of the Entrance Plaza as you enter, by Guest Relations.

Package Pickup
Ask the shop clerk to forward any large purchase you make to Guest Relations in the Entrance Plaza so that you won't have to carry it around all day. Allow three hours.

Shopping
World Showcase is nothing if not crammed with souvenirs—shopping is part of the entertainment. Many of the wares are also sold in shops and department stores around the United States. The hottest items these days are the commemorative millennium pins available throughout the park for purchase and trading, especially in front of Spaceship Earth, at $6–$12 per pin. There are exotic items as well: well-priced leather belts and purses in Morocco's **Tangier Traders;** Guerlain perfume and cosmetics at the **Guerlain Boutique,** in France; charming china in the **Magic of Wales,** in the United Kingdom; Armani Disney collectibles at the **Armani Shop,** in Italy; nutcrackers at **Die Weinachts Ecke,** in Germany; piñatas at **Plaza de los Amigos,** in Mexico; and kimonoed and obi-sashed dolls at **Mitsukoshi,** in Japan. Millennium Village is a bazaar of trinkets from throughout the world, which includes the **Village Marketplace,** where artists demonstrate and sell crafts from all corners of the globe.

If your shopping time is limited, check out the two shops at the entrance to World Showcase.

Disney Traders, as its name suggests, features Disney-character dolls dressed in the national costumes of the World Showcase participants and the requisite T-shirts and sweatshirts. Kids love the flags from around the world. Also sold here—and at some scattered kiosks throughout the park—is a great keepsake for youngsters: a World Showcase Passport ($9.95). At each pavilion, children can present their passports to be stamped—it's a great way to keep their interest up in this more adult area of Epcot. At **Port of Entry,** there are products from around the world. Its "Preserve and Protect" products—including a small topiary Mickey Mouse—strive to be ecologically sound.

Future World shopping will not tempt you to spend a lot of money. **Green Thumb Emporium,** a rare bright spot for acquisitive spirits in this part of Epcot, sells all sorts of kitchen- and garden-related knick-knacks—from hydroponic plants to vegetable refrigerator magnets. If you want the standard range of Epcot logo souvenirs, check out **Mouse Gear,** where you'll find more than 19,000 square ft of merchandise. You can pick up an aid to healthy living, including sweats emblazoned with Disney characters working up a sweat, at **Well & Goods Limited** in the Wonders of Life. For the more serious collector, **The Art of Disney** sells limited edition cels and figurines.

Visitor Information

Guest Relations, in Innoventions East, is the place to pick up schedules of live entertainment, park brochures, and the like. The computerized **WorldKey** information kiosks—in Innoventions East, on the bridge between Future World and World Showcase and near Germany—can come in handy. Using the touch-sensitive screens, you can obtain detailed information about every pavilion, leave messages for companions, and get answers to almost all of your questions. If the computer can't give you the answer, you can request the assistance of a host or hostess. International visitors can retrieve maps in their native language in dispensers located directly in front of Spaceship Earth right after they enter the turnstiles.

DISNEY–MGM STUDIOS THEME PARK

When Walt Disney company chairman Michael Eisner opened Disney–MGM Studios in May 1989, he welcomed visitors to "the Hollywood that never was and always will be." Inspired by southern California's highly successful Universal Studios tour, an even more successful version of which is a half hour's drive down I-4, Disney–MGM combined Disney detail with MGM's motion-picture expertise. The result is an amalgamation that blends theme park with fully functioning movie and television production center, breathtaking rides with instructional tours, nostalgia with high-tech wonders.

The rosy-hue view of the moviemaking business takes place in a dreamy stage set from the 1930s and 1940s, amid sleek Art Moderne buildings in pastel colors, funky diners, kitschy decorations, and sculptured gardens populated by roving actors playing, well, roving actors. Thanks to a rich library of film scores, the park is permeated with music, all familiar, all happy, all evoking the magic of the movies, and all constantly streaming from the camouflaged loudspeakers at a volume just right for humming along. And watching over all, like the penthouse suite of a benevolent genie, is the Earfful Tower, a 13-story water tower adorned with giant mouse ears.

THE BIRTH OF WALT DISNEY WORLD®

I T'D BE A GREAT QUESTION for Regis to ask: Florida was founded by A) Juan Ponce deLeon, B) Millard Fillmore, C) Danny Bonaduce, or D) Walt Disney. For travelers who can't fathom Florida without Walt Disney World, the final answer is D, in Central Florida at least. The theme park's arrival spawned a multi-billion-dollar tourism industry that begat a population boom that begat new highways, malls, and schools that begat a whole new culture.

So how did it happen? Why did Walt pin his hopes on forlorn Florida ranchlands 3,000 miles from Disneyland and the Disney Studios? In the 1950s, Walt Disney barely had enough money to open his theme park in California, and lacking the funds to buy a buffer zone, he couldn't prevent cheap hotels and tourist traps from setting up shop next door. This time he wanted land. And lots of it. Beginning in the early 1960s, Walt and his lieutenants embarked on a super secret four year project: they traveled the nation in search of a location that gave them them access to a major population center, good highways, a steady climate, and, most importantly, cheap and abundant land. Locations were narrowed down, and in the end Orlando, at the crossroads of Florida, was it.

In May 1965, major land transactions were being recorded a few miles southwest of Orlando in Osceola County. Two large tracts totalling $1.5 million were sold, and smaller tracts of flatlands and cattle pastures were purchased by exotic-sounding companies such as the Latin-American Development and Managers Corporation and the Reedy Creek Ranch Corporation. Although the sales reports were open to the public, the identity of the buyers were not.

Months passed and more land changed hands. By late June, the *Orlando Sentinel* reported that more than 27,000 acres had been sold so far. It wasn't until October when *Sentinel* reporter Emily Bavar broke the story, was it revealed that Walt Disney was the mastermind behind the purchases. Forcing his hand, Walt and his brother Roy hastily arranged a press conference and, with the governor by their side, admitted the land was theirs and could only hint at what Disney World would do for Florida. But once Walt described the $400 million project and mentioned the few thousand jobs it would create, Florida's government quickly gave Walt permission to establish the autonomous Reedy Creek Improvement District. With this, he could write his own zoning restrictions and building codes and plan his own roads, bridges, hotels, lakes, horse trails, airport, golf courses, night clubs, theaters, and a residential community for his employees.

Walt played a hands-on role in the planning of Disney World, but just over a year a later, in December 1966, he died. As expected, his faithful brother Roy took control and spent the following five years acting as his brother's executor, supervising the construction of the Magic Kingdom, two resort hotels, and a campground. Fittingly, before the park opened on October 1, 1971, Roy changed the name of his brother's park to "Walt" Disney World so the public would forever recognize who was responsible for bringing it to life. Sadly, Roy passed away three months after the park's opening, but by then Walt Disney World was hitting its stride. For the next decade, it became part of Florida's landscape. Families that once saw Orlando merely as a whistlestop on the way to Miami now made their vacation base at Walt Disney World.

Behind the scenes, however, a few cracks began to appear in the facade. In its first decade, growth was stagnant. There were no new hotels and the Magic Kingdom remained the flagship of the resort. Epcot, Walt's dream for a utopian city, was being built, however, it was no longer Walt's vision but an international

65

Close-Up

conglomeration of gift shops, Circlevision films, and quasi-futuristic displays. By the time Epcot opened in 1982, construction cost overruns and low attendance created a 19 percent drop in profits. Meanwhile, the Disney Channel and Disney's film division were also plodding along sluggishly. Eventually, in 1984, Michael Eisner came aboard as CEO and company chairman, along with Frank Wells as president and chief financial officer. Their arrival got Disney out of the doldrums.

Disney's unparalleled film catalog was brought out of storage with re-releases in theaters and on video. Jeffrey Katzenberg was put in charge of the Disney Studios, and suddenly the moribund movies the studio had been releasing were replaced by "new classics" such as *Aladdin, Beauty and the Beast, The Little Mermaid,* and the legendary *The Lion King.* At the theme parks, the release of the new films were supported by movie-themed parades and movie merchandise sold in the gift shops.

The Eisner Era accelerated Disney's—and Orlando's—growth. Even after Wells died in a helicopter accident in 1994 and Katzenburg left to form a company with David Geffen and Steven Spielberg, Walt Disney World expanded at a rate unheard of in the 1970s and early 1980s. In 1988 Walt Disney World premiered two new resorts: the Grand Floridian and Caribbean Beach. The following year, the Disney-MGM Studios theme park opened along with Typhoon Lagoon and Pleasure Island. Additional resort hotels opened in the early 1990s—the Yacht and Beach Club, Swan and Dolphin, Port Orleans, Disney's Old Key West and Dixie Landings resorts. By 1995 Walt Disney World had a new wedding pavilion; by 1997 Disney's Wide World of Sports, Downtown Disney West Side, and the Coronado Springs resort opened; and by 1998 the fourth theme park, Disney's Animal Kingdom, came to life. Also arriving in this decade of growth were new rides, parades, golf courses, stage shows, the planned community of Celebration, the Disney cruise lines, the book publishing arm of Hyperion, and Disney's purchase of Miramax Films and ABC television.

And it all started with a man who didn't have the cash to buy a little more land in Anaheim.

—Gary McKechnie

Although some of the attractions will interest young children, the park is really best for teenagers old enough to watch old movies on television and catch the cinematic references. Not quite as fantasy oriented as the Magic Kingdom or as earnestly educational as Epcot, the Studios could almost be said to have attitude—not a lot, mind you, but enough to add a little sizzle to the steak.

The park is divided into sightseeing clusters. **Hollywood Boulevard** is the main artery to the heart of the park: the glistening red-and-gold, multiturret replica of Grauman's Chinese Theater, home of the Great Movie Ride. Encircling it in a roughly counterclockwise fashion are **Sunset Boulevard,** where you'll find the Twilight Zone Tower of Terror II, the amphitheater in which Fantasmic! is staged every night, and the Rock 'n' Roller Coaster; the **Animation Courtyard,** which houses the Magic of Disney Animation, *Voyage of the Little Mermaid,* and *Bear in the Big Blue House*; **Mickey Avenue** is home to the Disney–MGM Studios PASS and the Studios Backlot Tour; the **New York Street** area has Jim Henson's Muppet*Vision 4-D, *Honey, I Shrunk the Kids* Movie Set Adventure playground, and the Backlot Theater; and **Echo Lake,** contains the Indiana Jones Epic Stunt Spectacular!, Star Tours, Disney's *Doug* Live!, and Sounds Dangerous.

Surprisingly, the entire park is rather small—only 110 acres, one-quarter the size of Universal Studios—with not even 20 major attractions, as opposed to nearly 50 in the Magic Kingdom. When waits are minimal you can easily cover the park in a day with time for repeat rides. And even when the lines seem to stretch clear to Epcot, a little careful planning will allow you to see everything on one ticket.

Numbers in the margin correspond to points of interest on the Disney–MGM Studios Theme Park map.

Hollywood Boulevard

With its palm trees, pastel buildings, and flashy neon, Hollywood Boulevard paints a rosy picture of Tinseltown in the 1930s. There's a sense of having walked right onto a movie set in the olden days, what with the art deco storefronts, strolling brass bands, and roving starlets and nefarious agents—actually costumed actors. These are frequently joined by characters from Disney movies new and old, who pose for pictures and sign autographs. *Beauty and the Beast*'s Belle is a favorite, as are Jafar, Princess Jasmine, and the Genie from *Aladdin,* the soldiers from *Toy Story,* and Esmeralda from *The Hunchback of Notre Dame.*

Hollywood Boulevard, like Main Street, has souvenir shops and memorabilia collections galore. **Oscar's Classic Car Souvenirs & Super Service Station** is crammed with fuel-pump bubble-gum machines, photos of antique cars, and other automotive knickknacks. At **Sid Cahuenga's One-of-a-Kind** antiques and curios store, you might find and acquire Meg Ryan's castoffs or at least autographed stars' photos. Down the street at **Cover Story,** don the appropriate costume and have your picture put on the cover of a major magazine. At the end of the street, at the corner of Sunset Boulevard, you'll find loads of child-size character clothing at **L.A. Cinema Storage.** The fortysomething crowd will also appreciate this shop's collection of old Mickey Mouse Club black-and-white production stills.

NEED A
BREAK?

For a sweet burst of energy, snag a cinnamon swirl at **Starring Rolls Bakery,** near the Brown Derby. Or try the croissants, turnovers, or almost-authentic bagels.

Disney–MGM Studios Theme Park

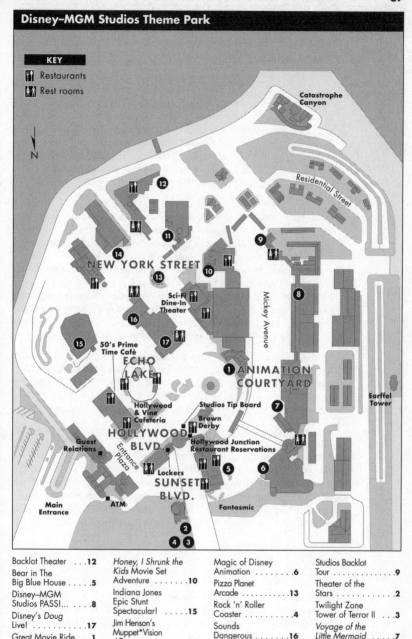

KEY

🚻 Restaurants
🚻 Rest rooms

N

Catastrophe Canyon

Residential Street

NEW YORK STREET

Sci-Fi Dine-In Theater

Mickey Avenue

50's Prime Time Café

ECHO LAKE

ANIMATION COURTYARD

Earffel Tower

Hollywood & Vine Cafeteria

Studios Tip Board

Brown Derby

HOLLYWOOD BLVD.

Hollywood Junction Restaurant Reservations

Guest Relations

Entrance Plaza

Lockers

SUNSET BLVD.

Main Entrance

ATM

Fantasmic

❶ **Great Movie Ride.** At the head of Hollywood Boulevard are the fire-engine-red pagodas of a replica of Grauman's Chinese Theater, which houses this attraction. The Imagineers pull out all the stops on this tour of great moments in film.

The lobby, really an ingenious way to spend time standing in line, slots you past such icons as Dorothy's ruby slippers from *The Wizard of Oz*, a carousel horse from *Mary Poppins*, and the piano played by Sam in *Casablanca*. You then shuffle into the preshow area, an enormous screening room with continuously running clips from *Mary Poppins, Raiders of the Lost Ark, Singin' in the Rain, Fantasia, Footlight Parade*, and, of course, *Casablanca*. The line continues snaking through the preshow, which itself is so much fun that you almost resent that you'll miss favorite clips once the great red doors swing open and it's your turn to ride.

Disney cast members dressed in 1920s newsboy costumes usher you onto open trams and you're off on a tour—through Audio-Animatronics, scrim, smoke, and Disney magic—of cinematic climaxes. First comes the world of musical entertainment with, among others, Gene Kelly clutching that immortal lamppost as he chimes "Singin' in the Rain" and Mary Poppins with her umbrella and her sooty admirers reprising "Chim-Chim-Cher-ee." The lights dim, and you move into either gangster land with James Cagney snarling in *Public Enemy* or a Western shoot-out à la John Wayne as Calamity Jane tries to rob the Miners' and Cattlemen's Bank and hijack the tram—and succeeds.

Nothing like a little time warp to bring justice. With pipes streaming fog and alarms whooping, the tram meets some of the slimier characters in *Alien*—look up for truly scary stuff—and then eases into the cobwebby, snake-ridden, and slithering set of the *Temple of Doom*, where Calamity Jane attempts to bluff an idol threat and gets vaporized.

Each time you think you've witnessed the best scene, the tram moves into another set: Tarzan yodels and swings on a vine overhead; then Bogey toasts Bergman in front of the plane to Lisbon. The finale has hundreds of robotic Munchkins cheerily enjoining you to "Follow the Yellow Brick Road," despite the cackling imprecations by the Wicked Witch of the West. Remember to check out Dorothy's tornado-tossed house—those on the right side of the tram can just spot the ruby slippers. The tram follows the Yellow Brick Road, and then there it is: Emerald City.

As icing on the cake, there's one more movie presentation with three screens all going at once to display yet more memorable moments, including great kisses ranging from Rhett Butler and Scarlett O'Hara's embrace to Roger and Jessica Rabbit's animated smooch. Then the lights come up, and the announcer calls you for the final scene: The Exit. *Duration: 22 mins. Crowds: Steady and large all day long; when the inside lines start spilling out the door, expect at least a 25-min wait. Strategy: Go first thing in the morning or at the end of the day. If the lines still look long, ask about the line's length before you slink away discouraged—Disney staffers often "stack" people up outside to clear up the crowds inside and to prepare for closing. Audience: All but young children, for whom it may be too intense. Rating:* ★★★

Sunset Boulevard

This avenue pays tribute to famous Hollywood monuments, with facades derived from the Cathay Circle, the Beverly Wilshire Theatre, and other City of Angels landmarks.

As you turn onto Sunset Boulevard from Hollywood Boulevard, you'll run smack into **Hollywood Junction Station,** where reservations can be made for restaurants throughout the park. Nearby **Legends of Hollywood** brims with books, videos, and posters of classic films, while **Once Upon a Time** showcases displays of vintage character toys.

② **Theater of the Stars.** The wildly popular stage show *Beauty and the Beast—Live on Stage* takes place in a re-creation of the famed Hollywood Bowl. The long-running production is a skillful condensation of the animated film. *Duration: 30 mins. Crowds: Almost always. Strategy: Queue up at least 30 mins prior to show time for good seats, especially with children. Audience: All ages. Rating:* ★★★

NEED A
BREAK?

Grab a quick bite on Sunset Boulevard at **Rosie's Red Hot Dogs, Catalina Eddie's Frozen Yogurt,** or, for a healthful snack, the **Anaheim Produce Company.**

③ **Twilight Zone Tower of Terror II.** Ominously overlooking Sunset Boulevard is a 13-story structure that's reputedly the now-deserted Hollywood Tower Hotel. You take an eerie stroll through the dimly lighted lobby and decaying library to the boiler room before boarding the hotel's giant elevator. As you head upward past seemingly deserted hallways, ghostly former residents appear in front of you, until suddenly—faster than you can say "Where's Rod Serling?"—the creaking vehicle plunges downward in a terrifying, 130-ft free-fall drop and then travels quickly up, down, up, down all over again. (The number of ups and downs was expanded in summer 1999—if you think the ride is wilder than last time, you're probably right.) Serling then warns, "The next time you check in to a deserted hotel on the dark side of Hollywood, make sure you know what vacancy you'll be filling, or you'll be a permanent member of . . . the Twilight Zone!" Serling's claim that you won't hear about this hotel in any guide book is wrong—you're hearing about it here. *Duration: 10 mins. Crowds: Yes! Strategy: Go early, wait until evening when the crowds thin out, or better yet, use your FAST-PASS advantage. Audience: Older children and adults. No pregnant women or guests with heart, back, or neck problems. Minimum height: 40″. Rating:* ★★★

④ **Rock 'n' Roller Coaster.** Opened in summer 1999, this is the first fairly straightforward roller coaster in Walt Disney World, and with its high-speed launch and multiple complete inversions, it is generating its fair share of screams. The vehicles look like limos and the track resembles the neck of an electric guitar that's been twisted; a hard-driving rock sound track by Aerosmith blasts from speakers mounted in each vehicle to accentuate the flips and turns. There's rock 'n' roll memorabilia in the queue area, and Aerosmith stars in the preshow. *Crowds: Huge. Strategy: Go early in the day. This is a definite FASTPASS candidate. Pick up your ticket first thing in the morning, then head over to do the animation tour. If the timing is right, then return to ride. Audience: Teens and adults. No guests with heart, back, or neck problems or motion sickness. Minimum height: 44″. Rating:* ★★★

Animation Courtyard

As you exit Sunset Boulevard, veer right through the high-arched gateway to the Animation Courtyard. You're now at one end of Mickey Avenue, and straight ahead are the **Magic of Disney Animation** and **Voyage of the Little Mermaid.** At the far end of the avenue are the popular **Disney–MGM Studios PASS** and **Studios Backlot Tour.**

⑤ Bear in the Big Blue House. The former Soundstage Restaurant is now home to the bears that are the newest rage among toddlers and preschoolers. In this interactive show, the stars of this hit TV program dance and sing popular songs all kids love. *Duration: 25 mins. Crowds: Not a problem, but lines tend to be very heavy in the mid-afternoon. Strategy: Go first thing in the morning, when your child is most alert. Audience: Toddlers, preschoolers. Rating:* ★★

⑥ Magic of Disney Animation. This self-guided tour through the Disney animation process is one of the park's funniest and most engaging attractions. More than any backstage tour, more than any revelation of stunt secrets, this tour truly takes you inside the magic as you follow the many steps of animation from concept to charisma. Disney's *Mulan, Tarzan,* and *Fantasia 2000* were all produced here in their entirety.

Although you can move at your own pace, the staff tries to keep crowds to a minimum, so groups assemble in the lobby. Take the opportunity to check out the collection of drawings and original cels, the clear celluloid sheets on which the characters were drawn for *Snow White, Fantasia,* and other Disney classics. Here, too, are the Academy Awards that Disney has won for its animated films.

From the lobby in the Animation Courtyard, you segue into the Disney Animation Theater for a hilarious eight-minute film in which Walter Cronkite and Robin Williams explain animation basics—a *Peter Pan* sequel called *Back to Neverland,* with Walter Cronkite as himself and his comic costar as a Little Lost Boy. The irrepressible Robin really wanted it to be called *Peter Pan: First Blood,* but the title was voted down. The film was almost impossible to complete because the steadfast, avuncular Cronkite kept cracking up. (You might, too, if you suddenly discovered Tinker Bell in your jacket pocket.) Robin Williams discovers the potential range of animation: "Hey," he proclaims as he's redrawn into a familiar rodent, "I can be a corporate symbol!" Meanwhile, we learn about cel-making, layout artists, background artists, cleanup artists, sound effects, and more. You also get to meet an animation artist who explains these animation process and answers any questions. From the theater, you follow walkways with windows overlooking the working animation studios, where you see Disney artists at their drafting tables doing everything you just learned about. Their desks are strewn with finished drawings of Simba, Scar, Aladdin, Genie, and other famous characters, and you can peer over their shoulders at soon-to-be-famous characters.

Meanwhile, Robin and Walter continue their banter on overhead monitors, explaining the processes as you saunter from the story room (where animators develop story lines), to the drawing boards (where ideas metamorphose from sketch to colorful characters), to the cleanup room, the special effects area, and the special camera that transfers drawings to cels. To produce one 24-minute film, the 70-plus members of the animation team must create 34,650 drawings and add scenes from at least 300 background paintings. No wonder everyone wears headphones, although it's doubtful they're listening to "Whistle While You Work."

The penultimate attraction on the tour is a continuously running video. "You believe the character *is* alive," confesses one of the geeky-looking animators who so identify with their characters that they can take on their personalities. Watching a low-key, pleasant Asian man become the blowsy, evil Scar from *The Lion King* right before your eyes makes you wonder if pixie dust really is in the air.

Upon completion of the tour there's a valedictory quip from Robin Williams, and you head into the Disney Classics Theater for a presentation of the best moments from animated films. It's fascinating to see the evolution of the art from the bright colors and straightforward drawings in *Snow White* and *Pinocchio* to the rainbow hues and complex panoramas of *Beauty and the Beast, Aladdin, The Lion King, Pocahontas,* and *Tarzan.* Best of all, you know that here the characters always will live happily ever after. *Duration: Usually around 40 mins. Crowds: Steady all day. Strategy: Go in the morning or late afternoon, when you can get in with less waiting and still see the animators at work (they get in at 9, have lunch around noon, leave by 6, and are not always around on weekends). The lowest crowds gather at around 5. Audience: All but young children. Rating:* ★★★

⑦ *Voyage of the Little Mermaid.* A boxy building on Mickey Avenue invites you to join Ariel, Sebastian, and the underwater gang in this stage show, which condenses the movie into a marathon presentation of the greatest hits. In an admirable effort at verisimilitude, a fine mist sprays the stage; if you're sitting in the front rows, expect to get refreshed. *Duration: 15 mins. Crowds: Perpetual. Strategy: If you decide not to ride the Rock 'n' Roller Coaster, go first thing in the morning, putting the FASTPASS to good use. Otherwise, wait until the stroller brigade's exodus after 5. Audience: All ages. Rating:* ★★

Mickey Avenue

A stroll down this street and you'll pass the soundstages that are used to produce some of today's television shows and motion pictures. On your left, there are several souvenir kiosks, as well as opportunities to mingle with Pooh and all of his friends, who each have a trailer parked along the street, for character meeting and greeting.

⑧ **Disney–MGM-Studios PASS!** This walking tour begins with a look at an exhibit of props, costumes, and sets from the hit television show *Home Improvement.* A guest is chosen to be a member of the *Tool Time* cast, and is videotaped acting "opposite" Tim Allen, whose face and voice are projected on an adjoining screen. The two elements are then edited together and shown as one scene to the audience. Then, you are taken to the Jim Henson Creature Shop, where many props and scaled-down scenery from previously produced Disney films are on display. You see models of the puppies that were in the film *101 Dalmatians* and learn how the real puppies were trained to perform. Next, you walk on catwalks and view soundstages of shows that are currently in production. Finally, you see the the DeVil Mansion and other special props from *101 Dalmatians,* along with a videotaped demonstration of how some stunt scenes were created. *Duration: 25 mins. Crowds: Moderate, unless the film being promoted has just hit theaters. Strategy: Go first thing in the morning if you have youngsters in tow; otherwise wait until near closing time. Because of all the walking involved, do not attempt if you're totally drained from the day. Audience: All but young children, who may be bored by the museum feel of much of the attraction; the payoff for them doesn't come until the very end. Rating:* ★★

⑨ **Studios Backlot Tour.** The first stop on this tour, which you enter at the far end of Mickey Avenue, in Animation Courtyard, is an outdoor special-effects water tank. Here, two willing, if unwary, audience members don bright yellow slickers to play the skipper of the ill-fated S.S. *Miss Fortune* and the submarine commander Captain Duck, about to pilot his craft into battle. As the audience watches, the skipper nearly gets drowned in a thunderstorm, and the doughty Duck gets strafed, torpedoed, and doused with 400 gallons of water from a depth charge while a video camera records the scenario and plays it back with music and background.

Then it's time to queue up for the tram ride for the back-lot tour. The wait is very interesting, because as you walk through the line, you are also touring a huge prop warehouse, which stores everything you could possibly imagine, from chairs to traffic lights to newspaper stands.

Board the tram for a tour of the back-lot building blocks of movies: set design, costumes, props, lighting, and the de rigueur**Catastrophe Canyon.** The tram's announcer swears that the film that's supposedly shooting in there is taking a break. Not! The next thing you know, the tram is bouncing up and down in a simulated earthquake, an oil tanker explodes in a mass of smoke and flame, and a water tower crashes to the ground, touching off a flash flood, which douses the tanker and threatens to drown the tram. Although the earthquake is more like a shimmy, the water and fire provoke genuine screams. As the tram pulls out, you see the backstage workings of the catastrophe: the canyon is actually a mammoth steel slide wrapped in copper-color cement, and the 70,000 gallons of flood water—enough to fill 10 Olympic-size swimming pools—are recycled 100 times a day, or every 3½ minutes.

Let your heartbeat slow down as the tram takes another pass through the Big Apple. This time you're close enough to see that brownstones, marble, brick, and stained glass are actually expertly painted two-dimensional facades of fiberglass and Styrofoam. Grips can slide the Empire State and Chrysler buildings out of the way anytime. Note the large airplane that Walt Disney used to search for the Florida theme park property.

Hop off the tram and walk through the **American Film Institute Museum,** a shop containing movie and television memorabilia of the past and present. *Duration: 60 mins. Crowds: Steady through the afternoon, but lines seem to move quickly. Strategy: As you enter the tram, remember that people sitting on the left get seared and wet; people on the right get crushed as the people on the left leap into their laps. Go early; it closes at dusk. Audience: All but young children; do not, repeat, do not take them on this ride, because they will be truly terrified in Catastrophe Canyon. Rating:* ★★★

New York Street

It's well worth touring the sets here on foot—as long as crews aren't filming—so that you can check out the windows of shops and apartments, the taxicabs, and other details.

⑩ *Honey, I Shrunk the Kids* **Movie Set Adventure.** Let your youngsters run free in this state-of-the-art playground based on the movie about Lilliputian kids in a larger-than-life world. They can slide down a gigantic blade of grass, crawl through caves, climb a mushroom mountain, inhale the scent of a humongous plant (which will then spit water back in their faces), and dodge sprinklers set in resilient flooring made of ground-up tires. All the requisite playground equipment is present: net climbs, ball crawls, caves, and slides. Because the area is enclosed, there's often a line to get in, which seems rather restrictive for a playground. *Duration: Up to you. Crowds: Steady. Strategy: Come early or come back when there's no line. Audience: Children and those who love them. Rating:* ★★★

⑪ **Jim Henson's Muppet*Vision 4-D.** You don't have to be a Miss Piggyphile to get a kick out of this combination 3-D movie and musical revue, although all the Muppet characters make appearances, including Miss

Piggy in the role of the Statue of Liberty. In the waiting area, Muppet movie posters advertise the world's most glamorous porker in *Star Chores* and *To Have and Have More,* and Kermit the Frog in an Arnold Schwarzenegger parody, *Kürmit the Amphibian,* who's "so mean, he's green." When the theater was constructed, special effects were built into the walls; the 3-D effects are coordinated with other sensory stimulation so you're never sure what's coming off the screen and what's being shot out of vents in the ceiling and walls. *Duration: 10-min preshow, 20-min show. Crowds: Steady from morning through late afternoon, and because the waiting area is carefully hidden, you don't know how long the line is until you've waited for too long. Strategy: Go early or late. And don't worry—there are no bad seats. Audience: All ages. Rating:* ★★★

⑫ Backlot Theater. Disney animated films are brought to life in productions with Broadway scope; in fact, the first show to be performed in the Backlot's original locale near the Brown Derby restaurant, *Beauty and the Beast: Live on Stage,* was actually a small-scale prototype for what eventually became the Broadway musical. (*Beauty and the Beast* proved so popular that it got its very own theater, the Theater of the Stars, when Sunset Boulevard was built.) Other productions have included *The Spirit of Pocahontas* and *The Hunchback of Notre Dame—A Musical Adventure. Duration: 30 mins. Crowds: Not a problem. Strategy: Arrive 15 mins before show time for a good seat—optimally the first two or three rows in the center of the theater. Audience: All ages. Rating:* ★★

⑬ Pizza Planet Arcade. Remember the Pizza Planet restaurant in *Toy Story?* This is a re-creation. Video games and machines with claws that give you a chance to win a stuffed animal are scattered throughout, and an area full of *Toy Story*–theme trinkets will almost certainly prompt cries of "I want one!" from your children. Food and drinks are also available to consume as your supply of quarters dwindles. *Duration: Up to you. Strategy: Go in the afternoon when you need a place to cool off. Audience: All but young children; most popular with preteens. Rating:* ★

Echo Lake

Segue from New York Street into Echo Lake, an idealized California. In the center is the cool, blue lake of the same name, an oasis fringed with trees and benches and ringed with landmarks: pink-and-aqua restaurants trimmed in chrome, presenting sassy waitresses and television sets at the tables; Min and Bill's Dockside Diner, which offers fast food in a shipshape atmosphere; and Gertie, a dinosaur that dispenses ice cream, Disney souvenirs, and the occasional puff of smoke in true magic-dragon fashion. Look for Gertie's giant footprints in the sidewalk. (Gertie, by the way, was the first animated animal to show emotion—an inspiration to the pre-Mickey Walt.) Here, too, you'll find two of the park's biggest attractions, the **Indiana Jones Epic Stunt Spectacular!** and **Star Tours,** while on the north side of the pond are **Disney's *Doug* Live!** and **Sounds Dangerous.**

⑭ Star Tours. Although the flight-simulator technology used for this ride was long ago surpassed on other thrill rides, most notably Universal Studios' *Back to the Future . . . The Ride,* this adventure inspired by the *Star Wars* films is still a pretty good trip. "May the force be with you," says the attendant on duty, "'cause I won't be!" Piloted by *Star Wars* characters R2D2 and C-3PO, the 40-passenger *StarSpeeder* that you board is supposed to take off on a routine flight to the moon of Endor. But with R2D2 at the helm, things quickly go awry: you shoot into deep space, dodge giant ice crystals and comet debris, innocently bumble into an intergalactic battle, and attempt to avoid laser-blasting fighters as you whiz through the canyons of some planetary city before coming to a heart-stopping halt. *Duration: 7 mins. Crowds: Can be substantial but occasionally are light. Lines swell periodically when Disney's Doug Live! and the Indiana Jones Epic Stunt Spectacular!, which are nearby, let out. Strategy: To make sure you'll walk right on, go shortly before closing or first thing in the morning. Otherwise cruise on with the help of a FASTPASS appointment. When you line up to enter the simulation chamber, keep to the far left to sit up front and closer to the screen for the most realistic sensations (the ride is rougher in back but the sensations of motion less exhilarating). Audience: Older children, Star Wars fans, and adults. No pregnant women, children under 3, or guests with heart, back, or neck problems or motion sickness; children under 7 must be accompanied by an adult. Rating:* ★★★

15 **Indiana Jones Epic Stunt Spectacular!** The rousing theme music from the Indiana Jones movies summons you to this great show featuring the stunt choreography of veteran coordinator Glenn Randall, whose credits include *Raiders of the Lost Ark, Indiana Jones and the Temple of Doom, E.T.,* and *Jewel of the Nile.* Presented in a 2,200-seat amphitheater, the show starts with a series of near-death encounters in an ancient Maya temple. Clad in his signature fedora and looking cute enough for front-row viewers to consider painting "Love You" on their eyelids, just like Professor Jones's adoring student did in *Raiders of the Lost Ark,* Indiana slides down a rope from the ceiling, dodges spears that shoot up from the floor, avoids getting chopped by booby-trapped idols, and snags a forbidden gemstone, setting off a gigantic boulder that threatens to render him two-dimensional.

It's hard to top that opener, but Randall and his pals do just that with the help of 10 audience participants. "Okay, I need some rowdy people," the casting director calls. While the lucky few demonstrate their rowdiness, behind them the set crew casually wheels off the entire temple: two people roll the boulder like a giant beach ball and replace it with a Cairo street, circa 1940. Nasty Ninja-Nazi stuntmen roll out a mat and bounce around performing flips and throws in the background. This is one of those times when it's better to be in the audience.

The scene they're working up to takes place on a busy Cairo street, down which saunter Indy and his redoubtable girlfriend, Marian Ravenwood, portrayed by a Karen Allen look-alike. She is to be kidnaped and tossed in a truck while Indy fights his way free with bullwhip and gun, and bad guys tumble from every corner and cornice. Motorcycles buzz around; the street becomes a shambles; and, as a stunning climax, the truck carrying Marian flips and bursts into flame.

Randall and his gang do a great job at explaining the stunts. You see how they are set up, watch the stars practice them in slow motion, and learn how cameras are camouflaged behind imitation rocks for trick shots. Only one stunt remains a secret: how do Indy and Marian escape the explosion? That's what keeps 'em coming back. *Duration: 30 mins. Crowds: Large, but the theater's high capacity means that everyone who wants to get in usually does. You can utilize your FASTPASS option here and avoid a 30- to 45-min wait to get a seat and walk right on in. Strategy: Go at night, when the idols' eyes glow red. If you sit up front, you can feel the heat when Marian's truck catches fire. Audience: All but young children. Rating:* ★★★

16 **Sounds Dangerous.** A multifaceted demonstration of the use of movie sound effects, this show features many of the gadgets created by sound master Jimmy MacDonald, who became the voice of Mickey Mouse during the 1940s and invented some 20,000 sound effects during his 45 years at Walt Disney Studios. Most qualify as gizmos—a metal sheet that, when rattled, sounds like thunder; a box of sand for footsteps on gravel; and other noises made from nails, straw, mud, leather, and other ordinary components. The premise of the show is that you will help Drew Carey, who portrays an undercover cop, find out who smuggled the diamonds from the snow globe. Then you don headphones to listen to the many sounds that go into the production of a movie or television show. Because the entire show takes place in the dark, it's extremely frightening for young children.

The Sounds Dangerous postshow is a treat consisting of hands-on exhibits called **SoundWorks.** There are buttons that go "boing" and knobs you push to alter your voice. Earie Encounters lets you imitate flying-saucer sounds from the 1956 film *Forbidden Planet.* At Movie Mimics you can try your chords at dubbing Mickey Mouse, Roger Rabbit, and other Disney heroes. *Duration: 30-min show; the rest is up to you. Crowds: Steady. Strategy: Arrive 15 mins before show time. Audience: All ages. Rating:* ★

NEED A BREAK?   Be sure to save room for Ice Cream of Extinction at the dinosaur-shape **Gertie's,** on the shore of Echo Lake.

---

⑰ Disney's *Doug* Live! Of the candidates screaming for attention when the casting director calls for volunteers, the most vociferous are chosen and perform alongside Doug, Patti Mayonnaise, Pork Chop, and the Gang in a mix of live theater and animation. To even the odds of getting chosen, go to the front of the waiting area, and let a staffer know that you would *love* to be in the show. Dressing outrageously and having a loud cheering section help. *Duration: 25 mins. Crowds: Large, but the large theater keeps waiting minimal. Strategy: Go anytime. Audience: Adults and grade-schoolers. Rating:* ★★

Strategies for Your Visit to Disney–MGM

When to Go

As at Epcot, it's best to go early in the week, while most other people are rushing through Disney's Animal Kingdom and the Magic Kingdom. If you're staying in a Disney hotel, you are entitled to early admission on Sunday and Wednesday, so schedule your visit accordingly. Be sure to arrive at the turnstiles about 15 minutes before the appointed hour so that you can take full advantage of this special perk. If you're *not* staying at a Disney hotel, make sure that you *don't* make your Studios visit on the early admission day—otherwise you'll go to a lot of trouble to show up early only to find that privileged Disney guests have already been there for an hour.

Blitz Tour

Arrive well before the park opens. When it does, run, don't walk, right up Hollywood Boulevard, hang a right at Sunset Boulevard, and dash to the 13-story **Twilight Zone Tower of Terror II.** You can make a FASTPASS appointment here. Next, head back to the Chinese Theater for the **Great Movie Ride.** It'll put you in the mood for a day at Disney–MGM like nothing else—and help you brush up on the songs pouring out of the hidden speakers. Return with your FASTPASS to ride **Tower of Terror .** Pick up your next FASTPASS now, this time for **Voyage of the Little Mermaid.** While you wait for your scheduled time, catch the **Studios' Backlot Tour** and **Disney–MGM Studios PASS!**

Grab a bite of early lunch at the **Studios Catering Company.** Return to see **Voyage of the Little Mermaid** with your appointed FASTPASS time. Then, head over to the **Indiana Jones Epic Stunt Spectacular!** pavilion and make another FASTPASS appointment and then check out the next time for the **Disney's *Doug* Live!** show. Zip over to **Sounds Dangerous** now, if there aren't too many people in line. Otherwise, catch the next performance of **Disney's *Doug* Live!** By now the time should have approached to head over to **Indiana Jones Epic Stunt Spectacular!**

Now, amble over to **Jim Henson's Muppet*Vision 4-D,** checking the lines at **Star Tours** on the way. If you can't see a line, nip in now. If the line looks appalling, the Muppets are a great consolation prize—especially because Muppet*Vision lets out in a back corner and while everyone is milling around and thinking of wandering up New York Street, you can whip right back to Star Tours for a second try. You could also try to catch a performance of the stage show at the **Backlot Theater.**

You'll need a little downtime after Star Tours. Take the opportunity to explore **Sunset Boulevard,** where the shops sell much of the same merchandise as those on Hollywood Boulevard but are less crowded. Grab a healthful snack at the Anaheim Produce Company, and try to catch a late-afternoon performance of *Beauty and the Beast* at the **Theater of the Stars.** That will put you in the right mood for the **Magic of Disney Animation,** and the time will be right, too—the crowds here will have begun to thin, but the animators won't have gone home yet. Spend all the time you want, but make sure that you catch the last show at the **Indiana Jones Epic Stunt Spectacular!** You'll want to catch the nighttime view. We love the way the idols' eyes glow in the dusk, and the gobs of flame from the exploding truck make you understand just why this attraction is called "spectacular." Then there's the music, which will carry you all the way back to the parking lots. Remember to turn at the gate for one last look at the Earfful Tower, whose perky appendages are outlined in gold lights.

On Rainy Days

Too much is outdoors here to make this a good bet on a rainy day.

Other Tips

- Plan to arrive in the parking lot a full hour ahead of the official opening time.

- Pick up an entertainment schedule on your way into the park.

- Set up a rendezvous point and time at the start of the day, just in case you and your companions get separated. Three excellent spots are in the garden in front of the Great Movie Ride, at the statue of Miss Piggy near the Muppets attraction, and on Mickey Avenue by the large Coke can that sprays water.

Disney–MGM Studios A to Z

Baby Care

At the small **Baby Care Center,** you'll find facilities for nursing as well as formula, baby food, pacifiers, and disposable diapers for sale. There are changing tables here and in all women's rooms and some men's rooms. You can also buy disposable diapers in the Guest Relations building. **Oscar's,** just inside the entrance turnstiles and to the right, is the place for stroller rentals ($7 rental fee; $1 deposit).

Cameras and Film

Walk through the aperture-shape door of the **Darkroom on Hollywood Boulevard,** where you can buy film and disposable Kodak Fun Saver cameras and get minor camera repairs. This is also the place to pick up pictures you want quickly. You can drop your film off here for one-hour developing or at any Photo Express container for two-hour developing. If you're staying on-site, you can even have the pictures delivered to your hotel. An extra-special memento is to have your picture taken in front of Grauman's Chinese Theater, or with Mickey Mouse on Sunset Boulevard near the Brown Derby ($7 for a 5" x 7" photo).

Dining
FULL-SERVICE RESTAURANTS

This park's full-service restaurants are so much fun that the magic continues—once you're inside, that is. Unfortunately, many diners never seem to want to leave their tables—after all, would you if you could watch television monitors airing '50s sitcoms while you chow down on veal-and-shiitake-mushroom meat loaf? Consequently, lines can be enormous.

To make reservations, call Disney dining reservations (☎ 407/939–3463) up to 60 days in advance, or stop in person at the restaurant or first thing in the morning at Hollywood Junction Restaurant Reservations, just to the right of the Studios Tip Board, at the intersection of Hollywood and Sunset boulevards.

With its staff in black tie and its airy, palm-fronded room positively exuding suave, the spacious **Brown Derby** is one of the nicest—if most expensive—places to eat in the park. The Cobb salad, salad greens enlivened by loads of tomato, bacon, turkey, egg, blue cheese, and avocado—invented at the restaurant's Hollywood namesake—is alive and well here, as you can see from the numerous orders being tossed tableside. The all-California wine list is wide-ranging enough to keep an oenophile happy. The butter comes in molds shaped like Mickey Mouse heads. On the day you want to see the show, if you request the Fantasmic! Dinner Package and make a reservation for no later than two hours before the start of the show, you can get priority seating for this big performance.

You'll certainly want to spend a leisurely lunch at the **'50s Prime Time Café**, where video screens constantly show sitcoms, where place mats pose television trivia quizzes, and where waitresses play "Mom" with convincing enthusiasm, insisting that you clean your plate. The menu is what your own mom might have made were she a character on one of those video screens—meat loaf, broiled chicken, pot roast, hot roast beef sandwiches—all to be washed down with root beer floats and ice cream sodas. Prime Time offers the Fantasmic! dinner package as well. Don't go to Star Tours immediately afterward—the time warp has been known to be too much to endure.

To replace the energy you've no doubt depleted by miles of theme-park walking, you can load up on carbs at **Mama Melrose's Ristorante Italiano.** The menu offers pasta, chicken, steak, and seafood dishes, as well as pizza baked in a brick oven. Ask for the Fantasmic! Dinner Package if you want priority seating for the show.

If you don't mind zombies leering at you while you slurp up sloppy joes, meat loaf, chef salads, and the like, then head to **Sci-Fi Dine-In Theater,** a re-creation of an actual drive-in. All the tables are contained within candy-color '50s vintage convertibles and face a large screen, where a 45-minute reel of the best and worst of science fiction trailers plays in a continuous loop. Only here would popcorn be considered an appropriate appetizer.

At the **Backlot Express,** in Echo Lake, you don't need a reservation to chow down on the burgers, fajitas, huge sandwiches, and chef salads.

More unusual fast foods such as baby back ribs, roasted chicken, and tortellini at lunch and prime rib, veal chops, and mesquite-grilled pork chops at dinner constitute the fare at **Hollywood & Vine Cafeteria of the Stars.** Minnie, Goofy, Pluto, and Chip and Dale put in appearances at breakfast and lunchtime character meals. There's a Hollywood theme to the place; characters and servers are just hoping to be discovered by some passing Hollywood screen agent, and the place is a real charmer—totally '50s and vaguely deco. In Echo Lake, **Min & Bill's Dockside Diner** is the spot for sandwiches. Step right up to the counter.

The **Studio Catering Company Commissary,** in Animation Courtyard, can provide you with sustenance for the next tour: hot dogs, burgers, pizza, and fries.

For Travelers with Disabilities

Almost everything in this park is wheelchair accessible.

Studio attractions are wheelchair accessible, with certain restrictions on the Star Tours thrill ride and Twilight Zone Tower of Terror II. Guests with hearing impairments can obtain a closed-captioning device for use with the monitors at preshow areas of some attractions.

To board the **Great Movie Ride,** on Hollywood Boulevard, you must transfer to a Disney wheelchair if you use an oversize model or a scooter; the gunshot, explosion, and fire effects make the attraction inappropriate for service animals.

At Sunset Boulevard, to board the **Twilight Zone Tower of Terror II** you must be able to walk unassisted to a seat on the ride and have full upper-body strength. The ride's free falls make it inappropriate for service animals. The **Theater of the Stars** is completely accessible to guests using wheelchairs. To ride the **Rock 'n' Roller Coaster,** guests who use wheelchairs must transfer to a ride vehicle.

At Animation Courtyard, the *Voyage of the Little Mermaid* and the **Magic of Disney Animation** are wheelchair accessible; both have preshow areas with TV monitors that are close-captioned for the hearing-impaired.

The **Studios' Backlot Tour** is wheelchair accessible, too. Guests with hearing impairments who lip-read should request a seat near the tour guide. The earthquake, fire, and water effects of the Catastrophe Canyon scene make the attraction inappropriate for some service animals. **Disney–MGM PASS** is accessible by those who use wheelchairs.

On New York Street, the *Honey, I Shrunk the Kids* **Movie Set Adventure** is barrier free for most guests using wheelchairs, although the uneven surface may make maneuvering difficult. **Jim Henson's Muppet*Vision 4-D** is also completely wheelchair accessible. Guests with hearing impairments may request a personal audio link that will amplify the sound here. A TV monitor in the preshow area is close-captioned.

At Echo Lake, the **Indiana Jones Epic Stunt Spectacular!** is completely wheelchair accessible. Explosions and gunfire may make it inappropriate for service animals. **Star Tours,** a turbulent ride, is accessible by guests who can transfer to a ride seat; those lacking upper-body strength should request an extra shoulder restraint. Service animals should not ride. **Disney's** *Doug* **Live!** is completely wheelchair accessible and has a TV monitor that is close-captioned for the hearing-impaired. **Sounds Dangerous** is also completely wheelchair accessible. However, the entertainment value is derived from the different sound effects, so guests with hearing impairments may decide to skip this one.

ENTERTAINMENT
Most live entertainment locations are completely wheelchair accessible. Certain sections of parade routes are always reserved for guests with disabilities. Tapings of television shows are wheelchair accessible, but none of the sound stages currently have sign-language interpreters. The noise and explosions in *Fantasmic!* may frighten service animals.

INFORMATION
See For Travelers with Disabilities *in* Walt Disney World A to Z, *below.*

RESTAURANTS AND SHOPS
All are fully wheelchair accessible, but there are no braille menus or sign-language interpreters.

WHEELCHAIR RENTALS
Oscar's, to your right in the Entrance Plaza, has standard chairs ($6; $1 deposit) as well as motor-powered chairs ($30; $10 deposit). No electric scooters are available in this park. If your rental needs replacing, ask a host or hostess.

Entertainment

The **daily parade** that wends its way up Hollywood Boulevard is also usually tied to the latest Disney hit film, most recently *Aladdin, Toy Story, Hercules,* and *Mulan,* with all the characters from the films appearing in larger-than-life incarnations.

The Studios' after-dark show, known as **Fantasmic!,** wows audiences of thousands with its 15 minutes of special effects and Disney's characters. Our omnipresent hero Mickey, in his Sorcerer's Apprentice costume, plays the embodiment of Good in the struggle against forces of Evil, personified by Disney villains and villainesses such as Cruella DeVil, Scar, and Maleficent. In some of the show's most interesting moments, animated clips of images of these famous bad guys alternate with clips of Disney nice guys (and dolls), projected onto screens made of water—high-tech fountains surging high in the air. Disney being Disney, it's Good that emerges triumphant, amid a veritable tidal wave of water effects and flames, explosions, and fireworks worthy of a Stallone shoot-'em-up. All the effects are so good that it's too bad the story doesn't rise to the same high level. If you don't think this will bother you, show up at the 6,500-seat Hollywood Hills Amphitheatre opposite the Twilight Zone Tower of Terror II on Friday or Saturday most of the year, nightly in busy periods. Curtain time varies seasonally: in winter when it gets dark early, the show goes on at about 6:30, and during the holidays there's an additional show at around 8:30. During spring break and in summer, start time is 8:15 or 9 and 10:30. Be sure to arrive about 90 minutes before start time (earlier is better); if this conflicts with your dinnertime, pick up fast food and bring it into the amphitheater. Where to sit? You get a better sense of the whole show if you're not too close, and you'll be able to exit most quickly if you take a seat near where you come in—the single way in is also the single nonemergency exit, and leaving the amphitheater is unbelievably tedious if you're on the left as you face the stage or up front. Besides, if you sit near the lagoon, spray from the fountains leaves droplets all over your glasses, if you wear them, and gives you a drenching that's not exactly pleasant when it's chilly.

First Aid

It's in the Entrance Plaza adjoining Guest Relations.

Getting Around
Inside this park, distances are short and walking is the optimal way to get around.

Guided Tours
If you want to learn more about the animation process, guests aged 16 and older can take the 2½-hour **Inside Animation** tour, offered Tuesday–Friday (🎫 $49; park admission is not required). At the end, you get to go backstage and paint your own animation cel. Reserve up to six weeks in advance by calling ☎ 407/939–8687.

Lockers
You'll find them alongside Oscar's Classic Car Souvenirs, to the right of the Entrance Plaza after you pass through the turnstiles. The cost is $3, with a $2 refundable key deposit.

Lost Things and People
If you're worried about your children getting lost, get name tags for them at Guest Relations, and instruct them to go to a Disney staffer, anyone wearing a name tag, if they can't find you. If the worst happens, ask any cast member before you panic; logbooks of lost children's names are kept at Guest Relations.

Guest Relations also has a computerized Message Center, where notes can be left for traveling companions not only at this park but also at others. Report any nonliving loss or find at Guest Relations in the Entrance Plaza. If nobody claims what you turn in, you may get to keep it.

Money Matters
There is an ATM near the Production Information Window, outside the park's Entrance Plaza. Currency exchange is available at the Guest Relations window.

Package Pickup
Ask the shop clerk to forward any large purchase you make to Guest Relations, in the Entrance Plaza, so you won't have to carry it around all day. Allow three hours.

Shopping
Many Studio attractions, including those related to any of the wildly successful Disney films, have strategically positioned shops and pushcarts that will have children clamoring for character merchandise. Genuine Indiana Jones bullwhips and fedoras are sold at the **Indiana Jones Adventure Outpost,** next to the stunt amphitheater. On your way out of Star Tours you're funneled through **Endor Vendors,** which stocks Darth Vader and Wookie masks as well as other out-of-this-world paraphernalia—remember, Halloween is just around the corner. Other shops are not so obviously tied to the attraction you were just at. Budding animators can hone their talents with Paint-a-Cel, a kit with two picture cels ready to be illustrated. It's sold at the **Animation Gallery** in the Animation Building. For movie memorabilia, check out **Sid Cahuenga's One-of-a-Kind** shop, to the left as you enter the park. Alongside old movie posters, autographed pictures, and assorted, one-of-a-kind knickknacks are original costumes once worn by stars in feature movies. **It's a Wonderful Shop,** tucked away in its own little corner in the New York Street area, is a great place to pick up very special Christmas decorations. Avid readers should browse in **The Writer's Stop,** where, if you happen to hit it right, you might get a book signed by a celebrity author. Who could resist a pair of Mickey Mitts, an easy-to-pick-up last-minute gift sold at **Legends of Hollywood** on Hollywood Boulevard? Use them to wave at the Earfful Tower on your way out.

Visitor Information

The **Crossroads of the World** kiosk in the Entrance Plaza dispenses maps, entertainment schedules, brochures, and the like. Foreign guests can pick up maps in their native tongue here as well, at the **International Relations** desk. Take specific questions to **Guest Relations,** inside the turnstiles on the left side of the Entrance Plaza.

The **Production Information Window** (☎ 407/560–4651), also in the Entrance Plaza, is the place to find out what's being taped when and how to get into the audience.

At the corner where Hollywood Boulevard intersects with Sunset Boulevard is the **Studios Tip Board,** a large chalkboard with constantly updated information about attractions' wait times—reliable except for those moments when everyone follows the "See It Now!" advice and the line immediately triples. Studio staffers are on hand.

DISNEY'S ANIMAL KINGDOM

Humankind's enduring love for animals is the inspiration for Disney's fourth theme park in Orlando, which opened in spring 1998 amid much controversy from animal rights activists over the deaths of several of the animals. Government investigations found no evidence of negligence on the part of Disney employees.

At 500 acres, the Animal Kingdom is the largest of all Disney theme parks worldwide and five times the size of the Magic Kingdom. So it gave Disney Imagineers plenty of scope for their creativity. The attraction explores the story of all animals—real, imaginary, and extinct. No castles gleam and sparkle as you enter. Instead, you're surrounded by a green grotto filled with waterfalls and gardens alive with exotic birds, reptiles, and mammals. In part it's like a very good zoo that displays animals in their natural habitats—but unlike most zoos, which open in mid-morning, this one opens early enough that you can do a lot of looking before its inhabitants settle down to snooze through the heat of the day.

But the Animal Kingdom is equal part entertainment complex. Beyond the entry area, the Oasis, the park proceeds in true Disney fashion, show-casing careful re-creations of natural and man-made landscapes that recall exotic lands ranging from Thailand and India to southern Africa, in the present and long ago. You'll also find rides, peppy musical shows, Disney logo merchandise, knickknacks from around the world, eateries, and, of course, Disney characters—where else does the Lion King truly belong? Cast members come from all over the world, Kenya and South Africa as often as Kentucky and South Carolina; you see them here and there, at every turn, ready to answer your questions, and you never know what accent you'll hear when they open their mouths. That's part of the charm of the place. All this is augmented by an earnest educational undercurrent that is meant to foster a renewed appreciation for the animal kingdom.

The park is laid out very much like its oldest sibling, the Magic Kingdom. The hub of this wheel is the spectacular **Tree of Life,** in **Safari Village.** Radiating from there are several spokes—the other "lands," each with a distinct personality. At the entrance is the **Oasis,** and to its right is **DinoLand U.S.A.** The northeast corner houses **Asia,** opened in March 1999; **Africa** is on the northwest side. South of Safari Village, immediately west of the Oasis, is **Camp Minnie-Mickey,** a character-greeting and show area.

Opening time for this park is earlier than for the others (8 AM) and for good reason: that's when many of the animals are most likely to be not only up and around but at their most active.

Numbers in the margin correspond to points of interest on the Disney's Animal Kingdom map.

The Oasis

At this lush entrance garden, you'll feel cool mist, smell the aroma of flowers, and see playful animals amid a miniature landscape of streams and grottoes, waterfalls, and glades fringed with banana leaves and jacaranda. At its best on those mystical Orlando mornings when the mists shroud the landscape, it's the scene-setter for the rest of your day. It's also the area to take care of essentials before entering the park. Here you'll find stroller and wheelchair rentals, Guest Relations, an ATM, and the ticket booths.

Safari Village

Primarily the site of the **Tree of Life,** this land is encircled by **Discovery River,** which is not an actual attraction, but can be viewed from a bridge in Harambe. Most of the visitor services that aren't in the Oasis are here, on the border with Harambe, including the Baby Care Center, First Aid Center, and Lost and Found.

❶ Tree of Life. The park centerpiece is an imposing 14 stories high and 50 ft wide at its base. Think of a Swiss Family Treehouse the height of the Twilight Zone Tower of Terror II, and add intricate animal forms symbolizing life on earth: roaring baboons, steeds rearing up, sharks swimming, chipmunks munching. Outside, paths tunnel underneath the roots as the fauna-encrusted trunk towers overhead. It's a rich and truly fascinating sight, as intriguing as a word-finder puzzle or a "Where's Waldo?" book; the more you look the more you see. Once inside, you get a bug's-eye view of life in the whimsical 3-D film adventure *It's Tough to Be a Bug!,* modeled vaguely on the animated film *A Bug's Life* from Disney and Pixar, the creators of *Toy Story.* In the Animal Kingdom, special effects in the film and in the theater leave you feeling that you've been sprayed with poison, zapped with bug spray, swatted at, and poked with a stinger. It's all in good fun—except, perhaps, at the end, when the cast member acting as emcee suggests that you stay in your seat until the cockroaches have left, and you feel a vague rustling around your ankles. *Duration: 20 mins. Crowds: Not a problem. Strategy: Since most people head to the safari first, if you're concerned about crowds, go early in the morning. Audience: All ages, but the bug show may frighten young children. Rating:* ★★★

DinoLand U.S.A.

Just as it sounds, this is the place to come in contact with creatures prehistoric at any of the different types of attractions typical of Disney parks. Here you can go on the thrilling **Dinosaur** ride, amble along the **Cretaceous Trail,** play in the **Boneyard,** or take in a show at the **Theater in t he Wild.** Kids will surely want to make a stop at **Chester and Hester's Dinosaur Treasures,** where objets d'inosaur are sold.

❷ Boneyard. Youngsters can slide, bounce, and slither around this archaeological dig site–cum–playground. There are twisting short and long slides, climbing nets, caves, and a jeep to climb on. *Duration: Up to you and your children. Crowds: Can be heavy mid-morning to early afternoon. Strategy: Go early in the morning. Audience: Elementary-school-age children and their families. Rating:* ★★

Disney's Animal Kingdom

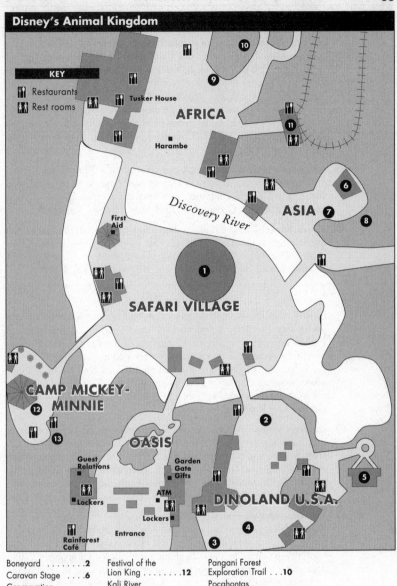

KEY

🚻 Restaurants

🚻 Rest rooms

Tusker House

AFRICA

Harambe

Discovery River

First
Aid

ASIA

SAFARI VILLAGE

**CAMP MICKEY-
MINNIE**

OASIS

Guest
Relations

Garden
Gate
Gifts

ATM

DINOLAND U.S.A.

Lockers

Lockers

Rainforest
Café

Entrance

❸ DINOSAUR. Disney's version of a quirky roadside attraction puts you face to face with huge dinosaurs who move and breathe with uncanny realism. When a carload of guests rouses a cantankerous Carnotaurus (pronounced "Car-no-*taw*-rus") from his Cretaceous slumber, it's show time. You travel back 65 million years on a twisting, start-stop adventure and try to save the "terrible lizards" as a massive asteroid hurtles toward Earth. Exciting Audio-Animatronics bring dinosaurs to life. *Duration: 10 mins. Crowds: Can get heavy mid-morning. Strategy: Go first thing in the morning or at the end of the day, and don't forget about the FASTPASS. Audience: All ages. Minimum height: 40". Rating:* ★★

❹ Cretaceous Trail. Walk through a re-creation of a primeval forest containing some of the survivors of the dinosaur age, such as soft-shelled turtles and Chinese alligators. *Duration: Up to you. Crowds: Not a problem. Strategy: Go anytime. Audience: All ages. Rating:* ★

❺ Tarzan Rocks! This live musical stage show based on the animated film features live acrobatics and stunts that are not to be believed. Don't miss it. *Duration: 30 mins. Crowds: Not a problem. Strategy: Arrive 15 mins before show time. Audience: All ages. Rating:* ★★★

Asia

Even before the Animal Kingdom opened, expansion was already under way. Featuring a typical rural Asian village, this land is full of rain-forest scenery and ruins. Groupings of trees grow from a crumbling tiger shrine and two massive towers, one representing Thailand, the other Nepal; these are the habitat for two families of gibbons whose hooting fills the air at all hours of the day. You'll be able to take the **Maharajah Jungle Trek,** see a bird show at the **Caravan Stage,** and raft the **Kali River Rapids Run.**

❻ Caravan Stage. This outdoor show area near the border with Africa presents Flights of Wonder, spectacular demonstrations of skill by falcons, hawks, and other rare and fascinating birds, which swoop down over the audience. *Duration: 30 mins. Crowds: Not a problem. Strategy: Arrive 15 mins before show time. Audience: All but young children, who might be frightened by the flying birds. Rating:* ★★

❼ Maharajah Jungle Trek. Get an up-close view of animals along this trail: Komodo dragons perched on rocks, Malayan tapirs near the wooden foot bridge, bat families in a dim cave, Bengal tigers in front of a maharajah's palace. The tigers have their own view of a group of Asian deer and a herd of black buck, an antelope species. At the end of the trek, you walk through an aviary set with a lotus pool. And Disney interpreters are on hand to answer any and all questions. *Duration: As long as you like. Crowds: Feels empty because people are constantly moving. Strategy: Go anytime. Audience: Older children and adults. Rating:* ★★

❽ Kali River Rapids Run. Asia's thrilling adventure is to the Animal Kingdom as Splash Mountain is to Frontierland. Aboard a round raft that seats 12, you run the Chakranadi River. After passing through a huge bamboo tunnel filled with jasmine-scent mist, your raft climbs 40 ft upriver, lurches and spins through a series of sharp twists and turns, and then approaches an immense waterfall, which curtains a giant carved tiger face. Past rain forests and temple ruins, you find yourself face to face with the denuded slope of a logged-out woodland burning out of control. There are many more thrills, but why spill the beans? *Duration: 7 mins. Crowds: Long lines all day. Strategy: Test out the FAST-*

PASS, or go at day's end, as close to park closing as possible. Audience: Older children and adults. No guests with heart, back, or neck problems, or motion sickness. Minimum height: 44". Rating: ★★★

Africa

This largest of the lands is an area of forests and grasslands, predominantly an enclave for wildlife from the continent. The focus is on live animals at the key attractions. **Harambe,** on the northern banks of Discovery River, is Africa's starting point. Inspired by the small town of Lamu, Kenya, this Disney version of a coastal village looks memorably foreign, just as you imagine you'd see in Africa. Signs on the apparently peeling stucco walls of the buildings are faded, as if bleached by the sun, and everything has a hot, dusty look. Even the shopping has an African theme. For souvenirs with both Disney and African themes, stop in **Safari Marketplace,** the Harambe shopping area. **Mombasa Marketplace/Ziwani Traders** sells African and safari apparel, decorative items for the home, and stuffed toys.

❾ Kilimanjaro Safaris. A giant baobab tree is the starting point for this adventure into the up-country. Although re-creating an African safari in the United States (or even Florida, for that matter) may not be a new idea, this safari goes a step beyond merely allowing you to observe elands, kudus, klipspringers, secretary birds, giraffes, zebras, elephants, lions, and the like. You'll find illustrated game-spotting guides on the backs of the seats in the open-side safari vehicles, and as you lurch and bump over some 100 acres of savanna, forest, rivers, and rocky hills, you'll see most of these animals. This being a theme park, dangers lurk, in the form of ivory poachers, and it suddenly becomes your mission to save a group of elephants from their would-be killers. To get the most from your adventure, do this early in the day, when the animals are awake—humans aren't the only creatures that want to be napping inside on a hot Central Florida afternoon. *Duration: 30 mins. Crowds: Heavy in the morning. Strategy: Arrive in the park first thing in the morning—it's worth the trouble—and come straight here from It's Tough to Be a Bug!, using the FASTPASS if necessary. If you arrive after 9 AM, save this for the end of the day, when it isn't so hot. You'll probably see about the same number of animals as in early morning and you won't wait quite as long. Audience: All but the most easily frightened young children, who may be put off by the jostling during an attempt to capture the poachers. Rating:* ★★★

❿ Pangani Forest Exploration Trail. Calling this a nature walk doesn't really do it justice. A path winds through dense vegetation, alongside streams, and past waterfalls. En route there are viewpoints where you can stop and watch lowland gorillas, hippos (which you can see underwater), meerkats, warthogs, exotic birds, and a bizarre colony of hairless, strange-looking mole rats. Interpreters are on hand at every viewpoint to answer questions—and ask a few of their own to get you thinking. This is much better than any zoo, where the only information about the animals is on plaques that never seem to tell you quite what you know. *Duration: Up to you. Crowds: Heavy in the morning, but there's room for a ll, it seems. Strategy: Go straight on in after the safari— it's a good place to be in the busiest part of the day. Audience: All ages, although young children who don't love animals may be bored. Rating:* ★★★

⓫ Conservation Station. Take the Wildlife Express steam train (or walk) to this unique center, where you can meet animal experts, learn about worldwide efforts to protect endangered species and their habitats, and hear about the park's behind-the-scenes operations, about Disney's own conservation programs, and about how to connect with efforts in your own community. And you don't have to be a kid to enjoy the **Affection Section,** where young children and adults who are giving their inner child free rein get face-to-face with goats and other small critters. *Duration: 5-min ride; the rest is up to you. Crowds: Can get heavy mid-morning. Strategy: Go in late afternoon. Audience: All ages. Rating:* ★★★

Camp Minnie-Mickey

This Adirondack-style land is a meet-and-greet area where characters from *The Lion King, The Jungle Book,* and other favorite Disney films gather for picture-taking and autographs. Very small children may be frightened by the larger-than-life renditions of Simba, Scar, et al., but everyone else will have a blast. Live performances are staged at the **Campside Circle** and **Grandmother Willow's Grove.**

⑫ Festival of the Lion King. This outdoor theater-in-the-round presents a delightful tribal celebration of song, dance, and specialty performances on huge moving stages. *Duration: 30 mins. Crowds: Not a problem. Strategy: Arrive 15 mins before show time. If you have a child who might want to go onstage, sit in one of the front rows to increase his or her chance of getting chosen. Audience: All ages. Rating:* ★★★

⑬ Pocahontas and Her Forest Friends. This is the venue for *Colors of the Wind,* a show starring live animals that is a lesson on nature and how to preserve endangered species. Pocahontas is your official hostess, talking on the subject and breaking out in song, "Just Around the River Bend." *Duration: 15 mins. Crowds: Not a problem. Strategy: Arrive 15 mins before show time. Audience: All ages. Rating:* ★★★

Strategies for Your Visit to Disney's Animal Kingdom

When to Go
This park is still experiencing its newness. It's crowded all week long, both at the beginning of the week and on weekends. Wednesday is probably the best day to go. Since the park opens early every day, there are no early admission days.

Blitz Tour
Whatever you do, arrive early. Count on arriving in the parking lot a half hour before the official park opening, an hour before opening if you want to grab some caffeine, with a snack, at the McDonald's outside the parking lot. That's 6:30 AM! Make a beeline for **Kilimanjaro Safaris** and make your FASTPASS appointment. Then, head over to *It's Tough to be a Bug!* When the show gets out, it will probably be time to return to the **Kilimanjaro Safaris.** It should still be early enough that the animals will be awake, mothers may be nursing their young, and it could prove to be very enjoyable and educational experience.

Proceed to the **Pangani Forest Exploration Trail,** stop at **Tusker House** for one of its huge and yummy hot cinnamon rolls, and then take a ride on the Wildlife Express to **Conservation Station.**

At about this point, head over to DinoLand U.S.A. to ride **Dinosaur.** You'll be able to make a FASTPASS appointment here. Let the children explore the **Boneyard** while you wait for the next performance of the *Tarzan Rocks!* stage show at the **Theater in the Wild.** By now, it should be time to return to **Dinosaur.** Upon leaving the ride, stop at the Restaurantosaurus to grab a bite. Next, head over to **Asia,** where you can make another FASTPASS appointment for the **Kali River Rapids Run.** Take in the next Flights of Wonder show at the **Caravan**

Stage and then check your FASTPASS time and see if you can now get VERY wet on the thrilling **Kali River Rapids Run.** Afterward, take a leisurely stroll along the **Maharajah Jungle Trek** making sure to take a look for the bats. Return to Africa for souvenir shopping at the Safari Marketplace, and have any bulky purchases sent to package pickup so you don't lug them around.

End your day by visiting **Camp Minnie-Mickey,** where you and the kids can have your pictures taken with the pride of *The Lion King* and catch the two stage shows. Have dinner at the Rainforest Café; the atmosphere alone is worth the visit.

On Rainy Days
If you want to see animals, skip this park.

Other Tips
- Expect big crowds.

- Go to bed early the night before, so you can arrive an hour before park opening. As at the other parks, this is a good way to get a jump on the crowds. In fact, if you don't come early, you won't see the wild animals at their friskiest—as they were meant to be seen—and you may miss out on some of the best reasons to come.

- Set up a rendezvous point and time at the start of the day, just in case you and your companions get separated. Some good places include the beginning or end of the queue line at *It's Tough to Be a Bug!,* in front of the Boneyard, at the entrance to the queuing area of the Conservation Train Station, or at the turnstile of the *Festival of the Lion King* show.

Disney's Animal Kingdom A to Z

Baby Care
The **Baby Care Center** is in Safari Village. You can buy disposable diapers, formula, baby food, and pacifiers. For stroller rentals ($7; $1 deposit), go to Garden Gate Gifts, in the Oasis.

Cameras and Film
Kodak's disposable Fun Saver cameras are widely available. For two-hour film developing, look for the Photo Express signs throughout the park. Photo pickup is at Garden Gate Gifts, in the Oasis.

Dining
Restaurants inside Disney's Animal Kingdom serve mostly foods of the fast variety.

FULL-SERVICE RESTAURANT

You don't have to pay park admission to dine at the **Rainforest Café,** which has entrances both inside the park and at the gate. It's the only full-service eatery in the Animal Kingdom area. Make reservations by phone (☎ 407/939–3463) up to 60 days in advance or in person first thing in the morning.

SELF-SERVICE RESTAURANTS

The **Restaurantosaurus** is the Animal Kingdom's McDonald's restaurant. It's open for counter-service breakfasts, lunches, and dinners. The theming isn't as great as at places such as Tusker House, but the food is identical to what your kids know and love. You can even get a McDonald's Happy Meal, with a special toy, different from what they get at home. Or come for the Donald's Prehistoric Breakfastosaurus character breakfast. Adult fast-food fans might be disappointed to discover that not all their McDonald's favorites are served here, so if you expect to find a Quarter Pounder with cheese, your taste buds might not be satisfied until after exiting the park.

Tusker House is a fast-food option in Harambe–but it's like no fast-food eatery you've ever seen. The cinnamon buns served at breakfast are scrumptious—and huge. The large area inside is hung with colorful draperies of African cloth, and there's a charming patio out back. Listen carefully and you'll overhear the goings-on from the upstairs guest house—just a bit of Disney atmosphere.

For Travelers with Disabilities

ATTRACTIONS

All attractions are completely wheelchair accessible, including the theater-in-the-round at Camp Minnie-Mickey and the Tree of Life theater showing *It's Tough to Be a Bug!,* which are also accessible to electric scooters. However, to fully experience all the bug movie's special effects, guests who use wheelchairs must transfer to one of the auditorium seats. Check the *Guidebook for Guests with Hearing Impairments* for information about closed-captioning boxes for the monitor-equipped attractions such as the Tree of Life. Scripts and story lines for all attractions are available. Personal translation units can be rented ($4; $40 deposit) to amplify sound in theaters.

RESTAURANTS AND SHOPS

All are wheelchair accessible.

WHEELCHAIR RENTALS

Garden Gate Gifts, in the Oasis, rents wheelchairs ($6; $1 deposit) and electric scooters ($30; $20 deposit).

First Aid

The park's first aid center, staffed by registered nurses, is in Safari Village.

Getting Around

You get around entirely on foot here, although you can take a train to Conservation Station.

Guided Tours

Backstage Safari (✉ $70 plus park admission) takes an in-depth look at animal conservation every Monday, Wednesday, and Friday 9:30–12:30, stopping at the animal hospital and other behind-the-scenes areas. Book at Guest Relations in the Oasis or by calling ☎ 407/939–8687 up to 60 days in advance. Guests must be at least 16 years old to participate.

Lockers

You can find them in Guest Relations ($3; $2 key deposit).

Lost Things and People

If you are worried about your children getting lost, get name tags for them at Safari Village. Instruct them to speak to someone with a Disney name tag if you become separated. If you do, immediately report your loss to any cast member. Lost-children logbooks are at Safari Village, which is also the location of the lost and found. After park closing, lost items are sent to the main **Lost and Found** in the Magic Kingdom (☎ 407/824–4245).

Money Matters

For cash and currency exchange, go to Guest Relations. There is an ATM in the Oasis to the right of the Entrance Plaza as you go into the park.

Package Pickup

You can have shop clerks forward any large purchases to Garden Gate Gifts, on the right side of the entrance plaza in the Oasis, so that you won't have to carry them around all day. Allow three hours.

Shopping

Before you pass through the turnstiles on your way into the Animal Kingdom, stop at the **Outpost Shop,** where you'll find stuffed character animals dressed up in safari gear. The must-have here is a safari hat with Mouse ears. Stores are scattered throughout the park, and **Harambe** village and its Safari Marketplace stock quite a selection of African imports and animal items—plush key chains, statues of various sizes and styles—as well as T-shirts, toys, and trinkets on various Disney and Animal Kingdom themes. Pick up extra film and disposable cameras at **Duka La Filimu,** in Harambe. African and safari apparel is across the street at **Mombasa Marketplace/Ziwani Traders.** At **Creature Comforts** (before you cross from Safari Village to Harambe), you can get a Minnie Mouse headband with a safari-style bow. **Island Mercantile,** to the left as you enter Safari Village, offers Animal Kingdom–logo goodies. **Disney Outfitters,** directly across from Island Mercantile and by the tip board, is another source of African-theme clothing and accessories. In Asia, **Mandala Gifts** carries clothing on a tiger theme, along with Asian umbrella stands and other souvenirs and gifts.

Visitor Information

Guest Relations, in the Oasis, is the place to pick up park maps and entertainment schedules and ask questions. Foreign visitors may collect maps in their language here.

TYPHOON LAGOON

Numbers in the margin correspond to points of interest on the Typhoon Lagoon map.

According to Disney legend, Typhoon Lagoon was created when the quaint, thatched-roof, lushly landscaped Placid Palms Resort was struck by a cataclysmic storm. It left a different world in its wake: surfboards sundered trees; once-upright palms imitated the Leaning Tower of Pisa; a great buoy crashed through the roof of one building; a small boat was blown through the roof of another; and part of the original lagoon was cut off, trapping thousands of tropical fish—and a few sharks. Nothing, however, topped the fate of *Miss Tilly,* a shrimp boat from "Safen Sound, Florida," which was hurled high in the air and became impaled on Mt. Mayday, a magical volcano that periodically tries to dislodge *Miss Tilly* with huge geysers of water.

Ordinary folks, the legend continues, would have been crushed by such devastation. But the resourceful residents of Placid Palms were made of hardier stuff—and from the wreckage they created 56-acre Typhoon Lagoon, the self-proclaimed "world's ultimate water park."

Four times the size of River Country (Disney's first water park), Typhoon Lagoon offers a full day's worth of activities. You can bob along in 4-ft waves in a surf lagoon the size of two football fields, speed down arrow-straight water slides and around twisty storm slides, bump through rapids, go snorkeling, and, for a mellow break, float in inner tubes along the 2,100-ft Castaway Creek, rubberneck from specially constructed grandstands as human cannonballs are ejected from the storm slides, or merely hunker down in one of the many hammocks or lounge chairs and read a book. A children's area replicates adult rides on a smaller scale. It's Disney's version of a day at the beach— complete with lifeguards in spiffy red-and-white-stripe T-shirts.

The layout is so simple that it is truly impossible to get lost. The eponymous wave and swimming lagoon is at the center of the park; the waves break on the beaches closest to the entrance and are born

Typhoon Lagoon

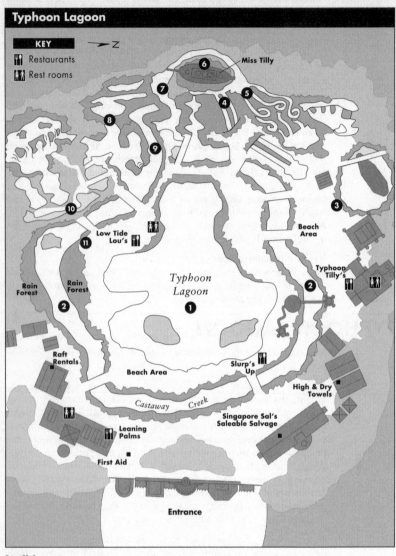

KEY →N

🚻 Restaurants
🚻 Rest rooms

Miss Tilly

⑥ Mt. Mayday
⑦ Mayday Falls
④ Humunga Kowabunga
⑤ Storm Slides
⑧ Keelhaul Falls
⑨ Gang Plank Falls
③ Shark Reef

⑩ Ketchakiddie Creek
⑪ Bay Slides

Low Tide Lou's

Beach Area

Typhoon Tilly's

Rain Forest

Rain Forest

② Castaway Creek

Typhoon Lagoon ①

② Castaway Creek

Raft Rentals

Beach Area

Slurp's Up

High & Dry Towels

Castaway Creek

Singapore Sal's Saleable Salvage

Leaning Palms

First Aid

Entrance

in Mt. Mayday at the other end of the park. Castaway Creek encircles the lagoon. Anything requiring a gravitational plunge—storm slides, speed slides, and raft trips down rapids—starts around the summit of Mt. Mayday. Shark Reef and Ketchakiddie Creek flank the head of the lagoon, to Mt. Mayday's right and left, respectively, as you enter the park.

❶ Typhoon Lagoon. This is the heart of the park, a swimming area that spreads out over 2½ acres and contains almost 3 million gallons of clear, chlorinated water. It's scalloped by lots of little coves, bays, and inlets, all edged with white-sand beaches—spread over a base of white concrete, as body surfers soon discover when they try to slide into shore. Ouch! The main attraction is the waves. Twelve huge water-collection chambers hidden in Mt. Mayday dump their load with a resounding "whoosh" into trapdoors to create waves large enough for Typhoon Lagoon to host amateur and professional surfing championships. A piercing double hoot from *Miss Tilly* signals the start and finish of wave action: every two hours, for 1½ hours, 4-ft-plus waves issue forth every 90 seconds; the next half hour is devoted to moderate bobbing waves. Even during the big-wave periods, however, the waters in Blustery Bay and Whitecap Cove are protected enough for timid swimmers.

❷ Castaway Creek. This circular, 15-ft-wide, 3-ft-deep waterway is everyone's water fantasy come true. Snag an inner tube and float along the creek that winds around the entire park, a wet version of the Magic Kingdom's Walt Disney World Railroad. You pass through a rain forest that showers you with mist and spray, you slide through caves and grottos, you burble by overhanging trees and flowering bushes, and you get dumped on at the Water Works, whose "broken" pipes the Typhoon Lagooners never got around to fixing. The current flows a gentle 2½ ft per second; it takes about 30 minutes to make a full circuit. Along the way there are exits where you can hop out and dry off or do something else—and then pick up another inner tube and jump right back in.

❸ Shark Reef. If you felt like leaping onto the stage at the Studios' *Voyage of the Little Mermaid* or jumping into the tank at Epcot's Living Seas, make tracks for this 360,000-gallon snorkeling tank. The coral reef is artificial, but the 4,000 tropical fish—including black-and-white-striped sergeant majors, sargassum trigger fish, yellowtail damselfish, and amiable nurse and bonnet-head sharks—are quite real. So are the southern stingrays that congregate in the warmer, shallower water by the entrance. To prevent algae growth, Shark Reef is kept at a brisk 72°F, which is 18 degrees colder than the rest of Typhoon Lagoon. A sunken tanker divides the reef; its portholes give landlubbers access to the underwater scene and let them go nose to nose with snorkelers. Unless the reef is practically deserted—almost never—you are supposed to swim in a counterclockwise circle around the tanker; one circuit takes about 15 minutes. Go first thing in the morning or at the end of the day if you want to spend more time. Chilly air and water temperatures close the reef from November through April. Children aged 7–10 can enjoy a personal snorkeling lesson at $20 per half hour. If your kids want to learn how to explore the depths of the ocean Disney style, sign them up at Guest Relations when you purchase your tickets.

❹ Humunga Kowabunga. There's no time to scream, but you'll hear just such vociferous reactions as the survivors emerge from the catch pool opposite Shark Reef. The basic question is: want to get scared out of your wits in three seconds flat—and like it enough to go back for more? The two side-by-side Humunga Kowabunga speed slides rightly deserve their acclaim among thrill lovers, as they drop more than 50 ft in a distance barely four times that amount. For nonmathematicians, that's very steep. Oh yes, and then you go through a cave. In the dark. The average speed is 30 mph; however, you can really fly if you lie flat on your back, cross your ankles, wrap your arms around your chest, and arch your back. Just remember to smile for the rubberneckers on the grandstand at the bottom. *No pregnant women or guests with heart, back, or neck problems or other physical limitations.*

5 Storm Slides. Each of these three body slides is about 300 ft long and snakes in and out of rock formations, through caves and tunnels, and under waterfalls, but each has a slightly different view and offers an idiosyncratic twist. The one in the middle has the longest tunnel; the others' secrets you'll have to discover for yourself. Maximum speed is about 20 mph, and the trip takes about 30 seconds.

6 Mt. Mayday. What goes down can also go up—and up and up and up and up. "It's likeclimbing Mt. Everest," wailed one teenager about a climb that seems a lot steeper than this 85-ft peak would warrant. However, it's Mt. Everest with hibiscus flowers, a shivering rope bridge, stepping stones set in plunging waters, and—remember that seminal typhoon?—a broken canoe scattered over the rocks near the top. The view encompasses the entire park.

Mayday Falls, Keelhaul Falls, Gang Plank Falls—white-water raft rides that you experience in oversize inner tubes—plunge down the left side of Mt. Mayday. Like the storm slides, they have caves, waterfalls, and intricate rock work, but with some extra elements.

7 Mayday Falls. The 460-ft slide over Mayday Falls in blue inner tubes is the longest and generally acclaimed the bumpiest; it's a straight slide over the falls into a catchment area, which gives you just enough time to catch your breath before the next plunge.

8 Keelhaul Falls. This spiraling, 400-ft ride in yellow inner tubes seems way faster than the purported 10 mph.

9 Gang Plank Falls. If you climb up Mt. Mayday for this ride, you'll go down in four-person, 6½-ft inner tubes that descend crazily through 300 ft of rapids.

10 Ketchakiddie Creek. Typhoon Lagoon's children's area has slides, minirapids, squirting whales and seals, bouncing barrels, waterfalls, sprinklers, and all the other ingredients of splash heaven. The bubbling sand ponds, where youngsters can sit in what seems like an enormous whirlpool bath, are special favorites. *All adults must be accompanied by a child under 48" and vice versa.*

11 Bay Slides. These are scaled-down versions of the Storm Slides geared toward younger kids.

Strategies for Your Visit to Typhoon Lagoon

There's really only one problem with Typhoon Lagoon—it's popular, and the presence of Blizzard Beach has shown no signs of eroding its popularity. In summer and on weekends, the park often reaches its capacity of 7,200 people by mid-morning. By this time Castaway Creek is a bank-to-bank carpet of tangled arms and legs; the Lagoon resembles the Times Square subway station at rush hour; and the lines for Humunga Kowabunga, the storm slides, and Shark Reef can top an hour. In that time, you could have driven to the Atlantic Ocean.

If you must visit in summer, go for a few hours during the dreamy late afternoon or when the weather clears up after a thundershower. Typically, rainstorms drive away the crowds, and lots of people simply don't come back. If you plan to make a whole day of it, avoid weekends—Typhoon Lagoon is big among locals as well as tourists. Instead, visit on a Monday, or on Sunday morning, when lots of potential castaways are in church. Arrive 30 minutes before opening time so you can park, buy tickets, rent towels, and snag inner tubes before the hordes descend. Set up camp and hit the slides, white-water rides, and Shark Reef first. Then bobble along Castaway Creek and save the lagoon itself for later.

If you're visiting at a quiet time of year, go in the afternoon, when the water will have warmed up a bit. Do Castaway Creek first to get a sense of the park.

There are plenty of lounge chairs and a number of hammocks but definitely not enough beach umbrellas. If you crave shade, commandeer a spot in the grassy area around Getaway Glen on the left side of the park just past the raft-rental concession. If you like moving about, people-watching, and having sand in your face, go front and center at the surf pool. For your own patch of sand and some peace and quiet, head for the coves and inlets on the left side of the lagoon.

Typhoon Lagoon A to Z

Dining
Standard beach fare—burgers, dogs, chef salads, and, of course, ice cream and frozen yogurt—is what's cooking at **Leaning Palms,** to your left as you enter the park. **Typhoon Tilly's Galley & Grog Shop,** on the right just south of Shark Reef, pours mostly sugary, nonalcoholic grog but also serves Davy Jones lager. **Let's Go Slurpin',** a beach shack on the edge of Typhoon Lagoon, dispenses frozen margaritas as well as wine and beer. Food carts purveying lemonade, soda, ices, and snow cones are scattered around the park.

For Travelers with Disabilities
The park is head and shoulders above River Country in the accessibility department. All paths that connect the different areas of Typhoon Lagoon are wheelchair accessible. Guests who use a wheelchair and who can transfer to a raft or inner tube can also float in Typhoon Lagoon and on Castaway Creek. Wheelchair rentals are available in the entrance turnstile area and are free with ID.

Facilities
There are men's and women's thatch-roof dressing rooms and two sizes of full-day lockers ($5 and $7) to the right of the entrance on your way into the park; a second, less-crowded set is near Typhoon Tilly's Galley & Grog Shop. The towels you can rent at the stand to the right of the main entrance (50¢) are a little skimpy; bring your own beach towel or buy one at Singapore Sal's if you care. The Typhoon Lagoon Imagineers thoughtfully placed rest rooms in every available nook and cranny. Most have showers and are much less crowded for clothes-changing than the main dressing rooms.

First Aid
The small first-aid stand is on your left as you enter the park, not far from the Leaning Palms food stand.

Lost Things and People
Ask about your misplaced people and things at the Guest Relations window near the entrance turnstiles, to your left as you enter the park. You'll be reunited with lost children at High and Dry Towels.

Picnicking

Picnicking is permitted. Tables are set up at Getaway Glen and Castaway Cove, near Shark Reef. Bring a box lunch from your hotel—and you'll eat well without having to line up with the masses.

Supplies

The **rental-rafts concession,** the building with the boat sticking through the roof to the left of the entrance, past the Leaning Palms food concession, also rents inner tubes. You need to rent them only for the lagoon; they are provided for Castaway Creek and all the white-water rides. You can borrow snorkels and masks at **Shark Reef.** Life vests are available at **High and Dry Towels** (25¢ deposit). You may not bring your own equipment into Typhoon Lagoon.

Singapore Sal's, to the right of the main entrance (on the way into the park), is the place to buy sunscreen, hats, sunglasses, and other beach paraphernalia.

Visitor Information

The staff at the **Guest Relations** window outside the entrance turnstiles, to your left, can answer many questions; a chalkboard inside gives water temperature and surfing information. During off-season, which encompasses October through April, the park is not open every day. Call Guest Relations (☎ 407/566–4141) for days of operation.

BLIZZARD BEACH

With its oxymoronic name, Blizzard Beach promises the seemingly impossible—a seaside playground with an alpine theme. As with its older cousin, Typhoon Lagoon, the Disney Imagineers have created an entire legend to explain the park's origin: after a freak winter storm dropped snow over the western side of Walt Disney World, entrepreneurs decided to create Florida's first downhill ski resort. Saunalike temperatures soon returned. But just as the resort's operators were ready to close up shop, they spotted a playful alligator sliding down the "liquid ice" slopes. The realization that the melting snow had created the tallest, fastest, and most exhilarating water-filled ski and toboggan runs in the world gave birth to the ski resort–cum–water park.

Disney Imagineers have gone all out here to create the paradox of a ski resort in the midst of a tropical lagoon. Lots of verbal puns and sight gags play with the snow-in-Florida motif. The park's centerpiece is Mt. Gushmore, which features the 120-ft-high Summit Plummet, as well as other toboggan and water-sled runs with names such as Teamboat Springs, a white-water raft ride; Toboggan Racer; Slush Gusher; and Runoff Rapids. Between Mt. Gushmore's base and its summit, swimskiers can also ride a chairlift converted from ski-resort to beach-resort use—with umbrellas and snow skis on their undersides.

Blizzard Beach Ski Patrol Training Camp. The preteens in your crowd may want to spend most of their time on the T-bar drop, bungee-cord slides, and culvert slides here. In addition, there's a chance to challenge **Mogul Mania,** a wide-open area where you can jump from one slippery mogul to the next. The moguls really look more like baby icebergs bobbing in a swimming pool.

Chair Lift. If you're waterlogged, take a ride from the beachfront base of Mt. Gushmore up over its face and on to the summit—and back down again, if you want.

Cross Country Creek. Just grab an inner tube and hop on, to circle the entire park on this creek. Along the way, you'll get doused with frigid water in an ice cave—almost heaven on a steamy Florida day.

Melt Away Bay. The park's main pool is a 1-acre oasis that's constantly fed by "melting snow" waterfalls. The man-made waves are positively oceanlike. If you're not a strong swimmer, stay away from the far end of the pool, where the waves originate. You can get temporarily stuck in a pocket—a feeling not unlike getting caught in an ocean's undertow—even if your head is still above water.

Downhill Double Dipper. These are side-by side racing slides where future Olympic hopefuls can compete against each other.

Mt. Gushmore. Slides off the top of this snowcapped peak at the center of the park include **Runoff Rapids, Slush Gusher, Snow Stormers, Summit Plummet, Teamboat Springs,** and **Toboggan Racer.**

Runoff Rapids. You have to steel your nerves to climb into these three twisting, turning flumes—even one that's in the dark. But once you're in, it's way more fun than scary.

Slush Gusher. This speed slide, which drops through a snow-banked mountain gully, is shorter and less severe than Summit Plummet but a real thriller nonetheless. *Minimum height: 48".*

Snow Stormers. No water park would be complete without a fancy water slide, and Blizzard Beach has one—actually three flumes that descend from the top of Mt. Gushmore along a switchback course of ski-type slalom gates.

Summit Plummet. This is Mt. Gushmore's big gun, which Disney bills as "the world's tallest, fastest, free-fall speed slide." From Summit Plummet's "ski jump" tower, it's a wild 55-mph plunge straight down to a splash landing at the base of the mountain. It looks almost like a straight vertical drop. If you're watching from the beach below, you can't hear the yells of the participants, but rest assured—they're screaming their heads off. *Minimum height: 48".*

Teamboat Springs. Six-passenger rafts zip along in the world's longest family white-water raft ride. In summer 2000, it doubled its speed of departure onto its twisting, 1,200-foot channel of rushing waterfalls. This is great for families—a good place for kids too big for Tike's Peak to test more grown-up waters.

Tike's Peak. Disney is never one to leave the little ones out of the fun, and this junior-size version of Blizzard Beach, set slightly apart from the rest of the park, features scaled-down elements of Mt. Gushmore.

Toboggan Racer. On this ride you slither down an eight-lane water slide over Mt. Gushmore's "snowy" slopes.

Winter Summerland. After a day in the sun, stop by this miniature golf course, which carries out the Blizzard Beach theme.

Strategies for Your Visit to Blizzard Beach

Blizzard Beach is just as popular as Typhoon Lagoon—it's a toss-up as to which is more crowded. As with every other mecca, your best bet is to get here early, before the gates fling open. Expect long lines at the Summit Plummet and other major attractions. If you go in summer, try to arrive in late afternoon, just after the daily thunderstorm. The air will be hot and humid, but you'll be cool as a cucumber because the hordes will have departed for indoor pursuits. If thrill rides aren't your top priority, though, there's always plenty of room in the wave pool at **Melt Away Bay.** A relaxing inner-tube ride on **Cross Country Creek** is a cool alternative as well.

Blizzard Beach A to Z

Dining
Stands around the park sell ice cream, soft drinks, bottled water, and beer. **Lottawatta Lodge**—a North American ski lodge with a Caribbean accent—is the park's main emporium of fast food. Lines are long at peak feeding times. Hot dogs, snow cones, and ice cream are on the menu at **Avalunch.** The **Warming Hut** has Italian-sausage heroes, popcorn, and ice. **Frostbite Freddie's** sells frozen drinks and spirits. Beer and soft drinks and bottled water can be purchased at **The Cooling Hut.**

For Travelers with Disabilities
Most paths are flat and level. If you use a wheelchair, you will also be able to float in Cross Country Creek, provided you can transfer to a large inner tube. Other guests with limited mobility might also be able to use the inner tubes at some of the park's tamer slides. A limited number of wheelchairs are available for rent ($6; $10 deposit) near the park entrance.

Facilities
Dressing rooms are in the Village area, just inside the main entrance. Here you'll find showers and rest rooms as well. Lockers are strategically located near the entrance, next to Snowless Joe's Rentals and near Tike's Peak, the children's area (more convenient if you have little swimskiers in tow). At Snowless Joe's it costs $5 to rent a small locker, $7 for a large one; $2 is refunded at the end of the day when you turn in your key. Only small lockers are available at Tike's Peak. Rest rooms are conveniently located throughout the park; there are facilities in the Village area near the entrance, in Lottawatta Lodge, at the Ski Patrol Training Camp, and just past the Melt Away Bay beach area. Towels are available for rent at Snowless Joe's ($1), but they're tiny. If you care, buy a proper beach towel there or bring your own.

First Aid
The first-aid stand is in the Village, between Lottawatta Lodge and the Beach Haus.

Lost Things and People
Start your visit by naming a specific meeting place and time. Instruct your youngsters to let any lifeguard know if they get lost. If they do get lost, don't panic: head for Snowless Joe's, local lost children central.

Picnicking
Alcoholic drinks and glass containers are not allowed, but picnicking is, and several areas are good, most notably the terrace outside Lottawatta Lodge and its environs.

Supplies
Personal flotation devices, better known as life jackets, are available free to children and adults at **Snowless Joe's.** A refundable deposit is required—$25 or a credit card imprint. You can't rent inner tubes here: they're provided at the rides.

Sunglasses, sunscreen, bathing suits, waterproof disposable cameras, and other sundries are available at the **Beach Haus,** along with Blizzard Beach logo merchandise. Check out the ski equipment hanging from the ceiling. The **Sled Cart,** a kiosk-style shop, sells souvenirs, suntan lotion, and water toys.

Visitor Information

Disney staffers at the **Guest Relations** window, to the left of the ticket booth as you enter the park, can answer most of your questions. During the off-season months of October through April, the park is not open on a daily basis. For the park's days of operation, call ☎ 407/560-3400.

RIVER COUNTRY

Imagine a mountain in Utah's red-rock country. Put a lake at the bottom, and add a verdant fuzz of maples and pines here and there on the sides. Then plant some water slides among the greenery, and call it a "good ole fashion' swimmin' hole." That's River Country.

It was the first of Walt Disney World's water parks. Whereas larger, glitzier Typhoon Lagoon is balmy and tropical, this one is rustic and rugged. Some of the activities are the same, but the mood is different. River Country is smaller and in many ways has more charm, and it's less crowded as a rule. Appropriately enough, it's the only one with an unobstructed view of Cinderella Castle. It's lovely to lie out in the sun and gaze at this icon glinting in the sunlight. In summer there are water games and character greetings at scattered times as part of River Country's All-American Water Party, which re-creates an old-fashioned Fourth of July picnic every day in summer.

When you're ready to get out of the water, follow one of the nature trails that begins at the edge of the property and skirts the shore of Bay Lake.

Bay Cove. Encompassing the roped-off corner of Bay Lake, this cove is the main section of River Country. Rope swings hang from a rustic boom, and there are various other woody contraptions from which kids perpetually dive and cannonball. Kids aged 7–10 may take snorkeling lessons here for $20 per half hour. Sign up at Guest Relations when you purchase your tickets.

Swimming Pool. This massive pool is bright blue and concrete paved, like something out of a more modern Midwest. There are a couple of short, steep water slides here.

White Water Rapids. For a leisurely trip down, follow the series of short chutes and swirling pools in a jumbo inner tube. Laughs, not thrills, are what this one is all about, as your tube gets caught in the pool's eddies and you spin around, stuck, until someone slides down and bumps you out. It's the closest thing to white-water rafting this side of the Great Smoky Mountains.

Whoop 'n' Holler Hollow. Consisting of the two big water slides—100 ft and 260 ft long—and descending from down the side of the mountain, this is truly the main event.

Strategies for Your Visit to River Country

Go early in the morning to avoid the crowds that sometimes close River Country altogether on busy days. Alternatively, in summer, wait until 4 and take advantage of the reduced-price admission ticket.

River Country A to Z

Dining

You can pick up burgers, hot dogs, and fries at **Pop's Place.** Picnicking is permitted but no alcoholic beverages or glass containers. There's seating near the concession stand, or you can eat at your towel.

For Travelers with Disabilities

Wheelchairs are available at Guest Relations at no charge (with ID as deposit), but very little of the park is wheelchair accessible; you're better off at Typhoon Lagoon or Blizzard Beach.

Facilities

There are dressing rooms for men and women near the entrance, with lockers ($5 and $7; $2 key deposit) and towel rentals ($1). Bring your own towel since the ones here are skimpy. Beach towels are for sale at a kiosk near the beach.

First Aid

It's in the white building next to the guest pay phone, but it's open only during Easter break and in summer. At any other time, go to Guest Relations, at the entrance turnstiles.

Lost Things and People

Lost youngsters are usually taken to the towel window and then walked around until they spot their folks. River Country is small enough that this system works well. Guest Relations is the spot to take finds and report losses.

Visitor Information

The staff at the **Guest Relations** window, at the entrance turnstiles, can answer most of your questions.

AND THERE'S MORE

Disney Quest

This five-story interactive indoor theme park, opened in June 1999 in Downtown Disney's West Side, is a virtual kingdom of attractions and adventures in a single building. Here Disney stories and characters come to life in a bold, new way—you not only make the magic, you are immersed in it. It's a wonderful, unique place to cool off on a hot summer day or to sit out an afternoon thunderstorm. To avoid crowds, arrive when it opens, at 10:30 AM. Its location in the middle of a nightlife complex ensures crowds after dark.

You begin your journey at the **Ventureport** after exiting the elevator, here known as the **Cybrolator.** The Ventureport serves as a crossroads within the complex, and from there you can go on to enter any one of four distinct entertainment environments, or "zones": the Explore Zone, the Score Zone, the Create Zone, and the Replay Zone. One price gains you admission to the building and allows you to play some of the games; at other games, you use a special debit card, which you can buy in increments of $5, $10, $20, and $30. The cost of each activity, which ranges from about $1 to $5, is deducted from the balance on your card. ⊠ *Downtown Disney,* ☎ *407/828–4600.* ☒ *$25, $20 children under 9.* ☉ *Daily 10:30 AM–midnight.*

The Explore Zone

In this virtual adventureland, you are immersed in exotic and ancient locales. You can fly through the streets of Agrabah on a hunt to release the genie on **Aladdin's Magic Carpet Ride.** Help Hercules battle Hades as you experience **Hercules in the Underworld.** Then take a **Virtual Jungle Cruise** down the rapids in a prehistoric world and paddle to adventure. End your stay in this area at **Pirates of the Caribbean: Battle for Buccaneer Gold,** where you can sink pirate ships to increase your treasure trove.

The Score Zone

Here you can match your game-playing skills against the best. Battle supervillains as you fly through a 3-D comic world in **Ride the Comix.** Rescue stranded colonists with your crew during **Invasion! An Ex- traTERRORestrial Alien Encounter.** Or hip-check your friends in a life-size **Mighty Ducks Pinball Slam** game.

The Create Zone

Let your creative juices flow in this studio of expression and inven- tion. You can learn the secrets of Disney animation at the **Animation Academy.** Create your own masterpiece at **Sid's Create-A-Toy.** Make yourself over with funny shapes at the **Magic Mirror.** Or, at **Living Easels,** create a *living* painting. On a TV screen you can choose from a num- ber of objects, including, say, the Cinderella Castle; then you can add flowers, candy, funny faces, and other objects of your choosing. De- sign your own roller coaster at **Cyberspace Mountain.** At **Songmaker,** produce your own hit in a soundbooth equipped with a computer and audio system that helps incorporate all kinds of sounds into your recording. You can buy what you've created in the Create Zone at **The Create Zone.**

The Replay Zone

The classic machines are here, with futuristic twists. Play SkeeBall, Don- key Kong, and **Whack A Alien.** Or sit in a bumper car and blast other guests inside their bumper cars with cannons at **Buzz Lightyear's As- troBlaster.** Cash in your winnings for candy, stuffed animals, mugs, T-shirts, and other prizes at the **Midway on the Moon.**

Food Quest

Here you'll find varied salads, sandwiches, pizza, and luscious-look- ing and surprisingly tasty desserts—cheesecake with strawberries and ice cream among them. Surf the Web at your table—there's a computer terminal in every booth—or play PacMan as you eat. The **Emporium,** at the exit, sells Disney Quest-theme merchandise.

Downtown Disney

Downtown Disney is really three parks in one featuring attractions, entertainment, shopping, and dining. First, there's the **West Side** with **Cirque du Soleil, House of Blues, Disney Quest, Planet Hollywood,** and the AMC movie theatres. Then, there's **Pleasure Island,** which is primarily an evening entertainment complex geared towards adults. You'll find destinations like the **Comedy Warehouse** and the **Wildhorse Saloon.** Finally, there's the **Marketplace,** which is home to a variety of shops and restaurants. What you haven't found in the theme parks you will probably find here. Visit **World of Disney,** the largest Disney char- acter store on the planet and let the kids play in the **Lego Imagination Center.**

WALT DISNEY WORLD® A TO Z

Admission

Visiting Walt Disney World is not cheap, especially if you have a child or two along. Everyone 10 and older pays adult price; reductions are available for children 3–9. No discounted family tickets are available. Prices change often, so be sure to call for the most up-to-date infor- mation.

Tickets and Passes

In Disneyspeak, "ticket" refers to a single day's admission to the Magic Kingdom, Epcot, the Studios, or the Animal Kingdom. If you want to spend two or three days at WDW, you have to buy a separate theme-park ticket each day. A ticket is good in the park for which you buy it only on the day you buy it.

If you want to spend more than three days, you have several options. The **Park Hopper Passes** allow unlimited visits to the four parks on any four or five days, depending on the length of the pass, with any combination of parks on a day. The five-, six-, and seven-day **Park Hopper PLUS** includes unlimited visits to the four theme parks on any five, six, or seven days, plus visits to, respectively, two, three, or four of WDW's minor parks, including Blizzard Beach, Pleasure Island, River Country, and Typhoon Lagoon. If you don't use your admissions to the minor attractions on this visit, you can use them next time around—they don't expire (but are not transferrable).

Although these passes don't represent a tremendous savings over the cost of one-day tickets, depending on the parks you plan to see and the number of days you have, they can save you money as well as time spent in line. A variety of **Annual Passes** are also available; if you plan to visit twice in a year, these are a good deal.

Staying at Disney-owned resorts gets you additional options. **Unlimited Magic Passes** are good from the time you arrive until midnight of the day you leave; buy them at the front desks of all resorts or in Guest Relations at the four theme parks. Prices, not including tax, are based upon the number of room nights and range from $115.54 for a one-night, two-day pass ($92.22 for children 3–9) to $306.37 for six nights, seven days ($244.89 for children 3–9). The pass is good for unlimited admission to all four theme parks, as well as unlimited admission to the three water parks and Pleasure Island. In addition, new **"E" Tickets** are available to guests at Disney-owned resorts for use on certain evenings, midweek once a month, during months that the Magic Kingdom closes early for everyone else. These tickets must be used in conjunction with a multiday pass used that day. You can ride the top rides over and over again, with nary a wait.

Imagine a trip to Disney and not ever having to wait in line? With FAST-PASS this is what will eventually happen, and it's included in regular park admission. You insert your theme park ticket into a special FAST-PASS turnstile. Out comes a FASTPASS ticket, complete with the time you should return to the attraction. In the meantime you are free to enjoy the other attractions in the park. At the appointed time you return to the attraction, head for the FASTPASS entrance, and proceed to the preshow or boarding area with little or no wait. At this writing, 15 attractions are using the system: Space Mountain, Splash Mountain, The Many Adventures of Winnie the Pooh, the Jungle Cruise, and Buzz Lightyear's Space Ranger Spin in Magic Kingdom; at Epcot, Test Track and *Honey, I Shrunk the Audience;* in Animal Kingdom, Kali River Rapids Run, Kilimanjaro Safaris, and Dinosaur; and at Disney–MGM Studios, Twilight Zone Tower of Terror II, Rock 'n' Roller Coaster, *Voyage of the Little Mermaid,* Star Tours, and the Indiana Jones Epic Stunt Spectacular!

Note that all Disney passes are nontransferable. The ID, once a photo, is now your fingerprint. Although you slide your pass through the reader like people with single-day tickets, you also have to slip your finger into a special v-shape fingerprint reader before you'll be admitted.

Prices

Disney changes its prices at least once a year and without much notice. For that reason, you may save yourself a few bucks if you buy your WDW tickets or passes as soon as you know for sure you'll be going. At press time, WDW admission prices, including 6% tax, were as follows:

		ADULTS	CHILDREN
One-Day Ticket		$ 48.76	$ 39.22
Park Hoppers	Four days	$186.56	$150.52
Five days		$218.36	$177.02
Park Hoppers PLUS	Five days	$250.16	$203.52
Six days		$281.96	$230.02
Seven days		$313.76	$266.52
Blizzard Beach and Typhoon Lagoon		$ 28.57	$ 22.79
River Country		$ 16.91	$ 13.25
Pleasure Island		$ 20.09	
Disney's Wide World of Sports (does not include events)		$ 8	$ 6.75

Purchasing Tickets and Passes

Tickets and passes to the Magic Kingdom, Epcot, the Studios, the Animal Kingdom, and the minor parks can be purchased at admission booths at the Transportation and Ticket Center (also known as the TCC), in all on-site resorts if you're a registered guest, at the Walt Disney World kiosk on the second floor of the main terminal at Orlando International Airport, and at various hotels and other sites around Orlando. American Express, Visa, and MasterCard are accepted, as are cash, personal checks with ID, and traveler's checks. Passes for five or more days are also available in many Disney Stores in malls throughout the country. Discounted tickets are available in varied locations. They're sold to members at many offices of the American Automobile Association, but check with your local office before you leave home. And you can get them from the Orlando Convention & Visitors' Bureau (✉ 8723 International Dr., ☎ 407/363–5871) and from a variety of visitor information stands not affiliated with the CVB. Note that some discounted tickets are available only if you agree to take a timeshare tour—you may want to pass up the opportunity.

By purchasing tickets before you leave for Orlando, you get a jump on your first day, while everyone else is lining up at Guest Services in the Disney hotels or at the theme-park ticket booths. You will, however, have to present yourself at Guest Services, near the park turnstiles, to have your pass processed—they'll record fingerprint information—so allow ample time when scheduling.

You can also buy your multiday passes by mail or on-line. Send a check or money order to Ticket Mail Order Dept., ✉ Walt Disney World, Box 10000, Lake Buena Vista, FL 32830. Allow four to six weeks for processing. On the Web, click onto www.disneyworld.com.

HAND STAMPS

If you want to leave any Disney park and return on the same day, be sure to have your hand stamped on the way out. You'll need both your ticket and the hand stamp to be readmitted.

Arriving and Departing by Car

Walt Disney World has four exits off I–4. For the Magic Kingdom, Disney–MGM Studios, Disney's Animal Kingdom, Fort Wilderness, and the rest of the Magic Kingdom resort area, take the one marked **Magic Kingdom–U.S. 192 (Exit 25)**. From here, it's a 4-mi drive along Disney's main entrance road to the toll gate, and another mile to the parking area; during peak vacation periods, be prepared for serious bumper-to-bumper traffic both on I–4 nearing the U.S. 192 exit and on U.S. 192 itself. A more direct and less-congested route to the theme parks and other WDW venues is via the exit marked **Disney World/ Animal Kingdom/ Epcot/ MGM/ Wide World of Sports (Exit 24D)**, 4 mi west of Exit 25. If I–4 traffic is not too heavy, it's worth it to go the extra distance.

For access to Downtown Disney (including the Marketplace, Pleasure Island, and Disney's West Side), as well as to Typhoon Lagoon, the Crossroads Shopping Center, and the establishments on Hotel Plaza Boulevard, get off at **Route 535–Lake Buena Vista (Exit 27)**.

The exit marked **Epcot–Downtown Disney (Exit 26)** is the one to use if you're bound for those destinations or for hotels in the Epcot and Downtown Disney resort areas; you can also get to the Studios from here.

Car Care
The gas islands at the **Disney Car Care Center** near the Magic Kingdom are open daily until 90 minutes after the Magic Kingdom closes. You can also gas up on Buena Vista Drive near Disney's BoardWalk, and in the Downtown Disney area across from Pleasure Island. Note that gas prices here are about 5¢–10¢ higher per gallon than off-property.

Parking
Every theme park has a parking lot—and all are huge. Sections of the Magic Kingdom lot are named for Disney characters; Epcot's highlight modes of exploration; those at the Studios are named "Stage," "Music," "Film," and "Dance"; and the Animal Kingdom's sound like Beanie Baby names—Unicorn, Butterfly, and so on. Although in theory Goofy 45 is unforgettable, by the end of the day, you'll be so goofy with eating and shopping and riding that you'll swear that you parked in Sleepy. Trams make frequent trips between the parking area and the parks' turnstile areas. No valet parking is available for Walt Disney World theme parks. Although valet parking is available at Downtown Disney, the congestion there is sometimes such that it may be faster to park in Siberia and walk. At Disney's BoardWalk, you park in the hotel lot, where valets are available as well.

FEES
For each major theme-park lot, admission is $6 for cars, $7 for RVs and campers, and free to Walt Disney World resort guests with ID. Save your receipt; if you want to visit another park the same day, you won't have to pay to park twice. Parking is always free at Typhoon Lagoon, River Country, and Blizzard Beach. Valet parking costs $8 at Downtown Disney and is free at Disney's BoardWalk.

Dining

Walt Disney World is full of places to snack and eat. The theme parks are chockablock with attractive, highly themed fast-food spots; all have not only fast food and cafeteria-style eateries but also full-service, sit-down restaurants, and, especially in Epcot's World Showcase, these eating-and-drinking spots are a big part of the show. On-site hotels offer still other options, including buffeterias as well as full-service restaurants.

This book does not describe and rate every eating spot. Best bets for quick snacks are described as "Need a Break?" in the theme-park sections of this chapter, and top options for meals are covered in the theme parks' Dining sections. For reviews of restaurants in Disney hotels and at Epcot, *see* Chapter 6.

Fresh fruits, salads, steamed vegetables, and low-fat foods are more widely available than you might expect. In full-service restaurants, for instance, you can usually get skim milk, and many fast-food operations have low-fat milk.

Beer, Wine, and Spirits

The Magic Kingdom's no-liquor policy, a Walt Disney tradition that seems almost quaint in this day and age, does not extend to the rest of Walt Disney World, and in fact, most restaurants and watering holes, particularly those in the on-site hotels, mix elaborate fantasy drinks based on fruit juices or flavored with liqueurs.

For Travelers with Disabilities

Attractions in all the Disney parks typically have both a visual element that makes them appealing without sound and an audio element whose charm remains even without the visuals; many are accessible by guests using wheelchairs, and most are accessible by guests with some mobility. Guide dogs and service animals are permitted, unless a ride or special effect could spook or traumatize the animal.

At many rides and attractions, guests with mobility, hearing, and visual impairments do not use the main entrance and sometimes even bypass lines; to find out where to enter or if you have specific questions, ask any host or hostess.

WDW's *Guidebook for Guests with Disabilities* details many specific challenges and identifies the special entrances. In addition, story notes, scripts, and song lyrics are covered in the *Guidebook for Guests with Hearing Impairments.* Both publications are available at the main visitor information locations in every park, along with **cassette tapes and portable players** that provide audio narration for most attractions (no charge, but refundable deposit required). There are also **wheelchair rentals** in every park.

Entertainment

Live entertainment adds texture to visits to the Disney theme parks and can often be a high point of the theme-park experience—even though you don't have to wait in line for your turn to board. Although the jokes may be occasionally silly, the humor broad, and the themes sometimes excessively wholesome, the level of professionalism is high and the energy of the performers unquestionable. Don't fail to pick up a performance schedule on your way into the theme parks, and keep the schedules in mind as you make your way around.

Getting Around

Walt Disney World has its own transportation system, which can get you wherever you want to go. It's fairly simple once you get the hang of it. Officially, all charges for transportation are included in the price of your multiday pass or are available for a small fee.

In general, allow an hour to travel between sites on Disney property. If you use your own car to get around, you will save a lot of time waiting for buses. Using your car could save up to 30 minutes overusing the WDW buses.

By Boat

Motor launches connect WDW destinations on waterways. Specifically, they operate between the Epcot resorts—except the Caribbean Beach—and the Studios and between Bay Lake and the Magic Kingdom, and also between Fort Wilderness, the Wilderness Lodge, and the Polynesian, Contemporary, and Grand Floridian resorts.

By Bus

Buses provide direct service from every on-site resort to both major and minor theme parks, and express buses go directly between the major theme parks. You can go directly from or make connections at the Downtown Disney, Epcot, and the Epcot resorts, including the Yacht and Beach Clubs, the BoardWalk, the Caribbean Beach Resort, the Swan, and the Dolphin, as well as to Disney's Animal Kingdom and the Animal Kingdom resorts (the All-Star and Coronado Springs resorts).

The buses to the Magic Kingdom all let you off at the TTC, where you have to change for a monorail or boat to get you to the turnstiles.

By Monorail

The elevated monorail serves many important destinations. It has two loops: one linking the Magic Kingdom, TTC, and a handful of resorts (including the Contemporary, the Grand Floridian, and the Polynesian); and the other looping from the TTC directly to Epcot. Before this monorail line pulls into the station, the elevated track circles through Future World—Epcot's northern half—and circles the giant silver geosphere housing the Spaceship Earth ride to give you a preview of what you'll see.

By Tram

From the Epcot resort area, trams operate to the International Gateway of the park's World Showcase. Trams also operate from the ticket and transportation center in each park. If you parked fairly close in, though, you may save time, especially at park closing time, by walking to your car.

Hours

The monorail, launches, buses, and trams all operate from early in the morning until at least midnight, although hours are shorter during early closing periods. Check on the operating hours of the service you need if you plan to be out later than that.

Lost and Found

There are **lost-and-found offices** in the Magic Kingdom at City Hall (☎ 407/824–4521), at Epcot (☎ 407/560–6166 or 407/560–6236), in Disney–MGM Studios (☎ 407/560–4668), and at Disney's Animal Kingdom (☎ 407/938–2265). After one day, all items are sent to the **Main Lost & Found** office at the TTC (☎ 407/824–4245).

Money Matters

The SunTrust branch in Lake Buena Vista is across the street from the Downtown Disney Marketplace (☎ 407/299–4786). Automatic teller machines are scattered throughout the Magic Kingdom, Epcot, the Studios, the Animal Kingdom, and Downtown Disney. Currency exchange services are available at Guest Services in each major theme park.

Opening and Closing Times

Major Theme Parks

Operating hours for the Magic Kingdom, Epcot, the Studios, and the Animal Kingdom vary throughout the year and change for school and legal holidays. In general, the longest days are during prime summer months and over the year-end holidays, when the Magic Kingdom is open until midnight, later on New Year's Eve; Epcot is open until 11, the Studios until 9. At other times, Epcot and the Studios are open until 8 and the Magic Kingdom until 7—but there are variations, so call ahead.

Animal Kingdom opens at 7 or 8 and closes at 7 or 8, depending on the season. Note that in general the Magic Kingdom, the Studios, and

Epcot's Future World officially open at 9 (Epcot's World Showcase opens at 11). The parking lots open at least an hour before the parks do. Arriving at the Magic Kingdom turnstiles before the official opening time, you can often breakfast in a restaurant on Main Street, which usually opens before the rest of the park, and be ready to dash to one of the popular attractions in other lands at Rope Drop, the Magic Kingdom's official opening time. The Studios and Epcot both have an early morning character breakfast; signing up ensures that you'll be close to the head of whatever line you want to charge to when your meal is over.

Guests who stay at an on-site Disney-owned hotel can enter one of the four parks on alternating days a full hour and a half before the official opening time.

In the Magic Kingdom, once a month at off-peak times of year, there are also "E" ticket evenings, in which Magic Kingdom entry is for Disney resort guests only.

Minor Parks
Hours at River Country, Typhoon Lagoon, and Blizzard Beach are 10–5 daily (until 7—occasionally 10—in summer).

Reservations

To make reservations at **restaurants** in Walt Disney World, including the heavily booked Epcot restaurants, call ☎ 407/939–3463. Plan early to avoid disappointment. To reserve **golf tee times and lessons** call ☎ 407/824–2270. Tours require reservations, too; booking information is given in the Guided Tours sections of the various theme parks' coverage.

Tips for Your Visit

The order in which you tour each of the Disney parks has everything to do with your priorities, the time of year you visit (which is in turn related to the opening and closing hours and the size of the crowds), the length you're staying in Walt Disney World, and whether you're staying on or off WDW property. The italicized "Crowds" and "Strategy" information that follows each attraction's review should help you draw up alternative plans. No matter where you go, you will have a smoother time if you follow certain basic rules.

- Plan to pull into the parking lot 50 minutes to an hour ahead of the published opening times—so that you can check belongings into lockers, rent strollers, and otherwise take care of business before everyone else. When you go to any theme park except the Magic Kingdom, count on being at the entrance turnstiles 45 minutes or more before official opening time.

- See the three-star attractions either first thing in the morning, at the end of the day, or during a parade.

- Whenever possible when you're visiting the theme parks, eat in a restaurant that takes reservations, bring your own food discreetly (a big money- *and* time-saver), or have meals before or after mealtime rush hours (from 11 AM to 2 PM and again from 6 to 8 PM). Or leave the theme parks altogether for a meal in one of the hotels. If you're in the Magic Kingdom, for instance, it's simple and fairly quick to head over to the Polynesian Village, the Grand Floridian, or the Contemporary. Early meals are particularly advantageous; you'll be resting up and cooling off while the rest of the world is waiting in line; then while they're all waiting to order, you'll be walking right into many attractions.

HOW TO REST UP AFTER WDW

ABOARD THE DISNEY *Magic,* Mickey's silhouette is on the funnels, Goofy clings to the stern, and the foghorn bellows "When You Wish Upon a Star." Styled like a classic liner, the *Magic* was a hit from Day One. Now it shares the seas with the nearly identical *Wonder.* Both are perfect places to kick back after your Disney marathon on a Bahamas cruise—and seven-day parks-and-cruise packages make everything miraculously easy. You check in just once: your Disney hotel room key becomes first your boarding pass at Disney's Port Canaveral terminal and later your stateroom key. Special buses ferry you between WDW hotels and the port; your luggage is transported from your hotel room to your cabin. When the cruise ends, you can check in for your flight at dockside. The cruises are winners for both families and adults. There are three pools, four cleverly themed restaurants, lavish shows with lots of special effects, a cinema that screens Disney films, and many nightclubs. And, as you'd expect, the kid's programs are carefully thought out, with separate spaces for teens, 9- to 12-year-olds, and 3- to 8-year-olds (parents with offspring here get a pager at drop-off). Your ultimate destination is Disney's private island, replete with lovely beaches and offshore "shipwrecks" created just for snorkelers. For details call ☎ 800/511–1333.

- Spend afternoons in high-capacity sit-down shows or catching live entertainment—or leave the theme parks entirely for a swim in your hotel pool. Don't forget to have your hand stamped on the way out.

- If you plan to take in Blizzard Beach, River Country, or Typhoon Lagoon, go early in your visit (but not on a weekend). You may like it so much that you'll want to go again.

- If you have small children and a meal with the characters is in your plans, save it for the end of your trip, when your youngsters will have become accustomed to these large, looming figures.

- Familiarize yourself with all age and height restrictions. Ideally, you should measure young children ahead of time so they won't get excited about rides they're too short to experience. However, most rides have premeasured signs at the entrance to the queuing area, so even if you don't know how tall your child is, you won't have to wait in line before finding out.

- Call ahead to check on operating hours and parade times, which vary greatly throughout the year.

- Have your children bring their Nintendos, Game Boys, or Giga Pets to play with while waiting in lines. Keeping them busy will cut down on whining.

Visitor Information

For general WDW information, contact **Guest Relations** (☎ 407/824–4321 or in any Disney resort) or the **WDW central switchboard** (☎ 407/

WALT DISNEY WORLD TIME-SAVING TIPS

CAN YOU IMAGINE A TRIP to a major theme park without experiencing the wait? FASTPASS is a new time saving device that can enable guests to experience two or more attractions in a single visit. (☞ Walt Disney World A to Z for details.) Aside from this scheduling innovation, there are other simple ways to save time and get more out of your Walt Disney World experience.

–If you are an on-site Disney resort guest, take advantage of early admission days.

–Visit during off-peak times. When crowds are sparse, so are the lines.

–Take your meals when everyone else is riding the rides and seeing the sites. A late lunch or early dinner will help you avoid peak lines.

–Arrive at the park about 30 minutes prior to opening so you can get a head start to the most popular attractions when guests are first let in.

–Make your dining reservations and purchase your park tickets before you leave home.

–When park-hopping, use your own car to save time. There can be 30-minute waits for park-provided bus transportation.

824–2222) if you want to speak directly to someone at a specific Disney location. For accommodations and shows, call **WDW Central Reservations** (☎ 407/934–7639). To inquire about specific resort facilities, call the individual property.

To get very detailed information, call the attraction or department directly: **Blizzard Beach** (☎ 407/560–4140), **Disney–MGM Studios TV-show tapings** (☎ 407/560–4651), **Disney Quest** (☎ 407/828–4600), **Downtown Disney's Marketplace** (☎ 407/828–3058), **Fort Wilderness** (☎ 407/824–2900), **KinderCare** child care (☎ 407/827–5444 for in-room; 407/827–5437 for drop-off), **Disney Institute** (☎ 407/827–4800), **Pleasure Island** (☎ 407/934–7781), **River Country** (☎ 407/560–9283), and **Typhoon Lagoon** (☎ 407/560–4141).

3 UNIVERSAL ORLANDO

The theme park formerly known as Universal Studios Escape had a rough beginning and is now easing into its next phase, and management is hoping a recent name change will alleviate confusion about the all-encompassing resort. Under any name, however, Universal Orlando has raised the stakes in its attempt to divert Disney guests through their own gates, and is certainly worth a two-day visit when in Orlando.

F OR MORE THAN A DECADE, Universal has remained one step behind Disney. The Disney–MGM Studios opened in 1989 whereas
Universal Studios Florida debuted in 1990. Disney was off to a
steady start, but Universal stumbled when its star attractions were literally down for years. In the last few seasons, however, an influx of
$3 billion has generated the largest expansion project in Orlando's his-
tory, and the results are clear: Universal's CityWalk is larger and arguably more colorful than Pleasure Island (although not Downtown
Disney as a whole), their Islands of Adventure is a stunning blend of
creativity and cutting-edge rides, and new hotels are turning what was
once a single park into a resort destination. The growing pains of the
expansion have been apparent, and guests were often confused with
name changes. Borrowing a concept from Walt Disney World Resort
(which encompasses theme parks and hotels), the "umbrella" is now
Universal Orlando, which contains Universal Studios (the original
movie theme park), Islands of Adventure (the second theme park), City-
Walk (the dining-shopping-nightclub complex), and the Portofino Bay
Hotel (which is soon to be joined by the Hard Rock Hotel and Royal
Pacific Resort). Although it's bordered by residential neighborhoods
and thickly trafficked International Drive, Universal Orlando is surprisingly expansive, yet intimate since two massive parking complexes
(7.5 million square ft), easy walks to all attractions, and a motor
launch that cruises to Portofino Bay make things fairly accessible. In
their promotional literature, Universal Orlando emphasizes "two
parks, two days, one great adventure." You may find that the caliber
of the parks' presentation, creativity, and cutting-edge technology may
bring you back for day three . . . or four.

Updated by
Gary
McKechnie

For pre-trip information, check out www.uescape.com.

UNIVERSAL STUDIOS

Although Disney does an extraordinary job when it comes to show-
manship, Universal Studios has taken advantage of their distinctly
non-Disney heritage to add attitude to their presentations. Universal
Studios performers aren't above tossing in a Calista "Ally McBeal" Flock-
hart joke when a skeleton is brought on stage, or mentioning noises a
duck might make (and not with their beaks) to get a cheap laugh.

Although this theme park caters to the masses, it appeals primarily to
people who like loud, fast, high-energy attractions. If you want to calm
down, there are quiet, shaded parks and a children's area where adults
can enjoy a respite while the kids are ripping through assorted play-
lands at 100 mph.

The park's 444 acres are a bewildering conglomeration of stage sets,
shops, reproductions of New York and San Francisco, and anonymous
soundstages housing theme attractions, as well as genuine moviemaking
paraphernalia. On the map, these sets are neatly divided into seven neighborhoods, which wrap themselves around a huge lagoon. The neighborhoods are **World Expo; Woody Woodpecker's KidZone,** a new area created
especially for toddlers and young children; the **Front Lot; Hollywood,** just
inside the Universal entrance; **New York,** with excellent street performances at 70 Delancey; New England-y **Amity;** and **Production Central,** which spreads over the entire left side of the Plaza of the Stars.

On a map it looks easy. On foot, a quick run through the park to hit
the top rides first is difficult since it involves a few long detours and
some backtracking. If you need help, theme park hosts are trained to

Universal Studios

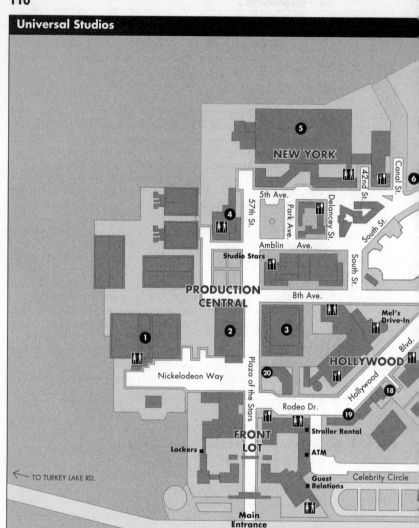

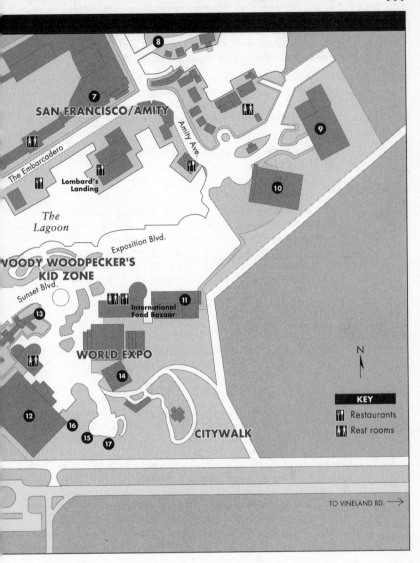

provide more information than you thought you needed. Look to them for advice on navigating the park. Also keep in mind that some rides—and many restaurants—don't open until 11:30 or noon, which may throw a kink in your perfectly laid-out plans.

Although Universal Studios may seem like a mix of movies and an old-fashioned carnival (beware of the cash-depleting midways), but over-all the thrills and casual attitude make Universal Studios an entertaining respite from the sometime synthetic worlds of entertainment you'll find in Orlando.

Numbers in the margin correspond to points of interest on the Universal Studios map.

The Front Lot

The cacophony of motion, sound, and sights when you enter the turn-stiles can be daunting, so before plunging into the park, take a moment to get your bearings. A few yards ahead to your right is Rodeo Drive–Hollywood Boulevard which is essentially a scene-setter, mood manipulator, and where the first of many kiosks and stores lie in wait to turn your vacation funds into snacks and souvenirs with a short shelf life. You'll be here soon enough. Straight ahead, you may be lured by several soundstage-size attractions.

Production Central

This area is composed of six huge warehouses containing working sound-stages, as well as several attractions. Follow Nickelodeon Way left from the Plaza of the Stars.

❶ **Nickelodeon Studios.** About 90% of Nickelodeon's original pro-gramming is produced on the soundstages you'll see here. The banks of lights, concrete floors, and general warehouse feel go a long way toward demystifying movie magic, but it's exactly that behind-the-scenes perspective that makes the tour interesting. You may get a peek at wardrobe and makeup studios, as well as a tour of the kitchen where Slime for the Slime Geyser is made, depending on how busy the park is on a given day. The Nickelodeon Studios tour winds up in the **Game Lab,** a theme-park version of a typical Nick game show, and ends with one lucky volunteer getting slimed, just for the spectacle of it all. Plan ahead and you can take in a taping—if squandering vacation time to fill seats for a cable program sounds like a good plan. *Duration: 30 mins. Crowds: Steady, long lines. Strategy: Skip it on a first-time visit or if no shows are taping. If you go, call 407/363–8500 for taping in-formation before leaving home, and get tickets at Guest Relations when you enter the park. Audience: All ages, but especially grade-school-ers. Rating:* ★★

❷ **FUNtastic World of Hanna-Barbera.** The first attraction you'll hit if you head straight on Plaza of the Stars, this is an animated motion simu-lator that's one of the park's most popular attractions. Before the doors open, Yogi Bear and his creators (Mr. Hanna and Mr. Barbera) appear on overhead video monitors to explain how cartoons are made. In the example, poor lil' Elroy Jetson is abducted by evil Dick Das-tardly and now you have a story line—and a cartoon kid—to follow. You're ushered into a large auditorium where your group sits in mo-tion simulators that'll take you through scenes from the Flintstones, Scooby Doo, and the Jetsons. It's a rocketing, rollicking ride and pretty fun since it's all seen in brilliant cartoon colors. Following the chase across time, the ride exits into an interactive electronic arcade where you (or your kids) can provide voice-overs and sounds to or color in the features of Hanna-Barbera characters. *Duration: 8 mins. Crowds: Usually stunning, despite high capacity. Strategy: Go as soon as the gates open or at night. Audience: All ages; may frighten some toddlers, and young children may want to go for stationary seats in the front of the theater. No pregnant women or guests with heart, back, or neck problems or motion sickness. Minimum height: 40". Rating:* ★★★

③ Alfred Hitchcock's 3-D Theatre. "Have you ever had a premonition?" asks the superbly cultured and ever-so-slightly spooky voice of Alfred Hitchcock, the star in the theater across the Plaza of the Stars from Hanna-Barbera. It starts off a dandy multimedia tribute to the master of suspense, who made 53 films for Universal Studios. Thanks to 3-D glasses, you learn what it's like to be a citizen of Bodega Bay on a day of abnormal avian activity. The audience is taken on a guided tour through a museum that highlights Hitchcock's many accomplishments. Unseen 3-D footage from *Dial M for Murder* is the highlight. As in any good Hitchcock film, this attraction engages your mind as well as your adrenaline—and has a characteristic twist of an ending. *Duration: 40 mins. Crowds: Sizable but fairly fast-moving because of the theater size. Strategy: Try to negotiate seats in the middle of the theater for best 3-D viewing. Audience: All but young children, who may be frightened. Rating:* ★★★

New York

This Universal take on the Big Apple recalls the original—right down to the cracked concrete and slightly stained cobblestones. The **Blues Brothers Bluesmobile** regularly cruises the neighborhood, and musicians hop out to give impromptu performances at 70 Delancey.

④ TWISTER: Ride It Out. This attraction accomplishes in a few minutes what it took the highly contrived 1996 movie to do in two long hours—and it's far more exciting. After enduring a slow line and a lecture from Helen Hunt and that other guy about the destructive force of tornadoes, you're eventually ushered into a standing-room theater where a bucolic country scene slowly transforms into a mighty scary make-believe windstorm. An ominous, five-story-high funnel cloud weaves in from the background to take center stage as 110 decibels of wind noise, crackling electrical lines, and shattered windows add to the confusion. A truck, signs, car, and cow are given frequent flyer points as they sail across the stage, and even though you know you're in a building and more guests are waiting patiently to get in, your first instinct is to head for the root cellar. Don't. Watch the whole thing and marvel at the special effects masters who put this together—and tear it apart every few minutes. *Duration: 15 mins. Crowds: Expect very long lines. Strategy: Go first thing in the morning or at closing. Audience: All but young children, who may be frightened. Rating:* ★★★

⑤ Kongfrontation. The 1976 film wasn't great, but the folks at Universal thought Kong was big enough to star in his own attraction. The waiting area reproduces a graffiti-filled 1970s New York subway station, and the story line involves potential victims (you) trying to escape King Kong by boarding a tram to Roosevelt Island. The tram guide keeps you posted on police sightings tracking the gorilla of your dreams, and when you round a corner, surprise! It's Kong snatching at your tram as helicopter gunships swoop in for a shot. There are a few more narrow escapes, but the contrived nature (not to mention the mistaken notion that gorillas are deadly) make this one a toss-up if the line's too long. You may be more impressed by the dimensions of the computerized ape that's more than four stories tall, weighs 6 tons, and has a 54-ft arm span. *Duration: 5 mins. Crowds: Lines ebb* *and flow throughout the day and move slowly because of the ride's small capacity. Strategy: Go early or late; if your time is limited, opt for Jaws and Earthquake, because they provide more thrill for the time spent in line. Audience: Older children and adults; Kong is too realistic for younger kids, who are easily frightened. No pregnant women or guests with heart, back, or neck problems or motion sickness. Minimum height: Without adult, 40". Rating:* ★★

Amity

This area combines two sets. One part is the wharves and warehouses of San Francisco's Embarcadero and Fisherman's Wharf districts, with cable-car tracks and the distinctive redbrick Ghirardelli chocolate factory; the other is the New England fishing village terrorized by the shark in *Jaws*.

❻ Beetlejuice's Graveyard Revue. You might wonder why someone gave the green light to this production since it's very weird in a "feel-sorry-for-the-poor-actors" kind of way. Then again, the majority of the audience seems to enjoy it because things explode and there's a lot of dancing action. Maybe you should judge for yourself: Beetlejuice is the host, and during the audience warm-up, he does a great job with quick jokes and snappy put-downs. Then he introduces the stars of the show: Frankenstein's monster (and his bride), the Phantom of the Opera, the Werewolf, and Dracula. For some reason, the monsters soon shed their traditional apparel for a set of groovy sequined threads straight from the Brady Bunch closet. Then they sing songs by artists as diverse as Sly and the Family Stone, Foreigner, and Jerry Lee Lewis. Keep in mind they do all this while still in full monster make-up and dancing like the Backstreet Boys. If you can forgive the convoluted and disjointed themes, you might get a kick out of it. *Duration: 25 mins. Crowds: Steady, but high capacity of amphitheater means no waiting. Strategy: Go when ride lines are at capacity or after dark on hot days. Audience: Older children and adults. Rating:* ★★★

❼ *Earthquake—*The Big One. Unless you volunteer as an extra, the preshow for onlookers can be a little slow. After Charlton Heston appears in a documentary about the 1973 movie and the preselected volunteers participate in the making of a short disaster scene, you board a train and take a brief ride into a darkened San Francisco subway tunnel. This is where the adrenaline kicks in very, very quickly. The idea is that you've been cast as an extra for the "final scene," and when the train parks at the station, a few lights flash, the ground starts to shake and suddenly you're smack dab in the middle of a two-minute, 8.3 Richter scale tremor that includes trembling earth, collapsing ceilings, blackouts, explosions, fire, and a massive underground flood coming from every angle. Don't miss it. If you're claustrophobic, though, this one might put you over the edge. *Duration: 20 mins. Crowds: Heavy. Strategy: As with most blockbusters, you will have to wait to ride. Go early or late. Audience: All but young children. No pregnant women or guests with heart, back, or neck problems or motion sickness. Minimum height: Without adult, 40". Rating:* ★★★

❽ Jaws. This popular ride around a 7-acre lagoon always has a long wait, so bide your time watching Amity TV on WJWS, a station piped into the waiting line, complete with commercials for used recreational vehicles and candied blowfish. And after you board your boat for a placid cruise around the bay, just what do you think's gonna happen? That's right. A 32-ft killer shark zeroes in at 20 mph, looking for a bite of your boat. Even though you know the shark is out there (and returns even after you've sought the safety of a boathouse), things can still get pretty frightening with surprise attacks, explosions, loud noises, and the teeth-grinding sounds on the side of your boat. The special effects on this ride really shine, especially the heat and fire from electrical explosions that could singe the eyebrows off Andy Rooney. Try it after dark for an extra thrill, then cancel the following day's trip to the beach. *Duration: 7 mins. Crowds: Lines stay long most of the day, but nothing like those at Back to the Future. Strategy: Go early or after dark for an even more terrifying experience—you can't see the attack as well but can certainly hear and feel it. For the shortest lines, cast off for Jaws during the stunt show. Audience: All but young children, who will be frightened. No pregnant women or guests with heart, back, or neck problems or motion sickness. Rating:* ★★★

❾ Wild, Wild, Wild West Stunt Show. The sign SQUARE DANCE AND HANGING, SATURDAY NIGHT lets you know what kind of town you've moseyed into, and the repeated playing of the theme from *Bonanza* confirms your hunch. The show involves trapdoors, fistfights, bullwhips, water gags, explosions, shoot-outs, horseback riding, and one tough mama who proclaims, "Listen, Pop-Tart, I've been falling off barns since I was three." She then demonstrates her inimitable style by hurling herself off the ridgepole. By the end of the show, the set is in shambles and every other theme park in Central Florida has been skewered in jokes and snide remarks: "Look, Ma, I'm Shamu," yells one sopping stuntman as he emerges, spitting water, from a well. The panting stuntpeople take time out from rebuilding the set for photographs, autographs, and questions. They will not, however, explain how you can replicate the stunt at home. *Duration: 16 mins. Crowds: Large, but its 2,000-seat amphitheater means no waiting. Strategy: On hot days go after dark, when it will be cooler in the amphitheater. Note the splash zone near the well, if you want to stay dry (or get wet). Audience: All ages. Rating:* ★★★

World Expo

The far corner of the park contains Universal Studios' most popular attraction, **Back to the Future . . . The Ride,** as well as the park's latest arrival, **Men In Black: Alien Attack.** These two make this the section to see for major thrills. When you're ready to kick back, stop at **Mel's Drive-In** for a thick chocolate shake.

❿ Men In Black: Alien Attack. This star attraction, which premiered April 2000, is billed as the world's first "ride-through video game." The preshow provides the story line: to earn membership into MIB, you and your colleagues have to round up aliens who have escaped when their shuttle crashed on earth. With this, you embark on a trip through New York streets, firing at aliens to rack up points. Keep in mind they can fire back at you and send your car spinning out of control. If you can stomach it, the ride wraps up inside a 30-ft-high bug that swallows your car, and to escape, you have to shoot your way out of the belly of the beast. Then you'll finish the adventure with one of 35 different ride endings, ranging from a hero's welcome to a loser's farewell. *Duration: 4 mins. 30 sec. Crowds: Bound to be out of this world. Strategy: Go during a Wild, Wild, Wild West Stunt Show, or first thing in the morning. Audience: Older children and adults. The spinning nature of the cars may cause dizziness, so use caution: no guests with heart, back, or neck problems or motion sickness. Tentative Rating:* ★★★

⓫ Back to the Future . . . The Ride. The ride that's been on top of everyone's list also seems to be popular with guys named Mike: Michael Jackson rode it three times in a row and Michael J. Fox, star of the 1985 movie, said it delivered what the script imagined. At heart, this is a motion simulator ride, with the twist being that following a very long wait, you are seated in a very cramped eight-passenger DeLorean that takes off into a series of past, present, and future scenes projected on a seven-story, one-of-a-kind Omnimax screen. Having no sense of perspective (or seat belts), makes this the rocking, rolling, pitching, and yawing equivalent of a hyperactive paint mixer. It is nonstop scary. If you like your rides shaken, not stirred, this one'll be worth the wait—and the queasy feeling that'll follow you around afterwards. *Duration: 5 mins. Crowds: Up to 2 hrs in busy seasons at peak times between 11 and 3; slightly less crowded first thing in the morning, when Twister siphons off the crowds. Strategy: Dash over when the gates open, or about a half hour afterward, or be prepared to wait (and wait . . . and wait). Alternatively, go late. Audience: Older children and adults. No pregnant women or guests with heart, back, or neck problems or motion sickness. Minimum height: 40″. Rating:* ★★★

Woody Woodpecker's KidZone

Universal Studios has addressed the lack of a kids (that is, preschoolers) play area with this compilation of rides, attractions, shows, and places where children can get sprayed, splashed, and soaked. **Fievel's Playland, A Day in the Park with Barney,** and the *E.T.* **Adventure** are now joined by **Animal Actors Stage,** the new **Woody Woodpecker's Nuthouse Coaster,** and **Curious George Goes to Town.** It's a great place for kids to burn out their last ounce of energy and give parents a much-needed break after nearly circling the park.

⓬ *E.T.* **Adventure.** Steven Spielberg puts one of his most beloved creations on display at this large structure adjoining Fievel's Playland. To the hoarsely murmured mantra of "Home, home," you board bicycles mounted on a movable platform and pedal through fantastic forests floating in mists of dry-ice fumes, magic gardens populated by such whimsical Spielberg characters as the Tickli Moot, and across the moon—remember to catch your shadow—in an attempt to help the endearing extraterrestrial find his way back to his home planet. The music is as tear-jerking as ever, and so is the little surprise when E.T. personally says good-bye at the end. Another surprise, the waiting area—a pine-scented forest complete with E.T. beckoning you on—is one of the most pleasant at this park, although small children may find the darkness a little scary. The score is by Academy Award–winning composer John Williams. *Duration: 5 mins. Crowds: Sometimes not bad, but up to a 2-hr wait during crowded periods. Strategy: Go early. Audience: All ages. No guests with heart, back, or neck problems or motion sickness. Rating:* ★★★

⓭ **AT&T at the Movies.** You can usually tell when a corporation sponsors an attraction because it often turns out to be a fairly boring commercial disguised as a fascinating presentation. This is no different. There are a few rooms of old microphones and recording devices and several computers where you can superimpose disguises on a picture of your face or hear your voice as it would have sounded on a Victrola. On the other hand, the environs are fairly cool on a hot day. *Duration: Up to you. Crowds: Busy but usually not too crowded. Strategy: Go any time. Audience: All ages. Rating:* ★

⓮ **A Day in the Park with Barney.** If you can't get enough of the big purple dinosaur, here he is again, in a theatre setting filled with brilliantly colored trees, clouds, and stars. The show, of course, is geared for preschoolers who love the fact that their TV playmate is right in front of them, dancing and singing. Although his star has dimmed a bit, little children still go crazy over the clap-along, sing-along songs including those monster classics "Mr. Knickerbocker," "If You're Happy and You Know It," and "I Love You." After the show, a play area featuring hands-on activities including a water harp, wood-pipe xylophone, and musical rocks will propel the now-excitable kids to even greater heights. *Duration: 20 mins. Crowds: Room for all. Strategy: Arrive 10– 15 mins early on crowded days for a good seat—up close and in the center. Audience: Young children. Rating:* ★★

⑮ Fievel's Playland. Another Spielberg movie spin-off, this playground features props and sets far larger than life, designed to make everyone feel mouse-sized. Boots, cans, and other ordinary objects are utilized to disguise tunnel slides, water play areas, ball crawls, and a gigantic net-climb equipped with tubes, ladders, and rope bridges. A harmonica slide plays music when you slide along the openings, and a 200-ft water slide gives kids (and a parent if they'd like) a chance to slide down in Fievel's signature sardine can. It should keep the kids entertained for hours. The downside? You might have to build one of these for your backyard when you get home. *Duration: Up to your preschooler. Crowds: Not significant, although waits do develop for the water slide. Strategy: On hot days, go after supper. Audience: Toddlers, preschoolers, and their parents. Rating:* ★★

⑯ Woody Woodpecker's Nuthouse Coaster. Far safer than the coasters featuring zero-G rolls and inversions, this low-speed, mild thrill version (top speed 22 mph) makes it a safe bet for younger kids and action-phobic adults. It races (a relative term) through a structure that looks like a factory with decorative gears and gadgetry; the coaster's cars look like shipping crates—some called "mixed nuts," some tagged as "salted nuts," and some labeled "certifiably nuts." Woody, a creation of animator Walter Lantz, takes you through his very own Nuthouse, with several ups and downs to reward you for the wait. *Duration: 1½ mins. Crowds: Heavy in mid-morning and early afternoon when the under-2 set is out in force. Strategy: Go at park closing, when most little ones have gone home. Audience: Young children and their parents. Rating:* ★★★

⑰ Curious George Goes to Town. The celebrated simian visits the Man with the Yellow Hat in a no-line, no-waiting alternative to other rides. The main town square is here with brightly colored building facades, and the plaza is an interactive aqua play area that adults avoid but kids are attracted to like fish to water. Yes, there's water, water everywhere, especially atop the clock tower, which periodically dumps a mighty huge 500 gallons down a roof and straight onto a screaming passel of preschoolers. They love it! They also love the levers, valves, pumps, and hoses that gush at the rate of 200 gallons per minute to spray, spritz, splash, and splatter themselves—and each other. At the head of the square, footprints lead to a dry play area, with a rope climb and a ball cage where youngsters can frolic among thousands of foam balls. Parents can get into the act, sit it out on nearby benches, or take a few minutes to buy souvenir towels to dry their waterlogged kids. *Duration: As long as you like. Crowds: Heavy in mid-morning. Strategy: Go in late afternoon, or early evening. Audience: Toddlers through preteens and their parents. Rating:* ★★★

Hollywood

Angling off to the right of Plaza of the Stars, Rodeo Drive forms the backbone of Hollywood.

⑱ Gory, Gruesome & Grotesque Horror Make-Up Show. The preshow area is fairly entertaining, showing plaster face masks of Lon Chaney Jr.,

Burgess Meredith, and Jim Backus, as well as methods early film-makers used to create special effect make-up. The real fun kicks off in the theater when a host brings out a "special effects expert" to describe what goes into (and what oozes out of) some of the creepiest effects in films. The actors have had time to work on the script and have taken the liberty to add their own jokes so the show becomes a completely entertaining mix of movie secrets and comedy club timing. Listen for throwaway lines and inside jokes (the kind so popular on shows like *The Simpsons*), that add to the enjoyment of what could have been merely another standard theme park show. *Duration: 25 mins. Crowds: Not daunting. Strategy: Go in the afternoon or evening. Audience: All but young children, who may be frightened; older children eat up the blood-and-guts stories. Rating:* ★★

⑲ **Terminator 2 3-D.** Arnold said he'd be back, and he is, along with the popular film's other main characters, including a buff Linda Hamilton. Universal's show, which combines 3-D cinematography and digital composite computer graphics, was directed by James "Titanic" Cameron and the skill shows. You've entered the headquarters of the futuristic consortium, Cyberdyne, and once inside the theater, a "community relations and media control" hostess greets your group and introduces their latest line of law-enforcing robots. Things go awry (of course), and the Schwarzenegger film, icy fog, live actors, gunfights, and a fantastically chilling grand finale keep the pace moving at 100 mph—although the 3-D effects seem few and far between. Kids may be scared silly and require some counseling, but if you can handle a few surprises then don't miss this one. *Duration: 12 mins. Crowds: Always. Strategy: Go first thing in the morning. Audience: All but very young children, who may be frightened. Rating:* ★★★

⑳ **Lucy: A Tribute.** If you smile when you recall Lucy stomping grapes, practicing ballet, gobbling chocolates, or wailing when Ricky won't let her be in the show, then you need to stop here. This minimuseum (and neighboring major gift shop) pays tribute to Lucille Ball with scripts, props, costumes, awards, and clips from the comedienne's estate. A challenging trivia quiz game has you trying to get Lucy, Ricky, Fred, and Ethel across country to Hollywood. A nice place to take a break and spend time with one of the funniest woman of television. *Duration: About 15 mins. Crowds: Seldom a problem. Strategy: Save this for a peek on your way out or for a hot afternoon. Audience: Adults. Rating:* ★

Strategies for Your Visit to Universal Studios

When to Go
Monday through Wednesday are the busiest days at Universal. The pace slows down on Thursday and Friday and builds again over the weekend. Saturday and Sunday are usually busy, especially during holiday weeks.

Blitz Tour
Universal estimates that at least 14 hours are needed to experience the entire park. If you want to attempt to see everything in one day, arrive early so that you can take care of business and see the fabled attractions before the park gets very crowded.

Don't be distracted by the faux Hollywood streets, and don't be lured into those shops calling to you as you go through the gate. But if you're one of the first people in the park and feel you have the stamina to circle the park twice to catch the A-list rides first and then pick up the B-list later, head to your right and start with **Terminator 2 3-D**; and then

UNIVERSAL:
THE SAGA OF CARL LAEMMLE

ALTHOUGH UNIVERSAL STUDIOS isn't as personality-driven as Walt Disney World, its heritage is every bit as interesting. What you see today—the theme parks, hotels, television programs, movie releases, records—all started on a crowded commercial street in Chicago in 1906. Carl Laemmle, a German immigrant and haberdasher, worked near a nickelodeon and noticed a curious fact: more people were waiting to watch silent films than to buy custom-tailored clothes. Laemmle had enough cash to rent a vacant building and open the White Front Theatre and within three years had created a chain of small theaters. However, Laemmle's streamlined operation soon ran up against the powerful force of Thomas Edison. Edison, who had invented most of the projection equipment used in America's theaters, had organized a monopoly of production companies that could control the production, distribution, and exhibition of movies. On principle, Laemmle resisted Edison's demand for patent and license fees and for showing only films produced by Edison and his partners. Not surprisingly, Laemmle soon stopped receiving movies. With no pictures to show, the film distributor had to get creative. In 1909 Laemmle struck back by forming the Independent Motion Picture Company and cranked out a series of silent shorts and features.

By 1912 he watched with satisfaction as a court order broke up Edison's monopoly. Two months later, Laemmle merged his forces with three other companies, and when it came time to select a name to reflect the new concern, he looked out his office window and saw the name "Universal Pipe Fittings" painted on the side of a cart. A few minutes later, the Universal Film Manufacturing Company was formed.

It wasn't long before Laemmle realized that shooting movies was far easier in Hollywood than in Chicago, and he consolidated his studios on the West Coast and produced 250 films in the first year. As the complex grew from the southern California ranchlands, Universal City was born, and on March 15, 1915, the studios were opened to the public for a gala grand opening. Twenty thousand people turned out. Recognizing the potential for profits, Laemmle began charging tourists 25¢ each to come to sit in the bleachers, eat a box lunch, and watch silent movies being made.

It was only after the arrival of talkies that Carl Laemmle, Jr.—now in charge of production—decided that Universal would scale down the number of productions in favor of improving their quality. The results were immediately noticeable when, in 1930, the classic *All Quiet on the Western Front* received the Academy Award for Best Picture. And when the nation slipped into the Great Depression, Universal maintained their standards by producing movies such as *Dracula* (1931), *Frankenstein* (1931), and *The Invisible Man* (1933).

It wasn't until the 1960s that Universal executives returned to Laemmles's concept that people would pay to see movies being made, and with Universal's involvement in television (Jack Benny, *Leave It To Beaver, The Munsters*, Alfred Hitchcock), there was always something happening at the Universal lot. The Hollywood tour became a consistent favorite for tourists in Southern California, and a spin-off was a natural. In 1990, Universal Studios Florida premiered on 840 acres just a few miles north of Walt Disney World in Orlando. Despite a rocky start, the theme park has expanded to become a full-fledged resort with an entertainment complex, luxury hotels, and an international reputation—all thanks to the vision of a moderately successful German tailor.

–Gary McKechnie

make tracks down the street to **Back to the Future . . . The Ride** while the lines are still at a minimum. Continuing counter-clockwise, the new **Men In Black: Alien Attack** is next, followed by must-see **Jaws, Earthquake— The Big One,** and, finally, near the entrance, **Twister: Ride It Out.**

You've just circled the park, and chances are the crowds have arrived. Based on your personal preferences, you can backtrack to pick up second-string attractions like **Alfred Hitchcock's 3-D Theatre,** the **FUNtastic World of Hanna-Barbera, Wild, Wild, Wild West Stunt Show,** and the **Gory, Gruesome & Grotesque Horror Make-Up Show.** The remaining rides and attractions are up to you. If the lines are short, all that remains are **Kongfrontation,** a tour of **Nickelodeon Studios,** the collection at **Woody Woodpecker's KidZone,** and **Lucy: A Tribute.** It's been a full day, and you just may have compressed 14 hours of fun into a 10-hour day.

On Rainy Days

Except during Christmas week, crowds are almost nonexistent at Universal Studios on rainy days—even though the park is in full operation and there are many places to take shelter from downpours. It's one of your best bets in the area in rainy weather. Only a couple of street shows are canceled because of bad weather.

Other Tips

- Hours change with the seasons and the park, so be sure to call the day before your visit to get official, up-to-the-minute information.

- The best way to see the top attractions is to stay at a Universal resort hotel. As a resort guest, you get the privilege of early admission—which may be two or three hours before anyone else enters the park. Not all rides will be open, but most of the more popular ones will be.

- Arrive in the parking lot 45 minutes early and see the biggest attractions first.

- Have a filling snack at 10:30, lunch after 2, and dinner at 8 or later. Or lunch on the early side at Lombard's Landing. Make your reservations ahead of time or, at the very least, when you enter the park, then dine at 5.

- If you're traveling with small children, avoid backtracking. Universal is just too big. Anticipate their getting wet at Fievel's Playland—and bring a bathing suit or change of clothing.

- Set up a rendezvous point and time at the start of the day, just in case you and your companions get separated. Good places are in front of the Slime Geyser by Nickelodeon Studios, by the stage area across from Mel's Drive-In, or by the seating area of Beetlejuice's Graveyard Revue.

- Be sure to write down your parking location. Aptly named after famous Universal movies, such as *Jaws* or *King Kong,* they may seem hard to forget. But a day of high-tech special effects will easily do the job, and you'll be glad to have the written note.

- When entering the park, many guests are taken by the towering soundstages to their left. Head to your right (bypassing shops and restaurants) to avoid crowds, especially early in the day.

Universal Studios A to Z

Baby Care

There are diaper-changing tables in both men's and women's rest rooms; nursing facilities are at Guest Relations (just inside Universal Studios Main Entrance and to the right), as well as at First Aid, adjoining Louie's Italian Restaurant between Amity's San Francisco and New York. No diapers are sold on the premises; instead, they're complimentary—to guests in need—at the Universal Studios Store and other locations. Strollers—which look like Jurassic Park jeeps—are for rent just inside the Main Entrance to the right, next to the First Union National Bank (singles $7, doubles $12; no deposit required). No formula or baby food is sold on the premises; the nearest sources are Kmart on Sand Lake Road, Walgreen on Kirkman Road, and Publix supermarkets on Sand Lake and Kirkman roads.

Baby Exchange

Many rides have Baby Exchange areas, so that one parent or adult party member can watch a baby or toddler while the other enjoys the ride or show. The adults then change roles, and the former caretaker rides without having to wait in line all over again.

Cameras and Film

At the **Lights, Camera, Action** shop in the Front Lot, just inside the Universal Studios Main Entrance, you'll find rental video cameras ($29.95 per day; deposit or credit-card imprint required). You must show a valid driver's license and a major credit card.

For minor camera repairs and one-hour film developing, go to the **Dark Room,** on Hollywood Boulevard.

Dining

Most eateries are on Plaza of the Stars and Hollywood Boulevard. Several restaurants accept reservations. To make them (as far in advance as you want), just call the restaurant or go there in person first thing in the morning.

FULL-SERVICE RESTAURANTS
Amity's **Lombard's Landing** (☎ 407/224–6400) is designed to resemble a warehouse from 19th-century San Francisco.

At the corner of Hollywood Boulevard and 8th Avenue—which turns into Sunset Boulevard along the bottom shore of the lagoon—is **Mel's Drive-In** (no reservations), a flashy '50s eatery with a menu and decorative muscle cars straight out of *American Graffiti*. For burgers and fries, this is one of the best choices in the park, and it comes complete with a roving doo-wop group. You're on vacation—go ahead and have that extra-thick shake. Mel's is also a great place to meet, in case you decide to go your separate ways in the park.

Production Central's **Classic Monsters Cafe** (☎ 407/363–8769) is the place for pizza and pasta. Frankenstein and other scary characters from vintage Universal films make the rounds of the tables as you eat. Be sure to check out the very funny monster-meets-celebrity pictures at the entrance.

SELF-SERVICE RESTAURANTS
The **International Food Bazaar,** near *Back to the Future . . .* The Ride, is an efficient, multiethnic food court serving Italian, American, German, Greek, and Chinese dishes at affordable prices (usually $5.95 or $6.75 per entrée). The Italian Caesar salad and Greek salads are especially welcome on a muggy day.

For Travelers with Disabilities

As in Walt Disney World's major parks, each attraction has an audio portion that appeals to those with visual impairments and a visual portion to interest those with hearing impairments. But Universal Studios also made an all-out effort not only to make the premises physically accessible for those with disabilities but also to lift attitudinal barriers. All employees now attend disability awareness workshops to remind them that people with disabilities are people first. And you can occasionally spot staffers using wheelchairs. Additionally, power-assist buttons make it easier to get past heavy, hard-to-open doors; lap tables are provided for guests in shops; and already accessible bathroom facilities have niceties such as insulated under-sink pipes and companion rest rooms. Parts of the park that once had cobblestone streets now have paved paths, and photo spots have been modified for wheelchair accessibility. Various attractions have been retrofitted (although Islands of Adventure was built with wheelchairs in mind) so that most can be boarded directly in a standard wheelchair; those using oversize vehicles or scooters must transfer to a standard model—these are available at the ride's entrance—or into the ride vehicle.

ATTRACTIONS

Alfred Hitchcock's 3-D Theatre, Animal Actors Stage Show, the **Gory, Gruesome & Grotesque Horror Make-Up Show, Beetlejuice's Graveyard Revue,** the **Wild, Wild, Wild West Stunt Show,** *Twister:* **Ride It Out,** and *Terminator 2* **3-D** are all completely wheelchair-accessible, theater-style attractions. Guests with visual impairments enjoy all of these shows, but sound and special effects make all but Alfred Hitchcock's 3-D Theatre inappropriate for service animals.

To ride *E.T.* **Adventure,** you must transfer to the ride vehicle or to a standard-size wheelchair if you're not already using one. Service animals are not permitted. There is some sudden tilting and accelerating, but anyone with heart, back, or neck problems can ride in E.T.'s orbs (the spaceships) instead of the flying bicycles. Guests who use wheelchairs must transfer to the ride vehicles to experience **Woody Woodpecker's Nuthouse Coaster,** but most of **Curious George Goes to Town** is barrier-free.

If you use a standard-size wheelchair or can transfer to one or to the ride vehicle directly, you can board **Kongfrontation,** *Earthquake—***The Big One,** *Jaws,* and *Men In Black* directly. If turbulence is a problem for you, you shouldn't ride, and service animals should not ride. Note that guests with visual impairments as well as those using wheelchairs should cross Amity's San Francisco with care.

The **Nickelodeon Studios** tour is also completely accessible by guests using wheelchairs and enjoyable for guests with other disabilities. If you lip-read, ask to stay up front. The **FUNtastic World of Hanna-Barbera** is completely accessible by guests using wheelchairs. However, your experience will be more intense if you can transfer to a ride seat and tolerate your vehicle's sudden sharp accelerations, climbs, stops, dives, and banked turns. If you can't, you can still experience the attraction, albeit from a stationary seat. Guests with other disabilities who enjoy other thrill rides will enjoy this one as well.

Lucy: A Tribute is wheelchair accessible, but the TV-show excerpts shown on overhead screens are not close-captioned. *Back to the Future . . .* **The Ride** is not accessible to people who use wheelchairs, nor are service animals permitted.

ENTERTAINMENT

There are special viewing areas at all of the outdoor shows.

RESTAURANTS

All restaurants are wheelchair accessible.

SERVICES

Many Universal Studios employees have had basic sign-language training; even some of the animated characters speak sign, albeit—because many have only four fingers—an adapted version. Like Walt Disney World, Universal supplements the visuals with a special guidebook containing story lines and scripts for the main attractions. The **"Studio Guide for Guests with Disabilities"** pinpoints special entrances available for those with disabilities; these routes often bypass the attraction's line. In addition, **cassettes** with narrative descriptions of the various attractions can be borrowed, along with portable tape players. You can get these and the various booklets at Guest Relations, just inside the Main Entrance and to the right. There is an **outgoing TTY** on the counter in Guest Relations.

WHEELCHAIR RENTALS

Wheelchairs ($7) and electric wheelchairs ($30) can be rented in Amity's New England and just inside the Main Entrance, to the right, next to the First Union National Bank. There's no deposit, but advance reservations for the motorized wheelchairs are recommended. If the wheelchair breaks down, disappears, or otherwise needs replacing, speak to any shop attendant.

Entertainment

If you're in Orlando at the right time of year, don't miss Universal's evening **seasonal parties**—most notably Mardi Gras and the wildly popular Halloween Horror Nights. Dazzling parades, live shows, and gastronomic delights are special features of these extravaganzas, which require a separate admission. Regular visitors are shooed out around 6; to get back in for the party, you need to buy another ticket. However, combination park-party tickets are available.

First Aid

Universal Studios' First Aid Center is between New York and Amity's San Francisco, next to Louie's Italian Restaurant.

Guided Tours

Universal has two **VIP Tours,** which offer what's called "back-door admission" or, in plain English, the right to jump the line. It's the ultimate capitalist fantasy and worthwhile if you're in a hurry, if the day is crowded, and if you have the money to burn—from $120 for an individual four-hour VIP tour, including park admission, to $1,700 for an eight-hour tour for up to 15 people, again including park admission—but not including tax. You will see Hanna-Barbera, *Twister,* Kongfrontation, *Earthquake, Jaws, Terminator 2, Back to the Future,* and *E.T.,* but if there are other attractions you'd like to see or some you'd like to skip, your guide will suggest something else. Best of all, the guides can answer practically any question you can throw at them—they're masters of Universal trivia.

Hours

Universal Studios is open 365 days a year from 9 to 7, with hours as late as 10 during summer and holiday periods. Since hours vary by season and park, make sure to call ahead.

Lockers

Lockers (50¢) are across from Guest Relations, with additional lockers located near the park exit (located on your left as you enter Universal Studios).

Lost Things and People

Misplaced possessions go to Guest Relations. If you lose your children or traveling companions, speak up immediately at Guest Relations or at Security—behind Louie's, between New York and San Francisco.

Money Matters

The First Union National Bank, just inside the Main Entrance, cashes traveler's checks, makes cash advances on credit cards, and exchanges foreign currency. There's one ATM at the bank and another outside the Main Entrance, to the right of the Guest Relations window; they're linked to Plus, Honor, Cirrus, Visa, and MasterCard.

Shopping

Every ride and every attraction has its affiliated theme shop; in addition, Rodeo Drive and Hollywood Boulevard are pockmarked with money pits. It's important to remember that few attraction-specific souvenirs are sold outside of their own shop, so if you're struck by Fred Flintstone "yabba dabba doo" boxer shorts at the Hanna-Barbera Shop, seize the moment—and the shorts. Other choice souvenirs include Universal Studios' trademark movie clipboard, available at the **Universal Studio Store**; sepia prints of Richard Gere, Mel Gibson, and Marilyn Monroe from **Silver Screen Collectibles**; supercool Blues Brothers sunglasses from **Shaiken's Souvenirs**; the little plush King Konglets from Kongfrontation, available at **Safari Outfitters, Ltd.**; and stuffed animals of Hanna-Barbera characters, sold at the **Hanna-Barbera Store.**

Stop by Hollywood's **Brown Derby** for the perfect topper, from fedoras to bush hats from *Jurassic Park*.

Visitor Information

Visit **Guest Relations,** in the Front Lot to the right after you pass through the turnstiles, for brochures, maps, and a schedule of the day's entertainment, tapings, and filmings.

Studio Information Boards in front of Studio Stars and Mel's Drive-In restaurants provide up-to-the-minute ride and show operating information—including the length of lines at the major attractions.

ISLANDS OF ADVENTURE

From the outset, the creators of Islands of Adventure sought to take the theme park as an entertainment form to a whole new level—and they've succeeded brilliantly. From Marvel Super Hero Island and Toon Lagoon to Seuss Landing, Jurassic Park, and the Lost Continent, every section of the park is very impressive, and, in shows and attractions and rides, they may have out-Disneyed Disney. Although it's not as easy to grasp as the logically laid out themes of other theme parks, IOA is more entertaining because it's doing what hasn't been done to death. If you can ignore the highly contrived story lines plastered onto every single ride, and try to forget that the designers try to put a positive spin on queues that can stretch more than ½ *mi* in length, then you're in for a day (or two) of fun. There are obviously some star attractions here, and a few that fall flat, but overall IOA has something to appeal to everyone. The park's five theme islands are connected by walkways and arranged around a large central lagoon, and the waterside setting is a good place to relax when the madding crowds descend in peak season or after you've exited an adrenaline-surging coaster. A minor warning: the relatively new park is still fine-tuning some sites. You may find restaurants closed, shows down, and attractions being replaced or repaired. Don't assume everything will be operating at peak performance.

After passing the turnstiles, you've arrived at the plaza called the Port of Entry. This international bazaar has selected bits and pieces of architecture, landscaping, music, and wares from a variety of sources, so you may see windmills and Indonesian pedicabs and African masks and Egyptian figurines in the mix. It's a visually stimulating area, and a massive archway inscribed with the statement "The Adventure Begins" seems to epitomize truth in advertising. There are bakeries and food carts and small restaurants where you are supposed to buy provisions for your journey, but this is the first of many unnecessary story lines you're supposed to follow. Just bypass the gift and food shops until later and head right into the park itself.

Numbers in the margin correspond to points of interest on the Islands of Adventure map.

Seuss Landing

The good doctor's eradication of a monotonous plague called "Dick and Jane" helped teach a nation of kids that reading could be fun. This single 10-acre island is the perfect tribute to Theodor Seuss Geisel, putting into three dimensions what we had only seen on the printed page. Adults arrive and instantly recall why Seuss was their favorite author, and kids are introduced to the Cat, Things One and Two, Horton, the Lorax, and Grinch. Visually, this is the most exciting parcel of real estate in America. From the topiary sculptures to the jumbo red-and-white striped hat near the entrance, the design is as whimsical as his books. Fencing is bent into curvy shapes, lampposts are lurching, and the Seussian characters that bristle atop the buildings seem to defy gravity. Even the trees grow in curves: a group of palm trees that had been growing sideways after Hurricane Andrew downed them a few years ago in southern Florida now wiggle happily skyward again in Seuss Landing. The sound track has the snargly feel of the pages of Seuss; the composer actually built some of the instruments played by Geisel's Whoville musicians and used them in the music. And everything, even the pavement, glows in what one of the park designers called "edible colors"—lavenders, pinks, peaches, and oranges. Flowers in the planters echo the sherbet hues of the pavement. In stores such as **Cats Hats & Things** and **Mulberry Store,** you'll find Seuss books and wonderful Seussian souvenirs, from funny hats to Cat-top pencils and bold red-and-white stripe coffee mugs. **Gertrude McFuzz' Fine-Feathered Finery** sells Seussian toppers. And when you're inspired to acquire a bit of two-dimensional Dr. Seuss, you can stop in to **Dr. Seuss' All the Books You Can Read.**

Don't miss **Sneetch Beach** (follow the sign near **Goose Juice**), where the Sneetches are frolicking in the lagoon alongside a strand littered with their beach things; the Seussonic boom box even has its own sound track, complete with commercials. Look carefully in the sand and you'll see where the Sneetches jumped the fence to get to the beach, fell flat on their faces, and finally started dragging their radio rather than carrying it. Nearby is the **Zax Bypass**—two Zaks facing off because neither one will budge. And keep an eye peeled for the characters—the grouchy Grinch, Thing One and Thing Two, and even the Cat himself.

❶ **Cat in the Hat.** Nostalgia strikes a chord when you enter the pages of the breakthrough reader. If you ever harbored a secret belief that a cat could actually come to your house to wreak havoc while your mom was out, then you get to live the experience here. After boarding a couch that soon spins, whirls, and rocks through the house, you roll past 18 scenes, 30 characters, and 130 effects that put you in the presence of the mischievous cat. He balances on a ball; hoists china on his umbrella, Thing 1, and his wild sibling, Thing 2; and flies kites in the house; and the voice of reason, the fish in the teapot, sounds the warning about

Islands of Adventure

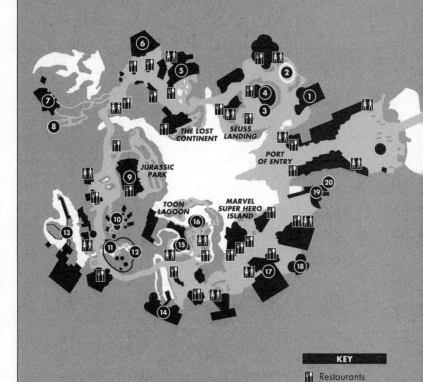

KEY

🍴 Restaurants

🚹🚺 Rest rooms

the impending return of the family matriarch. This is high drama—and more fun than you should be allowed to have. Don't miss it. *Crowds: Very heavy. Strategy: Go near the end of the day, when the children go home. Audience: All ages. Children under 48" must be accompanied by an adult. Rating:* ★★

❷ One Fish, Two Fish, Red Fish, Blue Fish. Dr. Seuss put elephants in trees and green eggs and ham on trains, so it doesn't seem far-fetched that fish can circle "squirting posts" to a Jamaican beat. After a rather lengthy wait, climb into your Seussian-style fish, and as it spins, you (or your child) control its up-and-down motion. The key is to follow the lyrics of the special song—if you go down when the song tells you to go up, you may be drenched courtesy of the afore-mentioned "squirting post." Mighty silly, mighty fun. *Crowds: Thick all day. Strategy: Go at the end of your visit when the tykes have left, so you can be a kid at heart. Otherwise, skip on your first visit. Audience: Young children. Children under 48" must be accompanied by an adult. Rating:* ★★

NEED A BREAK? | Inside **Circus McGurkus** fast-food eatery, you can grab a quick bite. Check out the walrus balancing on a whisker and the names on the booths: Tum-tumied Swumm, Rolf from the Ocean of Olf, the Remarkable Foon.

❸ If I Ran the Zoo. The best thing about kid-sized playgrounds is that they can ditch the adults and have fun at their level. In this Seussian maze, they encounter the trademarked fantasy creatures as they climb, jump, push buttons, and animate strange and wonderful animals. Park designers have learned that kids' basic needs include eating, sleeping, and getting splashed so they've thoughtfully added interactive fountains. *Duration: Up to you and your young ones. Crowds: Probably heaviest early in the day. Strategy: If you can talk your kids into waiting, come at the end of your visit. Audience: Young children. Rating:* ★★

❹ Caro-Seuss-el. The centerpiece of Seuss Landing could have come straight from the pages of a Seuss book. Ordinary horse-centered merry-go-rounds are extinct now that you've seen your new menagerie: the cowfish from *McElligott's Pool,* the elephant birds from *Horton Hatches the Egg,* and the Birthday Katroo from *Happy Birthday to You*— a veritable ark of imaginary animals. And because this is a 21st-century merry-go-round, the 54 mounts are interactive: the animals' eyes blink and their tails wag when you get on. It's a cliché to say you'll feel like a kid again, but you will when you hop aboard one of these fantastic creatures. *Crowds: Lines move pretty well, so don't be intimidated. Strategy: Make this a special end to your day. Audience: All ages. Children under 48" must be accompanied by an adult. Rating:* ★★

NEED A BREAK? | Pick up an ice cream at the **Hop on Pop Ice Cream Shop** or a fanciful drink at **Moose Juice Goose Juice**—the names are part of the fun here.

Lost Continent

Antique myths from around the world inspired this land. Pass the huge mythical birds guarding the entrances and the trees hung with weathered metal lanterns, and you hear distant booming thunder mixing with shimmering New Agey chimes and vaguely Celtic melodies. Farther along, the setting is like a sanitized version of a Renaissance Festival. Seers and fortune-tellers in a tent hung with silken draperies and carpeted with vintage Oriental carpets are on hand at **Mystics of the Seven Veils.** They read palms, tarot cards, and credit cards. **Tangles of**

Truth sells ingenious puzzles; it's fun just to stop and watch people as they try to extricate themselves from the $12 People Puzzles. The **Dragon's Keep** sells Celtic jewelry along with stuffed dragons, toy swords in various sizes and materials, and perfectly dreadful fake rats, mice, and body parts. And **Treasures of Poseidon** is stocked with shells and some baubles made from them. In one of the many nooks and crannies in this land, a **Talking Fountain** offers flip responses to guest questions, such as "Is there a God?" Answer: "Yes. He's from Trenton and his name is Julio." Watch out: you may get sprayed if you stand too close.

❺ **Poseidon's Fury: Escape from the Lost City.** The cool ruins of the Colossus of Rhodes will lure you into a darkened temple in which, after a long and winding wait, you enter an anteroom where you are joined by an old man who recounts the legend of the Lost City and battles between Poseidon and Zeus. The preshow continues in a larger, tiered theater in which a decorative medallion spins and unlocks a passage to a tunnel. Led by a guide, you walk through the tunnel, which is made all the more intriguing since the water that spins below and above(!) gives you a sensation similar to being sucked into a whirlpool—hard to describe, hard to forget. Finally, the third room is the payoff: the showdown between Poseidon and Zeus. This is when the fireworks (and waterworks) begin. Roughly 350,000 gallons of water, 200 flame effects, massive crashing waves, thick columns of water, and scorching fireballs are erupting all around you. Loud, powerful, hyperactive, and, if you stand in the splash zone, drenching. *Duration: 20 mins. Crowds: Heavy all the time. Strategy: Go toward the end of the day. Stay to the left against the wall as you enter and position yourself opposite the podium in the center of the room. In each succeeding section of the presentation, get into the very first row, particularly if you aren't tall. Audience: Older children and adults. Rating:* ★★★

❻ **Eighth Voyage of Sindbad.** It's impossible not to get a kick out of stunt shows, and here's another example (although Disney's Indiana Jones is still the winner). Here's the easy-to-follow story line: Sindbad and his sidekick arrive in search of treasure, get distracted by the beautiful princess, and are threatened by a sorceress. The good guy spends the whole 25 nonstop minutes punching, climbing, kicking, diving, leaping, and Douglas Fairbanks–ing his way through the performance that features water explosions, flames, and pyrotechnics. Kids love the action, women love Sindbad. The 1,700-seat theater is a welcome respite from the low-capacity attractions you've seen so far. A nice place to sit a spell and replenish your energy. *Duration: 25 mins. Crowds: Not a problem, due to size of the open-air auditorium. Strategy: Stake out seats about 15 mins prior to show time. Don't sit too close up front— you won't get the whole picture as well. Audience: Older children and adults. Rating:* ★★

NEED A
BREAK?   Pick up soft drinks at **Oasis Coolers.** Or head for **The Frozen Desert**—and be sure to check out the gleaming mosaic sign, with its gilded tiles, as you wait for your chance to order a swirled fruit-and-ice-cream sundae.

❼ **Dueling Dragons.** What you'll remember most about this ride is the fact you had to walk *3,180 ft* (more than a ½ mi!) before you settle into the red coaster (Fire Dragon) or blue coaster (Ice Dragon). The creative team says the forced march is because the preshow queue through Merlinwood Forest and Merlinwood Castle tells the story of the knights who inspired the Fire and Ice coasters. Eventually, you climb into cars suspended from the track so your feet are dangling freely, and as you whip through corkscrews and loops and are flung upside down and around, your legs are flying off into the wild blue yonder. With each coaster on a separate track, the thrill is in the near misses, which makes front-row seats a prized commodity. Coaster weights are checked by a computer, which programs the cars to have near-misses as close as 12 inches apart. Top speeds on the ride ranges 55–60 mph, with the Fire Dragon offering more inversions and the Ice Dragon providing more cornering. Either way, you'll want to take advantage of the small lockers where you can stash your stuff; wallets, glasses, change, and, perhaps, an air sickness bag. *Duration: 2 mins 25 secs. Crowds: Perpetual. Strategy: Ride after dark, when most visitors are going home; or go early. For the most exciting ride, go for the rear car of the Fire Dragon or the front car of the Ice Dragon; be aware that the queues for the front car of both coasters are much longer. Audience: Older children with roller-coaster experience and adults with cast-iron stomachs. No pregnant women or guests with heart, back, or neck problems. Minimum height: 54". Rating:* ★★★

⑧ Flying Unicorn. If you made the mistake of putting your kid on Dueling Dragons, the antidote may be this child-sized roller coaster which opened in the summer of 2000. Following a walk through a wizard's workshop, the low-key thrill ride places kids on the back of a unicorn for a ride through a mythical forest. *Duration: Not available at presstime. Crowds: Audience: Kids under 7, with adults riding along for moral support. Minimum height: Not available at presstime. Rating:* ★★★

NEED A BREAK?	If you're ready to toast your conquest of mortal fear, head straight across the plaza for the **Enchanted Oak Tavern,** ingeniously sprawled inside the huge base of a gnarled old oak tree. Order a glass of the park's own Dragon Scale Ale at the Alchemy Bar, or chow down on barbecued chicken and ribs or corn on the cob.

Jurassic Park

Walk through the arched gates of Jurassic Park and you'll detect a distinct difference in mood. The music is stirring and slightly ominous, the vegetation tropical and junglelike. All this, plus the high-tension wires and warning signs do a great job of re-creating the Jurassic Park of Steven Spielberg's blockbuster movie. The half-fun, half-frightening **Jurassic Park River Adventure** is the island's standout attraction, bringing to life key segments of the movie's climax.

⑨ Jurassic Park Discovery Center. If there's a scintilla of information your kids don't know about dinosaurs, they can learn it here. There are demonstration areas where a realistic raptor is being hatched and where you can see what you'd look like (or sound like) if you were a dino. In the Beasaurus area ("Be-a-Saurus"), you can look at the world from a dinosaur's point of view. There are numerous hands-on exhibits and a "Jeopardy!"-style quiz game where you can test your knowledge of dinosaur trivia. Upstairs is a casual restaurant. *Duration: As long as you like. Crowds: People mingle throughout, so that crowded feeling is almost extinct. Strategy: Go anytime. Audience: Older children and adults. Rating:* ★★

⑩ Triceratops Encounter. So far, you've seen stunning attractions that mix fact and fantasy, but this little walk-through exhibit seems the most surreal. No, this is *not* a real triceratops, but a 24-ft-long, 10-ft-high interactive robot that blinks and moves slightly when touched. Trainers fill you in on her family history, emotional state, and feeding habits.

Duration: Up to you. Crowds: Minimal. Strategy: Go anytime. Audience: All ages. Rating: ★

⓫ **Camp Jurassic.** Remember when you were a kid content with just a swing set and monkey bars? Well, those days have been replaced by fantastic play areas like this that are interwoven with the island's theme. Built primarily for kids, some adults join in, racing along footpaths through the forests, slithering down slides, clambering over swinging bridges and across boiling streams, scrambling up net climbs and rock formations, and exploring mysterious caves full of faux lava. Keep an eye open for the dinosaur footprints; when you jump on them, a dinosaur roars somewhere (different footprints are associated with different roars). Watch out for the watery cross fire nearby—or join in the shooting yourself. *Duration: As long as you want. Crowds: Sometimes more, sometimes less. Strategy: Go anytime. Audience: One and all. Rating:* ★★★

⓬ **Pteranodon Flyers.** These gondolas are eye-catching and can't help but tempt you to stand in line for a lift. The problem is that these wide wing-spanned chairs provide a very slow, very low capacity ride that will eat up a lot of your park time. Do it if you want a prehistoric bird's-eye view of the *Jurassic Park* compound. Otherwise, keep it moving. *Duration: 2 mins. Crowds: Perpetual, and since the ride loads slowly, waits can last 1 hr or more. Strategy: Skip this on your first few visits. Audience: All ages. Children under 48" must be accompanied by an adult. Rating:* ★

⓭ **Jurassic Park River Adventure.** Thanks to high-capacity rafts, the line moves fairly quickly to get you on a peaceful cruise on a mysterious river past friendly, vegetarian dinosaurs. Of course, something has to go amiss or it wouldn't be much fun at all. A wrong turn is what it takes, and when you enter one of the research departments and see that it's overrun by spitting dinosaurs and razor-clawed raptors, things get plenty scary. This is all a buildup to the big finish: a towering, roaring T Rex with teeth the size of hams that guards the exit. By some strange quirk of fate, a convenient escape arrives via a tremendously steep and watery 85-ft plunge that'll start you screaming. Smile! This is when the souvenir photos are shot. *Duration: 6 mins. Crowds: Huge all day long. Strategy: Go early or late. Audience: All but young children, who may be frightened. No pregnant women or guests with heart, back, or neck problems. Minimum height: 42". Rating:* ★★★

NEED A BREAK?   Watch your fellow travelers make their harrowing plunge from the **Thunder Falls Terrace.** One side is entirely glass for an optimal view. Or sit outdoors next to the river's thundering waterfall.

Toon Lagoon

It's an abrupt transition moving from Jurassic Park to Toon Lagoon, since the colors and theme between the two are worlds apart. Its main street, Comic Strip Lane, features cartoon characters that are instantly recognizable to anyone—anyone born before 1923, that is. Pert little Betty Boop, gangling Olive Oyl, muscle-bound Popeye, Krazy Kat, Mark Trail, Flash Gordon, Pogo, and Ally-Oop are featured, as are the relatively more contemporary Dudley Do-Right, Rocky, Bullwinkle, Beetle Bailey, Cathy, and Hagar the Horrible. Either way, the colorful backdrop and chirpy music is as cheerful as Jurassic Park is portentous. The merchandise is great, too. One whole store is devoted to Rocky and Bullwinkle trinkets, and you'll find a spate of clever Betty Boop items that are pretty hard to pass up.

⑭ **Dudley Do-Right's Ripsaw Falls.** Named after the fictional city from the popular 1960s animated pun-fest *Rocky and Bullwinkle,* this flume ride with a theme is definitely wet and wild. You're supposed to help Dudley rescue Nell, his belle, from the evil and conniving Snidely Whiplash, but by the time your mission is accomplished, you've dropped through the rooftop of a ramshackle dynamite shack and made an explosive dive 15 ft below water level into a 400,000-gallon lagoon, and you're not just damp—you're soaked to the skin. Actually, the final drop looks much scarier than it really is; the fact that the ride vehicles have no restraining devices at all cues you in to the danger quotient here. The beauty of the ride is that you never know quite what's ahead—and you're definitely not expecting the big thrill when the time comes. As you wait, check out the posters, which announce films coming to Rocky and Bullwinkle land: "The Silence of the Hams," "Nots Landing," and so on. By the way, if the weather is cold and you absolutely must stay dry, you can pick up a poncho at **Gasoline Alley,** opposite the entrance. *Crowds: Count on long lines all day. Strategy: Go in late afternoon, when you're hot as can be, or at day's end, when you're ready to head back to your car. There is no seat where you can stay dry. Audience: All but the youngest children. No pregnant women or guests with heart, back, or neck problems. Minimum height: 44"; children under 48" must be accompanied by an adult. Rating:* ★★★

⑮ **Popeye & Bluto's Bilge-Rat Barges.** At times this river ride is quiet, but often it's a bumping, churning, twisting, white-water raft ride that'll drench you and your fellow travelers. Like every ride at IOA, there's a story line here, but the real attraction is getting soaked, splashed, sprayed, or deluged. The degree of wetness varies since your circular raft may or may not spin in time to place you beneath torrents of water flooding from a shoreline water tower or streaming from water guns from an adjacent play area. There are lockers at the boarding area for anything you'd prefer to keep dry; and for a fee, towels are available at the exit. *Duration: 5 mins. Crowds: Heavy all day. Strategy: Go first thing in the morning or about 1 hr before closing. Audience: All but young children. No pregnant women or guests with heart, back, or neck problems or motion sickness. Minimum height: 48"; children under 48" must be accompanied by an adult. Rating:* ★★★

⑯ **Me Ship, the Olive.** From bow to stern, dozens of participatory activities keep families busy as they climb around this boat moored on the edge of Toon Lagoon. Toddlers enjoy crawling in Swee' Pea's Playpen, while older children and their parents take aim at unsuspecting riders locked into the Bilge-Rat Barges. Primarily, this is designed for kids, with hands-on activities such as whistles, bells, and organs to trigger, as well as narrow tunnels to climb through and ladders to climb up. Check out the view of the park from the top of the ship. *Duration: As long as you wish. Crowds: Fairly heavy all day. Strategy: If you are with young children, go in the morning or around dinnertime. Audience: Young children. Rating:* ★★

Marvel Super Hero Island

This island might return you to the halcyon days of yesteryear when you could name every hero and villain in a Marvel comic book. The facades along Stanley Boulevard (named for Marvel's famed editor and cocreator Stan Lee) put you smack in the middle of these adventures, with primary cartoony colors and signage ("Arcade" and "Food" and "Ice Cream" for instance, reveal the store's inventory). Although the spiky, horrific tower of **Doctor Doom's Fearfall** suggests the island's top attraction, the **Amazing Adventures of Spider-Man** is the one to

UNIVERSAL TIME SAVING TIPS

FOR BETTER OR WORSE, Universal Orlando isn't nearly the size of the Walt Disney World resort, so navigating it is much easier. There are also some hints at reducing wait times and accessing the park.

If you want to get to the best rides faster, skip the gargantuan parking garage and follow the signs to valet parking. For $12—just $5 more than the price of regular parking—you'll be in a lot just a few steps from the entrance to CityWalk and have a head start in reaching Universal Studios and Islands of Adventure, as well.

If you're toting a baby around with you, check out the baby exchange areas. Although you won't be able to ride with your spouse, one parent can enter the attraction, take a spin, and then return to take care of the baby while the other parent rides without having to wait in line again.

And when you stay at one of Universal's resort hotels (Portofino Bay, Hard Rock Hotel, Royal Pacific) you receive early admission to the parks, priority seating at some restaurants, and the option of an unlimited access ticket.

Do what you can to get into Universal Orlando's theme parks early—as early as 7 AM. When there are no crowds, you can accomplish in a few hours what it will take all day to do if you get here with everyone else.

see. Aside from rides, at various times Doctor Doom, Spider-Man, and the Incredible Hulk are available for photos, and sidewalk artists are on hand to paint your face like your favorite hero (or villain). Dominating the scenery is the Hulk's own coaster, its track colored a vivid lime green. Along with a hard-driving rock sound track, screams emanating from Doctor Doom's and from the Hulk Coaster set the mood for this sometimes pleasant, sometimes apocalyptic world.

⓱ **The Amazing Adventures of Spider-Man.** Even if you had never heard of Peter Parker or J. Jonah Jameson or had a clue what evil forces Spider-Man faces, the four and a half minutes spent in this building can validate the two hours you stood in line. This is unlike any ride at any theme park anywhere, combining moving vehicles, 3-D film, simulator technology, and special effects. In brief, after a turning and torturous wait in the *Daily Bugle's* offices, you learn that members of the Sinister Syndicate (Doctor Octopus (a.k.a. Doc Oc), Electro, Hobgoblin, Hydro Man, and deadly Scream) have used their Doomsday Anti-Gravity Gun to steal the Statue of Liberty. None of this matters, really, since once you board your car and don your 3-D glasses, you are instantly swept up into a weird cartoon battle between good and evil. When Spider-Man lands on your car, you feel the bump; when Electro runs overhead, you hear his footsteps following you. You feel the sizzle of electricity, a frigid spray of water from Hydro Man, and the heat from a flaming pumpkin tossed by the Hobgoblin. No matter how many times you visit this attraction, you'll cringe when Doc Oc breaks through a brick wall, raises your car to the top of a skyscraper, and then releases you for a 400-ft sensory free fall to the pavement below. We won't reveal how all this is done—just credit some genius engineers and gadgets—but the bizarre angles and perspective at which scenes are shown are so disorienting, you really do feel as if you've entered another dimension that blurs the border between ride and reality. *Do not miss this one. Duration: 4½ mins. Crowds: Inescapable. Strategy: Go early in the day or at dusk. Be sure to read the posters on the walls on your way in, to get a sense of who's who. Audience: All but timid young children; youngsters who are accustomed to action TV shows will be fine. No pregnant women or guests with heart, back, or neck problems. Minimum height: 40"; children under 48" must be accompanied by an adult. Rating:* ★★★

⓲ **Doctor Doom's Fearfall.** Although the 200-ft-tall twin towers look scary, the execution of the ride will make your pulse race only slightly. After being strapped into a chair, you're hoisted almost to the top and then dropped to earth. The process is repeated but with a little more force to make your plunge a little faster. Worth the wait only if there's no wait (but there usually is one) or if you want a panoramic view of the Orlando skyline. *Duration: 3 mins. Crowds: Heavy all day. Strategy: Go later in the day, when crowds are thinner, but not on a full stomach. Audience: Older children and adults. No pregnant women or guests with heart, back, or neck problems or motion sickness. Minimum height: 52". Rating:* ★★

⓳ **Incredible Hulk Coaster.** If you follow a clockwise tour of IOA, this is the first ride that'll catch your attention and the first you'll want to ride. The first third of the coaster is directly above the sidewalk and lagoon, so you can watch as cars are spit out from a 150-ft catapult that propels them from 0 to 40 mph in less than two seconds. If that's enough to pique your interest, then enter and endure the queue (and ever-present story line) and board the ride. This is when the experience you watched from the safety of the sidewalk is manifested through flesh-pressing G-forces that match those of an F-16 fighter. From here, things are enjoyable in a rough sort of way, since you are instantly whipped into an upside-down, zero-G, heart-line inverting position 110 ft above the ground. That's when you go into the roller coaster's traditional first dive—straight down toward the lagoon below at some 60 mph. Racing along the track, you then spin through seven rollovers in all and plunge into two deep, foggy subterranean enclosures. And just when you think it's over, it's not. It just keeps rolling along way after you've exhausted your supply of screams and shrieks. *Duration: 2 mins 15 secs. Crowds: All the time. Strategy: Make a beeline either to this coaster or to Dueling Dragons as soon as you arrive in the park. The fog effects are most vivid first thing in the morning; darkness enhances the launch effect, since you can't see the light at the end of the tunnel. Front and rear seats give you almost entirely different experiences. The ride is fastest in the rear and has fine views, but is roughest on the sides; the front row, with its fabulous view of that green track racing into your face, is truly awesome—but you have to wait even longer for it. Audience: Coaster lovers. No pregnant women or guests with heart, back, or neck problems. Minimum height: 54". Rating:* ★★★

㉔ Storm Force Accelatron. If you missed Hurricane Andrew, check out this new whirling indoor ride that uses sound, light, and other special effects to create a thunderstorm adventure that demonstrates the power of nature. Storm harnesses the power of weather to battle her archenemy Magneto (What?! *A storyline?*) by having people like you board "Power Orbs" which help convert human energy into electrical forces through the power of "cyclospin." The lowdown is an indoor storm. *Duration, Crowds, Strategy: Not available at presstime. Audience: Older children and adults. No pregnant women or guests with heart, back, or neck problems. Minimum height: 54". Rating:* ★★★

Strategies for Your Visit to Islands of Adventure

When to Go
Since the park is relatively new, most days are fairly busy. Park watchers predict that if any day is less populous, it might be Wednesday. Summer season and spring break can alter any predictions, however.

Blitz Tour
To see everything in Islands of Adventure, a full day is necessary, especially since the large number of thrill rides guarantees that long lines will greet you just about everywhere. To see the most without waiting, arrive in the parking lot 45 minutes before the park's official opening. When you validate your ticket, you'll be given an Islands of Adventure Passport, in which you can register a souvenir stamp from every "island" you visit. If you look at it closely, you'll see that it suggests an "itinerary," beginning with Seuss Landing. Skip that spot now, however, especially if you don't have young children in tow. Instead, head for the **Amazing Adventures of Spider-Man** and the **Incredible Hulk Coaster.** Then dash over to Lost Continent and ride **Dueling Dragons** and **Poseidon's Fury: Escape from the Lost City.** Check the schedule of show times and see if you can catch the **Eighth Voyage of Sindbad**; if the timing's not right for a show, stop to chat with the Talking Fountain outside the theater entrance before heading over to Jurassic Park and **Jurassic Park River Adventure**; if lines there are too huge, stop instead at the **Jurassic Park Discovery Center, Triceratops Encounter,** and **Camp Jurassic.** Skip **Pteranodon Flyers** unless there's no line.

Next, head over to Toon Lagoon. Line up for **Dudley Do-Right's Ripsaw Falls** and then hop aboard **Popeye & Bluto's Bilge-Rat Barges.** While you're drying off, walk to Marvel Super Hero Island, and queue up for **Doctor Doom's Fearfall.** If there's no line, you may want to take the opportunity to visit Spidey again.

By now, if you're in luck, the young Dr. Seuss fans and their families will have left the park, so it's time to hit Seuss Landing. Go to **Cat in the Hat** first, then on to **One Fish, Two Fish, Red Fish, Blue Fish.** Make a stop at the **Green Eggs and Ham Café** to see how those green eggs are made, even if you're not ready to chow down. **Caro-Seuss-el** will let you be a kid again. Before you exit, walk through *If I Ran the Zoo.* The animals really *are* totally strange and unusual.

On Rainy Days

Except during Christmas week, expect rainy days to be less crowded— even though the park is in full operation. (Coasters do run in the rain—although not in thunderstorms.) However, since most attractions are out in the open, you will get very wet.

Other Tips

- Maintaining their "one step behind Disney" status, shortly after Disney unveiled their FASTPASS, Universal Orlando introduced Universal Express. If you're a resort guest (although regular park guests could take advantage of this between April and September), you're granted admission to either Universal Studios or the Islands of Adventure as early as 7 AM, giving you a very generous head start on the day.

- If you plan to ride the Dueling Dragons or the Incredible Hulk Coaster, wear shoes that are strapped firmly onto your feet—no flip-flops or heel-less sandals. If you wear glasses, consider bringing or wearing a sports strap that will keep them firmly against your head when you're flung upside down. Neither coaster is so rough that you will absolutely lose your glasses, but it's better to be safe than sorry.

- Call the day before your visit to get official park hours, and arrive in the parking lot 45 minutes early. See the biggest attractions first.

- Be sure to write down your parking location.

- Just in case you and your companions get separated, set up a rendezvous point and time at the start of the day. Don't pick an obvious and crowded location (such as the Jurassic Discovery Center), but a small restaurant or bridge between two islands.

- Have a filling snack at 10:30, lunch after 2, and dinner at 8 or later. Or lunch on the early side at a place that takes reservations, such as Thunder Falls Terrace or Mythos, then have dinner at 5. Be sure to make your reservations ahead of time or, at the very least, when you enter the park.

Universal Studios Islands of Adventure A to Z

Baby Care

There are diaper-changing tables in both men's and women's rest rooms, and nursing areas in the women's rest rooms; stroller rentals ($7; $10 deposit) are at Guest Relations, in the Port of Entry. Disposable diapers are available at no charge at Health Services, inside Guest Services. They are also for sale at De Fotos Expedition and the Universal Studios Islands of Adventure Trading Company in Port of Entry, the Marvel Alterniverse Store in Marvel Super Hero Island, Gasoline Alley in Toon Lagoon, and Mulberry Street in Seuss Landing.

Baby Exchange

All rides have Baby Exchange areas, so that one parent or adult party member can watch a baby or toddler while the other enjoys the ride or show. The adults then do the baby swap, and the former caretaker rides without having to wait in line all over again.

Cameras and Film

DeFotos is a camera shop that offers rentals, repairs, and one-hour film developing. They're located in the Port of Entry on your right after the turnstiles.

Dining

Sit-down restaurants and fast-food eateries are scattered throughout Islands of Adventure. Several accept reservations. To make them (as far in advance as you want), just call the restaurant or go there in person first thing in the morning.

COUNTER-SERVICE RESTAURANTS

On Toon Lagoon, you can sample you-know-whats at **Blondie's Deli: Home of the Dagwood.** The jumbo sandwich that creates the restaurant's marquee is a hoot, and you can buy the real thing, by the inch, inside. The specialty of Seuss Landing's **Green Eggs and Ham Café** is, you guessed it, green eggs and ham! (The sunshades overhead are colossal versions of the above.) Don't worry—traditional breakfast fare is also available. In Jurassic Park, you can have Caesar salad on a pizza crust, along with more traditional versions of the Italian specialty, at **Pizza Predatoria.** Check out the rapacious raptors on the sign.

FULL-SERVICE RESTAURANTS

The park's fancy mealtime option is the startlingly sophisticated **Mythos Restaurant** (☎ 407/224–4534) in the Lost Continent. The cuisine is surprisingly ambitious—the menu offers such things as wood-roasted Maine lobster with corn and bacon stuffing and bourbon barbecue sauce, and blue-corn-crusted mahimahi with sweet baby bell peppers and tomatillo sauce—and the highly themed setting is gorgeous. Chicago restaurant designer Jordan Mozer seems to have placed the tables within a huge ivory grotto; windows look out onto the lagoon or into the back side of waterfalls, and the polished aluminum railings are supported by statuettes of the mythical strong men. Server names come straight from antique legends. The second full-service restaurant is **Confisco's Grill,** located near the lagoon at the intersection of Port of Entry and Seuss Landing. Meals include steaks, salads, sandwiches, soups, and pastas—and a neat little pub. The **Thunder Falls Terrace** (☎ 407/224–4461) in Jurassic Park serves rotisserie chicken and ribs.

For Travelers with Disabilities

As in Walt Disney World's major parks, each attraction has an audio portion that appeals to those with visual impairments and a visual portion to interest those with hearing impairments. But as at Universal Studios, Islands of Adventure has made an all-out effort not only to make the premises physically accessible for those with disabilities but also to lift attitudinal barriers. All employees attend disability awareness workshops to remind them that people with disabilities are people first. And you can occasionally spot staffers using wheelchairs.

ATTRACTIONS

All attractions are completely accessible to guests who use wheelchairs with the exception of the **Incredible Hulk Coaster, Doctor Doom's Fearfall,** and **Dueling Dragons,** for which you must transfer from your chair to ride.

RESTAURANTS

All restaurants are wheelchair accessible.

Many employees have had basic sign-language training; even some of the animated characters speak sign, albeit sometimes an adapted version. As at Universal Studios, Islands of Adventure visuals are supplemented by a special **guidebook** containing story lines and scripts for most attractions. In addition, **cassettes** with narrative descriptions of the various attractions can be borrowed, along with portable tape players. You can get these and the various booklets at Guest Relations, just inside the Main Entrance and to your right as you enter the park. There is an **outgoing TTY** on the counter in Guest Relations.

Wheelchairs ($7) and scooter rentals ($30) are handled at Guest Relations, in the Port of Entry. If the wheelchair breaks down, disappears, or otherwise needs replacing, speak to any shop attendant. If you need an electric wheelchair, make reservations in advance.

Entertainment

Throughout the day there are character greetings and shows in each of the Islands. In Toon Lagoon, you may run into **Toon Trolley. Ja Roo** does an acrobatic show in Jurassic Park. **Bandits Out of Time** appear in the Lost Continent. There's a **Seuss Street Show** in Seuss Landing. At Marvel Super Hero Island, the **X-Men** appear. During summer and holiday periods, when the park is open late, there's a big fireworks show, **Adventure to the Stars,** which can be seen anywhere along the lagoon bordering the islands—the lagoon-side terrace of Jurassic Park's Discovery Center has a fairly unimpeded view.

Guided Tours

Like Universal Studios, Islands of Adventure has VIP tours, which offer what's called "back-door admission"—you go straight to the head of the line. It's worthwhile if you're in a hurry, if the day is crowded, and if you have the money—from approximately $120 for an individual four-hour VIP tour, including park admission, to $1,700 for an eight-hour tour for up to 15 people, again including park admission. If you can't get enough of being pampered, they also offer a two-day, two-park tour for $3,000 for up to 15 people.

Hours

Islands of Adventure is open 365 days a year, from 9 to 7, with hours extended to 10 during summer and holiday periods.

Lockers

Lockers (50¢) are across from Guest Relations. There are also various Smart Lockers, which are free for up to an hour, scattered strategically throughout the park—notably at Dueling Dragons, the Incredible Hulk, Jurassic Park River Adventure, and Popeye & Bluto's Bilge-Rat Barges—where you can stash backpacks and cameras while you're being drenched or going through the spin cycle.

Lost Things and People

Misplaced possessions go to Guest Relations, in the Port of Entry. If you lose your children or traveling companions, speak up immediately at Guest Relations or Security.

Money Matters

There is an ATM outside the turnstiles leading into the Port of Entry.

Shopping

Be sure to check out the various theme shops and their treasures, ranging from a stuffed Cat in the Hat to a *Jurassic Park* dinosaur and a Blondie mug. In Toon Lagoon, you can pick up a poncho at **Gasoline**

Alley, along with clever blank books and cartoon character hats and wigs that recall Daisy Mae and others.

Nearby, pick up Bullwinkle stuffed animals and clothing at **Wossamotta U.** The **Dinostore** in Jurassic Park has a *Tyrannosaurus rex* that looks as if he is hatching from an egg, along with all manner of educational toys on the dino theme. The **Comics Shop** stocks Spider-Man memorabilia and toys. In the **Shop of Wonders** in the Lost Continent, Merlin wanna-bes c an buy things to make magic of their own. And the **Universal Studios Islands of Adventure Trading Company** store, in the Port of Entry, stocks just about every kind of souvenir you saw in the park.

WET 'N WILD

When Wet 'n Wild opened in 1977, it was actually the world's first water park. It quickly became known as the place to go for thrilling water slides, and although it's since been copied, Wet 'n Wild continues to have the most outrageously heart-stopping water slides and rides and tubing adventures around. This is the place to come if you want to experience one exhilarating slide ride after another. This mammoth water park is best known for rides like the totally scary Black Hole slide, which twists and turns through absolute darkness, and the Hydra Fighter, which combines bungee jumping with the thrill of firing a water cannon.

For those who don't relish being frightened half to death (or spending several minutes un-wedging your bathing suit from tight crevices), there are swimming pools and lazy river rides. An elaborate children's playground, for youngsters 4 ft and under, features miniature versions of the park's most popular rides. Bring a cooler and stop for lunch at one of the many picnic spots around the pools or on the lakeside beach or relax at one of several food courts. Pools are heated in cooler weather and Wet 'n Wild is one of the few water parks in the country to be open year round.

Black Hole. You'll be scared silly as you are enveloped in total darkness. A 1,000-gallon-a-minute blast of water shoots your two-person raft into 500 ft of a completely dark, twisting tunnel. Hang on tight. *Minimum height: 36", 48" without an adult.*

Blue Niagara. For a real thrill, head to the top of this giant, six-story-tall slide that's like a rushing waterfall inside a giant tube. Hold your breath as you jump into this tube of racing water. You'll slip and slide all the way down to the bottom, and splash out into a quiet pool. *Minimum height: 36", 48" without an adult.*

Bomb Bay. Challenge yourself to the ultimate free fall on this white-knuckle adventure. The slide is 76 ft long, and the drop, which is out of a capsule (you're like a bomb dropping out of a plane), is nearly vertical so you'll fall like a rock. *Minimum height: 36", 48" without an adult.*

Bubba Tub. The entire family can take this ride together. Just hop into the giant rubber inner tube and hang on. You'll all be laughing as your tube slips and slides up and down a triple-dip, six-story roller-coaster ride that ends in a watery pool. *Minimum height: 36", 48" without an adult.*

Bubble Up. Kids never tire of clambering up and then sliding back down this enormous, wet, magical bubble. It's surrounded by a pool of shallow water and stays inflated no matter how hard kids bounce on it.

Der Stuka. Der Stuka means "steep hill" in German, and, for sheer exhilaration, it's hard to beat this steep slide. After climbing up six stories, there's no turning back. It's your turn to let go and hurtle down a slippery, 250-ft-long speed slide. Luckily, the slide ends at a long, horizontal water runway, giving you time to glide to a graceful stop. *Minimum height: 36", 48" without an adult.*

Fuji Flyer. You'd better hang on when you take this thrilling slide. Tuck yourself into a seat in a four-person toboggan and try not to scream too loud as the in-line toboggan careens around watery curves. *Minimum height: 36", 48" without an adult.*

Hydra Fighter. Wet 'n Wild's first interactive water ride is a thrill a second. You're hanging from a tower on a bungee-type cord, buckled into a seat, back-to-back with a partner, and bouncing. Each time you face down a bounce, shoot water out of the cannon between your legs, and try to hit the ground. The stronger the stream of water, the higher and faster you go (and the farther you fall). *Minimum height: 36", 48" without an adult.*

Knee Ski. Even if you've never knee-skied you'll be a star. The kneeboard is attached to a cable, so just hop on, act like a pro, and let it take you on a thrilling ½-mile ride around the lake. *Minimum height: 36", 48" without an adult.*

Lazy River. Had enough? Then settle into an inner tube for a peaceful trip down a gently moving stream. Bask in the sun as you drift by colorful flowers and tropical greenery.

Mach 5. You'll think you're approaching the speed of sound on this quickie. Three water slides twist and turn with almost impossible curves. Choose one, hold your breath, and go. In just a moment you'll land with an abrupt splash. *Minimum height: 36", 48" without an adult.*

Raging Rapids. Here's your chance to experience white-water tubing. Settle into a tube with a group and be sure to hang on as the tube gets tangled in whirlpools and teeters in tumultuous wave pools. Be prepared, if you can, for the surprising waterfall plunge at the end.

Surf Lagoon. For sheer fun, jump into the surf here. It's hard to keep your position and even more difficult not to start laughing as you are buffeted about in this giant pool. Huge 4-ft-high waves toss all wouldbe surfers about.

The Surge. You'll be hanging onto each other during this exhilarating ride. Five of you hop in a giant inner tube and the fun begins. A surge of water takes the tube down five stories while twisting and turning through a series of steeply banked curves. *Minimum height: 36", 48" without an adult.*

The Wild One. Two of you at a time get to have your jollies on this bouncy ride. Just settle into a big tube and hang on. A boat tows you around the lake and it can get pretty bumpy. *Minimum height: 36", 48" without an adult.*

Strategies for your Visit to Wet 'n Wild

Wet 'n Wild is a must-stop spot for families and it can be really crowded, especially when the weather is hot. The park fills up as the day progresses, and your best bet, if you want to try to avoid the hordes, is to get here in the morning a half-hour before opening hours or to come on a cloudy day. In the summer, come before or after the daily afternoon thunderstorms. Be prepared for long lines at the most popular rides, such as the Hydra Fighter or the Black Hole.

Wet 'n Wild A to Z

Admission

Admission is $28.95 for adults and $22.95 for children ages 3–9 (half price after 5 in peak season, and at other times after 3). For information about the Orlando FlexTicket, a combination ticket for all of the Universal Studios parks, *see* Discounts *in* Universal Orlando A to Z, *below.* Parking is $5 for cars, $6 for RVs.

Dining

You'll find a variety of fare at the food courts sprinkled throughout Wet 'n Wild. For hamburgers, hot dogs, vegetarian burgers, salads, and sub sandwiches, head to the **Main Snack. Bubba's Chicken & BarBQ** specializes in lightly smoked ribs and chicken and barbecued beef sandwiches. **Pizza & Suds** is the place to go for calzones, spaghetti, or deep dish pizzas. When you just want something cool, you can't beat the sundaes and ice-cream cones at **Cookies & Cones.** For an unusual treat, try the funnel cakes or chilly dippin' dots, bite-size bits of ice cream in a candy coating, at **Funnel Cakes & Dippin' Dots.**

For Travelers with Disabilities

Slides are accessible via stairway towers that must be climbed. Guests with limited mobility might be able to bob about on a raft in **Surf Lagoon** or tube down the **Lazy River.** Many of the paths are flat and easily accessible in a wheelchair; however, no rides accommodate people using wheelchairs, and wheelchair rentals are not available.

Facilities

Dressing rooms (with lockers), showers, and rest rooms are at the front of the park, to the left after the main entrance. Towels can be rented ($2; $2 deposit). Additional dressing rooms, showers, and rest rooms are near the **Bubble Up** ride. Lockers for rent ($5; $2 deposit) can be found near the entrance and at handy locations throughout the park.

First Aid

The first aid stand is located at Guest Services, which is to the left just after you enter the park.

Lost Things and People

If you plan to split up, be sure everyone knows where and what time you plan to meet. Lifeguards look out for kids that might be lost. If they spot one, they'll take the child to Guest Services, which will page the parent or guardian. The Lost and Found is located at Guest Services, which is to the left just after you walk through the entrance to Wet 'n Wild.

Hours

Wet 'n Wild is open 365 days a year, from 10 to 6, with hours extending until 11 in the summer. Call for exact hours during holiday periods.

Picnicking

You are welcome to picnic and to bring coolers into the park. However, glass containers and alcoholic beverages are not permitted. There are many picnic areas scattered around Wet 'n Wild, in both covered and open areas.

Supplies

Personal flotation devices, also known as life jackets, are provided by the staff. If you are looking for sunscreen, sunglasses, bathing suits, camera film, and other necessities, stop in the **Trade Winds Gift Shop.**

Visitor Information

Guest Services (✉ 6200 International Dr., ☎ 407/351–3200 or 407/351–1800, 🖃) is to the left just after you enter the park.

UNIVERSAL ORLANDO A TO Z

Admission

One-day one-park tickets cost $48.76 for adults, $39.22 for children 3–9, including tax. **Escape Passes** sell for $84.75 for adults and $68.85 for children for two days, $121.85 and $100.65, respectively, for three days. Five-day tickets are your best bargain at $124.95 for adults and $99.95 for children. Tickets must be used on consecutive days. Multiday passes allow unlimited access to both parks during their period of validity. All admission media is available in advance by mail through **Ticketmaster** (☎ 800/745–5000).

DISCOUNTS

If you buy tickets at the **Orlando/Orange County Convention & Visitors Bureau** (✉ 8723 International Dr., ☎ 407/363–5871), you'll save about $4 per adult ticket ($3 on children's prices). American Automobile Association members get 10% off, sometimes more, at AAA offices. The Orlando FlexTicket, which covers the Universal parks (US, IOA, and Wet 'n Wild) as well as SeaWorld and Bush Gardens, Tampa, matches Walt Disney World's pass system. FlexTickets come in four-park versions that allow you seven days of unlimited admission to US, IOA, Wet 'n Wild, and SeaWorld ($169.55 adults, $135.63 children 3–9); and five-park versions that allow you 10 days of unlimited admission to all of the above plus Busch Gardens Tampa ($209.95 and $167.65).

HAND STAMPS

If you want to leave the park and come back the same day, have your hand stamped when you leave, and show your hand and your Studio Pass when you return.

Car Care

You can fill 'er up at the '40s-vintage pumps at the Texaco station at the Turkey Lake Road entrance. If you need a battery jump in the parking garage, raise your hood and speak to the nearest employee.

Getting There

Traveling east on I–4 (from WDW and the Tampa area), get off at **Universal Boulevard** (Exit 30A). Then take a left onto Universal Boulevard and follow the signs. Traveling west on I–4 (from the Daytona and Jacksonville areas), take **Universal Boulevard** (Exit 29B). Turn right onto Hollywood Way and follow the signs.

Parking

Universal's single parking garage complex, which serves both theme parks and CityWalk, is the world's largest car park. Because your vehicle is covered, it's not so sweltering at the end of the day, even when it's hot. The cost is $6 for cars, $8 for campers. Valet parking is available for $12.

Visitor Information

Contact **Universal Studios Escape** (✉ 1000 Universal Studios Plaza, Orlando 32819-7610, ☎ 407/363–8000; 888/331–9108; 407/363–8265 TTY, ✍).

4 SEAWORLD ORLANDO, BUSCH GARDENS, CYPRESS GARDENS

When Anheuser-Busch opened a small hospitality center adjacent to its Tampa brewery in 1959, the company couldn't foresee the day that a couple of somnolent koalas and a ride called Kumba would be more of a draw than a draft would be. Rising profits demanded the creation of a separate corporate umbrella, and Busch Entertainment Corporation (BEC) was spun off. Steady expansion and the 1989 acquisition of SeaWorld helped make BEC the second-largest theme-park owner and operator in the world.

By Catherine
Fredman

Updated by
Gary
McKechnie

B USCH GARDENS, as the tropical beer garden was called, was originally seen as a useful place to stash the Busch family's collection of exotic animals and birds while tending to the real
business: making and selling beer.

But in 1971, Disney opened the Magic Kingdom, Central Florida ex-
ploded, and by 1973 SeaWorld was established. In Tampa, the call of
the wild proved so strong that Anheuser-Busch began to develop Busch
Gardens into a multifaceted park and zoo on an Africa theme, with
the brewery increasingly a sideshow. The addition of Cypress Gardens
and SeaWorld to the Busch stable has made the company a key player
on the Central Florida attractions scene.

Each of the Busch parks has a personality and style of its own. SeaWorld
Orlando, 10 minutes from downtown, is for animal lovers and anyone
who favors a slower pace after the crowded, high-energy impact of Disney and Universal. Busch Gardens Tampa, about an hour from Orlando
on Florida's west coast, has become both a major zoological park and a
major thrill-ride park. Cypress Gardens, about a 40-minute drive from Orlando, is a throwback to another era in Central Florida life. Decidedly low-
tech, it's a celebration of the horticulturist's art spiced with a few carnival
rides that keep the grandchildren happy.

If you don't have much time to spend on a first visit to the Orlando
area, SeaWorld is the only one of the trio that's a must. At its new Discovery Cove, the highly publicized separate attraction that opened in
summer 2000, you can enjoy some of the features of a water park along
with a few of the more exclusive animal-encounter attractions available in the area. On subsequent visits or if you have enough time, you'll
definitely want to see how the Busch animal show stacks up against
the Animal Kingdom's, and it's fun to drop in on Cypress Garden to
sample its distinctive blend of kitsch, nostalgia, and natural beauty.

SEAWORLD ORLANDO

There's a whole lot more to SeaWorld than Shamu, its mammoth killer
whale mascot. Sure, you can be splashed by Shamu and his orca bud-
dies, but you can also stroke a stingray, see manatees face-to-snout,
learn to love an eel, and be spat upon by a walrus. But as the world's
largest marine adventure park, SeaWorld is devoted entirely to the mammals, birds, fish, and reptiles that live in the ocean and its tributaries.

Having been under the wing of the Busch Entertainment Corporation
for more than a decade, SeaWorld is bigger and better than ever. The
park rivals Disney properties for sparkling cleanliness, courteous staff,
and attention to detail—the nautical flags flying over the entrance
spell out "SeaWorld" in semaphore, and the strollers are shaped like
upended dolphins with tails as handles. Because there are more exhibits
and shows than rides, you can go at your own pace without that
hurry-up-and-wait feeling. And despite the park's size (200 acres),
touring it is actually a fairly calming experience.

Every attraction is designed to showcase the beauty of the marine
world and to demonstrate ways that humans can protect our waters
and wildlife. The presentations are never condescending—they are
gentle reminders of our responsibility to safeguard the environment.
From show to show, you'll find that SeaWorld's use of humor plays a
major role in this education.

First-timers may be slightly confused by the lack of distinct "lands" here—SeaWorld's performance venues, attractions, and activities surround a 17-acre lake, and the artful landscaping, curving paths, and concealing greenery sometimes lead to wrong turns. But armed with a map that lists show times, it's easy to plan a chronological approach that flows easily from one show and attraction to the next and allows enough time for you to take rest stops and meal breaks.

Although it's traditionally the third choice in Orlando's theme park trilogy, SeaWorld consistently offers a first-class experience. You won't be disappointed.

Numbers in the margin correspond to points of interest on the Sea-World map.

1 **Dolphin Nursery.** Capitalizing on the park's very successful breeding program, SeaWorld has a tank just for dolphin babies and their moms. Every hour, a staff member conducts a lecture followed by a question-and-answer period. *Crowds: Not a problem. Strategy: Go during a Shamu show so the kids can be up front. Audience: All ages. Rating:* ★★★

2 **Tropical Reef.** In this soothing indoor attraction, more than 30 separate aquariums are aswim with tropical fish from around the world. Each display seems more beautiful and imaginative than the next. Fish lay camouflaged on the bottom, dig holes, and glow in the dark. Printed descriptions reveal interesting facts about each tank's inhabitants, resulting in the oft-repeated, "Hey, cool, look at this one!" *Crowds: Not usually a problem. Strategy: Go at the end of the day—because it's near the entrance, most people stop here on their way in. Audience: All ages. Rating:* ★★★

3 **Turtle Point.** Many of the endangered specimens at this exhibit have been rescued from the wild and still live here because permanent injuries make it impossible for them to return. These lumbering beauties will peacefully live out their lengthy lives in the natural habitat here. *Crowds: Sporadically crowded, but generally enough space for all to get a good view. Strategy: Go anytime. Audience: All ages. Rating:* ★★★

4 **Stingray Lagoon.** In a broad, shallow pool, dozens of stingrays are close enough to touch, as evidenced by the guests surrounding the rim with outstretched hands. Smelts, available for $3 a tray at nearby concession stands, are a delicacy for the rays, and when they flap up for lunch you can feed them and stroke their velvety skin. It's one of the most rewarding experiences for everyone, and the snack-happy animals are obligingly hungry all day. If not, you have a cheap lunch. Look for the nursery pool with its baby rays. *Crowds: Can make it hard to get to the animals during busy seasons. Strategy: Go early—the smelt concession stand closes at dark. Audience: All ages. Rating:* ★★★

5 **Key West at SeaWorld.** This laid-back area is modeled after Key West, that southernmost Florida outpost famous for its spectacular sunsets and its Caribbean atmosphere. If you were thrilled silly feeding the rays, look for the huge pool that's home to a few dozen cute-as-Flipper Atlantic bottle-nosed dolphins—they're hungry, too. Each evening, Sea-World re-creates the real Key West's Sunset Celebration as children get their faces painted and have their pictures taken with a larger-than-human-size Shamu or Dolly Dolphin. A reggae beat gets things grooving, and even the dolphins seem to join the party. It's a fun place to end the day and a nice prelude to the nighttime Shamu show and pyrotechnics. *Crowds: Can get thick. Strategy: For premium access, attend a late Shamu show and hit Key West on your way out of the park*

SeaWorld Orlando

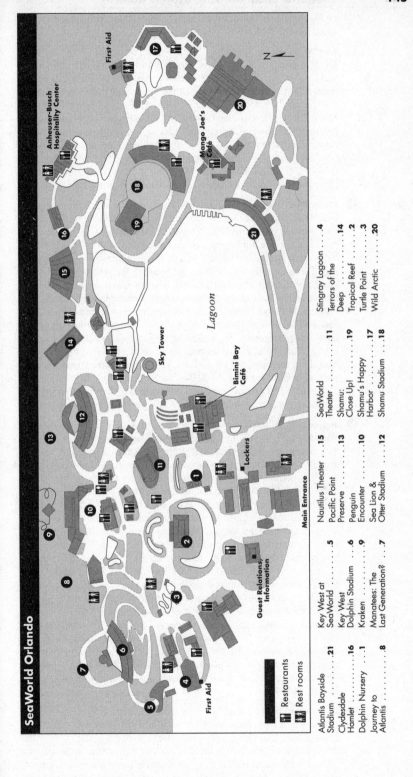

First Aid

First Aid

Anheuser-Busch Hospitality Center

Mango Joe's Café

Lagoon

Sky Tower

Bimini Bay Café

Lockers

Main Entrance

Guest Relations; Information

N

Restaurants

Rest rooms

Atlantis Bayside Stadium **21**
Clydesdale Hamlet **16**
Dolphin Nursery . . .**1**
Journey to Atlantis **8**

Key West at SeaWorld **5**
Key West Dolphin Stadium . .**6**
Kraken **9**
Manatees: The Last Generation? . . .**7**

Nautilus Theater . .**15**
Pacific Point Preserve **13**
Penguin Encounter **10**
Sea Lion & Otter Stadium . . .**12**

SeaWorld Theater **11**
Shamu: Close Up! **19**
Shamu's Happy Harbor **17**
Shamu Stadium . . .**18**

Stingray Lagoon . . .**4**
Terrors of the Deep **14**
Tropical Reef **2**
Turtle Point **3**
Wild Arctic **20**

or before the crowds thicken for the sunset celebration. Audience: All ages. Rating: ★★★

⑥ Key West Dolphin Stadium. In this thoroughly enjoyable show, bottle-nosed dolphins and a couple of Pseudorca whales (cousin to the Killers) wave, leap, and do back flips as the crowd oohs and aahs. In one sequence, a trainer rides on one of their backs and then gets torpedoed into the air. There's more entertainment in this 20-minute show than in a week of prime-time television. Make plans to get here early for a few reasons: a Jimmy Buffett–style crooner plays some soothing songs; and if you ask an attendant, your child may be chosen to help the trainer conduct a dolphin behavior (what we used to call "trick"). *Duration: 20 mins. Crowds: You'll always get in. Strategy: Sit in the first four rows if you want to get splashed. Audience: All ages. Rating:* ★★★

⑦ Manatees: The Last Generation? If you don't have time to explore Florida's springs in search of manatees in the wild, then don't miss the chance to see ones who were brought here after near-fatal brushes with motorboats. The lumbering, whiskered manatees look like a cross between walruses and oil barrels, and this display devoted to them is striking. Tramping down a clear tunnel beneath the naturalistic, 3½-acre lagoon, you enter **Manatee Theater,** where a film describes the lives of these gentle giants and how humans are threatening the species' survival. In **Manatee Habitat,** a 300,000-gallon tank with a 126-ft seamless acrylic viewing panel, you can look in on the lettuce-chomping creatures plus native fish, including tarpon, gar, and snook. Keep an eye out for mama manatees and their nursing calves. Other animals that share the manatee's world live in **Alligator Habitat,** a marsh display, and **Bird Habitat.** *Crowds: Since the area is fairly large, that "crowded" feeling is nonexistent. Strategy: Go during a Shamu show and not right after a dolphin show. Audience: All ages. Rating:* ★★★

⑧ Journey to Atlantis. SeaWorld's first entry in Florida's escalating "coaster wars" combines elements of a high-speed water ride and roller coaster with lavish special effects. Like most attractions, this has a story line that doesn't really matter, but here it is: the lost continent of Atlantis has risen in the harbor of a quaint Greek fishing village, and you board a rickety Greek fishing boat to explore it. Once inside, an ominous current tugs at your boat, and an old fisherman offers a golden sea horse (actually Hermes!) to protect you from the evil Sirens. That's it. There's supposed to be a battle between Hermes and Allura, but it's a ploy to crank up effects using LCD technology, lasers, and holographic illusions and present a wild, watery battle. There are frequent twists, turns, and short, shallow dives, but few hair-raising plunges except for the first drop that sends you careening nearly 60 ft into the main harbor (plan on getting soaked to the skin) and the final drop, which is a 60-ft nosedive into S-shape, bobsledlike curves. *Duration: 6 mins. Crowds: Large. Strategy: Make a beeline here first thing in the morning or go about an hour before closing; going at night is definitely awesome, and the wait, if there is one, will be cooler. Audience: Older children and adults; definitely not for the faint of heart or for anyone with a fear of dark, enclosed spaces. Minimum height: 42".
Rating:* ★★★

⑨ Kraken. SeaWorld rolled out their second coaster competitor in May 2000, with a new approach and a new story line. On thisone the big draw is that, like Universal's Hulk coaster, your legs dangle free and the cars are suspended on the track above you. More appealing for coaster enthusiasts is that this ride features seven inversions, zero-G rolls, and speeds up to 65 mph. And the story line? Kraken's a mythical sea beast whose energy and wildness is captured in this ride.

Crowds: Expect lines. Strategy: Get to the park when it opens and make a beeline to Kraken. Audience: Older children and adults. Tentative rating: ★★★

⑩ Penguin Encounter. In a large white building between Key West Dolphin Stadium and Sea Lion & Otter Stadium, 17 species of penguin scoot around a refrigerated re-creation of Antarctica. The lil' buggers are as cute as can be, waddling across icy promontories and diving into frigid waters to display aquatic skills you can witness through the thick, see-through walls. A moving walkway rolls you past at a slow pace, but you can also step off to an area where you can stand and marvel at these tuxedo-clad creatures. A similar viewing area for puffins and murres is just as entertaining. SeaWorld's penguin-breeding program has been so successful that it routinely supplies birds to other zoos. *Duration: Stay as long as you like. Crowds: Frequently gridlocked, despite a moving walkway tactfully nudging visitors past the glassed-in habitat. Strategy: Go while the dolphin and sea lion shows are on— and before you've gotten soaked at Journey to Atlantis or you'll feel as icy as the penguins' environment. Audience: All ages. Rating:* ★★

⑪ SeaWorld Theater. Between Penguin Encounter and the central lagoon, this theater is the venue for **"Pets on Stage."** This is where animals rescued from the local humane society perform. When the dogs are told to sit, they do! *Duration: 20–25 mins. Crowds: Not a problem. Strategy: Go when you want to sit down and cool off. Audience: All ages. Rating:* ★★

⑫ Sea Lion & Otter Stadium. Inside the sister to Key West Dolphin Stadium, a wildly inventive, multilevel pirate ship forms the set for **"Clyde and Seamore Take Pirate Island."** SeaWorld's celebrated sea lions, otters, and walruses prevail over pirate treachery in this swashbuckler of a saga. Show times are staggered so there's time to explore the attractions around the two stadiums between shows. Get here early to enjoy the preshow of the mime—he's definitely one of the best you'll ever see. *Duration: 40 mins, including the 15-min preshow. Crowds: No problem. Strategy: Sit toward the center for the best view, and don't miss the show's opening minutes. Audience: All ages. Rating:* ★★★

⑬ Pacific Point Preserve. A nonstop chorus of "aarrrps" and "yawps" leads the way to the 2½-acre home for California sea lions and harbor and fur seals, a naturalistic expanse of beaches, waves, and huge outcroppings of upturned rock designed to duplicate the rocky northern Pacific coast just behind Sea Lion & Otter Stadium. You can stroll around the edge of the surf zone, a favorite hangout for fun-loving pinnipeds, and peep at their underwater activities through the Plexiglas wall at one side of the tank. Buy some smelts and watch the sea lions sing for their supper from close up. *Crowds: Not a problem. Strategy: Go anytime. Audience: All ages. Rating:* ★★★

⑭ Terrors of the Deep. Within this large, innocuous white structure are some thoroughly nasty critters: eels, barracuda, sharks, and venomous and poisonous fish. SeaWorld wants to make you love them—or at least no longer be repulsed by them—so each animal is profiled via a video screen and educational posters. "There is little to love about the eel," one says, backing up its point by explaining how a slimy coat of mucus makes so-called blue eels appear green. Then you walk through a series of four Plexiglas tubes, surrounded by tanks containing the world's largest collection of such animals—a half dozen species of shark alone in some 660,000 gallons of water. The menacing creatures glide just feet overhead, and eels slither out from their hiding places. Stop to absorb this neatly contained underwater nightmare in a large viewing theater with benches. Even at its most crowded—this is another of Sea-World's most popular attractions—the walk-through tubes and over-head videos mean that even small children can get an eyeful. *Duration: Plan to spend 40 mins. Crowds: Most significant when adjacent sea lion show gets out. Strategy: Go during the sea lion shows. Audience: All ages. Rating:* ★★★

⑮ Nautilus Theater. This venue is home to a special stage show, which changes every year or so. The current production is popular *Cirque de la Mer*, or Circus of the Sea, a creative show on the model of small European circuses. Gymnastics, dance, and special effects highlight a theme that draws on the Peruvian background of its creator, comic Cesar Aedo, whose résumé also includes study with Marcel Marceau in Paris. Although the connection with the sea is pretty tenuous, the music is positively hypnotic. *Duration: 25 mins. Crowds: Not a problem. Strategy: Good when you need a rest. Audience: All ages. Rating:* ★★

⑯ Clydesdale Hamlet. A feature of all Anheuser-Busch parks, the walk-through hamlet houses hulking Clydesdale horses and provides a bucolic corral for their ponderous romping. A statue of a heroic stallion—which kids are encouraged to climb upon—makes a good theme-park photo opportunity. The Clydesdales are so incongruous in this marine-oriented setting that you have to agree with one teenager, who wisecracked, "Look, Dad, surf and turf." *Duration: You'll probably stay between 10 and 15 mins—it's up to you. Crowds: Never significant. Strategy: Go anytime. Audience: All ages. Rating:* ★

⑰ Shamu's Happy Harbor. If you want to take a break while your kids exhaust the last ounce of energy their little bodies possess, bring them here. This 3-acre outdoor play area has crawlable, climbable, explorable, bounceable, and get-wet activities. There's also a four-story net climb and adjacent arcade with midway games. Youngsters go wild for the tent with an air-mattress floor, pipes to crawl through, and "ball rooms," one for toddlers and one for grade-schoolers, with thousands of plastic balls to wade through. With big sailing ships to explore and water to play in and around, Happy Harbor is spacious and airy, and after a few minutes of this, they could qualify for the Navy Seals. *Crowds: Often a challenge. Strategy: Don't go first thing in the morning or you'll never drag your child away (but if you go mid-afternoon, expect plenty of hubbub). Bring a towel to dry them off. Audience: Toddlers through grade-schoolers. Rating:* ★★

⑱ Shamu Stadium. Home to SeaWorld's orca mascot, the stadium is hands-down the most popular feature in the park. Several performances daily give you a chance to marvel at the whales' fantastic flips, jumps, and other acrobatic antics. The preshow features a giant screen where your face may be shown (roughly the size of a Volkswagen), and a snapshot of your big-screen debut makes a unique souvenir. There's also video footage of orcas in the wild and a scattering of gently educational factoids. (Did you know that Shamu consumes 250 pounds of fish a day?) The show ends with a majestic bald eagle in a breath-taking free flight. In the funkier—and oddly enough, stirring—nighttime **"Shamu Rocks America,"** the famous orca jumps to the beat of "God Bless the USA"—not to be missed. During any Shamu show, there are always people who want to sit in the "splash zone" where Shamu uses his weight and massive fluke to flood the front rows. Wherever you sit, arrive early to get the seat of your choice. *Duration: 30 mins. Crowds: Sometimes a problem. Strategy: Go 45 mins early for the early afternoon show. Close-up encounters through the Plexiglas walls are not to be missed, so trot on down. Audience: All ages. Rating:* ★★★

⑲ **Shamu: Close Up!** For unprecedented up-close-and-personal underwater viewing of the breeding and nursery area, this is the place to be. Follow the signs around to the underground viewing stations for a unique glimpse of favorite whale pastimes: tummy-rubbing and back-scratching. The 1.7 million-gallon outdoor tanks are on the same level as the main pool in Shamu Stadium and have similar Plexiglas walls and viewing setups. SeaWorld can never predict when its whales will get pregnant, but its breeding program has been astonishingly successful. You should be able to see the latest baby Shamu cavorting after its mother. *Crowds: Sometimes so large you'll have to edge your way to viewing areas. Strategy: Ideal time is immediately after a Shamu show; although the crowds may be heavy, you'll have a better chance of seeing the whales. Otherwise, go early or late, or be patient. Audience: All ages. Rating:* ★★★

⑳ **Wild Arctic.** This pseudo ice station, with its flight-simulator helicopter ride and the interactive, educational elements that follow, is one of the best experiences in the park—provided your stomach can handle the motion simulation. At above- and below-water viewing stations you can take your time watching beluga whales blowing bubble rings, polar bears padding around with their toys, and groaning walruses trying to hoist themselves onto ½-inch-thick ice. You might even see a Sea-World staffer conducting a little research. *Crowds: Expect a wait during peak season. Strategy: Go early, late, or during a Shamu show. To see just the mammals, skip the simulated helicopter ride. Audience: All ages. Minimum height for motion option: 42". Rating:* ★★★

㉑ **Atlantis Bayside Stadium.** If you think a workout is changing channels without a remote, you'll be mighty impressed by the feats skiers do on water that gymnasts have difficulty doing on land. **"Intensity Games— Water Ski Challenge"** is an awesome display of athletic prowess, full of stupendous stunts and eye-opening jumps, in which two teams (Blue and Green) of waterborne tumblers try to outdo each other to snatch the day's title. Note the Blue and Green aren't for ocean colors—they represent corporate sponsors Pepsi and Mountain Dew. *Duration: 30 mins. Crowds: Not a problem. Strategy: Be warned—the splash factor is significant in the first 10 rows; the terrace at neighboring Mango Joe's Café and the deck at the Bimini Bay Café are alternative viewing spots. Audience: All ages. Rating:* ★★★

NEED A BREAK? End your visit with a sweets detour at **Cypress Bakery, Polar Parlor Ice Cream Shop,** or **Sweet Sailin' Confections,** their delectable treats hard to pass up.

Discovery Cove

Making a quantum leap from the traditional theme park, SeaWorld took a chance on opening Discovery Cove, a 32-acre limited-admission park where guests enter an extraordinary environment. Even before opening, they had booked families from all 50 states, with 20% of their guests coming from England. They're here to experience a re-creation of a Caribbean beach, complete with coral reefs, sandy beach, margaritas, and dolphins.

After walking through a huge thatched-roof tiki building, you register and are given a time to swim with the dolphins, the highlight of your Discovery Cove day. Your photo-ID allows you to charge drinks during the day, and that's all you need to worry about. With your admission, everything else is inclusive so you're not running to your locker (free) to get cash to buy suntan lotion (free), a towel (free), lunch (free), or a mask and fins (also free).

Even if you're aware of the neighboring interstate highway, you can't help feeling that you've entered a tropical oasis. Once inside, you are awash in rocky lagoons surrounded by lush landscaping, intricate coral reefs, and underwater ruins. A resort-style pool has cascading waterfalls, and white beaches are fringed with thatched huts, cabanas, and hammocks. Exciting encounters of animal species from the Bahamas, Tahiti, and Micronesia are part of the experience. A free-flight aviary is a riot of 300 exotic birds—and the fact that you swim beneath a waterfall to enter is even more exciting.

Although the price may seem steep ($179.99), when you consider that a dolphin swim in the Florida Keys runs approximately $125, and SeaWorld throws in a complimentary seven-day admission to their park (usually $48.76 a day), then it starts looking like a bargain.

Aviary. Swimmers emerge into the 100-ft-long, 35-ft-high aviary by passing under one of two waterfalls, discovering an unexpected tropical paradise on the other side. It provides a natural habitat for 30 species of tropical birds.

Beaches. Sugar-white beaches are lined with swaying palms, tropical foliage, and quaint thatched huts. Claim your own private spot in the sand with shady umbrellas, hammocks, lounges, or beach chairs.

Dolphin Lagoon. Following a training session beneath a cabana, you enter the water, and soon you'll feel the playful nudge from one of 28 dolphins as you swim together for 30 minutes in a deep-water lagoon surrounded by sandy beaches and lush tropical landscaping. SeaWorld trainers teach you about animal behaviors, and you discover the hand signals used to communicate with them. Even nonswimmers can handle this, courtesy of a flotation vest everyone must wear. Children older than six years may participate.

Coral Reef. Snorkelers follow clouds of thousands of tropical fish through this habitat. Swimmers can also snorkel beside an artificial sunken ship, peering through a nearly invisible glass partition at the barracudas and sharks.

Ray Lagoon. This is where you can wade and play with hundreds of southern and cow-nosed rays. Don't be afraid—they've had their barbs removed.

Tropical River. The Tropical River meanders its way throughout most of Discovery Cove. River swimmers travel through different environments—a sunny beach, a dense, tropical rain forest, an Amazon-like river, a tropical fishing village, an underwater cave, and the aviary.

Discovery Cove A to Z

ADMISSION
Tickets are $179.99 ($189.74 with tax) per person. The fee includes unlimited access to all swim and snorkeling areas and the flight aviary; a full meal; use of a mask, snorkel, swim vest, towel, locker, and other amenities; parking; and a pass for seven days of unlimited, come-and-go-as-you-please admission to SeaWorld Orlando. Gift certificates are available.

Other Tips
- If you wear glasses, don't worry. The masks at Discovery Cove can fit over your spectacles.

- If it becomes an all-day thunder and lightning rainstorm on your reserved day, they'll try to reschedule your visit when you're in town. If not, you'll have to settle for a refund.

- The earlier you make your reservations, the more latitude you have in selecting the time you want to swim with the dolphins.

RESERVATIONS

Reservations for Discovery Cove can be made by calling ☎ 877/434-7268 daily 9–8. Park hours are daily 9–5:30. Additional information can be found at www.discoverycove.com.

Strategies for Your Visit to SeaWorld Orlando

When to Go

Friday, Saturday, and Sunday are usually busier than the rest of the week, except during weeks that include Easter, July 4, and December 25, when every day is equally busy.

Blitz Tour

Although there's room for all at the stadiums, the other attractions—especially Penguin Encounter and Key West at SeaWorld—can get unpleasantly crowded, and there may be lines at Wild Arctic and Journey to Atlantis.

After passing the turnstiles, go straight ahead to the information desk for a park map and schedule of the day's shows. In this courtyard, take a moment to review show times and plan your day. Chances are you'll want to walk to the **SeaWorld Theater,** both to orient yourself and to get a sense of the larger vision of the park. If it's open and you're interested, whip over to **Kraken** and from there to **Penguin Encounter,** where you can literally chill out. While in this part of the park, visit—and feed—the sea lions at **Pacific Point Preserve,** either before or after (depending on show times) a raucous performance at **Sea Lion & Otter Stadium.** From here, see the sharks at **Terrors of the Deep,** on your way as you meander over to **Shamu Stadium** for a show. Afterward, you can go over to **Shamu: Close Up!**

By now you'll probably want a quick bite. Mango Joe's Café is conveniently located below Shamu Stadium. Let the young ones unwind at **Shamu's Happy Harbor** before heading to **Wild Arctic.** Stop in at the gift shop, and pick up the cuddly likeness of your favorite sea creature to go. Next, head to **Atlantis Bayside Stadium** to see the waterskiing show.

Cross back over the lagoon via the convenient walkway to see the **Dolphin Nursery** and the **Tropical Reef,** a cool indoor break from the afternoon sun. Pause at **Turtle Point** and **Stingray Lagoon** before your dolphin interaction at **Key West at SeaWorld.** Catch a show at **Key West Dolphin Stadium,** and visit **Manatees: The Last Generation?** By now, the lines at **Journey to Atlantis** should be shorter (you can only hope), but be prepared to get very, very, very wet!

If you've got the energy for nighttime festivities, grab dinner at **Mama Stella's Italian Kitchen** before returning to **Key West at SeaWorld** for the sunset celebration. Then it's on to **Shamu Stadium** for the funky **"Shamu Rocks America"** show and finally to the Red, White and Blue Spectacular **fireworks** show.

On Rainy Days

Although SeaWorld gives the impression of open-air roominess, almost a third of the attractions are actually indoors, and all the others are shielded from the elements by canopies, cantilevered roofs, or tautly stretched tarpaulins. Pick up a signature poncho—it's blue, with a black-

and-white orca on the back—at one of the ubiquitous concession stands, and dive right in.

Other Tips

- Try to arrive early for Shamu shows, which generally fill to capacity on even the slowest days.

- Pack a bathing suit or dry clothes for yourself and your children, since sooner or later, everyone will get soaked. (The culprits: Shamu's Happy Harbor, the up-close rows in the Shamu show, and Journey to Atlantis.)

- Budget ahead for food for the animals—a major part of SeaWorld charm. A small carton of fish is usually $2.

- As you get closer to the park, tune a radio to 1540 AM for SeaWorld information.

- If you're a park person who brings your own food, leave the plastic straws and lids behind—they can harm fish and birds.

- Wear comfortable sneakers—no heels or open sandals—since you may get your feet wet on the water rides.

SeaWorld Orlando A to Z

Admission

TICKETS

Regular one-day tickets cost $48.76 for adults, $39.22 for children 3–9, including tax.

DISCOUNTS

Two-day Value Tickets, which must be used within one week, are available. The cost is $59.36 for adults, $49.82 for children 3–9. However, sometimes you can get your second day free. The Orlando FlexTicket, which covers SeaWorld, other Busch parks, and the Universal parks, matches Walt Disney World's pass system. FlexTickets come in four-park versions that allow you seven days of unlimited admission to Universal Orlando parks, Wet 'n Wild, and SeaWorld ($169.55 adults, $135.63 children 3–9) and five-park versions that allow you 10 days of unlimited admission to all of the above plus Busch Gardens Tampa ($209.95 and $167.65). SeaWorld–Busch Gardens combination tickets, which include one day at each park, cost $83.74 for adults, $67.84 for children 3–9, including tax.

Baby Care

There are diaper-changing tables in or near most women's rest rooms and in the men's rest room at the front entrance, near Shamu's Emporium. You can buy diapers at machines in all changing areas and at Shamu's Emporium. A special area for nursing is alongside the women's rest room at Friends of the Wild gift shop, equidistant from SeaWorld Theater, Penguin Encounter, and Sea Lion & Otter Stadium. You will find stroller rentals at the Information Center ($6 for single, $12 for double; no deposit). However, no formula or baby food is sold on the premises; the nearest sources are a five-minute drive away at Gooding's Supermarket on International Drive, Publix supermarket and Eckerd Drug on Central Florida Parkway, and Kmart on Turkey Lake Road.

Cameras and Film

Disposable cameras are for sale on the premises, as are film and blank videotapes. There were neither camera nor camcorder rentals nor camera repairs on the premises at press time.

Dining

In addition to burgers, barbecue, and the usual burnt offerings sold at restaurants and concessions throughout the park, SeaWorld has two dandy places for lunch: **Mango Joe's Café** and **Bimini Bay Café**. At dinnertime, the luau takes over at Bimini Bay and Mango Joe's closes down, leaving a choice of the **Anheuser-Busch Hospitality Center,** the **Buccaneer Smokehouse,** or **Mama Stella's Italian Kitchen.**

DINNER SHOW

Entertainment comes in the form of the **Aloha! Polynesian Luau Dinner and Show** at Bimini Bay Café. In an Anheuser-Busch family version of *Blue Hawaii,* scantily clad dancers undulate across the floor, bearing lei-draped platters of roast pig, mahimahi, piña coladas, and hula pie. The food here is not the draw, but the show's nonstop entertainment makes up for any lack of taste. Reservations are required for this two-hour culinary island voyage and may be made the same day either at the luau reservations counter in the information center at the entrance or by telephone (☎ 407/327–2424 or 800/227–8048). The cost is $38.11 adults, $27.51 children 8–12, $16.91 children 3–7, including one cocktail and all nonalcoholic drinks. Although the restaurant is inside the park, you do not have to pay park admission to attend only the feast.

FULL-SERVICE RESTAURANT

The **Bimini Bay Café** dishes up light and tasty tropical cuisine in a pale pastel setting that would be refreshing even without the air-conditioning. The veranda tables have a great view of the floats where the water-ski tow boats pick up their next load of daredevil stuntmen and stuntwomen.

SELF-SERVICE RESTAURANTS

The **Anheuser-Busch Hospitality Center,** far from espousing the Teutonic overtones of its Busch Gardens cousin, is light and airy, combining cafeteria-style service with a bar serving Anheuser-Busch beverages. Learn how to brew your own beer at a free 30-minute beer-making class, offered every hour. Hot tip: You can also score two free beers here. **Buccaneer Smokehouse** serves up barbecued chicken and ribs. **Mama Stella's Italian Kitchen** is just that.

Chicken 'n' Biscuit serves chicken salads and crispy dinners with all the trimmings. **The Waterfront Sandwich Grill** has a selection of sandwiches that are carved to order, along with big, juicy hamburgers. At **Mango Joe's Café,** a cafeteria done in tropical hues between Shamu Stadium and Atlantis Bayside Stadium, the menu offers fresh fajitas, hefty salads, and delicious key lime pie. Many of the umbrella-shaded tables are right on the lake, and some have a great view of the water-skiing show.

For Travelers with Disabilities

ATTRACTIONS

Because many shows are in theaters and stadiums, you will have an easy day at SeaWorld if you use a wheelchair. With reserved seating areas, **Key West Dolphin Stadium,** the **Nautilus Theater, Sea Lion & Otter Stadium, SeaWorld Theater,** and **Shamu Stadium** are completely accessible, although entry usually requires an uphill climb along sloping ramps. The stadium shows usually fill to capacity, so plan to arrive 30–45 minutes before each show—45–60 minutes in peak seasons. At Shamu Stadium, the reserved seating area is inside the splash zone, so if you don't want to get soaking wet, get a host or hostess to recommend another place to sit. There is entertainment value in all of the theater and stadium shows for both hearing-impaired and visually impaired guests with a single exception: performances in the Nautilus Theater may be unrewarding for guests with visual impairments.

Penguin Encounter, Terrors of the Deep, Tropical Reef, and **Journey to Atlantis** are all wheelchair accessible. To ride the moving-sidewalk viewing areas in Penguin Encounter, Terrors of the Deep, and Journey to Atlantis, you must transfer to a standard wheelchair, available in the boarding area, if you do not already use one. Tropical Reef and Penguin Encounter have minimal entertainment value for guests with visual impairments. All are enjoyable for guests with hearing impairments. To ride **Kraken** you must be able to transfer to the ride vehicles.

Shamu's Happy Harbor has some activities that are accessible to children using wheelchairs and anyone else who wants to climb, crawl, or slide.

RESTAURANTS AND SHOPS
Restaurants are accessible, but drinking straws are not provided here out of concern for the safety of the animals. Shops are level, but many are so packed with merchandise that maneuvering in a wheelchair can be a challenge.

SERVICES
There's **outgoing TTY** at Bimini Bay Café and across from Key West Dolphin Stadium. Sign-language interpreters for the **guided tours** can be provided with advance notice.

WHEELCHAIR RENTALS
Both standard and electric wheelchairs are available at SeaWorld ($6 and $30 daily, respectively, with driver's license).

Entertainment
SeaWorld has had pyrotechnic shows since the beginning; themes change, but the operative word is always "spectacular," and the show is definitely worth staying for. Bringing back an old favorite, SeaWorld is once again presenting the "Red, White and Blue Spectacular."

First Aid
First-aid centers are behind Stingray Lagoon and near Shamu's Happy Harbor. Registered nurses are on duty.

Getting There
SeaWorld is just off the intersection of I–4 and the Beeline Expressway, 10 minutes south of downtown Orlando, and 15 minutes from Orlando International Airport. Of all the Central Florida theme parks, it's the easiest to find. If you're heading west on I–4 (toward Disney), take Exit 28 and follow signs a short distance to the parking lot. Heading east, take Exit 27A.

Guided Tours
Even if you already know the answer to the frequently asked question, "Do you paint Shamu?," it's worth spending the nominal extra fee to sign up for a SeaWorld behind-the-scenes guided tour. The 90-minute **Backstage Explorations** and **Animal Lover's Adventure** give broad overviews.

In the hour-long **Animal Training Discoveries** SeaWorld trainers discuss animal behavior and training techniques. The hour-long **To the Rescue** takes a look at such recently rescued animals as manatees and turtles. The 90-minute **Sharks Tour** teaches you about the care of sharks at the Terrors of the Deep attraction. The hour-long **Wild Arctic** tour gives you a close-up view of polar bears and penguins. All tours leave every 30 minutes until 3 and cost $6.95 for adults and $5.95 for children 3–

9. Register at the guided tour center to the left of the Guest Relations information center at the park entrance.

If you're serious—$349 worth of serious—about seeing how trainers work with animals, there are two slots a day open to tag along on the **Trainer for a Day Program** (TDP). You'll get a behind-the-scenes look at the day-to-day responsibilities of SeaWorld trainers by shadowing one of them throughout the day, and have a chance to touch and help feed the animals. Meeting time is 7 AM. Register in advance with the Education Department at 407/370–1382.

Hours
SeaWorld is open daily 9–7; in summer and on holidays the park may stay open as late as 10.

Lockers
Coin-operated lockers are available inside the park entrance and to the right as you enter, next to Shamu's Emporium. The cost is $1 or $1.50, depending on size. A change machine is nearby.

Lost Things and People
Go to the Information Center, just inside the park entrance, to report or meet up with lost parents or children or to reclaim your misplaced items or to drop off somebody else's. All employees who see lost-looking children will take them to the Information Center. A park-wide paging system helps reunite guests.

Money Matters
An ATM linked to various bank and credit-card networks is at the exit gate. Foreign currency can be exchanged at the Special Services window at the Main Gate (daily 10–3).

Package Pickup
When you make purchases anywhere in the park, your clerk can send them to Package Pickup, in Shamu's Emporium, on request. Allow an hour between making your purchase and departing.

Parking
Parking costs $6 per car, $7 per RV or camper. Preferred parking, which costs $10, allows you to park in the six rows closest to the front gate.

Shopping
As cuddly as the stuffed Shamus are the soft manatees sold at **Manatee Cove,** near the manatee exhibit; proceeds from the toys go to benefit a manatee preservation organization. The **Friends of the Wild** shop near Penguin Encounter carries various items, including tropical fish earrings and hair ornaments. Get a special souvenir photo at **Keyhole Photo,** near Shamu's Emporium. Key chains, mugs, and frames can be made with your picture while you wait, or you can pick them up at the end of the day. If you've left the park before realizing that your Aunt Betsy simply must have a Shamu slicker, visit **Shamu's Emporium,** just outside the entrance.

The SeaWorld visitor who can pass up plush Shamus is rare indeed—not in the least because they are available all over the park.

Visitor Information
Contact **SeaWorld Orlando** (✉ 7007 SeaWorld Dr., Orlando 32821, ☎ 407/351–3600 or 800/327–2424, ✑).

Inside the park, the main information center is **The Information Center,** near the park entrance. A large board at the entrance lists all show times.

BUSCH GARDENS

It's mighty strange, sheriff. Mighty strange. After you've endured an overdose of urban American density, you'll drive up to a fantastic, exotic park that blends the diverse regions of Africa on Florida's Gulf Coast. There's a chance that this combination thrill ride–adventure–botanical garden attraction would be a disjointed, subpar park, but that never happens. Busch Gardens is the land-based equivalent of Sea-World—it is quiet and calming, but it is also entertaining, intriguing, and wild.

There's an impressive roster of gut-wrenching roller coaster rides like Kumba and Gwazi scattered in and among the animal exhibits, along with water attractions, a sky ride, and shops galore. There are also exotic animals roaming the African veldt and rides scattered through a dozen areas that are loosely themed around turn-of-the-century Africa. The center of all this is **Timbuktu,** an open-air carnival and bazaar, with the main entrance taking you through **Morocco.** Walking counterclockwise along the winding paths, you'll also encounter **Myombe Reserve, Nairobi, the Congo, Stanleyville, Land of the Dragons,** and the **Bird Gardens.** Take a sharp right from Myombe Reserve and Nairobi and you'll find the **Crown Colony, Egypt, Edge of Africa,** and the **Serengeti Plain.** Although it's not as easy to navigate as the "hub-and-wheel" design of Disney's Magic Kingdom, each area is distinguished by its own distinctive architectural styles as well as regional music pumped through carefully camouflaged loudspeakers.

Despite the proliferation of rides, animals are the cornerstone of Busch Gardens' appeal. As a member of the American Association of Zoological Parks and Aquariums, Busch Gardens ranks among the top four zoos in the United States. More than 3,400 birds, mammals, and reptiles inhabit its 335 acres; the aviary houses some 600 rare and exotic birds; and about 500 African big-game animals roam uncaged on the 60-acre Serengeti Plain. Busch Gardens participates in the Species Survival Program, lending animals to other zoos for breeding, and has had tremendous success in breeding endangered animals on the premises. At the top of the program's wish list: hosting a pair of rare Chinese pandas. Animals are exhibited on islands, near concession stands, in spacious cages in the middle of a maze of lines, and in displays and shows in which they are the stars. There is little of the crowd and bustle of the Disney parks here, so relax and enjoy the beauty of nature spiced up by an occasional adrenaline-pumping adventure.

Numbers in the margin correspond to points of interest on the Busch Gardens map.

Morocco

The park's main entrance leads you through the gates of a tiled and turreted Moroccan fort, which houses the park administrative offices, and into a land of swirling colors and skirling music. Morocco itself contains two eateries—the Zagora Café and Sultan's Sweets—the Moroccan Palace Theater, and numerous souvenir stands, arranged in a replica of an open-air marketplace known as a souk. It's hard not to fall into the shekel-flinging mode; Middle Eastern music wails through the speakers, brightly colored wool tassels droop overhead, brass urns glimmer, bangles shimmer, veils waft in the wind, and mouthwatering smells issue from the bakery.

❶ Sultan's Tent. Follow the main drag to a raised platform hung with multicolor striped curtains, where a snake charmer snuggles up to a python and wraps it around her arms, waist, and neck. Show times are posted next to the tent. The snake charmer's main audience is a group of indifferent alligators, who loll about in a pond to the right. No hungry audience this: the alligators are so well fed and lazy that they ignore the plump koi fish that share their pond. *Crowds: Not a problem. Strategy: Pause to process the atmosphere before entering. Audience: All ages. Rating:* ★

❷ **Moroccan Palace Theater.** When you step into the blue-tiled, iron-fretted theater, catercorner to the alligators, you enter the cool comfort of an ice rink. An African-inspired park featuring an ice show? Go figure. Weird as it sounds, it works well. Ten skaters appear in "World Rhythms on Ice," a salute to songs from Brazil, Germany, Africa, Great Britain, Japan, America, and—Antarctica! This is one of the most interesting shows in the whole theme-park realm, and it offers a rare chance to see, close up, some Olympic-quality spins and jumps. *Duration: 25 mins. Crowd: Sizable, but there's always enough room. Strategy: Shows four times daily, six in high season; check schedules posted outside. Arrive 30–45 mins before show time to make sure you get a good seat. Audience: All ages. Rating:* ★★★

NEED A BREAK? **Sultan's Sweets** is the place for a cup of cappuccino and a *churro* (Mexican deep-fried sweet dough liberally dusted with confectioner's sugar). If your diet demands that you eat nothing but sugar-based foods, then you'll love the selection of candy, fudge, and ice cream. Breakfast is also available.

Crown Colony

This is a transportation and hospitality center with a distinctly non-African attraction that couldn't be accommodated elsewhere: BEC's signature Clydesdale horses—a staple at every BEC park. A station in Crown Colony serves as the terminus for one end of the Skyride, which connects to the Congo (☞ Serengeti Plain, *below,* for both).

❸ **Clydesdale Hamlet.** The usual batch of oversize beasts galumphs around a corral and stables; a particularly patient one is periodically led out for photographs, much to the delight of tykes and their parents. *Crowds: Never significant. Strategy: Go anytime. Audience: All ages. Rating:* ★

❹ **Akbar's Adventure Tours.** Motion simulator rides were extraordinary when they came out in the 1980s, so we can't promise the technology and experience will be anything you haven't already seen. The draw here is that Martin Short is Akbar, the "world's greatest tour guide," and to help keep his failing business afloat he takes you on a trip across Egypt with the requisite bouncing, drops, twists, and turns you've come to expect. Exotic Egyptian music sets the tone. *Duration: 5 mins. Crowds: Lines are virtually nonexistent. Strategy: Go anytime. Audience: All but young children. No guests with motion sickness or heart, neck, or back problems. Rating:* ★★

Egypt

Dominating this section of the park is the awesome roller coaster known as **Montu.** There are also plenty of shops and an interesting tour through a replica of the tomb of King Tutankhamen ("Tut" to his friends). You can also pick up the **Trans-Veldt Railroad** (☞ Nairobi, *below*) here.

158

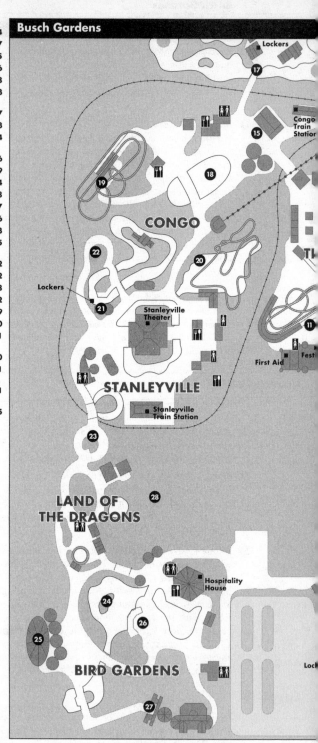

Busch Gardens

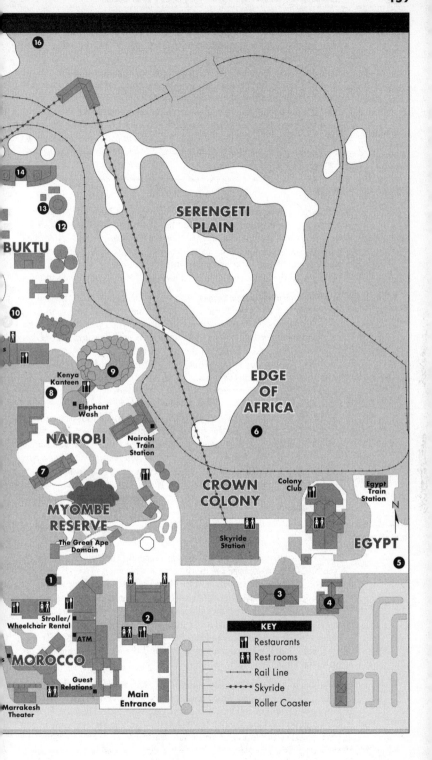

SERENGETI
PLAIN

BUKTU

Kenya
Kanteen

Elephant
Wash

NAIROBI

Nairobi
Train
Station

EDGE
OF
AFRICA

MYOMBE
RESERVE

The Great Ape
Domain

CROWN
COLONY

Colony
Club

Skyride
Station

Egypt
Train
Station

EGYPT

N

Stroller/
Wheelchair Rental

ATM

MOROCCO

Guest
Relations

Marrakesh
Theater

Main
Entrance

KEY

Restaurants
Rest rooms
—— Rail Line
••••• Skyride
—— Roller Coaster

❺ Montu. The entrance to this screaming-fast ride looks like it was taken from the set of *Cleopatra*. Past the towering Egyptian statues lies a snaking 4,000-ft-long roller coaster that—when you're locked down with no chance of escape—submits you to a G-force of 3.85 and speeds in excess of 60 mph. It's a gut-wrenching thrill ride that is not for the fainthearted or anyone who has the heebie-jeebies. As is true of its cousin Kumba, the mere sound and the sheer size of Montu are intimidating, but take the chance if you want to brag about it later. *Duration: 3 mins. Crowds: Lines can get long on busy days. Strategy: Go early in the morning or late in the day. Most of the time, settle in for a wait that will be worth it. Audience: Older children and adults. Minimum height: 54".* *Rating:* ★★★

Edge of Africa

On the southern edge of the Serengeti Plain, this 15-acre exhibit area showcases hippos, baboons, crocodiles, and various species of fish via above-surface and underwater viewing. In addition, there's an **African Village,** supposedly vacated by a Masai tribe that had been overtaken by lions and hyenas; a **Safari Encampment** with giraffes, zebras, and other denizens of the Serengeti Plain; and habitats for meerkats and vultures.

❻ Edge of Africa Welcome Center. You begin your walk-through experience here at a welcome center, where you learn about which animals were seen where during the previous 24 hours. Then you're off on your own for some personal encounters with lions, giraffes, and other creatures who make their home on the Serengeti Plain. The information in the Welcome Center is probably enough for most people, but if you love animals, it's probably worth your while to pay extra for the half-hour-long Edge of Africa **Safari Tour** in an open-air flatbed truck. You'll have a truly up-close and personal encounter with the animals, and the guides are very informative as they field as many questions as you want to ask. The highlight of the trip is getting to feed the animals yourself—caretakers give you branches or pieces of fruit—and watching a young giraffe being bottle-fed. *Tour times and cost: Five times daily; $20. Duration: Safari tour 30 mins; stay as long as you wish in the Welcome Center. Crowds: The wide-open Welcome Center usually doesn't feel crowded. Strategy: Visit anytime. Audience: All ages. Rating:* ★★★

Serengeti Plain

This is one of the must-sees at Busch Gardens: 500 animals running free on 500 acres that re-create their natural habitats (which turn out to look remarkably similar to Florida pastureland). Still, they're not confined by cages. Residents of the grasslands include zebras, camels, impalas, giraffes, lions, buffalo, ostriches, baboons, gazelles, Cape buffalo, and kudus (a heftier impala). In addition to the Safari Tour, there are a few other ways to see this area: the **Trans-Veldt Railroad,** which skirts the edge of the Serengeti; and the **Skyride,** which grants an aerial view.

Skyride. In addition to being a great shortcut to the far region of the park (Congo), this elevated tour places you five stories above the Serengeti and Timbuktu on a 1-mi one-way ride between Crown Colony and the Congo. The Skyride gives you a great overview of the park so you can plan your approach, but sometimes bad weather can close it down. *Duration: 7 mins. Crowds: Can get heavy in midday. Strategy: Ride in the morning or toward park closing time. Audience: All ages. Rating:* ★★★

Myombe Reserve: The Great Ape Domain

The entrance to this superbly luxuriant walk-through rain forest (opposite the Moroccan Palace Theater) is easily overlooked but shouldn't be missed. This is the park's most-heralded animal attraction, since it's home to an extended family of chimpanzees and another family of Western lowland gorillas. The gorillas (scientific name *Gorilla gorilla gorilla*) are just as magnificent as you'd expect, and the opportunity to see them in a somewhat natural setting and through a wide viewing area is undeniably thrilling. Guides will increase your gorilla IQ with information such as that gorillas rest 40% of the day and feed another 30%. There are also plaques and educational signage that will help you understand these fantastic animals. Check out the Aldabra tortoises, which can weigh more than 500 pounds and live to be 100. *Duration: As long as you like. Crowds: Not significant. Strategy: Visit either first thing in the morning or late in the afternoon; both are close to feeding time, when both apes and chimps are more active. Audience: All ages. Rating:* ★★★

Nairobi

Myombe's rain-forested path leads you to Nairobi, a collection of buildings containing the animal nursery, the petting zoo, the elephant display, and the Nairobi train station—a gingerbread clapboard structure straight out of *Out of Africa*.

➐ Animal Nursery. Within this long, low building are glass cages holding convalescing animals wrapped in nests of blankets; through the glass on the other side of the cages, you can see the laboratories and food preparation. Animals are fed at various times, so there's usually something going on. *Duration: As long as you like. Crowds: Not a problem. Strategy: Visit anytime. Audience: All ages. Rating:* ★★★

➑ Petting Zoo. Nubian and African pygmy goats, Barbados black-bellied sheep, ducks, rabbits, turtles, roosters, and hens are all gathered in this zoo. You are allowed to feed only the goats and sheep, both of which are rotated throughout the day to keep them from being overfed; food for the others is brought out on a tray twice daily. *Duration: As long as you like. Crowds: Never significant. Strategy: Go anytime. Audience: All ages. Rating:* ★

➒ Elephant Display. The big attraction in Nairobi is the building housing 22 Asian elephants; the most attractive part of the display is their swimming pool, in which elephant parents and children snort, swim, and clean off before getting dusty again. Every couple of hours, some of the elephants troop out to the Elephant Wash area next to the Kenya Kanteen, where a schedule is posted and where a caretaker keeps them cool with sprays from a garden house and explains their habits to guests. *Duration: As long as you like. Crowds: Can be significant for the Elephant Wash, but you can usually see. Strategy: Go anytime. Audience: All ages. Rating:* ★★

Trans-Veldt Railroad. The Kenya Kanteen is a good place to watch out for this authentic reproduction of an East African steam locomotive with, as the tour guide points out, an American cowcatcher in case the train encounters one of those pesky impala—none of which actually can come near the tracks. The train chugs around the Serengeti and then circumnavigates the park in a 2½-mi journey, with stops near the Congo River Rapids and in Stanleyville. *Duration: 20 mins; it's about 10 mins to the Congo Train Station and another 10 mins to Stanleyville. Crowds: Steady, but you almost always find a seat. Strategy: Since it comes only every 20 mins, watch the mother elephants dunking the* *little ones in the elephant pool until you hear the whistle; then dash for the station. Audience: All ages. Rating: ★★*

Timbuktu

The entrance to Timbuktu is a blindingly white mud fort, inside which is a claustrophobic walled area housing at least three rides that are guaranteed to make you lose your lunch. You'll also find a video arcade and numerous games of chance, a carousel and children's rides, the **Dolphin Theater**, and the **Festhaus**, an incongruous little piece of Germany.

⑩ Sandstorm. "The number one ride for making guests throw up" is how a Busch Gardens staffer eloquently describes this attraction. It doesn't look all that menacing, but the constant rotation of both your seat and the arm to which it's attached do the trick. *Duration: 2½ mins. Crowds: Not a problem. Strategy: Go anytime. Audience: Older children and adults. Rating: ★★*

⑪ Scorpion. This looming 1,805 ft of steel roller coaster is twisted into a gigantic hoop with a 65-ft drop and reaches a maximum speed of 50 mph. *Duration: 2 mins. Crowds: Lines can build at midday in busy periods. Strategy: Go early or late. Audience: Older children and adults. Minimum height: 42″. Rating: ★★*

⑫ Phoenix. Similar to the pendulum-like pirate ships you see at county fairs, this towering structure offers increasingly elevated crescent swings back and forth, higher and higher, until the whole thing swoops sickeningly over the top. Bon voyage! *Duration: 2 mins. Crowds: Lines can build at midday in busy periods. Strategy: Go early or late. Audience: Older children and adults. Minimum height: 48″. Rating: ★★*

⑬ Crazy Camel. This hopped-up carousel looks similar to a Mexican hat, with cars careening up and over bumps on the brim. Brightly painted camels dance alongside the traditional horses. Other enjoyable attractions nearby include children's rides and games of chance from basketball to fishing with a magnet, as well as a pint-size version of the Phoenix. For similar rides for little ones, check out **Land of the Dragons**, outside Stanleyville. *Crowds: Can get heavy in mid-afternoon. Strategy: Do the ride in early morning. Audience: All ages. Rating: ★★★*

⑭ Dolphin Theater. Although it's modeled after SeaWorld's theater, this dolphin tank is smaller and lacks the Plexiglas sides that let you peer at the underwater activities during the show. But *Dolphins of the Deep* is similarly delightful, and, in fact, the dolphins and trainers are borrowed from Busch Gardens' fishy cousin. Mick and Bud (Hmmmm, Busch Gardens . . . Michelob?! Budweiser?!) more than earn their 35 pounds of raw fish, jumping and waving their flippers and thoroughly enchanting everyone, including the one lucky child chosen to come up and play with them. If your child is between 5 and 8, outgoing, and not scared by dolphins, arrive 15 minutes early and ask an usher if your child can be picked. He or she will, however, be backstage learning the proper hand signals during a dandy bit when the trainer plays in the water with the dolphins. *Duration: 20 mins. Crowds: Never a problem. Strategy: Go at midday, when the other animals are snoozing; skip it if you've seen the show at SeaWorld and you're short on time. Audience: All ages. Rating: ★★★*

Congo

This area is practically indistinguishable from the real Congo. Unlike the open, dusty plains of the Serengeti and Nairobi, Congo and the adjacent Stanleyville are delightfully shaded by lush plantings and lofty, leafy trees, under whose branches nestle African fetish statues and piles of expedition-supply boxes for that "Dr. Livingstone, I presume" touch. A couple of thatched huts scattered throughout contain snakes in wire boxes and inquisitive parrots perched in cages. Keepers are on hand to explain their behavior and hold them for you to stroke. One end of the Skyride (☞ Serengeti Plain, *above*) and a stop on the Trans-Veldt Railroad (☞ Nairobi, *above*) can also be found here. Hysterical shrieks from the area's several thrill rides remind you that the visitors, if not the natives, are perpetually restless.

⑮ **Ubanga-Banga Bumper Cars.** Aptly named, this popular attraction has a carnival allure, and young kids, along with big kids who have never grown up, love them. *Duration: About 4 mins. Crowds: Never significant enough to cause a wait except in mid-afternoon during busy periods. Strategy: Go anytime—but if there's a line, don't wait. Audience: Older children and adults. Rating:* ★★

⑯ **Kumba.** The nearly 4,000 ft of twisting turquoise steel supports cars going up to 60 mph through three, first-of-a-kind coaster maneuvers: a "diving loop" that plunges you from 110 ft into a loop; a camelback, with a 360° spiral and three seconds of weightlessness; and the world's largest loop, with a height of 108 ft. That's in addition to spirals, cobra rolls, and a corkscrew in the dark. The ride is surprisingly smooth, totally free of the neck-wrenching you find on most similar adventures. Catch a replay of your screaming face on three TV monitors near the exit. *Duration: 3 mins. Crowds: Often. Strategy: Go as soon as the park opens. Audience: Older children and adults. Minimum height: 54".
Rating:* ★★★

⑰ **Congo River Rapids.** Everyone who loves water rides considers this one of the all-time best. Twelve people sit in each of several inner tube–like rafts and go for a bumper-car ride on a stream. As you go bumping and bucketing through nearly ¼ mi of rapids and waterfalls and through a dark cave, be sure your camera is wrapped in a waterproof bag—and remember to smile for the spectators taking pictures from the bridge. *Duration: 5 mins. Crowds: There's usually a line. Strategy: Go early to avoid waits and have the best time. Audience: Older children and adults. Children under 38" may ride when accompanied by an adult. Rating:* ★★★

⑱ **Claw Island.** Somehow all the hoopla at the park doesn't seem to bother the somnolent Bengal tigers. If you want to see them when they're most active, come in early morning or late afternoon. Some particularly pleasant shady benches overlook the island and are a nice place to recuperate before hitting the next rides. *Crowds: Nonexistent. Strategy: Go in the early morning, when the animals are awake. Audience: All ages. Rating:* ★★★

⑲ **Python.** When this ride premiered in the late 1970s, it was a cutting edge coaster. Today it's still thrilling, but takes a backseat to its wild siblings, Gwazi and Montu. Passengers are hurled through two hoops at 50 mph on the 1,250-ft track of this steel roller coaster. *Duration: 70 seconds. Crowds: Significant only in busy seasons. Strategy: Go early or late during holiday periods. Audience: Older children and adults. Children must ride with an adult. Minimum height: 48". Rating:* ★★

Stanleyville

Named for a city in Zaire now known as Kisangani, this area is very much akin to the Congo in flavor. Here, too, you are surrounded by lush tropical vegetation and animals native to that part of Africa, and you'll find the requisite rides and stores selling handicrafts. Yet another train station—a twin of Nairobi's—is located near the orangutans' island behind the Stanleyville Theater, where youngsters and the young at heart can listen to big band music.

㉑ Stanley Falls Log Flume Ride. Although somewhat dated as far as theme-park rides go, the Log Flume is still very popular because of its 40-ft drop. The ride may creak a little, and it's a little slow, but at least you're certain to get wet. *Duration: 3½ mins. Crowds: Significant, with lines even on average days. Strategy: Ride early in the morning or in the evening. Audience: Older children and adults. Minimum height: 42". Rating:* ★★★

㉑ Tanganyika Tidal Wave. The tidal wave actually offers two possibilities for dunking: the ride itself—a 55-ft drop sends you right into a splash pool—and, for those who are chicken, the viewing bridge at the bottom of the drop, where a recording of Tchaikovsky's *1812 Overture* heralds the next wave. A sign posted nearby politely reads, THIS BRIDGE IS PART OF A WATER ATTRACTION. YOU WILL GET SOAKED. THANK YOU. Either huddle behind the Plexiglas shelter on the bridge or skitter off—fast. *Duration: 6 mins. Crowds: Significant, with lines even on average days. Strategy: Ride early in the morning or in the evening. Audience: Older children and adults. Minimum height: 42". Rating:* ★★★

㉒ Orchid Canyon. This lovely 100-yard walk winds through 200-odd cascading orchids and bromeliads native to South Africa, the Philippines, and South America—it's a welcome respite from the sensory overload you'll get in the rest of the park. Meanwhile, placidly ignoring riders' screeches and distant pleas of "Aw, c'mon, Melissa, you need to go on this ride," lemurs, rhinoceroses, elands, and orangutans peacefully snooze away in spacious enclosures naturalized with rocks, trees, and, for the orangutans, gymnastic equipment. *Duration: Up to you. Crowds: Not a problem. Strategy: Go anytime. Audience: All ages. Rating:* ★★

Land of the Dragons

This cluster of kiddie-size attractions is one of the best children's areas in any theme park. Rope climbs and bouncing walkways fill the three-story **Tree House** at the center. Adults tromp along with their kids, loudspeakers belt out merry children's songs, and, several times daily, conservation specialists tell animal stories, sometimes with live animals as props. The youngsters' seats: fake toadstools. It's all wonderfully colorful and cheerful. *Crowds: Seldom a problem. Strategy: Wait until later in the day, or you may never get your youngsters away; or go at midday for a respite from the heat. Audience: Young children. Rating:* ★★★

Bird Gardens

Following the path from Stanleyville, past the orangutans, and onto the bridge over the train tracks brings you to this area, home to a sterling children's playground, a koala habitat, and more than 1,800 exotic birds representing 350 species. The flock of Caribbean flamingos is one of the largest in captivity; the hundred or so birds, vivid Caribbean flamingos and paler Chilean flamingos, are fed beta-carotene supplements to maintain their color.

㉓ Lory Landing. Named for the multicolored birds from Indonesia and the South Pacific, these aerialists fly freely beneath two sprawling live oaks just over the ramp from Stanleyville. This area is fascinating. For $1 you can feed the lorys Lorikeet Nectar, a special juice mixed just for them, and most birds will land on a shoulder or outstretched hand to take a sip. A trainer is usually on hand to answer questions such as, "How do I get this lory mess off my sweater?" *Duration: Up to you.*

Crowds: Not a problem. Strategy: Go in the morning, when the birds will be hungriest. Audience: All ages. Rating: ★★★

㉔ **Flamingo Island.** The dollar value on the flock of Caribbean flamingos nesting here is well over $1 million. The flamingos are part of a national breeding program, so the number of birds in the flock is constantly changing but may be as large as 100. *Duration: Up to you. Crowds: Not a problem. Strategy: Go early or late to see birds at their most active. Audience: All ages. Rating:* ★★

㉕ **Aviary.** Nearly 200 species of birds, including macaws and egrets, flutter freely among the trees and stalk along the ground of this lushly landscaped walk-through cage to your right of Flamingo Island as you come from Stanleyville. *Duration: Up to you. Crowds: Not a problem. Strategy: Go early or late to see birds at their most active. Audience: All ages. Rating:* ★★

㉖ **Bird Show Theater.** The open amphitheater just behind Flamingo Island displays macaws, condors, and eagles performing natural behaviors; bird enthusiasts rate *For The Birds* one of the best shows anywhere for the variety of birds and interesting stunts. You can have your photo taken with one of the squawking stars at the adjacent posing area just after each show. *Duration: 30 mins. Crowds: Sometimes significant during holiday periods. Strategy: Arrive 15 mins before show time in busy seasons. Audience: All ages. Rating:* ★★

㉗ **Koala House.** Down the boardwalk and past the aviary, an elaborate display with Chinese motifs once housed a pair of pandas; now it's home to a breeding group of four koalas—one male and three females, the marsupial version of the Playboy Mansion. You can usually spot some joeys (baby koalas), although a look at the impassive parents makes it hard to imagine that any two of them ever get worked up enough to procreate. For close-up viewing by visitors, the exhibit offers a people-mover and an elevated observation gallery. Also, pay a few quarters for pellets to feed the huge, decorative fish in the adjoining pool. They beg. Really. *Duration: Up to you. Crowds: Not a problem. Strategy: Go in late afternoon to see the animals at their most active. Audience: All ages. Rating:* ★

㉘ **Gwazi.** The two wooden roller coasters in Bird Gardens, which opened in June 1999, provide a rattling, clattering thrill a minute. Two trains depart the station in unison, separate, and then hurtle toward each other in an apparent headlong collision no fewer than six times. Although the cars' individual speeds are roughly 50 mph, staffers love to point out that the "fly-by" speed makes it seem more like 100! Add to this a 90-ft drop, and there's every reason to scream your lungs out. *Crowds: Expect heavy lines all day until the newness wears off. Strategy: Ride early or late. Leave your possessions with a nonrider or in lockers at the bottom of the ride. Audience: Older children and adults. Minimum height: 48". Rating:* ★★★

Strategies for Your Visit to Busch Gardens

When to Go

Monday is least crowded in summer and other times when local schools are out++re 2nd phrase above, when local schools are out it is also least crowded?++; any weekday is equally tranquil the rest of the year.

Blitz Tour

Figuring out the most efficient way to visit Busch Gardens is only slightly less complicated than planning a safari. Pick up a list of shows at the entrance gate and loosely schedule your day around them; they make welcome breaks in a full day on your feet, and some are even air-conditioned. Must-sees are the dolphin show, the bird show, the Elephant Wash, and the ice show. After passing right on through Morocco, head directly for **Gwazi** if you are a coaster enthusiast. If not, then head for the **Myombe Reserve.** Upon exiting you will be in Nairobi, where you can see the **Animal Nursery** and the **Elephant Display.** Before getting on the train, walk to Edge of Africa, then go over to Egypt. If you dare, ride **Montu,** then see **Tut's Tomb** and **Akbar's Adventure Tours.** Have lunch at the Crown Colony, then take the **Skyride** to the Congo. See the **Claw Island** tigers on your way to catch a show at the **Dolphin Theater.** Then ride the **Congo River Rapids, Kumba,** the **Tanganyika Tidal Wave,** and **Stanley Falls Log Flume Ride.** Now that you are soaked to the bone, change your clothes and head over to **Lory Landing.** If you have children, let them play for a while in the **Land of the Dragons** before the next presentation at the **Bird Show** theater. Walk through the Bird Gardens, being sure to check out the **Koala House.** Quench your thirst at the **Hospitality House** before heading back to Morocco to take in the last ice-show performance of the day at the **Moroccan Palace Theater.** It's a nice way to end your day, and you can hit the Moroccan souk on your way out.

On Rainy Days

The Skyride may close temporarily because of lightning or high winds, but otherwise it's business as usual in the park. However, you'll get wet, and since the animals seek shelter (as you will feel like doing), your experience may not be as rich as it would be when the sun is out.

Other Tips

- As soon as you arrive in the park, set up a specific rendezvous location and time in case you and your companions get separated. Good spots to meet are in front of the Moroccan Palace Theater, at the entrance to any of the train stations, by the Clydesdale Hamlet, at the Edge of Africa Welcome Center, or at a park bench in Land of the Dragons.

- Keep in mind that the animals nap through most of the day. You'll see the most action first thing in the morning and in the late afternoon.

- Water rides here are designed to get you wet—very wet. There is no dry seat on the rides. On cold or overcast days, if you don't want to freeze, bring rain gear or buy a plastic poncho (about $4). For that matter, you may want to bring a change of clothes—and stash it in a locker in case you need it.

- When kids and parents want to go their separate ways, you can rent Motorola radios to stay in touch. Fork over $10 (plus a $100 refundable deposit) and you've got a lifeline to the rest of your party.

- If you want to snap loved ones in mid-ride, look for photo staging spots at Congo River Rapids, Kumba, and the Tanganyika Tidal Wave.

Busch Gardens A to Z

Admission

TICKETS

Adults pay $45.68 and children 3–9 pay $36.74, not including tax.

DISCOUNTS

You can purchase a second-day ticket for $10.95; however, the ticket must be used the next day. Consider buying a Twilight Ticket if you enter the park after 3:30 PM. It is $33.70 for adults, $25.70 for children 3–9. Combination Busch Gardens–SeaWorld tickets, which allow one day in each park, cost $83.74 for adults, $67.84 for children 3–

9. The Orlando FlexTicket, which covers Busch Gardens and other parks, is also a money-saver (☞ Admission *in* SeaWorld Orlando A to Z, *above*).

Baby Care

Nursing facilities and diaper-changing tables are in Land of the Dragons; women's rest rooms also have changing tables. You'll find stroller rentals at Stroller and Wheelchair Rental, in Morocco ($6 for singles, $10 for doubles, including $1 deposit; doubles are safari trucks!). Disposable diapers are sold at Stroller and Wheelchair Rental. Baby food and formula are sold at the Food Lion on 50th Street and Busch Boulevard. Go down a little farther, to 56th Street, and you'll find a Kmart (on Busch Boulevard itself) as well as Publix and a Kash 'N' Karry, which are on 56th Street, left off Busch Boulevard.

Cameras and Film

Disposable cameras are for sale at **Safari Foto,** near the main entrance, as well as at other stores throughout the park.

Car Care

If you have car trouble, raise your hood and the parking patrol will assist you.

Dining

Most gustatory offerings are of the red-meat variety—smoked, wursted, or burgered. They are routinely washed down with Anheuser-Busch products, which are sold park-wide: Budweiser, Bud Light, Michelob, and nonalcoholic O'Doul's. Ice cream and popcorn stands are ubiquitous.

FULL-SERVICE RESTAURANTS

The Crown Colony's **Colony Club,** the fanciest place in the park, is done up to resemble a veddy British eatery from the good old *Out of Africa* days, with portraits of top-hatted sahibs, used polo mallets, and nicely faded Oriental carpets. Sandwiches, salad platters, and pizza are served downstairs, where it's counter service; upstairs, you can enjoy steak, chicken, and pasta dishes in white-tablecloth splendor, attended by proper waiters and waitresses, with huge windows and a great view of the Serengeti. The change in altitude affects the price only minimally, and the setting is one of the most relaxing in the park. Unfortunately, the number of window tables is limited, so you have to have lunch before noon and dinner around 4:30 to be sure of getting one without waiting. When the park closes early, seating may end around 4, although this varies.

Germany meets Timbuktu at the **Festhaus,** where dirndled maidens and lederhosen-clad youth dance around a beer-swilling, sausage-chomping crowd.

The **Hospitality House,** in Bird Gardens, provides free whistle-wetting brews (limit: two) on tap. After a full day at Busch Gardens, you'll need it. You can also order a delicious hero, the Tampa Sandwich Platter. Even the outdoor setting is pleasant, and there's music.

SELF-SERVICE RESTAURANTS

The **Bazaar Café** offers hearty barbecued beef sandwiches and, along with the Stanleyville Smokehouse, makes the Stanleyville air redolent of barbecue.

The **Stanleyville Smokehouse** serves slow-cooked chicken, beef, and ribs with corn on the cob and all the trimmings.

Morocco's **Zagora Café,** an enormous open-air cafeteria, dishes out basic burgers, fajitas, and turkey sandwiches.

For Travelers with Disabilities

To many wheelchair users, the Busch Gardens experience will be represented less by the wild rides than by the animals, which are on display at almost every turn. Of the rides that make up a significant part of the experience for many other visitors, almost all are accessible by guests who can transfer from their own wheelchair into the ride vehicles.

ATTRACTIONS

All attractions are wheelchair accessible in Morocco, Myombe Reserve, and Nairobi. **Akbar's Adventure Tours** is completely wheelchair accessible. To play in Land of the Dragons, children must be able to leave their wheelchairs, although they've provided an adjoining wheelchair-accessible playground to the side.

You must leave your wheelchair to board vehicles at **Montu** in Egypt; **Congo River Rapids, Ubanga-Banga Bumper Cars,** and **Python** in Congo; **Stanley Falls** and **Tanganyika Tidal Wave** in Stanleyville; **Crazy Camel, Phoenix, Sandstorm,** and **Scorpion** in Timbuktu; and **Gwazi** in Bird Gardens. For these, you must also be able to hold lap bars or railings, as well as sit upright and absorb sudden and dramatic movements. Timbuktu's other rides also cannot be boarded in a wheelchair. Transferring out of a wheelchair is required for **Congo kiddie rides,** too.

RESTAURANTS AND SHOPS

All shops and restaurants in Busch Gardens are wheelchair accessible.

SERVICES

The park publishes a leaflet describing each attraction's accessibility. It's available at Guest Relations.

WHEELCHAIR RENTALS

At **Stroller and Wheelchair Rental,** in Morocco, you can rent standard chairs ($5; $1 deposit) and motorized wheelchairs ($25; $5 deposit). If yours disappears and needs replacing, ask in any gift shop.

First Aid

The infirmary is alongside the Festhaus, in Timbuktu.

Getting There

Busch Gardens is at the corner of Busch Boulevard and 40th Street, 8 mi northeast of downtown Tampa, 2 mi east of I–275, and 2 mi west of I–75. It will take you an hour and 15 minutes to drive the 81 mi from Orlando on I–4. From Orlando, travel west on I–4, then north on I–75 to Fowler Avenue (Exit 54). This is also the exit for the University of South Florida. Bear left on the exit ramp, and it will lead you onto Fowler Avenue. Head west on Fowler Avenue to McKinley Avenue. (McKinley Avenue is the first light past the main entrance to the university.) Turn left on McKinley. Go south on McKinley to parking and the main entrance to the park.

Guided Tours

The **Serengeti Safari** ($20; ☎ 813/987–5212) leaves Edge of Africa five times a day on a 30-minute tour of the Serengeti Plain.

Hours

The park is open daily from 9:30 to 6, except during summer and some holidays, when hours are extended.

Lockers

You'll find them in the Moroccan village; in Stanleyville, near the Tanganyika Tidal Wave; and in the Congo, at the Kumba and Congo River Rapids rides. The cost is 50¢. There are change machines near the lockers.

Lost Things and People
Report losses and finds of material goods at Guest Relations at the main entrance. For lost companions, go to Security or speak to any of the security personnel, who wear white shirts, badges, and hats and look vaguely like sheriffs.

Money Matters
There are two ATMs—one just outside the main entrance and the other in Timbuktu's Festhaus. For currency exchange, go to the Guest Relations window near the main entrance in Morocco.

Package Pickup
If you'd rather not lug around your purchases all day, have them sent from any store in the park to **Sahara Traders,** in the Moroccan village area near the entrance. You can pick them up on your way out. The service is free, but do allow an hour for delivery.

Parking
The cost for parking is $6 for cars, $7 for trucks or campers, and $5 for motorcycles.

Shopping
There are three must-have stuffed animals on the Central Florida theme-park circuit, and two of them are here (the third being SeaWorld's plush killer whales). Cuddly gorillas are available at **J. R.'s Gorilla Hut,** just outside Myombe Reserve, along with a delightfully long-limbed chimpanzee whose Velcro palms attach in an everlasting hug. White-tiger puppets are sold at the **Stanleyville Bazaar.** You'll also find plenty of pseudo-African schlock—along with some authentic imported treasures. Craftspeople fashion their wares outside, and some interesting handcrafted items are available for sale. It's a good place to look for the perfect birthday trinket or Yuletide stocking stuffer, perhaps a set of carved wooden zoo animals or brilliantly colored, elephant-shape napkin rings. The stock in Stanleyville's **Air Africa** is similar to that of the Stanleyville Bazaar. **Continental Curios** in Morocco is the stop for inexpensive bangles, moderately priced brass, and exorbitantly priced Moroccan leather, not to mention a rainbow of gauze veils in which to swathe your own little Salome.

The Busch Gardens shopping is good enough that many a local resident comes here for birthday presents and such. If you leave the park without purchasing that beautiful bird key ring and want to run back for one, ask about one of the 30-minute **shopping passes,** available for a deposit equaling the price of admission.

Visitor Information
Contact **Busch Gardens** (⊠ Box 9158, Tampa 33674, ☎ 813/987–5082, ✎).

On-site park information is available at **Guest Relations,** near the main entrance, in Morocco. This is where you can find out if there will be any tapings of *Jack Hanna's Animal Adventures* in the park that day. Better yet, call in advance.

A large sign at the entrance lists each day's performance schedule; show times are also posted next to the individual stages and theaters.

CYPRESS GARDENS

If you're wondering what Florida attractions looked like in the beginning, swing by Cypress Gardens. A botanical garden, amusement park, and waterskiing show rolled into one, Cypress Gardens is a uniquely Floridian combination of natural beauty and utter kitsch. Working with a patch of swamp beside a pristine lake, Dick Pope (the "Father of Florida Tourism") and his wife Julie created Florida's first theme park. She was a Southern belle from Alabama with a green thumb, and he was a short, fast-talking real estate promoter and public relations whiz addicted to flashy jackets: "If I didn't wear the jackets," he once confided to *Life* magazine, "people would think I was a tall fire hydrant." They created their dream in a snake- and alligator-infested cypress swamp on the shores of Lake Eloise in what are euphemistically referred to as the Central Florida "highlands," and they opened for business on January 1, 1936. Ticket receipts that day totaled $38, not that much more than the price of a day's admission today. Cypress Gardens has been open ever since and is Central Florida's oldest continuously running attraction.

Despite Dick's self-designated status as "Swami of the Swamps" and "The Man Who Invented Florida," Cypress Gardens owes its two best-known traditions to Julie. In charge of the park during World War II while Dick was in the Armed Forces, Julie promised free water-ski shows for the soldiers at a nearby military base. What started with some stunts by Dick Jr. and his friends quickly expanded into a fully choreographed program with a bevy of "aquamaids" and stunt skiers, who originated the flips, barefoot skiing, and pyramids now a part of all waterskiing shows—both at Cypress Gardens and at other entertainment parks. When a winter storm devastated the plantings at the entrance to the park, Julie dressed the women on the staff in antebellum-style hoopskirts and had them stand in strategic locations, waving and smiling to draw visitors' attention away from the blighted blooms. These "Flowers of the South" provide photo-ops to this day.

The park now encompasses more than 200 acres and contains more than 8,000 varieties of plants gathered from 90 countries. More than half of the grounds are devoted to flora, ranging from natural landscaping to cutesy-poo topiary to chrysanthemum cascades. A staff of more than 40 horticulturists manages a 7-acre nursery complex, which turns out some 450,000 plants a year, and they produce annual chrysanthemum shows, poinsettia pageants, and a three-month spring flower extravaganza.

The main entrance funnels you straight through the main souvenir shop toward the Water Ski Stadiums. Once you get over your indignation at the blatant commercialism of this introduction, you'll spot the Botanical Gardens on the right; on the left are the Exhibition Gardens and the amusement area. Now you can relax and see what Florida looks like on a good day.

Numbers in the margin correspond to points of interest on the Cypress Gardens map.

❶ Botanical Gardens Cruise. One of the first things to do at Cypress Gardens is to get on the boat and float through the cypress-hung canals of the Botanical Gardens, passing waving belles, flowering shrubs, 27 different species of palm, and the occasional baby alligator. It's a calming experience and one of the first chances you'll have to see the Southern belles. *Duration: 30 mins. Crowds: Lines can get long in mid-afternoon. Strategy: Go first thing in the morning or at the end of the day. Audience: All ages. Rating:* ★★★

❷ Water Ski Stadiums. Don't miss one of Cypress Gardens' true specialties, the stunt-filled water-ski revue. Unlike the splashy song-and-dance extravaganzas at other parks, the Mardi Gras–theme show at Cypress Gardens is purely athletic—and those sitting in the front rows don't even get wet! Smiling aquamaids whiz along on one leg; the Ramp-

Cypress Gardens

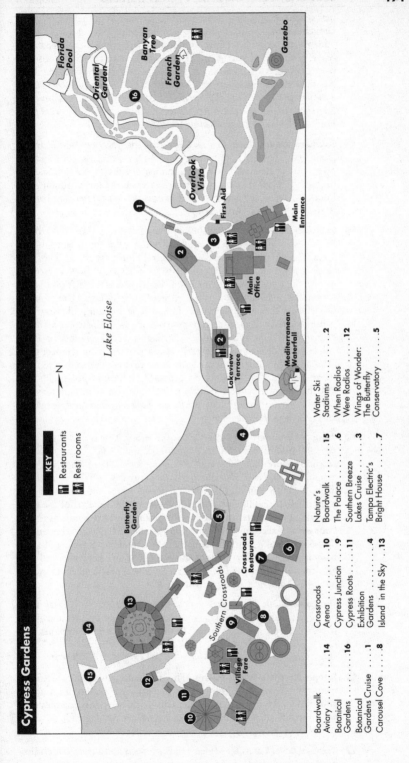

Lake Eloise

N

KEY
- Restaurants
- Rest rooms

Florida Pool
Oriental Garden
Banyan Tree
French Garden
Gazebo
Overlook Vista
First Aid
Main Entrance
Main Office
Lakeview Terrace
Mediterranean Waterfall
Butterfly Garden
Crossroads Restaurant
Southern Crossroads
Village Fare

Boardwalk Aviary **14**
Botanical Gardens **16**
Botanical Gardens Cruise . . . **1**
Carousel Cove **8**

Crossroads Arena **10**
Cypress Junction . . . **9**
Cypress Roots **11**
Exhibition Gardens **4**
Island in the Sky . . **13**

Nature's Boardwalk **15**
The Palace **6**
Southern Breeze Lakes Cruise . . **3**
Tampa Electric's Bright House **7**

Water Ski Stadiums **2**
When Radios Were Radios . . . **12**
Wings of Wonder: The Butterfly Conservatory **5**

masters pivot, flip, and jump over one another at 35 mph; Corky the Clown skis backward; and the grand finale involves a four-tier pyramid. The show can get a little corny, but it's lively enough to keep everyone entertained. If you're still at the park at night, catch the show at park closing; it's a must-see, as the skiers do their tricks in the dark, illuminated by some snazzy lighting. *Duration: 30 mins (presented every 2 hrs). Crowds: Not usually a problem. Strategy: Arrive 5–10 mins before show time and sit in either stadium; the view is equally good from both. Audience: All ages. Rating:* ★★★

❸ **Southern Breeze Lakes Cruise.** Replacing the pontoon boat is an authentic paddlewheel boat, which embarks on lake cruises lasting from 30-minute excursions to two-hour dinner cruises. Prices vary according to the length of cruise, which navigates lakes Eloise, Summit, and LuLu. *Departure times vary. Check at information for times and prices. Audience: All ages. Rating:* ★★

❹ **Exhibition Gardens.** A snapshot of one of Cypress Gardens' famous belles sashaying through here to freshen up at the Southern Mansion, a.k.a. Tara South, makes a classic Central Florida souvenir. The landscaping is heroic in intent, especially for the special flower festivals: during the annual November Mum Festival, 3 million(!) multicolor chrysanthemums cascade over the ledges of the 35-ft-high Mediterranean waterfall, decorate the walls of an Italian-style fountain, color four gargantuan floral hearts, and drape two topiary swans in an eye-spinning display of pink, purple, yellow, orange, and red. The Poinsettia Festival, from December through early January, stars flying-reindeer topiaries and Christmas trees made of more than 40,000 red, pink, and white blooms. The year-round Garden of Lights gilds the park's natural beauty with literally millions of bulbs on twinkling strands. *Crowds: Seldom a problem. Strategy: Walk through anytime. Audience: All ages. Rating:* ★★

❺ **Wings of Wonder: The Butterfly Conservatory.** This is one of the most peaceful places on earth. Enter and more than 1,000 butterflies representing more than 50 species flit about an enclosed Victorian-style greenhouse, whose 5,500 square ft contain three waterfalls, educational displays, and a couple of chrysalis chambers where you can watch new butterflies struggling out of their temporary homes. Part of the thrill is having them flutter around before making a gentle landing on you. Four gardens surround the conservatory: a butterfly garden constructed in the shape of a butterfly wing, which makes for great aerial shots from Island in the Sky; an herb and scent garden; a vegetable and fruit garden; and a rose garden. *Crowds: Seldom a problem. Strategy: Go anytime. Audience: All ages. Rating:* ★★

❻ **The Palace.** One of the park's most popular attractions is **Fairy Tales on Ice**, a dazzling ice extravaganza performed here by a troupe of European skaters, including former European and world champions. *Duration: 30 mins. Crowds: Not a problem. Strategy: Arrive 10 mins before show time for a good seat. Audience: All ages. Rating:* ★★★

❼ **Tampa Electric's Bright House.** This museum showcases electricity, from the turn of the century to the present. You'll see o ld-fashioned and modern-day appliances and get a historical perspective on how electricity affects all of us. *Crowds: Not a problem. Strategy: Go anytime. Audience: Older children and adults. Rating:* ★★

❽ **Carousel Cove.** Catering to fidgety kids who demand a reward for traipsing past antique radios and inanimate shrubbery, this attraction is perfectly geared to grandparents and grandchildren. Most rides are of the old-fashioned county-fair variety. There are six kiddie rides where the young-uns can work off excess energy, a shooting gallery, carousel, a miniature train, and similarly sized miniature golf. *Crowds: Seldom a problem. Strategy: Go anytime. Audience: Young children. Rating:* ★

9 **Cypress Junction.** One of the nation's most elaborate model railroad exhibits bridges the generation gap with its whistling freights, sleek expresses, tunnels, weather hazards, and all sorts of other knickknacks. At any given time, nearly two dozen trains operate on its 1,100 ft of track; nearly 5,000 miniature figures of people and animals add that extra bit of detail. Oddly enough, this menagerie of miniatures was originally created as a Christmas exhibit for the *National Enquirer* in Lantana, Florida. *Crowds: Not a problem. Strategy: Go anytime. Audience: All ages. Rating:* ★★★

10 **Crossroads Arena.** The far southern end of the park is home to circus acts starring highly skilled Russian performers. If you get there before the show, you can often watch the performers rehearse. *Duration: 25 mins, plus 15-min preshow. Crowds: Not significant. Strategy: Try for the first or last show of the day, because the tent gets wickedly hot at midday. Audience: All ages. Rating:* ★★★

11 **Cypress Roots.** This unprepossessing clapboard shack is chock-full of memorabilia about the "Maharaja of the Marshes" and his fair bride. Save a good 20 minutes for the video interview of the Popes and the same amount of time to read all the *Life* magazine clippings of Dick Sr.'s promotional exploits. *Crowds: Seldom a problem. Strategy: Go anytime. Audience: Older children and adults. Rating:* ★

12 **When Radios Were Radios.** Nostalgia gets a firm nudge at this antique radio museum, with its collection of hundreds of 1920s Philcos, Westinghouses, and their successors dating through the 1950s. This sounds a lot more boring than it actually is, so turn on and tune in. *Crowds: Seldom a problem. Strategy: Go anytime. Audience: Teens and adults. Rating:* ★★

13 **Island in the Sky.** A 153-ft-high revolving platform provides aerial views of the park's seasonal flower spectaculars and lush gardens, as well as views of nearby Winter Haven. *Duration: 1 min. Crowds: Lines can get long in mid-afternoon. Strategy: Go in the morning or at the end of the day. Audience: All ages. Rating:* ★★★

14 **Boardwalk Aviary.** At this interactive encounter, you can learn about a variety of birds native to Florida. An employee is on hand to answer your questions about the hand-raised lorys and lorikeets, pheasants, and muntjac deer. As at Busch Gardens, feeding nectar to the birds is part of the attraction. *Crowds: Seldom a problem. Strategy: Go anytime. Audience: All ages. Rating:* ★★★

15 **Nature's Boardwalk.** Take a leisurely stroll in this picturesque area with exhibits on animal habitats. Children enjoy the animal families. *Crowds: Seldom a problem. Strategy: Go anytime. Audience: All ages. Rating:* ★★★

16 **Botanical Gardens.** If you can, make this the last stop on your tour—for the same reason that you save room for dessert. Most of the plants are labeled, as part of the park's education program; the plantings are naturalized; and a saunter on winding paths beneath shady, live oaks or the quiet chamber created by a giant banyan's hanging roots provides a pleasant respite from the entertainment-park rush. Photo-ops abound. *Crowds: Never a problem. Strategy: Go anytime, especially at the end of your visit. Audience: Older children and adults. Rating:* ★★★

Strategies for Your Visit to Cypress Gardens

When to Go

Visit Cypress Gardens during the week, when most tourists are in other Orlando theme parks.

A Leisurely Tour

At Cypress Gardens the pace is slow partly because few people dash to gape at a banyan tree and partly because of the clientele, most of whom are older. In any case, there's no need to rush; even at a sedate pace, you can see just about everything in six hours. Keep in mind the hours here are usually opposite the major parks—when Disney is open until midnight, Cypress Gardens closes around 5 PM, staying open later only for holiday and special events, so you can arrive at noon and not miss anything. Lines are seldom a consideration. However, waits do build up at the **Botanical Gardens Cruise** in fine weather on weekends and during winter, a favorite traveling time for Cypress Gardens visitors. Therefore, start with the boat rides and save a pedestrian perambulation of the gardens for later in the day.

On Rainy Days

If the forecast is for rain, it's your call, since showers don't last very long in Florida. If it looks like an all-day affair, however, save the park for a sunny day.

Other Tips

- There are mailboxes near all exhibits with signs that say PLEASE TAKE ONE. Be sure to take one of the flyers inside, which contain interesting background on the attractions. You'll find Merlin, an audiotape recorder, at each attraction; it gives details of what you are seeing (free).

- If you have allergies, come prepared with antihistamines. The beautiful floral arrangements have been known to wreak havoc on susceptible sinuses.

- Set up a specific rendezvous location and time, in case you and your companions get separated. Good places are by the ticket booth for the Southern Breeze Lakes Cruise, at the gazebo in the Southern Crossroads, and in front of the Mediterranean waterfall.

Cypress Gardens A to Z

Admission

Daily rates, including tax, are $33.87 per adult, with one child (ages 6–12) admitted for each paying adult. If you have a passel of kids, admission is $15.85 per child.

Baby Care

You'll find stroller rentals at the Bazaar Gift Shop ($6.50; no deposit). Baby supplies are not sold on the premises; you can purchase baby food, formula, diapers, and wipes at the Winn-Dixie supermarket, across the street from the park. There are no designated facilities for nursing.

Dining

The food is fast and the service friendly. Since Cypress Gardens is plunk in the middle of Central Florida's citrus plantations, you can pick up freshly squeezed orange juice at most park food locations.

FULL-SERVICE RESTAURANT

The **Crossroads Restaurant** at the Southern Crossroads hub has a salad-quiche-sandwich menu with Southern touches.

The **Cypress Deli,** near Village Fare at Southern Crossroads, serves submarine sandwiches and big salads.

Open in peak season, **Lakeview Terrace,** on the upper level of the more southerly of the pair of water-ski stadiums, has a terrific view of the waterskiing show, as well as food that won't diminish your attention.

At **Village Fare,** a conglomeration of fast-food outlets at Southern Crossroads, you can get pizza, salads, burgers, and roast beef to eat at picnic tables covered with green-trellis tablecloths in an air-conditioned arena nearby.

For Travelers with Disabilities
All garden attractions at Cypress Gardens are wheelchair accessible, as are all restaurants and shops. Children with disabilities may not be able to negotiate some of the rides in Carousel Cove without assistance.

WHEELCHAIR RENTALS
You can rent standard wheelchairs ($6.50; no deposit) and motorized wheelchairs ($24 for three hours, $32 per day; $30 deposit).

First Aid
First aid is near the entrance to the Botanical Gardens.

Getting There
To get here, take I–4 west to the U.S. 27S exit. From there, the route is well signed: follow signs to Winter Haven; at Waverly, turn right (west) on Route 540, and go 5 mi. It's a 45-minute drive from Walt Disney World.

Guided Tours and Special Programs
Behind-the-scenes group tours of the nursery, as well as botanical tours of the gardens, are available by special request. Call the main park information number (☎ 941/324–2111) to arrange such tours.

A popular program for girls ages 5–12 is **Junior Belle.** The young lady will spend two hours living the life of Scarlett O'Hara, strolling around in one of those pretty dresses and having a formal picture taken. Cypress Gardens will then prepare the picture and press materials to deliver to your hometown newspaper and the placement rate for the cute-as-a-dickens pictures is fairly high. Arrangements can be made at the Junior Belle Boutique, in the Southern Crossroads. The cost is $39.95 in addition to regular park admission, and reservations are strongly suggested.

Hours
The park is open daily 9:30–5, longer during peak seasons.

Lockers
They're near the main office, just inside the park entrance, and cost 50¢.

Lost Things and People
Report lost children and adults as well as lost possessions at the main park office, just inside the main entrance.

Money Matters
An ATM is located near the rear entrance of the Bazaar Gift Shop.

Parking
The grassy parking area is divided into the North Lot and the South Lot; within these, rows are marked numerically. Unfortunately, free parking has given way to a $6 fee—$7 if you opt for the closer convenience of parking in the "sinkhole" (It's a real Florida sinkhole where the earth simply collapsed, leaving a bowl-shape depression.)

Shopping

Before entering the park, buy a straw fan at the **Bazaar Gift Shop** at the entrance—it's invaluable during hot afternoon performances at the Crossroads Arena and on steamy days. In Southern Crossroads pick up minitopiaries and tastefully flowered T-shirts and sweatshirts at **Gardening, Etc.** The **Butterfly Shop,** near Wings of Wonder, has a unique collection of fluttery fancies for collectors and some nifty things for bug-loving children.

Visitor Information

Contact **Cypress Gardens** (⊠ Box 1, Cypress Gardens 33884, ☎ 941/324–2111 or 800/237–4826; 800/282–2123 in FL, ✆).

Within the park, the principal **information booth** is just inside the main gate.

5 AWAY FROM THE THEME PARKS

There's much more to do in Orlando than wait in line and ride the rides. All around the area, smaller attractions allow for a change of pace. Parks and other natural areas provide moments of peace and quiet. Museums contain everything from Tiffany stained glass to airplanes, and a number of attractions hark back to the days of Old Florida.

Updated by
Pamela
Acheson

W HEN YOU'RE READY TO PUT SOME DISTANCE between you and Mickey, you'll find that Orlando and the surrounding Central Florida area offer much more than theme parks. Nature buffs like to escape to the Ocala National Forest or the Florida Audubon Society's Center for Birds of Prey, just north of Orlando in Maitland. Art devotees head for Winter Park and Rollins College's Cornell Fine Arts Museum or the Charles Hosmer Morse Museum of American Art. New Agers check out the town of Cassadaga—more than half the residents of this town are psychics, mediums, and healers. Attraction lovers seek out the additional rides and shows such as the Mystery Fun House and Wonderworks that are located along International Drive, halfway between WDW and Orlando. Indeed, you'll discover an abundance of sights—natural, unnatural, and supernatural—that are equally enjoyable and often less crowded and less expensive than those at the theme parks.

Take this opportunity to explore one or more of the many neighborhoods throughout Central Florida. But don't make the mistake of darting into a museum in one neighborhood and beelining it to a great restaurant in another or you could spend all your time in the car. These towns are spread out over quite a wide area.

Just to the southeast of Walt Disney World is the sprawling town of Kissimmee, which has a few sights of its own. Another group of things to do is clustered to the northeast of WDW, on International Drive, halfway to Orlando. In downtown Orlando you'll find a combination of skyscrapers, quiet parks and gardens, excellent museums, and the bustling shops and restaurants of Church Street Station. Next door is Winter Park, a quiet college town with old oak trees and several fine museums. Just north is Maitland, home to a bird sanctuary and an art center.

Farther afield lie parks, zoos, lakes, and the Ocala National Forest. So choose what you like, and linger for a while. This is your day off!

Numbers in the margin correspond to points of interest on the Away from the Theme Parks map.

ORLANDO AND ENVIRONS

Kissimmee

10 mi southeast of WDW; take I–4 Exit 25A.

Although Kissimmee is primarily known as being the gateway to Walt Disney World, its non-WDW attractions just might tickle your fancy.

❶ Long before Walt Disney World, there was **Gatorland.** This campy attraction south of Orlando on U.S. 441 has endured since 1949 without much change, despite competition from the major parks. Through the monstrous aqua gator-jaw doorway—a definite photo-op—await thrills and chills in the form of thousands of alligators and crocodiles, swimming and basking in the Florida sun. There is also a zoo that houses many other reptiles and mammals and an aviary where a bird might land on your shoulder. A free train ride provides an overview of the park, a water-level ride brings visitors eyeball-to-eyeball with gators, and a three-story observation tower overlooks the breeding marsh, swamped with gator grunts, especially come sundown during mating season.

For a glimpse of 37 giant rare and deadly crocodiles, check out the exhibit called **Jungle Crocs of the World** and be sure to catch the show, **Legends of Owen Godwin,** which reenacts the founder of Gatorland's

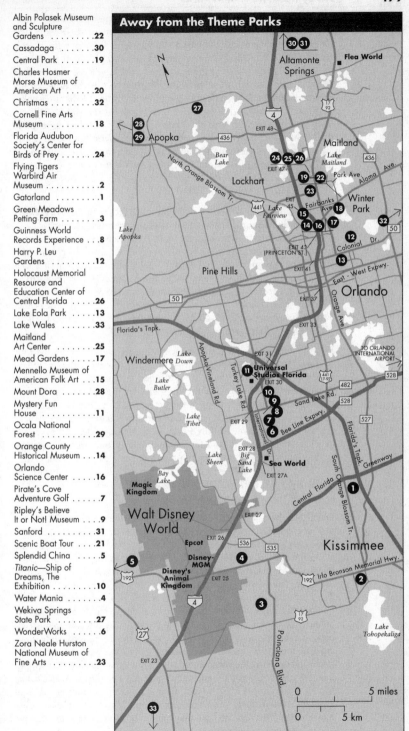

Away from the Theme Parks

worldwide travels in search of giant reptiles. Don't miss the **Gator Jumpa-roo Show,** in which gators leap out of the water for their food. The best is the first one in the morning, when the gators are hungriest. There's also a **Gator Wrestling Cracker-style Show,** and although there's no doubt who's going to win the match, it's still fun to see the handlers take on those tough guys with the beady eyes. In the educational **Snakes of Florida Show,** high drama is provided by the 30–40 rattlesnakes that fill the pit around the speaker. Don't look for scrupulous Disney-style cleanliness here, and the personnel aren't polished with pixie dust either. This is a real Florida experience, and you'll walk out those aqua gator jaws knowing the difference between a gator and a croc. ✉ *14501 S. Orange Blossom Trail, between Orlando and Kissimmee,* ☎ *407/855–5496 or 800/393–5297.* ⛋ *$16.93 adults, $7.48 children 3–12.* ☉ *Daily 9–dusk.*

❷ Old war birds never die—they just become attractions at the **Flying Tigers Warbird Air Museum.** The working aircraft restoration facility is nick-named Bombertown USA because most of the planes here are bombers. Once they are operational, they are usually flown away by private collectors, but the museum also houses a permanent collection of about 30 vintage planes in its hangar, with a few big ones out on the tarmac. Tour guides are full of facts and personality and have an infectious passion for the planes. From U.S. 192, turn south on Hoagland Boulevard, a.k.a. Airport Road. ✉ *231 Hoagland Blvd.,* ☎ *407/933–1942.* ⛋ *$8 adults, $6 children 5–12.* ☉ *Daily 9–5:30.*

Friendly farmhands keep things moving on the two-hour guided tour
❸ of **Green Meadows Petting Farm**—a 40-acre property with almost 200 animals. There's little chance to get bored and no waiting in line because tours, which take about two hours, are always starting. Everyone who wants to gets to milk the fat mama cow, and chickens and geese are turned loose in their yard to run and squawk while city slickers try to catch them. Children take a quick pony ride, and everyone gets jostled about on the old-fashioned hayride. Youngsters come away saying: "I milked a cow, caught a chicken, pet a pig, and fed a goat." Take U.S. 192 for 3 mi east of I–4 to Poinciana Boulevard; turn right and drive 5 mi. ✉ *1368 Poinciana Blvd.,* ☎ *407/846–0770.* ⛋ *$15 ages 3 and up.* ☉ *Daily 9:30–4.*

❹ **Water Mania** has all the requisite rides and slides without Walt Disney World aesthetics. However, it's the only water park around to have **Wipe Out,** a surfing simulator, where you grab a body board and ride a continuous wave form. The giant Pirate Ship in the **Rain Forest,** one of two children's play areas, is equipped with water slides and water cannons. The **Abyss,** similar to Wet 'n Wild's Black Hole (☞ Chapter 3), is an enclosed tube slide through which you twist and turn on a one- or two-person raft through 300 ft of deep-blue darkness. At this 36-acre park you'll also find a sandy beach, go-carts, a picnic area, snack bars, gift shops, and periodic concerts, which can be enjoyed while floating in an inner tube. Its 18-hole miniature golf course won't win any local prizes, considering the competition, but it does give you another way to pass the time while you're out of the water. It's 1½ mi from Walt Disney World, and from I–4 it's ¼ mi east. Bear in mind that the water rides are generally closed from mid-December to mid-March because of chilly weather and that all schedules may vary even more than stated below, due to weather and holidays. So be sure to call for exact opening and closing times. ✉ *6073 W. Irlo Bronson Memorial Hwy.,* ☎ *407/239–8448, 407/396–2626, or 800/527–3092.* ⛋ *$25.95 adults, $18.95 children 3–9 (half price after 3, after 4 in summer); parking $5.* ☉ *Nov.–Dec.*

21 and Jan. 4–early Mar., Wed.–Sat. 11–5; Dec. 22–Jan. 3, daily 10–5; early Mar.–Aug., daily 9:30–6; Sept.–Oct., Wed.–Sat. 10–5.

❺ More a superlative open-air museum than a theme park in the Mickey Mouse tradition, **Splendid China** is of most interest to older teens and adults. Here, in this 76-acre park, you can stroll among painstakingly re-created versions of China's greatest landmarks and watch artisans demonstrate traditional Chinese woodworking, weaving, and other crafts while tinkling meditative music plays in the background. It took $100 million and 120 Chinese craftspeople working for two years using, whenever possible, historically accurate building materials and techniques to create the 60-plus replicas. Both man-made structures and natural phenomena are represented—some life-size, others greatly reduced in scale. (The bricks in the Great Wall, for example, are only 2 inches long.) The emphasis is on tradition over technology; the most advanced electronics you'll see here are the tiny lights that glow inside the buildings after dark. To appeal to theme-park-savvy Western visitors, live entertainment and a playground are also on the grounds, and the shops and two restaurants in the Chinatown section are a cut above those at typical theme parks. The park is at its most magical at night, so the best time to arrive is after noon.

The park map numbers exhibits counterclockwise, but you'll finish with the most impressive sights if you travel clockwise. Although the ½-mi-long **Great Wall** cannot begin to replicate the size of the 1,500-mi-long original, it's nevertheless amazing—containing 6.5 million tiny bricks that were mortared into place by hand. Other exhibits of note include the **Imperial Palace,** the centerpiece of Beijing's famed Forbidden City; the **Leshan Buddha,** a 35-ft re-creation of the largest man-made statue in the world; **Potala Palace,** China's version of Venice; the **Summer Palace,** a representation of the traditional home of China's dowager empress; and the **Temple of Heaven,** a striking, blue-tile structure where the emperor, as high priest of his people, would spend time in fasting and prayer. Tuesday through Sunday, the Golden Peacock Theater presents a 90-minute live show, **Mysterious Kingdom of the Orient.** Besides the star attractions, Splendid China also has reproductions of Chinese temples, pagodas, typical Chinese homes, and grottoes filled with religious statuary. Each display is accompanied by a short written explanation, a recorded message, or both. To reach the park, take I–4 Exit 25B and continue west on U.S. 192 approximately 2½ mi, past all the Disney exits. Stay in the far-left lane and look for the dragon. ⊠ *3000 Splendid China Blvd.,* ☎ *407/397–8800 recording; 407/396–7111 or 800/244–6226.* ⊞ *$26.99 adults, $16.99 children 5–12 (admission includes live show); parking and Chinatown free.* ☉ *Daily 9:30–7, later in peak seasons, Chinatown shops and restaurants until 9.*

International Drive Area, Orlando

7 mi northeast of WDW; take I–4 Exit 28 or 29 unless otherwise noted.

A short drive northeast of WDW are several attractions that children adore but unfortunately may put some wear and tear on parents.

❻ Just up the street, the Ripley's Believe It or Not! building seems to be sinking into the ground, but true to Orlando tradition, the newer attraction, **WonderWorks,** one-ups the competition: it's sinking into the ground upside down. If the strange sight of a topsy-turvy facade complete with upended palm trees and simulated FedEx box doesn't catch your attention, the swirling "dust" and piped-out creaking sounds will. Inside, the upside-down theme continues only as far as the lobby. After that, it's a playground of 75 interactive experiences and demonstrations, some educational (similar to those at a science museum) and others just pure entertainment. Experience an earthquake or a hurricane, swim with sharks, play laser tag in the largest laser tag arena in the world, design and ride your own awesome roller coaster, or even play basketball with a 7-ft opponent. ✉ *9067 International Dr.,* ☎ *407/ 352–8655.* 🎟 *$14.95 adults, $10.95 children 4–12.* ☉ *Daily 9 AM– midnight.*

❼ You can play the crème de la crème of miniature golf at the two **Pirate's Cove Adventure Golf** locations. Each site offers two 18-hole courses that wind around artificial mountains, through caves, over waterfalls, and into lush foliage. The beginner's course is called Captain Kidd's Adventure; a more difficult game can be played on Blackbeard's Challenge. The courses are opposite Mercado Mediterranean Village and in the Crossroads of Lake Buena Vista shopping plaza. ✉ *8501 International Dr.,* ☎ *407/352–7378;* ✉ *Crossroads Center, I–4 Exit 27,* ☎ *407/827–1242.* 🎟 *Captain Kidd's Adventure $7 adults, $6.50 children 4–12; Blackbeard's Challenge $7.50 adults, $7 children 4–12; both courses $11.50 adults, $11 children 4–12; all-day (9–5) admission to one course $15.* ☉ *Daily 9 AM–11:30 PM.*

❽ Ever wonder how you could get to be a Guinness World Record Holder? Head over to the **Guinness World Records Experience** where interactive exhibits, film, and videos reveal what it takes to be a record holder and showcase some of the most bizarre accomplishments of people throughout the world. In the **Guinness World Theater,** you'll see a multimedia theater production that takes you to the brink of human endurance and endeavor and also looks at how and why so many people fail in their attempts to make the record. Try to attempt your own Guinness World Record in the **Micro-Technology Playground.** Walk down the multimedia streetscape of **Guinness Town** and see the Big and Tall Shop, Rain Woman, Blasting Zone, and Lightning Man. ✉ *8437 International Dr.,* ☎ *407/248–8891.* 🎟 *$12.95 adults, $7.95 children under 12.* ☉ *Daily 10 AM–11 PM.*

❾ **Ripley's Believe It or Not! Museum** challenges the imagination. A 10-ft-square section of the Berlin Wall. A pain and torture chamber. A Rolls-Royce constructed entirely of matchsticks. A 26- by 20-ft portrait of van Gogh made from 3,000 postcards. These and almost 200 other oddities speak for themselves in this museum-cum-attraction in the heart of tourist territory on International Drive. It is said that the fruits of Robert Ripley's explorations are to reality what Walt Disney World is to fantasy. The building itself is designed to appear as if it's sliding into one of Florida's notorious sinkholes. Give yourself an hour or two to soak up the weirdness here, but remember, this is a looking, not touching, experience, which may drive antsy youngsters—and their parents—crazy. The museum is ¼ mi south of Sand Lake Road. ✉ *8201 International Dr.,* ☎ *407/363–4418 or 800/998–4418.* 🎟 *$12.95 adults, $8.95 children 4–12.* ☉ *Daily 9 AM–midnight.*

Titania, a strong desire for all things related to the infamous voyage of the *Titanic* and James Cameron's mega-movie, continues to strike.

❿ This interactive attraction, **Titanic—Ship of Dreams, The Exhibition.** combines the best of *Titanic* fact and fantasy in a 25,000-square-ft multi-sensory adventure. Artifacts culled from the *Titanic*'s wreckage and the Hollywood movie set, such as a life jacket and Leonardo DiCaprio's costume, are displayed within carefully replicated rooms of the ship to inspire the feelings of excitement, glamour, and doom experienced by those onboard. As you approach a re-created 1912 ticket office, sounds of a bustling dock, crowds shouting "bon voyage," and a nearby foghorn set the scene as you are given a ticket with the name of an actual passenger. Before entering the ship, you pass through a simulated Belfast shipyard, complete with the aroma of oil and sea air, where actors playing shipbuilders explain the materials and progressive techniques used in the ship's design, and maybe admit to a few problems in its construction. Next, a White Star Line attendant in period costume greets you at the end of the gangway, inquiring whether or not you've crossed the Atlantic, if you have any baggage, or if you're prone to seasickness. Once inside, you'll stroll past the ship's remarkable full-size Grand Staircase, through the First Class parlor suite and the Verandah Café, to a deck deliberately chilled to 48°F where, just overboard, the notorious iceberg looms in the water. Check your ticket against a list of the 2,000 travelers who boarded the fated ship to see whether it was held by someone who was rescued or drowned. ⊠ *8445 International Dr.,* ☎ *407/248–1166.* ☞ *$16.95 adults, $11.95 children 6–12.* ☉ *Daily 10–9.*

⑪ There are a variety of ways to attack the **Mystery Fun House.** You might just want to bring your quarters and visit the video arcade (for which there's no admission charge). But a paid admission entitles you to a walk through the 18-chamber **Mystery Maze,** which comes with the warning that it is "90% dark" and full of gory and distorted images. Outside, there's the 18-hole **Jurassic Golf,** a basic putt-putt course, laid out flat and simple, with, as you might expect, a dinosaur motif. Groups of 10 or more can play **Laser Tag.** Equipped with laser guns and wearing reflector belts, players are transported on a simulated spaceship ride to the arena, where they score points by zapping one another and try to avoid being zapped by the UFO hovering overhead. Players also ride through an asteroid field. Underfoot, the playing surface feels like an air mattress, adding a simulated low-gravity element to the game. Take I–4 Exit 30B (Universal Studios). Turn right (north) on Kirkman Road and right again on Major Boulevard. ⊠ *5767 Major Blvd.,* ☎ *407/351–3357.* ☞ *Mystery Maze $10.95, Jurassic Golf $4.95, Laser Tag $4 per person (minimum 10 people).* ☉ *Daily 10–10; Mystery Maze Thurs.–Fri. 5–9, weekends 10–9; Laser Tag by appointment only.*

Downtown Orlando

15 mi northeast of WDW; take I–4 Exit 41 if you're heading westbound, Exit 40 if eastbound, or Exit 43 for Loch Haven Park sights.

Downtown Orlando is a dynamic community that's constantly growing and changing. Here you'll find new buildings under construction, interesting museums, and bustling Church Street Station. Numerous parks, many of which surround lakes, provide pleasant relief from the tall office buildings. Just a few steps away from downtown's tourist meccas are delightful residential neighborhoods with brick-paved streets and live oaks dripping with Spanish moss.

⑫ A visit to the **Harry P. Leu Gardens,** on the former lakefront estate of citrus entrepreneur Harry P. Leu, provides a quiet respite from the artificial world of the theme parks. On the grounds' 50 acres are a collection of historical blooms, many varieties of which were established before 1900. You'll see ancient oaks, a 50-ft floral clock, an orchid conservatory, and one of the largest camellia collections in eastern North America (in bloom October–March). **Mary Jane's Rose Garden,** named after Leu's wife, is filled with more than 1,000 bushes; it is the largest formal rose garden south of Atlanta. The simple 19th-century **Leu House Museum,** once the Leu family home, preserves the furnishings and appointments of a well-to-do, turn-of-the-20th-century Florida family. ⊠ *1920 N. Forest Ave.,* ☎ *407/246–2620.* ☞ *$4 adults, $1 children*

6–16. ☺ Garden Mon.–Sat. 9–8, Sun. 9–6; guided house tours daily on the hr and half hr 10–3:30.

⓭ In the heart of downtown you'll find **Lake Eola Park,** with its signature fountain in the center. The park represents an inner-city victory over decay. Established in 1892, the family park experienced a series of ups and downs that left it very run-down by the late '70s. With the support of determined citizens, the park gradually underwent a renovation, which restored the fountain and added a wide brick walkway around the lake. The security here is now such that families with young children use the well-lighted playground in the evening and downtown residents walk their dogs late at night in safety. The **Walt Disney Amphitheater,** perched on the lake, is a dramatic site for the annual Shakespeare Festival (April and May) as well as for weekend concerts and *FunnyEola,* a free, family comedy show performed the second Tuesday of every month. However, the most fun to be had in the park is a ride in a swan-shape pedal boat, one of which frequent Walt Disney World visitor Michael Jackson is reputed to have ordered for his personal use at his ranch. The view at dusk, as the fountain lights up in all its colors and the sun sets behind Orlando's ever-growing skyline, is spectacular. ⊠ *Robinson St. and Rosalind Ave.,* ☎ *407/246–2827 park; 407/839–8899 swan boats.* ◪ *Boat rental $7 per half hr, maximum 3 people per boat; children under 10 must be with an adult.* ☺ *Park daily 7–midnight; swan boats winter daily 11–6, summer daily 11–10; café weekdays 10–8, weekends 10–9.*

⓮ The **Orange County Historical Museum** is a storehouse of Orlando memorabilia, photographs, and antiques. Exhibits explore Native American and native Floridian culture, and they show off a country store, Victorian parlor, and print shop. Call for an update on the always-changing traveling exhibits. **Fire Station No. 3,** an actual 1926 brick firehouse behind the museum, houses antique fire trucks, fire-fighting memorabilia, and collectibles. Although most items are for looking only, there are some firefighters' bunks, hats, and jackets for youngsters to investigate. ⊠ *812 E. Rollins St.,* ☎ *407/897–6350.* ◪ *$4 adults, $2 children 6–12.* ☺ *Mon.–Sat. 9–5, Sun. noon–5.*

⓯ One of the few museums in the United States devoted to folk art and the only one in Florida, the **Mennello Museum of American Folk Art** is a welcome addition to Orlando. It features the nation's most extensive permanent collection of Earl Cunningham paintings, Paul Marco sculptures, John Gerdes paintings and sculptures, Virgil Norberg flat steel sculptures, and Gary Yost carvings of Uncle Sam. The **Museum Shop** features folk art books, toys, and unusual gifts. ⊠ *900 E. Princeton St.,* ☎ *407/246–4278.* ◪ *$2 adults, children under 12 free.* ☺ *Tues.–Sat. 10–5, Sun. noon–5.*

⓰ With all the high-tech glitz and imagined worlds of the theme parks, is it worth visiting the reality-based **Orlando Science Center,** in Orlando proper, closer to where most tourists stay? Absolutely. The action-packed, 207,000-square-ft, four-level building is the perfect antidote to long lines and overwhelming gimmickry. The 10 theme display halls house a multitude of exciting hands-on exhibits covering mechanics; electricity and magnetism; math; health and fitness; nature; the solar system; and light, lasers, and optics. The show "Good King Snooze" helps children understand how anesthesia works. Walk through an enormous open mouth (literally) and take a journey through the human body (figuratively). Raise a suspended VW bug with the help of a lever, and learn about physics while you're showing off (you don't need to tell the children it's educational if you don't want to). The **Dr. Phillips CineDome,** a movie theater with a giant eight-story screen, offers large-format IW-

ERKS films (Ub Iwerks was an associate of Walt Disney in the early days), as well as planetarium programs, and, on weekends, laser light shows. In addition, the **Darden Adventure Theater** features the center's in-house performance troupe, the Einstein Players. ✉ 777 E. *Princeton St.,* ☎ 407/514–2000. *Exhibits and Darden Adventure Theater $9.50 adults, $6.75 children 3–11; CineDome films $6 adults, $4.50 children; both $12 adults, $9.50 children; Ultimate Experience (all exhibits plus 2 CineDome films) $14.25 adults, $11 children; Orlando Science Center Experience (all exhibits plus 1 Cinedome film) $12.50 adults, $9.25 children; Planetarium only $4 adults and children; parking $3.50.* ⊙ *Tues.–Thurs. 9–5, Fri.–Sat. 9–9, Sun. noon–5.*

Winter Park

20 mi northeast of WDW; take I–4 Exit 45 and head east 3 mi on Fairbanks Ave.

This peaceful, upscale community may be just north of the hustle and bustle of Orlando, but it feels miles away. You can spend a pleasant day here shopping, eating, visiting museums, and taking in the scenery along Park Avenue. When you want a rest, look for a bench in the shady Central Park. Away from the avenue, the moss-covered trees form a canopy over brick streets, and old estates surround canal-linked lakes.

⓱ The 55 acres in the unusual park, **Mead Gardens,** have been intentionally left to grow as a natural preserve. Walkers and runners are attracted to the trails that wind around the creek, and a boardwalk provides a better view of the delicate wetlands. ✉ *S. Denning Ave.,* ☎ 407/599–3334. *Free.* ⊙ *Daily 8–sunset.*

Rollins College, a private liberal arts school, is in the heart of Winter Park's downtown. Among the school's alums are Mister (Fred) Rogers— yes, this was once his neighborhood. You'll see the **Knowles Memorial Chapel,** built in 1932, and the **Annie Russell Theatre,** a 1931 building that's often the venue for local theatrical productions.

⓲ On the Rollins College campus, the **Cornell Fine Arts Museum** is the oldest collection of art in Florida, with the first paintings acquired in 1896. It now houses a collection of more than 6,000 objects, including 19th- and 20th-century American and European paintings, decorative arts, and sculpture. Artists represented include William Merritt Chase, Childe Hassam, and Louis Comfort Tiffany. In addition, special exhibitions are scheduled throughout the year. Outside the museum, a small but charming garden overlooks Lake Virginia. ✉ *Rollins College, end of Holt Ave.,* ☎ 407/646–2526. *Free.* ⊙ *Tues.–Fri. 10–5, weekends 1–5.*

In the center of town is **Park Avenue,** facing a peaceful park and lined with a collection of chic boutiques, cozy cafés, restaurants serving a variety of cuisines, and hidden alleyways that lead to peaceful nooks and crannies as well as more restaurants and shops. Construction of a 7 Eleven raised the hackles of Winter Park's image-conscious city fathers, who feared an invasion of fast-food joints. Although their fears were groundless, an invasion of commercial chains such as Ann Taylor, B. Dalton, and Williams-Sonoma has hit the avenue. Regardless, it is still very tony and home to many one-of-a-kind shops. A recent streetscaping project that included the bricking of streets and new sidewalk plantings makes Park Avenue more appealing than ever for a peaceful stroll.

⓳ **Central Park** (✉ Park Ave.) is Winter Park's gathering place. This lovely green space with a stage and gazebo is often the scene of concerts. If you don't want to browse in the shops across the street, a walk through the park is a delightful alternative.

(20) You'll see the world's most comprehensive collection of the works of Louis Comfort Tiffany at the **Charles Hosmer Morse Museum of American Art,** including immense stained-glass windows, lamps, watercolors, and desk sets. Many of the items were made for Tiffany's mansion in Long Island, New York. The newest addition is the 8,000-square-ft Tiffany Chapel, originally built for the 1893 World's Fair. It took craftsmen 2½ years to painstakingly reassemble the chapel. Also housed here are collections of paintings by 19th- and 20th-century American artists, jewelry, and pottery, including a fine display of Rookwood. ⊠ *445 Park Ave. N,* ☎ *407/645–5311.* ☞ *$3 adults, $1 students and children.* ☉ *Tues.–Sat. 9:30–4, Sun. 1–4.*

(21) From the dock at the end of Morse Avenue, you can depart for the **Scenic Boat Tour,** a Winter Park tradition that has been in continuous operation for more than 60 years. The relaxing, narrated one-hour tour, which leaves hourly, cruises by 12 mi of Winter Park's opulent lakeside estates. ⊠ *312 E. Morse Blvd.,* ☎ *407/644–4056.* ☞ *$7 adults, $3 children 2–11.* ☉ *Daily 9–4.*

(22) Stroll through lush gardens showcasing the graceful sculptures created by internationally known sculptor Albin Polasek at the **Albin Polasek Museum and Sculpture Gardens.** The late artist's home, studio, galleries, and private chapel are centered on 3 acres of exquisitely tended lawns, colorful flower beds, and tropical foliage. Paths and walkways lead past classical life-size, figurative sculptures and whimsical mythological pieces. Inside the museum are works by Hawthorne, Chase, Mucha, and Saint-Gaudens. ⊠ *633 Osceola Ave.,* ☎ *407/647–6294.* ☞ *Free.* ☉ *Tues.–Sat. 10–4, Sun. 1–4.*

(23) Established in 1990, the **Zora Neale Hurston National Museum of Fine Arts** is designed to showcase creative works of artists of African descent. The museum holds five six-week long exhibits each year, with one reserved for promising, upcoming artists. The museum is named after local resident Zora Neale Hurston (1891–1960), a writer, folklorist, and anthropologist. ⊠ *227 E. Kennedy Blvd. Eatonville,* ☎ *407/ 647–3307.* ☞ *Donations accepted.* ☉ *Weekdays 9–4.*

Maitland

25 mi northeast of WDW; take I–4 Exit 47A, then Maitland Blvd. east, and turn right (south) on Maitland Ave.

An Orlando suburb with an interesting mix, Maitland is home to both the Florida Save the Manatee Society and one of Central Florida's larger office parks. A number of spectacular homes grace the shores of this town's various lakes, and there's a bird sanctuary and an art center.

(24) More than 20 bird species, including hawks, eagles, owls, falcons, and vultures, make their home at the **Florida Audubon Society's Center for Birds of Prey.** It is only partially open to the public because of ongoing improvements, including viewing windows into the labs, butterfly gardens, and walkways through the wetlands. There is an earnestness to this humble, working facility on Lake Sybelia in Maitland, which takes in 500–600 injured wild birds of prey each year. About 43% are able to return to the wild; permanently injured birds continue to live at the center and can be seen in the aviaries along the pathways and sitting on outdoor perches. The center also tracks eagles and occasionally sets up a closed-circuit monitor to observe a nest, so visitors can watch a genuine nature show. There's a nice spot to picnic here, too. From

Maitland Avenue, turn right on U.S. 17–92, right on Kennedy Boulevard, and right on Audubon Way. ⊠ *921 S. Lake Sybelia Dr.,* ☎ *407/ 644–0190.* 🎫 *Suggested donation $5 adults, $4 children 2–11.* ⊙ *Tues.–Sat. 10–4.*

㉕ It's local lore that the historic **Maitland Art Center,** near Lake Sybelia, is inhabited by the spirit of its architect-painter founder, André Smith. He began constructing his studio retreat in 1937, and the grounds and 23 buildings themselves are works of art. The seemingly infinite reliefs and other details on all the structures reflect Smith's fascination with Maya and Aztec influences and further account for the mystical aura. An outdoor chapel is a favorite spot for weddings, and romantic gardens blend harmoniously with the natural surroundings. Inside, galleries display an extensive collection of Smith's work as well as changing exhibits by local, regional, and national artists. Take Maitland Avenue ¾ mi south of Maitland Boulevard; turn right on Packwood Avenue. ⊠ *231 W. Packwood Ave.,* ☎ *407/539–2181.* 🎫 *Donation welcome.* ⊙ *Weekdays 9–4:30, weekends noon–4:30.*

㉖ The **Holocaust Memorial Resource and Education Center of Central Florida** chronicles ma jor events of the Holocaust. Exhibits are arranged in chronological order and include a large number of photographs and audiovisual presentations. The museum also contains a library and archives. ⊠ *851 N. Maitland Ave.,* ☎ *407/628–0555.* 🎫 *Free.* ⊙ *Mon.– Thurs. 9–4, Fri. 9–1, Sun. 1–4.*

SIDE TRIPS FROM ORLANDO

When you feel like venturing farther afield, hop in your car and within an hour or two you can be where you can celebrate Christmas year-round, canoe down a river, meet with a psychic, feed farm animals at a small zoo, or walk in a beautiful park. The areas below are arranged in a roughly clockwise fashion starting northwest of Orlando.

Apopka

13 mi northwest of Orlando and 28 mi north of WDW.

Orange groves used to cover this part of Florida, but housing developments continue to replace one grove after another. East of Apopka is a state park with pristine waterways and scenic drives through longleaf-pine forests.

Where the tannin-stained Wekiva River meets the crystal-clear Wekiva headspring, there is a curious and visible exchange—like strong tea infusing in water. Wekiva is a Creek Indian word meaning "flowing water,"
㉗ and the **Wekiva Springs State Park** sprawls around this area on 6,400 acres. The parkland is well suited to camping, hiking, and picnicking; the spring to swimming; and the river to canoeing and fishing. Canoe trips can range from a simple hour-long paddle around the lagoon to observe a colony of water turtles to a full-day excursion through the less-congested parts of the river that haven't changed much since the area was inhabited by the Timacuan Indians. Take I–4 Exit 49 (Longwood) and turn left on Route 434. Go 1¼ mi to Wekiva Springs Road; turn right and go 4½ mi to the entrance, on the right. ⊠ *1800 Wekiva Circle,* ☎ *407/884–2009.* 🎫 *$4 per vehicle.* ⊙ *Daily 8–sunset.*

En Route   As you drive northwest on U.S. 441, you head into aptly named Lake County, an area renowned for its pristine water and excellent fishing. Watch the flat countryside, thick with scrub pines, take on a gentle roll through citrus groves and pastures with live oaks.

Mount Dora

28 *35 mi (45 mins) northwest of Orlando and 50 mi (1 hr) north of WDW; take U.S. 441 (Orange Blossom Trail in Orlando) north or take I–4 to Exit 48, then Rte. 436 west to U.S. 441, and follow the signs.*

Built around the unspoiled Lake Harris chain of lakes, the quaint valley community of Mount Dora has a slow and easy pace, a rich history, New England–style charm, and excellent antiquing. Although the population of Mount Dora is less than 8,000, there is plenty of excitement here, especially in fall and winter. The first weekend in February is the annual Mount Dora Art Festival, which opens Central Florida's spring art fair season. Attracting more than 200,000 visitors over a three-day period, it is one of Central Florida's major outdoor events. During the year, there's a sailing regatta, a bicycle festival, a crafts fair, and many other happenings.

Take a walk down **Donnelly Street.** The yellow Queen Anne–style mansion is **Donnelly House** (✉ 515 Donnelly St.), an 1893 architectural gem. Notice the details on the lead-glass windows. Built in the 1920s, the **Dora Hotel** (✉ 413 Donnelly St.) is now used as a restaurant and office space. A historic train depot now serves as the offices of the **Mount Dora Chamber of Commerce.** Stop in and pick up a self-guided tour map that tells you everything you need to know—from historic landmarks to restaurants. ✉ *341 Alexander St., at 3rd Ave.,* ☎ *352/383–2165.* ☉ *Weekdays 9–5, Sat. 10–4; after hrs, maps on display at kiosk.*

Palm Island Park, on the shores of Lake Dora and within walking distance of downtown, gives nature lovers a close-up view of Florida's wildlife and foliage. Take a stroll along the boardwalks and watch out for blue and green herons, raccoons, otters, and even an alligator or two. You'll also see pond cypress, bald cypress, and many varieties of palm. Fishing in the lake is permitted, and well-placed picnic tables offer pleasant stops to enjoy a meal. ✉ *1 Liberty Ave.* ☉ *Daily 7:30–1 hr after sunset.*

Gilbert Park has a public dock and boat-launching ramp, a playground, and a large picnic pavilion with grills that offers a stunning view of the lake. ✉ *Tremain St. and Liberty Ave.* ☉ *Daily 7:30–1 hr after sunset.*

Stop in for tea or something stronger at the **Lakeside Inn** (✉ 100 N. Alexander St., ☎ 352/383–4104), a historic country inn built in 1883. A stroll around the grounds of this lakefront inn will make you feel as if you've stepped out of the pages of *The Great Gatsby*; there's even a croquet court.

If you walk along **5th Avenue,** you'll pass several of the town's historic buildings. The **Princess Gallery Theatre** (✉ 130 W. 5th Ave.) is a 1920s movie palace that's now home to several small boutiques. The **Simpson Hotel** (✉ 115 W. 5th Ave.) was built in 1925 by descendants of the Simpson family, Mount Dora's first homesteaders. Continue on 5th Avenue and you'll pass a number of charming gift and antiques shops. Along the way, you'll come upon the **Park Bench Restaurant** (✉ 116 E. 5th Ave., ☎ 352/383–7004), the perfect spot for a late lunch or early dinner.

Ocala National Forest

29 *60 mi northwest of WDW; take I–4 east to Exit 48, and head west on Rte. 436 to U.S. 441, which you take north to Rte. 19 north.*

Between the Oklawaha and the St. Johns rivers, the 366,000-acre Ocala National Forest is home to numerous species of vegetation. Clear streams wind through tall stands of pine or hardwoods. This spot is known for its canoeing, hiking, swimming, and camping and for its invigorating springs. Here you can walk beneath tall pine trees and canoe down meandering streams and across placid lakes. Stop in at the **Ocala National Forest Visitor Center** for general park information. ⊠ *45621 Rte. 19, Altoona,* ☎ *352/669–7495.* ⊙ *Daily 9–5.*

There are a number of developed recreation sites in the forest, including **Alexander Springs** (☎ 352/669–3522). This park is favored by the locals in the summer for its cold, fresh water. After hiking down to its small beach, swim out, preferably with a snorkel and fins, to the steep drop-off at the head of the spring, where the water rushes out from rock formations below. Although it's not unusual to see alligators sitting on the bank opposite the sandy beach, remember that they are still wild, can move very fast, and should not be provoked. You'll notice that the natives leave the water before sundown—feeding time! To get to Alexander Springs from the Ocala National Forest Visitor Center at Altoona, go north on Route 19 and turn right on Route 445. The entrance is on the left.

Cassadaga

㉚ *35 mi northeast of Orlando and 50 mi northeast of WDW; take I–4 to Exit 54 (Cassadaga and Lake Helen), turn right on Rte. 472 and right again at the first traffic light (Rte. 4139), and continue 2 mi.*

This tiny town is headquarters of the **Southern Cassadaga Spiritualist Camp Meeting Association** (⊠ Box 319, 32706, ☎ 904/228–3171). More than half of the 350 residents are psychics, mediums, and healers, which makes it the nation's largest such community. Pick up a brochure at the Information Center in the Andrew Jackson Davis Building (right in the center of town), which describes the history of the town and its philosophy of spiritualism. The pamphlet also lists certified mediums and their locations; you can book a full hour of consultation or opt for a mini 15-minute meeting. It is suggested that the best way to find a medium who is right for you is to walk or drive through this rustic, five-block by five-block neighborhood and see if you can find a house that is giving off the right energy. Then call ahead to schedule an appointment. After a reading, check out the tombstones in the **Lake Helen Cassadaga Cemetery** (⊠ North end of Stevens St.).

Church services are held at **Colby Memorial Temple,** and visitors are very welcome. Spiritualist services are nonsensational, meditative gatherings, with the most unconventional aspect being the "message" portion, during which certified mediums deliver specific messages to attendees from spirits in the beyond. ⊠ *1118 Stevens St.,* ☎ *904/228–3171.* ⊙ *Services Sun. 10:30–11:45 AM and Wed. 7:30–8:15 PM.*

This community rich in spirit doesn't offer much to the material world, except the modest **Southern Cassadaga Bookstore.** People here are friendly and wholesome and accustomed to curiosity seekers, but they do request respect. ⊠ *1112 Stevens St.,* ☎ *904/228–2880.* ⊙ *Weekdays 9:30–3:30, Sat. 9:30–5, Sun. noon–5.*

Sanford

㉛ *22 mi north of Orlando and 37 mi northeast of WDW; take I–4 to Exit 52.*

This growing community on the shores of Lake Monroe has attracted a number of Orlandoans seeking a respite from the burgeoning urban sprawl. A small collection of antiques stores, secondhand shops, and galleries, which date from the 1880s to the 1920s, are found in buildings along 1st Street.

A visit to the **Central Florida Zoological Park** will disappoint if you're expecting a grand metro zoo. However, this is a respectable display of about 230 animals, tucked under pine trees, and, like the city of Orlando, it continues to grow. The elephant exhibit is popular, as are the tortoises and the exotic and native snakes housed in the herpetarium. The zoo is becoming specialized in small and medium-size exotic cats, including servals, caracals, and jaguarundis, and there is an aviary that houses American bald eagles that have been grounded owing to injury. Children love the **Animal Adventure**, which has domestic and farm animals to pet and feed. Take I–4 Exit 52, and drive 1 mi east on U.S. 17–92 to the entrance, on the right. ⊠ 3755 N. U.S. 17–92, ☎ 407/ 323–4450. ☞ $7 adults, $3 children 3–12. ☼ Daily 9–5, pony rides weekends 10–4.

Christmas

32 33 mi northeast from WDW and 18 mi east of Orlando on Rte. 50 (Colonial Dr.).

There really is a Santa Claus in this tiny hamlet. Locals zipping to the beach or en route to Kennedy Space Center, on the coast near Cocoa Beach, can miss this town if they blink. But they flock here during December to have their holiday missives postmarked at the local post office. The headquarters of the Tosohatchee State Preserve, with more than 28,000 acres of woodlands, are also here.

If the children have been cooped up in the car for a while, the **Fort Christmas Museum** is a great place for them to let off steam. There's a large play area and picnic area, plus a restored 1837 fort, built during the Second Seminole War as part of preparations to take the fighting to South Florida. Inside the fort is a museum that details Florida pioneer life in the mid-19th century. There are also seven pioneer homes that have been restored and are now furnished in the style of the early 1800s. During the week the fort is often brimming with local schoolchildren who visit on Florida history field trips. ⊠ 2 mi north of Rte. 50 on Rte. 420 (Ft. Christmas Rd.), ☎ 407/568–4149. ☞ Free. ☼ Tues.–Sat. 10–5, Sun. 1–5.

Hop on a boat and take a thrilling ride through a real Florida swamp teeming with alligators. At **Jungle Adventures** pontoon boats bring you face-to-face with these slithery reptiles in their natural habitat. Daily wildlife shows at 10:30, 12:30, 2:30, and 4 feature the rare and endangered Florida panther, the Florida black bear, alligators, and various snakes. There are also daily alligator feeding demonstrations. Children delight in seeing the gentle animals in the petting zoo, and there are nature trails for the whole family to enjoy, including a one that takes you into a jungle. ⊠ 17 mi east of Orlando on Rte. 50, ☎ 407/568–2885. ☞ $14.50 adults, $8.50 children 3–11. ☼ Daily 9:30– 5:30.

The **Iron Bridge Easterly Wetlands** are the first large-scale man-made wetlands created and maintained with highly treated, reclaimed water, and they provide a habitat for wildlife. Created in 1987, they now are home to more than 150 species of birds, plus otters, foxes, deer, turtles, snakes, and alligators. There's a 2-mi bird viewing trail, many shorter trails that lead to good bird and wildlife viewing places, a hiking trail, and a lake. Don't expect to find a snack bar or crowds of people here. Unlike most central Florida attractions, this one is basically a show-case for nature. ✉ *From Rte. 50 go 2½ mi north on Rte. 420 (Ft. Christ-mas Rd.), turn east on Wheeler Rd., and drive 1½ mi east,* ☎ *407/246–2288.* 🎫 *Free.* ☉ *Feb.–Sept., daily 8–½ hr before sunset.*

Lake Wales

③③ *57 mi southwest of Orlando and 42 mi southwest of WDW.*

If, after several days at the theme parks, you find that you're in need of a back-to-nature fix, head south along U.S. 27. Along the way, you'll see what's left of Central Florida's citrus groves (there are still quite a lot of them) as well as a few RV parks, but the big bonus is getting away from the congestion of the city. If you just can't bear a day with-out a theme park, stop in at nearby Cypress Gardens (☞ Chapter 4).

Bok Tower Gardens is an appealing sanctuary of plants, flowers, trees, and wildlife that is overlooked by most visitors, but it's definitely worth a trip. Shady paths meander through pine forests in this peace-ful world of silvery moats, mockingbirds and swans, blooming thick-ets, and hidden sundials. You'll be able to boast that you stood on the highest measured point on Florida's peninsula, a colossal 298 ft above sea level. The majestic, 200-ft Bok Tower is constructed of coquina—from seashells—and pink, white, and gray marble. The tower houses a carillon with 57 bronze bells that ring every half hour after 10 AM. Each day at 3 PM there is a 45-minute recital, which may include early American folk songs, Appalachian tunes, Irish ballads, or Latin hymns. There are also moonlight recitals.

The landscape was designed in 1928 by Frederick Law Olmsted Jr., son of the planner of New York's Central Park. On the grounds you'll find the 20-room, Mediterranean Revival–style **Pinewood House,** built in 1930. Take I–4 to Exit 23, and head south on U.S. 27. About 5 mi past the Cypress Gardens turnoff, turn right on Route 17A to Alter-nate U.S. 27. Past the orange groves, turn left on Burns Avenue and follow it about 1½ mi to the gardens. ☎ *941/676–1408.* 🎫 *$6 adults, $2 children 5–12, free Sat. if you arrive 8 AM–9 AM; Pinewood House $5 suggested donation.* ☉ *Daily 8–6, Pinewood House tours Sept. 15–May 15, Tues. and Thurs. 12:30 and 2, Sun. 2.*

6   DINING

It's not hard to find just about any kind of cuisine at any kind of restaurant around Orlando. What's hard is deciding where to eat in the limited time you have.

Competition has bred a superlative selection of eateries, with every conceivable national chain opening outlets that are nearly always bigger, sometimes better, and often glitzier than you've ever seen, while a host of independents hold their own.

Updated by
Rowland
Stiteler

WALK INTO UNIVERSAL ORLANDO'S new entertainment and dining utopia, CityWalk, and you get an olfactory surprise. Instead of the traditional smell of hot grease cooking up another load of french fries, the compelling aroma of a wood-fire pizza oven performs its magic. This small fact symbolizes just how radically the Orlando restaurant picture has changed over the past few years. The competition for your dining dollar is as hot as the aforementioned pizza oven. That's the good news.

The bad news is that the restaurant marketing people seem to be calling the shots. And they have made a couple of decisions. First, they think that you want to eat in a restaurant with a name your neighbors will recognize when you get back home, not just a Hard Rock Cafe or a Planet Hollywood. Now so many famous people have restaurants bearing their names that you might well stop and ask yourself whether, say, forecasters on the Weather Channel and pitch men and women from the Home Shopping Network will be next.

The marketing wizards also seem to have decreed that every newcomer must have a theme, especially newcomers on tourist strips such as Kissimmee's Irlo Bronson Highway and Orlando's International Drive.

In addition, it has long been the case that Orlando has become something of a laboratory in which corporate America test-drives its new Burger Barns and Lasagna-on-a-Bun outlets to see if they'll make it. If they can batter it, fry it, microwave it, torture it, and serve it with a side of fries, you'll find it in Central Florida. In this kind of environment, it becomes hard for mom-and-pop restaurants to compete, and hard to find a menu that hasn't been subjected to a focus group before it's rolled out before the public. Nevertheless, the result is often good eating, as a sort of culinary Darwinism weeds out the bad food. That Darwinism is alive and well at Universal's CityWalk, where the wood ovens seem to have higher priority than the deep-fryers.

The same concept is applied to more upscale eateries in the mid-price range as well. Fabulous cuisine is available throughout Walt Disney World and the surrounding area, and it's getting progressively easier to find it. In recent years, the quality of food and the level of service have escalated, as Disney, Universal, and other big attractions upgraded their food scene. Now it's almost as easy to find a salade Niçoise as it is to find an order of fries.

Local Specialties
Grouper—fried, blackened, or broiled—is the closest thing Central Florida has to a local dish. Most natives don't eat much alligator tail—it's basically tourist bait—but almost every fish restaurant offers it for those who want to check it off their life experience list. What can we say? It tastes like chicken. Also worthy are some of the treats imported from the Florida Keys and billed as local fare. Try conch chowder, tasty Keys lobsters, and stone crabs, which are in season between October and March. Fresh hearts of palm, served in pricier restaurants, are also a treat. One tip on key lime pie: if it's green, especially fluorescent green, you've been had. Pie made from real key lime is yellowish, like the fruit itself.

Dinner Shows
Dinner shows are popular and quite numerous in Orlando, although the meal is not usually as memorable as the entertainment. Walt Disney World has several table-side extravaganzas, among them the perennially sold-out Hoop-Dee-Doo Revue at the Fort Wilderness Campground area. If you can't score a reservation for the Disney

hoop-along, check out the shows about Arabian nights, medieval knights, the Wild West, and Henry VIII, to name just a few. For our assessments and all the details, *see* Chapter 10.

Dress

Because tourism is king around Orlando, casual dress is the rule. Very few restaurants require jackets or other dress-up attire for men, and many that once did, like the popular Arthur's 27, are lightening up. Except in the priciest establishments, you can wear very casual clothing. And if your child is the only one wearing a hat with Goofy ears, you probably made a wrong turn and ended up in Georgia. In the reviews below, dress is mentioned only when men are required to wear a jacket.

Reservations

Reservations are always a good idea in a market where the phrase "Bus drivers eat free" is emblazoned on the city's coat of arms. Without reservations, the entire Ecuadorian soccer team or the senior class from Platt City High School may arrive moments before you and keep you waiting a long, long time. Many area restaurants accept what's known in these parts as requests for "priority seating"—they make no commitments to honor the time you both agree on. Still others don't take reservations at all.

If you plan to tackle one of these no-reservations spots, you can minimize your wait by using the same off-hours strategy that works in the theme parks: lunch at 11 AM, and have dinner before 5 PM. And if you must eat at peak hours, plan to arrive well before you think you'll want to eat, or have a snack before you leave home.

For restaurants within Walt Disney World, reservations are especially easy to make, thanks to its central reservations lines (☎ 407/939–3463 or 407/560–7277).

And, although you can't make reservations on-line at the Disney Web site, www.disney.go.com/DisneyWorld, you can certainly get a World of information about dining options throughout Disney, like the hours, price range, and specialties of all Disney eateries. Universal Orlando, which has become a major player in the culinary wars, also has its own reservation line (☎ 407/224–9255), and a diner-friendly Web site, www.uescape.com, from which you can surf your way to Web pages for all of the CityWalk restaurants.

Remember that although Orlando is not a big town, getting to places is frequently complicated, so always get directions, whether or not you need reservations.

In reviews below, reservations are mentioned only when they're essential or are not accepted. Unless otherwise noted, the restaurants listed are open daily for lunch and dinner.

IN WALT DISNEY WORLD

Don't worry—you won't go hungry here, you can't walk more than 100 yards on Disney property without seeing some variation of a food opportunity. Every theme park has its appropriate quota of counter-service eateries, and every one of them, even the McDonald's in Disney's Animal Kingdom, is beautifully themed. Moderately priced hotels each have a food court with a good variety of options ranging from burgers to stir-fries. The pricier hotels have full-service cafés, coffee shops, and buffets as well as sophisticated places that would hold their own among the best. Over the last few years, as Americans' taste in food

Paris, France.

Paris, Texas.

When it Comes to Getting Cash at an ATM,

Same Thing.

Whether you're in Yosemite or Yemen, using your Visa® card or ATM card with the PLUS symbol is the easiest and most convenient way to get cash. Even if your bank is in Minneapolis and you're in Miami, Visa/PLUS ATMs make getting cash so easy, you'll feel right at home. After all, Visa/PLUS ATMs are open 24 hours a day, 7 days a week, rain or shine. And if you need help finding one of Visa's 627,000 ATMs in 127 countries worldwide, visit **visa.com/pd/atm**. We'll make finding an ATM as easy as finding the Eiffel Tower, the Pyramids or even the Grand Canyon.

It's Everywhere You Want To Be.®

ONE LAST TRAVEL TIP:

Pack an easy way to reach the world.

123 456 7891 2345
J.D. SMITH

Wherever you travel, the MCI WorldCom Card℠ is the easiest way to stay in touch. You can use it to call to and from more than 125 countries worldwide. And you can earn bonus miles every time you use your card. So go ahead, travel the world. MCI WorldCom℠ makes it even more rewarding. For additional access codes, visit **www.wcom.com/worldphone.**

EASY TO CALL WORLDWIDE

1. Just dial the WorldPhone® access number of the country you're calling from.

2. Dial or give the operator your MCI WorldCom Card number.

3. Dial or give the number you're calling.

Aruba (A) ✛	800-888-8
Australia ◆	1-800-881-100
Bahamas ✛	1-800-888-8000
Barbados (A) ✛	1-800-888-8000
Bermuda ✛	1-800-888-8000
British Virgin Islands (A) ✛	1-800-888-8000
Canada	1-800-888-8000
Costa Rica (A) ◆	0800-012-2222
New Zealand	000-912
Puerto Rico	1-800-888-8000
United States	1-800-888-8000
U.S. Virgin Islands	1-800-888-8000

(A) Calls back to U.S. only. ✛ Limited availability. ◆ Public phones may require deposit of coin or phone card for dial tone.

EARN FREQUENT FLIER MILES

has evolved, so have the menu offerings across the board. Nowadays, every food spot, even the ones where fast food is king, offer a salad and a light sandwich or two. In the more elegant restaurants, the level of cooking has come up a couple of notches as well. No longer is the decor the only thing that will excite you—creativity in the kitchen also contributes consistently to the pleasure of a WDW meal.

Meals with Disney Characters

At these breakfasts, brunches, and dinners staged in hotel and theme-park restaurants all over Walt Disney World, kids can snuggle up to all the best-loved Disney characters. Sometimes the food is served buffet style; sometimes it's served to you banquet style. You'll find the cast of characters, times, and prices change as frequently as the Dow Jones Industrial Average (but locations of performances remain fairly constant) so be sure and call ahead if your child would be crushed if the Lion King characters show up instead of Mickey himself. Reservations are often required, even in some places that are not crowded, so show up on the early side if you hate to wait. Smoking is not permitted at any of these.

Breakfast

Reservations are not required for many of these events, but because characters rotate and mealtimes often change, call ahead.

You can drop in Sunday 8:30–10:30 at the **Wyndham Palace Suite Resort and Spa at WDW Resort** (☎ 407/827–2727, ☎ $16.95 adults, $8.95 children under 11); 7–11:30 daily for a no-holds-barred buffet at **Chef Mickey's at the Contemporary Resort** (☎ 407/939–3463, ☎ $14.95 adults, $7.95 children 3–11); 7–11:30 daily in the **Cape May Café at Disney's Beach Club** (☎ 407/939–3463, ☎ $14.95 adults, $8.50 children 3–11); 7:30–11 daily at the **Polynesian Resort's 'Ohana** (☎ 407/939–3463, ☎ $14.95 adults, $8.95 children 3–11); 7:30–11:30 daily at the **Artist Point restaurant at Disney's Wilderness Lodge** (☎ 407/939–3463, ☎ $14.50 adults, $8.75 children 3–11); Saturday 8–11 in the **Garden Grove at the Walt Disney World Swan** (☎ 407/934–1609, ☎ about $13 for adults, $8.50 for children 3–11, depending on whether you choose buffet or order from menu); 8:30–11:15 daily at **Hollywood & Vine at Disney–MGM Studios** (☎ 407/939–3463, ☎ $14.95 adults, $7.95 children 3–11); Sunday, Monday, and Wednesday from 7:30 to 10:15 at **Olivia's Cafe at Disney's Old Key West Resort** (☎ 407/939–3463, ☎ $13.95 adults, $8.50 children 3–11); and daily from park opening to 10:45 at the **Crystal Palace Buffet at Main Street, U.S.A.** (☎ 407/939–3463, ☎ $14.95 adults, $7.95 children 3–11); Sunday only from 8:30–11 at the **Hilton in the WDW Resort** (☎ 407/827–4000, ext. 3840, ☎ $14.95 adults, $7.95 children 4–11).

Reservations are required for other daily breakfasts, including the ones hosted by Cinderella, from 8 to 10 in the Magic Kingdom's **Cinderella's Royal Table** (☎ 407/939–3463, ☎ $14.95 adults, $7.95 children 3–11), and Mary Poppins, 7:30–11:30 in the **1900 Park Fare Restaurant in the Grand Floridian** (☎ 407/824–2383, ☎ $15.95 adults, $9.95 children 3–11). And Farmer Mickey is on hand in Future World between 8:40 and 11:10 (as well as later in the day) at the **Garden Grill in the Land** (☎ 407/939–3463, ☎ $14.95 adults, $8.25 children 3–11). The newest addition to the character breakfast menu is Donald's Breakfastosaurus, featuring appearances by Donald Duck and friends, at the **Restaurantosaurus** (☎ 407/939–3463, ☎ $14.95 adults, $8.95 children 3–11), in Disney's Animal Kingdom.

196

Dining

Apopka

Lockhart

Pine Hills

Windermere

Magic Kingdom

Walt Disney World see inset

Downtown Disney

Epcot

Disney's Animal Kingdom

Disney-MGM Studios

Bear Lake

Lake Apopka

Lake Down

Lake Butler

Lake Tibet

Lake Sheen

Big Sand Lake

Lake Maitland

Lake Fairview

North Orange Blossom Tr.

Florida's Tnpk.

Apopka-Vineland Rd.

Turkey Lake Rd.

International Dr.

Sand Lake Rd.

Bee Line

Central Florida

EXIT 48
EXIT 47
EXIT 45
EXIT 43
EXIT 47
EXIT 37
EXIT 33
EXIT 31
EXIT 30
EXIT 29
EXIT 28
EXIT 27A
EXIT 27
EXIT 26
EXIT 25

Fairbanks Ave.

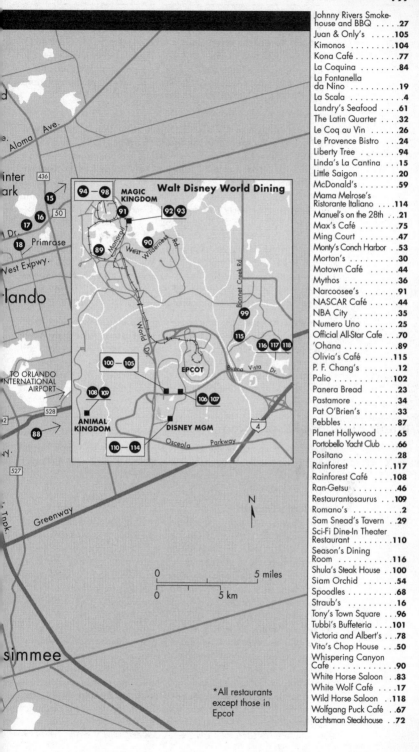

Sunday Brunch

The Disney characters show up for the lavish Sunday brunch 7:30–11 at the **Coral Café at the Walt Disney World Dolphin** (☎ 407/934–4025, ✉ $16.95 adults, $10.95 children 3–12). You can help yourself to everything from bacon and eggs and seafood crepes to pancakes and chocolate chip waffles in the distinctive circle-with-ears shape. Reservations are a good idea.

Dinner

Mickey and Minnie are at the buffet served from 5:30 to 9 daily at the **1900 Park Fare Restaurant in the Grand Floridian** (☎ 407/939–3463, ✉ $21.95 adults, $12.95 children 3–11). The eponymous chef stars during dinner, served 5 to 9:30 daily, at **Chef Mickey's at the Contemporary Resort** (☎ 407/939–3463, ✉ $19.95 adults, $8.95 children 3–11). The Mickster's zillionth daily appearance is at dinner, served from 5 to 7 daily at the **Liberty Tree Tavern in Liberty Square** (☎ 407/939–3463, ✉ $19.95 adults, $9.95 children 3–11). Farmer Mickey reprises his role in farmer garb at the **Garden Grill in the Land** (☎ 407/939–3463, ✉ $18.95 adults, $9.95 children 3–11) from 4:40 to 8:10 daily (as well as 11:30 AM to 4:20 PM). And Winnie the Pooh and friends appear at a nightly dinner buffet at the **Crystal Palace Buffet on Main Street, U.S.A.** (☎ 407/939–3463, ✉ $19.95 adults, $9.95 children 3–11). You need reservations for all of these.

Dinner with the *Lion King* characters is available from 6 to 10 on Tuesday and Saturday at **Gulliver's Grill Restaurant at the Walt Disney World Swan** (☎ 407/934–1609); the same restaurant is called Garden Grill at breakfast and lunch. Dinner guests pay à la carte prices from the standard menu. Every night at 8 (7 in winter months), near Fort Wilderness's Meadow Trading Post, there are a **Character Campfire** and free sing-along.

Magic Kingdom Resort Area

Restaurants here are in the Contemporary, Polynesian, and Grand Floridian hotels and the rustic Wilderness Lodge, as well as in the Magic Kingdom itself. To get to the area, your best bet is to take Exit 24C, 25B, or 26B off I–4.

American/Casual

$–$$ **Crystal Palace.** The name comes from the big glass atrium in which the restaurant is located, but experienced Disney visitors know it as a heavenly oasis, where the air-conditioning is turned up near meat-locker level in the summer, so you can rest your bones in a place exempt from the Florida heat. The buffet-style meal includes the full range of upscale mass-meal items, from roasted meats to soups of the day, with pasta, fresh-baked breads, and ice cream sundaes as part of the package. ⊠ *Main Street USA,* ☎ *407/939–3463. AE, MC, V.*

$–$$ **Liberty Tree Tavern.** Experienced Magic Kingdom visitors often follow a ritual that involves ducking into this place—with its prime spot on the parade route—an hour or so before a parade and then walking outside to watch the fanfare. Colonial period comfort food like roast turkey, honey-cured Virginia ham, and beef brisket are mainstays here, and you can sample all of them at the fixed-price, family-style meals, ranging from $4.75 for children at lunch to $19.95 for adults at dinner. Even though this eatery is called a tavern, don't expect to be served a beer—there's no alcohol flowing. ⊠ *Liberty Square,* ☎ *407/939–3463. AE, MC, V.*

$–$$ **Whispering Canyon Cafe.** There's no whispering in this place. In fact, the servers-cum-actors yell across the room things like "Ketchup! This guy needs some ketchup." The idea is to keep the atmosphere jovial in this family-style restaurant, where huge stacks of pancakes and big servings of spare ribs are the orders of the day. The dinner specialty here is barbecue, with a $21 all-you-can-eat meal that includes pork ribs, beef brisket, smoked sausage, and smoked turkey. The canyon part of the equation is the giant, totem-pole-laden hotel atrium onto which the dining area opens. Whispering Canyon makes a good alternative to the Wilderness Lodge's other restaurant, the highly acclaimed and often booked-up Artist Point. ⊠ *Wilderness Lodge,* ☎ *407/939–3463. AE, MC, V.*

$ **Aunt Polly's.** Getting to this walk-up eatery, supposedly operated by Tom Sawyer's Aunt Polly, is half the fun: to reach it, you have to jump on the raft ride in Frontierland and float on over. Although the menu is not exactly haute cuisine, once there you'll find fried chicken, "PB&J" sandwiches, cookies, ice cream, apple pie—all the ingredients of the quintessential American picnic. Plus, you get a great view of the river itself. ⊠ *Frontierland,* ☎ *407/939–3463. AE, MC, V.*

$ **Chef Mickey's.** At this mealtime extravaganza, you always get Mickey, Minnie, and Goofy presiding inside Disney's original on-property hotel. All the activity also means that this is not the place to go for a quiet bite to eat. The buffet-style meal includes eggs and pancakes for breakfast, and thick, oven-roasted prime rib, pasta, and mashed potatoes and gravy for lunch or dinner. If you don't like buffets, you can order from the menu, which is kid-driven, with dishes like macaroni and cheese, hot dogs, and pizza available at lunch and dinner, and an all-you-can-eat dessert bar with ice cream sundaes. ⊠ *Contemporary Resort,* ☎ *407/939–3463. AE, MC, V.*

$ **Tubbi's Buffeteria.** This buffet-service eatery in the Walt Disney World Dolphin would be pretty forgettable were it not for its hours, which are, as your kids might say, "24-7." Disney World has a dearth of late-night diners, with your best bet for food after midnight being room service in most hotels. But Tubbi's, which features sandwiches, pizza, and two daily blue plate specials, like meat loaf or barbecued chicken, serves up hot food round the clock. ⊠ *Walt Disney World Dolphin,* ☎ *407/934–4000. AE, MC, V.*

Contemporary

$$$$ ✕ **Victoria and Albert's.** Servers work in man-woman pairs, calling them-
★ selves Victoria and Albert and reciting specials in tandem. If this doesn't strike your fancy, you can't really shoo the thespian servers away. But the cuisine draws wows nevertheless. The intimate (seating just 45 people), lavish, and romantic Victorian-style room, considered Disney's top restaurant in its top hotel by many Disney execs, has a dome ceiling, fabric-covered walls, marbleized columns, and lots of flowers. A harpist adds an ethereal touch. The seven-course, prix-fixe menu ($85) changes from day to day. Appetizers might include veal sweetbreads or artichokes in duxelles (mushroom-based) sauce. Entrées range from poached lobster over creamed corn and couscous to grilled tenderloin with red wine risotto. Kosher and vegetarian meals can be ordered in advance. There's one seating (7–7:45) nightly. ⊠ *Grand Floridian,* ☎ *407/939–3463. Reservations essential. Jacket required. AE, MC, V.*

$$$–$$$$ ✕ **Citrico's.** There's nothing historic about the Grand Floridian's culinary centerpiece, and it's all the better for it. The setting is bright and cheerful, focused on an open central kitchen, in which chef Roland Muller's minions can be seen going about their work. But don't expect to be overwhelmed with citrus choices. Despite the restaurant name, the menu is not necessarily quintessential Florida but leans toward innovations like pan-seared wild striped sea bass and jumbo scallops, oak-grilled veal tenderloin, and a braised veal shank that's actually cooked for six hours. You can get a taste of the tender veal shank by ordering

it as an appetizer, served in a potato ravioli. And another appetizer, lobster crepes served with a vanilla-based sauce, is also worth sampling. Desserts include a citrus crème brûlée and a flourless chocolate torte with banana ice cream and Grand Marnier chocolate sauce. The wine list, one of WDW's largest, includes vintages from around the planet, and many are available by the glass. You'll be hard-pressed to get out for less than $40 a person. ⊠ *Grand Floridian,* ☎ *407/939–3463. AE, MC, V.*

$$–$$$$ ✕ **California Grill.** This viewful restaurant on the 15th floor of the Con-
★ temporary Resort is a shining example of the culinary revolution that has taken place at WDW in the last few years. The watchword here is "fresh food, simply prepared," in the words of restaurant manager George Miliotes. But those words hardly do justice to excellent offerings such as the pan-roasted grouper with herb dumplings and goat cheese ravioli with shiitake mushrooms, basil, and sun-dried tomatoes, the chili-braised venison steak, or the new brick oven–baked flatbreads topped with alderwood-smoked salmon and chive sour cream. Desserts are transcontinental, ranging from cappuccino quake, a fudge brownie with chocolate mousse, to angel food cake with strawberry compote and caramelized lemongrass custard. The restaurant has an extensive wine list. ⊠ *Contemporary Resort,* ☎ *407/939–3463. AE, MC, V.*

$–$$$ ✕ **Artist Point.** The Wilderness Lodge—a huge, brawny hotel straight
★ out of the Rocky Mountains—is definitely worth a look, and a meal here should be on your short list of things to do, if only because it's a good excuse to visit this tour de force of the Imagineer's art. The Northwestern salmon sampler or the elk and venison sausage sampler makes a good start, but you might also try the smoked duck breast, maple-glazed steak, sautéed elk sausage, or panfried rainbow trout, which probably traveled farther to get here than you did. And if you've never sampled buffalo meat (and actually want to), there's a grilled Colorado buffalo rib-eye steak. Good dessert choices include Pacific Northwest rhubarb and strawberry compote with vanilla ice cream, or berry cobbler, a blueberry biscuit with strawberries and crème fraîche. There's a good Northwestern wine list. ⊠ *Wilderness Lodge,* ☎ *407/939–3463. AE, MC, V.*

$–$$ **Cinderella's Royal Table.** What a difference a name can make. When this eatery, in the upper reaches of the trademark castle in the Magic Kingdom, was called King Stephan's Dining Hall, they could hardly give the food away. (King Stephan was Sleeping Beauty's father, but you probably knew that.) Now that it's Cinderella's Royal Table, with character appearances by Cinderella and her sisters, you need to book reservations 60 days in advance to be assured of a seating. The menu ranges from beef and barley soup to barbecued ribs to sautéed fish in a white wine sauce on pasta. If your kids don't feel up to anything as substantial as a balanced meal, there are cheeseburgers, chicken tenders, or the ubiquitous Disney mac and cheese for $4.95 a pop. Strawberry shortcake is a best bet for dessert. ⊠ *Walt Disney World Dolphin,* ☎ *407/934–4000. Reservations essential. AE, MC, V.*

$–$$ ✕ **Kona Cafe.** Desserts are the specialty at this eclectic restaurant in
★ WDW's Polynesian Resort. Pastry chef Isaac Tomada recently won the gold medal of the American Culinary Federation's pastry competition, and you will understand the accolades when you try his white chocolate guava cake or his Kahlúa torte—named after an active volcano, it's filled with warm hazelnut sauce and chocolate that spills out when you cut the pastry with your fork. The house specialty entrée, the Bag, consists of fish, clams, pork, and vegetables cooked in a roasting bag, which is ceremoniously cut open at the table by your server. The two-fisted chicken sandwich with roasted peppers and basil-infused mayonnaise is another standout. As the name of the place implies, coffee is a specialty. ⊠ *Polynesian Resort,* ☎ *407/939–3463. AE, MC, V.*

Italian

$$-$$$$ **Palio.** You can find some of the classic upscale Italian dishes here, like *saltimbocca alla Romana* (veal with prosciutto) and chicken *alla Marsala*. There's also a good pizza from the restaurant's wood-fired oven, and a house pasta specialty, tortellini stuffed with lobster and roasted garlic, that makes a great dinner choice. The dining experience is pretty upbeat, with strolling minstrels and a seemingly endless supply of fresh baked bread with roasted garlic spread to keep you happy until the entrées arrive. There's a good selection of fresh fish, with the best being the red snapper. Standout desserts include crème brûlée and a house specialty, Italian wedding cake. ⊠ *Walt Disney World Swan,* ☎ 407/934–3000. AE, MC, V.

$–$$ **Tony's Town Square Restaurant.** This Main Street USA Italian eatery was inspired by the animated movie classic *Lady and the Tramp* and offers everything from spaghetti and meat balls to more creative fare like wood-oven pizza and penne pasta with Italian sausage. But don't expect a straw-wrapped bottle of Chianti at the table. No alcohol is served, but the food is better than one might expect in this busy setting. A meal here makes a great way to pass the time while you are waiting for one of the big Main Street parades. ⊠ *Liberty Square,* ☎ 407/939–3463. AE, MC, V.

Polynesian

$–$$ **'Ohana.** A great place for carnivores, the only option here is an all-you-can-eat fixed-price meal ($21.95 for adults, $9.95 for kids) of grilled meats including pork, beef, chicken, or salmon. The restaurant is also a performance art palace of sorts. The chef performs in front of an 18-ft fire pit, grilling the meats as flames shoot up to sear in the flavors and entertain the diners. Special desserts include the coconut snowball and the guava cheesecake. ⊠ *Polynesian Resort,* ☎ 407/939–3463. AE, MC, V.

Seafood

$$–$$$$ **Narcoosee's.** This restaurant has one of the few weird names that Disney didn't make up: Narcoosee is a small central Florida town. The food is something of a salute to small-town central Florida fare, with an emphasis on seafood, such as panfried grouper, grilled shrimp, and crab with potato cakes. There are of course other items you'd never find in a small Florida town, like focaccia with duck pastrami and a nice tiramisu for dessert. The restaurant overlooks the water. ⊠ *Grand Floridian Resort,* ☎ 407/939–3463. AE, MC, V.

Steak

$–$$ **Concourse Steak House.** If you've always liked that trademark monorail that runs from the Magic Kingdom into the Contemporary Resort, you might want to consider having a meal under it. This steak house is set one story below the train itself, with the tracks running on each side above. The place isn't as noisy as it might seem. Steaks are the specialty here, with other entrées like mango-glazed barbecued pork ribs, oakwood-roasted chicken, and shrimp, chicken, and sausage jambalaya. Desserts include a good crème brûlée and a marbled cheesecake. ⊠ *Contemporary Resort,* ☎ 407/939–3463. AE, MC, V.

In Epcot

Epcot's World Showcase offers some of the finest dining in all Orlando. The problems are that you have to pay Epcot admission to eat in these establishments; the top-of-the-line places, such as those in the French, Italian, and Japanese pavilions, can be expensive; and reservations are hard to come by. On the other hand, most of them have a limited-selection children's menu with dramatically lower prices. Dress is informal—no one expects you to go all the way back to your hotel to tidy up. And if you have unruly youngsters in tow, you probably won't be alone. Kosher and vegetarian meals are available on request. (For other options in Future World, *see* Epcot A to Z *in* Chapter 2.)

Reservations

All restaurants, unless otherwise noted, are open for both lunch and dinner daily. For both meals, reservations are a must. At Epcot, there are two ways of making reservations: call the central reservations lines (☏ 407/939–3463 or 407/560–7277) or go to the restaurant directly and sign up.

Be flexible about your mealtimes. For the more popular establishments, it is much easier to get a reservation for lunch than for dinner, to get lunch reservations before noon, and to get dinner reservations for seatings before 6 and after 8. And it's always worth stopping by the restaurant of your choice during the day in hopes of a cancellation.

No matter how you book, show up a bit early to be sure of getting your table. You can pay with cash; charge with American Express, MasterCard, or Visa; or, if you're a guest at an on-site hotel on Disney property, charge the tab to your room.

Canadian

$$–$$$ ╳ **Le Cellier Steakhouse.** This comfortable eatery in Canada is the place to find well-prepared beef: it looks just like an old wine cellar—with dark woods and stone arches—even though it's above ground. Standouts are its tender steaks and prime rib; if you don't go for beef, try the maple-glazed salmon or the braised venison shank steak. Kids have a great option, too—burgers. The wine list contains as large a selection of Canadian vintages as you'll find in Florida. Good desserts include chocolate mousse, the maple Butterfinger mousse with raspberry sauce, and vanilla bean crème anglaise. Because eating Canadian may not be on every visitor's short list of priorities, this place can offer an alternative when other Epcot restaurants are too crowded.

Chinese

$–$$ ╳ **Nine Dragons Restaurant.** The specialty is Cantonese cuisine, from *moo goo gai pan* (a stir-fried chicken or vegetable dish) and sweet-and-sour pork to lobster. A good choice is Great Wall duck, shredded duck meat with red and green peppers, served with Chinese pancakes. However, the kitchen staff doesn't limit itself to one style of Chinese cooking; it also offers excellent Szechuan and Hunan style dishes, such as chicken, shrimp, and lobster prepared with hot peppers and fiery sauces. The menu even includes more obscure, Kiangche-style entrées, among them stir-fried scallops and vegetables with special sauces. Just next door, at the counter-service Lotus Blossom, you can get quick dishes like stir-fried beef, fried rice, and egg rolls.

English

$–$$ ╳ **Rose and Crown.** If you are an Anglophile and you love a good, thick beer, this is the place to soak up both the suds and the British street culture. (You can even go for the ale and beer sampler, five 4-ounce glasses for $8.25.) "Wenches" serve up just the type of traditional English fare you've always heard about—fish-and-chips, meat pies, Yorkshire pudding, and the ever-popular "bangers and mash," English sausage over mashed potatoes. At day's end, visitors mingle with Disney employees while knocking down pints of Bass Ale and Guinness Stout with Stilton cheese. At 4 PM a traditional tea is served. The food is relatively inexpensive, especially at lunch, and the terrace has a splendid view of IllumiNations. All things considered, it's one of the best bets in Epcot.

French

$$–$$$ ✕ **Bistro de Paris.** The great secret at the France pavilion—and, indeed,
★ in all of Epcot—is the Bistro de Paris, located around the back of Les Chefs de Paris and upstairs. The sophisticated menu changes regularly and reflects the cutting edge of French cooking. Come late, ask for a window seat, and plan to linger to watch IllumiNations, the dazzling Epcot light show. The French wines are moderately priced and available by the glass.

$$–$$$ ✕ **Les Chefs de France.** To create this sparkling French café-restaurant,
★ three of France's most famous culinary artists came together: Paul Bocuse, who operates one restaurant north of Lyon and two in Tokyo; Gaston Lenôtre, noted for his pastries and ice creams; and Roger Vergé, proprietor of France's celebrated Mougins, near Cannes. The three developed the menu, trained the chefs, and look in—apparently not as frequently as they should, according to some—to make sure the food and service stay up to snuff. Nevertheless, many Orlandoans consider this the best restaurant at Disney, even though it hasn't changed much over the years. Start with chicken-and-duck pâté, follow up with a classic coq au vin or roasted red snapper with lobster sauce, and end up with chocolate-doused, ice-cream-filled pastry shells.

German

$$ ✕ **Biergarten.** In this popular spot, Oktoberfest runs 365 days a year. The cheerful—some would say raucous—atmosphere is what you would expect in a place with an oompah band. Waitresses in typical Bavarian garb serve *breseln,* the hot German pretzels, which are made fresh daily on the premises. Other classic German fare in the one-price all-you-can-eat buffet includes sauerbraten and bratwurst, as well as good apple strudel and Black Forest cake. Patrons pound stout pitchers of all kinds of beer and wine on their long communal tables—even when the yodelers, singers, and dancers aren't egging them on.

Italian

$$–$$$ ✕ **L'Originale Alfredo di Roma Ristorante.** Waiters skip around singing
★ Italian songs and bellowing arias, a show in itself, so it's not surprising that this is the most popular restaurant at Epcot (try arriving at 11 if you don't have a lunch reservation). Nor should it startle you to hear that its namesake dish, made with mountains of butter flown in from Italy, is one of the principal reasons. The restaurant was created, with the help of Disney, by the descendants of Alfredo de Lelio, who in 1914 founded Rome's Alfredo all'Augusteo restaurant and invented the now-classic dish—fettuccine sauced with cream, butter, and loads of freshly grated, imported Parmesan cheese. But the true secret to the dish here is the butter. Pasta is your best bet aside from grouper *Veneziana* (with the grouper baked in a zesty sauce with a hint of garlic). Other standouts include the grilled veal chop with Chianti and black truffle sauce, and a couple of dessert offerings, the ricotta cheese cake and a credible cannoli.

Japanese

$$–$$$ ✕ **Mitsukoshi.** This complex of dining areas overlooking tranquil gardens is actually three restaurants. Yakitori House, a gussied-up fast-food stand in a small pavilion modeled on a teahouse in Kyoto's Katsura Summer Palace, offers broiled skewers of chicken basted with teriyaki sauce, and *gyudon* (paper-thin beef simmered in a spicy sauce and served with noodles). At the Tempura Kiku, two dozen diners sit around a central counter and watch the chefs prepare sushi, sashimi, and *tempura* (batter-dipped deep-fried shrimp, scallops, and vegeta-

bles). In the five Teppanyaki Dining Rooms, chefs skillfully chop vegetables, meat, and fish at lightning speed and then stir-fry them at grills set into communal dining tables. The Matsu No Ma Lounge to the right of this area pours Japanese sake, plum wine, and *saketinis* (martinis made with sake rather than vermouth). If you just want sushi, go to the lounge and you can usually avoid a wait.

Mexican

$$-$$$ ✕ **San Angel Inn.** The lush, tropical surroundings—cool, dark, and almost surreal—make this restaurant in the courtyard inside the Mexican pavilion perhaps the most exotic at WDW. It's popular among Disney execs as well as tourists, who treasure the respite it offers, especially when the humid weather outside makes Central Florida feel like equatorial Africa. Candlelighted tables are companionably close together, and the restaurant is open to a midnight-blue "sky" in the inside of the pavilion and filled with the music of folksingers, guitars, and marimbas. On the roster of authentic dishes, one specialty is *mole poblano* (chicken simmered until tender in a rich sauce of different kinds of chilies, green tomatoes, ground tortillas, cumin, and 11 other spices mixed with cocoa).

Moroccan

$$-$$$ ✕ **Marrakesh.** If you're worried about getting a table at Epcot, this is your best bet. It's the least popular of the World Showcase restaurants, not because the food isn't good—it is—but because the average American hasn't heard much about Moroccan cuisine. The food is mildly spicy and relatively inexpensive, and Disney has taken it quite seriously, bringing in chef Abrache Lahcen, who was personally recommended by King Hassan II of Morocco. Try the couscous, the national dish of Morocco, served with vegetables; or *bastilla* (an appetizer made of alternating layers of sweet-and-spicy pork and a thin pastry, redolent of almonds, saffron, and cinnamon). The building, painstakingly constructed and carved by artisans brought in from Morocco, is impressive. Inside, belly dancers and a three-piece Moroccan band set a North African mood that feels like the set of *Casablanca,* which, after all, was filmed in California.

Scandinavian

$$ ✕ **Restaurant Akershus.** Norway's tradition of seafood and cold-meat dishes is highlighted at the *koltbord* (Norwegian buffet) in this restaurant, comprising four dining rooms that occupy a copy of Oslo's Akershus Castle. Hosts and hostesses explain the dishes and suggest which ones go together, then send you off to the buffet table for the first of several trips—appetizers, which usually include herring done several ways. Then go for cold seafood such as gravlax, a cured salmon served with mustard sauce, and *fiskepudding,* a seafood mousse with herb dressing. Pick up cold salads and meats on your next trip, and on your last foray, fill up on hot lamb, veal, or venison. The selection of desserts, offered à la carte, includes cloudberries (a delicate fruit that grows on the tundra in season). Make sure you grab some of the *lefse,* a wonderful Norwegian flatbread made from potatoes and wheat flour, even if you have to ask your server for it. The lefse goes quickly at the buffet line, and it's wonderful for using the same way you'd use a tortilla. Considering that you can eat all the expensive fish you want for a fixed, moderate price, this is one of Disney's real bargains.

Seafood

$$-$$$ ✕ **Coral Reef Restaurant.** Not all of the good eating in Epcot is in the World Showcase, as the popularity of this fish house at the Living Seas Pavilion attests. Part of the attraction of this place is the view of the giant aquarium (part of the Living Seas exhibit itself), which you see

from a three-tiered seating area that gives every diner a good view. Stand-outs include the wood-grilled salmon (flown in fresh from Chile), the oven-baked sea bass, and the pan-seared scallops with a truffle vinai-grette. A great appetizer, incidentally, is the lobster and corn beignet, with spicy chili sauce. And if you want to be able to tell the folks back home you tried alligator, you can sample it here; there's a grilled alli-gator sausage served in a Creole vinaigrette.

Epcot Resort Area

These restaurants are in hotels and nightlife complexes clustered around Epcot, Disney's BoardWalk, the Yacht and Beach Club, and the Swan and Dolphin hotels. To get to the area, take I–4 and use Exit 25B or 26B.

American/Casual

$–$$ **ESPN Sports Club.** Sports fan? Not only is the restaurant filled with big-screen TVs showing virtually every important sporting event on the planet, it's a place from which sports shows are beamed to your liv-ing room. Local sports radio shows regularly shoot here, and ESPN broadcasters periodically film here as well. There are also live sports trivia contests when the bar is not doubling as a broadcast studio. The menu is not extensive, but the burgers are big and juicy, and you can sample unusual beers like J. W. Dundee Honey Wheat. This place is open quite late by Disney standards—until 2 AM on Friday and Sat-urday. ⊠ *Disney's BoardWalk,* ☎ *407/939–5100. AE, MC, V.*

$ **Big River Grille & Brewing Co.** If you like microbrews with esoteric-sounding names, like Pale Rocket Red Ale, Wowzers Wheat, and Tilt, this place is worth an hour or two of your time. You can dine inside among the giant copper brewing tanks, both functional and decora-tive, or sit outside and sip your suds on the lake-view patio. The menu tends to be red-meat-oriented, with baby-back ribs, barbecued pork, and a house special steak called a Drunken Ribeye, but there's also a worthwhile sautéed chicken dish and pan-seared salmon fillet. ⊠ *Dis-ney's BoardWalk,* ☎ *407/560–0253. AE, MC, V.*

Contemporary

$–$$$ **Gulliver's Grill at Garden Grove.** The legend here—and of course, every Disney area restaurant has one—is that this eatery was founded by Peter Miles Gulliver, a direct descendent of the Jonathan Swift character. Eat among tall palms and lush greenery even on one of Cen-tral Florida's few chilly days thanks to the restaurant's setting in a giant greenhouse. The menu has everything from grilled salmon to BLT sandwiches, with some Italian entrées and a good Caesar salad. If your kids can forget Mickey for a second, this is a good place to catch the *Legend of the Lion King* characters on Tuesday and Saturday. ⊠ *Walt Disney World Swan,* ☎ *407/934–3000. AE, D, DC, MC, V. No lunch.*

Japanese

$–$$ **Kimonos.** Knife-wielding sushi chefs prepare world-class sushi and sashimi, but also excellent beef teriyaki and other Japanese treats good for a full dinner or just a snack. The steamed dumplings, stuffed with pork, are quite good, as is their Japanese spin on a Florida delicacy, soft-shell crab. ⊠ *Walt Disney World Swan,* ☎ *407/934–1621. AE, D, DC, MC, V. No lunch.*

Mediterranean

$$–$$$$ ✕ **Spoodles.** Chef David Reynoso, a native of Mexico who studied in
★ the United States and Italy, has blended all the best foods of the Mediterranean into a taste that can be sampled through the tapas-style menu (small portions on small plates, and a lot of them). The result-ing mixture is so international you can almost hear "It's a Small

World" playing. (Thankfully, it isn't.) Perhaps the best dish is *rotollo,* a Moroccan flat bread rolled up like a burrito and filled with succulent roasted vegetables, hummus, cucumbers, and yogurtlike *tzatziki.* High recommendations also go to the barbecued Moroccan beef skewers with raisin and almond couscous, the spicy black mussel and pepperoni soup with Greek orzo and tomato fennel broth, and the duck sausage pizza. Fittingly, desserts are pan-Mediterranean, too. A $21 sampler lets you taste them all, but if you want to settle on just one, high marks go to the chocolate "Mount Vesuvius," with raspberries and warm liquid fudge. The children's menu includes macaroni and cheese and pepperoni pizza ($7). Although the decor is hardly reminiscent of the Mediterranean, little else would disqualify Spoodles from being one of the best restaurants in Orlando. ⊠ *Disney's Board-Walk,* ☎ 407/939–3463. AE, MC, V.

Mexican

$ **Juan and Only's Bar and Jail.** No, you can't do "time" here, but the concept is intriguing. Actually, the bar–jail packaging gives this fine Mexican eatery a kind of Pancho Villa feeling. The menu devotes a fair amount of space developing the myth of Juan and his partner. It's a nice place for a few margaritas and some Tex-Mex treasures like the house specialty, an excellent version of chiles rellenos. ⊠ *Walt Disney World Dolphin,* ☎ 407/934–4000. AE, D, DC, MC, V.

Seafood

$–$$$ ✕ **Flying Fish.** One of Disney's better new restaurants, this fine fish house was created by Martin Dorf, who is responsible for two other eateries on Disney's A-list, the California Grill and Citrico's (☞ *above*). You can get a good sense of the kitchen's way with seafood by starting with the Flying Fish sampler appetizer, which includes peeky-toe crab cakes, tuna tartare with cucumbers, and asparagus with Maine lobster, garlic butter, and Manchego cheese. The best of the house specialties are the potato-wrapped Florida red snapper served with leek-fennel fondue, and the oak-grilled scallops with corn-bacon risotto and chive blossoms. And if you love chocolate, save room for a house specialty dessert, "Lava Cake," a fine chocolate cake served warm with a liquid chocolate center, topped with pomegranate ice cream. ⊠ *Disney's BoardWalk,* ☎ 407/939–3463. AE, MC, V.

Steak

$$–$$$$ **Shula's Steak House.** The most expensive menu item here is the menu itself. It's printed on a Don Shula–autographed NFL regulation football, just like the ones available at the cashier's station for $300. This place is not just a shrine to an NFL coaching legend, however. The expertly cooked beef would be enough to fill this semiformal feeling eatery even if it didn't have a Florida household name attached. Among the best selections are the porterhouse and prime rib. If you want to eschew red meat, go for the lobster or the catch of the day. As it is with the upscale-beef business, veggies will cost you a little extra, like $8 for some asparagus or $5 for a baked potato. With white linen tablecloths and extremely attentive servers, this place makes a more than worthy replacement for Harry's Safari Bar and Grille, the whimsical WDW Dolphin eatery supplanted by Shula's. ⊠ *Walt Disney World Dolphin,* ☎ 407/934–1362. AE, D, DC, MC, V. No lunch.

$–$$ ✕ **Yachtsman Steakhouse.** The key at this steak house in the ultrapolished Yacht and Beach Club is aged beef, which you can see mellowing in a giant glassed-in butcher shop that greets you as you enter. The prime rib is superb. Go for the admiral's cut if you feel you can handle about 2 pounds of prime beef, or try the smaller captain's cut. If you want a good cross section of all that the restaurant does well, order the mixed grill—a small fillet of beef, plus a lamb chop and a chicken breast, all carefully prepared. If you prefer a good steak, try the Kansas City strip, also tender and moist. For dessert, don't miss the tasty Jack Daniels cake, chocolate mousse seasoned with high-octane Tennessee whiskey. The decor is an odd mix of nautical and Big Sky Country motifs. ⊠ *Yacht and Beach Club,* ☎ *407/939–3463. AE, MC, V. No lunch.*

Disney–MGM Studios

The Studios tends to offer more casual American cuisine (a.k.a. cheese-burger city) than the other parks, but has some good, imaginative of-ferings in the park.

American

$ **'50s Prime Time Cafe.** Who says you can't go home again? If you hap-pened to grow up in middle America in the 1950s, just step inside. While "I Love Lucy" plays on a television screen, you can feast on meat loaf, pot roast, or fried chicken served up on a Formica table top, of course. Follow it up with chocolate cake or a thick milk shake. Baby Boomers grew up on this familiar food so it's no wonder that it's difficult to get a seat during the prime lunch and dinner hours. ⊠ *Disney–MGM Stu-dios,* ☎ *407/939–3463. AE, MC, V.*

American/Casual

$–$$ **Sci-Fi Dine-In Theater Restaurant.** Now that drive-in theaters have all but disappeared in America, this place is something of a cultural trea-sure. In a faux drive-in where it's always dark, you can sit in fake cars and watch classics like *Attack of the Fifty-foot Woman* while you munch burgers and fries and other drive-in goodies. The milk shakes are delicious, and all told, this place is a tad more entertaining than the old drive-ins anyway. Of course, you don't get those steamy win-dows. ⊠ *Disney–MGM Studios,* ☎ *407/939–3463. AE, MC, V.*

$ **Hollywood & Vine.** This Disney–MGM Studios buffet-style restaurant is designed for those who like lots of food and lots of choices. You can have everything from frittatas to fried rice at the same meal. Even though the buffet is all-you-can-eat at a relatively low price, it does offer some upscale entrées like smoked salmon and oven-roasted pork. ⊠ *Disney–MGM Studios,* ☎ *407/939–3463. AE, MC, V.*

Contemporary

$–$$ **Hollywood Brown Derby.** Disney is masterful at creating exact repli-cas of famous pieces of Americana, and they've done just that with the Florida re-creation of this famous Hollywood restaurant from the 1940s. Inside, white linen tablecloths and potted palms, along with a host of movie star caricatures lining the walls, re-create the interior of the real Brown Derby. The house specialty is the Cobb salad, a dish originally created at the California restaurant. Other menu standouts include fettuccine with shrimp or chicken, and a good New York strip steak. ⊠ *Disney–MGM Studios,* ☎ *407/939–3463. AE, MC, V.*

Italian

$–$$ **Mama Melrose's Ristorante Italiano.** Mama's is a casual, comfy approach to Italian dining, with red-checkered tablecloths, red vinyl booths, and a menu filled with hearty dishes like lasagna and fettuccine Alfredo. Other standouts include the rock shrimp risotto with artichoke hearts and the oak-grilled pork tenderloin with a sweet wine sauce. You get fresh-baked bread and olive oil almost the minute you sit down, and you can feast on it as long as you like. Cheesecake is the way to go for dessert. ⊠ *Disney–MGM Studios,* ☎ *407/939–3463. AE, MC, V.*

Disney's Wide World of Sports

Disney's Wide World of Sports has a huge array of sporting facilities that are the site of major as well as local competitions. To get there, take I–4 Exit 25B.

American/Casual

$–$$ ✕ **Official All-Star Cafe.** You can't go wrong with cuisine created by renowned gastronomic experts Shaquille O'Neill, Monica Seles, Joe Montana, Tiger Woods, Andre Agassi, Wayne Gretzky, and Ken Griffey Jr. And for an atmosphere that brings the dining experience to its zenith, there's nothing better than 16 big-screen TVs playing sports clips nonstop as loud rock music blares, spotlights roam around the room and across the tables, and strobe lights periodically blind you. If you agree, you're going to love this celeb-brand eatery. The food, ranging from burgers to steaks to pasta, is nothing special. Among the best offerings are Wayne's Cracked Ribs (barbecued spare ribs), Shaq's Slammin' Smoked Turkey Sandwich, and Bull Penne Pasta. The best dessert is the Banana Split Decision Cheesecake. At $5.95, the white chocolate chip cookie may be the most expensive cookie in North America. ⊠ *690 S. Victory Way,* ☎ *407/827–8326. AE, MC, V.*

Downtown Disney/Lake Buena Vista Area

Downtown Disney has three sections: the Marketplace, a small shopping-and-dining area; Pleasure Island, a nightlife complex with a hefty admission after dark; and Disney's West Side, another group of hipper-than-hip entertainment, dining, and shopping spots nearby. The edge of Disney property is about a block away; just on the other side of the highway that marks the border are clustered a huge variety of restaurants and hotels, freestanding and in small malls. This constitutes what's known as the Lake Buena Vista area. There are some wonderful mealtime options here, along with a great Gooding's supermarket, a fantasy in itself if you come from a small city. To get to the Lake Buena Vista/Downtown Disney area, take I–4 Exit 27.

American/Casual

$$ ✕ **Planet Hollywood.** Patrons come to this Downtown Disney landmark to see the movie memorabilia assembled by owners Schwarzenegger, Stallone, Willis, and the biggest showman among the partners, restaurateur Robert Earl. You can shop for T-shirts at the Planet Hollywood retail store just outside while you wonder when you'll actually get inside. The wait, once a guaranteed two hours at peak periods, has abated somewhat, except when movies at the multiplex next door let out. Food is secondary to the sets—20,000 square ft, complete with an indoor waterfall; the building cost $15 million, as much as a theme-park attraction. The menu offers burgers, smoked and grilled meats, and unusual pastas and salads. Among the better offerings are the Creole pizza with shrimp, chicken, and Cajun sausage, and the tasty $7.50 burger, a bargain in these parts. ⊠ *Downtown Disney West Side, at entrance to Pleasure Island,* ☎ *407/827–7827. Reservations not accepted. AE, D, DC, MC, V.*

$–$$ **Boatwright's Dining Hall.** Here, you are a boatwright on your lunch or dinner break inside a giant riverboat that you're helping to build. And you must be building it in New Orleans, because the cuisine is Cajun influenced, with a fine étouffée, jambalaya, and of course, red beans and rice. You can also grab a variety of other eats, from grilled steaks to broiled grouper. Crescent City pork chops—two chops glazed with honey mustard sauce, also makes a good bet. ⊠ *Dixie Landings Resort,* ☎ *407/934–6000. AE, MC, V.*

$–$$ ✕ **Olivia's Café.** If you frequently find yourself trying to decide what kind of cuisine you want, this place could be the answer. It has just about everything, from a smattering of seafood—fried shrimp and grilled grouper—to fried chicken with mash potatoes and gravy. You can even get Cuban black beans and rice or Mexican guacamole and tortilla chips. There's also a strange but tasty mixture of cuisines: black bean and roasted corn ravioli, with an avocado cream sauce. Good dessert options include the chocolate chip pecan pie and the white chocolate key lime cheesecake. The setting is pleasant, with indoor palms and rough wood walls like an old Key West house, but not necessarily special. Except in mid-summer, outdoor seating, which overlooks a waterway, is a pleasant option. ⊠ *Old Key West Resort,* ☎ *407/939–3463. AE, D, DC, MC, V.*

$–$$ ✕ **Rainforest Café.** People start queuing up half an hour before the 10:30
★ AM opening of this 30,000-square-ft jungle fantasy in Downtown Disney's Marketplace. A pump system creates periodic "rain storms," and a 3½-story man-made volcano, forming the roof, erupts frequently. The food, an eclectic mix of American fare with imaginative names, is also an attraction. Good choices include Eyes of the Ocelot, a nice meat loaf topped with sautéed mushrooms; Rasta Pasta, bow-tie pasta with grilled chicken and pesto sauce; and Mojo Bones, tender ribs with barbecue sauce. A branch just outside the gates of Animal Kingdom is open for breakfast at 7:30 AM daily; the Downtown Disney location serves lunch and dinner only. Disney's main restaurant reservation service (407/939–3463) takes priority seating reservations for both Rainforest locations. ⊠ *Downtown Disney Marketplace,* ☎ *407/827–8500 or 407/939–3463;* ⊠ *Disney's Animal Kingdom,* ☎ *407/938–9100 or 407/939–3463. AE, D, DC, MC, V.*

$–$$ **Wild Horse Saloon.** Not to be confused with the White Horse Saloon, just up the road at the Hyatt Regency Grand Cypress, this country dancing and barbecue palace replaced the Fireworks Factory in the Downtown Disney Marketplace. They barbecue everything here, from steaks to spare ribs to salmon, and do a good job of it. The country music is live (and loud). ⊠ *Downtown Disney Marketplace,* ☎ *407/939–3463. AE, MC, V.*

Cajun/Creole

$–$$ ✕ **House of Blues.** From the outside, this cavernous, rusted tin building in Downtown Disney looks like an old factory; the inside looks like an old church converted into an eatery, complete with angelic fresco. But it's all a cover-up for what's really a darn good little Southern cookin' restaurant and bar with a separate concert hall, a prime Orlando live-music venue, just up the sidewalk. The best bets on the menu are catfish, pork chops, and the New Orleans–style étouffée. The gospel Sunday brunch is righteous and so popular you'll need reservations. Suffused with the Downtown Disney "If you're here, you must be cool" attitude, the place gets even noisier when the live music plays (11 PM–2 AM); lunches can be almost serene. Reservations are essential for Sunday brunch but aren't accepted for lunch on weekdays. ⊠ *Downtown Disney West Side,* ☎ *407/934–2583. AE, D, MC, V.*

Contemporary

$–$$$ ✕ **Wolfgang Puck Café.** You almost need a road map to find all the
★ parts of this elegant eatery in Downtown Disney. There's a Wolfgang Puck Express in the Marketplace area where you will find excellent light fare such as wood-fire minipizzas, in addition to the main Puckarama in Disney's West Side, which also has a Puck Express. However, the latter is attached to a two-story restaurant with a more elegant dining room upstairs and a sushi bar and semicasual café downstairs. The café is a good choice if you want to sample the fa-

mous Puck fare without going too upscale. Must-tries include the pizzas, with toppings such as grilled chicken and salmon, and various inspired pastas whose sauces are sublimely laced with chunks of lobster,
salmon, or chicken. ⊠ *Downtown Disney West Side,* ☎ *407/938–9653.
AE, MC, V.*

$–$$ ✕ **Pebbles.** This is California cuisine, dude, with a Florida touch that
brings grouper and other regional favorites into the picture. Orlandoans
are lapping it up to such an extent that the restaurant, whose original
is at the Crossroads shopping area just outside Disney property, now
has four other locations. The original in Lake Buena Vista is your chance
to see how locals live. Good entrées include angel-hair pasta smoth-
ered with smoked duck, scallops, and Asian spices, and the Mediterranean salad, in which sun-dried tomatoes put in an obligatory
appearance. The Caesar salad, tossed table-side, is consistently one of
the best choices. Burgers with excellent cheeses are also served, and
the wine list is thoughtful but reasonably priced. ⊠ *Crossroads of Lake
Buena Vista, Orlando,* ☎ *407/827–1111;* ⊠ *17 W. Church St., Orlando,* ☎ *407/839–0892. No lunch weekends;* ⊠ *2516 Aloma Ave.,
Winter Park,* ☎ *407/678–7001;* ⊠ *2110 Rte. 434, Altamonte Springs,*
☎ *407/774–7111. Reservations not accepted. AE, D, DC, MC, V.*

Continental

$$$–$$$$ ✕ **Arthur's 27.** Critics and diners have raved over the years about the
combination of imaginative cuisine and the world-class view you get
with your meal—the restaurant is on the 27th floor of the Wyndham
Palace Resort, overlooking all of Walt Disney World and its environs.
The relentless stiffness, the only sticking point, has softened, and men
no longer need a jacket and tie—something that's casual-elegant is fine.
All entrées come with a heavenly sauce, like the rich, creamy cognac-
based mixture spooned over the beef tenderloin and the herb-rich gar-
lic sauce that accompanies roast loin of lamb. Desserts include a
credible crème brûlée with raspberries and a chocolate cake well worth
the calories. You can choose among three prix-fixe dinner options: $60
for a six-course meal, $55 for a five-course meal, or $49 for a four-
course special; à la carte costs a lot more. ⊠ *Wyndham Palace Resort
& Spa, 1900 Buena Vista Dr., Lake Buena Vista (I–4 Exit 27),* ☎ *407/
827–3450. Reservations essential. AE, D, DC, MC, V.*

Cuban

$–$$$ ✕ **Bongos Cuban Café.** Gloria Estefan's Cuban eatery is tucked inside
a two-story Downtown Disney building shaped like a pineapple. Al-
though it looks a little silly by day, it looks great when bathed in just
the right lighting at night. The menu won't make any of the chefs along
Miami's Calle Ocho jealous, but the choices are relatively solid. There's
a decent but pricey paella and a fine rice and chicken casserole jazzed
up with other morsels, such as lobster or black beans. Other familiar
Cuban offerings include arroz con pollo, *churrasco* (skirt steak), and
tasty ham croquettes. The eclectic wine list ranges from a Chilean
chardonnay by the glass to Louis-Jadot Pouilly-Fuissé. Try one of three
varieties of flan for dessert along with good Cuban coffee, also available at a walk-up bar outside. There's live music at night. ⊠ *Downtown Disney West Side,* ☎ *407/828–0999. Reservations not accepted.
AE, D, DC, MC, V.*

Eclectic

$–$$ **Seasons Dining Room.** If you want to go to a different restaurant every
night but don't really have the energy, this place is for you. Here, the
seasons change not every three months, but every 24 hours, and each
season brings a new cuisine type. One night it might be New Orleans–
style cooking, with étouffée and jambalaya; the next night it might be

Polynesian, with grilled mahimahi. A particularly good "season" to catch is Northwest night, when there's plenty of grilled salmon, venison, and desserts with fresh berries. ⊠ *Disney Institute,* ☎ *407/939–3463. AE, MC, V.*

French

$$$–$$$$ ✕ **La Coquina.** This restaurant just off Disney property in the Hyatt Regency Grand Cypress bills itself as French with an Asian influence, and if you sample the pheasant and truffle wonton with foie gras and chives, you'll approve. The best meal here is Sunday brunch, whose generous selection of goodies makes the price ($38) seem like a bargain. The restaurant is a showcase for the hotel's culinary staff. As part of the fanfare guests walk through the kitchen to choose their food, which is then prepared table-side; for a closer look, contact the restaurant manager about sitting at the special chef's table in the kitchen. Lose your tank tops: men must wear shirts with collars, and women must dress "appropriately." ⊠ *Hyatt Regency Grand Cypress, 1 Grand Cypress Blvd.,* ☎ *407/239–1234. AE, D, DC, MC, V.*

Italian

$$–$$$$ ✕ **Portobello Yacht Club.** Operated by Chicago's venerable Levy brothers, this eatery on the edge of Pleasure Island has a much better lineage than the one Disney made up—that the building was the home of Merriweather Adam Pleasure, eponym of Pleasure Island. Of course, Pleasure is fictitious, but pleasurable dining is not. The northern Italian cuisine here is uniformly good. Start with something simple— chewy sourdough bread with roast garlic. Then move on to *spaghettini alla Portobello,* a stick-to-your-ribs pasta dish with scallops, clams, shrimp, mussels, tomatoes, garlic, Portobello mushrooms, and herbs. There's always a fresh-catch special, and a wood-oven pizza has been added—not quite as good as Wolfgang Puck's (☞ *above*), but tasty. ⊠ *Pleasure Island,* ☎ *407/934–8888. AE, MC, V.*

Mexican

$–$$ ✕ **Chevy's.** It defies logic to think you'd find anything original across from hotel row just off Disney property, where garish neon signs advertise "bargain" T-shirts and gasoline sells for 20¢ a gallon more than you'd pay in downtown Orlando. Sure enough, Chevy's is a chain out of California, occupying an ersatz cantina that looks like every Mexican restaurant in every suburb you've ever seen. But the food on your plate is a real shocker. It's good. Really good. The menu promises that everything is made from fresh ingredients, and it's not just hyperbole. Try the hot tamales, a simple dish made perfect by a fresh cornmeal shell and the piquant taste of the chicken, pork, or beef. The menu also includes some gringo creativity, like chicken with Dijon mustard wrapped in a tortilla; a huge burrito made with barbecue and black beans; and a good flan and some fetching cream pies. ⊠ *12547 Rte. 535, Lake Buena Vista,* ☎ *407/827–1052. AE, MC, V.*

Seafood

$$–$$$$ ✕ **Fulton's Crab House.** Run by Levy Restaurants, the Chicago company that also operates the nearby Portobello Yacht Club, this nautical eatery is in a faux riverboat docked in a lagoon between Pleasure Island and the Marketplace. Fulton's is a first-class fish house, with lovely views from the windows lining its three dining decks and polished, unhurried service. Crab is the specialty, and just like the tourists who consume it, the crab at Fulton's flies in daily from all over North America. Dungeness crab from the Atlantic banks, Alaskan king crab, Florida stone crab: It's all served fresh. A crab sampler offers a taste of just about every variety on the menu. ⊠ *Downtown Disney Marketplace,* ☎ *407/934–2628. AE, MC, V.*

$$\text{-}$$$ ✕ **Landry's Seafood House.** What appears from the outside to be an old warehouse converted into a restaurant—a popular architectural trick in Central Florida—is actually a brand-new building, just off Disney property, virtually identical to the restaurants this fast-growing chain has built in 15 other states. The food here is first-rate, especially some of the Cajun specialties like the fresh-caught Pontchartrain, a broiled fish with slightly spicy seasoning and a creamy white-wine sauce, topped with a lump of crabmeat. Good appetizers include the shrimp quesadilla and the seafood-stuffed jalapeños. A $15 seafood platter lets you sample many Landry's specialties, including crab fingers, fried oysters, and shrimp. ⊠ *8800 Vineland Ave. (Rte. 535),* ☎ *407/827–6466. AE, D, DC, MC, V.*

$-$$$ **Cap'n Jack's Oyster Bar.** This nautical-theme restaurant adjacent to the lagoon near the Downtown Disney Marketplace serves a variety of fresh seafood, and it's not difficult to keep your check in the reasonable range (if you don't opt for the Maine lobster). New England clam chowder is the specialty here, as is a variety of fresh fish, including grouper and tuna. You can also make a tasty meal out of the fresh oyster and steamed clams. Pumpkin cheesecake is among the best of the desserts. *Downtown Disney Marketplace,* ☎ *407/939–3463. AE, MC, V.*

Steak

$$\text{-}$$$ ✕ **White Horse Saloon.** Cattle ranchers would love this, the only hoedown kind of place we know of in a top-notch hotel—one that is otherwise decorated with Ming dynasty artwork, no less. If you hanker for that dude ranch feeling, you'll be mighty pleased at the way this Western-theme saloon in the Hyatt Regency Grand Cypress sells its products: you can get a barbecued half chicken for 20 bucks or pay $1 more for prime rib. If you want to go for the 28-ounce beef worshiper's cut— that's 1½ pounds of corn-fed beef—it's $46. All entrées come with sourdough bread, baked or mashed potatoes, and your choice of creamed spinach or corn on the cob. A hearty apple pie served hot with cinnamon-raisin sauce awaits those desperadoes who can still handle dessert. ⊠ *Hyatt Regency Grand Cypress, 1 Grand Cypress Blvd.,* ☎ *407/239–1234. AE, DC, MC, V.*

Disney's Animal Kingdom

The Animal Kingdom, Disney's newest park, is not quite as restaurant-laden as some of the other parks yet, but it's off to a good start nevertheless.

American/Casual

$-$$ ✕ **Rainforest Café.** This location is similar to the Rainforest in Downtown Disney Marketplace, complete with the long line outside the door as soon as the place opens, so it's best to go early or late. A wide range of choices includes Eyes of the Ocelot, a hearty meat loaf topped with sautéed mushrooms; Rasta Pasta, bow-tie pasta with grilled chicken and pesto sauce; and Mojo Bones, tender ribs with barbecue sauce. This location begins serving breakfast at 7:30 daily. ⊠ *Disney's Animal Kingdom,* ☎ *407/938–9100 or 407/939–3463. AE, D, DC, MC, V.*

$ ✕ **Restaurantosaurus.** Only through the corporate power of Disney can this magic occur: this diner is a Restaurantosaurus for breakfast, and then, shortly before noon, becomes a McDonald's. The breakfast is a massive buffet affair, with everything from pancakes to omelets. Come in the morning and you'll find a group of college archaeology students have set up camp here to live during a dig. Their clothes are even hanging on a line outside. You can catch the "college students" along with Donald Duck and others at the daily character breakfast.

⊠ *Disney's Animal Kingdom,* ☎ *407/939–3463. Reservations not accepted. AE, D, DC, MC, V.*

INTERNATIONAL DRIVE

Among the hotels that line landscaped, manicured International Drive you'll find a fair number of restaurants. Many are branches of chains that run the gamut from fast-food spots to theme coffee shops and up, and sometimes the food is quite good. To get to the area, take I–4 Exit 28 or 29. Count on traveling about half an hour from the Kissimmee area or from WDW property.

American/Casual

$–$$$ ✕ **Dan Marino's Town Tavern.** Being a macho kind of eatery, with a giant-screen TV tuned into ESPN at all times, and more photos of Miami Dolphins quarterback Dan Marino than you'd probably find at his mother's house, it's no surprise that this sports bar offers some carnivore-pleasing dishes. There's the house specialty, a 28-ounce cowboy steak, and a hearty meat loaf, but Marino, and the people who planned his menu, is clearly not oblivious to culinary trends: you'll also find trendy light fare such as sesame-seared tuna and wood-roasted, barbecue-rubbed salmon. The best of the good desserts is the almond basket, a caramelized almond cookie with whipped cream, raspberry sauce, and raspberry sorbet. ⊠ *Pointe*Orlando, 9101 International Dr.,* ☎ *407/363–1013. AE, MC, V.*

$–$$ ✕ **Beeline Diner.** As you might expect from its location in the Peabody Orlando, this slick, 1950s-style diner with red vinyl counter seats is not exactly cheap, but the salads, sandwiches, and griddle foods are tops. They do a great job preparing the greatest combo ever—thick, juicy burgers served with fries and heavenly milk shakes. Open 24 hours. ⊠ *Peabody Orlando, 9801 International Dr.,* ☎ *407/352–4000. AE, D, DC, MC, V.*

Steak

$$–$$$$ ✕ **Vito's Chop House.** There's a reason they keep the blinds closed most of the time at this restaurant. First, it's a little classier inside than its I-Drive surroundings. And second, the restaurant seems to double as the cellar for its 500-wine list, with literally hundreds of bottles stacked all over the dining area. If you sample the beef offerings, you won't be in the dark about the quality of the steaks, which are superb. If you don't mind laying out $94.95 for what's labeled "Vito's Ultimate Surf n' Turf," you can feast on a 50-ounce porterhouse and a 1½-pound lobster (which will feed at least two people). Other good bets include the T-bone, the filet mignon, and the rib eye, each for less than $20. Also of note are the wood-grilled pork chops di Vito, promised on the menu as 1½ inches thick. Stone crabs are available in season. Worthwhile desserts include grilled peach di Vito, an excellent key lime pie, and Italian wedding cake, a house specialty. ⊠ *6633 International Dr.,* ☎ *407/354–2467. AE, D, DC, MC, V. No lunch.*

Caribbean

$–$$ ✕ **Bahama Breeze.** This is no mom-and-pop out-island outfit but an offering from Darden Restaurants, the General Mills spin-off that brought you Red Lobster and the Olive Garden. Even though the lineage is corporate, the menu is creative and tasty. Lush palm trees and bright, island-style artwork keep things relaxed—a good thing, since your wait may be lengthy. You're issued a beeper on arrival and buzzed when your table is ready. Meanwhile, you can sip piña coladas and other West Indian delights on a big wooden porch. The food is worth the wait. Start with *tostones con pollo* (plantain chips topped with chicken and cheese), followed by coconut curry chicken or paella. ⊠ *499 E. Altamonte Dr., Altamonte Springs,* ☎ *407/831–2929. Reservations not accepted. AE, D, DC, MC.*

Chinese

$$–$$$$ ✕ **Ming Court.** Even though this place is on International Drive, a truly great wall designed to look like a dragon's back blocks out the hubbub and gives an enclosed courtyardlike serenity to this Chinese palace of a restaurant. A pool with carp greets you at the entrance, and the elegance continues inside, where you can look out through glass walls over a beautifully arranged series of floating gardens. The prices are probably a little higher than what you're used to paying at your local strip mall, but then the food is probably better, too. Ming Court is within walking distance of the Orange County Convention Center and can be quite busy at lunchtime. ⊠ *9188 International Dr.,* ☎ *407/351–9988. AE, D, DC, MC, V.*

Contemporary

$–$$$ ✕ **Cafe Tu Tu Tango.** Multiple kitchens here bombard you with different courses, which arrive in waves if you follow the house custom and order a series of appetizers. Actually, you end up doing this anyway, since the entrées are appetizer-size. The menu gives the address—on International Drive—a new meaning. Try the Cajun chicken egg rolls, for instance, with blackened chicken, Greek goat cheese, Creole mustard, and tomato salsa, if you want to get a compendium of world cuisines at one go. For added atmosphere, artists paint at easels while diners sip drinks like Matisse margaritas and Renoir rum runners. Even though nothing on the menu costs more than $8, it's not hard to spend $50 for lunch for two. ⊠ *8625 International Dr.,* ☎ *407/248–2222. Reservations not accepted. AE, D, DC, MC, V.*

Fast Food

$ ✕ **McDonald's.** McDonald's-o-philes sometimes argue about the status of this shrine. No, it's not the world's largest McDonald's, despite the claims of the billboards on I–4 and its three-story french-fries sculpture outside. The one on Arbat Street in Moscow is bigger, but for the moment this is *America's* largest. It also has more frills than any other burger joint on the planet. How many other McDonald's, for instance, have a place to buy airline tickets . . . or socks? That's right, socks. (They're required in the huge indoor playground.) There's also a theater with musicians and magicians and a gift shop brimming with T-shirts (and socks). As for dining rooms, you can chow down in the tiki bar–style Sunset Terrace; the Maui Room, with a 600-gallon saltwater aquarium; or the Rock and Roll Room, featuring '50s memorabilia and a jukebox. ⊠ *6875 Sand Lake Rd., at International Dr.,* ☎ *407/351–2185. Reservations not accepted. AE, DC, MC, V.*

Italian

$$–$$$$ ✕ **Ciao Italia.** In the shadow of SeaWorld, this charming mom-and-pop eatery is in the middle of tourism's fast lane. Still, nothing is hurried. Every item is made to order, so you might want to bring along a copy of *War and Peace*. Your patience will be rewarded. The Italian-speaking proprietors have re-created a piece of their native southern Italy in Central Florida. The proof is in the sweet New Zealand mussels, served with either white garlic or marinara sauce, and the light, colorful *pollo alla Tonino* (chicken breast with red and yellow peppers). The standout appetizer is Tony's special—a meal in itself—with butterfly shrimp, a big mushroom stuffed with lobster, sautéed calamari, and white beans with a white-wine sauce. ⊠ *6149 Westwood Blvd.,* ☎ *407/354–0770. AE, D, DC, MC, V. Beer and wine only. No lunch.*

$$–$$$ ✕ **Capriccio's.** Corporate executives and conventioneers, who make up much of the Peabody's clientele, like the relaxed atmosphere of this hotel restaurant. The marble-top tables are arranged so that everyone can view the open kitchen and the wood-burning pizza ovens, which turn out whole-wheat-flour pies ranging from pizza *margherita* (with sun-dried tomatoes and smoked mozzarella, fontina, provolone, and Parmesan cheeses) to pizza *blanca* (with mozzarella, goat cheese, and fresh thyme). If you're not in the mood for pizza, try one of the mesquite-grilled fish, beef, or chicken entrées, like the *pollo gonzo* (chicken in a lemon sage sauce). If you don't mind spending $7 for dessert, try the imported-from-Italy lady fingers with amaretto sauce. ⊠ *Peabody Orlando, 9801 International Dr.,* ☎ *407/352–4000. AE, DC, MC, V. Closed Mon.*

Japanese

$–$$$ ✕ **Ran-Getsu.** The surroundings are a Disney version of the Orient, but the food is fresh and carefully prepared, much of it table-side. Sit at the curved, dragon-tail-shape sushi bar and order the *matsu* platter (an assortment of *nigiri-* and *maki*-style sushi). Or, unless you're alone, you can have your meal Japanese-style at the low tables overlooking a carp-filled pond and decorative gardens. Specialties include sukiyaki, *shabu-shabu* (thinly sliced beef prepared table-side in a simmering seasoned broth and served with vegetables), and *kushiyaki* (grilled skewers of shrimp, beef, chicken, and scallops). If you feel more adventurous, try the deep-fried alligator tail, but skip the key lime pie. ⊠ *8400 International Dr.,* ☎ *407/345–0044. AE, DC, MC, V. No lunch.*

Mexican

$–$$ ✕ **Don Pablo's.** If you're in dire need of an enchilada fix, this place is for you. Although the big, barnlike building doesn't actually look like a border cantina, it still qualifies as one of the best Tex-Mex places this far from the Rio Grande. Particularly worthwhile are the chicken enchiladas, made with slow-simmered chicken wrapped in corn tortillas, and the beef fajitas, marinated steak served sizzling on a cast-iron platter, with sides of frijoles, rice, and flour tortillas. ⊠ *8717 International Dr.,* ☎ *407/354–1345;* ⊠ *4645 S. Semoran Blvd., Orlando,* ☎ *407/208–0801;* ⊠ *100 Towne Center Blvd., Sanford,* ☎ *407/ 328–1885;* ⊠ *900 E. South Rte. 436, Casselberry,* ☎ *407/834–4421. Reservations not accepted. AE, DC, MC, V.*

Seafood

$$–$$$$ ✕ **Atlantis.** Waiters bring entrées on silver-domed trays, and the dark-wood paneling, frescoes overhead, and plush green carpet underfoot in this dining room in the Renaissance Orlando Resort clearly imply that cutoffs belong back in your suitcase. Specialties include various lobster dishes and grilled fish such as yellowfin tuna and salmon. There are also worthy red-meat dishes, including roast loin of lamb, and the obligatory surf-and-turf combo—a good sirloin served with scallops. Desserts include some fine soufflés, which must be ordered 30 minutes in advance. A harpist begins playing each evening at 7. Reserve with the hotel concierge when Atlantis is closed. ⊠ *Renaissance Orlando Resort, 6677 Sea Harbor Dr.,* ☎ *407/351–5555. AE, MC, V. No lunch.*

$–$$$ ✕ **Monty's Conch Harbor.** The quality of the decor is childlike—complete with whimsical, giant fiberglass sea creatures lurking above the dining area. But there's no child's play involved in the menu of this fine, Florida-style fish house, an offshoot of a restaurant that's been a Miami-area standout for years. Among the best offerings are the stone-crab claws, although at $25 for four claws they're pricey; the tasty dolphin (the fish, not Flipper) served with a ginger glaze; and the swordfish, served with an interesting roasted-corn tomato salsa. If you're not going to make it to Key West on this trip, try Monty's conch chowder, some of the best available this far north. Also worth a try is the she-crab soup. The house specialty drink, called a Pain Killer, is priced based on how much rum you want in your 16-ounce glass. The restaurant automatically adds a 15% tip to your tab no matter what size your party, so the servers have no real incentive to be nice to you—but most are anyway. ⊠ *Pointe*Orlando, 9101 International Dr.,* ☎ *407/354–1122. AE, MC, V.*

Thai

$–$$ ✕ **Siam Orchid.** One of Orlando's several elegant Asian restaurants, Siam Orchid occupies a gorgeous structure a bit off International Drive. Waitresses, who wear costumes from their homeland, serve authentic fare such as Siam wings, a chicken wing stuffed to look like a drumstick, and *pla rad prik* (a whole, deep-fried fish covered with a sauce flavored with red chilies, bell peppers, and garlic). If you like your food spicy, say "Thai hot" and grab a fire extinguisher. ⊠ *7575 Republic Dr.,* ☎ *407/351–0821. AE, DC, MC, V.*

UNIVERSAL ORLANDO

In 1999 Universal became a culinary contender overnight. The opening of Universal Orlando's CityWalk added seven restaurants and a vastly bigger and more elaborate Hard Rock Cafe; at Islands of Adventure, each of the six lands has between two and six eateries—not all of them strictly burgers-and-fries affairs. Universal has done a good job of providing information and access to these eateries, with a special reservation and information line (☎ 407/224–9255) and a Web site, www.uescape.com, that includes menus for many of the restaurants.

To get to Universal, take I–4 Exit 30A from eastbound lanes, Exit 29B when you're westbound.

Character Breakfasts

Universal now offers its own character breakfasts, featuring the Dr. Seuss characters, including Cat in the Hat, at **Circus McGurkus Café Stoopendous** in **Seuss Landing** (8–10 on Monday and Wednesday, 8:45–10:30 all other days) and at the **Confisco Grille** from noon to 2 PM every day ($14.95 for adults and $8.95 for kids 12 and under). To reserve, call ☎ 407/224–9255.

CityWalk

American/Casual

$–$$$ ✕ **Hard Rock Cafe Orlando.** The new CityWalk location is the biggest of all (and gets the lion's share of the memorabilia that rotates among Hard Rocks worldwide). Built to resemble Rome's Coliseum, it can seat 800 in the restaurant and another 2,000 in the giant attached concert hall. Yet it's still tough to get a seat at meal times without waiting. The menu hasn't changed much; standouts still include the popular $8.29 burger, along with the baby-back ribs and homemade-style meat loaf. There are a fair number of other choices, however, ranging from pasta to fajitas. Best dessert is the $5 chocolate chip cookie (it's big) covered with ice cream. Try for the viewful balcony on the second floor. ⊠ *6000 Universal Blvd., at Universal Orlando's CityWalk,* ☎ *407/ 351–7625. Reservations not accepted. AE, D, DC, MC, V.*

$–$$ ✕ **Jimmy Buffett's Margaritaville.** If you are a Parrot-head, you can probably name the top two items on the menu before you ever walk in the door. You've got your cheeseburger, featured in the song "Cheeseburger in Paradise," and your Ultimate Margarita, from "Wasted Away Again in Margaritaville." The single about the tasty fried fish platter or the stone crab claws never quite hit the charts, and *Billboard* hasn't yet noticed quite how extensive the menu is compared to those at similar entertainment-oriented spots—you can get everything from quesadillas to chowder to crab cakes and a pretty decent steak as well. Although the place won't remind you of Key West if you've spent much time there, it does try for the Florida Keys feeling, what with the giant plastic replica of a seaplane hanging from the ceiling and all the memorabilia. ⊠ *6000 Universal Blvd., at Universal Orlando's CityWalk,* ☎ *407/224–9255. AE, D, MC, V.*

$–$$ ✕ **Motown Café Orlando.** This place is a shrine to Motown music, and at night, when there's a $3.25 cover charge, it's jumping with the sounds that made Motown Records one of the legends of American music. By day, if you want a quiet and uncrowded place to grab a good meal, this is the spot. The menu is eclectic, ranging from the vaguely Asian Jackson 5 pot stickers to Smokey's ribs. Some offerings defy categorization, like the fried chicken and Belgian waffles combo. On the walls and in glass cases, clothes worn by Marvin Gaye, the Commodores, and other Motown stars give the place kind of a Hard Rock Cafe of soul music ambience, but it's a lot easier to get seated here in the daytime. ⊠ *6000 Universal Blvd., at Universal Orlando's CityWalk,* ☎ *407/224–9255. AE, D, MC, V.*

$–$$ ✕ **NASCAR Café Orlando.** Crowded and loud, this two-story eatery has some of the qualities that draw millions to one of America's most popular spectator sports, NASCAR racing. And if the racing memorabilia on the walls is not enough for you, there are a couple of actual race cars hanging from the ceilings. The food is better than you might think. Sure, there are some less-than-memorable items like the Dipstick fried cheese and Talladega chicken tenders, but there are actually some substantial elements such as a good chicken mushroom soup with grilled chicken and shiitake mushrooms, the remarkably ungreasy popcorn shrimp, and the Thunder Road burger, with melted pimento cheese and sautéed onions. Desserts are largely forgettable. ⊠ *6000 Universal Blvd., at Universal Orlando's CityWalk,* ☎ *407/224–9255. AE, D, MC, V.*

$–$$ ✕ **NBA City.** Drop into this place to see the Wilt Chamberlain memorabilia or shoot a few hoops on the computerized basketball games, but the food alone would be worth the stopover. The menu includes a range of trendy offerings like a quesadilla stuffed with barbecued chicken, Monterey Jack cheese, and cilantro and a 12-ounce pork chop glazed with maple-mustard sauce. There's also a variety of brick-oven pizzas, including a house special, the BLT pizza. The big-screen TVs with nonstop basketball action probably won't surprise you, but the relatively quiet bar upstairs, with elegant-looking blond-wood furniture, probably will. ⊠ *6000 Universal Blvd., at Universal Orlando's CityWalk,* ☎ *407/363–5919. AE, D, MC, V.*

$–$$ ✕ **Pat O'Brien's Orlando.** This watering hole and eatery is a replica of the famous New Orleans bar, complete with a brick-walled courtyard and outdoor tables—a perfect spot to sip the Crescent City's famous drink, the hurricane, and to munch on some bayou-inspired snacks like crawfish nachos, Cajun shrimp, and alligator bites. Although the menu isn't lengthy, you can still chow down on staple Louisiana French-bread sandwiches like po'boys, filled with tangy shrimp and sausage, and muffelettas, made with salami, ham, provolone, and olives. This being a celebration of New Orleans, there's also a good jambalaya, the spicy stew of sausage and chicken breast meat. With a side of red beans and rice, plus the house specialty dessert, strawberry hurricane cheesecake, you've got a hearty meal. There's live music at night and a $2 cover charge. ⊠ *6000 Universal Blvd., at Universal Orlando's City-Walk,* ☎ *407/224–9255. AE, D, MC, V.*

Caribbean

$–$$ ✕ **Bob Marley's, A Tribute to Freedom.** This informal restaurant and reggae club, which runs live music almost all day long, seems more like a tribute to tolerance—that is, how loud a noise the human ear can tolerate. Suffice it to say that you will need to scream your order to your dreadlock-wearing server. The good news is that the music is quite good. Best to reach for the authentic Jamaican beer, Red Stripe, early and often. Once you get past the decibel level, you may notice that the food is quite tasty, notably the spicy jerk chicken on a stick and the typical "Jamaican patties," spicy ground pork, lamb, and other meats. ⊠ *6000 Universal Blvd., at Universal Orlando's CityWalk,* ☎ *407/ 224–9255. AE, D, MC, V.*

Contemporary

$$$–$$$$ ✕ **Emeril's.** This ambitious restaurant from famed TV chef Emeril La-gasse has already nailed down a spot on every local critic's short list of the best restaurants in town for its rendition of the innovative Cajun cooking that Lagasse perfected in his New Orleans original, in a ware-house. In the Orlando rendition the gleaming dark wood paneling and the crisp white napery are as polished as they come, although metal alloy chairs and an exposed-pipe ceiling recall its predecessor. And the food is, as one bite reveals, the genuine article. Not surprisingly, the Louisiana treats shine: smoked chicken and andouille sausage, gumbo, and shrimp remoulade. The creative factor takes the rest of the menu way beyond typical bayou-style fare. Consider, for instance, a dish called "A Study of Duck," which features seared duck breast, seared Hud-son Valley foie gras, and a leg of duck confit, served with wild mush-room bread pudding, duck reduction, and a drizzle of port wine extraction. It's definitely an intellectual creation, but it's also a great meal. Even the wood-baked pizza is stellar, topped with wild and ex-otic mushrooms and a potato sauce spiked with chives and truffles. The desserts are great, including a triple-chocolate cheesecake and a traditional New Orleans bread pudding. If your whole family or group is up for a culinary adventure, try the meal called "Emeril's Degusta-tion," a six-course sampling of the high points of the day's offerings. (The price varies depending on what's included.) The cellar stocks 12,000 bottles. Reservations are a must. ⊠ *6000 Universal Blvd., at Univer-sal Orlando's CityWalk,* ☎ *407/224–2424. AE, D, MC, V.*

Italian

$–$$ ✕ **Pastamore.** One of CityWalk's sleepers, this does not have a theme or a celebrity front man. Pastamore has to make it in the restaurant derby the old-fashioned way—on the strength of good food and a cre-ative menu. And it does just that, with its wood-fire pizza, fresh pasta, and Italian beer and wines. Especially notable are the huge Italian sand-wiches that are pricey ($10) but tasty, with ingredients like marinated chicken, peppers, and sun-dried tomatoes. There's a selection of gelato, and an unusual touch, Italian breakfast breads—the place opens at 8 AM. ⊠ *6000 Universal Blvd., at Universal Orlando's CityWalk,* ☎ *407/ 224–9255. AE, D, MC, V.*

Latin

$–$$ ✕ **The Latin Quarter.** This grottolike restaurant and club, with domed ceilings and stone walls, is another one of those jumping-by-night, dor-mant-by-day spots at which you can get an excellent meal anytime but with little competition for your server's attention during daylight hours. The focus is on the music and cuisine of 21 Latin nations, and visiting chefs and musicians rotate through from everywhere south of the Rio Grande. Consistently the menu offers *churrasco* (skirt steak), *puerco asada* (slow-roasted pork), *pollo rostistado* (slow-roasted chicken), and an outstanding fried snapper with tomato salsa. Most entrées are served with black beans and rice. Best bets for dessert include the crepes and the mango and guava cheesecakes. You'll find a wide selection of South American beers, like Polar from Venezuela and Rio Crystal from Brazil. ✉ *6000 Universal Blvd., at Universal Orlando's CityWalk,* ☎ *407/224–9255. AE, D, MC, V.*

Islands of Adventure

Universal's newest endeavor has done more than bring a few more gravity-defying thrills to the already crowded Orlando theme park. Islands of Adventure, where it's as easy to get a glass of Merlot and a croissant as it is to get a burger and fries, offers a few culinary adventures as well. There are only a couple of full-service, sit-down restaurants in the park at this point, but the offerings at several of the cafeteria-style eateries are pretty creative and tasty as well.

American/Casual

$ ✕ **Enchanted Oak Tavern.** Step into this cavernous, faux oak tree to escape the Florida heat. Cafeteria-style meals include chicken and spare ribs platters, and most entrées are served with homemade-style corn muffins. You can make a meal of two à la carte items, the smoked turkey leg and roasted corn on the cob. Universal's own home brew, Dragon Scale Ale, is on tap. The adjacent Alchemy Bar can be a convenient, kid-free zone. ✉ *6000 Universal Blvd., Seuss Landing section at Universal Studios Islands of Adventure,* ☎ *407/224–9255. AE, D, MC, V.*

$ ✕ **Green Eggs and Ham Cafe.** The name alone will attract you to this place if you are a Dr. Seuss devotee. The green eggs come in the form of an egg and ham sandwich, the most popular item at this walk-up, outdoor eatery, which looks something like a hallucinatory McDonald's. There is also a fairly tasty "green" garden salad, as well as some other conventional fare like a garden variety cheeseburger, fries, and "frings," a combo of fries and onion rings. ✉ *6000 Universal Blvd., Seuss Landing section at Universal Studios Islands of Adventure,* ☎ *407/224–9255. AE, D, MC, V.*

American

$-$$ ✕ **Confisco Grille.** You could walk right past the outside of this Mediterranean-looking eatery in the Port of Entry section of the park, but if you want a good meal and sit-down service, you'd best not pass by too quickly. Entrées like the pan-roasted pork chops, wood-grilled salmon steaks, and (a house specialty) homemade macaroni and cheese with ham will fill you up quickly, but save room for desserts like chocolate-banana bread pudding or the crème brûlée. The restaurant offers character meals with the Dr. Seuss and Marvel comic characters from noon to 2 PM. ✉ *6000 Universal Blvd., Port of Entry section at Universal Studios Islands of Adventure,* ☎ *407/224–9255. AE, D, MC, V.*

Contemporary

$-$$ ✕ **Mythos.** The restaurant name sounds Greek (and the waiters have all taken Greek names like "Adonis" and "Aristotle"), but the menu is eclectic and creative. Standouts include blue corn–crusted mahimahi with sweet baby bell peppers and tomatillo salsa, wood-roasted lobster with corn, and wild mushroom risotto. Creative desserts include a fine pumpkin cheesecake. But the building itself is enough to grab your attention. It looks like a giant rock formation from the outside and a huge cave (albeit one with plush upholstered seating) from the inside. It also has a waterfront view of the big lagoon in the center of the theme park. ⊠ *6000 Universal Blvd., Lost Continent at Universal Studios Islands of Adventure,* ☎ *407/224–9255. AE, D, MC, V.*

CELEBRATION

This Disney-created community, in which every blade of grass in every lawn is just right, reminds some locals of something out of the 1970s film the *Stepford Wives*. But Celebration, which draws on vernacular architecture from all over the United States and was based on ideas from some of America's top architects and planners, offers a great retreat from the theme parks and from the garish reality of the U.S. 192 tourist strip just 1 mi to the east. The shell of it is as faux as Main Street, U.S.A., but as the town evolves, you see signs that real life is being lived here—and a good life it is. The charming little downtown area, which could be a movie set, faces a small lagoon, and all four of the town's restaurants have sidewalk seating with lake views. After dinner, take your youngsters over to the huge interactive fountain, and have fun getting sopping wet.

To get there take I–4 to Exit 25A, and follow the "Celebration" signs.

American/Casual

$–$$$ ✕ **Front Street Grill.** This urbane spot has sophisticated dark wood paneling but a family-friendly menu full of casual, homey fare such as bacon cheeseburgers, chicken potpie, turkey meat loaf, chicken-salad sandwiches, and barbecued pork ribs, along with slightly more creative maple-glazed salmon and crème brûlée. Other specialties include rotisserie chicken, marinated with rosemary and garlic and cooked over mesquite wood. If you want an uptown twist on a popular Florida mainstay dish, try the pistachio-crusted grouper with vanilla rum–butter and sweet potato–jalapeño smash. And if your youngsters want to stick with the familiar, there are four flavors of premium ice cream on the dessert menu. As with all of the Celebration eateries, there's an excellent sidewalk seating area under an awning. ⊠ *721 Front St.,* ☎ *407/566–1141. AE, D, MC, V.*

$–$$$ ✕ **Max's Café.** Looking like a classic 1950s diner, complete with tile floors that you thought they stopped manufacturing decades ago, this informal eatery features an eclectic menu ranging from shepherd's pie to the house special baked-potato omelet (served only until 4:30 PM). In addition to a good, hearty version of the quintessential American hamburger, there's also a salmon burger and a veggie burger for the cholesterol-wary. Another good choice is the nachos, with a variety of zesty toppings on multicolored tortilla chips. The sidewalk café makes a good place to pop in after dinner elsewhere for dessert (like hot apple pie à la mode) and a latte. If you hit the place on one of those hot and humid Florida days, there's plenty of air-conditioned seating inside in '50s-style diner booths. ⊠ *701 Front St.,* ☎ *407/566–1144. Reservations not accepted. AE, D, MC, V.*

Italian

$–$$$ ✕ **Café d' Antonio.** They keep the wood-burning oven and grill pretty busy in this place, and the mountains of hardwood they go through every week in the open kitchen at the rear of the dining room flavor most of the menu, or at least the best of it—the pizza, the grilled fish and chicken, even the steaks and chops. Standouts include salmon from the grill and *pizza Mediterranea,* topped primarily with grilled vegetables. Even the lasagna comes from the wood-fired oven. For dessert, try the hazelnut chocolate cake or the ricotta cheesecake. Italian vintages make up the better part of the wine list. Like the rest of Celebration's restaurants, this one has an awning-covered terrace overlooking the lagoon; should you need respite from the summer heat, grab one of the tables in the pleasant dining room. The paneling is as dark and soothing as the napery is white and starched. ⊠ *691 Front St.,* ☎ *407/566–2233. AE, D, MC, V.*

Latin
$$–$$$ ✕ **Columbia Restaurant.** This brand-new building creates an illusion of its own—it looks like an old Spanish mansion, with gold stucco walls set off with dark wood and fine Spanish tile work. But no one would ever accuse the Columbia Restaurant, a venerable Florida dining institution in Tampa's Ybor City, of fakery. Celebration's branch offers a dining experience not unlike the one you would find there (minus the flamenco dancers) as well as the fine Latin cuisine. If you know anything about Latin cuisine, zero in on the paella—either the *paella à la Valenciana,* with clams, shrimp, scallops, chicken, pork, and even calamari mixed into tasty yellow rice; or the all-seafood version, *paella verde,* which also includes lobster in the mix. Or try Columbia's excellent version of a basic Latin arroz con pollo—rice with chicken, served with black beans on the side and fresh Cuban bread. Desserts include a good Cuban flan and a credible key lime pie. ⊠ *649 Front St.,* ☎ *407/566–1505. AE, D, DC, MC, V.*

ELSEWHERE IN ORLANDO

Downtown Orlando

Downtown Orlando, located north of Walt Disney World and slightly north of the International Drive area, is a thriving business district with a tourist fringe in the form of Church Street Station. Restaurants mainly serve weekday workers, sports fans attending events in the nearby arena, and tourists who head for the station area to party hearty. If you want a glimpse of the city that is markedly less tourist-oriented and frenetic, especially at night, downtown Orlando is worth the 15- to 25-mi drive from the heart of Disney. If you go during the day, wait until after morning rush hour. To get there take Exit 41 off I–4 if you're heading westbound, Exit 40 if eastbound, unless otherwise noted.

Contemporary
$$$–$$$$ ✕ **Manuel's on the 28th.** How's this for one-upmanship? For a decade,
★ Arthur's 27 was Orlando's loftiest restaurant in terms of altitude, with a spot on the 27th floor of what is now the Wyndham Palace. Then in 1994, Manuel's on the 28th opened its doors on the 28th floor of the BankAmerica Building and was almost immediately hailed by local dining critics as a culinary landmark. In many cases, restaurants with a view offer only that, but the cuisine here is excellent, with stellar entrées like phyllo-wrapped loin of lamb in roasted shallot rosemary sauce, green curry and ginger-crusted yellowfin tuna, and oak-roasted Black Angus fillet with shrimp. The small list of appetizers includes macadamia-crusted Atlantic sea scallops and oak-grilled Hudson Valley foie gras. For dessert, try the baked apples wrapped up in pastry, beggar's purse style, and served with caramel sauce. There's an extensive wine list and even wines by the half glass. ⊠ *390 N. Orange Ave., Suite 2800,* ☎ *407/246–6580. AE, D, DC, MC, V. Closed Sun.–Mon. No lunch.*

$–$$$ ✕ **Harvey's Bistro.** In the Bank of America building, within walking distance of the arena and the Centroplex, this clubby café with paneled walls and white tablecloths has collected an enthusiastic business crowd at lunch and draws concert-, theater-, and arena goers after dark. The menu offers a good selection of bistro and comfort foods. Soups are good, as are the oven-roasted saffron scallops, the duck cassoulet with white and black beans, and the thin-crust pizza with caramelized onions, fresh spinach, and goat cheese. If you're a red-meat fan, rejoice. Harvey's has a good pot roast, a pan-seared tenderloin, and a decent porterhouse. The bistro is open until 11 PM on weekends, and the late hours are a plus, as is its proximity to several hot nightclubs. ⊠ *390 N. Orlando Ave.,* ☎ *407/246–6560. AE, D, DC, MC, V. Closed Sun. No lunch Sat.*

French

$$–$$$$　　✕ **Le Provence Bistro Français.** This charming, two-story restaurant in the heart of downtown does a fine imitation of an out-of-the-way bistro on the Left Bank in Paris—that is, as long as you don't spot the palm trees out the window. Reasonable prices and first-rate service make the experience even more delightful, and the food is excellent. For lunch try the salade Niçoise, made with fresh grilled tuna, French string beans, and hard-boiled eggs; or the cassoulet *toulousain,* a hearty mixture of white beans, lamb, pork, and sausage. At dinner you can choose between a six-course prix-fixe menu, a less pricey four-course version, or à la carte options. ⊠ *50 E. Pine St.,* ☎ *407/843–1320. AE, DC, MC, V. Closed Sun. No lunch Sat.*

Central Orlando

The central part of Orlando shows the character of what the town was before it became a big theme park. Quiet streets are lined with huge oaks covered with Spanish moss. Museums and galleries are found along main thoroughfares, as are dozens of tiny lakes. The restaurants in this area, a good half hour from the Disney tourism area via I–4, tend to have more of their own sense of character and style than the eateries going full tilt for your dollars in Kissimmee or on International Drive.

American/Casual

$–$$　　✕ **White Wolf Café.** The centuries collide in this quaint restaurant
★　　hung with Tiffany lamps (all for sale) in Orlando's small but vibrant antiques and art gallery district. The fare is generally light and includes about a dozen salads. One solid choice is the Moroccan, made with chicken, almonds, raisins, and bananas tossed in honey curry mustard dressing on a bed of romaine. A great appetizer is the sun-dried tomato lavosh, a Mediterranean style cracker bread topped with artichoke hearts, sun-dried tomatoes, and mozzarella cheese. Sandwich mainstays include turkey clubs and BLTs as well as a strange but worthy pita sandwich called the Mighty Joe Mango, concocted with fresh fruits, vegetables, and mango salsa. Entrées change often but usually include a deep-dish lasagna; there's also an excellent lasagna variation baked into French bread instead of pasta. Drinks range from specialty coffees to wines by the glass. White Wolf was named for Casper, the owner's now-deceased German shepherd. ⊠ *1829 N. Orange Ave.,* ☎ *407/895–5590. AE, MC, V.*

$　　**Panera Bread.** If you speak any European language besides English, you may think the name of this place is a bit redundant, but what this informal eatery overlooking Lake Eola lacks in nomenclature, it more than makes up for with cuisine. Best bets are the specialty breads, available by the loaf at the in-house bakery shop. Everything from Asiago cheese bread to well-textured nine-grain loaf is available fresh daily, and the fresh-baked breads provide the key ingredient in the house specialty, sandwiches. Choices range from the Tuscan chicken on rosemary and onion focaccia to roast beef and cheddar on an Asiago baguette. Take I–4 Exit 40 or 41. ⊠ *227 N. Eola Dr.,* ☎ *407/481–1060. AE, MC, V.*

Barbecue

$–$$ Johnny Rivers Smokehouse and BBQ. No, he's not a pop star who hit the charts a lot in the 1960s. This Johnny Rivers, an Orlando native who spent years as head chef at Disney before going out on his own, is locally more famous than the singer. His fame comes from his talent with food, and you'll likely agree that he's earned it when you bite into the barbecue at this west Orlando eatery. The roasted tater quesadilla appetizer, actually nothing like a quesadilla at all, but delicious just the same, has smoked chicken, pork, and beef layered in slices of baked potato and covered with jack cheese and sour cream. With three meats on it, the quesadilla gives you a sampling of all the major specialties of the restaurant, but it's so big, you may not want to order an entrée. If you are up for putting away a whole week's worth of calories in one meal, move boldly ahead to the smoked baby-back rib feast or the smoked rib and Maine lobster combo. ⊠ *5370 W. Colonial Dr.,* ☎ *407/293–5803. MC, V.*

Chinese

$–$$ ✕ Forbidden City. The Hunan-style food at this restaurant in a reconstructed gas station is terrific. Start with the diced chicken with pine nuts in a package—icy lettuce cups wrapped around spicy chicken, which offers a delightful mix of cold and hot sensations. The sesame chicken—large chunks of sesame-coated poultry sautéed in a sweet sauce—goes perfectly with bright-green broccoli in a subtle garlic sauce. The traditional 10-ingredient lo mein is full of fresh shrimp, chicken, beef, and pork. ⊠ *948 N. Mills Ave.,* ☎ *407/894–5005. MC, V. Closed Sun. No lunch Sat.*

$–$$ ✕ 4-5-6. With its mirrored walls and emerald green carpet, this restaurant is sleek and clean-looking, setting the stage for the food, which is made without MSG or preservatives. Dumplings sautéed in hot peanut butter sauce is a must for peanut butter fans. Specialties include "Five Fresh Herbs Steamed Fresh Fish," made with sea bass, and "Chicken-Three-Ways," with portions of General Tso's chicken, lemon chicken, and sliced chicken breast with snow peas on a single platter. The friendly staff tries hard to accommodate, so be sure to speak up if you want your food spicy or served in a special casserole to keep it warmer longer. ⊠ *657 N. Primrose Dr.,* ☎ *407/898–1899. AE, MC, V. Beer and wine only.*

Cuban

$–$$ ✕ Numero Uno. To the followers of this long-popular Latin restaurant,
★ the name is quite appropriate. Downtowners have been filling the place up at lunch for years. It bills itself as "the home of paella," and that's probably the best choice. If you have an hour and 15 minutes to wait and a good appetite, try the *paella Valenciana*, made with yellow rice, sausage, chicken, fish, and Spanish spices and served with a side order of plantains. If you don't have that long, go for traditional Cuban fare like shredded flank steak or the dish that half of Latin America eats daily, arroz con pollo. Take I–4 Exit 34 or 35A. ⊠ *2499 S. Orange Ave.,* ☎ *407/841–3840. AE, D, DC, MC, V.*

French

$$–$$$ ✕ Le Coq au Vin. Although Louis Perrotte could run a stuffed-shirt kind
★ of place—his food is as expertly prepared as any in town—he chooses to be self-effacing and to run a modest little kitchen in a small but charming house in south Orlando. Perrotte and his wife, Magdalena, who acts as hostess, make the place warm and homey, and it is usually filled with friendly Orlando residents, who appreciate the lovely traditional French fare: homemade chicken liver pâté, fresh rainbow trout with champagne sauce, and Long Island duck with green peppercorns. For

dessert, try crème brûlée, and pat yourself on the back for discovering a place that few tourists know about. Ask to be seated in the main dining room—it's the center of action. Take I–4 Exit 34 or 35. ☒ *4800 S. Orange Ave.,* ☏ *407/851–6980. AE, DC, MC, V. Closed Mon.*

Italian

$$–$$$ ✗ **La Fontanella da Nino.** This lovely Neapolitan-style Italian eatery was formerly called just "La Fontanella," after the little fountain in its quiet courtyard, a wonderful place for a leisurely lunch. But when chef Nino Carrera also became the owner, he added his name and some of his own personal touches that brought this spot to its current high level. Because the open-air seating area is perfect for enjoying a few glasses of pinot grigio or chardonnay (it's beer and wine only here), the menu calls for *stuzzichini,* a name from a Neapolitan phrase which means "something to nibble on." The *peperoni saltati* (roasted peppers sautéed with garlic, black olives, and capers) makes a good choice, as does the *melenzane all griglia* (grilled marinated eggplant). Standout entrées include *vitello Marsala* (veal cutlet sautéed with mushrooms and wine) and *pollo Scarpariello* (pasta with chicken, grilled sausage, and mushroom in a cream sauce). ☒ *900 E. Washington St.,* ☏ *407/ 425–0033. AE, MC, V. No lunch Sun.*

$$ ✗ **Gargi's Italian Restaurant.** When Amtrak rolls by on the nearby tracks, it seems like you're still on the *Earthquake* ride at Universal Studios. If you don't mind a tremor or two, you're in for some of the best pasta in Florida at this mom-and-pop eatery across the street from a quiet Orlando lake, immediately north of downtown. If you crave old-fashioned spaghetti and meatballs, lasagna, or manicotti made with sauces that you know have been simmering all day, this storefront hole-in-the-wall is the place. If you want more than basic pasta, try some of the specialties, like the veal marsala or tasty shrimp with marinara sauce and peppers over linguine. The place is notorious for slow service—but worth it. Take I–4 Exit 42. ☒ *1421 N. Orange Ave.,* ☏ *407/894– 7907. AE, MC, V. Beer and wine only. Closed Sun.*

$–$$ ✗ **Alfonso's Pizza & More.** The bad news, if you value tranquility, is
★ that this stellar neighborhood pizza parlor is located about 60 yards from the front door of Orlando's Edgewater High School, and things can get a little frenzied at lunchtime. The good news is that this is a strong contender for best pizza in Orlando, a prohibitive favorite in the non–wood-fired-oven division, and the demeanor of the dining room can be quite placid at night. Its strong suit is the pizza, hand-tossed with a variety of toppings ranging from pepperoni to pineapple, but the calzones and some of the pasta dishes, like fettuccine Alfredo, are quite worthy as well. All the sauces and pizza dough are made from scratch daily. Take I–4 Exit 42 to the College Park neighborhood area. ☒ *3231 Edgewater Dr.,* ☏ *407/827–7324. MC, V.*

$–$$ ✗ **Tiramisu Cafe.** As the name implies, this is a great place to pop in for a quick Italian dessert and a cup of cappuccino. But this small bistro on the edge of Lake Ivanhoe in Orlando's antiques and gallery district offers a lot more, including a sidewalk seating area and some great light Italian cooking. Focaccia pizzas—individual minipizzas served on Italian flatbread—are among the better specialties here, as are the Italian soups and some worthy smoked and grilled fish selections. If tiramisu is not quite exotic enough for your dessert tastes, try the tiralese, a cherry-flavored chocolate mousse cake coated with a hard, semisweet chocolate shell. Take I–4 Exit 42. ☒ *399 Ivanhoe Blvd., at Orange Ave.,* ☏ *407/228–0303. AE, MC, V.*

Seafood

$–$$ ✕ **Straub's Fine Seafood.** One school of economic thought in Orlando is that the farther you drive from Disney, the less you pay. Straub's proves the point with items like escargots for $6—less than the price of a burger in Kissimmee. The emphasis here is on food, not atmosphere. Owner Robert Straub, a fishmonger of many years, prepares a fine mesquite-grilled Atlantic salmon with béarnaise on the side. He fillets all his own fish and won't serve anything he can't get fresh. Blackened dolphin Cajun style is quite good, as is the angel-hair pasta with sautéed shrimp, pine nuts, capers, artichoke hearts, and fresh spinach. The menu states the calorie count and fat content of every fish item, but for the coconut-banana cream pie, made on the premises, you just don't want to know. ✉ *5101 E. Colonial Dr.,* ☎ *407/273–9330;* ✉ *512 E. Altamonte Dr., Altamonte Springs,* ☎ *407/831–2250;* ✉ *Straub's Boatyard, 743 Lee Rd., Orlando,* ☎ *407/628–0067. AE, D, DC, MC, V.*

Steak

$$–$$$ ✕ **Del Frisco's Prime Steak House.** In this genuine New York–style steak house, you can hear the sound of Ol' Blue Eyes belting out the standards throughout a clubby dining room where big, juicy sirloins and porterhouses are the entrées of choice. Scalloped potatoes and chopped spinach mixed with melted cheddar cheese and bacon bits come with the steaks and are sure to blow your low-fat diet. Take I–4 Exit 46. ✉ *729 Lee Rd.,* ☎ *407/645–4443. AE, D, DC, MC, V. Closed Sun. No lunch.*

$–$$$ ✕ **Linda's La Cantina.** This place takes beef very seriously, as you can tell by the disclaimer on the menu: "We cannot be responsible for steaks cooked medium-well and well done." Despite that stuffy-sounding caveat, this down-home eatery has been a favorite among locals since the Eisenhower administration. The menu is short and to the point, including about a dozen steaks and just enough ancillary items to fill up a page. Among the best is the La Cantina large T-bone—more beef than most can handle, for $22. With every entrée you get a heaping order of spaghetti or a baked potato. ✉ *4721 E. Colonial Dr.,* ☎ *407/894–4491. AE, D, MC, V.*

Vietnamese

$
★ ✕ **Little Saigon.** As Orlando flourishes, so do its ethnic restaurants. The friendly folks here love to introduce novices to their healthy and delicious national cuisine. Sample the spring rolls or the summer rolls (spring-roll filling in a soft wrapper). Then move on to the grilled pork and egg, served atop rice and noodles, or the traditional soup, filled with noodles, rice, vegetables, and your choice of either chicken or seafood; ask to have extra meat in the soup if you're hungry, and be sure they bring you the mint and bean sprouts to sprinkle in. ✉ *1106 E. Colonial Dr.,* ☎ *407/423–8539. MC, V. Beer and wine only.*

Southwestern Orlando

This is the part of the city nearest the main Disney tourism area, a mere five minutes or so northeast of International Drive or Universal Orlando. Because the neighborhood has lots of expensive homes, with incomes to match, it tends to offer the more upscale goods including some of the city's better restaurants.

Contemporary

$$–$$$$
★ ✕ **Chatham's Place.** In Florida, grouper is about as ubiquitous as Coca-Cola, but to discover its full potential, try the grouper here, sautéed in pecan butter and flavored with cayenne. It's a strong contender for the best dish in Orlando today. A close second is another house specialty—pan-roasted rack of lamb flavored with rosemary. This

place perennially appears on the "best" lists of virtually every Florida publication. The setting is a nondescript office building, so it's a good thing the food is worthy of a palace, and the service is as good as it gets in Central Florida. Take I–4 Exit 29. ☒ *7575 Dr. Phillips Blvd.,* ☎ *407/345–2992. AE, D, DC, MC, V.*

$–$$$ ✕ **Sam Snead's Tavern.** The prototype for a golf-theme grill, this lively restaurant is a tribute to the venerable pro champion Sam Snead. The wood-paneled walls are chockablock with pictures and memorabilia of his illustrious career. The kitchen does well with an eclectic variety of foods ranging from hamburgers and grilled chicken to veal chops and fish. The Caesar salad is excellent, as are the barbecued spareribs. Chocolate Sack sounds weird but isn't: it's pound cake, ice cream, strawberries, and whipped cream packed into what looks like a paper bag made of chocolate, and it's much too much for one person. This is one of the few restaurants in town open as late as 1 AM. Take I–4 Exit 30. ☒ *2461 S. Hiawassee Rd.,* ☎ *407/295–9999. AE, D, DC, MC, V.*

Italian

$$$ ✕ **Christini's.** Orlando is short on the kind of upscale Italian restaurant you find so often in New York, so locals, tourists, and Disney execs gladly pay the price at Christini's, one of the city's best for northern Italian cuisine. As a result, the place always feels as if there's a party going on, particularly in the center of the room. Owner Chris Christini is on hand nightly to make sure that everything is perfect. Try the pasta with lobster, shrimp, and clams or the huge veal chops, perfumed with fresh sage. Note: This is no place to be in a hurry; dinner, with its various courses, will often take a couple of hours or more. Take I–4 Exit 29. ☒ *Marketplace, 7600 Dr. Phillips Blvd.,* ☎ *407/345–8770. AE, D, DC, MC, V.*

$$–$$$ ✕ **Positano.** One side of this cheerful restaurant is a bustling family-style
★   pizza parlor; the other is a more formal dining room. Although you can't order pizza in the dining room, you can get anything on the entire menu in the pizzeria, which serves some of the best New York–style pies in Central Florida. Try the unusual and piquant *ziti aum* (mozzarella, Parmesan, eggplant, and basil in a tomato sauce). ☒ *Good Homes Plaza, 8995 W. Colonial Dr.,* ☎ *407/291–0602. AE, D, DC, MC, V.*

Steak

$$–$$$$ ✕ **Morton's of Chicago.** Beef is not only good food, it's good theater at this upscale steak house, where you can see the kitchen staff at work from a seat in the main dining room. Center stage is a huge broiler, kept at 900°F to sear in the flavor of the porterhouses, sirloins, T-bones, and other cuts of aged beef that make up Morton's specialties. Although the beef is the star of the show, some of the supporting cast, such as the potatoes Lyonnaise, turn in a great performance. The ambience here is that of a sophisticated city club, and youngsters with mouse caps are not common among the clientele. The prices could be a reason for the adult nature of the crowd. With side dishes, it's not unusual for your check to hit $65 a person, but if beef is your passion, this is the place. The wine list offers about 500 vintages, include selections from Australia and Chile as well as France, Italy, and California. Take I–4 Exit 29. ☒ *Marketplace, 7600 Dr. Phillips Blvd., Suite 132,* ☎ *407/248–3485. AE, DC, MC, V.*

Orlando International Airport

Italian

$$–$$$ ✕ **Hemisphere.** The name doesn't give you a clue, but this airport restaurant specializes in northern Italian cuisine and does a good job of it. On the ninth floor of the Hyatt Regency Orlando International hotel, the restaurant overlooks a major runway, but it's far enough removed

that you don't get any jet noise, just a nice air show. House specialties include sautéed shrimp and sea scallops on saffron risotto, rack of lamb with cannelloni and roasted potatoes, and an "everything-but-the-kitchen-sink" dish with shrimp, mussels, and scallops with linguine, olives, capers, and tomatoes. Desserts vary daily, but there's always a good tiramisu. Because the hotel is built right into the atrium of the airport's B-Airside Terminal, the restaurant offers easy access for a good meal between flights. ⊠ *Hyatt Regency Orlando International Airport,* ☎ *407/825–1234, ext. 1900. AE, DC, MC, V.*

OUTLYING TOWNS

Altamonte Springs

This suburb is a good 45 minutes and 30 mi from Disney, but it has one thing making it worth the drive—the inverse relationship between prices and proximity to the Magic Kingdom. And it's not just the restaurants; everything from a gallon of gas to a pair of sunglasses will cost you significantly less in Altamonte than in, say, Kissimmee. To get to the area, follow I–4 to Exit 48.

Italian

$$ ✕ **La Scala.** Mirrored walls and gracious, sophisticated decor make this one of Orlando's most romantic restaurants. The fact that owner Joseph del Vento, a former opera singer who once worked in New York's Tre Scalini, breaks into song every so often only adds to the charm. For pasta, order the dish called Chop, Chop, Chop (fresh seafood sautéed tableside, doused in marinara sauce, and served over fettuccine). ⊠ *205 Loraine Dr.,* ☎ *407/862–3257. AE, DC, MC, V. Closed Sun. No lunch Sat.*

Mexican

$ ✕ **Amigo's.** There are those who say the best Mexican food in Central Florida is at Amigo's, a local chain of restaurants run by a family of transplanted Texans. They start with good basics, like refried beans that would play well in San Antonio. Go for the Santa Fe dinner, so big it almost takes a burro to bring it to your table; you'll be able to sample tamales, enchiladas, chiles rellenos, and those heavenly frijoles, and wash it all down with a Mexican beer. Plan to wait in line if you hit the Altamonte Springs location during the noon hour or around 8 PM. ⊠ *120 N. Westmonte,* ☎ *407/774–4334;* ⊠ *494 N. Semoran, Winter Park,* ☎ *407/657–8111;* ⊠ *6036 S. Orange Blossom Trail, Orlando,* ☎ *407/857–3144;* ⊠ *4250 Alafaya Trail, Oviedo,* ☎ *407/359–1333. Reservations not accepted. AE, MC, V.*

Seafood

$$ ✕ **Gina's on the Water.** The waterfront location is almost a technicality; the postage stamp–size Crane's Roost Lake is actually across the street. But guests don't come for the proximity to the water. They come because the Italian seafood restaurant is one of the best way-too-small eateries around. It serves all sorts of tasty tuna, grouper, snapper, and salmon entrées, as well as some decent landlubber options, like the excellent minipizza with barbecued chicken. Traditional Italian pasta dishes are dispensed from an open-air, stage-front-style upstairs kitchen, while a quiet downstairs bar area affords views of the lake or the current football game (on several TVs). ⊠ *309 N. Lake Blvd.,* ☎ *407/ 834–5880. AE, D, MC, V.*

Kissimmee

Although Orlando is the focus of most theme-park visitors, Kissimmee is actually closer to Walt Disney World. To get into the area, follow I–4 to Exit 25A, and allow about 15 or 20 minutes to get from WDW or anyplace in the Kissimmee area, or about 30 minutes from I-Drive.

Italian

$–$$ ✕ **Romano's Macaroni Grill.** Any one of the three local locations of this prolific chain is a good bet for good but not great cuisine Italiano. They're friendly, they're casual, and they're comfortable. They spin out popular pastas with toppings and sauces made with everything from sausage to eggplant. The specialty is *scallopini de pollo Romano,* which is made with chicken instead of the traditional veal, featuring artichokes and capers, and served with angel-hair pasta. House wines are brought to the table in gallon bottles. You serve yourself and then report how many glasses you had. ⊠ *5320 W. Irlo Bronson Memorial Hwy.,* ☎ *407/396–6155;* ⊠ *884 W. Rte. 436, Altamonte Springs,* ☎ *407/682–2577;* ⊠ *12148 S. Apopka–Vineland Rd., Lake Buena Vista,* ☎ *407/239–6676. AE, D, DC, MC, V.*

Lake Wales

A tiny hamlet about an hour southwest of Walt Disney World, Lake Wales offers no particular reason to visit, except for its lush orange groves, an off-beat attraction (Cypress Gardens), and one outstanding Continental restaurant. To get into the area, follow I–4 to Exit 23 and U.S. 27 south.

Continental

$$$$ ✕ **Chalet Suzanne.** If you like to drive, are on your way south, or are
★   visiting Cypress Gardens or Bok Tower Gardens, consider making time for a scrumptious and relaxing meal at this family-owned country inn. Because of its charm and originality, Chalet Suzanne has earned praise from restaurant critics and might provide one of the most memorable dining experiences of your stay. Expanded bit by quirky bit since it opened in the 1930s, this unlikely inn looks like a small Swiss village plopped in the middle of orange groves by way of the Mediterranean. Come for the traditional six-course dinner (all meals are prix fixe) or for a sophisticated breakfast of eggs Benedict or Swedish pancakes with lingonberries. Sitting in the antiques-filled dining room and watching turtles play in the lake or ibis meander on the lawn is the perfect way to start your day. The restaurant is about 2 mi south of the Cypress Gardens turnoff on U.S. 27. ⊠ *3800 Chalet Suzanne Dr.,* ☎ *863/676–6011. AE, DC, MC, V. Closed Mon. in summer.*

Longwood

A northern suburb 30–45 minutes from Disney, Longwood residents choose it because it's a long way from the tourism treadmill. The community has some worthy restaurants as well. To get into the area, follow I–4 to Exit 49.

Italian

$$–$$$ ✕ **Enzo's on the Lake.** Enzo's is one of Orlando foodies' favorite
★   restaurants, even though it's on a tacky stretch of highway filled with used-car lots. The Roman charmer who owns the place, Enzo Perlini, has turned a rather ordinary lakefront house into an Italian villa. It's worth the trip, about 30 minutes from I-Drive, to sample the antipasti. Mussels, cooked in a heady broth of white wine and garlic, and the mild *buffalo* mozzarella cheese, flown in from Italy, make equally good starters. The *bucatini à la Enzo* (sautéed bacon, mushrooms, and peas served over long hollow noodles) is a very popular house specialty. ⊠ *1130 S. U.S. 17–92,* ☎ *407/834–9872. AE, DC, MC, V. Closed Sun.*

Maitland

Not quite as far from Disney as the northernmost Orlando suburbs, this town, 25 minutes from Disney and 5 mi north of downtown Orlando, is still more like reality than you'll find on I–Drive. And like most Orlando residential areas, it's dotted with serene lakes shaded by stately oaks and worthwhile shopping and dining as well. To get into the area, follow I–4 to Exit 47.

Italian

$$–$$$$ ✕ **Buca di Beppo.** Located in the building that formerly housed The Bubble Room, this profusely decorated Italian eatery makes a great place to take to take the family, but a very expensive place to dine alone. Reason: Everything is served in family-sized portions, and at family-sized prices, and they don't cut you a break for dining solo. It's $10 for a small green salad, $8 for an order of mashed potatoes that one person could never eat, and $10 for three meat balls. But if you've got your family with you, the fine southern Italian cooking becomes a good deal, with entrees like chicken marsala and veal parmigiana, which will easily feed a couple of people per serving, ranging from $17 to $20. Wood-baked pizzas offer a wide variety of toppings, from a pedestrian pepperoni to a more creative eggplant, escarole, and artichoke with provolone. ✉ *1351 S. Orlando Ave.,* ☎ *407/622–7663. AE, D, MC, V.*

$–$$$ ✕ **Antonio's La Fiamma.** The wood-burning grill and oven give the place a delightful smell, but they aren't just for ambience. They're used to turn out great grilled fish dishes, gourmet pizzas, and homemade bread. In the main section, upstairs, diners can watch the cooks at the back of the building working away. Try the *sogliola al forno* (a light fillet of sole with fresh leeks, garlic, basil, and lemon) or the equally compelling *pollo all'aglio e rosmarino* (chicken basted with Antonio's own recipe of fresh rosemary, garlic, and olive oil, then roasted over a wood-burning rotisserie). The *linguine alla cine di rapa* (with sautéed bitter greens, sausage, and slivered garlic) is a tantalizing marriage of tastes and textures. If you don't have time for a leisurely sit-down meal, visit the deli-style version downstairs, which has many of the same menu items both at lunch and dinner. ✉ *611 S. Orlando Ave. (U.S. 17–92),* ☎ *407/645–5523. AE, MC, V. Closed Sun.*

Winter Park

Winter Park is a charming suburb on the northern end of Orlando, 25 minutes from Disney. It's affluent, understated, and sophisticated—and can be a pleasure after many days in the theme parks when you need a break. To get into the area, follow I–4 to Exit 45.

Chinese

$–$$$ **P. F. Chang's.** A look at the outside of this place, where two huge, stone Ming dynasty–style statues of horses stand guard, makes you think it could be a museum. The interior continues the theme, with replicas of sculptures found in the ancient Chinese city of Xi'an, and a big mural depicting 12th-century China over the bar. But this is no museum (the horses are actually hollow, imitation stone), it's one of a highly themed Chinese eatery chain that seems more influenced by California than Canton. There's a lengthy wine list, for instance, and very un-Asian desserts like chocolate macadamia nut pie and fruit tortes. But the array of Chinese dishes, which represent virtually all of the major Chinese cuisine types, is also impressive. Standouts include the Cantonese duck, Chang's spicy chicken, and salt and pepper shrimp. A house appetizer is called "soothing lettuce wraps," basically a neatly cut pile of lettuce leaves, in which you wrap an assortment of stir-fried meat and vegetables, kind of like rolling your own burrito. ⊠ *423 N. Orlando Ave. (U.S. 17–92),* ☎ *407/622–0188. AE, MC, V.*

Contemporary

$–$$ ✗ **Dexter's.** This hip college favorite, which draws much of its clientele from Rollins College just a block away, almost blends into the coin laundry next door. You don't expect it to be as trendy and sophisticated as it is: it even has its own wine label and publishes a monthly newsletter for those who appreciate a good vintage. There's often jazz at night, and you won't feel out of place if you're over 40. One of the best entrées is chicken tortilla pie, a stack of cheese-laden tortillas that looks more like a spaceship than a pie. Still, if you're not up for an evening among the coeds, try Dexter's of Thornton Park, in gentrified Thornton Park, just east of downtown Orlando. You may be the only tourist there. ⊠ *200 W. Fairbanks Ave.,* ☎ *407/629–1150;* ⊠ *808 E. Washington St., Orlando,* ☎ *407/648–2777. Reservations not accepted. AE, D, DC, MC, V.*

$–$$ ✗ **Houston's.** It took this Atlanta-based chain to seize the obvious and
★   build an eatery on big Lake Killarney, with a spectacular view. As you watch the egrets and herons (but no alligators, since city authorities periodically remove them), you can savor a good range of meaty fare. The fancy wood-grilled burger acquits itself well, but there's nothing like the steaks, cooked precisely to your specifications. A variety of hardwood-grilled fish entrées like tuna and salmon offer tasty alternatives. Of the excellent soups, the baked potato creation is the best; gargantuan salads round out a fulfilling soup-and-salad meal. Houston's is also a great place for a drink around sunset, when you can enjoy the view either from the outdoor patio or the small dock. ⊠ *215 S. Orlando Ave. (U.S. 17–92),* ☎ *407/740–4005. Reservations not accepted. AE, MC, V.*

Italian

$–$$ ✗ **Brio Tuscan Grille.** This place is trendy, both in its location—the new Winter Park Village—and its menu, which includes such vogue Italian cooking as wood-grilled pizzas and oak-grilled meats, including steaks, lamb chops, and even lobster. Another house specialty, "chicken under the brick," is a whole chicken breast, slow-roasted with a weight on top to flatten it out. It's then served with a tasty, mushroom-laden marsala sauce. Italian flatbreads are also a specialty, with a good appetizer choice being the brio bruschetta, a wood-baked flatbread covered with shrimp scampi, mozzarella, and roasted peppers. The dining room has quite an upscale feeling with Italian archways, but the sidewalk tables are also a good option. A take-home bakery adjoins the restaurant. ⊠ *480 N. Orlando Ave.,* ☎ *407/662–5611. AE, MC, V.*

7 LODGING

New hotels sprout like weeds in Orlando, providing visitors with a dizzying array of choices. There's someplace for everyone, from basic motels with rock-bottom rates to elaborate themed resorts with every facility imaginable and nightly charges that exceed the annual per-capita income in many Third World countries.

Updated by
Rowland
Stiteler

THERE WAS A TIME WHEN SIMPLY BEING in the midst of the world's largest concentration of theme parks was enough of a selling point to make most Orlando hotels thrive. But somewhere along the way, as the room inventory topped 100,000 (more hotel rooms than New York City or Los Angeles), the competition became so intense that hotels needed to become attractions unto themselves in order to compete. At the Portofino Bay Resort at Universal Orlando, for instance, the hotel has been crafted to re-create every detail of the Italian oceanside resort village of Portofino. On the Orlando resort's waterfront (actually on a small, man-made lake) Italian "fishermen" mend their nets to add to the atmosphere, even though they never actually fish. It's all part of the show.

Simple in-house game arcades for the kids became a minimum standard at Orlando hotels years ago. Now most of the larger hotels have their own in-house children's clubs, many of which provide live entertainment, such as clown shows, magic shows, and performances by Disney characters. The hotels have learned that you've got to have a bit of on-property showbiz to survive, and the traveler benefits by having hotel choices that are anything but ordinary.

The biggest hotel spectacle—or at least the biggest to be announced yet—will come in 2003 with the opening of the 1,400-room Opryland Hotel & Convention Center in Kissimmee, which will feature a 50-ft-tall lighthouse, a 60-ft-long Florida shrimp boat, a re-creation of the historic district of old St. Augustine, and a Florida Keys waterscape—all indoors under a huge glass roof. At the same time the Opryland opens, Disney will be opening a new 5,800-room economy-priced hotel complex, similar to the All-Star Resorts.

At the end of 2000, another highly themed hotel, the 650-room Hard Rock Hotel, became the second on-property hotel at Universal. More will follow. It's safe to assume that the most elaborate hotel for the Orlando market has yet to be announced, and more themed hotels, designed to entertain you as much as provide lodging, will spring up in the next few years. Most of the bigger, fancier hotels will of course have room rates commensurate with their huge construction budgets. But even so, because of the vast array of choices in every price range, it will likely be easy in the foreseeable future to find a lodging that suits your budget. That's because with 100,000 hotel rooms, and another 40,000 on the horizon by 2010, there will always be plenty of competition.

One rule of thumb in selecting a hotel—assuming you plan far enough in advance—is to request a brochure. If it has lots of pictures of Walt Disney World and no pictures of the hotel, it's probably a dump. Because the market is so competitive, hotels are obliged to spend millions on frequent renovations. Those which don't update fall behind and usually rely on simply being near Disney as the mainstay of their marketing plan. And, with most of the bigger hotels and a lot of the smaller ones having their own Web sites, you can get a virtual tour of the place before you invest your money and time.

Your first big decision, however, is whether to stay at a hostelry within WDW or one outside the property. There are advantages to each option. To help in finding your perfect room, we've reviewed hundreds of offerings throughout the main hotel hubs both in and surrounding WDW.

How to Choose

When examining your options, give careful thought to the kind of vacation you want. Consider what you want to see during your Orlando visit and how long you want to stay. Within a given price category, compare the facilities of the available establishments to make sure that you get exactly what you want; our charts (☞ *below*) will help you do this. Don't overlook the savings to be gained from cooking your own breakfast and maybe a few other meals as well, which you can do if you choose an establishment with cooking facilities. If you're traveling with children, remember to ask about the cutoff age, the age at which the management considers your offspring to be adults—and makes you pay accordingly, even when they share your room. Finally, don't overlook time spent in transit; if you're not staying at a property in or near WDW, you can waste a few hours a day sitting in traffic.

Staying in WDW

If you're coming to Orlando for only a few days and are interested solely in the Magic Kingdom, Epcot, and the other Disney attractions, the resorts on Disney property—whether or not they're owned by Disney—are the most convenient. Put aside your car keys, because Walt Disney World buses and monorails are efficient enough to make it possible to visit one park in the morning and another after lunch, with a Park- or All-in-One Hopper admission ticket. You have the freedom to return to your hotel for R&R when the crowds are thickest, and if it turns out that half the family wants to spend the afternoon in one of the parks and the other half wants to float around Typhoon Lagoon, it's not a problem.

On-site hotels were built with families in mind. Older children can travel on their own on the transportation system without inviting trouble. Younger children get a thrill from knowing that they're actually living in Walt Disney World. Rooms in the more expensive Disney-owned properties are large enough to accommodate up to five; villas sleep six or seven. All accommodations offer cable TV with the Disney Channel and a daily events channel.

If you're an on-site guest at a Disney hotel, a major perk is early admission: each day guests at Disney-owned hotels can get in to one of the three parks one hour before regular park opening—and even when the theme parks or water parks have reached capacity, as Blizzard Beach, Typhoon Lagoon, and Disney–MGM Studios sometimes do, on-site guests are guaranteed entry. Then there are the small conveniences: guests at Disney-owned properties are able to charge to their room most meals and purchases throughout WDW. To golfers, it's important to know that Disney guests get first choice of tee times at the golf courses and can also reserve them up to 30 days in advance.

Staying Around Orlando

If you're planning to visit attractions other than WDW or if the Disney resorts seem too rich for your blood, then staying off-site holds a number of advantages. You'll enjoy more peace and quiet and may have easier access to SeaWorld and Universal—as well as to Orlando's shopping, dining, and entertainment facilities. You're almost certain to save money.

The hotels closest to Walt Disney World are clustered in several principal areas: along International Drive within Orlando city limits; the U.S. 192 area, which includes the boundaries of Kissimmee, the town that is actually closest to Walt Disney World and with hotels that tend to be small and cheap; and in the Downtown Disney–Lake Buena Vista area around WDW's northernmost entrance, just off I-4 at Exit 27. Nearly every hotel in these areas provides frequent transportation to and from Walt Disney World. In addition, there are some noteworthy—if far-flung—options in the suburbs and in the Greater Orlando area. Since the city isn't so big, even apparently distant properties are seldom much more than 45 minutes' drive from Disney toll plazas, when traffic is running smoothly. If you're willing to make the commute, you're likely to save a bundle: whereas accommodations at the Hilton on Hotel Plaza Boulevard, near Downtown Disney, will cost you upwards of $190 a night in season, another Hilton about 45 minutes away in Altamonte Springs has rates that start $75 lower. Some of the simpler motels with Kissimmee addresses, only 10 minutes from Disney, will put you up for $40 a night or even less.

Reservations

All on-site Disney accommodations may be booked through the **Walt Disney World Central Reservations Office** (✉ Box 10100, Suite 300, Lake Buena Vista 32830, ☎ 407/934–7639); persons with disabilities can call **WDW Special Request Reservations** (☎ 407/939–7807; 407/939–7670 TTY) to get information or book rooms. Rooms at most non-Disney chain hotels can be reserved by calling either the hotel itself or the toll-free number for the entire chain. Be sure to tell the reservations clerk exactly what you are looking for—Disney-owned property or not, price range, the number of people in your party, and the dates of your visit. When you book a room, be sure to mention whether you have a disability or are traveling with children and whether you prefer a certain type of bed or have any other concerns. If possible, stay flexible about dates; many hotels and attractions offer seasonal discounts of up to 40%.

Deposits

You must give a deposit for your first night's stay within three weeks of making your reservation. At many hotels you can get a refund if you cancel at least five days before your scheduled arrival. However, individual hotel policies vary, and some properties may require up to 15 days' notice for a full refund. Check before booking.

When to Book

Reserve your WDW or non-Disney hotel several months in advance—as much as a year ahead if you want to snag the best rooms during high season.

Other Options

If neither the WDW Central Reservations Office nor the off-site hotels have space on your preferred dates, look into packages from American Express, Delta, or other operators, which have been allotted whole blocks of rooms. In addition, because there are always cancellations, it's worth trying even at the last minute; for same-day bookings, call the property directly. Numbers for Disney properties are given in the reviews below.

Packages, including cruises, car rentals, and hotels both on and off Disney property, can be arranged through your travel agent or **Walt Disney Travel Co.** (✉ 1675 Buena Vista Dr., Lake Buena Vista 32830, ☎ 800/828–0228).

Rates

Rates are lowest from early January to mid-February, from mid-April to mid-June, and from mid-August to the third week in December; low rates often remain in place longer at non-Disney properties. Always call several places—availability and special deals can often drive room rates at a $$$$ hotel down into the $$ range—and don't forget to ask if you're eligible for a discount. Many hotels offer special rates for members of, for example, the American Automobile Association (AAA) or the American Association of Retired Persons (AARP). We always list the facilities that are available, but we don't specify whether you'll be charged extra to use them. When pricing accommodations, always ask what's included.

IN WALT DISNEY WORLD®: DISNEY-OWNED HOTELS

Traditionally, guests have had to take a heavy hit in the wallet to stay in Disney-owned hotels. During the past several years, however, the number of moderately priced properties has boomed. With a wide selection of price ranges available, most lodging decisions come down to what area of WDW or what style of hotel strikes your fancy. Resort hotels predominate, but there are also campsites, trailers, and kitchen-equipped suites and villas. These accommodations are clustered together in four sections of Walt Disney World.

The Magic Kingdom resort area has ritzy hotels, all of which lie on the Magic Kingdom monorail route and are only minutes away from the park. Fort Wilderness Resort and Campground, with trailers and RV and tent sites, is just southeast of this area. The Epcot resort area, south of the park, includes the luxurious Yacht and Beach Club Resorts as well as the popular Caribbean Beach Resort and Coronado Springs Resort, and a popular high-end property, the BoardWalk Inn and Villas. The Downtown Disney/Lake Buena Vista resort area, east of Epcot, is near Pleasure Island and the Downtown Disney shopping and entertainment complex. Accommodations include two mid-price resorts with an Old South theme as well as the Villas at Disney Institute, made up of town houses and villas equipped with kitchens. The newest complex, All-Star Village, is in the park's southwest corner, not far from U.S. 192.

Magic Kingdom Resort Area

Take I–4 Exit 24C, 25B, or 26B.

Resort Hotels

$$$$ 🏨 **Contemporary Resort.** Even though this awkwardly modern, 15-story, flat-topped pyramid is old enough for some parents to have dreamed of riding into it on the monorail when they were kids (it was built in 1971), it remains current. Looking like an intergalactic docking bay, the ideally situated resort bustles from dawn to after midnight. Half the rooms are in the Tower, the main building; you'll have to pay extra for their spectacular views. Those in front look out on Cinderella Castle and Space Mountain, flaming sunsets, and the fireworks show; those in back have ringside views of the Electrical Water Pageant and sunrise over misty Bay Lake. All have a small terrace. A hop on the monorail, which comes right into the main lobby, takes you to the Magic Kingdom and Epcot; other destinations are reached by motor launch and bus. One of the hotel's three restaurants, Chef Mickey's, is the mecca of character meals, and a great experience with your kids. Its 15th-floor gourmet restaurant, the California Grill, is one of Disney's best. With a 72,000-square-ft convention center adjacent to the hotel, the clientele tends to be more business-oriented here than at the other resorts. ☎ 407/824–1000, FAX 407/824–3539. *1,005 rooms, 36 suites. 3 restaurants, 2 lobby lounges, snack bar, room service, 3 pools, beauty salon, 6 tennis courts, health club, shuffleboard, volleyball, beach, marina, boating, waterskiing, baby-sitting, children's programs (ages 4–10), playground, coin laundry, laundry service, concierge, convention center. AE, MC, V.*

236

Lodging

Florida's Tnpk.

435

EXIT 31

1

2

8

Universal
Studios **9**

Kirkman Rd.

EXIT 30

439

International Dr.

Lake
Down

10

EXIT 29

11 **12** **13**

16 **14**

15

Lake
Butler

18

Turkey Lake Rd.

Little
Sand
Lake

Lake
Tibet

535

EXIT 2

Apopka - Vineland Rd.

Big
Sand
Lake

Lake
Sheen

33 **34**

Winter Garden Vineland Rd.

64

Lake
Mabel

35

535

36

Hotel Plaza Blvd.

26

28 **27**

Buena Vista Dr.

3

Magic
Kingdom **37**

Vista Blvd.

29

30 **32**

Buena Vista
Lagoon

Downtown
Disney

**For Walt Disney World Hotels,
See Walt Disney World Map,
Chapter 2**

Epcot Center Dr.

Epcot

Disney's Animal
Kingdom

40

41

Buena Vista Dr.

Disney–MGM
Studios

N

48

46

0   3 miles

0   3 km

EXIT

4

42

192

43 **44** **45**

61

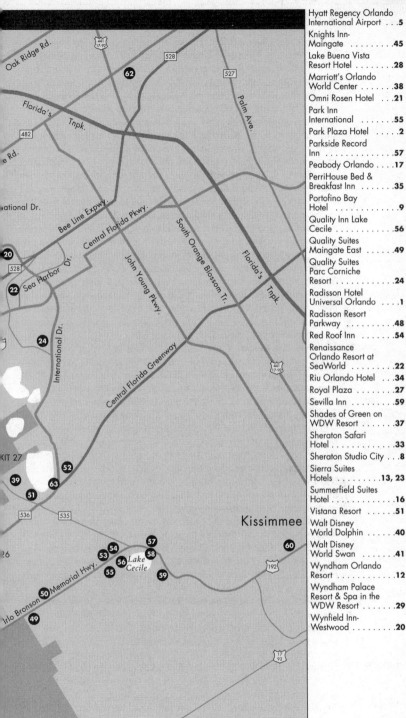

237

$$$$
★ ⊡ **Grand Floridian.** Although the Contemporary is more of a traditional first-class ritual, this place is what Disney considers its top hotel, as you'll see from the rates. This Disney fantasy appears to have been transported brick by brick from some Victorian-era coastal hot spot to the shores of the Seven Seas Lagoon. Actually, the gabled red roof, brick chimneys, rambling verandas, and delicate gingerbread are grand-old yet brand-new. Serious attention was paid to each detail, from the crystal chandeliers and stained-glass domes to the ornate balconies and aviary. Although equipped with every modern convenience, the moss-green and salmon-pink rooms, with Victorian wallpaper and wall hangings, have real vintage charm, especially the attic nooks. For those who want to invest in the top-echelon treatment, the hotel offers 74 concierge suites, complete with in-room wet bars, in a section with its own private entrance elevator. Add a dinner or two at Victoria and Albert's or Citrico's (☞ Chapter 6), and you'll probably spend more here in four days than on an average mortgage payment, but you'll have the memory of the best Disney offers. And if you find you want still more pampering, you can try a lake cruise on the *Grand 1,* a 44-ft yacht that can take hotel guests on Seven Seas Lagoon for an experience complete with butler service and gourmet dining on board. ☎ 407/824–3000, FAX 407/824–3186. *900 rooms, 90 suites. 5 restaurants, 4 lounges, room service, pool, beauty salon, hot tub, 2 tennis courts, croquet, health club, volleyball, beach, marina, boating, waterskiing, baby-sitting, children's programs (ages 4–10), playground, coin laundry, laundry service, concierge. AE, MC, V.*

$$$$
⊡ **Polynesian Resort.** If it weren't for the kids in Mickey Mouse caps, you might think you were in Fiji. A three-story tropical atrium fills the lobby. Orchids bloom alongside coconut palms and banana trees, and water cascades from volcanic rock fountains. A mainstay of the activities here is the nightly luau, complete with Polynesian dancers and a feast featuring Hawaiian-style roast pork. A new restaurant at the resort, 'Ohana, features a 16-ft-long open fire pit, where meats are roasted on skewers. 'Ohana also features Minnie's Menehune character breakfast. In the rooms, two queen-size beds and a twin bed in the living room accommodate five. Lagoon-view rooms—which overlook the Electrical Water Pageant—are the most peaceful and the priciest, and most units have a balcony or patio. Both pools—one an extravagantly landscaped, free-form affair with rocks and caverns—are beloved by children; for quiet, head for the beach. Monorail, bus, and motor launch lines network at this always popular resort. ☎ 407/824–2000, FAX 407/824–3174. *848 rooms, 5 suites. 3 restaurants, lobby lounge, snack bar, room service, 2 pools, volleyball, beach, boating, waterskiing, baby-sitting, children's programs (ages 4–10), playground, coin laundry, laundry service, concierge floor. AE, MC, V.*

$$$–$$$$
★ ⊡ **Walt Disney World Wilderness Lodge.** Even though other Disney hotels are more expensive by a couple hundred dollars a night, this property is one of the most spectacular, thanks to its architecture. The seven-story hostelry was modeled after the turn-of-the-century lodges of national parks out West. Of course, Disney does everything bigger and grander than does history. Supported by great tree trunks, the towering, five-story lobby features an 82-ft-high, three-sided fireplace made of rocks from the Grand Canyon, illuminated by enormous tepee-shape chandeliers. Two 55-ft-tall, hand-carved totem poles, inspired by Northwest Indian tribes, complete the movie-set quality of the lobby area. Rooms have Western motifs—leather chairs, patchwork quilts, and cowboy art. Each has a balcony or a patio and two queen beds or, on request, a queen and two bunk beds. The hotel's showstopper is its Fire Rock Geyser, a sort of faux Old Faithful, near the large pool, which itself begins as a hot spring in the lobby. (Most rooms have views

of the faux geyser, the pine forests around the place, or nearby Bay Lake.) One of the hotel's restaurants, Artist Point, serves Pacific Northwest cuisine and is considered one of the top restaurants in Orlando. Motor launches transport guests across Seven Seas Lagoon, also nearby, to the Magic Kingdom, and buses connect you to the other parks. ☎ 407/824-3200, FAX 407/824-3232. *728 rooms, 31 suites. 2 restaurants, 2 lobby lounges, room service, pool, wading pool, beach, boating, waterskiing, bicycles, baby-sitting, children's programs (ages 4–10), coin laundry, laundry service. AE, MC, V.*

Fort Wilderness Resort and Campground

If you're seeking a calm spot amid the theme-park storm, you need go no farther than these 700 acres of scrubby pine, tiny streams, and peaceful canals on the shore of subtropical Bay Lake, about a mile from the Wilderness Lodge. This is about as relaxed as it gets in Walt Disney World. Sports facilities abound, bike trails are popular, and there's a marina where you can rent a sailboat. To experience this property, you can bring your own tent or RV or rent one of the fully equipped, air-conditioned Disney trailers, known as Wilderness Homes, parked on the property. All facilities are available to all Fort Wilderness guests.

$$$–$$$$ ⚠ **Wilderness Homes.** In the old days people usually stayed in one of these when the rest of moderately priced Orlando was booked up. Then the word got out: cheap family accommodations available in a beautifully forested area. Now people are calling months in advance and requesting the same Wilderness Home they had last year. You won't find *House Beautiful* decor, but these perfectly comfortable accommodations put the relaxed friendliness of Fort Wilderness within reach of families who haven't brought their own RV and don't want to camp out. The larger trailers can accommodate four grown-ups and two youngsters; the bedroom has a double bed and a bunk bed, and the living room has a double sleeper sofa or Murphy bed. The smaller trailers, without the bunk beds, sleep four. ☎ 407/824–2900, FAX 407/824–3508. *408 60- and 80-ft trailers. Cafeteria, grocery, snack bar, 2 pools, 2 tennis courts, basketball, horseback riding, shuffleboard, volleyball, beach, boating, bicycles, playground, coin laundry. AE, MC, V.*

$–$$ ⚠ **RV and Tent Sites.** Bringing a tent or RV to Walt Disney World is one of the cheapest ways actually to stay on WDW property, especially considering that sites accommodate up to 10. Tent sites with water and electricity are real bargains. RV sites cost more but come equipped with electric, water, and sewage hookups as well as outdoor charcoal grills and picnic tables; you can even get maid service for your trailer. ☎ 407/824–2900. *307 preferred tent sites; 90 tent sites with water and electric hookups; 386 trailer sites with water, electric, and sewage hookups. Cafeteria, grocery, snack bar, 2 pools, 2 tennis courts, basketball, horseback riding, shuffleboard, volleyball, beach, boating, bicycles, playground, coin laundry. AE, MC, V.*

Epcot Resort Area

Take I–4 Exit 25B or 26B.

Resort Hotels

$$$$ ▦ **BoardWalk Inn and Villas.** Long before Disneyland ever existed, American vacationers loosened their starched collars at amusement piers that
★ dazzled with elaborate gingerbread structures, cotton-candy colors, and pavilions of extravagant design. The most famous was at Atlantic City, re-created by Disney at its BoardWalk area. As part of the complex, WDW's noted architectural master, Robert A. M. Stern, has designed this inn, WDW's smallest and most intimate deluxe hotel, which features 19th-century New England architecture. The pool complex in-

cludes a 200-ft water slide in the form of a classic wooden roller coaster. Bus, tram, and motor launch lines access the parks, and you can walk to Epcot. Concierge-level rooms offer extra perks like a private club, wine and cheese every evening, and free breakfast. The proximity to the BoardWalk dining and entertainment area is no small benefit; it offers some of Disney's better restaurants and the popular ESPN Sports Club. ☎ 407/939–5100 inn; 407/939–6200 villas, ℻ 407/939–5150. 378 rooms, 20 suites, 383 villas. 3 restaurants, lobby lounge, room service, pool, tennis court, croquet, exercise room, nightclub, baby-sitting, laundry service, concierge, convention center. AE, MC, V.

$$$$ ⊞ **Walt Disney World Yacht and Beach Club Resorts.** Straight out of a
★ Cape Cod summer, these properties—across a 25-acre lake from the BoardWalk—are coastal inns on a grand Disney scale. The five-story Yacht Club recalls turn-of-the-century New England seacoast resorts, with its hardwood floors, lobby full of gleaming brass and polished leather, oyster-gray clapboard facade, and evergreen landscaping; there's even a lighthouse on its pier. Rooms are similarly nautical, with white-and-blue naval flags on the bedspreads and a small ship's wheel on the headboard. Drawing on similar inspirations is the blue-and-white, three- to five-story Beach Club, where a croquet lawn and cabana-dotted, white-sand beach set the scene. The Beach Club has a particular attraction for kids that's been added in the recent past, Stormalong Bay, a 3-acre water park, complete with water slides and whirlpools. Guest rooms are summery, with wicker and pastel furnishings. Both establishments are refreshingly unstuffy, just right for families. ☎ 407/934–8000 Beach Club; 407/934–7000 Yacht Club, ℻ 407/934–3850 Beach Club; 407/934–3450 Yacht Club. 1,213 rooms, 112 suites. 4 restaurants, 3 lobby lounges, snack bar, room service, 3 pools, beauty salon, 2 tennis courts, croquet, health club, volleyball, beach, boating, baby-sitting, laundry service, concierge. AE, MC, V.

$$$ ⊞ **Caribbean Beach Resort.** Talk about tropical punch! Awash in dizzy-
★ ing Caribbean colors, this hotel was the first of Disney's moderately priced accommodations. Just east of Epcot and Disney–MGM and surrounding 45-acre Barefoot Bay, this property comprises five palm-studded "villages" named for Caribbean islands. Each has its own small, rectangular pool; all share a white-sand beach. Bridges over the lake connect to the 1-acre, path-crossed Parrot Cay, where there's a play area. A 1½-mi-long promenade circling the lake attracts bikers, joggers, and romantic strollers. The hub of the resort is a complex called Old Port Royale, decorated with pirates' cannons and tropical birds and housing stores, a food court, and a tropical lounge. The large guest rooms have soft pastel colors and white wood furniture, with coffeemakers standard and refrigerators available for $6 a day. On-property dining isn't fancy, but it's not expensive, either. ☎ 407/934–3400, ℻ 407/934–3288. 2,112 rooms. Restaurant, food court, lobby lounge, wading pool, hot tub, jogging, beach, boating, bicycles, baby-sitting, playground, coin laundry, laundry service. AE, MC, V.

$$$ ⊞ **Coronado Springs Resort.** Opened in 1997, this moderately priced
★ hotel on yet another Disney-made lake serves two constituencies. Because of its on-property, 95,000-square-ft convention center, it's popular with business groups. But its casual Southwestern architectural style; its wonderful, lively, Mexican-style Pepper Market food court; and its elaborate swimming pool complex, complete with a Maya pyramid with a big water slide, attract a good number of family vacationers as well. The lobby is a Victorian treasure, filled with big columns and arches, and recreation options are plentiful. There's a 3,000-square-ft, full-service health club, but if you like jogging, walking, or biking you're in the right place. A sidewalk circles the property's 15-acre lake. The hotel is close to both Epcot and Disney's Animal King-

dom. ☎ *407/939–1000,* FAX *407/939–1001. 1,967 rooms. 2 restaurants, bar, food court, room service, 4 pools, beauty salon, health club, boating, bicycles, laundry service, convention center. AE, MC, V.*

Downtown Disney/Lake Buena Vista/WDW Resort Area

Take I–4 Exit 27.

Resort Hotels

$$$ ⊞ **Dixie Landings Resort.** Disney's Imagineers drew inspiration from the Old South for this sprawling, moderately priced resort northwest of Downtown Disney and Lake Buena Vista. Rooms, in three-story plantation-style mansions and two-story, rustic bayou dwellings, are all the same size and accommodate up to four in two double beds. Elegantly decorated, they have wooden armoires and gleaming brass faucets; a few rooms have king-size beds. In addition, about half of them are designated nosmoking. Guest registration looks like a steamboat interior, and a 3½-acre, old-fashioned swimming-hole complex called Ol' Man Island is, in fact, a pool with slides, rope swings, and an adjacent play area. ☎ *407/934–6000,* FAX *407/934–5777. 2,048 rooms. Restaurant, food court, lobby lounge, 6 pools, wading pool, hot tub, boating, video games, baby-sitting, playground, coin laundry, laundry service. AE, MC, V.*

$$$ ⊞ **Port Orleans Resort.** Disney's version of New Orleans's French Quarter emulates the charm and romance of the original. Ornate row houses with wrought-iron balconies overgrown with vines are clustered around squares lushly planted with magnolias. Walking on the lamplighted sidewalks that edge the complex's alleyways, you might find yourself on Bourbon Street, since routes are named for French Quarter thoroughfares. The food court serves up such Crescent City specialties as jambalaya and beignets (fritters), in addition to standards (like pizza and burgers), and Bonfamille's Café offers varied Louisianastyle fare, plus such American favorites as prime rib and spit-roasted chicken. Kids love the large, free-form Doubloon Lagoon, one of Disney's most exotic pools, with its "sea serpent" (actually a creative water slide) that "swallows" swimmers and spits them into the water. ☎ *407/ 934–5000,* FAX *407/934–5353. 1,008 rooms. Restaurant, food court, lobby lounge, pool, wading pool, hot tub, croquet, boating, bicycles, baby-sitting, coin laundry, laundry service, concierge. AE, MC, V.*

Villas with Kitchens

$$$$ ⊞ **Old Key West Resort.** A red-and-white lighthouse helps you find your way through this marina-style resort. Freestanding villas resemble turn-of-the-century Key West houses, with white clapboard siding and private balconies that overlook the waterways winding through the grounds. The one-, two-, or three-bedroom houses have whirlpools in the master bedrooms, full-size kitchens, full-size washers and dryers, and outdoor patios. The huge, 2,265-square-ft grand villas accommodate up to 12 adults—so grab some friends. ☎ *407/827–7700,* FAX *407/827–7710. 704 units. Restaurant, lobby lounge, snack bar, 4 pools, spa, 3 tennis courts, basketball, health club, jogging, shuffleboard, boating, bicycles, video games, baby-sitting, playground, coin laundry, laundry service. AE, MC, V.*

$$$$ ⊞ **Villas at Disney Institute.** The secret's out: you don't have to stay at a hotel when you come to WDW. If you're holidaying with your family or a group of friends, you might favor this good-value, self-catering option—the five clusters of villas in the Downtown Disney/Lake Buena Vista area (☞ *below*). These share a single check-in point. To get around within the area, a car or rented bike or golf cart is necessary, and buses offer transport to the parks. The accommodations are not quite as plush as those in the resort hotels but are more personal and homey than hotel rooms. And you get plenty of living space: lodgings range from one-story bungalows to two-story town houses. The following five villa complexes—all but the Old Key West Resort—are part of the Disney Institute.

Bungalows. The smallest and least expensive of the villas, these were designed to meet the needs of businesspeople attending meetings at the nearby WDW Conference Center. The accommodations are built of cedar and have one bedroom with two queen-size beds, a daybed in an adjacent parlor, a microwave, a tea- and coffeemaker, and a wet bar, but no kitchen—they're the only villas without one. A few deluxe units with whirlpools sleep six, but most of the suites accommodate five. *316 units.*

Fairway Villas. The name hints at this complex's proximity to the links: these officially titled "Two-Bedroom Deluxe Villas" sit beside the Lake Buena Vista Golf Course, one of WDW's best. Built of cedar like the One- and Two-Bedroom Townhouses (☞ *below*), these spacious guest quarters are more tastefully decorated than those of some of the other Disney Institute villas. Done in muted mauves and blues, each sleeps eight in two bedrooms with two double beds each, a loft with a queen-size bed, and a living room with a Murphy bed. *64 units.*

Grand Vista Homes. These attractively furnished accommodations, originally designed as two-story, 2,000-square-ft condominiums for a housing development, are now available to rent through WDW. All the comforts of a luxury hotel are offered, including nightly turndown service and stocked refrigerators. *4 units.*

One- and Two-Bedroom Townhouses. These facilities have fully equipped kitchens and either one or two bedrooms. The one-bedroom units have a king-size bed in one room and a double Murphy bed in the living room and sleep up to four. The two-bedroom units, which sleep six, have a sofa bed in the living room, a king-size bed in one bedroom, and a queen-size or two doubles in the other. *44 1-bedroom units, 94 2-bedroom units.*

★ **Treehouse Villas.** Take your vacation experience to a whole new level with these out-of-the-way forest retreats on stilts, officially known as the "Two-Bedroom Resort Villas with Study." Isolated within a heavily wooded area ribboned with canals, these won't exactly make you feel like Tarzan or Jane, but the woods do occasionally reverberate with a howl or two late at night. Each villa accommodates six and has a kitchen and breakfast bar, two bathrooms, and two bedrooms with queen-size beds on the main level, plus a double-bedded study. There is a utility room with washer and dryer on a lower level. *60 units.*

For all villas: ☎ 407/934–7639 or 407/827–1100, ⒻⒶⓍ 407/934–2741. *Restaurant, lobby lounge, room service, 5 pools, hot tubs, health club, bicycles, boating, baby-sitting, playground, coin laundry, laundry service. AE, MC, V.*

All-Star Village

Take I–4 Exit 25B.

Resort Hotels

$$–$$$ 🏨 **All-Star Sports, All-Star Music, and All-Star Movies Resorts.** What could Americans possibly love more than Mickey Mouse? Sports and music, perhaps. The two original buildings here carry out five sports themes (baseball, football, tennis, surfing, and basketball) and five music themes (Broadway, country, jazz, rock, and calypso). And in early 1999, a third, 1,920-room resort was added—All-Star Movies, complete with extravagant salutes to *Fantasia, Toy Story, 101 Dalmatians,*

The Mighty Ducks, and *The Love Bug.* Don't worry about being able to tell them apart; gargantuan exterior ornamentation defines each theme. Stairwells shaped like giant bongos frame Calypso, at Sports, you'll find 30-ft tennis rackets striking balls the size of small cars, and in Movies, giant icons of Pongo and Perdita from *101 Dalmatians* and Buzz Lightyear from *Toy Story* fit at the end of each building like giant book-ends. These resorts mark Disney's entry into the economy-priced hotel market, and so, beneath the elaborate packaging, they're basically well-maintained motels. Each room has two double beds, a closet rod, an armoire, and a desk. The End Zone and Intermission food courts offer a predictable selection of fast foods. ☎ *407/939–5000 Sports; 407/939–6000 Music; 407/939–7000 Movies,* FAX *407/939–7333 Sports; 407/939–7222 Music; 407/939–7111 Movies. 1,920 rooms at each. 2 bars, 2 food courts, 4 pools, playground, baby-sitting, coin laundry, laundry service. AE, MC, V.*

IN WALT DISNEY WORLD: OTHER HOTELS

Although not operated by the Disney organization, the Swan and the Dolphin just outside Epcot, the military's Shades of Green Resort near the Magic Kingdom, and the seven hotels along Hotel Plaza Boulevard near Downtown Disney call themselves "official" Walt Disney World hotels. Although the Swan, Dolphin, and Shades of Green hostelries offer the special privileges of on-site Disney hotels, such as free transportation to and from the parks and early park entry, the Downtown Disney resorts simply offer their own transport systems to shuttle hotel guests to the park.

✎ following the text of a review is your signal that the property has a Web site, where you will find details and, usually, images; for a link, visit www.fodors.com/urls.

Magic Kingdom Resort Area

Take I–4 Exit 25B or 26B.

$–$$ ⊞ **Shades of Green on Walt Disney World Resort.** Formerly the Dis-ney Inn, this quiet resort, only two minutes by car from the Magic King-dom, is now operated by the U.S. Armed Forces Recreation Center. Vacationing active-duty and retired personnel from all branches of the armed forces, as well as those in the reserves, National Guard, and ac-tive civilian employees of the Department of Defense, are eligible to stay here, and rates vary with your rank. Flanked by three world-class golf courses, the hotel offers spacious, country-style rooms that ac-commodate up to five in two queen-size beds and a comfortable sleeper sofa. Choose among views of the fairways, lush gardens, or pools. Guests have access to all 99 holes of Disney golf on six courses—Disney's Mag-nolia and Palm golf courses are right next door. ⊠ *1950 W. Magno-lia Palm Dr., Lake Buena Vista 32830-2789,* ☎ *407/824–3600,* FAX *407/ 824–3665. 287 rooms. 2 restaurants, 2 lobby lounges, room service, 2 pools, wading pool, golf privileges, 2 tennis courts, health club, coin laundry, laundry service. AE, D, MC, V.*

Epcot Resort Area

Take I–4 Exit 25B or 26B.

$$$$ ⊞ **Walt Disney World Dolphin.** Two mythical, 56-ft sea creatures
★ bracket the 25-story glass pyramid—one of the tallest structures at WDW—that is the central part of this Michael Graves–designed hotel.

Although this pyramid hardly qualifies as a Wonder of the World, it's a wonder nonetheless. Outside, a waterfall cascades down from seashell to seashell into a 54-ft-wide clamshell supported by giant dolphin sculptures. A mural sprouts giant banana leaves on the coral-and-turquoise facade. Inside, the fabric-draped lobby resembles a giant sultan's tent, and monkey-shape chandeliers are matched by equally jocular palm tree–shape lamps in rooms. The best units overlook Epcot and its nightly fireworks. All rooms have either two queen beds or one king and bright, beach-inspired bedspreads and drapes, along with the Nintendo-equipped television your child probably insists upon. A special club/concierge level has been created, with its own private lounge and plenty of pampering for the guests—at a price. The hotel has an extensive program designed to entertain your kids while you steal some child-free moments, including the Camp Dolphin summer camp and a five-hour evening program called the Dolphin Dinner Club. But you may have difficulty tearing them away from the Grotto Pool and its high-speed water slide. ⊠ *1500 Epcot Resorts Blvd., Lake Buena Vista 32830-2653,* ☎ *407/934–4000 or 800/227–1500,* 𝖥𝖠𝖷 *407/934–4884. 1,369 rooms, 140 suites. 7 restaurants, 3 lobby lounges, room service, 4 pools, beauty salon, 4 tennis courts, exercise room, beach, boating, children's programs (ages 4–10), concierge. AE, D, MC, V.* ☜

$$$$ 🏨 **Walt Disney World Swan.** Facing its twin, the Dolphin, across Crescent Lake, this is another example of the postmodern "Learning from Las Vegas" school of entertainment architecture characteristic of Michael Graves. Two 46-ft swans grace the rooftop of this coral-and-aquamarine hotel, connected to the Dolphin by a covered causeway. (In the middle, you can catch a ferry to Epcot or Disney–MGM.) Guest rooms, in a 12-story main building and two 7-story wings, are quirkily decorated with floral and geometric patterns, pineapples painted on furniture, and exotic bird-shape lamps. Rooms are a bit plusher than at the Dolphin, but the price reflects that. A quiet piano bar near the lobby takes a slightly different approach—most patrons sip rich coffee rather than brandy or highballs. Every guest room has two queen beds or one king, two phone lines (one data port), a Nintendo-equipped television, and a coffeemaker; some have balconies. One of the benefits of the Swan is that guests can avail themselves of all of the facilities and services of the Dolphin as well, including Camp Dolphin, the summer kid's camp, and the Dolphin Dinner club, which will feed and entertain your children for five hours nightly. The newest extra at this big hotel complex is Fantasia Gardens, the 36-hole miniature golf wonderland just across the street. ⊠ *1200 Epcot Resorts Blvd., Lake Buena Vista 32830,* ☎ *407/934–3000 or 800/248–7926,* 𝖥𝖠𝖷 *407/934–4499. 649 rooms, 109 suites. 5 restaurants, 3 lobby lounges, room service, 2 pools, 4 tennis courts, health club, beach, boating, babysitting, concierge. AE, DC, MC, V.* ☜

Downtown Disney/Lake Buena Vista/WDW Resort Area

Take I–4 Exit 27.

$$$–$$$$ 🏨 **DoubleTree Guest Suites in the WDW Resort.** It's probably no accident that there's no picture of the hotel's exterior—lavender and pink with dark blue awnings—on the brochure. The interior is another story. Comfortable one- and two-bedroom suites are decorated in tasteful hues, with gray carpeting and blond-wood furniture. Each bedroom has either a king bed or two doubles, and living rooms have a foldout sofa, so it's possible to sleep 10 if you can stand a spring break–style crowd. Units come with a TV in each room plus another (black-and-white) in the bathroom, a refrigerator, wet bar, and cof-

feemaker; microwaves are available on request. The smallish lobby has a charming feature—a small aviary with birds from South America and Africa. ✉ *2305 Hotel Plaza Blvd., 32830,* ☎ *407/934–1000 or 800/222–8733,* FAX *407/934–1015. 229 units. Restaurant, 2 bars, pool, wading pool, hot tub, 2 tennis courts, exercise room, coin laundry, laundry service. AE, DC, MC, V.*

$$$–$$$$ 🏨 **Hilton at WDW Resort.** Although this isn't the palatial type of property where the Sultan of Brunei stays, it is still a fine, upscale hotel that is well worth what you pay. An ingeniously designed waterfall tumbles off the covered entrance and into a stone fountain surrounded by palm trees so hefty you'd think they were on steroids. Another fountain adorns the lobby, enlivened by shell-shape cornices and two large tanks of tropical fish. Although not huge, guest rooms in bright yellow and mauve are cheery, cozy, and contemporary. Prices vary dramatically from one floor, location, and season to another. A nice new touch is the seafood buffet in the lobby (around 6 PM), which tantalizes with wonderful smells of shrimp and salmon. The Vacation Station, a hotel within a hotel, is aimed at kids. ✉ *1751 Hotel Plaza Blvd., 32830,* ☎ *407/827–4000; 800/782–4414 reservations,* FAX *407/827–6369. 812 rooms, 27 suites. 7 restaurants, lobby lounge, room service, 3 pools, outdoor hot tub, health club, baby-sitting, children's programs (ages 3–12), coin laundry, laundry service, business center. AE, DC, MC, V.*

$$$–$$$$ 🏨 **Royal Plaza.** The hotel bills itself as the place where Burt Reynolds and Barbara Mandrell (apparently experts on what makes a fine hotel) stay when in Orlando. Although it's hard to tell why. It's nice and comfortable and convenient, but it is not, as they say, to die for. You can book the suites where the two celebrities stay—with photos, gold records, and other memorabilia they donated. Otherwise, you'll get a comfortable but not extravagant unit decorated in earth tones with multicolor bedspreads. Each has a terrace or balcony, and the best overlook the pool. The casual, lively hotel is popular with families, and now that its raucous club has been replaced by a quieter bar, it's easier to sleep. If you're a golfer, you'll like the advance reservation privileges at five nearby courses. ✉ *1905 Hotel Plaza Blvd., 32830,* ☎ *407/828–2828 or 800/248–7890,* FAX *407/828–8046. 394 rooms, 21 suites. Restaurant, 2 bars, grill, pool, hot tub, sauna, golf privileges, 4 tennis courts, baby-sitting, laundry service. AE, D, DC, MC, V.*

$$$–$$$$ 🏨 **Wyndham Palace Resort & Spa in the WDW Resort.** This sand-color
★ tower, the largest hotel at Lake Buena Vista, has gone through several identity changes over the years, from adding the Orlando area's biggest health spa a few years ago to becoming Wyndham's flagship property in Orlando in 1998 (before that it was the Buena Vista Palace). The hotel completed a massive refurbishment in 2000 that included a renovation of all guest rooms, plus the construction of huge new meeting and conference facilities, but they didn't change the name this time. No matter what you call it, it deserves the label "luxury" hotel for its on-site charms alone, not to mention that it's in a great neighborhood—about 100 yards from the nearest Wolfgang Puck's (in Downtown Disney). Upper-floor rooms in the main hotel are more expensive; the best ones look out toward Epcot's Spaceship Earth. Suites in the adjacent Island Resort accommodate up to eight. All rooms have balconies or patios. At the Top of the Palace, the club-bar on the 27th floor, anyone there at sunset receives a free glass of champagne and a wonderful view of the sun sinking into the Disney complex. With the change to the Wyndham name, the hotel has added a number of touches, including the Wyndy Harbor Kid's Klub, which will feed and entertain your kids while you dance the night away at Pleasure Island or do whatever else inspires you. ✉ *1900 Buena Vista Dr., 32830,* ☎ *407/827–2727 or 800/327–2990,* FAX *407/827–6034. 1,014 rooms. 4 restaurants,*

4 lobby lounges, patisserie, snack bar, room service, 2 pools, wading pool, hot tub, spa, 3 tennis courts, health club, volleyball, baby-sitting, children's programs (ages 4–12), playground, coin laundry, laundry service, business services. AE, D, DC, MC, V. ✍

$$$ 🏨 **Grosvenor Resort.** The nondescript pink high-rise across from Downtown Disney looks like a Department of Veterans Affairs hospital on the outside but is quite pleasant on the inside. Offering a wealth of facilities and comfortable rooms for a fair price, this resort, designated "an official Walt Disney World property" (not to be confused with the hotels Disney operates itself), is a good deal in the neighborhood. Rooms are average in size but colorfully decorated and filled with amenities, such as an in-room VCR. (Other amenities come à la carte, such as a mini-refrigerator for $6 a night.) Blond-wood furniture and rose-color carpeting give the rooms a homey feeling, and spacious public areas have colonial Caribbean decor. Baskerville's, festooned with Sherlock Holmes memorabilia, hosts a Saturday murder-mystery dinner show. The hotel provides a free shuttle service to all Disney theme parks, and it's within walking distance of Downtown Disney. ⊠ *1850 Hotel Plaza Blvd., 32830,* ☎ *407/828–4444 or 800/624–4109,* ℻ *407/828–8192. 626 rooms, 7 suites. 3 restaurants, lobby lounge, room service, 2 pools, wading pool, hot tub, 2 tennis courts, basketball, volleyball, playground, coin laundry, laundry service. AE, DC, MC, V.* ✍

$$–$$$ 🏨 **Courtyard by Marriott at WDW Resort.** In the tranquil 14-story atrium, accented with gazebos, white-tile trim, and tropical gardens, you can enjoy a gourmet breakfast under white umbrellas. By evening, activity has shifted to the Tipsy Parrot, the hotel's welcoming bar. Guest rooms here are Marriott-modern and feature handy coffeemakers. ⊠ *1805 Hotel Plaza Blvd., 32830,* ☎ *407/828–8888 or 800/223–9930,* ℻ *407/827–4623. 323 rooms. Restaurant, lobby lounge, 2 pools, wading pool, hot tub, exercise room, playground, coin laundry, laundry service. AE, DC, MC, V.*

$$–$$$ 🏨 **Lake Buena Vista Resort Hotel.** Formerly one of the nicest Travelodges you'd ever want to see, this 18-story property changed its name and reinvented itself in 1999, but still offers great amenities for its price range (to become even nicer). Among the best touches are the tropical rain-forest look from its patio restaurant—screened in to keep the mosquitoes from carrying you away—and the great Disney view from its rooftop lounge. Like all the hotels along "Hotel Row" in Buena Vista, this property offers shuttle transportation to Disney resorts, but you can easily walk to Downtown Disney if you want to shop and soak up the nightlife. ⊠ *2000 Hotel Plaza Blvd., 32830,* ☎ *407/828–2424 or 800/348–3765,* ℻ *407/828–8933. 325 rooms. Restaurant, lobby lounge, snack bar, pool, wading pool, playground, coin laundry, laundry service. AE, D, DC, MC, V.*

ORLANDO

Universal Orlando

Take I–4 to Exit 30A.

On a property at Universal Orlando, with an easy hotel entrance off Kirkman Road, this hotel is the first of five planned at Universal, and will shuttle you to the theme park along a man-made canal on a water taxi.

$$$$ 🏨 **Portofino Bay Hotel.** This hotel is not exactly Italy, and it's not exactly a five-star property, but it tries hard to be both, and comes quite close. Picture the Italian Riviera and you might conjure up images of Portofino, with Italian fishermen along the waterfront mending their nets. At Universal's first on-property hotel, there's a faux waterfront on a man-made lake, with a dozen faux fishing boats moored on the 1 acre or so it covers. You'll see the Italian "fishermen" (actually costumed actors) sitting around mending their nets, but these probably won't see fish anytime soon. It's all about atmosphere here. Other Italian touches make a bit more sense, like the gelato machines around the pool that dispense tasty Italian ices, a wood-fire pizzeria, and two great Italian restaurants. And of course, the architecture of the resort will give you that Portofino feeling—it's an exact copy of the little Italian village, complete with the same brightly colored stucco buildings. (One of the great touches is a poolside water slide designed to look like a Roman aqueduct.) With 42,000 square ft of meeting space, the hotel caters to corporate meetings and conventions, and you'll find a lot of unusual amenities, such as poolside cabanas with fax machines and Internet hookups. But this new luxury hotel is also attentive to tourists' needs—some more particular than others: for about $300 a night, you can stay in a "butler" villa and get your own butler to mix your drinks, fix your bed, or pack and unpack your suitcases. If you want to be in a section of the hotel that is a little more kid-free than normal for a theme-park hotel, go for the more expensive villa section. Perks include one-hour early entry to Universal Studios and Islands of Adventure and special VIP access to popular rides. Two of the hotel's restaurants, Mamma Della's and Delfino Riviera, have established themselves as among the better Italian eateries in Orlando. ✉ *1000 Universal Studios Plaza, Orlando 32819,* ☎ *407/224–7117. 750 rooms. 3 restaurants, bar, pizzeria, room service, spa, health club, laundry service, meeting rooms. AE, D, DC, MC, V.*

International Drive

Take I–4 Exit 28 or 29 unless otherwise noted.

If you plan to visit Universal Orlando theme parks or other nearby attractions besides Walt Disney World, the sprawl of newish hotels, restaurants, and shopping malls known as International Drive—"I-Drive" to locals—makes a convenient base. Parallel to I–4, this four-lane boulevard with a grassy, landscaped median punctuated with palm trees is just a few minutes south of downtown Orlando. It stretches from just south of SeaWorld on the south as far north as Universal Orlando on the north, passing Wet 'n Wild, several popular dinner theaters, and the local convention center en route.

Each part of I-Drive has its own personality. The southern end is classier, and south of SeaWorld there's still, amazingly, quite a lot of wide-open space just waiting for new hotels and restaurants to open up; the concentration of cheaper restaurants, fast-food joints, garish T-shirt shops, and inexpensive malls increases as you go north. Universal Orlando is up there but is increasingly a self-contained enclave. For reasonably priced groceries, try the Publix supermarket just east of I–4 at Exit 30 or the Goodings just outside the Disney state line near Downtown Disney.

$$$$ ⊞ **Peabody Orlando.** At 11 AM, the celebrated Peabody ducks exit a
★ private elevator into the marble-floor lobby and waddle across a red carpet to the little marble fountain where they pass the day, basking in high-class fame: eat your heart out, Donald. At 5, to the crowd's delight, the marching mallards repeat the ritual in reverse. Built by the owners of the landmark Peabody Hotel in Memphis, this 27-story structure looks like three high-rise offices from afar, but don't be put off by its austere exterior. The interior is impressive and handsome. The most panoramic of the oversize upper-floor rooms have views of WDW. Across from the Orange County Convention Center, the hotel attracts rock

stars and other performers, conventioneers, and duck lovers. The hotel is expanding and will add 1,000 rooms by the year 2003, and will be connected via an enclosed walkway to the newly expanded Orange County Convention Center. If you are into the health thing, the hotel goes beyond the traditional fitness center. In conjunction with an Orlando hospital, there's actually an in-house wellness center where you can get a complete check-up and analysis of your health. ⊠ *9801 International Dr., 32819,* ☎ *407/352–4000 or 800/732–2639,* FAX *407/ 351–9177. 891 rooms. 3 restaurants, 2 lobby lounges, room service, pool, wading pool, hot tub, spa, golf privileges, 4 tennis courts, health club, baby-sitting, concierge. AE, D, DC, MC, V.*

$$$–$$$$ 🏨 **Caribe Royale Resort Suites & Villas.** This big pink palace of a hotel, with flowing palm trees and massive, man-made waterfalls, looks like a Las Vegas casino hotel. The lobby has a quirky open walkway that looks down on what appear to be restaurant steam tables— a missed opportunity for a garden. Huge ballrooms are designed to attract one of the hotel's two constituencies, corporate conferences. The other marketing target is vacationing families. Key family-friendly ingredients are free transportation to Disney World, 10 minutes away; a huge children's recreation area, including a big pool with a 65-ft water slide; and a full breakfast buffet that features all you can eat of everything from eggs to hot oatmeal. For weary parents, the hotel offers a kids program on Thursday through Saturday nights for $40 per child. The suites all have a TV in each room, a wet bar, and microwave, refrigerator, and coffeemaker in each kitchen area. Plus the resort recently added 120 two-bedroom villas and a 50,000-square-ft meeting center. Take I–4 Exit 26. ⊠ *8101 World Center Dr., 32821,* ☎ *407/238–8000 or 800/823–8300,* FAX *407/238–8088. 1,218 suites, 120 villas. 3 restaurants, lobby lounge, room service, pool, wading pool, 2 tennis courts, coin laundry, laundry service, concierge, convention center. AE, D, DC, MC, V.* 🐕

$$$–$$$$ 🏨 **Embassy Suites Hotel at Plaza International.** The concept of an all-suite hotel that serves a free buffet breakfast and complimentary cocktails, pioneered by the Embassy Suites chain, has proved very popular in Orlando. This particular Embassy Suites has a central atrium with a lounge where a player piano sets the mood. Rooms are comfortably arranged—each unit has a bedroom and a full living room equipped with wet bar, refrigerator, pullout sofa, and two TVs—and, more to the point, the cost is less than that of many single rooms in the area. Two-room suites can sleep up to six. ⊠ *8250 Jamaican Ct., 32819,* ☎ *407/345–8250 or 800/327–9797,* FAX *407/352–1463. 246 rooms. Lobby lounge, indoor-outdoor pool, hot tub, sauna, steam room, exercise room, baby-sitting. AE, D, DC, MC, V.*

$$$–$$$$ 🏨 **Embassy Suites International Drive South.** Another of the all-suite chain of hotels, this member has an expansive lobby with marble floors, pillars, hanging lamps, and old-fashioned ceiling fans. Tropical gardens with mossy rock fountains and palm trees add to the atrium's distinctive Southern ambience. Elsewhere, ceramic tile walkways and brick arches complement the tropical mood. The hotel offers a good number of little extras, like a health club with a fine steam room, free shuttle service to all four Disney parks and Universal Orlando, and free hot breakfast. ⊠ *8978 International Dr., 32819,* ☎ *407/352–1400 or 800/433–7275,* FAX *407/363–1120. 244 suites. Restaurant, lobby lounge, indoor pool, outdoor pool, hot tub, health club, sauna, steam room. AE, D, DC, MC, V.* 🐕

$$$–$$$$ 🏨 **Omni Rosen Hotel.** Created for convention delegates and business travelers, this 24-story, 1,334-room palace is immediately adjacent to the Orange Convention Center but makes a great spot for tourists as well. It's only a five-minute drive from SeaWorld or Universal Orlando,

and it's within easy walking distance of some of International Drive's newer treasures, like the Pointe*Orlando shopping and entertainment center and Ripley's Believe It or Not! There's a massive pool area surrounded by tropical vegetation and a couple of good Caribbean restaurants, including the Everglades Room and Cafe Gauguin, where you can admire a big Gauguin-inspired mural while you eat. If dollars are not something you cling to, the hotel offers three big presidential suites, from which you can see Walt Disney World (a good 10 mi away), but those suites are often booked by visiting corporate chieftains there to use the hotel's own 100,000-square-ft convention center, or the 1-million-square-ft public convention factory next door. Microwaves don't come standard in the rooms, but are available for a fee. ✉ 9840 International Dr., 32819, ☎ 407/996–9480 or 800/204–7234, FAX 407/996–3169. 1,174 rooms, 160 suites. 3 restaurants, lobby lounge, room service, pool, hot tub, massage, health club, laundry service. AE, D, DC, MC, V.

$$$–$$$$ 🏨 **Quality Suites Parc Corniche Resort.** A good bet for golf enthusiasts, the resort is framed by a Joe Lee–designed course. Each of the one- and two-bedroom suites is full of pastels and tropical patterns and has a patio or balcony with a golf course view, as well as a kitchen. The largest accommodations, with two bedrooms and two baths, can sleep up to six. A complimentary full buffet breakfast is served daily, and SeaWorld is only a few blocks away. Located on the newer section of I-Drive that's about 3 mi southwest of the Orlando Convention Center, the hotel is in a little less busy area than some of the properties closer to Orlando. ✉ 6300 Parc Corniche Dr., 32821, ☎ 407/239–7100 or 800/446–2721, FAX 407/239–8501. 210 suites. Restaurant, lobby lounge, pool, wading pool, hot tub, 18-hole golf course, baby-sitting, playground, coin laundry, laundry service. AE, D, DC, MC, V. ✍

$$$–$$$$ 🏨 **Renaissance Orlando Resort at SeaWorld.** Occupying the entire core of the building, the hotel's 10-story atrium is full of waterfalls, goldfish ponds, and palm trees; as guests shoot skyward in sleek, glass elevators, exotic birds—on loan from SeaWorld across the street—twitter in a large, hand-carved, gilded Venetian aviary. It's nice to be greeted with a glass of champagne when you register, but the spacious guest rooms—Central Florida's largest—and luxurious marble bathrooms are even more pleasant. With 185,000 square ft of meeting space in the hotel, the place can sometimes seem like a busy convention hall, but it's in a section of International Drive that is not nearly as crowded (or tacky) as the hotels only a mile up the street. Atlantis (☞ Chapter 6), the formal restaurant, is something of an undiscovered gem. ✉ 6677 Sea Harbor Dr., 32821, ☎ 407/351–5555 or 800/468–3571, FAX 407/351–4618. 778 rooms. 5 restaurants, 2 lobby lounges, room service, pool, wading pool, beauty salon, hot tub, massage, sauna, golf privileges, 4 tennis courts, health club, volleyball, baby-sitting, laundry service, concierge. AE, D, DC, MC, V.

$$$–$$$$ 🏨 **Sheraton Studio City.** The most striking new feature of this renovated, former Quality Inn is a giant silver globe on the roof that makes it look like something suited for Times Square on New Year's Eve. But the hotel takes a Hollywood-theme approach, with ubiquitous movie posters and black-and-white art-deco decor throughout. Because this 21-story building is round, the rooms are a little odd in shape (although your kids may not notice with the in-room video game play stations), but everything above the fourth floor tends to have a great view. The 20th floor has plush luxury suites for those ready to spring for $300 a night for a good view of Universal Studios (directly across I–4) and International Drive (just out the front door). You can easily walk to Wet 'n Wild and half a dozen other International Drive attractions. Or you can mosey up to the top floor bar and enjoy the view from there.

✉ *5905 International Dr., 32819,* ☎ *407/351–2100 or 800/327–1366,* ℻ *407/248–0266. 302 rooms. 2 restaurants, 2 bars, lobby lounge, room service, pool, wading pool, beauty salon, hot tub, laundry service, concierge. AE, D, DC, MC, V.* 🐕

$$$–$$$$ 🏨 **Summerfield Suites Hotel.** "Time to go to bed, kids—yes!—in your own room." How many times have you wanted to say that on your vacation? Sleeping from four to eight people, the one- and two-bedroom units at the all-suites Summerfield are a great option for families. Parents relish the chance for a little peace, and youngsters enjoy the feeling of grown-up privacy and, more important, the chance to control their own TV fate—there's a set in each room. Two-bedroom units, the most popular, have fully equipped kitchens, plus a living room with TV and VCR. Plush landscaping manages to give the place a secluded feel even though it's on International Drive. The hotel frequently offers specials, like a fifth night free, or a free rental car with overnight stays, which are always listed on the hotel's Web site. ✉ *8480 International Dr., 32819,* ☎ *407/352–2400 or 800/830–4964,* ℻ *407/352–4631. 146 suites. Grocery, lobby lounge, pool, wading pool, hot tub, exercise room, coin laundry, laundry service. AE, D, DC, MC, V.* 🐕

$$–$$$$ 🏨 **Enclave Suites at Orlando.** With three 10-story buildings surrounding an office, restaurant, and recreation area, this all-suite lodging is less a hotel than a condominium complex. Here, what you would spend for a room in a fancy hotel gets you a complete apartment, with significantly more space than you'll find in other all-suite hotels. Accommodating up to six, the units have full kitchens, living rooms, two bedrooms, and small terraces with a view of a nearby lake. There's free transportation to SeaWorld, Wet 'n Wild, and Universal Orlando, but Wet 'n Wild is an easy walk from the hotel. ✉ *6165 Carrier Dr., 32819,* ☎ *407/351–1155 or 800/457–0077,* ℻ *407/351–2001. 352 suites. Grocery, 1 indoor pool, 2 outdoor pools, 2 wading pools, hot tub, tennis court, exercise room, playground, coin laundry, laundry service. AE, D, DC, MC, V.*

$$–$$$$ 🏨 **Radisson Hotel Universal Orlando.** When it opened in the mid-1970s, this was the largest convention hotel between Miami and Atlanta. The hotel has undergone a lot of changes since then, including refurbishing all guest rooms, which was completed at the same time Universal's Islands of Adventure opened in 1990. It's still a hotbed of business-trippers, but it's now mixed with a large percentage of theme-park visitors. The we-try-harder attitude and the great location right at the entrance to Universal Orlando make this hotel very attractive to tourists. And don't worry about noisy conventioneers—the meeting and convention facilities are completely isolated from the guest towers. If you happen to be at the hotel on business, the hotel offers a new teleconferencing center from which you can originate live video links with points all over the world. Take I–4 Exit 30B. ✉ *5780 Major Blvd., 32819,* ☎ *407/351–1000 or 800/327–2110,* ℻ *407/363–0106. 742 rooms, 15 suites. Restaurant, deli, lobby lounge, room service, pool, wading pool, hot tub, exercise room, baby-sitting, playground, coin laundry, dry cleaning. AE, D, DC, MC, V.*

$$–$$$$ 🏨 **Sierra Suites Hotel.** The two new Orlando locations of this all-suite hotel chain are designed for the business traveler: personal voice mail, two phone lines, speaker phone, and a good-size work table in each room, plus on-property copy and fax service. Another nice touch is the free local phone calls. But the benefit for families is that you get a lot for your money. Consequently, the Sierra Suites seem ideal for either someone who is in the Witness Protection Program and wants to disappear in Orlando or a family on a budget who wants to maximize what they can spend at the attractions. The full kitchen lives up to the word "full," with a two-burner stove, refrigerator, freezer, coffeemaker, toaster, ice maker, and dishwasher, plus pots, pans, and silverware, everything you'll need to avoid restaurant tabs for as long as you like. The earth-tone decor is warm if not stunning, and the suites all have two queen- or one king-size bed, plus a sofa bed. ⊠ *8750 Universal Blvd., Orlando (I–4 Exit 29) 32819,* ☎ *407/903–1500,* FAX *407/903–1555. 137 suites. Kitchenettes, in-room safes, pool, hot tub, exercise room, coin laundry, laundry service. AE, D, DC, MC, V.* ⊠ *8100 Palm Pkwy., Orlando (I–4 Exit 27) 32836,* ☎ *407/239–4300,* FAX *407/239– 4446. 125 suites. Kitchenettes, in-room safes, pool, hot tub, exercise room, coin laundry, laundry service. AE, D, DC, MC, V.*

$$$ 🖅 **Buena Vista Suites.** This all-suite property, a 10-minute shuttle ride from the Disney parks, is set up to be a headquarters for families on vacation, with some convention and business trade on the side. All suites include two rooms (a bedroom and a living room with a fold-out sofa bed); a small kitchen area with microwave, sink, coffeemaker and refrigerator; two TVs (one with a video player); and two phones. King suites feature a single king bed and an in-room whirlpool bath instead of a second bed. The hotel offers multinight packages that include multiday all-park passes to Disney, typically costing about $500 for four days, including lodging. There's a free hot breakfast buffet, and you can always stock your refrigerator 24 hours a day from the 7 Eleven across the street. ⊠ *8203 World Center Dr., Lake Buena Vista 32830,* ☎ *407/239–8588 or 800/537–7737,* FAX *407/239–1401. 280 suites. Restaurant, room service, outdoor pool, wading pool, 2 tennis courts, hot tub, exercise room, coin laundry. AE, D, DC, MC, V.* ✧

$$$ 🖅 **The Castle DoubleTree Resort.** Although this mid-price hotel is big with U.K. tourists, you won't necessarily think you're in Scotland despite the castlelike qualities, like the tall gold-and-silver color spires and ornate iron gates. With purple carpets and drapes, medieval-style mosaics and arched doorways, the hotel has a pleasant ambience that makes you feel like playing Dungeons and Dragons. And it has its own homespun folklore, including an alleged castle creature, a life-size version of which is found in the hotel lobby. (Smaller versions are for sale in the gift shop, along with all sorts of Disney character dolls.) Of course, there is no dungeon, but there is a great rooftop terrace and an inviting courtyard with a big, round swimming pool. The rooms all have a refrigerator—good for keeping the leftovers from the hotel's Cafe Tu Tu Tango, one of the better restaurants in this part of Orlando. Your kids can eat them in front of the room's Sony Playstation. Because this property hosts a fair number of small-business meetings, it has such amenities as three phone lines in each room, data ports, and personal voice mail. It also has location going for it: it's on a section of I-Drive that's close to Universal Orlando and a good selection of newer, smaller attractions like Ripley's Believe It or Not! ⊠ *8629 International Dr., 32819,* ☎ *407/352–0233 or 800/952–2785,* FAX *407/352–8028. 214 rooms. 2 restaurants, lobby lounge, room service, pool, hot tub, exercise room, laundry service. AE, D, DC, MC, V.* ✧

$$$ 🖅 **Clarion Plaza Hotel.** You'll see no shortage of wide-eye conventioneers sporting name tags at this 12-story hotel alongside the Orange County Convention Center. Yet leisure travelers are gradually discovering both the hotel's prime location and its long list of amenities. Guest rooms are simple but large, with two queen-size beds and a nice little extra: a video-game unit hooked up to the TV. The dining lineup is unusually diverse for a hotel in this price range—there's a new pizzeria, Rossini's—as is the presence of coin laundries on every floor. Harris Rosen, the self-made millionaire who owns this and several other big Orlando hotels, got rich by saving money and figures you might want to as well. The hotel also has a popular nightclub, Backstage, which frequently offers live music. ⊠ *9700 International Dr., 32819,* ☎ *407/352–9700* or 800/627–8258, FAX 407/352–9710. 810 rooms. 2 restaurants, bar, coffee shop, lobby lounge, room service, pool, hot tub, nightclub, baby-sitting, coin laundry, laundry service. AE, D, DC, MC, V.

$$–$$$ 🏨 **Wyndham Orlando Resort.** Originally opened as a big convention hotel more than a decade ago, this former Marriott reconstituted itself as a Wyndham in early 1999 and announced a $36 million expansion and renovation to help it assume its new identity as an upscale resort. In 2000, the hotel opened six new restaurants and lounges, a children's entertainment center, and an upscale shopping court, and completed the refurbishment of all 1,064 guest rooms. What's made this quarter-century-old hotel worth spending all those millions on is the same thing that makes it attractive to vacationers these days: you could almost throw a baseball from the driveway of the hotel and have it land inside the brand-new, $2.6 billion Universal Orlando complex. Hotel management expects room rates to go up once all that new paint and plaster have dried, but for now, the place is a relative bargain. ⊠ 8001 International Dr., 32819, ☎ 407/351–2420 or 800/996–3426, FAX 407/351–5016. 1,064 rooms. 2 restaurants, lobby lounge, room service, 3 pools, hot tub, 4 tennis courts, health club, laundry service. AE, D, DC, MC, V.

$–$$$ 🏨 **Wynfield Inn–Westwood.** If you don't want a room with just the bare essentials yet don't have the budget for luxury, this two-story motel is a find. The rooms are comfy if not spectacular; most have two double beds. Children 17 and under stay free in their parents' room (with a maximum of four guests per room). The hotel is ¼ mi from SeaWorld. ⊠ 6263 Westwood Blvd., 32821, ☎ 407/345–8000 or 800/346–1551, FAX 407/345–1508. 299 rooms. Restaurant, 2 bars, 2 pools, coin laundry, laundry service. AE, D, DC, MC, V.

$–$$ 🏨 **Fairfield Inn by Marriott.** This understated, few-frills, three-story hotel—the Marriott Corporation's answer to the Motel 6 and EconoLodge chains—is a natural for single travelers or small families on a tight budget. It's squeezed between International Drive and the highway and doesn't have the amenities of top-of-the-line Marriott properties, but nice perks such as complimentary coffee and tea, free local phone calls, and cable TV give a sense of being at a much fancier property. ⊠ 8342 Jamaican Ct., 32819, ☎ FAX 407/363–1944, ☎ 800/228–2800. 134 rooms. Pool. AE, D, DC, MC, V.

Downtown Disney/Lake Buena Vista Area

Take I–4 Exit 27.

In addition to the Disney-owned and non-Disney-owned resorts clustered on Disney property not far from Downtown Disney, there are a number of nearby hotels unaffiliated with Walt Disney World. Just outside the park's northernmost entrance, they tend to be sprawling, high-quality resorts catering to Walt Disney World vacationers. Although they share a certain sameness with resorts the world over, they vary in size and price. As a rule, the bigger the resort and the more extensive the facilities, the more you can expect to pay. If you're looking for a clean, modern room, you cannot go wrong with any of them. All are equally convenient to Walt Disney World. One may emphasize one recreational activity more than another, so your ultimate decision may depend on how much time you plan to spend at your hotel and which of your strokes—your drive or your backhand—requires the most attention.

$$$$ 🏨 **Hyatt Regency Grand Cypress Resort.** On more than 1,500 acres,
★   Orlando's most spectacular resort offers virtually every amenity and facility and then some—even a 45-acre nature preserve. Golf facilities, including a high-tech golf school, are first-class. The huge, 800,000-

gallon pool resembles an enormous grotto, has a 45-ft water slide, and is fed by 12 waterfalls. A striking 18-story atrium is filled with tropical plants, ancient Chinese sculptures, and live, tropical birds. Accommodations are divided between the Hyatt Regency Grand Cypress and the **Villas of Grand Cypress** (⊠ 1 N. Jacaranda Dr., Orlando 32836, ☎ 407/239–4700 or 800/835–7377; 146 villas). In the higher price range, this place provides tremendous value. There's just one drawback: the king-size conventions the resort commonly attracts. ⊠ *1 Grand Cypress Blvd., Orlando 32836,* ☎ *407/239–1234 or 800/233–1234,* FAX *407/239–3800. 750 rooms. 5 restaurants, 4 lobby lounges, room service, 2 pools, 4 hot tubs, massage, 2 18-hole and 1 9-hole golf courses, 12 tennis courts, croquet, health club, horseback riding, jogging, boating, bicycles, baby-sitting, children's programs (ages 4–12), laundry service. AE, D, DC, MC, V.* ☜

$$$–$$$$ 🏨 **Embassy Suites Resort Lake Buena Vista.** This is a typical example of the popular all-suite chain. Some locals are shocked by the wild turquoise, pink, and peach facade (clearly visible from I–4, it has become something of a local landmark), but the Embassy Suites Resort is an attractive option for other reasons. It's just 1 mi from Walt Disney World, 3 mi from SeaWorld, and 7 mi from Universal Orlando. The central atrium lobby, loaded with tropical vegetation and soothed by the sounds of a rushing fountain, is a great place to enjoy the complimentary breakfast and evening cocktails. All suites have a separate living room with a sofa that folds out into a bed. ⊠ *8100 Lake Ave., Lake Buena Vista 32836,* ☎ *407/239–1144, 800/257–8483, or 800/ 362–2779,* FAX *407/239–1718. 330 suites. Restaurant, deli, lobby lounge, indoor-outdoor pool, wading pool, hot tub, tennis court, basketball, exercise room, shuffleboard, volleyball, baby-sitting, children's programs (ages 4–10), playground. AE, D, DC, MC, V.*

$$$–$$$$ 🏨 **Vistana Resort.** Consider this peaceful resort if you're interested in tennis. Its clay and all-weather courts can be used without charge, and private or semiprivate lessons are available for a fee. It's also a good bet if your family is large or you're traveling with friends. Spread over 135 landscaped acres, the spacious, tastefully decorated villas and town houses have two bedrooms each plus a living room and all the comforts of home, including a full kitchen and a washer and dryer. This resort, just across I–4 from Downtown Disney, is clearly a hit: in 1999, it added another 239 units, expanding the property by 20%. ⊠ *8800 Vistana Center Dr., Orlando 32821,* ☎ *407/239–3100 or 800/877– 8787,* FAX *407/239–3111. 1,539 units. 2 restaurants, grocery, lobby lounge, 7 outdoor pools, 5 wading pools, 7 hot tubs, miniature golf, 13 tennis courts, basketball, health club, shuffleboard, baby-sitting, children's programs (ages 4–12). AE, D, DC, MC, V.* ☜

$$–$$$$ 🏨 **Holiday Inn SunSpree Resort Lake Buena Vista.** Proving that if children are happy, their parents are happy, this place is as kid-oriented as it gets. Upon arrival, you check in and so do your little ones—at their own registration desk. Off the lobby are a small theater; the CyberArcade; a buffet restaurant, where kids accompanied by adults eat free at their own little picnic tables; and Camp Holiday, a free supervised program (beeper rental available). The family-friendly focus continues in the guest rooms, many of them Kidsuites. A playhouse-style room within a larger room, each Kidsuite has a fun-inspiring theme: magic castles, tree houses, igloos, space capsules, etc. (At night, Max, the hotel's raccoon mascot, will even tuck in kids.) Add a refrigerator, microwave, and coffeemaker, and you have a reasonably priced alternative to typical suites that still provides some privacy. ⊠ *13351 Rte. 535, 32821,* ☎ *407/239–4500 or 800/366–6299,* FAX *407/239–7713. 507 rooms. Restaurant, bar, grocery, lobby lounge, pool, wading pool, 2 hot tubs, basketball, exercise room, Ping-Pong, theater, video games,*

children's programs (ages 4–12), playground, coin laundry, laundry service. AE, D, DC, MC, V.

$$–$$$ 🏨 **Country Inn & Suites by Carlson** The signature lobby fireplace looks a little ridiculous in the Orlando location of this hotel chain, but the in-room amenities and the proximity to Downtown Disney (½ mi) make this place a good bet for either families or adult couples. If you are among the latter groups, there's a one-bedroom suite with in-room hot tub for about $100, or, for families, the same $100 will get you what the hotel calls a one bedroom "Country Kids Suite," with two beds, two TVs (one of which is hooked up for video games), along with a refrigerator and a microwave. Another nice touch can add up to big bucks—free local phone calls, very important if you are calling all over Orlando asking for directions and making reservations. Guests enjoy a free Continental breakfast buffet. There's no full-service restaurant, but the hotel is next door to two restaurants, and within walking distance of a dozen. Shuttle service to Disney parks is provided. ✉ *12191 S. Apopka Vineland Rd., Lake Buena Vista 32836,* ☎ *407/239–1115 or 800/456–4000,* FAX *407/239–8882. 170 rooms and 50 suites. Pool, wading pool, hot tub, exercise room, coin laundry. AE, D, DC, MC, V.* 🍃

$$–$$$ 🏨 **PerriHouse Bed & Breakfast Inn.** Exactly 1 mi from the Magic King-
★   dom as the crow flies, this eight-room bed-and-breakfast on a serene bird sanctuary makes a unique lodging experience in build-it-bigger-and-they-will-come Orlando. PerriHouse offers a chance to split your time between experiencing the nearby attractions and spending quiet moments bird-watching: the 13-acre sanctuary is complete with observation paths, a pond, a feeding station, and a small birdhouse museum. About 200 trees and more than 1,500 bushes have been planted, making it an extremely bird-friendly environment. Here you can awaken to the cries of bobwhites, downy woodpeckers, red-tail hawks, and an occasional bald eagle. Nick and Angi Perretti planned and built the circular house so that each room has an outside entrance. In 1999, they added birdhouse vacation cottages, complete with fireplaces, whirlpool tubs, and king-size canopy beds. A house specialty is a Mimosa cocktail, served to you at the hot tub. ✉ *10417 Centurion Ct., Lake Buena Vista 32836,* ☎ *407/876–4830 or 800/780–4830,* FAX *407/876–0241. 8 rooms. Pool, hot tub. AE, D, DC, MC, V.* 🍃

$$–$$$ 🏨 **Riu Orlando Hotel.** What looks like a brown-brick office building from the outside is actually quite comfortable inside. After traipsing through Orlando's theme parks and malls, what many visitors may want most is to lounge around their living room just the way they do at home. The guest rooms in this six-story complex let you do just that: providing you with big, comfy couches, with a better-than-at-home, big-screen TV fitted with a Nintendo unit. (Rooms also have coffeemakers, irons and ironing boards, and a hair dryer; in-room refrigerators are available for a small fee.) Although there are no cooking facilities in the brightly colored rooms, the hotel operates a big buffet downstairs—a full breakfast, lunch, and dinner at prices ranging from $8 to $16. ✉ *8688 Palm Pkwy., Orlando 32836,* ☎ *407/239–8500 or 888/222–9963,* FAX *407/239–8591. 167 rooms. Restaurant, lobby lounge, pool, hot tub. AE, D, DC, MC, V.*

$$–$$$ 🏨 **Sheraton Safari Hotel.** Sometimes just being different doesn't work, but in this case, management's decision to bring a little piece of Nairobi into the hotel district adjacent to Downtown Disney is a bona fide success. From the pool's jungle motif to the bamboo enclosures around the lobby pay phones, this place feels like Africa. But you'll be happy to know that they didn't go too far. The new conference center will keep some people all business, and guest rooms are tastefully contemporary, with no leopard skins for bedspreads or elephant tusks for furniture. Watch your kids slide down the giant snake water slide in the pool area while you sip drinks at the poolside Zanzibar. ⊠ *12205 Apopka–Vineland Rd., Orlando 32836,* ☎ *407/239–0444 or 800/423–3297,* FAX *407/239–1778. 496 rooms, 96 suites. Restaurant, lobby lounge, room service, pool, hot tub, health club. AE, D, DC, MC, V.* ♨

Orlando International Airport

$$$–$$$$ 🏨 **Hyatt Regency Orlando International Airport.** If you have to catch an early morning flight, this hotel, inside the main terminal complex, is a good idea. Counting the time you spend waiting for the elevator, you're just a five-minute walk from your guest room to the nearest airline ticket counter. And for the bleary-eyed traveler, there's a Starbucks inside the terminal, about 50 yards from the front door of the hotel. Guest rooms have views of either the runways or a 10-story-tall atrium area that's part of the terminal. (The terminal-side rooms all have balconies.) A good northern Italian restaurant on the ninth floor offers both fine pasta and a good view of the 747s coming down the runway, and an in-house health club and swimming pool offer a chance to unwind. Considering the hotel's location it's amazingly quiet. Although no jet engines can be heard, if you leave your sliding glass door open in a room facing the terminal atrium, you'll hear that classic "Mr. Jones, please pick up the green courtesy phone." ⊠ *9300 Airport Blvd., 32827,* ☎ *407/825–1234,* FAX *407/856–1672. 446 rooms. 2 restaurants, lounge, room service, pool, hot tub, health club, laundry service, meeting rooms. AE, D, DC, MC, V.*

$$–$$$ 🏨 **Adam's Mark Orlando.** Located about 5 mi from the airport gates, this hotel is conveniently located between Orlando International and International Drive. And if you like to shop in non-tourist-driven stores, there's a real bonus here. The hotel is connected to one of Orlando's biggest shopping centers, the Florida Mall, an upscale venue with stores such as Ann Taylor and Saks Fifth Avenue, as well as your standard Sears Roebuck, JC Penny, and, of course, a Disney store. The hotel feels quite upscale with its polished marble floors and fountains in the lobby, a good in-house restaurant called Le Jardin, and a pleasant outdoor pool area that seems serene, even though the hotel complex is surrounded by the shopping center parking lot. Typical rooms have either two queen beds or a king and a fold-out sofa, and microwaves and refrigerators are available for a small fee. All rooms have coffeemakers and irons and ironing boards. ⊠ *1500 Sand Lake Rd., at S. Orange Blossom Trail, 32809,* ☎ *407/859–1500,* FAX *407/855–1585. 510 rooms. Restaurant, lounge, room service, pool, hot tub, health club, laundry service, meeting rooms. AE, D, DC, MC, V.*

$$ 🏨 **Best Western Airport Inn & Suites.** Located just over a mile from the front gates of Orlando International, this new hotel (opened in spring 2000) is a good bet for experienced travelers who know the tricks of saving money on travel. The suites can easily sleep four, and have minikitchens, including microwaves and refrigerators. There's no in-house restaurant, but a Waffle House is next door and half a dozen other restaurants are within walking distance. The hotel is about 10 minutes from International Drive. ⊠ *8101 Aircenter Ct., at McCoy Rd., 32809 (Exit 8 from Hwy. 528 W).* ☎ *407/581–2800,* FAX *407/581–2810. 95 rooms. Pool, laundry service, meeting room. AE, D, DC, MC, V.*

KISSIMMEE

Take I–4 Exit 25A unless otherwise noted.

If you're looking for anything remotely quaint, charming, or sophisticated, move on. With a few exceptions, the U.S. 192 strip—a.k.a. the Irlo Bronson Memorial Highway, the Spacecoast Parkway, and Kissimmee—is a neon-and-plastic theme park crammed with mom-and-pop motels, bargain-basement hotels, cheap restaurants, fast-food spots, nickel-and-dime attractions, gas stations, and minimarts in mind-numbing profusion. But if all you want is a decent room with perhaps a few extras for a manageable price, this is Wonderland. Room rates start at $20 a night—lower at the right time of year, if you can cut the right deal—with most costing $30 to $70 a night, depending on facilities and proximity to Walt Disney World. Among the chain hotels—Best Western, Comfort Inn, Econolodge, Holiday Inn, Radisson, Sheraton, Travelodge, and so on—are a pride of family-owned properties, many of which are run by recent immigrants.

Whatever your choice, you will find basic rooms, grounds, and public spaces that vary little from one establishment to the next. Keep in mind that the newer the property, the more comfortable your surroundings. Of course, the greater the distance from Walt Disney World, the lower the room rates. A few additional minutes' drive may save you a significant amount of money, so shop around. And if you wait until arrival to find a place, don't be bashful about asking to see the rooms. It's a buyer's market.

$$$–$$$$ ★ 🏨 **Celebration Hotel.** If it looks like a magnificent hotel built at the turn of the century it is—but in this case in 1999, not 1899. Like everything else in the charming, Disney-created, little town of Celebration, Florida, this 115-room hotel weds the best of the 19th and 20th centuries in one concept. The entrance lobby is what you would find in one of the grand hotels of the Victorian era, with hardwood floors and classic, decorative millwork on the walls and ceilings. Although the rooms have ceiling fans and furniture reminiscent of the early 1900s, they also have a 25-inch television, three phone lines, dedicated data ports, and a six-channel stereo sound system. The "dormer rooms" have romantic little seating areas with a great view of the picturesque downtown and the nearby lake. The three-story property, with a signature lighthouse tower and another old Florida touch—a tin roof—overlooks the lake in the center of downtown Celebration. Within easy walking distance of four very popular restaurants, the hotel also offers its own eateries, the Orange Grove Breakfast Room and the Plantation Dining Room. Guests can enjoy the 65,000-square-ft Celebration Health Fitness Center and the Robert Trent Jones–designed Celebration Golf Course. Even though it's less than a mile south of the U.S. 192 tourist strip in Kissimmee, the setting for this hotel is serene. ✉ *700 Bloom St., Celebration (I–4 Exit 25A) 34747,* ☎ *407/566–6000,* FAX *407/566–1844. 115 rooms. 2 restaurants, lobby lounge, pool, hot tub, exercise room, golf privileges, laundry service. AE, D, DC, MC, V.*

$$$–$$$$ 🏨 **Marriott's Orlando World Center.** To call this hotel massive would be an understatement—at 2,000 rooms, it's one of the largest in Orlando. The lineup of amenities and facilities seems endless—there's even on-site photo processing—but it's a plus for tourists that mitigates the presence of all those conventioneers, who largely pay the freight here. One of the four pools is Florida's largest, and the lobby is a huge, opulent atrium, adorned with 16th-century Asian artifacts. Luxurious villas—the Royal Palms and Sabal Palms—are available for daily and weekly rentals. Take I–4 Exit 26A. ✉ *8701 World Center Dr., Orlando 32821,* ☎ *407/239–4200 or 800/228–9290,* FAX *407/238–8777. 2,000 rooms, 98 suites. 6 restaurants, ice cream parlor, 2 lobby lounges, room service, indoor pool, 3 outdoor pools, wading pool, beauty salon, 4 hot tubs, 18-hole golf course, 8 tennis courts, health club, baby-sitting, children's programs (ages 4–12), coin laundry, laundry service. AE, D, DC, MC, V.*

$$–$$$$ 🏨 **Best Western Suites & Resort Hotel on Lake Cecile.** Of the all-suite hotels on U.S. 192, this complex of four-unit town houses is probably the best. One side of the complex faces the highway; the other overlooks an attractive lake, where you can sail, water-ski, jet-ski, and fish. (Water-sport rentals are operated by vendors next door to the hotel.) Forty units are split-level suites accommodating six persons, with complete kitchens, small living rooms, loft bedrooms, and fireplaces. All others accommodate two and are similar to studio apartments but still have full kitchens and fireplaces. The hotel, formerly a Residence Inn by Marriott, was extensively renovated in late 1998 when it became a Best Western. ✉ *4786 W. Irlo Bronson Memorial Hwy., 34746,* ☎ *407/396–2056 or 800/468–3027,* 𝖥𝖠𝖷 *407/396–2296. 158 units. Pool, hot tub, basketball, playground, coin laundry, laundry service. AE, D, DC, MC, V.*

$$–$$$$ 🏨 **Four Points Hotel Sheraton Lakeside.** This formerly bland property underwent a name change and extensive upgrade in early 1999, giving it new zest. The complex of 15 two-story balconied buildings spread over 27 acres by a small man-made lake offers quite a few recreational facilities from pedal boating to tennis. Each room, available in two double- or one king-size-bed configurations, has a refrigerator and safe. The children's program offers arts and crafts, movies, and miniature golf in a comfortable play area. ✉ *7769 W. Irlo Bronson Memorial Hwy., 34747,* ☎ *407/396–2222 or 800/848–0801,* 𝖥𝖠𝖷 *407/239–2650. 651 rooms. 2 restaurants, deli, lobby lounge, room service, 3 pools, wading pool, miniature golf, 4 tennis courts, exercise room, boating, fishing, children's programs (ages 4–12), coin laundry, laundry service. AE, D, DC, MC, V.*

$$–$$$$ 🏨 **Holiday Inn Hotel & Suites Main Gate East.** Everything seems to be the biggest something in Orlando, and this property is the world's largest two-story Holiday Inn. The service is good, despite the size, but that's not the only reason to stay here. All rooms have TVs with VCRs and kitchenettes. You can rent videotapes and buy snacks and groceries in the lobby, and some of the restaurants serve buffet-style—an added convenience. For kids there's Camp Holiday's kids' program. ✉ *5678 W. Irlo Bronson Memorial Hwy., 34746,* ☎ *407/396–4488, 800/366–5437, or 800/465–4329,* 𝖥𝖠𝖷 *407/396–1296. 614 rooms, 110 suites. Restaurant, bar, food court, grocery, kitchenettes, room service, in-room VCRs, 2 pools, wading pool, 2 hot tubs, 2 tennis courts, basketball, volleyball, video games, children's programs (ages 3–12), playground, coin laundry, dry cleaning. AE, D, DC, MC, V.*

$$$ 🏨 **DoubleTree Guest Suites Orlando Maingate.** The brochure on this resort-hotel complex stretches a point when it says it has the charm of a small village in the Spanish region of Andalusia. The red-tile-and-stucco villas and palm-studded grounds are indeed attractive, but it's the spacious accommodations that are truly noteworthy. Each of the one-, two-, and three-bedroom units has a living and dining area, a kitchen, and two TVs; the three-bedroom villa has 1,200 square ft of living space and sleeps up to eight comfortably. A wonderful small touch are the "welcome" chocolate chip cookies. ✉ *4787 W. Irlo Bronson Memorial Hwy., 34746,* ☎ *407/397–0555,* 𝖥𝖠𝖷 *407/397–0553. 150 villas. Restaurant, grocery, lobby lounge, pool, wading pool, hot tub, tennis court, health club, coin laundry. AE, D, DC, MC, V.*

$$$ 🏨 **Hyatt Orlando Hotel.** Instead of a single tower, this very large hotel consists of 10 two-story buildings surrounding four courts on 56 landscaped acres. Each court is a community with its own heated pool, hot tub, park, and playground at its center. The rooms are spacious but otherwise not memorable. The lobby is vast and mall-like, with numerous shops and restaurants; Fio-Fio is upscale Italian, and there is also a very good deli. If you'll be spending most of your time attack-

ing Orlando attractions, the reasonable rates and convenience—it's the closest independent property to WDW—will more than make up for the unremarkable nature of the place. ⊠ *6375 W. Irlo Bronson Memorial Hwy., 34747,* ☎ *407/396–1234 or 800/233–1234,* FAX *407/396–5090. 922 rooms, 17 suites. 3 restaurants, deli, lobby lounge, sports bar, 4 outdoor pools, beauty salon, 4 hot tubs, 2 tennis courts, exercise room, jogging, playground, coin laundry, laundry service. AE, D, DC, MC, V.* ✎

$$–$$$ ⚑ **DoubleTree Resort & Conference Center.** This sleek, twin-tower, seven-story modern hotel, just a few minutes from WDW's front door, has cheerful guest rooms, large bathrooms, and plenty of extras for the price. It's not fancy, but it is perfectly adequate. Plus there's a special, kids-oriented perk: free cookies for all guests. The best rooms are those with a view of the pool. Two floors in each tower are reserved for nonsmokers. A fair amount of conference business led to its recent name change from the "Inn at Maingate." ⊠ *3011 Maingate La., 34747,* ☎ *407/396–1400 or 800/239–6478,* FAX *407/396–0660. 577 rooms, 6 suites. Restaurant, deli, lobby lounge, room service, pool, hot tub, 2 tennis courts, basketball, exercise room, jogging, baby-sitting, coin laundry, laundry service, meeting rooms. AE, D, DC, MC, V.*

$$–$$$ ⚑ **Quality Suites Maingate East.** This hotel is an excellent option for a large family or group of friends. The spacious rooms, designed to sleep 6 or 10, come equipped with a microwave, refrigerator, and dishwasher. Suites have two bedrooms with two double beds each and a living room with a double pullout couch. A complimentary Continental breakfast is offered, and free beer and wine are served afternoons at the poolside bar. As a bonus, guests get buy-one, get-one-free coupons to Cypress Gardens, Water Mania, Wild Bill's Dinner Theater, and King Henry's Feast. Kids will enjoy the motel's restaurant: a toy train chugs along overhead. No-smoking suites are available. ⊠ *5876 W. Irlo Bronson Memorial Hwy., 34746,* ☎ *407/396–8040 or 800/848–4148,* FAX *407/396–6766. 225 suites. Restaurant, bar, lobby lounge, pool, wading pool, hot tub, playground, laundry service. AE, D, DC, MC, V.*

$$–$$$ ⚑ **Radisson Resort Parkway.** This bright, spacious Radisson may offer
★ the best deal in the neighborhood: attractive setting (amid 1½ acres of lush tropical foliage), good facilities, and competitive prices. Its delicatessen comes in handy when you want to assemble a picnic. Generously proportioned rooms are decked out in tropical patterns, with pastel colors and pineapple shapes carved in white wooden furniture; rooms with the best view and light face the pool with its 40-ft water slide. ⊠ *2900 Parkway Blvd., 34746,* ☎ *407/396–7000 or 800/634–4774,* FAX *407/396–6792. 712 rooms, 6 suites. Restaurant, deli, lobby lounge, snack bar, 2 pools, wading pool, 2 hot tubs, sauna, 2 tennis courts, exercise room, volleyball, coin laundry, laundry service, business services. AE, D, DC, MC, V.* ✎

$–$$$ ⚑ **Best Western Kissimmee.** You certainly can't complain about the price at this hotel overlooking a nine-hole, par-3 public golf course, immediately next door to the property itself. Not surprisingly, this independently owned and operated three-story lodging is a hit with golf-loving senior citizens as well as families. The pools in the garden courtyard are amply shaded to protect tender skin from the sizzling sun. Spacious rooms are done in soft pastels, with light-wood furniture and attractive wall hangings. Units with king-size beds and kitchenettes are available. The hotel's restaurant, Casual Cuisine, serves breakfast and dinner buffet-style, as well as from a varied, full-service menu. ⊠ *2261 E. Irlo Bronson Memorial Hwy., 34744,* ☎ *407/846–2221 or 800/944–0062,* FAX *407/846–1095. 282 rooms. Restaurant, bar, lobby lounge, picnic area, 2 pools, shop, playground. AE, D, DC, MC, V.*

$–$$ ☷ **Comfort Inn Maingate.** This hotel is close to Walt Disney World—just 1 mi away—so you can save a bundle without unduly inconveniencing yourself. Standard rooms are light and airy with a mauve-and-soft-blue color scheme; deluxe rooms, overlooking a landscaped garden, have refrigerators, coffeemakers, and hair dryers. Children 18 and under stay free, and those 10 and under eat free as well. ✉ *7571 W. Irlo Bronson Memorial Hwy., 34747,* ☎ *407/396–7500 or 800/223–1628; 800/432–0887 in FL,* 🖷 *407/396–7497. 282 rooms. Restaurant, lobby lounge, pool, coin laundry. AE, D, DC, MC, V.*

$–$$ ☷ **Parkside Record Inn.** There are campgrounds in these parts that cost more than this simple property—the kind of mom-and-pop operation with few frills and the type of rock-bottom rates that made U.S. 192 famous. Most of the remodeled, clean rooms have refrigerators and microwaves, and all have free HBO and ESPN. Plus there's a Continental breakfast and a heated pool. What the place lacks in luxuries and ambience it more than makes up for with the friendliness of its staff, who'll gladly direct you to equally inexpensive restaurants. And in a recent, if somewhat modest, upgrade, the motel has added a couple of picnic tables and some charming decorations like painted concrete deer, ducks, puppies, and even an ersatz alligator to keep you company on the lawn. In that sense, this is a piece of Old Florida that is fading away. ✉ *4651 W. Irlo Bronson Memorial Hwy., 34746,* ☎ *407/396–8400 or 800/874–4555,* 🖷 *407/396–8415. 57 rooms. Pool. AE, D, MC, V.*

$–$$ ☷ **Quality Inn Lake Cecile.** Although this may not be the Ritz-Carlton, it's quite a pleasant little property and offers some nice amenities for its price range, like a white-sand beach on the lake adjacent to the hotel, plus Jet-Ski rentals and waterskiing. Recent renovations have included new carpeting, mattresses, bedspreads, and 25-inch color TVs in all rooms. And the hotel is 4 mi from WDW. ✉ *4944 W. Irlo Bronson Memorial Hwy., 34746,* ☎ *407/396–4455 or 800/864–4855,* 🖷 *407/ 396–4182. 222 rooms. Food court, pool, beach, coin laundry. AE, D, DC, MC, V.*

$–$$ ☷ **Red Roof Inn.** If you want a clean, quiet room but don't want to gamble on an independent, this three-story chain motel delivers consistently. The small, comfortable rooms are decorated in blues and grays. A big plus are the many fast-food and budget-priced eateries within walking distance. The complimentary daily newspaper and coffee each morning are pleasant surprises. ✉ *4970 Kyng's Heath Rd., 34746,* ☎ *407/396–0065 or 800/843–7663,* 🖷 *407/396–0245. 102 rooms. Pool, hot tub, coin laundry. AE, D, DC, MC, V.*

$ ☷ **Knights Inn–Maingate.** Part of a national chain, this one-story motel, with a prefab, old-world facade, is not exactly an English charmer, but it does offer spacious, clean rooms at budget prices. There are kitchenettes in some rooms. ✉ *7475 W. Irlo Bronson Memorial Hwy., 34746,* ☎ *407/396–4200 or 800/944–0062,* 🖷 *407/396–8838. 120 rooms. Pool, coin laundry. AE, D, MC, V.*

$ ☷ **Park Inn International.** The Mediterranean-style architecture of this property on Cedar Lake is not likely to charm you off your feet, but the friendly staff might. Ask for a room as close to the water as possible. There is a restaurant, but for an extra $10 you can get a room with a refrigerator and microwave. ✉ *4960 W. Irlo Bronson Memorial Hwy., 34741,* ☎ *407/396–1376 or 800/327–0072,* 🖷 *407/396– 0716. 192 rooms. Restaurant, grocery, pool, hot tub, beach, coin laundry. AE, D, DC, MC, V.*

$ ☷ **Sevilla Inn.** This family-operated motel offers good lodging at a great price. Stucco and wood on the outside, the three-story building has standard rooms with cable TV. If you need a place just to drop your bags and get some rest between theme parks, this is a good bet. The pool area is encircled by palm trees and tropical shrubs. ⊠ *4640 W. Irlo Bronson Memorial Hwy., 34746,* ☎ *407/396–4135 or 800/367–1363,* 𝖥𝖠𝖷 *407/396–4942. 50 rooms. Pool, coin laundry. AE, D, MC, V.*

Downtown Orlando

Downtown Orlando, north of Walt Disney World and slightly north of the International Drive area, is a thriving business district with a tourist fringe in the form of Church Street Station. To get there take Exit 41 off I–4 if you're heading westbound, Exit 40 if eastbound.

$$$–$$$$ 🏨 **Four Points Hotel Orlando Downtown by Sheraton.** For 37 years,
★ this hotel was essentially just an adequate property called the Harley (not after the motorcycle), which relied on its location in the middle of downtown, just across the street from Lake Eola—a pleasant place to get away from the tourism district's mayhem. But the hotel changed owners in 1999 and reopened in April 2000 with a massive makeover. The new exterior has 14 gold-leaf domes that give it a distinctive Mediterranean look. The rooms include 48 suites, many of which offer a splendid view of the lake. A club-level floor offers concierge services, and the property is within easy walking distance of any place in downtown Orlando (which isn't very big) including Church Street Station and the Orlando Arena. ⊠ *151 Washington Ave., 33801,* ☎ *407/841–3220,* 𝖥𝖠𝖷 *407/424–7074. 203 rooms, 48 suites. Restaurant, lounge, pool, laundry service, meeting rooms. AE, D, MC, V.*

OUTLYING TOWNS

Travel farther afield and you can get more comforts and facilities for the money, and maybe even some genuine Orlando charm—of the warm, cozy, one-of-a-kind country inn variety.

Altamonte Springs

Take I–4 Exit 48.

Staying among the suburban developments, office parks, and shopping malls of Altamonte Springs may not be as glamorous as dwelling with the Disney characters, but accommodations in this suburb, 45 minutes' drive from the theme parks, cost on average one-third less than comparable lodgings elsewhere in the Orlando area. The suburban atmosphere offers relief from the frantic tourist scene farther south. In addition, the area is convenient to Enzo's on the Lake, one of Orlando's best restaurants, as well as to the jumbo Altamonte Mall. One warning: much of the metro area population lives in this northeastern sector and works in central Orlando; I–4 rush hours can be a big problem.

$$$ 🏨 **Embassy Suites Orlando–North.** What makes this hotel different from others in its chain is its location on the edge of Crane's Roost Lake, which offers fishing and a 1-mi jogging trail around its perimeter. Otherwise, suites are up to the high Embassy Suites standard and look out on a lush, tropical atrium. Although the sound of the waterfalls is soothing, the same can't be said for that of the conventioneers at the tables around them. So for guaranteed quiet, choose a suite on an upper floor. Accommodations are spacious and flawlessly kept, the staff friendly and helpful, and the complimentary cooked-to-order breakfast a great send-off for your busy day. ⊠ *225 E. Altamonte Dr., 32701,* ☎ *407/ 834–2400 or 800/362–2779,* 𝖥𝖠𝖷 *407/834–2117. 227 suites. Restaurant, lobby lounge, room service, indoor pool, exercise room, coin laundry, laundry service, business services. AE, D, DC, MC, V.*

$$–$$$ 🏨 **Hilton Orlando/Altamonte Springs.** Although the emphasis at this eight-story, concrete-and-glass tower is on the business traveler, tourists will also appreciate the hotel's quiet elegance. The comfortable rooms are decorated with dark-green florals and prints. This hotel also has two floors of more pricey one- and two-bedroom executive suites and individual rooms with concierge service; all rooms have ironing boards and hair dryers. An extensive renovation in early 1999 refurbished the guest rooms, lobby, restaurant, and lobby lounge. Weekend specials include Continental breakfast. ✉ *350 S. Northlake Blvd., 32715,* ☎ *407/830–1985 or 800/445–8667,* ℻ *407/331–2911. 322 rooms, 5 suites. Restaurant, lobby lounge, room service, pool, hot tub, health club, laundry service. AE, D, DC, MC, V.*

Lake Wales

Take I–4 Exit 23 and U.S. 27 south.

South of Greater Orlando, this town in the middle of orange country is primarily a good base for visiting Cypress Gardens or Bok Tower Gardens or for people on their way to or from South Florida. It's also a good place to get away from the fast pace and congestion of Orlando and Walt Disney World while still being within about 45 minutes of the parks.

$$$–$$$$ 🏨 **Chalet Suzanne.** This quiet, family-owned B&B is a world away from the world of Disney, a perfect retreat when you've had enough of crowds, noise, and hubbub. Drive past RV parks and orange groves to this little country inn with a style you can't put your finger on. Constructed over time since the 1930s, buildings resemble a Swiss village but are painted in tropical pink and aqua and accented with Near Eastern tiles. The grounds contain everything from a serene "autograph garden" (lined with tiles made by guests in the resort's own ceramic studio) that's a popular spot for weddings to a soup cannery. Some of the lovely antiques-dotted guest rooms have original tile baths, whereas others have whirlpools. The best look out on a lake or garden. But perhaps the biggest treat is a meal in the inn's elegant restaurant, where a six-course dinner is the house specialty and, lucky for guests, breakfast is included. The inn is about 2 mi south of the Cypress Gardens turnoff on U.S. 27. ✉ *3800 Chalet Suzanne Dr., 33853,* ☎ *863/676–6011 or 800/433–6011,* ℻ *863/676–1814. 30 rooms. Restaurant, bar, lake, pool, badminton, croquet, volleyball, private airstrip. AE, D, DC, MC, V.* 🐾

Winter Park

Take I–4 Exit 45.

Winter Park, a small college town and Orlando's poshest and best-established neighborhood, is full of chichi shops and restaurants. If its heart is the main thoroughfare of Park Avenue, then its soul must be Central Park, an inviting greensward dotted with huge trees hung with Spanish moss. It feels a million miles away from Orlando's tourist track, but it's just a short drive from the major attractions.

$$$ 🏨 **Park Plaza Hotel.** Small and intimate, this 1922-vintage establishment—complete with wrought-iron balcony—feels almost like a private home, with such nice touches as complimentary breakfast brought to your room and free valet parking, an important perk in Winter Park, where parking places are as scarce as in midtown Manhattan. The key to a special stay is a front garden suite with a living room. These open onto a long balcony usually abloom with impatiens and bougainvillea and punctuated by wicker tables and chairs to enhance people-watching. Balconies are so covered with shrubs and ferns that they are somewhat private, inspiring more than a few romantic interludes, a member of management confided. This old-fashioned hotel is definitely not for people who want recreational facilities or other amenities—nor is it suitable for young children. Aside from these things, the only downside is the proximity of Amtrak. If you feel the earth move while on a romantic getaway, it could be your companion, or it could just be the train. ⊠ *307 Park Ave. S, 32789,* ☎ *407/647–1072 or 800/228–7220,* ℻ *407/647–4081. 27 rooms. Restaurant, lobby lounge, room service, jogging, laundry service. AE, DC, MC, V.*

8   SHOPPING

When you visit Orlando, you'll notice some less-than-subtle reminders that your return trip may include a moving van loaded with souvenirs: there are billboards, kiosks, street vendors, small gift shops, and massive shopping malls that dwarf the Great Pyramids. The signs are clear that 95% of your vacation budget will end up in a gift-shop cash register. Ca-ching!

S HOPPING IS PART OF THE ENTERTAINMENT at Walt Disney World and throughout the Greater Orlando area. There's something in every price range in virtually every store, so even youngsters on allowances can get in on the act. You'll find everything from specialty stores, gift shops, and flea markets to factory outlets, department stores, and—of course—malls. Shop-'til-you-drop types will be delighted to know that Orlando is packed with malls—and every year there are more and more. It is virtually impossible to step outside your hotel room without seeing a mall or a sign advertising one. Whatever your shopping interests—Pongo and Perdita stuffed toys, Ralph Lauren blue jeans, flea-market finds—the area provides a great opportunity to do a lifetime of shopping in a few days. Most stores accept traveler's checks and major credit cards. And cash.

Updated by
Gary
McKechnie

WALT DISNEY WORLD ®

Naturally, you'll be able to find a surfeit of Disney trinkets in every park. And do you think it's coincidence that Disney merchandisers route guest exits directly into a gift shop? Beyond the obvious Disney film tie-ins, there are more unusual items to be found, such as the Western-style gifts at the Magic Kingdom's Frontier Trading Post. Lookin' sporty in that coonskin cap! For top suggestions within the parks— such as the Emporium, the Magic Kingdom's largest gift shop—*see* Chapter 2, especially the shopping descriptions in the A to Z sections. Outside the parks, there's perhaps even more shopping, offering a wealth of wonderful finds for all sorts of interests. Tennis balls with Mickey Mouse logos, for instance, are available in the pro shops at the Contemporary and other hotels. Keep in mind most Disney stores will hold your merchandise and deliver it free to your room—provided you're staying at a Disney resort.

Shopping Districts

The largest concentration of stores on Disney property is found in the three-in-one shopping and entertainment complex known as **Downtown Disney,** which comprises the Marketplace, West Side, and Pleasure Island, known primarily for its clubs.

Downtown Disney Marketplace

Before it was swept up into what is now Downtown Disney, this pleasant complex of lakeside shops was known as the Disney Village Marketplace (hours generally 9:30 AM–11 PM). Although there are plenty of shopping-only establishments, you can find treasures at other venues, too. (Check out the glow-in-the-dark bats, displayed in a black-lighted room, at either Rainforest Café, for example.) But for pure shopping pleasure, the Marketplace is the best bet at Downtown Disney—or anywhere else in the whole wide World. Here you can find shops selling chocolates and pastries, Disney housewares and artwork, silver and gold, cut crystal, as well as quiet cafés. Two of the larger stores are the family-style **LEGO Imagination Center** (☎ 407/828–0065), featuring an impressive backdrop of large and elaborate LEGO sculptures (sea monsters, tourists, etc.) and piles of colorful LEGO pieces waiting for children and their parents to construct something. The **World of Disney** (☎ 407/828–1451), a Disney superstore to end all Disney superstores, pushes you into sensory overload with nearly a half-million Disney items from Tinkerbell wings to Tigger hats. Of course, there is also Disney as art. There are elegant watches, limited edition artwork, and stylish furniture pieces with a Disney twist.

For those out of cash, there are instant Disney credit applications next to each register. How convenient.

Downtown Disney West Side

Among the standout stores here is **Guitar Gallery** (☎ 407/827–0118), which sells videos, music books, accessories, and guitars, guitars, and more guitars, ranging in price from $199 to $15,000. Keep an eye open for the guitar heroes who drop in prior to gigs at the neighboring House of Blues. **Magnetron** (☎ 407/827–0108), as the name implies, sells magnets—some 20,000 of them. So what's the big attraction? Well, they light up, change color, glow in the dark, and come in every shape, size, color, and character (check out magneto-Elvis). Cigars are kicking ash at the **Sosa Family Cigar Company** (☎ 407/827–0114), a family-owned business with a fella rolling stogies by hand in the front window and a humidor room filled with see-gars. If you're comfortable paying $1,900 for a framed, autographed picture of the cast of *Bonanza*, stop by **Starabilia's** (☎ 407/827–0104). Although prices for the memorabilia run high—you can pay from $195 for a Pee Wee Herman autograph to $15,500 for a rare "Norma Jean" (later Marilyn Monroe) signature—you can't lose any money window-shopping. At 49,000 square ft, the enormous **Virgin Megastore** (☎ 407/828–0222) has a selection as large as its prices. You can find better deals elsewhere, but not every record store has around 150,000 music titles, more than 300 listening stations, 20,000 videos, a 10,000-square-ft book department, 4,500 DVD titles, 2,000 software titles, and a full-service café. Stop by and help Branson make another billion.

UNIVERSAL ORLANDO

Universal Orlando's CityWalk

To spice up the mix of CityWalk's entertainment and nightlife, Universal added a range of stores geared to trendy teens and middle-age conventioneers who can't go back home without a little something. Most stores are tucked between buildings on your left and right when you exit the moving walkway that rolls in from the parking garages, and a few are hidden upstairs. Hours vary but are generally 11 AM–11 PM, closing at midnight on weekends. You can call the shops direct or get complete theme park, nightlife, and shopping information from **Universal Orlando** (☎ 407/363–8000).

Considering someone paid $3 million for Mark McGwire's 70th home-run ball, maybe there *is* a market for sports collectibles. **All Star Collectibles** (☎ 407/224–2380) appeals to sports junkies with one-of-a-kind items and the paraphernalia that professional autograph hounds hound athletes into signing. If you follow Florida sports, the state's college and professional teams are well represented.

It's a shame the '70s had to come back to haunt us but they have, and they're here at **Captain Crackers** (☎ 407/224–2468). This disco fantasyland is bursting with lights and the novelty toys and T-shirts you thought were funny in high school. For a more current twist, it also carries funky Jams World clothing. *Funky.*

When the children are still running 100 mph but the din of Universal has worn you adults down, take a break at CityJazz (a cool club) or duck upstairs to **Cigarz** (☎ 407/370–2999) to smoke a hand-rolled cigar and sip a coffee, cordial, or single malt scotch. So what if it's the middle of the day?

If you can't find a lava lamp at your local mall, you'll find one at **Dapy** (☏ 407/224–2411)—as well as novelty clocks and other trendy items that display a European flair.

Still can't tell if your wedding ring is a cubic zirconia or a 48-carat diamond? Then you won't mind shopping at **Elegant Illusions** (☏ 407/224–2347), where the faux jewelry has creative and nostalgic designs. Only your jeweler will know for sure.

If you appreciate the spectacular designs that nature creates, you're not alone. Merchandise at **Endangered Species** (☏ 407/224–2310) is designed to raise awareness of endangered species, ecosystems, and cultures worldwide. Another draw is periodic appearances by artists, authors, and educators who discuss issues regarding the preservation of the planet. The store sells stuffed animals and T-shirts, prints, and figurines—all with an animal theme.

Tired of asking people the time? Invest in a watch, you cheapskate. **Fossil** (☏ 407/226–1705) has hundreds of hip watches, such as the futuristic, limited edition Brain watch that can save messages and memos, and other more retro designs. There are also leather goods, apparel, and sunglasses.

The idea at **Fresh Produce Sportswear** (☏ 407/363–9363) is to take the color and designs of produce and use them to create bright, comfortable styles for men, women, and children. The style is casual resort wear, all 100 percent cotton.

Borrowing on the magnetic appeal of Downtown Disney's Magnetron (all magnets), **Glow!** (☏ 407/224–2401) sells everything that shines, glows, reflects, or illuminates, from apparel to home decor.

If you absolutely *must* buy a Jimmy Buffett souvenir and can't make it to Key West, then **Jimmy Buffett's Margaritaville** (☏ 407/224–2144) is the next best thing. Although his merchandise is as hard to find as Starbucks coffee, you can stock up on JB T-shirts, books, guitars, margarita glasses, sunglasses, picture frames, license plates, and theme hats (shark, cheeseburger, parrot, and toucan).

Florida has managed to turn a natural detriment (small waves) into an asset—Florida's Cocoa Beach is the "Small Wave Capital of the World." Thus explains **Quiet Flight** (☏ 407/224–2126), where surf- and beachwear and accessories will either confirm you're over the hill or motivate you to take up the sport. It opens earlier than most, at 8:30 AM.

Silver (☏ 407/224–2300) has a great interior—it's designed like the 1930s ship *The Normandie*—and swing music on the speakers creates an Art Deco–era feeling. This store has an impressive line of silver jewelry and accessories such as watches, wallets, silver-plated handbags, and hair clips.

The mother lode of Universal icons can be found at the **Universal Studios Store** (☏ 407/224–2207), located next to Pastamore. Items are branded with recognizable images from TV, theater, and classic films: monsters, Woody Woodpecker, Babe, Curious George, Jurassic Park, Hercules . . . you want 'em, they got 'em.

THE ORLANDO AREA

Factory Outlets

Orlando

The International Drive area is filled with factory outlet stores, most on the northeast end. These outlets are clumped together in expansive malls or scattered along the drive, and much of the merchandise is discounted 20%–75%. You can find just about anything, some of it top quality, but be advised: retailers have learned that they can fool shoppers into believing they must be getting a deal because they're at a stripped-down outlet store. Actually, prices may be the same as or higher than those at other locations.

✎ following the text of a review is your signal that the property has a Web site, where you will find details and, usually, images; for a link, visit www.fodors.com/urls.

Belz Factory Outlet World is the area's largest collection of outlet stores—more than 180—in two malls and four nearby annexes, plus a third set of shops, the Belz Designers Outlet, which opened in 1999. A good place to find discount name-brand clothes for the whole family, the complex includes such stores as Maidenform, Danskin, Jonathan Logan, Calvin Klein, Van Heusen, Burlington Brands, Bugle Boy, Gap, OshKosh, Bally Shoes, Bass Shoes, Etienne Aigner, and Banister. Especially popular are the outlets for athletic shoes: Converse, Reebok, Foot Locker, and Nike. There are also good buys in housewares and linens in such outlets as Pfaltzgraff, Corning/Revere, Mikasa, and Fitz & Floyd. Don't worry about carting home breakable or cumbersome items; these stores will ship your purchases anywhere in the United States by UPS. Although the mall isn't fancy, it is clean and pleasant. Mall 2 offers a carousel for children and an adequate food court. The information booth sells discount tickets to all the non-Disney theme parks. ✉ 5401 W. Oak Ridge Rd., at northern tip of International Dr., ☎ 407/354–0126 or 407/352–9611. ☉ Mon.–Sat. 10–9, Sun. 10–6. ✎

Duffers, both foreign and domestic, love all the locations of the **Edwin Watts Golf Shop,** a no-handicap shop for golfing equipment. ✉ 7501 Turkey Lake Rd., ☎ 407/345–8451; ✉ 7024 International Dr., ☎ 407/352–2535; ✉ 8330 S. International Dr., ☎ 407/351–1444. ☉ Weekdays 9:30–8, Sat. 9:30–6, Sun. noon–5.

Quality Outlet Center and Quality Center East, two interconnected strip shopping centers, contain more than 20 brand-name, factory-outlet stores, including Samsonite, Great Western Boots, Corning/Revere, Royal Doulton, Dockside Imports, Florsheim Shoes, Laura Ashley, and Mikasa. ✉ 5409 and 5529 International Dr., 1 block north of Kirkman Rd. ☉ Mon.–Sat. 9:30–9, Sun. 11–6.

Special Tee Golf sells discounted golf and tennis equipment and sportswear at several locations, two of which are along the I-Drive tourist corridor. ✉ 5400 International Dr., ☎ 407/352–3673; ✉ 8747 International Dr., ☎ 407/363–1281; ✉ 1233 W. Sand Lake Rd., ☎ 407/251–6363. ☉ Mon.–Sat. 9:30–8, Sun. 11–5. ✎

The huge, multilevel **Sports Dominator** could probably equip all the players of Major League Baseball and the NFL, NBA, and NHL combined. Each sport receives its own section, crowding the floor with soccer balls, golf clubs, catcher's mitts, jerseys, bows, and a few thousand more sports items. The prices may not be less than anywhere else, but the selection is a winner. ✉ 6464 International Dr., ☎ 407/354–2100. ☉ Daily 9 AM–10 PM.

A great place for jeans, the **World of Denim** carries Levi's, Lee, Chaps, Ralph Lauren, DKNY, Tommy Hilfiger, Wrangler, Guess?, and Calvin Klein. Although the selection in children's sizes is limited, most women's and men's sizes can be found, especially with the assistance of the many sales clerks, who are ready to help you dig through the stacks. A seamstress will make free alterations while you wait; it takes only 10 minutes if you're first, but much longer if there's a line. The Mercado location

268

Shopping

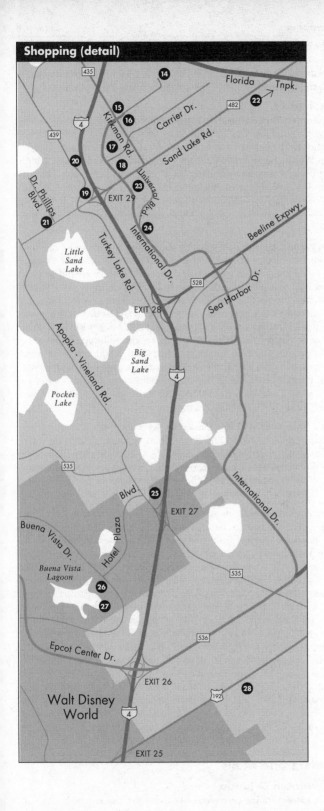

Shopping (detail)

is the largest of the three and, strangely, the Pointe*Orlando location's name is **Denim Place.** ✉ 7623 International Dr., ☎ 407/351–5704; ✉ 8255 International Dr. (Mercado), ☎ 407/345–0263; ✉ 9101 International Dr. (Pointe*Orlando), ☎ 407/248–8444. ⊙ Daily 9 AM–midnight.

Kissimmee

Kissimmee Manufacturers' Outlet Mall doesn't look too appealing from the road, but this strip shopping center contains a nice selection of shops. The nearly 25 stores include Bass, Samsonite, Van Heusen, Bon Worth, Bugle Boy, Publisher's Outlet, Nike, Fieldcrest Cannon, and Brand Name Shoes, carriers of Reebok and L.A. Gear. The mall is off U.S. 192, 1 mi east of Route 535. ✉ 4673 W. Hwy. 192, ☎ 407/396–8900. ⊙ Mon.–Sat. 10–9, Sun. 11–5.

Flea Markets

Flea World claims to be America's largest flea market under one roof. More than 1,600 booths lend credence to the claim, but so much abundance sometimes means only that good bargains are hiding under unusually large piles of junk. Unlike flea markets in some areas, this one sells only new merchandise—everything from car tires, Ginsu knives, and pet tarantulas to gourmet coffee, leather lingerie, and beaded evening gowns. It's also a great place to buy cheap Florida and Mickey Mouse T-shirts. A free newspaper, distributed at the parking lot entrance, contains a map and directory. Children are entertained at Fun World next door, which offers two unusual miniature golf courses, arcade games, go-carts, bumper cars, bumper boats, kiddie rides, and batting cages. ✉ 3 mi east of I–4 Exit 50 on Lake Mary Blvd., then 1 mi south on U.S. 17–92, Sanford, ☎ 407/321–1792. 🎟 Free. ⊙ Fri.–Sun. 9–6.

With 400 booths, **192 Flea Market Outlet** is about one-quarter the size of Sanford's Flea World, but it's much more convenient to the major Orlando attractions and is open daily. The all-new merchandise includes "tons of items": toys, luggage, sunglasses, jewelry, clothes, beach towels, sneakers, electronics, and the obligatory T-shirts. ✉ 4301 W. Vine St. (Hwy. 192), Kissimmee, ☎ 407/396–4555. ⊙ Daily 9–6.

Renninger's Twin Markets may be Florida's largest gathering of antiques and collectibles dealers. At the top of the hill, 400 flea market dealers sell household items, thingamabobs, garage sale surplus, produce, baked goods, pets, and anything else you can think of. At the bottom of the hill, 200 antiques dealers set up shop to sell ephemera, old phonographs, Deco fixtures, antique furniture, and other stuff Granny had in her attic. If you're smart, you'll hit the flea market first, because that's where antiques dealers find many of their treasures. Both markets are open every weekend, but on certain weekends, the antiques market has Antique Fairs, attracting about 500 dealers. The really big shows, however, are the three-day Extravaganzas, which draw 1,400 dealers. These events can be all-day affairs; otherwise spend the morning at Renninger's and then move on to downtown Mount Dora in time for lunch. ✉ U.S. 441, Mount Dora, ☎ 352/383–8393. 🎟 Markets and Antique Fairs free, Extravaganzas $10 Fri., $5 Sat., $3 Sun. ⊙ Markets weekends 9–5; Antique Fairs Mar.–Oct., 3rd weekend of month 7–5; Extravaganzas Nov., Jan., and Feb. (3rd weekend), Fri. 10–5, weekends 7–5. 🍽

Shopping Centers and Malls

Downtown Orlando
Church Street Station Exchange came to life as a decorative, brassy, Victorian-theme "festival marketplace." Although the fittings are still in

place, the arrival of CityWalk and Downtown Disney have siphoned off many of the shoppers. The result is vacant storefronts that the new owners, a British concern, hope to fill when they open a haunted house on the third floor. In the meantime, some stores such as Victoria's Secret still occupy the first floor and across the street is Bumby Emporium, a Church Street souvenir shop, and Buffalo Trading Company, where you can buy string ties, cowboy hats, and snakeskin boots. Daytime is slow as molasses, so you may enjoy shopping here at night better. ⊠ *Church St. Station, 129 W. Church St.,* ☎ *407/422–2434.* ⊘ *Daily 11–11.*

Church Street Marketplace is an outdoor mall-style collection of stores and restaurants such as Brookstone and the Sharper Image. Along with a smattering of jewelry, hot dog, and coffee kiosks, there are other retailers such as B. Dalton, Behr's Chocolates, Cigarz, and Hit or Miss. Dining and drinking options include the Olive Garden, Hooter's, Amura Sushi Bar, Friday's American Bar, and Jungle Jim's. For entertainment, there's Howl at the Moon, a sing-along nightclub—but the free show's just watching the crowds on Church Street. ⊠ *55 W. Church St.,* ☎ *407/841–8000.* ⊘ *Weekdays 10–10, weekends 10–6 (but actually much later); restaurant and bar hrs vary.*

At **Orlando Fashion Square,** Dillard's, JCPenney, and Sears Roebuck are the anchors for 165 specialty shops, including such chain stores as Camelot Music, Gap, Lerner, and Lechters. Wicks N' Sticks sells candles; local entrepreneur Selma serves delicious (and eponymous) Selma's Cookies; and, just in case you missed something at the home of the Mouse, there's a large Disney Store. If you didn't get lunch, there's a large, popular food court. The mall is 3 mi east of I–4 Exit 41. ⊠ *3201 E. Colonial Dr.,* ☎ *407/896–1131.* ⊘ *Mon.–Sat. 10–9, Sun. 11–6.*

International Drive Area, Orlando

Florida Mall was the largest mall in Central Florida, and when they tacked on an additional ½-million square ft it became even larger. There's 1.6 million square ft of shopping action here, friends, and here's what you'll get: Burdines; Sears Roebuck; JCPenney; Parisian; Dillard's; Saks Fifth Avenue; 250 specialty shops, kiosks, and carts; seven theaters; and a 17-restaurant food court as well as four sit-down restaurants including Ruby Tuesday, California Cafe, Paradise Bakery, and a Pebbles Cafe in Saks Fifth Avenue. Of the 48 new stores, roughly half are new to the Orlando area, such as Restoration Hardware, J. Crew, Pottery Barn, Brooks Brothers, Cutter & Buck, Harry & David Gourmet Foods, Swarovski, and Mystique. The huge Warner Bros. Store is another example of Bugs Bunny's quest to outshine Mickey. There are concierge service and stroller and wheelchair rentals, and because the mall attracts crowds of Brazilian and Puerto Rican tourists, there is foreign language assistance, too. The mall is minutes from the Orlando International Airport and 4½ mi east of I–4 and International Drive at the corner of Sand Lake Road and South Orange Blossom Trail. If you can't get enough shopping in, stay the night at the 510-room Adam's Mark Hotel, which has its own mall entrance. ⊠ *8001 S. Orange Blossom Trail,* ☎ *407/851–6255.* ⊘ *Mon.–Sat. 10–9:30, Sun. 11–6.* ⊛

A neighborhood shopping center not to be confused with Downtown Disney's Marketplace, this **Marketplace** is closer to I-Drive and provides all the basic necessities in one spot. Stores include a pharmacy, post office, one-hour film processor, stationery and card store, bakery, dry cleaner, hair salon, optical shop, natural-food grocery, and 24-hour supermarket. Also in the Marketplace are three popular restaurants: Christini's, Enzo's, and the Phoenician. Take the I–4 Sand Lake Road exit and head west. ⊠ *7600 Dr. Phillips Blvd.,* ☎ *no phone.* ⊘ *Hrs vary.*

The Mercado is a Mediterranean-style relaxation stop for bus tours and tourists meandering along International Drive. It houses more than 60 specialty shops, such as American Cola Company, which offers Coca-Cola and Anheuser-Busch memorabilia; and Earth Matters, a shop for environmentalists that sells items with a wildlife theme. An international food court plus seven restaurants are found along the walkway that circles the festival courtyard, where live entertainment can be enjoyed at various times throughout the day. The Mercado's latest arrival, *Titanic*—Ship of Dreams, The Exhibition (☎ 407/248–1166), tells the story of the doomed ship and passengers with meticulously crafted full-scale reproductions and rare artifacts. At $16.95 for adults and $11.95 for children 6–12, you'd expect them to throw in DiCaprio. ✉ *8445 International Dr.,* ☎ *407/345-9337.* ⊙ *Daily 10–10.*

Pointe*Orlando is the latest arrival to the I-Drive corridor and a "lifestyle entertainment center" (also known as an outdoor mall) that is trying to turn International Drive—long considered a strip of substandard tourist shops—into Florida's 5th Avenue. In addition to WonderWorks and the enormous Muvico Pointe 21 theater, the massive complex near the Peabody Orlando and Orange County Convention Center is home to 70 specialty shops, including A/X Armani Exchange, Abercrombie & Fitch, Foot Locker Superstore, Chico's, Dan Marino's Town Tavern, and Johnny Rockets, and a few dozen pushcart vendors selling hair ribbons, sunglasses, and other small items. The focal point, however, is the mighty impressive F. A. O. Schwarz, the legendary store that features every toy you can imagine—75% of them exclusive to F. A. O. Considering you'll have to pay to park, the nearby ATM is more than convenient. ✉ *9101 International Dr.,* ☎ *407/248-2838.* ⊙ *Daily 10 AM–11 PM.* ✎

Kissimmee

The **Old Town** shopping-entertainment complex features more than 70 specialty shops and restaurants, re-creating a turn-of-the-20th-century Florida village. You can buy a 25¢ Pepsi at the General Store, watch the taffy maker at Coffelt's Taffy & Chocolates or the candle maker at Kandlestix, and, at Black Market Minerals, pan for gemstones and sharks' teeth or buy agate, onyx, quartz, or even dinosaur fossils. Every Saturday night there is a parade of 300–500 classic automobiles. ✉ *5770 W. Irlo Bronson Memorial Hwy.,* ☎ *407/396-4888 or 800/843-4202.* ⊙ *Daily 10 AM–11 PM.*

Lake Buena Vista

Directly across from the Lake Buena Vista Village entrance to Walt Disney World, the conveniently located **Crossroads of Lake Buena Vista** contains 11 restaurants and more than 25 shops catering primarily to tourists. Upscale and casual shops are geared toward sun and surf, electronics, and children, but the necessities, such as the carpeted 24-hour Gooding's supermarket, post office, bank, and cleaners, are also here. Although you'll find the usual franchised restaurants, there are also some local spots, such as the casual Pebbles. While you shop, your offspring can entertain themselves at Pirate's Cove Adventure Golf. Take I-4 Exit 27. ✉ *12545–12551 Rte. 535,* ☎ *407/827-7300.* ⊙ *Stores daily 10–10; restaurant hrs vary.*

Northern Suburbs

Seminole Towne Center answers the shopping needs of Orlando's burgeoning northern suburbs. Anchored by Dillard's, Sears Roebuck, JCPenney, Burdines, and Parisian, the mall contains more than 120 retailers, including branches of major chain stores such as Ann Taylor, Eddie Bauer, Gap, Foot Locker, and Victoria's Secret. For something tropical, try A Shop Called Mango, owned by singer Jimmy Buffett.

And just in case you missed something in the theme parks, there's a branch of the Disney Store here. Strollers and wheelchairs are available for rent. There's a pretty good food court, too, and the surrounding strip malls aren't as unappealing as others in Orlando. The mall is ¼ mi east of I–4 Exit 51 and south of Route 46. ⊠ *200 Towne Center Circle, Sanford,* ☎ *407/323–2262.* ⊙ *Mon.–Sat. 10–9, Sun. noon–6.*

Shopping Districts

Orlando's Antique Row

Although not known as a mecca for antiques hunters, Orlando has a small but thriving antiques row just north of downtown on North Orange Avenue. This is a great spot to spend a Saturday afternoon before hitting downtown nightclubs. Get off I–4 at Exit 43, take Princeton Avenue east to North Orange Avenue, and turn right.

A&T Antiques prides itself on having the area's largest selection of antiques, although that doesn't matter unless you're looking for European and country pine furniture and decorative pieces. ⊠ *1620 N. Orange Ave.,* ☎ *407/896–9831.* ⊙ *Weekdays 9–6, Sat. 10–5.*

A wonderful neighborhood store, **Flo's Attic** sells furniture, pottery, china, jewelry, and other treasures. There's lots of stuff to sort through. ⊠ *1800 N. Orange Ave.,* ☎ *407/895–1800.* ⊙ *Mon.–Sat. 9–5.*

Ivanhoe Row, a group of shops near downtown Orlando, sells mostly delightful but pricey antiques. The Fly Fisherman specializes in accoutrements for the angler; you can often spot salesperson and customer testing out a rod and reel in Lake Ivanhoe, across the street. Swanson's Antiques carries a fine selection of 19th- and 20th-century furniture and bric-a-brac. Wildlife Gallery offers paintings and sculptures of various members of the animal kingdom. Other shops include the William Moseley Gallery (19th-century oil paintings), Tim's Wine Mart (hundreds of labels), Jarboe (upscale women's fashions), and Christopher Jude (upscale men's clothing). After antiquing, cross the street and take a stroll in the beautiful park surrounding Lake Ivanhoe. ⊠ *1211–1231 N. Orange Ave.,* ☎ *407/898–6050.* ⊙ *Weekdays 10–6, Sat. 10–5.*

If you're wondering where old vinyl records have gone, they're at **Rock 'n' Roll Heaven.** Crammed with rare albums, 45s, rock paraphernalia, board games, and sheet music, the shop is fun for the curious and a must-see for collectors. The Ehmen brothers are devoted to the genre and take pride in selling only mint-condition platters. ⊠ *1814 N. Orange Ave.,* ☎ *407/896–1952.* ⊙ *Mon.–Sat. 10–7:30.* ✎

Mount Dora

If you love antiques or if you're just tired of theme parks, treat yourself to a day here. Founded by homesteaders in 1874, this charming little town has 19th-century stores and houses tucked into rolling hills that overlook Lake Dora. The New England–style village is recognized as the Antiques Capital of Florida and also Festival City for its art, antiques, and crafts shows that take place nearly every weekend in the fall, winter, and spring. There are dozens of crafts shops, boutiques, galleries, and antiques shops here—and more opening nearly every day. Country Pine Newtiques, in the renovated Princess Theatre, has an extensive selection of Tom Clark gnomes, scented candles, peaceful music, and other collectibles.

When you're done shopping, get a bite at any of Mount Dora's varied eating establishments, from the Windsor Rose Tea Room and the

Beauclaire Dining Room, in the historic Lakeside Inn (sit on the wide veranda and watch the sun set over Lake Dora), to the Goblin Market (creative cuisine in a renovated garage) and Eduardo's Mexican & American Cantina, whose open-air setting is better than its food. Look for Shiraz bistro, which serves tasty urban cuisine in a nice, quiet setting. It's hidden upstairs in a retail complex. Mount Dora is west of U.S. 441 on Old U.S. 441 or Route 44B. Contact the **Chamber of Commerce** (☎ 352/383–2165, ✍) for more information.

Winter Park

In the more than 100 years since rich northern families started building grand estates in this swank Orlando suburb, **Park Avenue** has become a favorite for tony shopping. Although longtime residents complain that the avenue is beginning to resemble a mall—as local one-of-a-kind stores are replaced by chains such as a ladies-only Banana Republic, Gap, and Ann Taylor—visitors are usually charmed by this posh shopping district, with its tiny courtyards ringed by chic restaurants (perfect for people-watching), galleries, bookstores, and other little shops.

In the summer of 1999, a multimillion-dollar restoration of the avenue was completed, adding wider sidewalks, hanging plants, vintage street-lamps, spruced up landscaping, and red bricks replacing black asphalt.

For shoppers and nonshoppers alike the real fun of Park Avenue is exploring the little nooks and crannies that divert you from the main drag. Between Welbourne and Morse avenues, around the corner from Barnie's Coffee, you'll find Greeneda Court. A walk to the back reveals a delightful fountain and wrought-iron tables and chairs where you can sit and relax with a cappuccino from Barnie's. Of course, the antiques store hidden there could keep you on your feet. In the middle of the next block, wedged in between Victorian Joy (No. 316), a children's boutique with designer clothing, and the Rune Stone, a European toy store that adults enjoy as much as the kids, is the Hidden Garden Shops, which houses Pooh's Corner, a delightful children's bookstore specializing in hard-to-find titles. Also look for Wood, Stone and Steel, which carries culinary tools and tabletop items. Scott Laurent Gallery showcases the works of more than 150 Central Florida artists and artisans, including paintings, original jewelry, original and limited-edition framed art, sculpture, art glass, fountains, and decorative gifts. The third weekend in March brings the Winter Park Sidewalk Art Festival. More than 40 years after its debut, it still attracts thousands of art aficionados and a few hundred of America's better artists. ⊠ *Park Ave., between Fairbanks and Canton Aves.* ☉ *Most shops Mon.–Sat. 10–5, some also Sun. noon–5.*

If you happen to be in town on Saturday morning, you might want to walk over to the **Farmers' Market,** next to the downtown train depot, two blocks west of Park Avenue. A long-standing tradition, this market shows the real community that exists behind the upper-crust facade. Friends and neighbors gather to shop for fresh fruits and vegetables, breads and pastas, fish, sausage, herbs and spices, and a colorful array of fresh flowers and tropical plants. Early risers nibble on tangerines, oranges, avocados, and strawberries or drop by for a breakfast of pastries, bagels, rolls, or crepes served with a cup of hot chocolate, espresso, or spiced tea. ⊠ *New England and New York Aves.,* ☎ *407/ 623-3358.* ☉ *Sat. 7–1.*

9 SPORTS AND THE OUTDOORS

There's more to an Orlando workout than walking 10 miles a day in the theme parks and swimming in the hotel pool. Warm Florida weather encourages outdoor sports, with golf, tennis, boating, and fishing leading the way.

Updated by
Rowland
Stiteler

O RLANDO IS THE PLACE TO VISIT if you want to be outside, whether you canoe, hike, fish, or beachcomb. You'll find just about every outdoor sports opportunity here—unless it involves a ski lift—that you'll find anywhere else in the country. There are plenty of tennis courts and more than 130 golf courses in a 40-mi radius, staffed by nearly three dozen PGA pros, and some of the world's best-known golfing champions—huge names such as Arnold Palmer and Tiger Woods—have homes in the Orlando area. Anglers have their own place in the Orlando sun as well, on the dozens of small lakes, and the metropolitan area is home to as many big-league professional bass fishermen as it is to big-league baseball stars and PGA golf luminaries. Predictably, boating is popular, both on the literally hundreds of lakes and on the scores of backcountry rivers fed by clear, warm springs.

Orlando also holds a hot ticket as a professional sports town. The Orlando Magic basketball team is big time, and now the city has a team in the Women's National Basketball Association (WNBA), the Orlando Miracle, which plays a summer schedule in the Orlando Arena. True baseball fans have plenty of minor-league action to enjoy. The five-year-old International Hockey League franchise, the Orlando Solar Bears, has already established a rabid fan base, and in 1996 Disney started upping the ante. It added the Walt Disney Speedway, the home of Indy 200 as well as of the Richard Petty Driving Experience, followed, in 1997, by Disney's Wide World of Sports. This complex accommodates tournament-type events in more than 25 individual and team sports, serves as the spring-training home of the Atlanta Braves, and offers participatory sports—basketball, softball, and track and field events—for visiting groups. Two key sources for sports information on all things Disney are the **sports information/reservations hot line** (☎ 407/939–7529) and the **Disney sports and recreation Web site** (☜).

☜ following the text of a review is your signal that the property has a Web site, where you will find details and, usually, images; for a link, visit www.fodors.com/urls.

ACTION!

Auto Racing

If you've always wanted to ride in or even drive a NASCAR-style stock car on a real race track, head to the **Richard Petty Driving Experience** (⊠ Walt Disney Speedway, ☎ 800/237–3889, ☜). Depending on what you're willing to spend—and the cost ranges from $90 to $2,200—you can do everything from being a passenger for three laps on the 1-mi track to taking 1½ days of lessons, culminating in your very own solo behind the wheel. Although even the cheapest option works out to $30 per mi—about the cost of a New York City cab and somewhat less dangerous—it's a one-of-a-kind experience. The Richard Petty organization recently opened a second Central Florida location at the Daytona International Speedway, but it could best be termed as the "Richard Petty Riding Experience," since it involves riding in the car with an experienced race car driver, rather than driving a car yourself.

Biking

Walt Disney World

The most scenic bike riding in Orlando is on Walt Disney World property, along roads that take you past forests, lakes, golf courses, and Disney's wooded resort villas and campgrounds. Most rental locations not only have regular bikes for adults but smaller bikes with training wheels for children and bikes with baby seats. And Disney's lawyers are always watching out for liability problems—helmets are free with all bike rentals, and management asks that you wear them. Bikes are available for rent at **Caribbean Beach Resort Marina** (☎ 407/934–2850) for $6 per hour. Rentals at Disney's **Coronado Springs Resort** (☎ 407/939–1000) are $5.66 per hour, $13.20 per day. Coronado Springs has an odd collection of other rental bikes you don't find at other locations. A two-seat surrey bike, a four-wheel bike designed to look like an old-fashioned carriage, rents for $14.98 per half hour. A four-seat surrey bike rents for $17.12 per half hour. You must be at least 18 to sign a rental agreement. At **Fort Wilderness Bike Barn** (☎ 407/824–2742), bicycles cost $5.66 per hour, $13.20 a day.

Theoretically, bike rentals are only for those lodging on WDW property; in practice, rental outfits usually check ID's only in busy seasons. However, bikes must be used only in the area in which you rent them. Although you have to be 18 to rent a bike at other Disney locations, the Fort Wilderness Bike Barn will rent you one when you've reached the Old Testament marrying age—12. Rentals at the **Villas at Disney Institute** (☎ 407/827–6905) run $5.66 an hour, $13.20 a day.

Elsewhere
For years, Orlando was not much of a bicyclist's town, with no bike trails to speak of and a tough stand on riding bikes on sidewalks. But things have changed. The city now has two good bike trails that have been created from former railroad lines.

The biggest, the **West Orange Trail,** runs some 19 mi through western Orlando and the neighboring towns of Winter Garden and Apopka. The best place to access the trail is at **Clarcona Horseman's Park** (✉ 3535 Damon Rd., Apopka, ☎ 407/654–5144).

A shorter bikeway, the **Cady Way Trail,** connects east Orlando with the well-manicured enclave suburb of Winter Park. The trail is only 3½ mi long, but it's quite pleasant and has water fountains and shaded seating along the route. The best place to access the trail is at the small park at its west end, immediately east of the parking lot of the **Orlando Fashion Square Mall** (✉ 3201 E. Colonial Dr.; I–4 Exit 41).

Information about Orlando bike trails can be obtained from the **city transportation planning bureau** (☎ 407/246–2775).

The area near **Rollins College,** in Winter Park, offers views of lakes, tree-lined streets, and the homes of much of the area's old money. Most riders prefer to go west of town to the **Clermont–Lake County** area. Since it's out in the boonies, there isn't much traffic. Orange groves offer great scenery, and some hills offer a challenge.

Florida Backroad, by Robert Howard ($14.95 in bookstores), contains detailed descriptions of biking areas, plus maps with mileage markers and routes for 40 excursions.

Fishing

Central Florida is covered with freshwater lakes and rivers teeming with all kinds of fish, especially largemouth black bass, but also perch, catfish, sunfish, and pike.

Licenses
To fish in most Florida waters—but not at Walt Disney World—anglers over 16 need a fishing license, available at bait-and-tackle shops, fishing camps, most sporting-goods stores, and Wal-Marts and Kmarts.

Some of these locations may not sell saltwater licenses, or they may serve non-Florida residents only; call ahead to be on the safe side. (Information on obtaining licenses is available from the **Florida Game & Fish Commission** at ☎ 800/282–8002.) The cost is $17 for seven days, and $32 for one year (fresh- and saltwater). Florida residents get a price break; a fresh- or saltwater license is $14 per year, and residents over 65 need no license.

Walt Disney World

Bay Lake Fishing Trips takes two-hour fishing excursions on regularly stocked Bay Lake and Seven Seas Lagoon. Departing from Fort Wilderness, Wilderness Lodge, Contemporary, Polynesian, and Grand Floridian resort marinas, trips include boat, equipment, coffee and pastries, and a guide for up to five anglers. These organized outings are the only way you're allowed to fish on the lakes, which are brimming with fish. Reservations are required. Yacht and Beach Club and Disney's Boardwalk Hotel guests can book a similar fishing excursion on Crescent Lake for the same fee as the Bay Lake trip. ☎ 407/939–7529. ☞ $171.20 for a 2-hr trip, and $51.40 for each additional hr. ☉ Daily 8, 11:30, and 3.

Bass specialists head for **Captain Jack's Guided Bass Tours.** These two-hour fishing expeditions on Lake Buena Vista for up to five anglers depart from the Downtown Disney's Marketplace marina. ☎ 407/828–2461. ☞ $68.50 per person, or $137 for a group of 2–5 people. ☉ Daily 6:30 and 9 AM.

Fishing without a guide is permitted in the canals around the Dixie Landings and Port Orleans resorts and at Fort Wilderness Resort and Campground. Poles and tackle can be rented at the **Fort Wilderness Bike Barn.** You must be at least age 12 to rent a rod and reel. ☎ 407/824–2742. ☞ Cane pole with tackle $2 per hr, $4 per day; family special, 4–6 poles with tackle for $12.50 per hr; rod and reel with tackle $4 per hr, $8 per day. ☉ Daily 8–5.

Disney now also offers special **kids-only fishing trips** in which adult Disney staff members drive the boats and serve as guides for children ages 6–12. ☎ 407/939–7529. ☞ Cost of 2-hr excursions $21.40 per child. ☉ Daily 8–4.

There is fishing off the dock at the **Ol' Man Island Fishing Hole.** Catch and release is encouraged, but you can have your fish packed in ice to take home, although you'll have to clean them yourself. Excursions are also available. ✉ Dixie Landings, ☎ 407/934–5409. ☞ Cane poles and bait $4 per hr per person, $12.50 per hr for family of up to 6; no fee to use dock with pole rental; trips $60 per person, reservations required. ☉ Daily 9–3.

A two-hour fishing trip down the **Sassagoula River** at Dixie Landings includes guide, rod, bait, and soft drinks. Reservations must be made in advance. ✉ Dixie Landings, ☎ 407/939–7529. ☞ $50 per party boat, up to 5 anglers. ☉ Daily 6:30 and 8:30 AM.

Elsewhere

Top Central Florida fishing waters include Lake Kissimmee, the Butler and Conway chains of lakes, and Lake Tohopekaliga—a Native American name that means "Sleeping Tiger." (Locals call it Lake Toho.) The lake got its centuries-old name because it becomes incredibly rough during thunderstorms and has sent more than a few fishermen to a watery grave. Be careful in summer when you see storm clouds. Your best chance for trophy fish is between November and April on Toho or Kissimmee; for good creels, the best producer is usually the Butler area, which has the additional advantage of its scenery—lots of live oaks and

cypresses, plus the occasional osprey or bald eagle. Toho and Kissimmee are also good for largemouth bass and crappie. The Butler chain
yields largemouth, some pickerel, and the occasional huge catfish. A
variety of services are available, from equipment and boat rental to full-
day trips with guides and guarantees.

FISHING CAMPS

A number of excellent fishing camps in the form of lakeside campgrounds
draw a more outdoorsy crowd than you'll find elsewhere in the area.

East Lake Fish Camp, on East Lake Tohopekaliga, has a restaurant and
country store, sells live bait and propane, and rents boats. You can also
take a ride on an airboat. It has 243 RV sites and 24 cabins. Try to
make reservations for the cabins at least two weeks in advance during
the winter and spring. ⊠ *3705 Big Bass Rd., Kissimmee,* ☎ *407/348–
2040.* ☜ *RV sites $20 (2 people) and cabins $50 (2 people, $5 each
additional, up to 5 persons per cabin).*

Red's Fish Camp, on West Lake Tohopekaliga, has 69 RV sites. Most
of the full hookups are booked year-round, but electrical and water
hookups are usually available, as are live bait, food, and drinks. ⊠ *4715
Kissimmee Park Rd., St. Cloud,* ☎ *407/892–8795.* ☜ *RV sites $12
per night, $200 per month plus electricity.*

Richardson's Fish Camp, on West Lake Tohopekaliga, has nine cabins
with kitchenettes, 16 RV sites, 12 tent sites, boat slips, and a bait shop.
⊠ *1550 Scotty's Rd., Kissimmee,* ☎ *407/846–6540.* ☜ *RV sites
$22.50; tent sites $17; 1-bedroom cabins $40; 2-bedroom cabins $61;
3-bedroom cabins $72.*

GUIDES

Guides fish out of the area's fishing camps, and you can usually make
arrangements to hire them through the camp office. Rates vary, but
for two people $150 for a half day and $225 for a full day are good
rules of thumb. Many area guides are part-timers who fish on weekends or take a day off from their full-time job to guide, hitting a variety of local state and private lakes.

Bass America, in business 18 years, provides boat, tackle, transportation, and ice and soft drinks for bass fishing on local lakes. Live bait
is an extra charge—and Bass America guarantees fish. ⊠ *5935 Swoffield
Dr., Orlando 32812,* ☎ *407/281–0845.* ☜ *Half day from $175, full
day from $225, additional adult $50, children 6 or under free.*

Bass Challenger Guide (BCG) takes you out in Ranger boats equipped
with tackle, license, bait, and ice. Transportation can be arranged between fishing spots and local hotels. Bass is the only quarry, and the
company guarantees "No bass, no pay!" ⊠ *Box 679155, Orlando
32867,* ☎ *407/273–8045 or 800/241–5314.* ☜ *Half day from $200
plus license and bait, full day from $275.*

Cutting Loose Expeditions goes after bass but also arranges saltwater
expeditions to the Indian River flats to light-tackle-cast for redfish, sea
trout, tarpon, and snook. It'll arrange deep-sea charters out of Port
Canaveral, too. All trips can include everything but food. They will
even pick you up at the hotel and take you to the fishing hole. ⊠ *Box
447, Winter Park 32790,* ☎ *407/629–4700 or 800/533–4746.* ☜
Half day from $225, full day from $325, offshore $750. ✑

Golf

With sunny weather practically year-round, Central Florida is a golfer's
haven, with about 130 golf courses within a 45-minute drive of Or-

lando International Airport. Most of Florida is extremely flat, but many of the courses listed here have man-made rolling hills that make them more challenging. Many resort hotels let nonguests use their golf facilities. Some country clubs are affiliated with particular hotels, and their guests can play at preferred rates. If you're staying near a course you'd like to use, call and inquire. And because hotels have become so attuned to the popularity of golf recently, many hotels that don't even have golf courses nearby have golf privileges or discounts for hotel guests at courses around town. If you like golf, it's always good to check with your hotel about what it offers before you set out on your own.

In general, even public courses have dress codes—most courses would just about as soon see you stark nude as wearing a tank top, for instance—so call to find out the specifics at each; and be sure to reserve tee times in advance. The yardages quoted are those from the blue tees. Greens fees usually vary by season, but the highest and lowest figures are provided, and virtually all include mandatory cart rental, except for the few nine-hole walking courses.

Golfpac (⊠ Box 162366, Altamonte Springs 32716-2366, ☎ 407/260–2288 or 800/327–0878) packages golf vacations and prearranges tee times at more than 40 courses around Orlando. Rates vary based on hotel and course, and at least 60–90 days' advance notice is recommended to set up a vacation.

Walt Disney World

Where else would you find a sand trap shaped like the head of a well-known mouse? Walt Disney World has 99 holes of golf on five championship courses—all on the PGA Tour route, plus a nine-hole walking course. Eagle Pines and Osprey Ridge are the newcomers, flanking the Bonnet Creek Golf Club just east of Fort Wilderness. They join WDW's original courses, the Palm and the Magnolia, which flank the Shades of Green Resort, to the west, and the Lake Buena Vista course, near Downtown Disney's Marketplace. All courses are full-service facilities, including driving range, pro shop, locker room, snack bar–restaurant, and PGA-staffed teaching and training program.

GREENS FEES

There are lots of variables here, with prices ranging from $5.35 for a youngster 17 or under to play nine holes at Oak Trail walking course to an adult non–hotel guest paying $172 to play 18 holes at one of Disney's newer courses in peak season. The three original Disney courses have the same fees and discount policies: guests at WDW resorts pay $100; all others pay $155 (summer rates, in effect May 1–September 30, are $91 for WDW guests and $96 for all others). Fees at Eagle Pines and Osprey Ridge change throughout the year and are a little more expensive. All offer a twilight discount rate, $22–$80, which goes into effect at 2 PM between October and February and at 3 PM April–October 2. If you are on a tight budget, the best bargain is golf after 5 PM in summer (May 22–September 30), when adults can play the nine-hole Oak Trail walking course for $10.70 and youngsters 17 and under can play for $5.35.

TEE TIMES AND RESERVATIONS

Tee times are available from 7:30 AM until dark on weekdays and from 7 until dark on weekends. You can book them up to 60 days in advance if you're staying at a WDW-owned hotel, seven days ahead if you're staying elsewhere from May to December, and four days in advance from January to April. For tee times and private lessons at any course, call ☎ 407/939–4653.

GOLF INSTRUCTION

One-on-one instruction from PGA-accredited professionals at any Disney course is available for $54 for adults and $34 for youngsters 17 and under. Lesson time is 30 minutes. For private lessons at any course, call ☎ 407/939–4653.

COURSES

Eagle Pines, one of two newer courses, was designed by golf-course architect Pete Dye. Greens are small and undulating, and fairways are lined with pines and punctuated by bunkers that broaden the challenge. ⊠ *Bonnet View Golf Club. 6,772 yards. Par: 72. USGA rating: 72.3. 18 holes.*

The **Lake Buena Vista** course winds among Downtown Disney–area town houses and villas; greens are narrow—and hitting straight is important, since errant balls risk ending up in someone's bedroom. ⊠ *Lake Buena Vista Dr. 6,819 yards. Par: 72. USGA rating: 72.7. 18 holes.*

The **Magnolia,** played by the pros in the Disney/Oldsmobile Golf Classic, is long but forgiving, with extra-wide fairways. ⊠ *Shades of Green. 7,190 yards. Par: 72. USGA rating: 73.9. 18 holes.*

Oak Trail is a walking course designed to be fun for the entire family. It was designed by Ron Garl and is noted for its small, undulating greens. Oak Trail is close to the Magnolia golf course. ⊠ *Shades of Green. 2,913 yards. Par: 36. 9 holes.*

Designer Tom Fazio leavened the challenge of **Osprey Ridge** with a relaxing tour into some of the still-forested portions of the huge WDW acreage. However, tees and greens as much as 20 ft above the fairways keep competitive players from getting too comfortable. ⊠ *Bonnet Creek Golf Club. 7,101 yards. Par: 72. USGA rating: 73.9. 18 holes.*

The **Palm,** one of WDW's original courses, has been confounding the pros as part of the annual Disney/Oldsmobile Golf Classic for years. It's not as long as the Magnolia, or as wide, and there are more trees. And don't go near the water! ⊠ *Shades of Green. 6,957 yards. Par: 72. USGA rating: 73. 18 holes.*

Elsewhere

Greens fees at most non-Disney courses fluctuate with the season. A twilight discount applies after 2 PM in busy seasons and after 3 PM during the rest of the year; the discount is usually half off the normal rate. Because golf is so incredibly popular around Orlando, a good number of courses have raised their rates in the past year.

The only way for the general public to get onto **Arnold Palmer's Bay Hill Club** course is to be invited by a member or to book lodging at the club's 64-room hotel. But with double-occupancy rates for rooms overlooking the course—*and* including a round of golf—running as low as $155 per person a night in summer, many consider staying at the club a real bargain. The course is the site of the annual Nestlé Invitational, and its par-4 18th hole is considered one of the toughest on the PGA tour. ⊠ *9000 Bay Hill Rd., Orlando,* ☎ *407/876–2429 or 888/ 422–9445. 7,207 yards. Par: 72. USGA rating: 75.1. 18 holes; 3,409 yards. Par: 36. 9 holes.* ⛳ *Greens fees included in room rates, $155 single; $250 double. Restaurant, private lessons, club rental.* ✍

Perhaps the best thing about pretty **Barnett Park Golf Practice Facility** is its price: it's free. All a golfer has to do is show up to use the net-enclosed driving range (with 10 pads), the three chipping holes with grass and sand surroundings, and the nine-hole putting green. As a special bonus, children ages 7–13 can spend time with a pro—for free—

from 3 to 4:30 PM on Wednesday. ⊠ *4801 W. Colonial Dr., Orlando,* ☎ *407/836–6248.* ☜ *Free.*

In addition to having a great pedigree (designed by Robert Trent Jones Jr. and Sr.), **Celebration Golf Club,** a lovely wooded course, has the same thing going for it that the Disney-created town of Celebration, Florida has: it's just 1 mi off the U.S. 192 tourist strip (and therefore a 10-minute drive from Walt Disney World), yet it is as serene and bucolic as any spot in Florida. In addition to the 18-hole course, driving range, and three-hole junior course, the club includes a quaint, tin-roof clubhouse with a pro shop and restaurant, flanked by a tall, wooden windmill that is a local landmark. ⊠ *700 Golf Park Dr., Celebration,* ☎ *407/ 566–4653. 6,783 yards. Par: 72. USGA rating: 73. 18 holes.* ☜ *Rates vary, depending on time of year, time of day you start playing, whether you're a Florida resident, and whether you're a Celebration resident, but you can pay as little as $55 and as much as $110, including cart rental, depending on the variables. Daily discount rates begin at 1* PM. *Restaurant, pro shop, private lessons, club rental.*

Cypress Creek Country Club is a demanding course with 16 water holes and lots of trees. ⊠ *5353 Vineland Rd., Orlando,* ☎ *407/351– 2187. 7,014 yards. Par: 72. USGA rating: 73.6. 18 holes.* ☜ *Greens fees $32–$50. Tee times 7 days in advance. Restaurants, private lessons, club rental.* ♨

Diamond Players Club Clermont. This hilly course, a half-hour drive west of Orlando, bills itself as "Florida's Mountain Golf Course" because it involves altitude changes of 190 ft, with its highest point at 250 ft above sea level—the Alps by Florida standards. Water plays into seven of the 18 holes. The Clermont area gives you a good look at Florida at a less frenetic pace. ⊠ *2601 Diamond Club Dr., Clermont,* ☎ *352/ 243–0411. 6,911 yards. Par: 71. USGA rating: 73.7. 18 holes.* ☜ *Greens fees $35–$45 Florida residents; $39–$49 nonresidents. Restaurant, private lessons, club rental, lockers, driving range, putting green.* ♨

Falcon's Fire Golf Club, designed by golf-course architect Rees Jones, has strategically placed fairway bunkers that demand accuracy off the tee. ⊠ *3200 Seralago Blvd., Kissimmee,* ☎ *407/239–5445. 6,901 yards. Par: 72. USGA rating: 72.5. 18 holes.* ☜ *Greens fees $79–$110. Tee times 7 days in advance. Restaurants, private and group lessons, club rental, lockers, driving range, putting green.* ♨

World-famous golf pro Nick Faldo and Marriott Corp. have joined up to create the **Faldo Golf Institute by Marriott,** an extensive-curriculum golf school and nine-hole golf course on the grounds of the corporation's biggest time-share complex, Marriott's Grande Vista. Here you can do anything from taking a one-hour, $150 lesson with a Faldo-trained pro (although not the great Faldo himself, of course) to immersing yourself in a $1,175, three-day extravaganza in which you learn more about golf than your spouse probably ever would want to hear about. Among the high-tech teaching methods at the school is the Faldo Swing Studio, in which instructors tape you doing your current, paltry swing, analyze the tape, and then teach you how to reform your physical skills the Faldo Way. The course, designed by Ron Garl, is geared to make you use every club in your bag (and perhaps a few you may elect to buy in the pro shop), according to the Garlster himself. As with virtually everything else in Florida, prices go up in peak seasonal months, but there's always a group discount at the Faldo Institute, even for groups as small as two people. ⊠ *12001 Avenida Verde, Orlando 32821,* ☎ *407/238–7677. 2,308 yards. Par: 32. 9 holes.* ♨

Grenelefe Golf and Tennis Resort, about 45 minutes from Orlando, has three 18-hole courses amid gentle hills. Length is the key here. The West Course, designed by Robert Trent Jones Sr., plays to 7,325 yards from the championship tees. An absence of water hazards—there are just two ponds—softens the course somewhat. The East Course is very tight, with small greens and lots of changes in elevation. Designed by Ed Seay, it requires accuracy. The South, designed by Ron Garl and Andy Beane, has plenty of sand and water but wider fairways and larger greens. The resort has 800 villas and offers three- to seven-day lodging and golf packages that range from $410 to $1,000. ✉ *3200 Rte. 546, Haines City 33844,* ☎ *941/422–7511 or 800/237–9549. West Course: 7,325 yards. Par: 71. USGA rating: 75. 18 holes. East Course: 6,802 yards. Par: 72. USGA rating: 72.5. 18 holes. South Course: 6,869 yards. Par: 71. USGA rating: 73.1. 18 holes. ⛳ Greens fees $40–$130. Tee times 3 days in advance, but courses often closed to public at busiest time of year (Jan.– Apr.). Restaurants, private lessons, club and shoe rental.* ✎

Hawk's Landing Golf Course at Marriott's Orlando World Center, originally designed by Joe Lee, was extensively upgraded with a new, Robert E. Cupp III design in early 1999. The course includes 16 water holes, lots of sand, and lots of exotic new landscaping. ✉ *1 World Center Dr., Orlando 32821,* ☎ *407/238–8660. 6,307 yards. Par: 71. USGA rating: 73.2. 18 holes. ⛳ Greens fees $65–$160. Tee times 7 days in advance for public, 90 days in advance for World Center guests. Restaurants, private and group lessons, club and shoe rental.*

Hunter's Creek Golf Course, a Lloyd Clifton–designed course, has large greens and 14 water holes. ✉ *14401 Sports Club Way, Orlando 32837,* ☎ *407/240–4653. 7,432 yards. Par: 72. USGA rating: 75.2. 18 holes. ⛳ Greens fees $30–$80. Tee times 3 days in advance. Snack bar, private lessons, club rental.*

MetroWest Country Club has a rolling Robert Trent Jones Sr. course, with few trees but lots of sand. ✉ *2100 S. Hiawassee Rd., Orlando 32835,* ☎ *407/299–1099. 7,051 yards. Par: 72. USGA rating: 73.1. 18 holes. ⛳ Greens fees $38–$75 residents, $70–$90 nonresidents. Tee times 7 days in advance. Restaurants (lunch only), private and group lessons, club rental.* ✎

Orange Lake Country Club, about five minutes from Walt Disney World's main entrance, has three nine-hole courses, all very similar. Distances aren't long, but fairways are very narrow, and there's a great deal of water, making the course very difficult. The fourth course was designed by Arnold Palmer. Standard practice is to play two of the three 9-hole courses, the Orange, Lake and Cypress courses in combination for a single round of golf, yielding the same experience as playing a single, par-72 course. ✉ *8505 W. Irlo Bronson Memorial Hwy., Kissimmee 34747,* ☎ *407/239–0000 or 800/877–6522. Lake/Orange: 6,531 yards. Par: 72. USGA rating: 72.2. Orange/Cypress: 6,670 yards. Par: 72. USGA rating: 72.6. Cypress/Lake: 6,571 yards. Par: 72. USGA rating: 72.3. 27 holes. ⛳ Greens fees $20–$125. Tee times 2 days in advance. Restaurants, private and group lessons, club rental, driving range, putting green.*

Poinciana Golf & Racquet Resort, about 18 mi southeast of Walt Disney World, near Kissimmee, has 69 bunkers and water on 12 holes nestled in a cypress forest. ✉ *500 E. Cypress Pkwy., Poinciana 34759,* ☎ *407/933–5300 or 800/331–7743. 6,700 yards. Par: 72. USGA rating: 72.2. 18 holes. ⛳ Greens fees $24–$65. Tee times 7 days in advance, proper dress required, discount coupons accepted off-season.*

Restaurants, private and group lessons, club rental, driving range, putting green.

Timacuan Golf and Country Club has a two-part course designed by Ron Garl. Part I, the front nine, is open, with lots of sand; Part II, the back nine, is heavily wooded. ⊠ *550 Timacuan Blvd., Lake Mary 32746,* ☎ *407/321–0010. 6,915 yards. Par: 71. USGA rating: 73.2. 18 holes.* 🖃 *Greens fees $32–$92. Tee times 5 days in advance. Restaurants, club rental, driving range, putting green.*

In 1997 voters saved the charming **Winter Park Municipal Golf Club** from destruction by voting to tax themselves. Opened in 1914, the inexpensive nine-hole course features narrow fairways, a low-key approach (no carts here), and a cozy clubhouse where you can buy everything from a 50¢ candy bar to a $200 golf bag. ⊠ *761 Old England Ave., Winter Park 32789,* ☎ *407/623–3339. 2,400 yards. Par: 35. 9 holes.* 🖃 *Greens fees $8.75. Wed.–Thurs. 8:45–10 reserved for members. Club rental, putting green.*

Health Clubs

Walt Disney World

Although most of the Walt Disney World health clubs accept only guests at Walt Disney World hotels—and some accept only guests of that particular hotel—it's not difficult to find a hotel fitness center or spa that will take nonguests. In fact, the number of hotels adding public spas grows each year. Because massage therapy schools are turning out hundreds of new graduates every year in Orlando, competition has increased, and getting rubbed the right way has become more and more of a bargain. Some hotel spas have even—gasp—lowered their rates (minimally) for an hour of massage.

Body by Jake, at the Dolphin, has step and water aerobics classes, hand weights, personal trainers, treadmills, and stationary bikes. ⊠ *Walt Disney World Dolphin,* ☎ *407/934–4264.* 🖃 *Free for Dolphin guests, $10 per person for nonguests; massage $45 per 25 mins for Swedish massage, $50 for deep massage, $70 per 50 mins for Swedish massage, $75 for deep massage, $110 per 1½ hrs for Swedish, $115 for deep massage.* ☉ *Daily 6 AM–9 PM. Guests at other hotels admitted only by the day. Dry sauna, coed Jacuzzi.*

The glittering **Grand Floridian Spa and Health Club** has Cybex and cardiovascular equipment, treadmills, stair steppers, free weights, and saunas. The Grand Floridian Spa offers children's services called "My First" treatments for ages 10 and up. Couples rooms are available. There is an 18% service charge on all therapies. Spa packages are available. ⊠ *Grand Floridian,* ☎ *407/824–2332.* 🖃 *$12 per person per day, $30 per person for length of stay; massage $52 per 25 mins, $98 per 50 mins, $143 per 80 mins.* ☉ *Daily 6 AM–9 PM. Saunas, steam rooms, whirlpools, personal training, body treatments, facials.*

Muscles and Bustles Health Club, at Disney's BoardWalk Inn and Villas, offers Cybex equipment, circuit training, tanning, steam rooms, and massage services. ⊠ *BoardWalk Inn and Villas,* ☎ *407/939–2370.* 🖃 *$12 per person per day, $20 per person or $40 per family for length of stay; massage $45 per 25 mins, $70 per 50 mins, $115 for 75 mins.* ☉ *Daily 6 AM–9 PM. Steam rooms.*

Old Key West Resort Exercise Room, open only to Disney resort guests, has Nautilus equipment, free weights, and massage services. ⊠ *Old Key West Resort,* ☎ *407/827–7700.* 🖃 *Free; massage $35 per 25 mins, $55 per 50 mins.* ☉ *Daily 6:30 AM–midnight.*

Olympiad Fitness Center, open to all Disney guests, has Nautilus and hand weights, stair climbers, stationary bikes, cross-country ski machines, and treadmills, plus a tanning bed. Massages are offered at the club or in your room. ⊠ *Contemporary Resort,* ☎ *407/824–3410.* ▣ *$12 per person per day, $20 per person or $40 per family for length of stay; massage $45 per half hr, $70 per hr, $90 per hr in-room; aroma therapy in addition to any massage is $15.* ☉ *Daily 6 AM–9 PM. Dry sauna.*

Ship Shape Health Club has Nautilus, cardiovascular equipment, free weights, a sauna, a spa, and a steam room. ⊠ *Yacht and Beach Club Resorts,* ☎ *407/934–3256.* ▣ *$12 per person per day, $20 per person or $40 per family for length of stay; massage $45 per half hr, $70 per hr.* ☉ *Daily 6 AM–9 PM. Sauna, steam room.*

Villas at Disney Institute Sports and Fitness Center has just about anything you could want: a weight and cardiovascular room with Cybex equipment, an indoor exercise pool, and an NBA-size gymnasium among other numerous offerings. There are 10 private treatment rooms and men's and women's steam rooms. The à la carte menu of treatments includes body therapies and massages. ⊠ *Villas at Disney Institute,* ☎ *407/827–4455.* ▣ *$15 per person per day, $35 per person or $50 per family for length of stay, free with purchase of spa treatment; massage and other therapy rates vary.* ☉ *Daily 6 AM–8 PM. Saunas, steam rooms, whirlpools, pool, body treatments, facials.*

Wyndham Palace Resort and Spa in the WDW Resort has a fitness center containing the entire spectrum of fitness equipment, including Nautilus machines, weights, stair climbers, stationary bikes, and treadmills. There's also a lap pool. Massages and 60 other health and beauty therapies are offered in the full-service spa, the largest in the Disney area. If you want to get your body treated with seaweed, mud, mustard, or a variety of liquids or semisolids that will astound you, this is the place. And if you buy a spa treatment, you can use the fitness center all day for free. ⊠ *1900 Buena Vista Dr., Lake Buena Vista,* ☎ *407/827–2727.* ▣ *Free for hotel guests, $10 per person for nonguests, free with purchase of massage; massage $53 per 25 mins, $88.50 per 50 mins, $105–$115 per 80 mins.* ☉ *Spa daily 8–7, massage daily 8–8. Dry sauna, steam bath, whirlpool, lap pool, body treatments.*

Elsewhere

To find out what's hot in exercise facilities when you visit, the best bet is to ask at your hotel, because clubs outside WDW come and go. And don't forget about the local YMCAs, longtime favorites. To find the one nearest where you're staying, phone the Metropolitan YMCA office (☎ 407/896–9220). Most accept guests on a single-visit basis, for $10–$15, and you don't have to be a Y member.

Downtown YMCA Family Center has Nautilus, Cybex machines, free weights, racquetball, a half-Olympic-size pool, two gyms, and aerobics classes. It's an older property, but the weight room facilities have been revamped. ⊠ *433 N. Mills Ave., Orlando,* ☎ *407/896–6901.* ▣ *$12 per person per day, $6 to YMCA members from outside Orlando (first 2 visits free to prospective members).* ☉ *Weekdays 5 AM–9:30 PM, Sat. 8–6, Sun. 1–5.*

International Drive YMCA is definitely more posh than the Downtown Y. It has Nautilus, free weights, racquetball, two swimming pools (one Olympic-size), and a diving well. Members can call ahead to reserve racquetball courts. ⊠ *8422 International Dr., Orlando,* ☎ *407/363–1911.* ▣ *$10 per person per day, $50 per person per wk.* ☉ *Weekdays 6 AM–9 PM, Sat. 8–5, Sun. noon–4.*

Horseback Riding

Walt Disney World

Fort Wilderness Resort and Campground offers tame trail rides through backwoods. Children must be at least nine, and adults must weigh less than 250 pounds. The campground is open to the public. ☎ 407/824–2832. ⚏ *Trail rides $25 for 45 mins.* ☼ *Rides daily; times vary according to season. Reservations essential. Check in 30 mins prior to ride.*

Elsewhere

Grand Cypress Equestrian Center gives private lessons in hunter, jumper, dressage, and combined training. Supervised novice and advanced group trail rides are also available. Call at least a week ahead for reservations in winter and spring. ✉ *Hyatt Regency Grand Cypress Resort, 1 Equestrian Dr., Orlando,* ☎ *407/239–4608.* ⚏ *Trail rides $45 per hr for novice, $100 per hr for advanced; private lessons $55 per half hr, $100 per hr.* ☼ *Daily 8:30–5.*

Horse World Riding Stables offers basic and longer, more advanced nature-trail tours along beautifully wooded trails near Kissimmee. Pony rides are also available, and the stables area has picnic tables, farm animals you can pet, and a pond to fish in. Reservations a day in advance are recommended for the popular advanced trails. ✉ *3705 S. Poinciana Blvd., Kissimmee,* ☎ *407/847–4343.* ⚏ *Trail rides $29.95 for basic, $40 for intermediate, $45 for advanced; pony rides $6 for children under 6.* ☼ *Daily 9–5.*

Ice-Skating

Orlando sees frost only about once every other year, so ice-skating fever is not taking the city by storm. But there is a public rink, if you feel the urge to chill out.

Orlando Ice-Plex is definitely spiffy but seems touristy. ✉ *Dowdy Pavilion, 7500 Canada Ave., Orlando,* ☎ *407/352–6667.* ⚏ *Skate rental $2; admission prices and open-skating times vary; call for information.*

Miniature Golf

Winter Summerland and Fantasia Gardens Miniature Golf Courses. Disney likes to promote the 99 holes of golf it has created on property over the last couple of decades, but for those who aren't cut out to be Arnold Palmer and like their golfing experience a little more on the whimsical (and smaller) side, WDW has carved out 72 holes in two miniature golf complexes. The Winter Summerland course, which probably got its inspiration from nearby Blizzard Beach, involves everything from sand castles to snow banks and allegedly is where Santa and his elves spend their summer vacation playing. The course is close to Disney's Animal Kingdom and the Coronado Springs and All-Star Resorts. The Fantasia course, heavily themed in imagery from Disney's *Fantasia,* is adjacent to the Swan and Dolphin Resort complex and is near the Disney–MGM Studios. ☎ *407/939–7529.* ⚏ *$9.25 adults, $7.50 children 3–9, with a 50% discount for the second consecutive round played.*

Rock Climbing

With topography that gives definition to the old adage "flat as the top of a pool table," you wouldn't think you'd find a good place for rock climbing around Orlando. But Orlando is a place where they make their own mountains on a regular basis, and the **Aiguille Rock Climbing Center,** in the Orlando suburb of Longwood, has all the cliffs you can handle—on 6,500 square ft of rock-studded walls. Climbers reach a height of 45 ft, and different areas of the indoor, air-conditioned facility are set up to provide varying levels of challenges to match your rock-climbing skill level. For safety, all climbers are tethered to a rope controlled by someone on the ground level. ⌧ *999 Charles St., Longwood,* ☎ *407/332–1430.* ⌨ *Day passes $21 adults, $16 students 12–18, $14 children under 12.* ☉ *Weekdays 10–10; Sat. 10 AM–midnight; Sun. 10–7.*

Sky Diving

If you've always wanted to try sky diving, but could never quite get up the courage to jump out of an airplane, you might try **Sky Venture,** a 120-mph vertical-lift wind tunnel that allows you to experience everything sky divers enjoy, all within an airblast that only covers 12 ft of height. The experience starts with sky-diving instruction, after which you suit up and hit the wind tunnel, where you soar like a bird, all under the watchful eye of your instructor. While you are "falling" on the wind stream, you even experience what divers called "ground rush" because you are surrounded by a video depiction of a real sky dive. The experience is so realistic that sky diving clubs come to Sky Venture, just across the street from Wet 'n Wild, to hone their skills. ⌧ *6805 Visitors Circle, Orlando,* ☎ *407/903–1150.* ⌨ *$35 adults, $20 children 12 and under.* ☉ *Weekdays 4 PM–midnight, weekends noon–midnight.* ✎

Running

Walt Disney World

Walt Disney World has several scenic running trails. Pick up maps at any Disney resort. At the **Caribbean Beach Resort** (☎ 407/934–3400), there is a 1½-mi running promenade around Barefoot Bay. **Fort Wilderness Campground** (☎ 407/824–2900) has a 2⅓-mi running course with plenty of fresh air and woods, as well as numerous exercise stations along the way. Early in the morning all the roads are fairly uncrowded, however, and make for good running. The roads that wiggle through Downtown Disney resorts are pleasant, as are the cart paths on the golf courses.

Elsewhere

Orlando now has two excellent bike trails that are also good for running (☞ Biking, *above*).

Turkey Lake Park (⌧ 3401 S. Hiawassee Rd., Orlando, ☎ 407/299–5581), not far from Disney, has a 3-mi biking trail that's popular with runners. Several wooded hiking trails also make for a good run. The park closes at 7:30 PM, and fees are $2 adults, $1 children ages 3–12.

In Winter Park, around **Rollins College,** you can run along the shady streets and around the lakes, inhaling the aroma of old money. The **Orlando Runners Club** meets in the area every Sunday morning at 7 for 3-, 6-, and 12-mi jaunts; for details, call the Track Shack (⌧ 1104 N. Mills Ave., Orlando, ☎ 407/898–1313), open weekdays 10–7, Saturday 10–5.

Sporting Clays

Set on an 11,000-acre family-owned ranch a short drive from Orlando International Airport, the new **TM Ranch Shooting Sports** offers wild turkey hunting (March 20–April 25) as well as year-round action in the increasingly popular sport, sporting clays, in which you use shotguns to shoot a variety of targets, including clay discs (about the size and shape of a hockey puck), launched into the air in patterns that mimic the flight characteristics of wild game birds. A big part of the appeal of a sporting clays course is its natural backdrop, and TM Ranch offers a good one, with pine, cypress, and palmettos surrounding the course. Expert marksmanship instruction is available at the Remington Shooting School, which operates on the property in winter. The facility, which features a pro shop and catered barbecue lunches, also has a meeting pavilion that can handle groups of up to 500 people, as well as a camping area with 90 RV hookups. TM Ranch also has a package deal with the Orlando Renaissance Hotel–Airport, in which you get a night at the hotel and 100 rounds of clay shots at the ranch for as little as $140. ⊠ *15520 TM Ranch Rd., Orlando 32832,* ☎ *407/ 384–1715.* 🖾 *A round of 50 clay shots $22; 100-shot rounds $38; gun rental $8; ammunition $6 per box. Turkey hunting $500 a day; quail hunting starts at $220 a half-day per person for groups of 2 or more or $400 for a full day.*

Tennis

Walt Disney World

You can play tennis at any number of Disney hotels, and you'll find the courts a pleasant respite from the milling throngs in the parks. All have lights and are open from 7 AM to 8 PM, unless otherwise noted, and most have lockers and rental rackets ($3–$5 a day). There seems to be a long-term plan to move from hard courts to clay, and the Contemporary has already converted. All courts are open to all players, but court staff can opt to turn away nonguests when things get busy (however, that doesn't often happen). The tennis pros are employees of Peter Burwash, Inc., and will travel to any Disney resort to give lessons.

The **Contemporary Resort** is the center of Disney's tennis program, with its sprawl of six clay courts. It has two backboards and an automatic ball machine. Reservations are available up to 24 hours in advance, and there is an arrange-a-game service. ☎ *407/939–7529 reservations; 407/824–3578 pro shop.* 🖾 *$15 per hr, $50 for length of stay; clinics $25; private lessons $50 per hr, $30 per half hr, five 1-hr private lessons $225; ball machines $25 per hr, $12.50 per half hr; racket rental $5 per day.*

The **Dolphin and Swan** share four asphalt courts. There is no instruction available; balls may be purchased at the Body by Jake (☞ *above*) health center. ☎ *407/934–4264.* 🖾 *Free to hotel guests; racket rental $10 per day.* ☉ *Daily 8 AM–6 PM.*

Fort Wilderness Resort and Campground has two courts out in the middle of a field. They're popular with youngsters, and if you hate players who are too free about letting their balls stray across their neighbors' court, this is not the place for you. There are no court reservations and no instruction. ☎ *407/824–2742.* 🖾 *Free; racket rental $3 per hr.*

At the **Grand Floridian,** the two clay courts attract a somewhat serious tennis-minded crowd. Court reservations are available up to 24 hours in advance. ☎ *407/939–7529 reservations; 407/824–2433 pro shop.* 🖾 *$15 per hr, private lessons $50 per hr, ball machine $25 per hr.*

The **Yacht and Beach Club Resorts** have two blacktop courts. Court reservations are not required. Equipment is available for use at the towel window at no charge. ☎ *407/934–3256.* 🖾 *Free.* ☉ *Daily 7 AM–10 PM.*

Elsewhere

Lake Cane Tennis Center has 13 lighted hard courts. Six pros provide private and group lessons. ⊠ *5108 Turkey Lake Rd., Orlando,* ☎ *407/ 352–4913.* 🖾 *$3 per hr weekdays during day, $5 per hr weekends and* *evenings; lessons $35 per hr, $18 per half hr.* ⊙ *Weekdays 8 AM–10 PM, weekends 8–6.*

In addition to its golf courses, **Orange Lake Country Club** has seven all-weather hard tennis courts, all of them lighted. It is five minutes from Walt Disney World's main entrance. Court reservations are necessary. ✉ *8505 W. Irlo Bronson Memorial Hwy., Kissimmee,* ☎ *407/239–0000 or 800/877–6522.* ▧ *Free for guests, $4 per hr for nonguests; private lessons $30 per hr; racket rental $2 per hr, $5 per day.* ⊙ *Daily dawn–11 PM for guests, 8–5 for nonguests.*

Orlando Tennis Center offers 16 lighted tennis courts (nine HarTru and seven asphalt), two outdoor racquetball courts, and three teaching tennis pros. Call in advance for court availability. ✉ *649 W. Livingston St., Orlando,* ☎ *407/246–2162.* ▧ *Tennis $5.80 per person for 1½ hrs on HarTru, $3.68 per person for 1½ hrs on asphalt; racquetball $2.62 per person per hr; private lessons $35 per hr, $18 per half hr, group lessons $7.* ⊙ *Weekdays 8 AM–10 PM, weekends 8–6.*

Red Bug Park has 16 lighted hard courts and eight outdoor covered four-wall racquetball courts. Court reservations are available up to 24 hours in advance. ✉ *3600 Red Bug Lake Rd., Casselberry,* ☎ *407/695–7113.* ▧ *Tennis $2 per hr before 5, $4 per hr after 5; racquetball $4 per hr; private lessons $34 per hr.* ⊙ *Daily 8 AM–10 PM.*

Sanlando Park has 25 lighted hard courts and eight covered, fan-cooled racquetball courts. Call for court reservations by 9:30 AM the day before. ✉ *401 W. Highland St., Altamonte Springs,* ☎ *407/869–5966.* ▧ *Tennis $2 per hr before 5, $4 per hr after 5; racquetball $4 per hr; private lessons $40 per hr with head pro, $32 per hr with assistant pros, $16 per half hr.* ⊙ *Daily 8 AM–10 PM.*

Water Sports

Walt Disney World

Boating is big at Disney, with the largest fleet of for-rent pleasure craft in the nation. There are marinas at the Caribbean Beach Resort, Contemporary Resort, Dixie Landings Resort, Downtown Disney Marketplace, Fort Wilderness Resort and Campground, Grand Floridian, Old Key West Resort, Polynesian Resort, Port Orleans Resort, Wilderness Lodge, and the Yacht and Beach Clubs, where you can rent Sunfish sailboats, catamarans, motor-powered pontoon boats, pedal boats, and tiny two-passenger Water Sprites—a hit with children—for use on Bay Lake and the adjoining Seven Seas Lagoon, Club Lake, Lake Buena Vista, or Buena Vista Lagoon. Most rent Water Sprites; otherwise, each hotel has its own rental roster, and you're sure to find something of interest. The Polynesian Resort marina rents outrigger canoes. Fort Wilderness rents canoes for paddling along the placid canals in the area. And you can sail and water-ski on Bay Lake and the Seven Seas Lagoon; stop at the Fort Wilderness, Contemporary, Polynesian, or Grand Floridian marina.

At Disney's Contemporary Resort, **Sammy Duvall's Water Sports Centre** (☎ *407/939–7529,* ✈) offers waterskiing, wakeboarding, and parasailing on Bay Lake. Waterskiing (maximum of five people) and wakeboarding (maximum of four people) include boat and equipment rental, plus the services of an expert instructor. Each costs $130 per hour, plus tax. Parasailing, at $80 per outing, reaches a height of 450 ft for a flight that lasts from 7 to 10 minutes. Individual participants must weigh at least 100 pounds, but youngsters may go aloft accompanied by an adult. (Tandem flights cost $120.)

Elsewhere

Alexander Creek and **Juniper Creek,** in Ocala National Forest just north of the greater Orlando area, offer wonderful wilderness canoeing, with abundant wildlife and moss-draped oaks and bald cypresses canopying the clean, clear waters. Some of these runs are quite rough—lots of ducking under brush and maneuvering around trees. You must pack out what you pack in. **Alexander Springs Canoe Rental** (✉ 49525 Rte. 445, Altoona, ☎ 352/669–3522) rents canoes for $16 per half day, $23 per full-day (with $20 cash deposit and ID), daily 8–1:45 PM. All canoes must be returned to the beach by 3:45 PM. **Juniper Springs Canoe Rental** (✉ Rte. 40, Silver Springs, ☎ 352/625–2808) has canoes for $23–$26 (with $20 cash deposit and ID). Rentals are available daily 8–noon.

Orange Lake, a private lake at the Orange Lake Country Club, next to Walt Disney World, has all types of boating—in rowboats, paddleboats, canoes, wave runners, waterskiing, and jet boats. You can even sign up for waterskiing school. Rentals are available at **Orange Lake Water Sports** (✉ 8505 W. Irlo Bronson Memorial Hwy., Kissimmee, ☎ 407/239–0000): $8 per half hour for canoes; $10 per hour for paddleboats and rowboats; $40 per half hour or $60 per hour for wave runners; $40 per half hour or $60 per hour for jet boats; and $40 per half hour or $63 per hour for waterskiing. It's open daily 10–6.

The **St. Johns River** winds through pine and cypress woods and past pastures where cows graze placidly, skirting the occasional housing development. There's good bird- and wildlife-watching; herons, ibis, storks, and sometimes bald eagles can be spotted, along with alligators and manatees. It's a favored local boating spot, for everything from a day of waterskiing to a weeklong trip in a houseboat. Rentals are available in Deland (west of I–4 Exit 56 via U.S. 44). **Hontoon Landing Resort and Marina** (✉ 2317 River Ridge Rd., Deland, ☎ 904/734–2474; 800/248–2474 in FL) rents luxury houseboats ($425–$975 per day, $1,095–$2,595 per week [October–March], $1,495–$2,595 per week [April–September]), pontoons ($100 per day on weekdays, $135 on weekends), 16-ft fishing boats ($75 per day), and canoes ($3 per hour, $15 per day). The marina also offers coupon specials during the off season, cutting an additional $200 off a weekly houseboat rental. **Holly Bluff** (✉ 2280 Hontoon Rd., Deland, ☎ 904/822–9992 or 800/237–5105) rents pontoon boats ($700 per weekend); full-week boats, which range in capacity from 4 to 12 people, cost from $1,000 to $2,400, with rates lower December–February.

A boat ride on **Shingle Creek** provides views of giant cypress trees dripping with Spanish moss. You can get around by airboat or rent a quiet electric swamp boat or a canoe from **Airboat Rentals** (✉ 4266 Irlo Bronson Memorial Hwy., Kissimmee, ☎ 407/847–3672), open daily 9–5. Airboats are $25 per hour, swamp boats and electric boats run $45 per day, and canoes cost $15 per day.

Another great waterway for nature lovers is the **Wekiva River,** which runs through 6,397-acre Wekiva State Park into the St. Johns River. Bordered by cypress marshlands, its clear, spring-fed waters showcase a rich array of Florida wildlife, including otters, raccoons, alligators, bobcats, deer, turtles, and numerous birds. Canoes and battery-powered motorboats, whose quiet engines don't disturb the wildlife, are the best way to get around; they're available for rent from **Katie's Wekiva River and Campground** (✉ 190 Katie's Cove, Sanford, ☎ 407/628–1482, ✍). Canoes cost $14.50 for the first two hours with a two-hour minimum, $2 each additional hour, or $25 per day. One-way trips, in which you can leave the canoe downstream and get a shuttle ride back to the campground, leave on the hour and cost $16.50 per adult and $8.25 for children under 12. Riverfront cabin rentals range from $60 a day to $375 a week.

FROM THE SIDELINES

Walt Disney World

Disney doesn't do anything unless it does it in a big way, and **Disney's Wide World of Sports Complex** (☎ 407/363–6600) is no exception. The huge new complex contains a 7,500-seat baseball stadium—housed in a giant stucco structure that from the outside looks like a Moroccan palace—a 5,000-seat field house, and a number of fan-oriented commercial ventures such as the Official All-Star Cafe and shops that sell clothing and other items sanctioned by Major League Baseball, the NBA, and the NFL. During spring training, the stadium is home to the perennially great Atlanta Braves, and in 1999 the complex added minor-league baseball with the addition of Orlando Rays games. But that's just the tip of the iceberg. The complex hosts all manner of individual and team competitions, including big-ticket tennis tournaments. In all, some 30 spectator sports are represented among the annual events presented, including Harlem Globetrotters basketball games and fantasy camps (☎ 407/828–3267) and track events ranging from the Walt Disney World Marathon to dozens of annual Amateur Athletic Union (AAU) championships. Additionally, groups from family reunions to corporate meetings can arrange to play softball, basketball, and other games at the complex.

Elsewhere

Not everything in Orlando is wholesome, Disney-style family fun. Wagering a wad of cash at the jai-alai fronton or the dog track is guaranteed to wipe the refrain from "It's a Small World" right out of your head. Most of the tracks and frontons now have closed-circuit TV links with major horse-racing tracks, so you can bet on the ponies and then watch the race on a big-screen TV. And even if you bet and lose steadily, you won't necessarily spend more than you would at most of the attractions. In addition, there are teams in various sports and leagues that play their regular seasons in and around Orlando, as well as Major League Baseball clubs that make their spring-training homes in the area.

Auto Racing

The Indy 200 is held in late January at the **Walt Disney Speedway** (✉ Adjacent to Disney's Wide World of Sports Complex, ☎ 407/839–3900 tickets; 407/939–7810 vacation packages). The facility has a 1-mi trioval track and accommodates 51,000 fans. When there isn't racing, would-be drivers can take the Richard Petty Driving Experience (☞ *above*).

Baseball

Watching a minor-league or spring-training game in a small ballpark can take you back to a time when going to a game didn't mean bringing binoculars or watching the big screen to see what was happening. Minor-league teams play April–September, and spring training lasts only a few weeks, usually February–March, but it can be a thrill to watch stars up close while you, and they, enjoy a spring break before getting back to work. Tickets to the minors usually run $3–$6; spring training seats, except for the Braves, cost $8–$10.

Minor Leagues

The **Kissimmee Cobras** (✉ 1000 Bill Beck Blvd., Kissimmee, ☎ 407/933–2520 tickets; 407/933–5500 administrative office), Houston's Class A team in the Florida State League, play at Osceola County Stadium, 12 mi east of I–4 Exit 25. Arrive early because tickets are sold only at the stadium on a same-day, first-come basis. Call for schedule and ticket information.

The **Orlando Rays** (✉ 700 W. Victory Way, Kissimmee, ☎ 407/363–6600) are the Tampa Bay Devil Rays' Class AA Southern League affiliate. They play 70 home games April–August at Disney's Wide World of Sports stadium. Call for schedule and ticket information.

Spring Training

The **Atlanta Braves** (☎ 407/363–6600) hold spring training and exhibition baseball games with other major-league teams during February and March at Disney's Wide World of Sports Complex. Tickets are $10.50–$15.50. Tickets are available through **Ticketmaster** at ☎ 407/839–3900 or at the stadium box office. The Braves offer an instructional training season for rookie prospects in September and October. Call for admission prices and game schedules. Baseball fans who attend the games will find Disney's own set of rules apply to their conduct. A sign outside the stadium proclaims NO UNAUTHORIZED BANNERS OR FLAGS. WEAPONS OF ANY KIND ARE STRICTLY PROHIBITED. SMOKING IN LINES, AREAS AND SEATING AREAS IS PROHIBITED. STANDING OR DANCING ON SEATS, STAIRS OR AISLES IS NOT ALLOWED. THE THROWING OF ANY OBJECTS IS PROHIBITED. IDENTIFICATION FOR BEER AND WINE PURPOSES IS REQUIRED FOR PURCHASES. HELIUM BALLOONS ARE NOT ALLOWED. It's always good to know that the lawyers got to the stadium long before the first fan arrived.

A few other teams hold spring training in the immediate area. The **Kansas City Royals** (☎ 941/424–2500) play at the aptly named Baseball City, south of Orlando. The **Houston Astros** (☎ 407/933–5500) call Osceola County Stadium in Kissimmee their spring-training home. For dates and more information, get a copy of the free *Florida Spring Training Guide,* published each year in early February by the Florida Sports Foundation (✉ 2964 Wellington Circle N, Tallahassee 32308, ☎ 850/488–8347).

Basketball

The **Orlando Magic** (✉ 600 W. Amelia St., Orlando, ☎ 407/839–3900 Ticketmaster; 407/916–2255 box office; 407/896–2442 season tickets), which has driven the city to new heights of hoop fanaticism, play in the 15,820-seat Orlando Arena, two blocks west of I–4 Exit 41. Tickets ($17–$125) are next to impossible to get—your best bet for seeing a game is probably a sports bar. For a summer season that begins in early June, the Orlando Arena is home to the city's new Women's National Basketball Association (WNBA) team, the **Orlando Miracle.** Tickets are available for $8 to $85 and can also be purchased at the arena box office (☎ 407/916–9622) or through **Ticketmaster** (☎ 407/839–3900, ✍).

Dog Racing

Sanford Orlando Kennel Club has dog racing and betting, as well as South Florida horse-racing simulcasts and betting. ✉ *301 Dog Track Rd., Longwood,* ☎ *407/831–1600.* ✍ *$1 general admission.* ☉ *Nov.–Apr., Mon.–Sat. 7:30 PM; matinees Mon., Wed., and Sat. 12:30.*

Seminole Greyhound Park, a newer, larger, and prettier track, lets you wager on greyhounds and simulcast horse racing. ✉ *2000 Seminola Blvd., Casselberry,* ☎ *407/699–4510.* 🎫 *$1 general, $2 clubhouse, children half price, grandstand free.* ☉ *May–Oct., Mon.–Sat. 7:30 PM; matinees Mon., Wed., and Sat. 12:30.*

Football

The **Orlando Predators** (✉ 600 W. Amelia St., Orlando, ☎ 407/648–4444; 407/872–7362 season ticket information) play in the indoor Arena Football League, which differs from the National Football League in that teams have only eight players, each of whom holds both offensive and defensive positions. Games are held May–August at the Orlando Arena, and tickets cost $5–$32.

Ice Hockey

Hockey in Florida? You bet! The **Orlando Solar Bears** (✉ 600 W. Amelia St., Orlando, ☎ 407/872–7825, 🏒), the city's own International Hockey League team, established in 1995, have taken the community by storm. The regular hockey season is October–April. The Solar Bears skate their 41 home games at the Orlando Arena, and tickets are $6–$28.

Jai Alai

Orlando-Seminole Jai-Alai, about 20 minutes north of Orlando off I–4 Exit 48, offers South Florida horse-racing simulcasts and betting in addition to jai alai at the fronton. ✉ *6405 S. U.S. 17–92, Fern Park,* ☎ *407/331–9191.* 🎫 *$1 general, $2 reserved seating.* ☉ *Wed.–Sat. 7:30 PM; matinees Thurs. and Sat. noon, Sun. 1.*

Soccer

Among its cornucopia of events, **Disney's Wide World of Sports Complex** presents soccer matches and tournaments, including the annual Disney Soccer Classic, an October match that attracts men's and women's teams from around the world. For information, call ☎ 407/363–6600.

10 AFTER DARK

Mickey and his friends have a decidedly nocturnal side, as do all sorts of party animals around Orlando. A wide variety of bars, clubs, and shows—many based on those ever-present themes that made the area famous—cater to families as well as adults.

Updated by
Gary
McKechnie

F OR SOME, ORLANDO IS simply a factory town, and the factories just happen to be theme parks. To others, it's a backwater burg that lacks sophistication and culture. Then there are the preteen girls who see it as the breeding ground for synthetic bubblegum boy groups. Orlando might be all of this, but it is an entertainment capital of the world and as such is obligated to provide evening diversions to everyone who visits.

There are about 13 million travelers who come to Orlando each year, and many are adults traveling without children. After years of denial, Disney heeded the command of the profits and created Pleasure Island and later West Side to create the Downtown Disney entertainment complex. In response, Universal Orlando opened CityWalk to siphon off what Disney had siphoned off from downtown Orlando, which is now trying to find its footing amidst the new competition.

If you're here for at least two nights and don't mind losing some sleep, reserve one evening for Downtown Disney and the next for CityWalk. They are both well worth seeing. If you want a one-night blowout, however, head to Disney—believe it or not! By virtue of Disney's status as essentially a separate governmental entity, clubs on Disney property are allowed to stay open later than bars elsewhere; you can get served here until 2:45 AM—if you have the energy for it.

WALT DISNEY WORLD® RESORT

When you enter the fiefdom known as Walt Disney World, chances are you'll see as many watering holes as cartoon characters. After beating your feet around a theme park all day, there are lounges, bars, speakeasies, pubs, sports bars, and brewpubs where you can settle down with a soothing libation. Your choice of nightlife can be found at various Disney shopping and entertainment complexes—from the casual down-by-the-shore BoardWalk to the much larger multiarea Downtown Disney, which comprises the Marketplace, Pleasure Island, and West Side. Everywhere you look, jazz trios and bluesmen, DJs and rockers are tuning up and turning on their amps after dinner's done. Plus, two long-running dinner shows provide an evening of song, dance, and dining, all for a single price. As with the parks, you can get information on WDW nightlife by calling ☎ 407/824–2222 or 407/824–4500 or checking on-line at www.disney.com. Disney nightspots accept American Express, MasterCard, and Visa. And cash. Lots of it.

Disney's BoardWalk

At the turn of the 20th century, Americans escaping the cities for the seaside spent their days enjoying the pleasures of breeze-swept boardwalks above the strand, where the earliest thrill rides kept company with band concerts and other activities. Here, across Crescent Lake from Disney's Yacht and Beach Club Resorts, WDW has created its own version of these amusement areas, a shoreside complex cleaner than Atlantic City that's complete with restaurants, bars and clubs, souvenir sellers, surreys, saltwater taffy vendors, and shops. When the lights go on after sunset, the mood is festive—a nice, nostalgic setting for plentiful diversions and a romantic stroll. For information on events call the BoardWalk entertainment hot line, ☎ 407/939–3492 or 407/939–2444.

Atlantic Dance started life as a hypercool room recalling the Swing Era, with martinis, cigars, and Sinatra soundalikes. A brief flirtation with techno pop ended when a certain khaki commercial showed up. Now they're swinging again Monday through Thursday, offering dance lessons Tuesday through Thursday, holding contests periodically, and hosting live bands Friday through Monday. Ages 17 and under are allowed, but they must be accompanied by an adult. ☎ 407/939–2444 or 407/939–2430. ▨ $5 cover. ☉ Daily 9 PM–2 AM.

The lovely **Belle Vue Room,** upstairs in the BoardWalk Inn, is a cozy, comfortable 1930s-style sitting room where you can get away from the crowds for a quiet drink. Step out onto the balcony for a soothing view of the village green and lake. ☎ 407/939–5100, ext. 3565. ▨ No cover. ☉ Daily 5 PM–midnight.

Big River Grille & Brewing Works, Walt Disney World's first brewpub, signals that America's good-beer movement has gone mainstream. You can see the stainless-steel vats and watch the brewmasters tending their potions. Pub grub, sandwiches, and cigars round out the offerings, and a sidewalk café is a great place for people-watching. ☎ 407/560–0253. ▨ No cover. ☉ Mon.–Thurs. 11:30 AM–1 AM, Fri.–Sun. 11:30 AM–2 AM.

ESPN Club is a sports fan's dream come true. As with all things Disney, the sports motif is carried into every nook and cranny. The main dining area looks like a sports arena, with a basketball-court hardwood floor and a giant scoreboard that projects the big game of the day. Sportscasters originate programs from a TV and radio broadcast booth, and there are more than 70 TV monitors throughout the facility, even in the rest rooms. If you want to watch NFL games on Sunday, get there about two hours before kickoff, because the place is packed. ☎ 407/939–1177. ▨ No cover. ☉ Sun.–Thurs. 11:30 AM–1 AM, Fri.–Sat. 11:30 AM–2 AM.

Jellyrolls features comedians at dueling grand pianos in a setting that's rugged and boisterous. The sing-along piano-bar concept is popping up throughout Orlando, but conventioneers make this one unusually interesting. Where else could you watch CEOs conga to Barry Manilow's "Lola"? ☎ 407/560–8770. ▨ Sun.–Thurs. $3, Fri.–Sat. $5. ☉ Daily 7 PM–2 AM.

Downtown Disney

West Side

Disney's West Side is a pleasantly hip outdoor complex of shopping, dining, and entertainment with the main venues being the House of Blues, DisneyQuest, and Cirque du Soleil. Other than for this trio, there are no covers (except for the HOB which changes for special performances). The laid-back feeling, waterside setting, wide promenade, and diverse degree of shopping and dining make West Side worth a visit whether you're club-hopping or not. Opening time is 11 AM, closing time around 2 AM, and crowds vary with the season, but weeknights tend to be less busy.

For **entertainment times** and more information, call ☎ 407/824–4500 or 407/824–2222.

You'll find Latin rhythms at **Bongos Cuban Café,** an enterprise of pop singer Gloria Estefan. The pre-Castro Havana decor and Arquitectonica designs are eye-popping, and the entertainment (a Desi Arnaz look-alike and Cuban bands) is fun. But since the food is less fun, come for a beer and a baba-lu. ☎ 407/828–0999. ☉ Daily 10:30 AM–2 AM.

The surreal show at **Cirque du Soleil** (☎ 407/939–7600 for reservations) starts at 100 mph and accelerates from there. Althoughthe ticket price is high compared to other local shows, you'll be hard-pressed to hear anyone complain. It is 90 minutes of extraordinary acrobatics, avant-garde stagings, costumes, choreography, and a grand finale that'll thrill you silly and make you double-check Newton's laws of gravity. A cast of 72 international performers takes the stage in this specially constructed, 70,000-square-ft venue. A few hints: call well in advance for tickets to improve your chances of getting front row seats; they are closed Mondays and Tuesdays; and hire a baby sitter if necessary—they charge admission for infants. ☎ *$65.72 adults, $40.28 children ages 0–9.* ☉ *Performances Wed.–Sun. 6 and 9 PM.*

DisneyQuest is a five-floor video–virtual reality arcade near the entrance to Pleasure Island. Escape from brick and mortar with larger-than-life games (such as human pinball), and, for us old folks, circa-1970s games such as Asteroids, Tron, and Space Invaders. One admission buys an all-day arcade experience, although the novelty can wear off before the sticker shock does. ☎ *407/828–4600.* ☎ *$27 adults, $21 children 3–9.* ☉ *Daily 10:30 AM–midnight.*

Adjacent to the **House of Blues** restaurant, which itself showcases cool blues alongside its Mississippi Delta cooking, HOB's concert venue brings local and nationally known artists playing everything from reggae to rock to R&B. This is arguably the best live-music venue in Orlando, and the chance to stand a few feet from your guitar heroes is the way music should be seen and heard. The entertainment continues into Sunday morning with the Sunday Gospel Brunch. ☎ *407/934–2583.* ☎ *Covers vary for shows, Gospel Brunch $28 adults, $15 children 4–12.* ☉ *Gospel Brunch Sun. 10:30–1.*

Downtown Disney Marketplace
Drop in at **Cap'n Jack's Oyster Bar,** which overlooks the water, for huge, beautiful strawberry margaritas laced with strawberry tequila. Oh yeah—it serves oysters, too. ☎ *407/828–3870.* ☉ *Daily 11:30–10:30.*

Pleasure Island
Pleasure Island was Disney's first foray into a nighttime complex, and judging by the crowds, the combination of clubs and stores and entertainment remains an attractive mix. The 6-acre park is home to eight clubs—all of which can be accessed with a single admission.

If you're wondering if you'll find people like you here, don't worry—you will. There are college-aged kids, young married couples, middle-aged business travelers, mom and pop who snuck out for an evening sans kids (although kids are allowed—with adults—to all clubs except Mannequins and BET SoundStage Club), and an assortment of foreign tourists from Europe, South America, and Asia. If you arrive on Thursday evening, chances are you'll rub elbows with Disney World cast members arriving to spend their just-issued paychecks. ✉ *Off Buena Vista Dr.,* ☎ *407/934–7781 or 407/824–2222.* ☎ *Pay-one-price admission $20, shops and restaurants free Sun.–Wed. 10:30 AM–11 PM, Thurs.–Sat. 10:30 AM–midnight.* ☉ *Clubs daily 7 PM–2 AM, shops and restaurants daily 10:30 AM–2 AM.*

The **Adventurers Club** is supposed to re-create a private club of the cabaret-happy 1930s. The walls are practically paved with memorabilia from exotic places (with the occasional faux animal head), and servers entertain you with their patter while the lead actors share tall tales from their adventures. You can simply stop for a drink and enjoy the scenery or visit the Library for a slapstick show—either is fun.

BET SoundStage Club, backed by Black Entertainment Television, pays tribute to all genres of black music through videos, live performances, and shows by BET's own dance troupe. As the evening progresses, sounds shift from BET's Top 10 to old R&B to hip-hop—a blend that's attracted legions of locals who proclaim this the funkiest nightspot in Central Florida (perhaps also the loudest). You must be at least 21 to be admitted.

Preceding the popularity of ABC's improvisational hit *Whose Line Is It Anyway?*, the gifted comedians at the **Comedy Warehouse** perform various improv games, sing improvised songs, and create off-the-cuff sketches based largely on suggestions from the audience. Each of the evening's five performances is different, but the cast is usually on target. Drop by—it's always refreshing to watch a gifted comedy troupe work without profanity.

In case the lava lamps and disco balls don't tip you off, the '70s are back at **8TRAX.** Slip on your bell-bottoms, strap on your platform shoes, and groove to Chic, the Village People, or Donna Summer on disk. After a while, it'll seem like you're in your own Quentin Tarantino film.

Thanks to **Mannequins,** the earth will stay in balance because of the speed at which Walt Disney is spinning in his grave. Here Disney dancers go over the top with suggestive bump-and-grind moves apparently inspired by the less-than-inspiring film *Showgirls*. Still, enough guests love the high-tech New York–style dance palace atmosphere, the Top-40 hits, the revolving dance floor, the elaborate lighting, and the special effects—such things as bubbles and snow. You must be at least 21 to be admitted.

One of the better places for jazz in Central Florida, the **Pleasure Island Jazz Company** presents nightly performances by accomplished soloists or six- or seven-piece bands. The decor recalls a '30s speakeasy, and the well-stocked tapas bar and assorted wines by the glass add a smooth '90s touch. The songs of Dinah Washington, Billie Holiday, and friends played between sets keep the mood mellow.

The three-tier **Rock & Roll Beach Club** is always crowded and throbbing with rock music of the 1950s and '60s. The live band and disc jockeys never let the action die down. Another plus are the pool tables, pinball machines, Foosball, darts, and video games that make this seem less like Disney and more like Blue Collarville, USA.

Wildhorse Saloon is a retro Western hangout that hits the bull's-eye with daily (and nightly) dance lessons, kickin' barbecue, and up-and-coming country singers. The dance floor's large enough for a few laps of line dancing. You can go here for a $5 cover without paying to enter Pleasure Island. ☎ 407/827–9453 or 407/827–4947 (concert line). ✉ *No cover Sun.–Mon., $5 Tue.–Sat., concert prices $8–$15.*

Hotel Bars
Now that Walt Disney World has added about a dozen new resort hotels to accommodate guests and conventioneers that once stayed off property, the lounges of some can be surprisingly active. Depending on whether the resort is geared toward business or romance, the lounges can be soothing or boisterous—or both. If you happen to be staying at a Walt Disney World hotel, here's what you may encounter. To reach any of these hotel bars direct, you can call the Disney operator at ☎ 407/824–4500 or 407/824–2222.

The **Ale and Compass Lounge** is a cappuccino-coffee bar that also serves ales and spirits in a serene, nautical setting. ✉ *Yacht Club Resort.* ☉ *Daily 4 PM–midnight.*

Disney's Wide World of Sports Complex is suspiciously empty when no games are being played, but when the games begin there's just as much action over at the **All-Star Cafe.** Within this stadium-size space is a restaurant and souvenir equipment donated by Andre Agassi, Monica Seles, Tiger Woods, Lou Holtz, and company. For a drink, skip the restaurant and head to the bar in front, and afterward check out the huge billiard room in back. If you subscribe to 48 premium sports channels, then this place is a must-see. Otherwise, take a look if you're here on game day. ☎ 407/824–8326. ☉ *Daily 11–11, bar until midnight.*

The lounge adjoining the **California Grill** offers a pleasant view of the Magic Kingdom. The great view is enhanced when the sun goes down and the tiny white lights on Main Street start to twinkle. Add to this nightly fireworks (usually at 10 PM), and there's no better place to order a glass of wine and enjoy the show. ⊠ *Contemporary Resort,* ☎ 407/ 939–3463. ☉ *Daily 5:30 PM–midnight.*

Befitting its location, **Captain's Tavern** has tropical drinks, beer, wine, and cocktails. Old Port Royale is an island market–style setting and the tavern follows suit. It may not be Margaritaville, but it's close enough. ⊠ *Caribbean Beach Resort,* ☎ 407/939–3463. ☉ *Daily 5 PM–10 PM.*

At the **Copa Banana,** a DJ, karaoke, and specialty drinks keep the clientele entertained and tipsy. Because the Dolphin is a business hotel, count on sharing a fruit-slice shape table with after-hours suits. If you're annoyed by Peterson from accounting, the large screen TV may keep you occupied. Note: if you want to relax in a Disney bar, skip this one— although it's on property, the Dolphin is not a Disney hotel. ⊠ *Dolphin Hotel,* ☎ 407/934–4000. ☉ *Daily 8 PM–2 AM.*

Heading south, you'll find the sprawling New Mexican/Mexican– theme Coronado Springs Resort. To slake the thirst of conventioneers, Disney added **Francisco's Lounge,** an open-air cantina-style drinkery near the convention hall entrance. Cool tile floors, umbrellas, and traditional accents are only a backdrop for house specialty margaritas. If you're on a corporate expense account, bottoms up. ⊠ *Coronado Springs Resort.* ☉ *Weekdays 1 PM–midnight, weekends 1–1.*

A short drive or bus ride away at the non-Disney hotels of Walt Disney World, the **Giraffe Tavern & Grille** is a casual lounge whose contemporary look, oak bar, and low lighting are designed for relaxed conversation. ⊠ *Royal Plaza, Lake Buena Vista,* ☎ 407/828–2828. ☉ *Daily noon–2 AM.*

Lively entertainment and good drink specials draw a lively young crowd of Disney cast members to the Palace's less-refined nightspot, the **Laughing Kookaburra.** Tuesday and Thursday, your standard party bar hosts "Ladies Night," and live music is performed Tuesday through Saturday. ⊠ *Wyndham Palace, Lake Buena Vista,* ☎ 407/827–3722. ☉ *Weekdays 5 PM–2 AM, weekends 7 PM–2 AM.*

Martha's Vineyard Lounge is a cozy, refined hideaway where you can settle back and sip a variety of domestic and European wines. Each evening 18 wines are poured for tasting. After facing the madding crowd, it's worth a detour if you're looking for a quiet retreat and a soothing glass of zinfandel. ⊠ *Beach Club Resort.* ☉ *Daily 5:30 PM–10 PM.*

At the stylish Grand Floridian, **Mizner's** is tucked away at the far end of the second floor of the main lobby. Even on steroids, this place wouldn't approach rowdy—it's a tasteful getaway where you can unwind with ports, brandies, and mixed drinks while overlooking the beach and the elegant setting that surrounds you. ⊠ *Grand Floridian.* ☉ *Daily 5 PM–1 AM.*

Narcoossee's is a restaurant with a bar inside that serves ordinary beer in expensive yard glasses, but the porch-side views of the Seven Seas

Lagoon (and the nightly Electrical Water Pageant) are worth the premium you'll pay. Find a nice spot and you can also watch the Magic Kingdom Fireworks. ⊠ *Grand Floridian.* ⌚ *Daily 5 PM–10 PM.*

At the **Tambu Lounge** beside 'Ohana's restaurant, Disney bartenders ring up all the variations on rum punch and piña coladas. Festooned with South Seas–style masks, totems, and Easter Island head replicas, the setting is exotic—with the exception of the large screen TV. ⊠ *Polynesian Resort.* ⌚ *Daily 1 PM–midnight.*

Nestled within a carbon copy of the magnificent Yellowstone Lodge, the **Territory Lounge** at the Wilderness Lodge is a frontier-theme sanctuary that pays tribute to the Corps of Discovery (look overhead for the trail map of Lewis and Clark). A full liquor bar (plus beers, of course) is offered—but you may get just as big a kick looking at the props on display: surveying equipment, daguerreotypes, large log beams, parka mittens, maps, and what they claim are a pair of Teddy Roosevelt's boots. ⊠ *Wilderness Lodge.* ⌚ *Weekdays 4 PM–midnight, weekends 3 PM–1 AM.*

The 27th-floor **Top of the Palace Lounge** offers not only a dazzling view of the Disney empire but also a complimentary champagne toast at sunset each evening—a clock in the lobby lets you know when that is. Considering that this is the highest vista at WDW, file this one away under "worth a detour"—it's a pleasant precursor to dinner at the stylish Arthur's 27 (right next door). ⊠ *Wyndham Palace Resort & Spa, Lake Buena Vista,* ☎ *407/827–3591.* ⌚ *Daily 5 PM–1 AM.*

Dinner Shows

The **Hoop-Dee-Doo Revue,** staged at Fort Wilderness's rustic Pioneer Hall, may be corny, but it is also the liveliest dinner show in Walt Disney World. A troupe of jokers called the Pioneer Hall Players stomp their feet, wisecrack, and otherwise make merry while the audience chows down on barbecued ribs, fried chicken, corn on the cob, strawberry shortcake, and all the fixin's. There are three shows nightly, and the prime times sell out months in advance in busy seasons. But you're better off eating dinner too early or too late rather than missing the fun altogether—so take what you can get. And if you arrive in Orlando with no reservations, try for a cancellation. ⊠ *Fort Wilderness Resort,* ☎ *407/939–3463 in advance; 407/824–2803 day of show.* ▣ *$46.33 adults, $23.78 children 3–11, includes tax and gratuities.* ⌚ *Daily 5, 7:15, and 9:30. No smoking.*

The **Polynesian Luau** is an outdoor barbecue with entertainment appropriate to its colorful South Pacific setting at the Polynesian Resort. Its fire jugglers and hula-drum dancers are entertaining for the whole family, if never quite as endearing as the napkin twirlers at the Hoop-Dee-Doo Revue—although the hula dancers' navel maneuvers are something to see. Reservations a month in advance are essential. ⊠ *Polynesian Resort,* ☎ *407/939–3463 in advance; 407/824–1593 day of show.* ▣ *$46.33 adults, $23.78 children 3–11, includes tax and gratuities.* ⌚ *Tues.–Sat. 5:15 and 8. No smoking.*

Light Shows, Fireworks, and Parades

Both in the theme parks and around the hotel-side waterways, Walt Disney World offers up a wealth of fabulous sound-and-light shows after the sun goes down. In fact, WDW is one of the earth's largest single consumers of fireworks—perhaps even rivaling mainland China. Traditionally, sensational short shows have been held at the Magic Kingdom at 10. Times vary during the year, so check with Guest Services just to be certain. You can also find them at Pleasure Island as part of the every-night-is-New-Year's-Eve celebrations—an event that's worth the wait into the wee hours. For a great, unobstructed view of the fireworks above Cinderella Castle at the Magic Kingdom, head to the second floor of the Main Street Train Station—but get there early.

Until January 1, 2001, the biggest blowout is IllumiNations 2000: Reflections of Earth at Epcot, part of its 15-month opulent Millennium Celebration. If you're only here one evening, this is the one to see.

Electrical Water Pageant
This is one of Disney's small wonders, a 10-minute floating parade of sea creatures outlined in tiny lights, with an electronic score highlighted by Handel's *Water Music*. Don't go out of your way, but if you're by Bay Lake and the Seven Seas Lagoon, look for it from the beaches at the Polynesian (at 9), the Grand Floridian (9:15), Wilderness Lodge (9:35), Fort Wilderness (9:45), the Contemporary (10:05), and, in busy seasons, the Magic Kingdom (10:20). Times occasionally vary, so check with Guest Services.

Fantasmic!
Fantasmic!, the Disney–MGM big after-dark show, is held once nightly (twice in peak season) in a 6,500-seat amphitheater. The special effects are superlative indeed, as Mickey Mouse in the guise of the sorcerer's apprentice emcees a revue full of song and dance, pyrotechnics, and special effects. For the best seats, arrive very early (☞ Disney–MGM Studios *in* Chapter 2).

IllumiNations 2000: Reflections of Earth
Each evening until January 1, 2001, the grand finale of Walt Disney World's Millennium Celebration takes place on the lagoon of the World Showcase. This is no mere fireworks display; it is a symphony of lasers, dancing waters, neon images, and a stirring musical score that prompts a chorus of "ooohs" and "aaaahs" from onlookers. The story line focuses on the Earth Globe, a 28-ft diameter sphere that displays images and icons to celebrate human diversity and the unified spirit of mankind. Even if you miss the message, the combination of fire and water and music should kindle your spirit. It may sound silly, but check the wind direction before staking a claim since smoke can cloak some views. Some of the better vantage points are the Matsu No Ma Lounge in the Japan pavilion, the patios of the Rose and Crown in the United Kingdom pavilion, and Cantina de San Angel in Mexico. Another good spot is the World Showcase Plaza between the boat docks at the Showcase entrance, but this is often crowded with visitors who want to make a quick exit after the show. If you want to join them here, claim your seat at least an hour in advance (☞ Epcot *in* Chapter 2).

The Main Street Electrical Parade
Disney characters galore, from Cinderella and Alice to Minnie and Mickey, proceed down Main Street and through Frontierland on floats that are essentially black steel frameworks encrusted with thousands of tiny lights. Some of the characters' costumes are also wired with lights. The effect is truly splendid, and the parade is one of the Magic Kingdom's don't-miss attractions. It runs only when the park is open late and at times that vary from day to day; check before you leave home or ask any Disney staffer while you're in the park. The early showing is for parents with children, and the later ones get night owls and others with the stamina and the know-how to enjoy the Magic Kingdom's most pleasant, least-crowded time of day. For the early show, stake out a spot at least 30 minutes before the scheduled start of the parade (☞ Magic Kingdom *in*

Chapter 2). At press time, the parade was scheduled to run through summer 2000, but after that, its future was uncertain.

Tapestry of Nations

It's no secret that Disney puts on some of the most spectacular parades in the country, but this one manages to go beyond spectacular. Backed by the talent of the Lion King's Michael Curry, 120 towering puppets (attached to parading performers) march around the World Showcase accompanied by 720 drums and 30 drummers. Giant torch towers set the stage for this event, which, although filled with some hard to understand symbolism, is a mighty impressive eclectic collection of costumes, colors, motion, and music. Don't panic if you miss the first one—it steps off twice each evening at 6:30 and 8:10 (☞ Epcot *in* Chapter 2).

Movies

With all the only-in-WDW activities, it seems a shame to do what you can always do at home. But there are nights when your feet won't walk even one more step. Try the **AMC 24 Theatres** (⊠ Downtown Disney West Side, ☎ 407/827–1309 ticket office; 407/298–4488 show times). The cinema is state-of-the-art and plays all the latest films.

UNIVERSAL ORLANDO

Now that Universal has put Dynamite Nights Stuntacular on hiatus, evening action has been shifting to the eclectic and eccentric CityWalk, a 30-acre pastiche of shops, restaurants, clubs, and concert venues. The attitude here is as hip and sassy as elsewhere in the Universal domain.

✍ following the text of a review is your signal that the property has a Web site, where you will find details and, usually, images; for a link, visit www.fodors.com/urls.

Universal Orlando's CityWalk

Aside from having a catchy headline ("Get a Nightlife"), CityWalk has met the challenge of diverting the lucrative youth market from Disney and downtown Orlando. It did it by creating an open and airy gathering place that includes clubs ranging from quiet jazz retreats to over-the-top discotheques. On weeknights the crowd is a mix of families and conventioneers; weekends draw a decidedly younger crowd, and they're still arriving while the rest of us are getting our beauty sleep.

Several changes have occurred at CityWalk, mostly relating to admission prices—changes that work in your favor. The steep $16.95 cover and $6 parking fee is now a more reasonable $7.95 Party Pass (a one price–all clubs admission), and parking is now free after 6 PM, and if you'd like to see a movie, add $4 to your Party Pass. It's a long walk from the parking garage to CityWalk, and it's even longer when you stumble out at 2 AM and realize it's a ¼ mi back to your car. Then again, you shouldn't be driving when you feel like this anyway, so have a good time and call a cab. Taxis run at all hours. If you don't go for the Party Pass, keep in mind that covers vary depending on the entertainment and that each club serves some type of food. For information about any of these places call ☎ 407/363–8000 (Universal main line) or 407/224–2683 or 407/224–2600 (CityWalk guest services) or check on-line at www.uescape.com.

Why spend your time watching a movie when you're on vacation? Who cares? It's your vacation. The 20-screen, 5,000-seat **Loew's Universal Cineplex** (☎ 407/354–5998 tickets; 407/354–3374 box office) can offer an escape from the crowds. You can purchase tickets in advance by telephone.

The beauty of **Bob Marley–A Tribute to Freedom** is that even if you can't dance, you can pretend by simply swaying to syncopated reggae rhythms. The museum-club is modeled after "The King of Reggae's" home in Kingston, complete with intimate low ceilings and more than 100 photographs and paintings reflecting pivotal moment's in Marley's life. Off the cozy bar is a neat patio area where you can be jammin' to a (loud) live band nightly. You must be 21 and over on Friday and Saturday after 10 PM. 💸 *$4.25 cover after 8 PM.* ☽ *Daily 4 PM–2 AM.*

CityWalk hasn't forsaken the needs of older folks who prefer a quiet, cool, sophisticated place to chill out. Fortunately, **CityJazz** isn't exclusively progressive jazz but a celebration of all types. You can tell this once you enter the beautiful, tiered room where soft lighting, rich woods, and candlelight create a perfect backdrop. To pay tribute to members of the Down Beat Hall of Fame, there's also memorabilia from Ella Fitzgerald, Duke Ellington, Lionel Hampton, Count Basie, and other legends. For a quiet martini and live entertainment, you can't do much better than this. 💸 *$3.25 cover, special performance ticket prices $6–$26.50.* ☽ *Sun.–Thurs. 6 PM–1 AM, Fri.–Sat. 6 PM–2 AM.*

As at Pleasure Island's Mannequins, you must be 21 to enter **the groove** (note the hip lowercase lettering), a cavernous hall where every nook and cranny is filled with techno-pop and the decor can switch suddenly from '60s Retro to Victorian. The very sound of the place can be terrifying to the uninitiated, and the rapidly flickering images on several screens, designed as visual stimulation, only compound matters. Apparently the combination of music, light, and mayhem appeals to a younger group. They know enough to escape the dance floor into three rooms: the Green Room, a '70s-style setting filled with beanbag chairs and everything you threw out when Duran Duran hit; the sci-fi Blue Room; and the Red Room, which is hot and romantic in a bordello sort of way. Lots of fog, lots of swirling lights, lots of motion. 💸 *$5.25 cover.* ☽ *Daily 9 PM–2 AM.*

You could travel all over the world, but you'll never find a larger **Hard Rock Cafe,** where there's great food, loud music, and lots of eye candy. Start with dinner and stay for the show since much of the attraction here is at the adjoining **Hard Rock Live.** If you feel that you're growing old, get your reality check via the Cafe's "archival" punk rock posters and gear. The best items adorn a room on the second floor: Beatles rarities such as cutouts from the Sgt. Pepper cover, John Lennon's famous "New York City" T-shirt, plenty of autographs, Paul's original lyrics for "Let It Be," and the doors from London's Abbey Road studios. Wow. The adjoining concert hall, **Hard Rock Live** resembles Rome's Colosseum, and almost every evening an entertainer performs here; occasionally it's one you recognize (Ringo, Elvis Costello, Jerry Lee Lewis, etc.). Although the seats are hard and two-thirds don't face the stage, it's one of Orlando's top venues. Warning: they don't allow large purses or bags inside and there are no lockers at CityWalk, so leave big baggage in your car. 💸 *Varying cover for concerts.* ☽ *Daily from 11 AM, with a varying closing time.*

Jimmy Buffett may be the most savvy businessman in America. He took a concept, wrapped it up in a catchy tune, and parlayed it into books, clothing, musicals, and **Jimmy Buffett's Margaritaville.** Florida law requires residents play Buffett music 24 hours a day, but if you're from out of state you might still not be over cheeseburgers in paradise. Attached to the restaurant are three bars (Volcano, Land Shark, and 12 Volt) that bring Buffett songs to life. There's a Pan Am Clipper suspended from the ceiling, music videos projected onto sails, fishing poles sticking out from booths, live entertainment, limbo and hula hoop contests, a huge margarita blender that erupts "when the volcano blows," live music nightly, and all the other subtleties that give Parrotheads a place to roost. ▨ *$3.25 cover after 10 PM.* ☉ *Daily 11 AM–2 AM.*

Florida's Hispanic population is the fastest-growing in the state, and the **Latin Quarter** seems to have attracted all who live in Orlando. Crowded, pulsing, and filled with women in skin-tight fabric that passes for clothing, the club feels like a 21st-century version of Ricky Ricardo's Tropicana, although the design is based on a mix of Aztec, Incan, and Maya architecture. This boasts the highest cover of all CityWalk clubs ($10), which you can offset with a one-price-buys-all Party Pass. If you can get your hips working overtime, pick a rhumba from 1 to 10 and swivel . . . and tango and merengue and salsa . . . ▨ *$10 cover.* ☉ *Daily 11 AM–2 AM.*

The **Motown Cafe,** the club closest to the parking lot, is more restaurant than bar, but still worth seeing. You'll find the usual retinue of rock star stuff (such as the Jackson 5's basketball uniforms), as well as great statues of Little Stevie Wonder and the Supremes. Each evening, the house band (alternating between Supremes or Temptation look-alikes) rekindles Motown hits, and even folks from Dubuque find it hard to stay seated through a good Smokey Robinson song. There's lots of hand-clapping, finger-snapping, and groove-shaking going on here. ▨ *$3.25 cover after 9 PM Sun.–Thurs., after 10 PM Fri.–Sat.* ☉ *Sun.–Thurs. 11:30 AM–midnight, Fri.–Sat. 11:30 AM–2 AM.*

It's a legend in New Orleans, and it's doing all right in Orlando. Over at **Pat O'Brien's,** you'll find an exact replica of the original. The flaming fountain is going strong, dueling pianists are shooting it out, the balcony re-creates the Crescent City, and yet another barroom is perfectly suited for conversation. The draw here is the Patio Bar, where abundant tables and chairs allow you to take a break from vacation and do nothing but enjoy a respite from the madding crowd—and drink a Hurricane. ▨ *$2.25 after 9 PM.* ☉ *Daily 4 PM–2 AM.*

ORLANDO AND KISSIMMEE

For several years, downtown Orlando clubs had a monopoly on night-time entertainment—which came to a close when Disney and Universal muscled their way in. Nightspots still attract office workers after hours, but the cool clubs are now sitting beside grungy tattoo and piercing parlors that are making the downtown area look tired and seedy. Add to this thinning crowds at Church Street Station and it gets a little more depressing. Still, there are evenings when downtown sparkles—special events and holiday weekends for instance—and the absence of wall-to-wall crowds might make a visit worth the trip.

The Arts

When the fantasy starts wearing thin, check out the Orlando arts scene in *The Weekly,* a local entertainment and opinion newspaper that accurately tracks Orlando culture, lifestyles, and nightlife. In Friday's *Orlando Sentinel,* the "Calendar" section carries reviews on plays, nightclubs, live music venues, restaurants, and attractions. Both newspapers provide a wealth of information and are available at any newsstand. For some reason, local theater has the mistaken impression it presents Broadway-caliber shows, and tickets are often overpriced. To make prices even steeper, traveling Broadway shows actually do come to the Carr Performing Arts Centre.

The area has an active agenda of dance, classical music, opera, and theater, much of which takes place at the **Carr Performing Arts Centre** (⌧ 401 W. Livingston St., Orlando, ☎ 407/849–2577, ✇). The Broadway Series (☎ 407/839–3900 Ticketmaster) features top-notch touring shows such as *Beauty and the Beast, Fame,* and *Fosse.* The **Civic Theaters of Central Florida** (⌧ 1001 E. Princeton St., Orlando, ☎ 407/896–7365) comprises three theaters: the Main Stage, which features Broadway-style shows with evening performances Thursday through Saturday and Sunday matinees; the Second Stage, which offers off-Broadway and contemporary plays; and the Family Classics, which has, as the name implies, weekend shows for the whole family. In early 2000, the theatre was in danger of bankruptcy, so call in advance. **Orange County Convention and Civic Center** (⌧ South end of International Dr., Orlando, ☎ 407/345–9800) is primarily the site for corporate conventions but is sometimes the venue for local concerts by top artists. The downtown Orlando Arena (nicknamed the O-rena by Magic basketball fans) was given a new name thanks to a large check from a major corporation. The clunkily named **TD Waterhouse Centre** (⌧ 600 W. Amelia St., Orlando, ☎ 407/849–2020) plays host to many big-name performers and sports events such as arena football and hockey, and is a popular venue for wrestling.

During the school year, the Bach Festival organization at **Rollins College** (⌧ Winter Park, ☎ 407/646–2233) has a three-part concert series that is open to the public and is usually free. The choral series is held at Rollins' Knowles Memorial Chapel, and the second part, the visiting artists series at the Annie Russell Theater features internationally celebrated artists who have performed at venues such as Carnegie Hall. The last week in February, internationally recognized artists appear at the **Bach Music Festival** (☎ 407/646–2182, ✇), a Winter Park tradition for more than 60 years and the last in the trilogy. The festival is held at the Annie Russell Theater and the Knowles Memorial Chapel and culminates on Sunday afternoon with "Highlights," which includes short features by several of the artists who appeared during the week. Also contact the **Annie Russell Theater** (☎ 407/646–2501) for information about its regular series of student productions.

Church Street Station

Orlando's original entertainment complex, Church Street Station was created in the 1970s when ex-Navy pilot Bob Snow transformed run-down buildings into a downtown complex of old-fashioned saloons, dance halls, dining rooms, and shopping arcades. When Bob Snow left, however, corporations with little finesse nearly finished it off. Annual attendance of nearly 2 million now hovers around 500,000, and there are empty storefronts in the shopping area, Church Street Exchange. Still, appearances count for something: the 19th-century steam engine, calliope, and horse-drawn carriages add a special ambience.

Several themed clubs are here, and even on quiet nights there are usually street musicians, singers, and balloon-bending clowns hitting the bricks. On weekend evenings, the pace picks up, with crowds heaviest from 10 to 11. The complex and the street is most popular on fall weekends, when a big football game is going on at the Citrus Bowl, and during theme parties on holidays such as St. Patrick's Day, May's Island Fest, Halloween, and New Year's Eve. Call ahead around holidays to check events, especially if you're thinking of taking the children. ⌧ *129 W. Church St., Orlando,* ☎ *407/422–2434.* ⌹ *$17.95 adult cover after 6 PM, $11.95 children ages 4–12. AE, MC, V.* ✇

Quiet **Apple Annie's Courtyard** offers recorded, easy-listening music from Jimmy Buffett to James Taylor for your enjoyment either before or after dinner. With nice high-back chairs, paddle fans, and a tropical feel, this is a good place to rest your feet and sip a drink. ☉ *Sun.– Thurs. 11 AM–1 AM, Fri.–Sat. 11 AM–2 AM.*

The **Cheyenne Saloon and Opera House** is the biggest, fanciest, rootin'-tootin'est saloon you may ever see. Occupying a tri-level former opera house, the place is full of moose racks, steer horns, buffalo heads, and Remington rifles; the seven-piece country-and-western band that plays here darn near brings the house down. With all the pickin', strummin', fiddlin', hollerin', and do-si-do-in', it's a fun place to people-watch. It's also one of the few places at Church Street to draw a big crowd every night. The upstairs restaurant serves chicken-and-ribs fare. ☉ *Sun.– Thurs. 5 PM–1 AM, Fri.–Sat. 5 PM–2 AM; dinner daily 5–11; shows daily 8:15, 10:15, and 11:25, Fri.–Sat. also 12:45 AM.*

Cracker's Seafood Restaurant, next to the Orchid Garden, is a good place to get a meal of fresh Florida seafood and pasta or slam down a few oysters with a beer chaser. ☉ *Daily 11 AM–midnight, lunch Sun.–Fri. 11–4, dinner daily 4–11.*

Lili Marlene's Aviator's Pub and Restaurant has the finest dining on Church Street and the relaxed atmosphere of an English pub. Food is hearty, upscale, and very American—mostly steaks and seafood. Walls are wood-paneled and decked with biplane-era memorabilia; from the ceiling hang model aircraft. There's no music and no cover. Check out Al Capone's dining room table. ☉ *Lunch daily 11–4, dinner daily 5:30– 11:30, Fri. until midnight.*

The **Orchid Garden Ballroom** began as a venue for '30s and '40s music but surrendered to the more popular '50s–'90s music that the house band plays throughout the evening. Although the music is hot, the decorative Victorian lamps, iron latticework, arched ceilings, and stained-glass windows are now out of place. Why they haven't redecorated to fit the music is a mystery, but since you've already paid admission, drop by and enjoy. ☉ *Sun.–Thurs. 7:15 PM–1 AM, Fri.–Sat. 7:15 PM–2 AM; first show daily 8.*

A throbbing disco, **Phineas Phogg's** has a sound system that will blow your argyle socks off. Perhaps because there's no cover, the nightspot is packed with a good-looking yuppie tourist crowd, young singles, a sprinkling of old-timers, and local talent showing off dance moves. The Backstreet Boys got their start here. Sorry. The place is packed by midnight and may be the only club still jamming until closing. You must be at least 21 to enter. ☉ *Sun.–Thurs. 8 PM–1 AM, Fri.–Sat. 8 PM–2 AM.*

Rosie O'Grady's Good Time Emporium, the original bar on Church Street, is a turn-of-the-20th-century saloon with dark wood, brass trim, and jazz reviews from Dixieland to contemporary. Multidecker sandwiches and hot dogs are served, along with sodas and such drinks as a Flaming Hurricane. A jazz band plays at night and is usually the time when Rosie's recalls past glories. ☉ *Sun.–Thurs. 7:15 PM–1 AM, Fri.–Sat. 7:15 PM–2 AM; shows at 7:15, 8:40, and 10:15 PM.*

Downtown Orlando Clubs and Bars

:08 is a country-theme nightclub with rather unusual attractions. In addition to presenting such country artists as Trisha Yearwood and Marty Stuart, the club sponsors Buck and Bull Night on Saturday, when professional cowboys entertain the crowd by ridin' real live snortin' bulls. Frontier Fridays are highlighted by dance lessons, ladies' drink specials, monster truck events, country karaoke, and music by a live country band. A little bit of country in the heart of downtown. ⊠ *100 W. Livingston St.,* ☎ *407/839–4800.* 🎫 *$5 ages 21 and older, $7 ages 18–20.* ⊙ *Fri.–Sat. 8 PM–3 AM. AE, MC, V.*

Howl at the Moon was Orlando's first sing-along bar, and it continues to encourage patrons to warble the pop classics of yesteryear or favorites such as the "Time Warp" and "Hokey Pokey." This isn't karaoke: everybody sings at once, so the noise level is just below a sonic boom. Toss back a couple of long-neck beers or one of the house specialty drinks—served in souvenir glasses—and you won't care anymore. Piano players keep the music rolling in the evening, and the World's Most Dangerous Wait Staff adds to the entertainment. No food is served, but the management encourages you to bring your own or order out; several nearby restaurants deliver. You must be 21 or older. ⊠ *Church St. Marketplace, 55 W. Church St., 2nd floor,* ☎ *407/841–4695 or 407/841–9118.* 🎫 *Wed. and Fri.–Sat. $4, Thurs. $2, Sun.–Tues. free.* ⊙ *Sun.–Thurs. 6 PM–2 AM, Fri.–Sat. 4 PM–2 AM. AE, D, MC, V.*

As popular as any other place in the area, **Mulvaney's** is clearly downtown's most-frequented Irish pub. Seven nights a week the wood-panel bar is packed with pub crawlers fond of simple fare, imported ales, and live entertainment, especially authentic Irish folk music. ⊠ *27 W. Church St.,* ☎ *407/872–3296.* 🎫 *Free.* ⊙ *Weekdays 11 AM–2 AM, Sat. noon–2 AM, Sun. 1 PM–2 AM. AE, MC, V.*

Refreshingly free of stand-up comedians, lively **Sak Comedy Lab** is home to Orlando's premier comedy troupe. Deserving of its regular first-place finishes in a national improv competition, it plays to sold-out audiences, so get here early. Duel of Fools is the regular cast; the Sak Comedy Lab Rats are apprentices with potential. Wayne Brady, star of *Whose Line Is It Anyway?*, got his start here. ⊠ *380 W. Amelia Ave.,* ☎ *407/648–0001.* 🎫 *Duel of Fools and Improv Jam $12, Lab Rats $3.* ⊙ *Duel of Fools Thurs.–Sat. 8 PM; Improv Jam Fri.–Sat. 10 PM; Lab Rats Tues. 9 PM. No credit cards.*

The **Sapphire Supper Club** is perhaps the locals' favorite live music venue, and a good place to go to see touring—and local—musicians. It serves full dinners Wednesday through Saturday and offers up live music seven nights a week. You can sip trademark martinis while listening to anything from alternative rock to rockabilly to undiluted jazz. Several now-national acts got their start here, including Matchbox 20 and Seven Mary Three. ⊠ *54 N. Orange Ave.,* ☎ *407/246–1419 or 407/249–1380.* 🎫 *$5–$18 depending on entertainment.* ⊙ *Sat.–Thurs. 8 PM–2 AM, Fri. 5 PM–2 AM. AE, D, MC, V.* 🍴

At **Zuma Beach,** a sun-and-surf-theme dance club, up to 1,200 young adults a night take advantage of the club's changing entertainment. Every evening is a Ride the Wave Beach Blast Celebration that ranges from Sunday evening ECW wrestling matches to Tuesday male revues to Ladies' Night on Thursday when women can drink for free. Adults 18 and older are welcome, but you must be 21 to drink. ⊠ *46 N. Orange Ave.,* ☎ *407/648–8363.* 🎫 *$6.* ⊙ *Daily 9 PM–3 AM. AE, MC, V. Closed Mon..* 🍴

Clubs and Bars Around I-Drive

A favorite hangout of people who work along I-Drive and at SeaWorld, **Bennigan's** draws crowds from 2 to 7 PM and again from 10 PM to closing. Food is served almost until closing. ⊠ *6324 International Dr.,* ☎ *407/351–4436.* 🎫 *No cover.* ⊙ *Daily 11 AM–2 AM. AE, D, MC, V.*

There are actually three piano-pounders in **Blazing Pianos,** a large hall that's usually filled with visitors and locals screaming along to songs they remember from their childhood. On weekends, this may be the most active club in town, and even though there's no minimum, many people end up losing their fear of singing in public by ordering many specialty drinks and beers. Families are welcome Sunday through Thursday, when the mood is more PG than R. ⊠ *In the Mercado, 8445 International Dr.,* ☎ *407/363–5104.* ▣ *Cover $7 Fri.–Sat., $5 Sun.– Thurs.* ☉ *Weekdays 7 PM–12:30 AM, weekends 7 PM–1:30 AM; shows daily 8 PM. AE, D, MC, V.* ✎

If pubs could be reinvented in America instead of England, then the perfect prototype would be the **Cricketers Arms,** which is tucked in a back alley of the Mercado shopping complex. Locals crowd this English-style, American-looking pub to hear good Florida bands. Tables are small and closely packed inside, but you can always grab one outside on the sidewalk (nice at night) or go to the back patio. This is a great place to experience Britain—with a cold beer. ⊠ *In the Mercado, 8445 International Dr.,* ☎ *407/354–0686.* ▣ *No cover except for soccer matches ($10).* ☉ *Daily 11 AM–2 AM. AE, MC, V.* ✎

He never won a Super Bowl (probably because he wore unlucky number 13), but Miami Dolphin quarterback Dan Marino has had better luck with **Dan Marino's Town Tavern.** More sophisticated than a locker room, it has secluded booths and an oblong, football-shape bar that seems to have struck a chord with locals who linger over the house specialty, Marino Margaritas (no, they don't contain Gatorade). This is more restaurant than bar—until around 9 PM, when the bar comes to life. It's not wild, just a calming place for a quiet drink. Be sure to have your server validate your parking ticket. ⊠ *In the Pointe*Orlando, 9101 International Dr.,* ☎ *407/363–1013.* ▣ *No cover; parking $2, free with validation.* ☉ *Daily 11–11. AE, MC, V.*

Friday's national scope explains how they could afford to build a sports bar the size of Delaware, **Friday's Front Row Sports Grille & Restaurant.** You enter on an incline to give you the sense you're walking into a sports stadium. To the right is the dining area; if you're here for drinks, walk past the bleachers toward the back and join the locals, who come here to play trivia games, eat the bar food, talk stats, and ogle autographed pictures. The fun continues upstairs, and upstairs beyond that. ⊠ *8126 International Dr.,* ☎ *407/363–1414.* ▣ *No cover.* ☉ *Daily 11 AM–2 AM. AE, D, DC, MC, V.*

JB's Sports Bar & Restaurant has been around for years, surviving on the sports-mindedness of Universal employees, Disney cast members, and locals. You're welcome, too. Weeknights are fine, but on weekends and during big games, the place is like a frat-house party, with 28 TVs broadcasting the action and grog flowing nonstop. You can shoot some darts during commercials. And head for the enclosed patio if you need a break from the noise. The setting (in a shopping plaza) is as basic as the bar food: hot dogs, wings, and sandwiches. ⊠ *4880 S. Kirkman Rd.,* ☎ *407/293–8881.* ▣ *No cover except for special pay-per-view events.* ☉ *Daily 11 AM–2 AM. AE, D, DC, MC, V.*

The **Orlando Ale House** would look so much better if it weren't in a strip mall since it's a nice retreat for a beer. It's large and gracious inside, with booths and brass rails and standard-issue pool tables, dart boards, and TV screens. There's a raw bar, and you can order sandwiches, burgers, pastas, and fried foods. Beer is the big seller here, especially on Monday and Thursday, when you can buy a bucket for $5; the $1 drafts and $1 margaritas are a good deal as well. ⊠ *5573 S.*

Kirkman Rd., ☎ *407/248–0000* ✉ *No cover.* ☉ *Daily 11* AM*–2* AM. *AE, D, MC, V.*

The **Players Grill,** one of several drinkeries at Pointe*Orlando, is ostensibly the "Home of the NFL Players." Whatever. At least you will see their artifacts on display en route to the upscale restaurant upstairs or the sports bar on the ground level. Drink specials change with the sporting event; the pool tables, pinball machines, and darts are staples. ✉ *In Pointe*Orlando, 9101 International Dr.,* ☎ *407/903–1974.* ✉ *No cover.* ☉ *Weekdays 4–10:30, weekends 11* AM*–midnight. AE, D, DC, MC, V.*

Dinner Shows

Dinner shows are immensely popular nighttime entertainment around Orlando. For a single price, these hybrid eatery-entertainment complexes deliver a theatrical production and a multicourse dinner. Performances run the gamut from jousting to jamboree tunes and tend to be better than the standard forgettable meal; unlimited beer, wine, and soda are usually included, but mixed drinks (and often *any* drinks before dinner) will cost extra. What the shows lack in substance and depth they make up for in color and the enthusiasm of the performers. The result is an evening of light entertainment, which youngsters in particular will enjoy. Seatings are usually between 7 and 9:30, and there are usually one or two performances a night, with an extra show during peak periods. At most, you sit with strangers at tables for 10 or more; that's part of the fun. Always reserve in advance, especially for weekends. If you're in Orlando in an off-season, try to take in these dinner shows on a busy night—a show playing to a small audience can be pathetic and embarrassing. Also be on the lookout for discount coupons: you'll find them in brochure racks in malls, in hotels, and at the Orlando/Orange County Convention & Visitors Bureau. Since performance schedules can vary depending on the tourist season, it's always smart to call in advance to verify show times.

Orlando

Mark Two, Orlando's first true dinner theater, stages complete Broadway shows and, during the Christmas holidays, musical revues chockfull of Broadway tunes. Prior to the show, the audience grazes on ordinary food, and dessert arrives during intermission. It's a local effort, with sets, costumes, music, choreography, and direction created by employees; under the circumstances, you wouldn't expect the world's best *Oklahoma!,* and you don't get it. But it can be a pleasure to revisit these old favorites while sitting comfortably with a drink in hand. Each show runs for six to eight weeks. Unlike other dinner theaters, the Mark Two offers only tables for two and four. Young children usually find it impossible to sit through the shows, and the steep charge provides ample reason to leave them with a baby-sitter. Ask about discounts. The theater is in an ordinary shopping plaza west of I–4 Exit 44. ✉ *Edgewater Center, 3376 Edgewater Dr.,* ☎ *407/843–6275 or 800/726–6275.* ✉ *Matinees $30.50–$38; evenings $35.50–$43; children 15 and under receive a $10 discount.* ☉ *Wed.–Thurs. and Sat. 1:15 and 8, Fri. 8, Sun. 6:30. AE, D, MC, V.* ✎

If Sherlock Holmes has always intrigued you, head for **Sleuths Mystery Dinner Show,** where your four-course meal is served up with a healthy dose of conspiracy. Each of the seven whodunit performances rotated throughout the year stops short of revealing the perpetrator. You get to question the characters and attempt to solve the mystery. Did the butler do it? ✉ *7508 Universal Blvd.,* ☎ *407/363–1985 or 800/393–*

1985. ⊞ *$38.95 adults, $22.95 children 3–11.* ⊙ *Mon.–Sat. 6, 7:30, and 9, Sun. 7:30. AE, D, MC, V.* ⊛

Kissimmee

An elaborate palace outside, **Arabian Nights** is more like an arena within, with seating for more than 1,200. The show features eerie fog, an Arabian princess, and a buffoonish genie, but the real stars are the 60 fabulous horses (and a cast of 30 performers) that create acts representing horse-loving cultures from around the world: bareback acrobatics by gypsies, an intricate Western square dance on horseback, a chariot race, and Walter Farley's *Black Stallion.* The three-course dinners are prime rib or vegetarian lasagna, but you don't end up paying much attention to the food, since you're served during the show. Locals have voted this the best dinner show in town, and extra shows are added in the summer. Call ahead. ⊠ *6225 W. Irlo Bronson Memorial Hwy., Kissimmee,* ☎ *407/239–9223 or 800/553–6116; 800/533–3615 in Canada.* ⊞ *$36.95 adults, $23.95 children 3–11.* ⊙ *Daily 7:30. AE, D, MC, V.* ⊛

Capone's Dinner and Show returns to the gangland Chicago of 1931, when mobsters and their dames represented the height of underworld society. The evening begins in an old-fashioned ice cream parlor, but say the secret password and you'll be ushered inside Al Capone's private Underworld Cabaret and Speakeasy. Dinner is an unlimited Italian buffet that's heavy on pasta. ⊠ *4740 W. IrloBronson Memorial Hwy.,* ☎ *407/397–2378.* ⊞ *$39.95 adults, $23.95 children 4–12.* ⊙ *Daily 8. AE, D, MC, V.* ⊛

Medieval Times, in a huge, ersatz-medieval manor house, portrays a tournament of sword fights, jousting matches, and other games on a good-versus-evil theme, featuring no fewer than 30 charging horses and a cast of 75 knights, nobles, and maidens. Sound silly? It is. Yet if you view it through the eyes of your children, this two-hour extravaganza is super. That the show takes precedence over the hearty meat-and-potatoes fare is obvious from the dining setup: everyone sits facing forward at long, narrow banquet tables stepped auditorium-style above the tournament area. Additional diversions in the Medieval Life area include a dungeon and torture chamber to tour and demonstrations of antique blacksmithing, woodworking, and pottery making. ⊠ *4510 W. Irlo Bronson Memorial Hwy.,* ☎ *407/239–0214 or 800/229–8300.* ⊞ *$39.95 adults, $24.50 children 3–11.* ⊙ *Castle daily 9–4, village daily 4:30–8, performances usually daily at 8 but call ahead to check. AE, D, MC, V.* ⊛

Movies

If you didn't come to Orlando just to see a "regular" movie at one of the megaplexes, check out the impressive **Muvico Pointe 21** (⊠ Pointe*Orlando, 9101 International Dr., Orlando, ☎ 407/903–0555). It not only has 21 screens and stadium seating but also a six-story theater for IMAX 3-D films, which are viewed with state-of-the-art liquid-crystal headsets.

11 THE COCOA BEACH AREA

This section of Florida, known as the Space Coast, provides the pleasures that both of those words imply. A hop, skip, and a jump from Orlando, you can thrill to attractions based on real, not imagined, space travel and relax on genuine wave-lapped ocean beaches.

T**HE MOST DIRECT ROUTE** from Greater Orlando to the coast, the
Beeline Expressway (Route 528), is arrow-straight, cut through
forests of long-needle pine and laid across the yawning savannas

Updated by
Pamela
Acheson

at the very southern tip of the south-to-north St. Johns River, which
begins life as a tiny stream in a place called Hell and Blazes, Florida.
In this extremely flat countryside of cedars, red maples, and palmettos, American egrets, blue herons, and shy limpkins wade and fish for
dinner; ibises tend their chicks; and graceful anhingas perch where they
can, spreading their wings to dry. High above watery prairies yellow
with wild mustard and butterflies, hawks hunt and ospreys soar over
their nests that crown stately sabal palms, Florida's official tree. It feels
a million miles from the artificial worlds of the theme parks, and it's
one good reason to make the trip from Orlando to Brevard County,
on the east coast, only an hour away.

The laid-back beach communities are another reason to venture out
of Orlando. Moreover, the area is home to the Kennedy Space Center
and offers water sports, fishing, golf, nature, nightlife, a great zoo, and
some distinctive shopping.

Accommodations, restaurants, and shopping are relatively close to
one another and to all the region's points of interest. And if you're lucky
enough to be in town during a space shot, you'll be treated to a spectacular sight.

Pleasures and Pastimes

Beaches

On Florida's mid-Atlantic coast from Canaveral National Seashore south
to Sebastian Inlet, there are about 100 mi of wide, sandy beaches. Although the winter season alone counts about 600,000 vacationers, the
area's beaches are much less densely developed than Daytona's. Sun
worshipers don't have to worry about being run over as they frolic or
stroll—no cars are allowed on these sands. Although Central Florida's
Atlantic beaches have some wave action, those looking for big surf will
be much happier on the West Coast—of the United States, not of
Florida. Generally, beaches below Satellite Beach, south of Cocoa
Beach, tend to be rocky, with an uneven bottom.

Dining

If you like fresh seafood, the Space Coast is your kind of place. The
area is dotted with casual eateries with a heavy emphasis on the fruits
of the sea. There are a few upscale dining establishments in Cocoa and
Cocoa Beach, but for the most part the eatin' is easy. At some places,
you can just walk up to a beachside window and order a basket of fried
shrimp and a brew. For approximate costs, *see* the dining price chart
in Smart Travel Tips A to Z.

Fishing

There are many hot spots for local fishing. Check *Florida Today,* the
local newspaper, or bait-and-tackle shops to find out what's biting where.
You can surf cast for bluefish, pompano, sea bass, and flounder; success is mixed and depends on the season. Or try your hand at pier fishing. (All major beach towns have lighted piers, and admission is usually
$1–$4.) Here anglers sometimes pull in mackerel, trout, sheepshead,
and tarpon. Because it's on the inland waterway rather than the Atlantic, the Titusville pier has good shrimping, too. You can also fish
from some of the bridges that cross the inland waterway.

Cocoa Beach Area

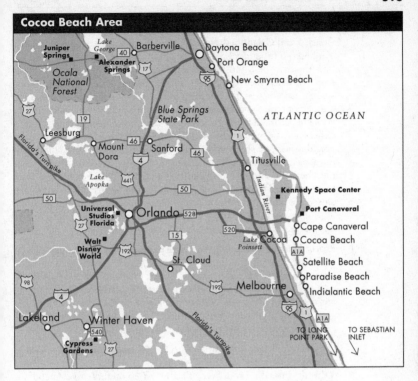

Lodging

Most lodging in Cocoa Beach is on Route A1A around its intersection with Route 520. Small motels abound; the few larger hotels are part of popular chains. For approximate costs, *see* the lodging price chart *in* Smart Travel Tips A to Z.

Surfing

Cocoa Beach is the self-proclaimed East Coast Surfing Capital. Those who like to hang ten in the Pacific, however, will find the waves here quite tame. But when there's a storm brewing and surf's up, you can get quite a ride. Cocoa Beach's main tourist attractions, the collection of Ron Jon Surf Shops, is a tribute to the town's principal claim to fame.

Exploring the Cocoa Beach Area

Although just 50 mi separate the Space Coast and Orlando, they're a world apart. In the small oceanfront towns of Cocoa Beach, Titusville, and Cape Canaveral, you won't find a lot of glitz, glamour, or giddy attractions. Mainly, it's sun, sand, and surf. If you're looking to get away from it all, this could be the place.

Besides the beach, there is one major attraction in the area: Kennedy Space Center Visitor Complex. The other sights tend to be rather low-key, funky, and offbeat. Still, there's plenty to see and do—or not do. Probably the nicest thing about Cocoa Beach and its neighbors is their laid-back style, which is very easy to get used to.

Great Itineraries

If you have the time, the best plan is to set aside two or three days to enjoy the area. But the Space Coast can also be enjoyed as one- or two-day trips from Orlando.

IF YOU HAVE 2 DAYS

For a reprieve from Disney take this surf-and-turf tour of the Space Coast. From Orlando, drive the Beeline Expressway (Route 528) east. You'll pay a total of $2.50 in tolls, and then, just past mile marker 30, take the exit for Route 520. Watch carefully for the exit; during the summer, when the trees aren't pruned, the direction sign is often obscured. Take 520 east about 9½ mi to the **Lone Cabbage Fish Camp** for a touch of real down-home Florida. Here you can fish from the dock, get some gator tail for lunch, and take an airboat ride—a genuine Florida experience. Continue east on 520 to **Cocoa Village,** a quaint restored neighborhood of shops and restaurants nestled on the west side of the Intracoastal Waterway. If you want to shop, it's best to come here sometime between mid-morning and mid-afternoon. Saturday tends to be more crowded than weekdays, and on Sunday almost all the shops are closed. To walk the entire Cocoa Village area, allow at least 45 minutes; if you plan to do some serious browsing in the shops or stop for a bite to eat, allow about two hours.

Proceed farther east on 520 to **Cocoa Beach.** At the intersection of 520 and A1A, known as Atlantic Avenue in Cocoa Beach, make a right (south) and then an almost immediate left turn into **Ron Jon Surf Shop,** a tribute to marketing genius and tourists' insatiable need for T-shirts and beach toys. It's a two-story display of all the surfing and beach gear you could ever use, and it's open 24 hours a day. Check into your hotel and spend the rest of the day soaking up the sun.

On day two, head north on A1A to the **Kennedy Space Center Visitor Complex.** Follow the signs to 528 (Orlando) and take the exit for Route 3 (heading north). From here, it's about a 20-minute drive. Spend the day learning the story of America's exploration of space. Be sure to include a stop at the **United States Astronaut Hall of Fame,** where you can test your skills landing the shuttle on a simulator. On your way back, retrace your route; at the end of Route 528, follow the signs for **Port Canaveral.** You'll probably get to see several giant cruise ships at dock, and you'll get another good view of Kennedy Space Center's launchpads.

IF YOU HAVE 4 DAYS

Allowing yourself that extra day or two will give you an opportunity to explore this lovely piece of Florida leisurely. This itinerary picks up on day three—your day to get back to nature. From the beach head north on A1A to U.S. 1 on the mainland and go north to Route 406. Turn east on Route 406 and then right on Route 402 and look for signs to the **Merritt Island Wildlife Refuge.** Take a drive through the refuge (just continue on Route 402) before heading to one of the beaches at the **Canaveral National Seashore,** where you should spend the day. Be sure to look down the beach; you'll get some great views of the launchpads. Return to Cocoa Beach for day four. Jump-start the day with a brisk walk or jog along the beach to witness a spectacular sunrise. When you've had enough sun and sand, head for the shops and restaurants of **Cocoa Beach Pier.**

Cocoa

50 mi east of downtown Orlando, 60 mi east of WDW.

The small town of Cocoa is on mainland Florida and fronts the Intracoastal Waterway. There's a planetarium and a museum worth stopping at, as well as a rustic fish camp nearby. Perhaps Cocoa's most interesting feature is restored **Cocoa Village,** which folks in a rush to get to the beach tend to overlook. A welcome return to reality after the stage sets of the theme parks, the Victorian-style village is a cluster of restored turn-of-the-20th-century buildings and cobblestone walkways, where visitors can enjoy several restaurants, indoor and outdoor cafés, snack and ice cream shops, and almost 50 specialty stores.

The **Astronaut Memorial Planetarium and Observatory,** one of the largest public-access observatories in Florida, and considered to be one of the best planetariums in the world, features a 24-inch telescope through which visitors can view objects in the solar system and deep space. The planetarium presents evening star shows; ever-changing, large-format films in the **IWERKS Discovery Theater;** and weekend laser light shows. The **Science Quest Demonstration Hall** features hands-on exhibits, including scales calibrated to other planets, which weight watchers find thrilling. The **International Hall of Space Explorers** displays exhibits on space travel. During the course of the year schedules sometimes vary slightly from those described below, so it is best to call before you attend. Travel 2½ mi east of I–95 Exit 75 on Route 520, and take Route 501 north for 1¾ mi. ✉ *1519 Clearlake Rd.,* ☎ *321/634-3732.* ✑ *Observatory and exhibit hall free; star show or film $5 adults, $3 children under 12; laser show $6 adults and children.* ☉ *Tues. and Fri. (sometimes Thurs.)–Sat. 6:30 PM–9:30 PM; star shows 7, films 8, laser light shows Fri.–Sat. 9.*

To see what the land was like in other eras, check out the **Brevard Museum of History and Natural Science.** Hands-on activities for children are the draw here. Not to be missed is the **Windover Archaeological Exhibit** of 7,000-year-old artifacts indigenous to the region. Don't overlook the hands-on discovery rooms and the **Collection of Victoriana.** The museum's **nature center** has 22 acres of trails encompassing three distinct ecosystems—sand pine hills, lake lands, and marshlands. ✉ *2201 Michigan Ave.,* ☎ *321/632-1830.* ✑ *$4 adults, $2.50 children under 17.* ☉ *Tues.–Sat. 10–4; Nov.–Apr., also Sun. 1–4.*

A riverfront restaurant and attraction, **Lone Cabbage Fish Camp** is offbeat and extremely casual. It's the natural habitat of wildlife (such as alligators) and local characters—even Arnold Palmer loves the place, as photos of him on the wall attest. This one-of-a-kind spot also has a dock where you can buy bait and fish, as well as secure an airboat ride with guides who are very informed about the river and all its flora and scaly fauna. The camp is 9 mi north of Cocoa's city limits, 4 mi west of I–95. ✉ *8199 Rte. 520,* ☎ *321/632-4199.* ✑ *Airboat ride $15 adults, $7.50 children under 12.* ☉ *Airboat rides daily 10–6:30.*

To get to **Cocoa Village,** head east on Route 520—named King Street in Cocoa—and make a right onto Brevard Avenue; follow the signs for the free municipal parking lot. As its name suggests, **Porcher House** was the home of E. P. Porcher, one of Cocoa's original pioneers and the founder of the Deerfield Citrus groves. The Porcher Home, built in 1916 and now a national historic landmark, is an example of 20th-century classical revival–style architecture incorporating local coquina rock. The house is open to the public for unguided tours. ✉ *434 Delannoy Ave., Cocoa Village,* ☎ *321/639-3500.* ✑ *Donation welcome.* ☉ *Weekdays 9–5.*

Dining and Lodging

$$–$$$ ✕ **Café Margaux.** Choose a table outside in a charming courtyard or indoors in a cozy, flower-decorated dining room at this small, intimate spot in restored Cocoa Village. The menu is an eclectic mix of French and Italian cuisine prepared with some creative twists. For starters, try the snails over couscous or the duck liver, Armagnac, and truffle paté. For an entrée choose from a wide range of selections, including lamb served with a black truffle polenta, and veal tenderloin with crabmeat,

tiger shrimp, and hollandaise sauce. ⊠ *220 Brevard Ave.*, ☎ *321/639–8343. AE, DC, MC, V. Closed Tues.*

$$ ✕ **Black Tulip Restaurant.** A tree provides the centerpiece in one of the two intimate dining rooms of this romantic bistro in pleasant Cocoa Village. Appetizers include broiled oysters with scallions and dill sauce, escargots over fresh spinach, and a delicious black-bean soup. Select from such entrées as roast duckling with apples and cashews, filet mignon medallions with a tangy mustard and artichoke sauce, or grouper stuffed with crab and wrapped in puff pastry. Lunch selections are lighter and include sandwiches, salads, and quiches. ⊠ *207 Brevard Ave.*, ☎ *321/631–1133. AE, DC, MC, V.*

$ ✕ **Lone Cabbage Fish Camp.** No-nonsense catfish, frogs' legs, turtle, country ham, and alligator (as well as burgers and hot dogs) make the drive from either the beach or Orlando worthwhile. On the first and third Sunday of every month, there's a fish fry and spirited country-and-western hoedown—definitely not for the shy. ⊠ *8199 Rte. 520*, ☎ *321/632–4199. AE, MC, V.*

$$ ▥ **Indian River House Bed & Breakfast..** This charming 1910 house, is nestled in tropical foliage behind a white picket fence and faces the Intracoastal Waterway, known locally as the Indian River. The two-story frame building has dormer windows and a small covered porch. Three rooms have views of the river, and all of them are individually and comfortably decorated with an eclectic mix of furnishings. You can spot the space shuttle as well as dolphins, manatees, and egrets from the dock, where canoes and kayaks are available for guests. ⊠ *3113 Indian River Dr., 32922*, ☎ *321/631–5660. 4 rooms. Dock, boating, bicycles. MC, V.*

Nightlife and the Arts

A restored 1924 brick building that's a registered national landmark, **Cocoa Village Playhouse** (⊠ 300 Brevard Ave., ☎ 321/636–5050) was originally the Aladdin Theater, a vaudeville house, and then did a turn as a movie theater before being purchased by Brevard Community College. Today it's the area's community theater. From September through March, it mounts plays and musicals featuring local talent. The rest of the year the stage hosts touring professional productions, concerts, and, in summer, shows geared toward children on vacation.

Shopping

You could spend hours browsing in the many boutiques and shops of **Cocoa Village,** along Brevard Avenue and Harrison Street, where you'll find the densest concentration of shops. If you like to cook, or even just like to eat, spend some time wandering through the huge array of kitchen and cooking items—handsome ceramic bowls, colorful glassware, regional cookbooks, exotic soup mixes—at the **Gourmet Experience** (⊠ 316 Brevard Ave., ☎ 321/636–5480). For a choice of gourmet ingredients, or delicious takeout, try the **Chef's Corner** (⊠ 12 Oleander St., ☎ 321/631–8578). It's the catering arm of the well-known **Black Tulip Restaurant** (☞ *above*). The shelves here are stocked with a tempting assortment of unusual canned, jarred, and packaged foods, and the take-out counter specializes in fresh salads and several daily specials. Doll house devotees come to a screeching halt when they catch sight of the perfectly decorated doll houses displayed in the storefront windows of the **Toy Box** (⊠ 419 Brevard Ave., ☎ 321/632–2411). Inside it's even better, with shelves and walls jam-packed with miniature items, from tiny sets of silverware to mini-drapes and chairs to teensy sets of outdoor swings.

The **Bath Cottage** (⊠ 300 Brevard Ave., ☎ 321/690–2284) carries just about everything you might want in your bathroom, from fine soaps to aromatherapy candles, plush towels, one-of-a-kind bath rugs, and a large assortment of elegant shower curtains. For some terrific sculptures of fish, follow the brick path back to the **Harry Phillips Gallery** (⊠ 116-B Harrison St., ☎ 321/636–4160). Fins and tails bend, capturing angelfish, dolphins, and marlins in motion. Take a break from the heat with a hand-packed ice-cream cone from the **Village Ice Cream & Sandwich Shop** (⊠ 120 Harrison St., ☎ 321/632–2311).

Cocoa Beach

65 mi east of Orlando, 70 mi east of WDW.

On a barrier island across from Cocoa, **Cocoa Beach** (⊠ Rte. A1A) is one of the Space Coast's nicest beaches, with many wide stretches that are excellent for biking, jogging, power walking, or strolling leisurely. (Begin your walk north of the 520 extension, and head for the Cocoa Beach Pier, where you can take a break at one of several watering holes.) In some places there are dressing rooms, showers, playgrounds, picnic areas with grills, snack shops, and surf-side parking lots. Beach vendors offer necessities, and guards are on duty in summer. Cocoa Beach is considered the capital of Florida's surfing community.

Stretching 800 ft into the Atlantic, the **Cocoa Beach Pier** (⊠ 401 Meade Ave., ☎ 321/783–7549) is a local gathering spot as well as a beachside grandstand for space shuttle launches. There are several souvenir shops, bars, and restaurants, as well as a bait-and-tackle shop.

When the children have had enough of the beach, take them to **Jungle Village Family Fun Center** to tire them out. There are mazes to climb around and get lost in, go-carts for children and adults, a "soft play" playground, batting cages for both softball and hard ball; laser tag, and 36 holes of miniature golf with a jungle theme featuring Pinky, a life-size elephant who sports pachyderm-size sunglasses. Hey, it's Florida. Don't go in the middle of the day in summer; you could wilt from the drop-dead heat. ⊠ *Rte. A1A, 2½ mi north of Rte. 520,* ☎ *321/783–0595.* 🎟 *Park free; go-carts $6.10 people over 57", $4.88 40"–57", $3.66 under 40"; miniature golf and laser tag $6.10 adults, $4.88 children under 12.* ☉ *Sun.–Thurs. 10 AM–midnight, Fri.–Sat. 10 AM–1 AM.*

Dining and Lodging

$$–$$$$ ✕ **Mango Tree Restaurant.** Candles, fresh flowers, white linen table-
★   cloths, rattan basket chairs with fluffy cushions, and eggshell-color walls set a romantic mood here. Well-spaced tables in the intimate dining room overlook a waterfall and garden aviary that is home to pheasants, swans, and ducks. The baked Brie, the escargots with garlic butter, or the fresh seared tuna are good appetizer choices. For the main course, try the fresh local fillet of grouper du jour or the veal loin chop with Portobello mushroom sauce. ⊠ *118 N. Atlantic Ave.,* ☎ *321/799–0513. AE, MC, V. Closed Mon. No lunch.*

$$–$$$ ✕ **Bernard's Surf.** A Cocoa Beach tradition, Bernard's, which opened
★   in 1948, is a family operation that has a faithful following of locals and seasonal visitors. The menu features a wide variety of seafood entrées, including fresh grouper, swordfish, cobia, pompano, lobster, mussels, scallops, and shrimp. The house specialty is snapper topped with a creamy seafood sauce of crab, shrimp, and scallops. Landlubbers can choose from pork chops, ribs, and many cuts of steak. Be sure to try the Caesar salad, prepared right at your table, and save room for dessert: the cheesecake, topped with raspberries and chocolate, is unbeatable. ⊠ *2 S. Atlantic Ave.,* ☎ *321/783–2401. AE, D, DC, MC, V. No lunch.*

$$-$$$ ✕ **Heidelberg.** As the name suggests, the cuisine here is definitely German, from the sauerbraten served with potato dumplings and red cabbage to the beef Stroganoff and spaetzle to the classically prepared Wiener schnitzel. All the soups and desserts are homemade; try the apple strudel and the rum-zapped almond-cream tortes. The atmosphere here is elegant, with crisp linens, fresh flowers, and a dark-red color scheme. ⊠ *7 N. Orlando Ave., opposite City Hall,* ☎ *321/783–6806. AE, MC, V. Closed Mon. No lunch Sun.*

$$ ✕ **Pier Restaurant.** Right on the water in the shopping, dining, and entertainment complex on Cocoa Beach Pier, this restaurant has floor-to-ceiling windows that overlook the ocean. Among the excellent fresh-fish options are mahimahi and grouper, which you can order broiled, blackened, grilled, or fried. ⊠ *401 Meade Ave.,* ☎ *321/783–7549. AE, D, DC, MC, V.*

$-$$ ✕ **Alma's Italian Restaurant.** A local favorite for more than 30 years, Alma's is crowded on weekends, but five separate dining rooms keep the place from feeling jammed. The specialties of the house are fresh-caught grouper Italian style and veal Parmesan. The cellar stocks more than 200 imported and domestic wines, and the atmosphere is warm and casual, courtesy of red-checked tablecloths, stone floors, dim lighting, and a large stained-glass window. ⊠ *306 N. Orlando Ave.,* ☎ *321/ 783–1981. AE, DC, MC, V. No lunch.*

$ ✕ **The Boardwalk.** At this popular open-air bar on Cocoa Beach Pier, finger food reigns and you can count on live entertainment Monday, Wednesday, and Friday through Sunday evenings. At the Friday-night Boardwalk Bash there's $7 lobster and $2 ribs. ⊠ *401 Meade Ave.,* ☎ *321/783–7549. AE, D, DC, MC, V.*

$ ✕ **Fischer's Bar and Grill.** This casual eatery, owned by the same family that runs the more upscale Bernard's Surf (☞ *above*), is a perfect spot for winding down after a tough day at the beach. Although complete dinners are available, people tend to come for the salads, pasta, burgers, and platters of tasty fried shrimp. There's a happy hour from 4 to 7. ⊠ *2 S. Atlantic Ave.,* ☎ *321/783–2401. AE, DC, MC, V.*

$ ✕ **Oh, Shucks!** In this open-air bar on Cocoa Beach Pier, the main item is—you guessed it—oysters, served on the half shell. It also offers burgers plus live entertainment nightly. ⊠ *401 Meade Ave.,* ☎ *321/ 783–7549. AE, D, DC, MC, V.*

$ ✕ **Rusty's Seafood & Oyster Bar.** Oysters, prepared raw, steamed, or casino style, are just one of the draws at this casual eatery with a Hooter's motif—waitresses are dressed in very short shorts. Other popular menu items include seafood gumbo, spicy wings, steamed crab legs, burgers, and baskets of fish-and-chips, clam strips, or fried calamari. It's a popular spot with the locals. There are two locations: the first is in the same building as Bernard's Surf; the other is at Port Canaveral. ⊠ *2 S. Atlantic Ave.,* ☎ *321/783–2401;* ⊠ *628 Glen Cheek Dr., Port Canaveral,* ☎ *321/783–2033. AE, D, DC, MC, V.*

$$$-$$$$ 🏨 **Inn at Cocoa Beach.** The finest accommodations in Cocoa Beach are
★ in this charming oceanfront inn. Each spacious room is decorated differently, but all have some combination of reproduction 18th- and 19th-century armoires, four-poster beds, and comfortably upholstered chairs and sofas. All units have balconies or patios and views of the ocean. Several have whirlpool baths. Included in the rate are an evening spread of wine and cheese and a sumptuous Continental breakfast with delicious homemade muffins and breads, served in the sunny breakfast room. ⊠ *4300 Ocean Beach Blvd., 32931,* ☎ *321/799–3460; 800/ 343–5307 outside FL,* 𝔽𝔸𝕏 *321/784–8632. 50 rooms. Breakfast room, pool, beach. AE, D, MC, V.*

$$$ 🏨 **Cocoa Beach Hilton Oceanfront.** At seven stories, this hotel is one of the tallest buildings in Cocoa Beach. Dense natural foliage separates the property from the roadway. Rooms are comfortably but not lavishly furnished. Most have ocean views, but for true drama get a room on the east end, facing the water: the floor-to-ceiling windows really show off the scenery. The hotel's best feature is its location, right on the beach. A band plays reggae music poolside on weekends. ⊠ *1550 N. Atlantic Ave., 32931,* ☎ *321/799–0003 or 800/526–2609,* FAX *321/ 799–0344. 296 rooms. Restaurant, bar, pool, beach, video games, baby-sitting. AE, D, DC, MC, V.*

$$$ 🏨 **Doubletree Oceanfront Hotel.** Rooms here are light and airy and comfortably furnished in pastel prints; many are oceanfront with superb water views and private balconies. This well-maintained five-story hotel is popular with families and is also a favorite of Orlandoans as a weekend getaway. ⊠ *2080 N. Atlantic Ave., 32931,* ☎ *321/783– 9222,* FAX *321/783–6514. 138 rooms, 10 suites. Restaurant, bar, 2 pools, wading pool, exercise room. AE, DC, MC, V.*

$$–$$$ 🏨 **Cocoa Beach Oceanside Inn.** The name says it all: this five-story property is right on the beach and all rooms, have an oceanfront balcony. You can swim in the heated pool and still have a view of the ocean without getting salt in your eyes. ⊠ *1 Hendry Ave., 32931,* ☎ *321/ 784–3126 or 800/874–7958,* FAX *321/799–0883. 76 rooms. Restaurant, bar, pool, beach, laundry service. AE, D, MC, V.*

$$–$$$ 🏨 **Comfort Inn and Suite Resort.** This six-story hostelry is across the street from the ocean and within walking distance of more than a dozen restaurants. You can choose from standard double rooms, minisuites, one-bedroom ocean-view suites, and fully equipped efficiencies. The poolside bar has a waterfall, and there's a pond full of tropical fish, in addition to the many facilities. ⊠ *3901 N. Atlantic Ave., 32931,* ☎ *321/783–2221,* FAX *321/783–0461. 40 rooms, 64 suites, 40 efficiencies. Bar, pool, hot tub, Ping-Pong, shuffleboard, volleyball, playground. AE, D, DC, MC, V.*

$$–$$$ 🏨 **Holiday Inn Cocoa Beach Resort.** When two adjacent beach hotels were redesigned and a promenade park landscaped between them, the low-rise, 30-acre Holiday Inn Cocoa Beach Resort was born. Public rooms are plush and modern, and there are many facilities. Options include standard, king, and oceanfront suites, which have a living room with sleeper sofa, or you can opt for a villa or bi-level loft. ⊠ *1300 N. Atlantic Ave., 32931,* ☎ *321/783–2271,* FAX *321/784–8878. 500 rooms. Restaurant, 2 bars, snack bar, pool, 2 tennis courts, shuffleboard, volleyball, baby-sitting, children's programs (ages 3–12). AE, DC, MC, V.*

$$–$$$ 🏨 **Ocean Suite Hotel.** A five-story building with a great location, this property is just a half block south of Cocoa Beach Pier. Ideal for families, each unit is a two-room suite with a refrigerator and microwave. ⊠ *5500 Ocean Beach Blvd., 32931,* ☎ *321/784–4343,* FAX *321/783– 6514. 50 suites. Restaurant, bar, pool. AE, D, DC, MC, V.*

$$–$$$ 🏨 **Wakulla Motel.** This popular, two-story motel is clean and comfortable and just off the beach. Some rooms are a block away from the water, and a few are just a walk down the boardwalk. The bright rooms are decorated in tropical prints, mirroring the extraordinary courtyard filled with tropical plants. Completely furnished five-room suites, designed to sleep six, are great for families; they comprise two bedrooms, a living room, dining room, and fully equipped kitchen. ⊠ *3550 N. Atlantic Ave., 32931,* ☎ *321/783–2230,* FAX *321/783–0980. 116 suites. 2 pools, shuffleboard, volleyball. AE, D, DC, MC, V.*

$$ 🏨 **Best Western Ocean Inn.** Popular with families, this no-nonsense motel doesn't have a lot of frills. You'll have to walk a half block to get to the beach, but the trek can be worth it to save your vacation dollars

for things besides an oceanfront room. ⊠ *5500 N. Atlantic Ave.,
32931,* ☎ *321/784–2550 or 800/245–5225,* FAX *321/868-7124. 103
rooms, 1 suite, 14 efficiencies. Pool, exercise room, coin laundry. AE,
D, DC, MC, V.*

$$ 🏨 **Pelican Landing Resort on the Ocean.** This two-story beachfront motel
is friendly and warm. Rooms have ocean views, kitchenettes with mi-
crowaves, and TVs with cable and HBO; one even has a screened porch.
Boardwalks to the beach, picnic tables, and a grill round out the
amenities. ⊠ *1201 S. Atlantic Ave., 32931,* ☎ *321/783–7197. 11
units. Picnic area, beach. D, MC, V.*

Nightlife

The **Cocoa Beach Pier** (⊠ 401 Mead Ave., ☎ 321/783–7549) is a hap-
pening spot. Come to **The Boardwalk** (☞ *above*) Friday night for the
Boardwalk Bash, with live acoustic and rock-and-roll music; drop in
Saturday for more live music; and come back Wednesday evening to
catch the reggae band. At **Oh, Shucks!** (☞ *above*) you can count on
finding live bands Friday and Saturday nights. **Coconuts on the Beach**
(⊠ 2 Minuteman Causeway, ☎ 321/784–1422), a beachfront hang-
out that's long been the local party place, is popular with the younger
crowd. There are karaoke nights, ladies' nights, 25¢ beer nights, and
volleyball tournaments, plus live music on Thursday, Friday, and Sat-
urday. Burgers, salads, and sandwiches are on the menu. For some great
live jazz, head to **Heidi's Jazz Club** (⊠ 7 Orlando Ave., ☎ 321/783–
4559). Music begins at 5, except on Sunday, when a jam session starts
at 7 and sit-in musicians are welcome, so bring your instrument and
join in.

Outdoor Activities and Sports

The **Cocoa Beach Country Club** (⊠ 5000 Tom Warriner Blvd., ☎ 321/
868–3351) is actually an extensive public sports complex that's owned
by the city and open to anyone. Set against the banks of the Banana
River, it offers a variety of facilities, including a 27-hole championship
golf course, which touches the shores of 17 lakes and is home to much
wildlife; an Olympic-size swimming pool; 10 lighted tennis courts; a
restaurant; and a riverside pavilion with picnic tables.

BIKING

Although there are no bike trails as such in the area, cycling is allowed
on the beaches and the Cocoa Beach Causeway. Bikes can be rented
hourly, daily, or weekly at **Ron Jon Surf Shop** (⊠ 4151 N. Atlantic Ave.
[Rte. A1A], ☎ 321/799–8888).

FISHING

The **Cocoa Beach Pier** (⊠ 401 Meade Ave., ☎ 321/783–7549) has a
bait-and-tackle shop and a fishing area. Although most of the pier is
free to walk on, there's a 50¢ charge to enter the fishing area at the
end and $3.50 if you plan to fish.

Shopping

Cocoa Beach may seem an unlikely place for a shop with a South Pa-
cific theme, but, hey, why not? High-quality Tiki carvings, masks, and
sculptures are offered at **Mai Tiki Gallery** (⊠ 1 N. Atlantic Ave. [Rte.
A1A], ☎ 321/783–6890). There's also a selection of souvenirs the chil-
dren will love.

Merritt Square Mall (⊠ 777 E. Merritt Island Causeway [Rte. 520],
Merritt Island, ☎ 321/452–3272), the area's only major shopping
mall, is about a 20-minute ride from the beach. Stores include Dillard's,
JCPenney, Sears Roebuck, Bath & Body Works, Foot Locker, and
Waldenbooks. There are two six-screen multiplexes, along with a food

court and several popular restaurant chains—Ruby Tuesday's and the Outback Steak House.

It's impossible to miss the **Ron Jon Surf Shop** (⊠ 4151 N. Atlantic Ave. [Rte. A1A], ☎ 321/799–8888). With a giant surfboard and an aqua, teal, and pink art-deco facade that looks like Cinderella Castle on acid, Ron Jon takes up nearly two blocks along A1A. What started in 1963 as a small T-shirt and bathing-suit shop has evolved into a 52,000-square-ft superstore that's open every day 'round the clock. Inside you'll find every kind of beachwear, plus the requisite T-shirts and flip-flops. There's also a wide variety of merchandise from Australia, including boomerangs. In the center of the store there's a waterfall and pond that can be viewed from within a glass elevator. For up-to-the-minute surfing conditions call the store and press 3 and then 7 for the **Ron Jon Surf and Weather Report.**

Ron Jon Watersports (⊠ 4151 N. A1A, ☎ 321/799–8888) features the latest in surfing rentals, including glass and foam surfboards, body boards, scuba equipment, and kayaks.

Melbourne

20 mi south of Cocoa.

Despite its dependence on the high-tech space industry, this town has a decidedly laid-back atmosphere.

Exhibits of contemporary art and presentations of decorative arts, ethnographic works, photography, and experimental art forms as well as hands-on activities for children are the draw at the **Brevard Museum of Arts and Science.** ⊠ *1463 Highland Ave.,* ☎ *321/242–0737.* ☞ *$5 adults, $2 children under 12.* ☉ *Tues.–Sat. 10–5, Sun. 1–5.*

★ Stroll along the shaded boardwalks at the 56-acre **Brevard Zoo** and get a close-up look at alligators, crocodiles, giant anteaters, marmosets, jaguars, eagles, river otters, kangaroos, exotic birds, and kookaburras. Stop by **Paws-On,** an interactive learning playground; get cozy with a wide range of domestic animals in **Animal Encounters;** have a bird hop on your shoulder in the **Australian Free Flight Aviary,** and step up to the **Wetlands Outpost,** an elevated pavilion that is a gateway to 22 acres of wetlands through which you can paddle kayaks. A seven-minute train ride loops around Lemur Island and stops at all the main attractions. Visitors can feed certain birds or animals at scheduled times on some days. Picnic tables, a snack bar, and a gift shop complete the picture. ⊠ *8225 N. Wickham Rd.,* ☎ *321/254–9453.* ☞ *$6.50 adults, $4.50 children 2–12; kayaks $4 per person; train ride $1.50.* ☉ *Daily 10–5, kayaks available weekdays 1–4, weekends 11–4.*

OFF THE BEATEN PATH

SATELLITE BEACH – The beaches of this sleepy little community just south of Patrick Air Force Base, about 15 mi south of Cocoa Beach, are almost always uncrowded. The only amenities are several picnic areas.

PARADISE BEACH – Small and scenic, this 1,600-ft stretch of sand is part of a 10-acre park north of Indialantic, about 20 mi south of Cocoa Beach on A1A. It has showers, rest rooms, picnic tables, a refreshment stand, and lifeguards in summer.

Outdoor Activities and Sports

Even though they play at South Florida's Pro Player Stadium during the season, baseball's **Florida Marlins** (⊠ 5800 Stadium Pkwy., ☎ 321/633–9200) use Melbourne's Space Coast Stadium for their spring-

training site. For the rest of the season, the facility is home to the Brevard County Manatees, one of the Marlins' minor-league teams.

Sebastian

22 mi south of Melbourne.

One of only a few sparsely populated areas on Florida's east coast, this
little fishing village has as remote a feeling as you'll find anywhere between Jacksonville and Miami Beach.

The 578-acre **Sebastian Inlet State Recreation Area** offers 3 mi of interesting beach that's good for swimming, surfing, and snorkeling. The
beach is rocky and the sand coarser than elsewhere along the coast,
and the underwater drop-off is often sharp. It's fun for treasure hunters,
because storms occasionally wash up coins known as pieces of eight
from the area's ancient Spanish shipwrecks. Sebastian is also a favorite
destination for Florida anglers. Warning: Come seriously prepared for
what Floridians call their state bird—the ubiquitous mosquito. The park
has a bathhouse, a concession, a fishing jetty, a boat ramp, and camp-
sites. ⊠ *9700 S. Rte. A1A, Melbourne Beach,* ☎ *321/984–4852.* 🖼
$3.25. ☉ *Daily 24 hrs, bait and tackle shop daily 8–6, concession stand
daily 9–5.*

The **McLarty Treasure Museum** was built to commemorate the loss of
a fleet of Spanish treasure ships in a hurricane. Don't miss the dramatic
movie *The Queen's Jewels and the 1715 Fleet.* Filmed by the Arts &
Entertainment television network, it's a riveting tale of the 11 ships
that sank in 1715 in a devastating hurricane. These ships are the source
of most of the treasure that still washes ashore along this part of the
Florida coastline. The museum is 1½ mi south of the south entrance
to the Sebastian Inlet State Recreation Area. ⊠ *9700 Rte. A1A,* ☎ *561/
589–2147.* 🖼 *$1 ages 6 and older.* ☉ *Daily 10–4:30.*

Port Canaveral

5 mi north of Cocoa.

This once bustling commercial fishing area is still home to a small shrimping fleet, charter boats, and party fishing boats. In recent years, a
growing number of cruise ships have called Port Canaveral home, and
the port has been expanded several times. It's now a great place to catch
a glimpse of these giant ships, even if you're not headed out on a cruise.

A place where friendly conversations are unavoidable, **Jetty Maritime
Park** is a campground and picnic area that offers a wonderful taste of
the real Florida. A long fishing pier juts out into the ocean, making it
a great place to watch the space shuttle take off. A jetty constructed
of giant boulders adds to the landscape, and a walkway that crosses
it provides access to a less populated stretch of beach. Shops offer area
souvenirs. ⊠ *400 E. Jetty Rd., Cape Canaveral,* ☎ *321/783–7111.* 🖼
$3 per car for either fishing or beach. ☉ *Daily 7 AM–9 PM.*

Dining and Lodging

$$ ✕ **Flamingos.** Wicker furniture and paintings of flamingos give a
Caribbean feel to this casual spot, which features what the chef calls
"Floribbean" cuisine. It's a true blend of Caribbean and Florida specialties,
such as the Floribbean Paella, which includes alligator along with the
traditional ingredients of clams, mussels, and andouille sausage. Other
house favorites are chicken kabobs, fried calamari, crawfish with sweet
potato cakes, and alligator and conch fritters. ⊠ *Radisson Resort at the
Port, 8701 Astronaut Blvd.,* ☎ *321/784–0000. AE, D, MC, V.*

$$$ 🏨 **Radisson Resort at the Port.** This resort directly across the bay from Port Canaveral is not on the ocean, but it does provide complimentary transportation to the beach, Ron Jon Surf Shop, and the cruise ship terminals at Port Canaveral. Rooms have wicker furniture, hand-painted wallpaper, coffeemakers, and ceiling fans; they come with one king-size or two double beds and have TVs with cable and HBO. The pool is tropically landscaped and replete with a cascading 95-ft mountain waterfall. ✉ *8701 Astronaut Blvd., 32920,* 🕿 *321/784–0000 or 800/333–3333,* 🖷 *321/784–3737. 200 rooms. Restaurant, 2 pools, hot tub, 2 tennis courts, health club, playground, laundry service, business services, convention center, airport shuttle. AE, DC, MC, V.*

Outdoor Activities and Sports
Cape Marina (✉ 800 Scallop Dr., 🕿 321/783–8410) offers half- and full-day fishing charters.

Titusville

17 mi north of Cocoa.

This small community is home to the Kennedy Space Center, the nerve center of the U.S. space program. Here you'll find several attractions that are devoted to the history of space exploration.

The **Kennedy Space Center Visitor Complex,** just southeast of Titusville, is one of Central Florida's most popular sights. Many of the attractions are free, including parking (sections of the lot are named after the various space shuttles). Within the facility is the outdoor **Rocket Garden,** its lawns bristling with rockets; a museum filled with exhibits on spacecraft that have explored the last frontier; and a theater showing several short films. Outside, there's also a full-scale replica of a space shuttle, *Explorer,* where you can view the payload bay, cockpit, and crew quarters. Children love the space playground, with a ⅕-scale space shuttle–space station gym.

The most moving exhibit is the **Astronauts Memorial,** a tribute to those who have died while in pursuit of space exploration. Dedicated in May 1991, the memorial was financed mostly by Floridians who purchased *Challenger* license plates. The 42½-ft-high by 50-ft-wide "Space Mirror" tracks the movement of the sun throughout the day, using reflected sunlight to illuminate brilliantly the names of the 16 fallen astronauts that are carved into the monument's 70,400-pound polished granite surface.

To get the most out of a visit to the space center, you should take at least one of the two bus tours offered. These are the only way to see much of the working part of the facility up close. The **Cape Canaveral Tour** visits the launch pad where Alan Shepard took America's first trip into space as well as other historic pads where Mercury and Gemini spacecraft were launched. You'll also see modern launch pads where unmanned rockets carry commercial, scientific, and military spacecraft into orbit. The **Kennedy Space Center Tour** covers NASA's space shuttle facilities, including the launch pads and the enormous Vehicle Assembly Building, one of the largest buildings in the world. Security concerns mandate that many sights be viewed through a tour bus window. However, live and recorded narrations are provided during both tours, and there are historical exhibits at camera stops. Depending on launch schedules, not all sights may be included in the tours. The new, special-interest tour **Cape Canaveral: Now and Then** visits historical sights seldom accessible to the public, such as training facilities, launch sites, the Cape Canaveral Lighthouse, and the Mercury Memorial. Your choice of the Kennedy Space Center or Cape Canaveral bus tour is also included (🎫 $35 per person, ⊙ Tues. and Fri., 11 and 2:30).

IMAX films are projected onto 5½-story screens in the only back-to-back twin **IMAX theater complex** in the world. In the IMAX I Theater, two films alternate all day long, beginning with *The Dream Is Alive,* an awesome 40-minute film shot mostly by the astronauts, which takes you from astronaut training and a thundering shuttle launch to an astronaut's-eye view of life aboard the shuttle while in space. Also showing is *Mission to Mir. L-5: The First City in Space,* a fantasy of the futuristic experiences of a family living in space, is shown in 3-D IMAX format in the IMAX II Theater. On Kennedy Space Center grounds, tune your car radio to AM 1320 for attraction information. ⊠ *Rte. 405, Kennedy Space Center,* ☎ *321/452–2121 or 800/572–4636.* ☒ *Space Center free; Mission Pass (choice of one bus tour and two IMAX movies) $21.35 adults, $16.25 children 3–11; bus tours $14 adults, $10 children 3–11; IMAX I and II Theaters $7.50 adults, $5.50 children 3–11.* ☉ *Space Center daily 9 AM–7:30 PM, last tour 2 hrs before closing; closed certain launch dates, so call ahead; IMAX I and II Theaters daily 10–5:40.*

At the **United States Astronaut Hall of Fame** you can enter the world of virtual reality, thanks to an interactive display where you can lose your breath because of the 3-G pull of a mock G-force trainer. Highlights of the **The Astronaut Adventure** includes a simulated liftoff experience, a hair-raising simulated jet aircraft dogfight complete with 360° barrel rolls, and a shuttle landing simulator that lets you try your hand at landing the cumbersome craft. For a quiet interlude, view videotapes of historic moments in the space program. The exhibit, **First on the Moon,** focuses on crew selection for Apollo 11 and the Soviet Union's role in the space race. This is also home to **U.S. Space Camp,** which offers young people a hands-on learning environment that budding astronauts will love. ⊠ *6225 Vectorspace Blvd., off Rte. 405, Kennedy Space Center,* ☎ *321/269–6100.* ☒ *$13.95 adults, $9.95 children 6–12.* ☉ *Daily 9–5.*

Aviation buffs won't want to miss the **Valiant Air Command Warbird Air Museum.** The museum is filled with aviation memorabilia from both world wars, Korea, and Vietnam, as well as extensive displays of vintage military flying gear and uniforms. ⊠ *6600 Tico Rd.,* ☎ *321/268–1941.* ☒ *$7.50 adults, $4 children 4–12.* ☉ *Daily 10–6.*

The 57,000-acre **Canaveral National Seashore,** home to more than 250 species of birds and other animals, is an unspoiled area of hilly sand dunes, grassy marshes, and shell-sprinkled beaches. The beach itself is sprinkled with seashells. Surf and lagoon fishing are available, and a hiking trail leads to the top of a Native American shell midden at Turtle Mound. A visitor center is on Route A1A. Weekends are busy, and parts of the park are closed before launches, sometimes as much as two weeks in advance, so call ahead.

Part of the national seashore, remote **Playalinda Beach** has pristine sands and is the longest stretch of undeveloped coast on Florida's Atlantic seaboard. Hundreds of giant sea turtles come ashore here from May through August to lay their eggs. There are no lifeguards, but park rangers patrol. Eight parking lots anchor the beach at 1-mi intervals. Take bug repellent in case of horseflies. To get here, follow U.S. 1 north into Titusville to Route 406 (I–95 Exit 80), follow Route 406 east across the Indian River, and then take Route 402 east for 12 mi. *Southern end:* ⊠ *Rte. 402,* ☎ *904/267–1110; northern end:* ⊠ *7611 S. Atlantic Ave., New Smyrna Beach,* ☎ *904/428–3384.* ☒ *$5 per car.* ☉ *Daily 6 AM–8 PM.*

At the 140,000-acre **Merritt Island National Wildlife Refuge,** which adjoins the Canaveral National Seashore, you can see wildlife and rivers of grass up close. Wander along nature trails at this habitat for wintering migratory waterfowl, and take a self-guided, 7-mi driving tour along **Black Point Wildlife Drive.** On the **Oak Hammock Foot Trail,** you can learn about the plants of a hammock community. ⊠ *Rte. 402, across Titusville causeway,* ☎ *321/861–0667.* ⛋ *Free.* ☉ *Daily sunrise–sunset.*

If you're interested in getting closer to the wildlife of the Merritt Island National Wildlife Refuge or other local scenic waterways, check out **A Day Away Kayaking Tours** with Rick Shafer. He leads guided eco-tours for all levels of experience in which you might paddle alongside dolphins, manatees, and herons, and other birds. Tours are 1 to 5 hours and start at $25 per person–lunch included. ⊠ *306 Parker Drive, Titusville, FL 32780,* ☎ *321/268–2655.* ⬙

Dining and Lodging

$–$$
★
✕ **Dixie Crossroads.** This sprawling restaurant is always crowded and festive, but it's not just the atmosphere that draws the throngs; it's the basic but uniformly excellent seafood. The specialty is the difficult-to-cook rock shrimp, which the Crossroads crew shells and fries or broils to perfection. Other standouts include the clam strips and the all-you-can-eat catfish. If you don't have time to wait for a table, you can order takeout. ⊠ *1475 Garden St., 2 mi east of I–95 Exit 80,* ☎ *321/268–5000. Reservations not accepted. AE, D, DC, MC, V.*

$$–$$$
⌸ **Holiday Inn–Kennedy Space Center.** Because it offers great views of liftoffs, this hotel on the Indian River books up fast when a launch at the Kennedy Space Center is scheduled. Rooms are comfortable but modestly furnished. The beach is a car ride away, but there is a big pool. ⊠ *4951 S. Washington Ave., 32780,* ☎ *321/269–2121,* ℻ *321/267–4739. 120 rooms. Restaurant, lounge, pool, wading pool, playground. AE, D, DC, MC, V.*

COCOA BEACH AREA A TO Z

Arriving and Departing

By Car

The Beeline Expressway (Route 528) is accessible from either I–4 or Florida's Turnpike. Tolls for the trip from Orlando add up to $2.50 for a car. If you take the Beeline directly to the coast, you will end up in Port Canaveral, about 6 mi north of Cocoa Beach. The coast is about 90 minutes from WDW and 60 minutes from Orlando.

Route 520, which is reached from the Beeline—exit just past mile marker 30—is a slightly less direct but more scenic route to Cocoa Beach. Continuing east on 520 will take you through the town of Cocoa and on to Cocoa Beach and Route A1A, the beach's main artery.

Route 50, known in Orlando as Colonial Drive, is also a straight shot to the coast. You'll have to get through some traffic, but once you're on the outskirts of Orlando, it's smooth sailing as long as it's not during the morning or evening rush hours. Route 50 dead-ends at A1A in Titusville, just north of the access road to the Kennedy Space Center Visitor Complex. If you're going to the center for the day, Route 50 is actually a more direct route than the Beeline.

By Plane

The nearest major airport is **Orlando International Airport** (☎ 321/825–2001), about a one-hour ride. The **Cocoa Beach Shuttle** (☎ 321/784–3831) provides transportation to and from the airport. Reservations are required.

American Eagle, Continental, Delta, Spirit, and US Airways provide some service to **Melbourne International Airport** (☎ 321/723–6227), approximately a half-hour ride from Cocoa. The **Melbourne Airport Shuttle** (☎ 321/724–1600) ferries arriving and departing passengers.

Getting Around

By Bus

Space Coast Area Transit (☎ 321/633–1878) is the provider of local bus service. The fare is $1 adults, 50¢ for senior citizens, people with disabilities, or students with valid ID. Route 9 runs between Merritt Square Mall and all major points along the beaches between Port Canaveral and Cocoa Beach.

By Car

The Space Coast is very easy to navigate. On the beach, the main thoroughfare is A1A, known as Atlantic Avenue in Cocoa Beach and by other names in other beach towns. The area around the intersection of A1A and Route 520 tends to be congested at almost all hours. In general, however, traffic here can be somewhat lighter than in other towns along the coast. The principal route on the "mainland" is U.S. 1, which goes by various local names such as Dixie Highway.

Contacts and Resources

Car Rentals

If you are driving from Orlando International Airport, you will find that although a few major car rental companies are in the main terminal on Level 1, many are a bus ride away (although buses run quite frequently). Several car rental companies also have offices on the Space Coast. Call these numbers for the location nearest to where you'll be staying: **Avis** (☎ 800/331–2112), **Budget** (☎ 800/527–0700), **Hertz** (☎ 800/654–3131).

Emergencies

Dial **911** for police, fire, or ambulance.

HOSPITAL

Cape Canaveral Hospital (✉ 701 W. Cocoa Beach Causeway [Rte. 520], Cocoa Beach, ☎ 321/799–7111) has a 24-hour emergency room.

Guided Tours

AIRBOAT TOURS

Daily from 10 to 6, 30-minute airboat rides on the St. Johns River are available at **Lone Cabbage Fish Camp** (✉ 8199 Rte. 520, Cocoa, ☎ 321/632–4199) for $15 adults, $7.50 children under 12. Reservations are essential.

Visitor Information

The **Cocoa Beach Area Chamber of Commerce** (✉ 400 Fortenberry Rd., Merritt Island 32952, ☎ 321/459–2200 or 800/572–4636) provides general information as well as dates for rocket launches. To find out more information about Cocoa Village, call or write the **Cocoa Village Association** (✉ Brevard Ave., south of Rte. 520, Box 1, Cocoa Village 32923, ☎ 321/631–9075). A good source for launch information and area information is the **Space Coast Office of Tourism** (✉ 2725 St. Johns St., Melbourne 32940, ☎ 321/633–2110 or 800/872–1969).

For information on Titusville, call the **Titusville Area Chamber of Commerce** (✉ 2000 S. Washington Ave., Titusville 32780, ☎ 321/267–3036).

INDEX

NOTES

NOTES